# Readings in Modern Philosophy
## Volume I

Descartes, Spinoza, Leibniz
and Associated Texts

# Readings in Modern Philosophy
## Volume I

### Descartes, Spinoza, Leibniz
### and Associated Texts

Edited by
Roger Ariew
and
Eric Watkins

Hackett Publishing Company, Inc.
Indianapolis/Cambridge

*For David, Daniel, Christa, and Nicholas,*
*who we hope will find this anthology of use someday*

For further information, please address:

Hackett Publishing Company, Inc.
P.O. Box 44937
Indianapolis, IN 46244-0937

www.hackettpublishing.com

Cover design by Abigail Coyle

**Library of Congress Cataloging-in-Publication Data**

Readings in modern philosophy / edited by Roger Ariew and Eric Watkins.
    p. cm.
   Includes bibliographical references.
   Contents: v. 1. Descartes, Spinoza, Leibniz, and associated texts—v. 2. Locke,
Berkeley, Hume, and associated texts.
   ISBN 0-87220-535-5 (cloth: v. 1)—ISBN 0-87220-534-7 (paper: v. 1)—ISBN
0-87220-533-9 (cloth: v. 2)—ISBN 0-87220-532-0 (paper: v. 2)
   1. Philosophy, Modern. I. Ariew, Roger. II. Watkins, Eric, 1964–
B791.M65 2000
190–dc21
                                                    00-038860

# CONTENTS

# GENERAL INTRODUCTION

When G. W. Leibniz traveled to Paris in 1672, he found an intellectual environment in great turmoil. Leibniz had been trained in Aristotelian (or scholastic) philosophy, which had dominated European thought ever since the thirteenth century, when the majority of the Aristotelian corpus was rediscovered and translated from Greek and Arabic into Latin, and then was made compatible with Christian doctrine (by Thomas Aquinas and others). Until his trip to Paris, Leibniz's properly philosophical works consisted primarily of a thesis on the scholastic problem of the principle of individuation and the publication of a new edition of an obscure sixteenth-century philosopher who had attempted to rehabilitate a more authentic Aristotelian philosophy from the "barbarism" of the scholastics. But a philosophical revolution was taking place in mid-seventeenth-century Paris. New scientific and philosophical doctrines had emerged from Galileo Galilei, from René Descartes and his followers, from Francis Bacon, Blaise Pascal, Thomas Hobbes, and countless others. Scholastics had fought back fiercely against the new philosophy and science; they had succeeded in getting Galileo's work condemned by the Catholic Church in 1633 and in putting Descartes's works on the *Index of Prohibited Books* in 1663. Still, the substantial forms and primary matter of the scholastics were giving way to a new mechanistic world of geometrical bodies, corpuscles, or atoms in motion. With this world came novel mathematical tools and scientific methods for dealing with its newly conceived entities. Old problems that seemed to have been resolved within a scholastic framework were raised again, and with new urgency: what can one say about necessity, contingency, and freedom in a world of atoms governed by laws of motion? The structure of the universe, whether it is finite or infinite, and the concepts of space and time were up for grabs. Other basic philosophical issues were also keenly debated, including the location of the soul, its immortality, God's purpose in the creation, and his relation to the universe. With such a great intellectual upheaval came the questioning as to whether humans even have knowledge at all. Leibniz, of course, became a major contributor to this intellectual movement that defined the modern world. In Paris, he read and copied Descartes's manuscripts and sought out proponents of the new philosophy, such as Antoine Arnauld and Nicholas Malebranche; Leibniz's own later work was often precipitated by the correspondence he maintained with them and others, such as Pierre Bayle. He traveled to London and met members of the Royal Society (Henry Oldenburg and Robert Boyle, among others, though not Isaac Newton, with whom he later corresponded). On his way back to Lower Saxony, he visited Baruch Spinoza in the Netherlands.

It is our hope that this anthology will provide a glimpse of that intellectual ferment, that is, the radical movement of thought from Descartes and his contemporaries to Leibniz and his contemporaries. For that process, we have tried, as much as possible, to provide whole texts—that is, Descartes's *Meditations*, Leibniz's *Discourse* and *Monadology*; Spinoza's *Ethics* has been excerpted. We have attempted to surround these works with additional texts that will assist instructors in teaching the primary sources—for example, selections from Hobbes's *Leviathan* and Malebranche's *Search after Truth*, or portions of Descartes's *Discourse* and the *Objections* and *Replies* to his *Meditations*. Along the way, we have tried to provide alternatives to the "main" texts, which instructors might prefer to teach. Of course, we have had to make many difficult choices; we hope that we have supplied most, if not all, the desired selections and have not cast off too many of our readers' favorites.

Another goal was to achieve some consistency among texts. With Descartes, Spinoza, and Leibniz, this was accomplished, we hope, by the use of the same translator for the various works of the given philosopher (Donald Cress for Descartes, Samuel Shirley for Spinoza, and Roger Ariew and Daniel Garber for Leibniz). We modernized and Americanized those primary texts originally written in English; in particular, we have adopted an open style of punctuation. A modernization we did not undertake is the discarding of italics and the use of uppercase words for emphasis, mention, and so on. This early modern practice does not seem to be a significant bar to comprehension for twenty-first-century students. We also did not attempt to render historical texts into gender-neutral language. Of course, some will inevitably feel that our modernization has been too extensive, whereas others might have wished that we had made even greater emendations. We hope to have avoided both extremes, bearing in mind the needs of the readers for whom this anthology is intended.

This anthology is designed for the one-semester or one-quarter course often called "The Rationalists." It is a slightly revised and expanded version of approximately the first third of our anthology, *Modern Philosophy: An Anthology of Primary Sources*. We have included the selection from Malebranche (from the second third of that anthology), along with a new selection of Descartes's *Principles* and a bit more of Newton's works (the "General Scholium" from the second edition of the *Principia* and "Query 31" from the *Optics*).

We are very grateful to the authors and translators named in the footnotes at the start of each selection for permission to reproduce their materials.[1] We would also like to thank Karl Ameriks, Daniel Garber, Marjorie Grene, Patricia Kitcher, Nelson Lande, Joseph Pitt, Tad Schmaltz, and Kenneth Winkler for their many helpful suggestions concerning what selections to include. Finally, we wish to thank Deborah Wilkes at Hackett, who once again has been tremendously helpful and supportive.

---

1. In all selections except Malebranche, footnotes are those of the editors or translators.

# 1. DESCARTES'S *MEDITATIONS* AND ASSOCIATED TEXTS

René Descartes was born in 1596 at La Haye, in Touraine, France. He became one of the central intellectual figures of the seventeenth century, making major contributions to metaphysics, natural philosophy, and mathematics. Descartes was educated at the Jesuit College of La Flèche (in Anjou) from about 1607 to about 1615; he received a master's degree in law from Poitier in 1616. The next year he went to the Netherlands and joined the army of Prince Maurice of Nassau; at Breda he made the acquaintance of Isaac Beeckman, who introduced him to a "physico-mathematical" way of doing natural philosophy. When traveling in Germany, he had a series of dreams (on November 10, 1619) about the unity of science; his first major philosophical project, the *Rules for the Direction of the Mind*, which he composed (ca. 1618–28) but did not finish, was devoted to that theme. Instead, Descartes turned his thoughts to physical and astronomical topics and worked on *The World or Treatise on Light*; unfortunately, he suppressed the publication of this treatise when he learned of Galileo's condemnation in 1633. His first printed work was the *Discourse on Method* (1637) to which he appended the less controversial scientific essays, *Dioptrics*, *Meteors*, and *Geometry*. A few years

later, he expanded Part IV of the *Discourse* into *Meditations on First Philosophy*, which he published with sets of objections and replies (1641). In 1644, Descartes further revised his philosophy into textbook form and disseminated it with his physics as *Principles of Philosophy*. Although he spent most of his adult life in seclusion in the Netherlands, in 1649, he went to Sweden at the invitation of Queen Christina, but he did not last the winter, dying in Stockholm in 1650.[1]

1. Descartes's philosophical works, most of his mathematical and scientific treatises, and much of his correspondence are available in English translation. References to Descartes's works are to the standard edition by Charles Adam and Paul Tannery, *Oeuvres de Descartes* (2nd ed., Paris: Vrin, 1964–74); references to this edition are abbreviated as AT volume, page. For more on Descartes's philosophy, see Margaret Wilson, *Descartes* (London: Routledge and Kegan Paul, 1978); Edwin M. Curley, *Descartes against the Skeptics* (Cambridge, Mass.: Harvard University Press, 1978); Martial Gueroult, *Descartes's Philosophy Interpreted According to the Order of Reasons*, trans. R. Ariew (Minneapolis: University of Minnesota Press, 1984–85), 2 vols.; Marjorie Grene, *Descartes* (Indianapolis: Hackett Publishing Company, 1998); John Cottingham, ed., *The Cambridge Companion to Descartes* (New York: Cambridge University Press, 1992). For the relation between Descartes's philosophy and his physics, see Daniel Garber, *Descartes's Metaphysical Physics* (Chicago: University of Chicago Press, 1992). To situate Descartes's philosophy among that of his contemporaries, see Roger

The *Meditations* is one of the great works of philosophy, a seminal treatise for subsequent philosophers. In its compact form, it raises most of the problems that they will need to address: skepticism, the existence and nature of the self, the existence of God, the possibility of error, the nature of truth, including the truth of mathematics, the essence and existence of bodies, and so on. The great Cartesian commentator Martial Gueroult described the *Meditations* as a diptych, a work of art in two panels. He saw the first three Meditations as the first panel, ruled by the darkness of the principle of universal deception, with a battle being fought against it by the truth of the existence of the self—a mere point of light—a narrow but piercing exception to the principle of doubt, culminating with the defeat of the principle and the victory of the exception. The second panel is then ruled by the blinding light of God's absolute veracity—that is, the principle of universal truth—and fought against by the existence of error, a narrow point of darkness and seeming exception to that principle, puncturing the light of universal veracity in the same way that the existence of the self punctured the darkness of universal deception. However, here the battle culminates with the victory of the principle, the triumph of light over darkness. Gueroult saw the Cartesian movement as unified in that its perspectives are complementary from beginning to end: to the hypothesis of the evil genius, which plays a role of segregation, elimination, and purification in the first three Meditations, corresponds the dogma of divine veracity, which is a heuristic principle, an organ of reintegration, and a rule of discipline in the last three Meditations. Thus, Gueroult thought of the *Meditations* as a single block of certainty, in which everything is so arranged that nothing can be taken away without the whole thing's dissolving.

But beyond the tight composition of the *Meditations* and its closely woven fabric, one might ask about the purpose of the work, what it was intended to do. Here one can point to the integration of the argument

of the *Meditations* into a larger framework as the foundation of the new sciences. As Descartes said to his close correspondent Marin Mersenne, "I may tell you, between ourselves, that these six Meditations contain all the foundations of my physics. But please do not tell people, for that might make it harder for supporters of Aristotle to approve of them. I hope that readers will gradually get used to my principles, and recognize their truth, before they notice that they destroy the principles of Aristotle" (January 18, 1641). The *Meditations* attempts a complete intellectual revolution: the replacement of Aristotelian philosophy with a new philosophy in order to replace Aristotelian science with a new science. For a seventeenth-century Aristotelian, a body is matter informed by substantial and accidental forms, and change is explained by the gain or loss of such forms: in mutation by the acquisition of a substantial form, and in what Aristotelians would call true motion (that is, augmentation and diminution, alteration, or local motion) by the successive acquisition of places or of qualitative or quantitative forms. The mechanist program consisted of doing away with qualitative forms and reducing all changes to something mathematically quantifiable: matter in motion. As Descartes said in *The World*, not only the four qualities called heat, cold, moistness, and dryness, "but also all the others (and even all the forms of inanimate bodies) can be explained without the need of supposing for that purpose anything in their matter other than the motion, size, shape, and arrangement of its parts" (*The World*, chap. 5). Accordingly, Descartes does not need substantial forms and does not explain mutation as change of form, whether substantial or accidental. He finds no forms other than the ones he has described quantitatively. For Descartes, the only motion is local motion; hence he states, "The philosophers also suppose several motions that they think can be accomplished without any body changing place. . . . As for me, I know of none except the one which is easiest to conceive . . . , the motion by which bodies pass from one place to another" (*The World*, chap. 7).

One can glimpse the mechanist project in the *Discourse on Method*, in which an earlier version of the *Meditations* is embedded together with a method of philosophizing and a few scientific treatises as samples

Ariew, John Cottingham, and Tom Sorell, eds. and trans., *Cambridge Texts in Context: Descartes's Meditations* (Cambridge: Cambridge University Press, 1998).

of the method. Thus the context of the *Meditations* is the same as Francis Bacon's and Galileo Galilei's, except that Descartes does not champion induction, and although he advances the corpuscularian or mechanical philosophy to the extent that he reduces physical objects to matter in motion, he makes it clear that he does not accept the reality of atoms as ultimate indivisible constituents of matter.

The *Meditations* solicited many objections, from those of Thomas Hobbes, Antoine Arnauld, and Pierre Gassendi, which are published with the work, to subsequent ones from G. W. Leibniz and Blaise Pascal to Baruch Spinoza, John Locke, and the rest. Indeed, it would not be an exaggeration to state that all of modern philosophy constitutes reactions to and criticisms of Descartes's *Meditations*.

# Francis Bacon, *New Organon* (1620)[1]

*Francis Bacon was born in London in 1561; he was a successful lawyer, politician, and essayist. Bacon entered parliament in 1584 and held various administrative political and judicial offices; he rose to Lord Chancellor, was knighted, became Lord Verulam and ultimately Viscount St. Albans. His political career ended in 1621 when he confessed to bribery. He died in London in 1626. His philosophical views, in particular* The Advancement of Learning *(1605) and* Novum Organum[2] *(1620), were enormously influential on later seventeenth-century thought, especially with scientific institutions such as the Royal Society. From his earliest days at Trinity College, Cambridge, Bacon was preoccupied with a philosophy and scientific method that would entail a decisive break with the past. He came to believe that the traditional process of deduction from supposedly self-evident principles had produced little new scientific knowledge; it either gave back what we already knew or else led us astray by giving illusory support to our confusions. What was needed was a confrontation with various obstacles to knowledge, with various idols, that is, false appearances. Also needed was the systematic understanding and control of nature based on an empirical method. The axioms of Bacon's philosophy would be statements of natural causes and laws derived by induction from scientific observation and experiment.[3]*

1. Man, being the servant and interpreter of Nature, can do and understand so much and so much only as he has observed in fact or in thought of the course of nature; beyond this he neither knows anything nor can do anything.

2. Neither the naked hand nor the understanding left to itself can effect much. It is by instruments and helps that the work is done, which are as much wanted for the understanding as for the hand. And as the instruments of hand either give motion or guide it, so the instruments of the mind supply either suggestions for the understanding or cautions.

3. Human knowledge and human power meet in one; for where the cause is not known, the effect cannot be produced. Nature to be commanded must be obeyed; and that which is in contemplation is as the cause is in operation as the rule. [ . . . ]

11. As the sciences we now have do not help us in finding out new works, so neither does the logic we now have help us in finding out new sciences.

1. From *Works*, ed. J. M. Robertson (London: Routledge, 1905), English, modified.
2. That is, *New Organon* or new scientific method, contrasting to Aristotle's logical and methodological works, known collectively as the Organon.

3. For more about Bacon, see Antonio Perez-Ramos, *Francis Bacon's Idea of Science and the Maker's Knowledge Tradition* (Oxford: Oxford University Press, 1988) or Markku Peltonen, ed., *The Cambridge Companion to Bacon* (Cambridge: Cambridge University Press, 1996).

12. The logic now in use serves rather to fix and give stability to the errors which have their foundation in commonly received notions than to help the search for truth. So it does more harm than good.

13. The syllogism is not applied to the first principles of science, and is applied in vain to intermediate axioms, being no match for the subtlety of nature. It commands assent therefore to the proposition, but does not take hold of the thing.

14. The syllogism consists of propositions, propositions consist of words, words are symbols of notions. Therefore, if the notions themselves (which is the root of the matter) are confused and too hastily abstracted from the facts, there can be no firmness in the superstructure. Our only hope therefore lies in a true induction.

15. There is no soundness in our notions, whether logical or physical. Substance, quality, passion, essence itself are not sound notions; much less are heavy, light, dense, rare, moist, dry, generation, corruption, attraction, repulsion, element, matter, form, and the like. But all are fantastical and ill defined.

16. Our notions of less general species, as man, dog, dove, and of the intermediate perceptions of the sense, as hot, cold, black, white, do not materially mislead us; yet even these are sometimes confused by the flux and alteration of matter and the mixing of one thing with another. All the others which men have adopted up to now are but wanderings, not being abstracted and formed from things by proper methods.

17. Nor is there less willfulness and wandering in the construction of axioms than in the formation of notions, not excepting even those very principles which are obtained by common induction, but much more in the axioms and lower propositions educed by the syllogism.

18. The discoveries which have been made in the sciences up to now are such as lie close to vulgar notions, scarcely beneath the surface. In order to penetrate into the inner and further recesses of nature, it is necessary that both notions and axioms be derived from things by a more sure and guarded way, and that a method of intellectual operation be introduced altogether better and more certain.

19. There are and can be only two ways of searching into and discovering truth. The one flies from the senses and particulars to the most general axioms, and from these principles, the truth of which it takes for settled and immovable, proceeds to judgment and to the discovery of middle axioms. And this way is now in fashion. The other derives axioms from the senses and particulars, rising by a gradual and unbroken ascent, so that it arrives at the most general axioms last of all. This is the true way, but as yet untried.

20. The understanding left to itself takes the same course (namely the former) which it takes in accordance with logical order. For the mind longs to spring up to positions of higher generality, that it may find rest there, and so after a little while wearies of experiment. But this evil is increased by logic, because of the order and solemnity of its disputations.

21. The understanding left to itself, in a sober, patient, and grave mind, especially if it is not hindered by received doctrines, tries a little that other way, which is the right one, but with little progress; for the understanding, unless directed and assisted, is a thing unequal, and quite unfit to contend with the obscurity of things.

22. Both ways set out from the senses and particulars, and rest in the lightest generalities, but the difference between them is infinite. For the one just glances at experiment and particulars in passing, the other dwells duly and orderly among them. The one, again, begins at once by establishing certain abstract and useless generalities, the other rises by gradual steps to that which is prior and better known in the order of nature.

23. There is a great difference between the idols of the human mind and the ideas of the divine, that is to say, between certain empty dogmas, and the true signatures and marks set upon the worlds of creation as they are found in nature.

24. It cannot be that axioms established by argumentation should avail for the discovery of new works, for the subtlety of nature is greater many times over than the subtlety of argument. But axioms duly and orderly formed from particulars easily discover the way to new particulars, and thus render sciences active.

25. The axioms now in use, having been suggested by a scanty and manipular experience and a few particulars of most general occurrence, are made for

the most part just large enough to fit and take these in; and therefore it is no wonder if they do not lead to new particulars. And if some opposite instance, not observed or not known before, chances to come in the way, the axiom is rescued and preserved by some frivolous distinction; whereas the truer course would be to correct the axiom itself.

26. The conclusions of human reasoning as ordinarily applied in matters of nature, I call for the sake of distinction *anticipations of nature* (as something rash or premature). That reason which is elicited from facts by a just and methodical process, I call *interpretation of nature.*

27. Anticipations are a sufficiently firm ground for consent; for even if men went mad all after the same fashion, they might agree with one another well enough.

28. For the winning of assent, indeed, anticipations are far more powerful than interpretations, because being collected from a few instances, and those for the most part of familiar occurrence, they straightway touch the understanding and fill the imagination; whereas interpretations, on the other hand, being gathered here and there from very various and widely dispersed facts, cannot suddenly strike the understanding; and therefore they must necessarily, in respect of the opinions of the time, seem harsh and out of tune, much as the mysteries of faith do.

29. In sciences founded on opinions and dogmas, the use of anticipations and logic is good; for in them the object is to command assent to the propositions, not to master the thing.

30. Though all the wits of all the ages should meet together and combine and transmit their labors, yet great progress will never be made in science by means of anticipations; for radical errors in the first concoction of the mind are not to be cured by the excellence of subsequent functions and remedies.

31. It is idle to expect any great advancement in science from the superinducing and engrafting of new things upon old. We must begin anew from the very foundations, unless we would revolve forever in a circle with mean and contemptible progress. [. . .]

36. One method of discovery alone remains to us, which is simply this: We must lead men to the particulars themselves, and their series and order, while men on their side must force themselves for a while to lay their notions by and begin to familiarize themselves with facts.

37. The doctrine of those who have denied certainty could be attained at all has some agreement with my way of proceeding at the first setting out, but they end in being infinitely separated and opposed. For the holders of that doctrine assert simply that nothing can be known. I also assert that not much can be known in nature by the way which is now in use. But then they go on to destroy the authority of the senses and understanding; whereas I proceed to devise and supply helps for the same.

38. The idols and false notions which are now in possession of the human understanding, and have taken deep root in there, not only so beset men's minds that truth can hardly find entrance, but even after entrance is obtained, they will again, in the very instauration of the sciences, meet and trouble us, unless men being forewarned of the danger fortify themselves as far as may be against their assaults.

39. There are four classes of idols that beset men's minds. To these for distinction's sake I have assigned names, calling the first class *idols of the tribe*; the second, *idols of the cave*; the third, *idols of the market place*; the fourth, *idols of the theater.*

40. The formation of ideas and axioms by induction is without doubt the proper remedy to be applied for the keeping off and clearing away of idols. To point them out, however, is of great use; for the doctrine of idols is to the interpretation of nature what the doctrine of the refutation of sophisms is to common logic.

41. The idols of the tribe have their foundation in human nature itself, and in the tribe or race of men. For it is a false assertion that the sense of man is the measure of things. On the contrary, all perceptions both of the sense and of the mind are according to the measure of the individual, and not according to the measure of the universe. And the human understanding is like a false mirror, which, receiving rays irregularly, distorts and discolors the nature of things by mingling its own nature with it.

42. The idols of the cave are the idols of the individual man. For every one (besides the errors common to human nature in general) has a cave or den of his own, which refracts and discolors the light of nature, owing either to his own proper and peculiar nature;

or to his education and conversation with others; or to the reading of books and the authority of those whom he esteems and admires; or to the differences of impressions, accordingly as they take place in a mind preoccupied and predisposed or in a mind indifferent and settled; or the like. So that the spirit of man (according as it is meted out to different individuals) is in fact a thing variable and full of perturbation, and governed as it were by chance. Whence it was well observed by Heraclitus that men look for sciences in their own lesser worlds, and not in the greater or common world.

43. There are also idols formed by the intercourse and association of men with each other, which I call idols of the market place, on account of the commerce and consort of men there. For it is by discourse that men associate; and words are imposed according to the apprehension of the vulgar. And therefore the ill and unfit choice of words wonderfully obstructs the understanding. Nor do the definitions or explanations, with what in some things learned men are accustomed to guard and defend themselves, by any means set the matter right. But words plainly force and overrule the understanding, and throw all into confusion, and lead men away into numberless empty controversies and idle fancies.

44. Lastly, there are idols which have immigrated into men's minds from the various dogmas of philosophies, and also from wrong laws of demonstration. These I call idols of the theater, because in my judgment all the received systems are but so many stage plays, representing worlds of their own creation after an unreal and scenic fashion. Nor is it only of the systems now in vogue or only of the ancient sects and philosophies that I speak; for many more plays of the same kind may yet be composed and in like artificial manner set forth, seeing that the most widely different errors have causes which are for the most part alike. Neither again do I mean this only of entire systems, but also of many principles and axioms in science which by tradition, credulity, and negligence have come to be received.

But of these several kinds of idols I must speak more largely and exactly, that the understanding may be duly cautioned.

45. The human understanding is of its own nature prone to suppose the existence of more order and regularity in the world than it finds. And though there may be things in nature which are singular and unmatched, yet it devises for them parallels and conjugates relatives which do not exist. Hence the fiction that all the celestial bodies move in perfect circles, spirals, and dragons being (except in name) utterly rejected. Hence too the element of fire with its own orb is brought in to make up the square with the other three which the sense perceives. Hence also the ratio of the density of the so-called elements is arbitrarily fixed at ten to one. And so on of the other dreams. And these fancies affect not only dogmas, but also simple notions.

46. The human understanding when it has once adopted an opinion (either as being the received opinion or as being agreeable to itself) draws all other things to support and agree with it. And though there is a greater number and weight of instances to be found on the other side, yet it either neglects and despises these, or else by some distinction sets aside and rejects, in order that by this great and pernicious predetermination the authority of its former conclusions may remain inviolate. And therefore it was a good answer that was made by one who, when they showed him hanging in a temple a picture of those who had paid their vows as having escaped shipwreck, and would have him say whether he did not now acknowledge the power of the gods; "Yes," he asked again, "but where are the pictures of those who were drowned after their vows?" And such is the way of all superstition, whether in astrology, dreams, omens, divine judgments, or the like, in which men, having a delight in such vanities, notice the events where they are fulfilled, but where they fail, though this happens much more often, neglect and pass them by. But this mischief insinuates itself with much more subtlety into philosophy and the sciences, in which the first conclusion colors and brings into conformity with itself all that come after, though far sounder and better. Besides, independently of that delight and vanity which I have described, it is the peculiar and perpetual error of the human intellect to be more moved and excited by affirmatives than by negatives, whereas it ought properly to hold itself indifferently disposed towards both alike. Indeed, in the establishment of any true axiom, the negative instance is the more forcible of the two.

# Galileo Galilei, *The Assayer* (1623), "Corpuscularianism"[1]

Galileo Galilei was born in Pisa in 1564. He studied at the University of Pisa, became lecturer in mathematics there in 1592, and then lectured at the University of Padua from 1592 to 1610. In 1610, he constructed a telescope and made observations of the moon and of the satellites of Jupiter, describing his findings in Sidereal Messenger (1610). As a result of the great popularity of that work, he moved to Florence as "Chief Philosopher and Mathematician" to the court of the Cosimo of Medici, Grand Duke of Tuscany (1610–42). In 1615, he was denounced by the Inquisition for his support of Copernican astronomy (or heliocentrism) and went to Rome to defend it, but it was condemned by the Church in 1616. Years later, in 1633, he was summoned to Rome, forced to retract his views, and placed under permanent house arrest at Arcetri (near Florence). He died there in 1642. Galileo realized that a successful defense of Copernican astronomy, as suggested by his Sidereal Messenger and Letters on Sunspots (1613) and as discussed in his Dialogues Concerning the Two Chief World Systems (1632), would require a new physics, together with an altered philosophy and theology. He sketched some aspects of the new physics in Discourse on the Two New Sci-

ences (1638) and argued for a change in relations between theology and science in the Letter to the Grand Duchess Christina on the Use of Biblical Quotations in Matters of Science (1615); in The Assayer (1623), Galileo advanced corpuscularian perspectives in the methodology of science and sketched some philosophical views about causality, perception, and ontology.[2] However interesting and well-fashioned is the corpuscularian section of The Assayer—especially coming from so important a figure in the history of science—it should be noted that there were very many disparate sources for corpuscularian ideas in the early seventeenth century.[3]

In accordance with the promise which I made to Your Excellency, I shall certainly state my ideas concerning the proposition "Motion is the cause of heat," explain-

1. Editors' title. Translated from the Italian by A. C. Danto. From *Sources in Western Civilization*, by permission of Arthur Danto and Columbia University Press.

2. English translations are available for all of Galileo's major works: *Sidereal Messenger, Letters on Sunspots, The Assayer, Two Chief World Systems,* and *Two New Sciences*. For more about Galileo, see Pietro Redondi, *Galileo Heretic* (Princeton: Princeton University Press, 1987); Richard J. Blackwell, *Galileo, Bellarmine, and the Bible* (Notre Dame, Ind.: University of Notre Dame Press, 1991); or Mario Biaggioli, *Galileo Courtier* (Chicago: The University of Chicago Press, 1993).

3. Lucretius's *De rerum natura* (*On the Nature of Things*) was probably the most widely available source for corpuscularianism; Descartes most likely learned his corpuscularianism from Isaac Beeckman.

ing in what way it appears to me to be true. But first it will be necessary for me to say a few words concerning that which we call "heat," for I strongly suspect that the commonly held conception of the matter is very far from the truth, inasmuch as heat is generally believed to be a true accident, affection, or quality which actually resides in the material which we feel to be heated.

Now, whenever I conceive of any material or corporeal substance, I am necessarily constrained to conceive of that substance as bounded and as possessing this or that shape, as large or small in relationship to some other body, as in this or that place during this or that time, as in motion or at rest, as in contact or not in contact with some other body, as being one, many, or few—and by no stretch of imagination can I conceive of any corporeal body apart from these conditions. But I do not at all feel myself compelled to conceive of bodies as necessarily conjoined with such further conditions as being red or white, bitter or sweet, having sound or being mute, or possessing a pleasant or unpleasant fragrance. On the contrary, were they not escorted by our physical senses, perhaps neither reason nor understanding would ever, by themselves, arrive at such notions. I think, therefore, that these tastes, odors, colors, etc., so far as their objective existence is concerned, are nothing but mere names for something which resides exclusively in our sensitive body *(corpo sensitivo)*, so that if the perceiving creatures were removed, all of these qualities would be annihilated and abolished from existence. But just because we have given special names to these qualities, different from the names we have given to the primary and real properties, we are tempted into believing that the former really and truly exist as well as the latter.

An example, I believe, will clearly explain my concept. Suppose I pass my hand, first over a marble statue, then over a living man. So far as the hand, considered in itself, is concerned, it will act in an identical way upon each of these objects; that is, the primary qualities of motion and contact will similarly affect the two objects, and we would use identical language to describe this in each case. But the living body, which I subject to this experiment, will feel itself affected in various ways, depending upon the

part of the body I happen to touch; for example, should it be touched on the sole of the foot or the kneecap, or under the armpit, it will feel, in addition to simple contact, a further affection to which we have given a special name: we call it "tickling." This latter affection is altogether our own, and is not at all a property of the hand itself. And it seems to me that he would be gravely in error who would assert that the hand, in addition to movement and contact, intrinsically possesses another and different faculty which we might call the "tickling faculty," as though tickling were a resident property of the hand *per se*. Again, a piece of paper or a feather, when gently rubbed over any part of our body whatsoever, will in itself act everywhere in an identical way; it will, namely, move and contact. But we, should we be touched between the eyes, on the tip of the nose, or under the nostrils, will feel an almost intolerable titillation—while if touched in other places, we will scarcely feel anything at all. Now this titillation is completely ours and not the feather's, so that if the living, sensing body were removed, nothing would remain of the titillation but an empty name. And I believe that many other qualities, such as taste, odor, color, and so on, often predicated of natural bodies, have a similar and no greater existence than this.

A solid body and, so to speak, one that is sufficiently heavy, when moved and applied against any part of my body whatsoever, will produce in me the sensation which we call "touch." Although this sense is to be found in every part of the body, it appears principally to reside in the palm of the hand, and even more so in the fingertips, with which we can feel the most minute differences of roughness, texture, and softness and hardness—differences which the other parts of the body are less capable of distinguishing. Some among these tactile sensations are more pleasing than others, depending upon the differences of configuration of tangible bodies; that is to say, in accordance with whether they are smooth or irregular, sharp or dull, flexible or rigid. And the sense of touch, being more material than the other senses and being produced by the mass of the material itself, seems to correspond to the element of earth.

Since certain material bodies are continually resolving themselves into tiny particles, some of the particles, because they are heavier than air, will descend; and some of them, because they are lighter than air, will ascend. From this, perhaps, two further senses are born, for certain of the particles penetrate two parts of our body which are effectively more sensitive than the skin, which is incapable of feeling the incursion of materials which are too fine, subtle, or flexible. The descending particles are received by the upper surface of the tongue, and penetrating, they blend with its substance and moisture. Thus our tastes are caused, pleasant or harsh in accordance with variations in the contact of diversely shaped particles, and depending upon whether they are few or many, and whether they have high or low velocity. Other particles ascend, and entering the nostrils they penetrate the various nodes (*mammilule*) which are the instruments of smell; and these particles, in like manner through contact and motion, produce savoriness or unsavoriness—again depending upon whether the particles have this or that shape, high or low velocity, and whether they are many or few. It is remarkable how providently the tongue and nasal passages are situated and disposed, the former stretched beneath to receive the ingression of descending particles, and the latter so arranged as to receive those which ascend. The arrangement whereby the sense of taste is excited in us is perhaps analogous to the way in which fluids descend through the air, and the stimulation of the sense of smell may be compared to the manner in which flames ascend in it.

There remains the element of air, which corresponds to the sense of sound. Sounds come to us indiscriminately, from above and below and from either side, since we are so constituted as to be equally disposed to every direction of the air's movement; and the ear is so situated as to accommodate itself in the highest possible degree to any position in space. Sounds, then, are produced in us and felt when (without any special quality of harmoniousness or dissonance) there is a rapid vibration of air, forming minutely small waves, which move certain cartilages of a certain drum which is in our ear. The various external ways in which this wave-motion of the air is produced are manifold, but can in large part be reduced to the vibrating of bodies which strike the air and form the waves which spread out with great velocity. High

frequencies give rise to high tones; low frequencies give rise to low tones, but I cannot believe that there exists in external bodies anything, other than their size, shape, or motion (slow or rapid), which could excite in us our tastes, sounds, and odors. And indeed I should judge that, if ears, tongues, and noses be taken away, the number, shape, and motion of bodies would remain, but not their tastes, sounds, and odors. The latter, external to the living creature, I believe to be nothing but mere names, just as (a few lines back) I asserted tickling and titillation to be, if the armpit or the sensitive skin inside the nose were removed. As to the comparison between the four senses which we have mentioned and the four elements, I believe that the sense of sight, most excellent and noble of all the senses, is like light itself. It stands to the others in the same measure of comparative excellence as the finite stands to the infinite, the gradual to the instantaneous, the divisible to the indivisible, the darkness to the light. Of this sense, and all that pertains to it, I can pretend to understand but little; yet a great deal of time would not suffice for me to set forth even this little bit that I know, or (to put it more exactly) for me to sketch it out on paper. Therefore I shall ponder it in silence.

I return to my first proposition, having now shown how some affections, often reputed to be indwelling properties of some external body, have really no existence save in us, and apart from us are mere names. I confess myself to be very much inclined to believe that heat, too, is of this sort, and that those materials which produce and make felt in us the sense of heat and to which we give the general name "fire" consist of a multitude of tiny particles of such and such a shape, and having such and such a velocity. These, when they encounter our body, penetrate it by means of their extreme subtlety; and it is their contact, felt by us in their passage through our substance, which is the affection we call "heat." It will be pleasantly warm or unpleasantly hot depending upon the number and the velocity (greater or lesser) of these pricking, penetrating particles—pleasant if by their penetration our necessary perspiring is facilitated, unpleasant if their penetrating effects too great a division and dissolution of our substance. In sum, the operation of fire, considered in itself, is nothing but movement, or the penetration of bodies by its extreme subtlety, quickly or slowly, depending upon the number and velocity of tiny corpuscles of flame (*ignicoli*) and upon the greater or lesser density of the bodies concerned. Many bodies dissolve in such a manner that the major part of them becomes transformed into further corpuscles of flame; and this dissolution continues as further dissolvable material is encountered. But that there exists in fire, apart from shape, number, movement, penetration, and contact, some further quality which we call "heat," I cannot believe. And I again judge that heat is altogether subjective, so that if the living, sensitive body is removed, what we call heat would be nothing but a simple word. Since it is the case that this affection is produced in us by passage of tiny corpuscles of flame through our substance and their contact with it, it is obvious that once this motion ceases, their operation upon us will be null. It is thus that we perceive that a quantity of fire, retained in the pores and pits of a piece of calcified stone, does not heat—even if we hold it in the palm of our hand—because the flame remains stationary in the stone. But should we swish the stone in water where, because of its weight, it has greater propensity for movement and where the pits of the stone open somewhat, the corpuscles of flame will escape and, encountering our hand, will penetrate it, so that we will feel heat. Since, in order for heat to be stimulated in us, the mere presence of corpuscles of flame is not by itself sufficient, and since movement is required in addition, it is with considerable reason that I declare motion to be the cause of heat.

This or that movement by which a scantling or other piece of wood is burned up or by which lead and other metals are melted will continue so long as the corpuscles of flame, moved either by their own velocity or (if this be insufficient) aided by a strong blast from a bellows, continue to penetrate the body in question; the former will resolve itself into further corpuscles of flame or into ash; the latter will liquefy and be rendered fluid like water. From a common-sense point of view, to assert that that which moves a stone, piece of iron, or a stick, is what *heats* it, seems like an extreme vanity. But the friction produced when two hard bodies are rubbed together, which either reduces them to fine flying particles or permits the corpuscles of flame contained in them to escape, can finally be analyzed as motion. And the particles, when they encounter our body and penetrate and tear through it, are felt, in their motion and contact, by the living creature, who thus feels those pleasant or unpleasant affections which we call "heat," "burning," or "scorching."

Perhaps while this pulverizing and attrition continue, and remain confined to the particles themselves, their motion will be temporary and their operation will be merely that of heating. But once we arrive at the point of ultimate and maximum dissolution into truly indivisible atoms, light itself may be created, with an instantaneous motion or (I should rather say) an instantaneous diffusion and expansion, capable—I do not know if by the atoms' subtlety, rarity, immateriality, or by different and as yet unspecifiable conditions—capable, I say, of filling vast spaces.

But I should not like, Your Excellency, inadvertently to engulf myself in an infinite ocean without the means to find my way back to port. Nor should I like, while removing one doubt, to give birth to a hundred more, as I fear might in part be the case even in this timid venture from shore. Therefore, I shall await a more opportune moment to re-embark.

# René Descartes, *Discourse on the Method for Conducting One's Reason Well and for Seeking the Truth in the Sciences* (1637)[1]

## [Author's Preface]

*If this discourse seems too long to be read at one time, it may be divided into six parts. In the first part, you will find various considerations concerning the sciences; in the second part, the chief rules of the method which the author has sought; in the third part, some of the rules of morality which he has derived from this method; in the fourth part, the arguments by which he proves the existence of God and of the human soul, which are the foundations of his metaphysics; in the fifth part, the order of the questions in physics that he has investigated, and particularly the explanation of the movement of the heart and of other difficulties that pertain to medicine, as well as the difference between our soul and that of beasts; and in the final part, what things the author believes are required in order to advance further in the investigation of nature than the author has done, and what reasons have made him write.*

## Part I

Good sense is the best distributed thing in the world, for everyone thinks himself to be so well endowed with it that even those who are the most difficult to please in everything else are not at all wont to desire more of it than they have. It is not likely that everyone is mistaken in this. Rather, it provides evidence that the power of judging well and of distinguishing the true from the false (which is, properly speaking, what people call "good sense" or "reason") is naturally equal in all men, and that the diversity of our opinions does not arise from the fact that some people are more reasonable than others, but solely from the fact that we lead our thoughts along different paths and do not take the same things into consideration. For it is not enough to have a good mind; the main thing is to apply it well. The greatest souls are capable of the greatest vices as well as of the greatest virtues. And those who proceed only very slowly can make much greater progress, provided they always follow the right path, than do those who hurry and stray from it.

For myself, I have never presumed that my mind was in any respect more perfect than that of ordinary men. In fact, I have often desired to have as quick a wit, or as keen and distinct an imagination, or as full and responsive a memory as some other people. And other than these I know of no qualities that serve in the perfecting of the mind, for as to reason or sense, inasmuch as it alone makes us men and distinguishes

---

1. Translated from the French by Donald Cress in René Descartes, *Discourse on Method* (Indianapolis: Hackett Publishing Company, 1980).

us from the beasts, I prefer to believe that it exists whole and entire in each of us, and in this to follow the opinion commonly held by the philosophers, who say that there are differences of degree only between accidents, but not at all between forms or natures of individuals of the same species.

But I shall have no fear of saying that I think I have been rather fortunate to have, since my youth, found myself on certain paths that have led me to considerations and maxims from which I have formed a method by which, it seems to me, I have the means to increase my knowledge by degrees and to raise it little by little to the highest point which the mediocrity of my mind and the short duration of my life will be able to allow it to attain. For I have already reaped from it such a harvest that, although I try, in judgments I make of myself, always to lean more on the side of diffidence than of presumption, and although, looking with a philosopher's eye at the various actions and enterprises of all men, there is hardly one of them that does not seem to me vain and useless, I cannot but take immense satisfaction in the progress that I think I have already made in the search for truth, and I cannot but envisage such hopes for the future that if, among the occupations of men purely as men, there is one that is solidly good and important, I dare to believe that it is the one I have chosen.

All the same, it could be that I am mistaken, and what I take for gold and diamonds is perhaps nothing but a bit of copper and glass. I know how much we are prone to err in what affects us, and also how much the judgments made by our friends should be distrusted when these judgments are in our favor. But I will be very happy to show in this discourse what paths I have followed and to represent my life in it as if in a picture, so that everyone may judge it for himself; and that, learning from the common response the opinions one will have of it, this may be a new means of teaching myself, which I shall add to those that I am accustomed to using.

Thus my purpose here is not to teach the method that everyone ought to follow in order to conduct his reason well, but merely to show how I have tried to conduct my own. Those who take it upon themselves to give precepts must regard themselves as more competent than those to whom they give them; and if

they are found wanting in the least detail, they are to blame. But putting forward this essay merely as a story or, if you prefer, as a fable in which, among some examples one can imitate, one will perhaps also find many others which one will have reason not to follow, I hope that it will be useful to some without being harmful to anyone, and that everyone will be grateful to me for my frankness.

I have been nourished on letters since my childhood, and because I was convinced that by means of them one could acquire a clear and assured knowledge of everything that is useful in life, I had a tremendous desire to master them. But as soon as I had completed this entire course of study, at the end of which one is ordinarily received into the ranks of the learned, I completely changed my mind. For I found myself confounded by so many doubts and errors that it seemed to me that I had not gained any profit from my attempt to teach myself, except that more and more I had discovered my ignorance. And yet I was at one of the most renowned schools of Europe, where I thought there must be learned men, if in fact any such men existed anywhere on earth. There I had learned everything the others were learning; and, not content with the disciplines we were taught there, I had gone through all the books I could lay my hands on that treated those disciplines considered the most curious and most unusual. Moreover, I knew what judgments the others were making about me; and I did not at all see that I was rated inferior to my fellow students, even though there already were some among them who were destined to take the place of our teachers. And finally our age seemed to me to be just as flourishing and as fertile in good minds as any of the preceding ones. This made me feel free to judge all others by myself, and to think that there was no doctrine in the world that was of the sort that I had previously been led to hope for.

I did not, however, cease to hold in high regard the academic exercises with which we occupy ourselves in the schools. I knew that the languages learned there are necessary for the understanding of classical texts; that the charm of fables awakens the mind; that the memorable deeds recounted in histories uplift it, and, if read with discretion, aid in forming one's judgment; that the reading of all good books is like a conversation with the most honorable people of past ages, who were their authors, indeed, even like a set conversation in which they reveal to us only the best of their thoughts; that oratory has incomparable power and beauty; that poetry has quite ravishing delicacy and sweetness; that mathematics has some very subtle stratagems that can serve as much to satisfy the curious as to facilitate all the arts and to lessen men's labor; that writings dealing with morals contain many lessons and many exhortations to virtue that are very useful; that theology teaches one how to reach heaven; that philosophy provides the means of speaking plausibly about all things and of making oneself admired by the less learned; that jurisprudence, medicine, and the other sciences bring honors and riches to those who cultivate them; and, finally, that it is good to have examined all these disciplines, even the most superstition-ridden and the most false of them, in order to know their true worth and to guard against being deceived by them.

But I believed I had already given enough time to languages, and also to the reading of classical texts, both to their histories and to their fables. For conversing with those of other ages is about the same thing as traveling. It is good to know something of the customs of various peoples, so as to judge our own more soundly and so as not to think that everything that is contrary to our ways is ridiculous and against reason, as those who have seen nothing have a habit of doing. But when one takes too much time traveling, one eventually becomes a stranger in one's own country; and when one is too curious about what commonly took place in past ages, one usually remains quite ignorant of what is taking place in one's own country. Moreover, fables make one imagine many events to be possible which are not so at all. And even the most accurate histories, if they neither alter nor exaggerate the significance of things in order to render them more worthy of being read, almost always at least omit the baser and less noteworthy details. Consequently, the rest do not appear as they really are, and those who govern their own conduct by means of examples drawn from these texts are liable to fall into the extravagances of the knights of our romances and to conceive plans that are beyond their powers.

I held oratory in high regard and was enamored of poetry, but I thought both were gifts of the mind rather than fruits of study. Those who possess the strongest reasoning and who best order their thoughts in order to make them clear and intelligible can always best persuade others of what they are proposing, even if they were to speak only Low Breton[2] and had never learned rhetoric. And those who have the most pleasing rhetorical devices and who know how to express themselves with the most embellishment and sweetness would not fail to be the greatest poets, even if the art of poetry were unknown to them.

I delighted most of all in mathematics because of the certainty and the evidence of its reasonings. But I did not yet notice its true use, and, thinking that it was of service merely to the mechanical arts, I was astonished by the fact that no one had built anything more noble upon its foundations, given that they were so solid and firm. On the other hand, I compared the writings of the ancient pagans that deal with morals to very proud and very magnificent palaces that were built on nothing but sand and mud. They place virtues on a high plateau and make them appear to be valued more than anything else in the world, but they do not sufficiently instruct us about how to recognize them; and often what they call by so fine-sounding a name is nothing more than a kind of insensibility, pride, desperation, or parricide.

I revered our theology, and I desired as much as anyone else to reach heaven; but having learned as something very certain that the road to heaven is open no less to the most ignorant than to the most learned, and that the revealed truths guiding us there are beyond our understanding, I would not have dared to submit them to the frailty of my reasonings. And I thought that, in order to undertake an examination of these truths and to succeed in doing so, it would be necessary to have some extraordinary assistance from heaven and to be more than a man.

Concerning philosophy I shall say only that, seeing that it has been cultivated for many centuries by the most excellent minds that have ever lived and that, nevertheless, there still is nothing in it about which

2. This dialect was considered rather barbarous and hardly suitable for sophisticated literary endeavors.

there is not some dispute, and consequently nothing that is not doubtful, I was not at all so presumptuous as to hope to fare any better there than the others; and that, considering how many opinions there can be about the very same matter that are held by learned people without there ever being the possibility of more than one opinion being true, I deemed everything that was merely probable to be well nigh false.

Then, as for the other sciences, I judged that, insofar as they borrow their principles from philosophy, one could not have built anything solid upon such unstable foundations. And neither the honor nor the monetary gain they promised was sufficient to induce me to master them, for I did not perceive myself, thank God, to be in a condition that obliged me to make a career out of science in order to enhance my fortune. And although I did not make a point of rejecting glory after the manner of a Cynic, nevertheless I placed very little value on the glory that I could not hope to acquire except through false pretenses. And finally, as to the false doctrines, I thought I already knew well enough what they were worth, so as not to be liable to be deceived either by the promises of an alchemist, the predictions of an astrologer, the tricks of a magician, or the ruses or boasts of any of those who profess to know more than they do.

That is why, as soon as age permitted me to emerge from the supervision of my teachers, I completely abandoned the study of letters. And resolving to search for no knowledge other than what could be found within myself, or else in the great book of the world, I spent the rest of my youth traveling, seeing courts and armies, mingling with people of diverse temperaments and circumstances, gathering various experiences, testing myself in the encounters that fortune offered me, and everywhere engaging in such reflection upon the things that presented themselves that I was able to derive some profit from them. For it seemed to me that I could find much more truth in the reasonings that each person makes concerning matters that are important to him, and whose outcome ought to cost him dearly later on if he has judged badly, than in those reasonings engaged in by a man of letters in his study, which touch on speculations that produce no effect and are of no other consequence to him except perhaps that, the more they

are removed from common sense, the more pride he will take in them, for he will have to employ that much more wit and ingenuity in attempting to render them plausible. And I have always had an especially great desire to learn to distinguish the true from the false, in order to see my way clearly in my actions, and to go forward with confidence in this life.

It is true that, so long as I merely considered the customs of other men, I found hardly anything there about which to be confident, and that I noticed there was about as much diversity as I had previously found among the opinions of philosophers. Thus the greatest profit I derived from this was that, on seeing many things that, although they seem to us very extravagant and ridiculous, do not cease to be commonly accepted and approved among other great peoples, I learned not to believe anything too firmly of which I had been persuaded only by example and custom; and thus I little by little freed myself from many errors that can darken our natural light and render us less able to listen to reason. But after I had spent some years thus studying in the book of the world and in trying to gain some experience, I resolved one day to study within myself too and to spend all the powers of my mind in choosing the paths that I should follow. In this I had much more success, it seems to me, than had I never left either my country or my books.

## Part II

I was then in Germany, where the occasion of the wars which are not yet over there[3] had called me; and as I was returning to the army from the coronation of the emperor, the onset of winter detained me in quarters where, finding no conversation to divert me and fortunately having no worries or passions to trouble me, I remained for an entire day shut up by myself in a stove-heated room,[4] where I was completely free to converse with myself about my thoughts. Among them, one of the first was that it occurred to me to consider that there is often not as much perfection

3. Thirty Years War (1618–48).
4. There is no need to allege that Descartes sat in or on a stove. A *poêle* is simply a room heated by an earthenware stove. Cf. E. Gilson, *Discours de la méthode: texte et commentaire* (Paris: Vrin, 1967), p. 157.

in works composed of many pieces and made by the hands of various master craftsmen as there is in those works on which but a single individual has worked. Thus one sees that buildings undertaken and completed by a single architect are usually more attractive and better ordered than those which many architects have tried to patch up by using old walls that had been built for other purposes. Thus those ancient cities that were once mere villages and in the course of time have become large towns are usually so poorly laid out, compared to those well-ordered places that an engineer traces out on a vacant plain as it suits his fancy, that even though, upon considering each building one by one in the former sort, one often finds as much, if not more art, than one finds in those of the latter; still, upon seeing how the buildings are arranged—here a large one, there a small one—and how they make the streets crooked and uneven, one would say that it is chance rather than the will of some men using reason that has arranged them thus. And if one considers that there have nevertheless always been officials responsible for seeing that private buildings contribute to the attractiveness of public areas, one will well understand that it is difficult to make things that are very finely crafted by laboring only on the works of others. Thus I imagined that peoples who, having once been half-savages and having been civilized only little by little, have made their laws only to the extent that the inconvenience due to crimes and quarrels forced them to do so, could not be as well ordered as those who, from the very beginning of their coming together, have followed the fundamental precepts of some prudent legislator. Likewise, it is quite certain that the state of the true religion, whose ordinances were made by God alone, must be incomparably better ordered than all the others. And, speaking of things human, I believe that if Sparta was at one time very flourishing, this was not because of the goodness of each one of its laws taken by itself, seeing that many of them were very strange and even contrary to good morals, but because, having been devised by a single individual, they all tended toward the same end. And thus I thought that book learning, at least the kind whose reasonings are merely probable and that do not have

any demonstrations, having been composed and enlarged little by little from the opinions of many different persons, does not draw nearly so close to the truth as the simple reasonings that a man of good sense can naturally make about the things he encounters. And thus, too, I thought that, because we were all children before being men and because for a long time it was necessary for us to be governed by our appetites and our teachers (which were frequently in conflict with one another, and of which perhaps neither always gave us the best advice), it is nearly impossible for our judgments to be as pure or as solid as they would have been if we had had the full use of our reason from the moment of our birth and if we had always been guided by it alone.

It is true that we never see anyone pulling down all the houses in a city for the sole purpose of rebuilding them in a different style and of making the streets more attractive; but one does see very well that many people tear down their own houses in order to rebuild them, and that in some cases they are even forced to do so when their houses are in danger of collapsing and when the foundations are not very secure. This example persuaded me that it would not really be at all reasonable for a single individual to plan to reform a state by changing everything in it from the foundations up and by toppling it in order to set it up again; nor even also to reform the body of the sciences or the order established in the schools for teaching them; but that, as regards all the opinions to which I had until now given credence, I could not do better than to try to get rid of them once and for all, in order to replace them later on, either with other ones that are better, or even with the same ones once I had reconciled them to the level of reason. And I firmly believed that by this means I would succeed in conducting my life much better than if I were to build only upon old foundations and if I were to rely only on the principles of which I had allowed myself to be persuaded in my youth without ever having examined whether they were true. For although I noticed various difficulties in this undertaking, still they were not irremediable, nor were they comparable to those difficulties occurring in the reform of the least things that affect the public. These great bodies are too difficult to raise up once they have been knocked down, or even to hold up once they have been shaken; and their fall can only be very violent. Moreover, as to their imperfections, if they have any (and the mere fact of the diversity that exists among them suffices to assure one that many do have imperfections), custom has doubtless greatly mitigated them and has even prevented or imperceptibly corrected many of them, against which prudence could not provide so well. And finally, these imperfections are almost always more tolerable than changing them would be; similarly, the great roads that wind through mountains little by little become so smooth and so convenient by dint of being frequently used that it is much better to follow them than to try to take a more direct route by climbing over rocks and descending to the bottom of precipices.

That is why I could in no way approve of those troublemaking and restless personalities who, called neither by their birth nor by their fortune to manage public affairs, are forever coming up with an idea for some new reform in this matter. And if I thought there were in this writing the slightest thing by means of which one might suspect me of such folly, I would be very sorry to permit its publication. My plan has never gone beyond trying to reform my own thoughts and building upon a foundation which is completely my own. And if, my work having pleased me sufficiently, I here show you a model of it, it is not for the reason that I would wish to advise anyone to imitate it. Perhaps those with whom God has better shared his graces will have more lofty plans; but I fear that even this one here may already be too daring for many. The single resolution to rid oneself of all the opinions to which one has heretofore given credence is not an example that everyone ought to follow; and the world consists almost exclusively of two kinds of minds for whom it is not at all suitable. First, there are those who, believing themselves more capable than they are, are unable to avoid being hasty in their judgments or have enough patience to conduct all their thoughts in an orderly manner; as a result, if they have once taken the liberty of doubting the principles they had accepted and of straying from the common path, they could never keep to the path one

must take in order to go in a more straightforward direction, and they would remain lost all their lives. Second, there are those who have enough reason or modesty to judge that they are less capable of distinguishing the true from the false than certain others by whom they can be instructed; such people should content themselves more with following the opinions of these others than with looking for better ones themselves.

And as for myself, I would unquestionably have been counted among these latter persons if I had always had only one master or if I had not known at all the differences that have always existed among the opinions of the most learned. But I had learned in my college days that one cannot imagine anything so strange or so little believable that it has not been said by one of the philosophers, and since then, I had recognized in my travels that all those who have sentiments quite contrary to our own are not for that reason barbarians or savages, but that many of them use their reason as much as or more than we do. And I considered how one and the same man with the very same mind, were he brought up from infancy among the French or the Germans, would become different from what he would be had he always lived among the Chinese or the cannibals; and how, even down to the styles of our clothing, the same thing that pleased us ten years ago, and that perhaps will again please us ten years hence, now seems to us extravagant and ridiculous. Thus it is more custom and example that persuades us than any certain knowledge; and yet the majority opinion is worthless as a proof of truths that are at all difficult to discover, since it is much more likely that one man would have found them than a whole multitude of people. Hence I could not choose anyone whose opinions seemed to me preferable over those of the others, and I found myself, as it were, constrained to try to guide myself on my own.

But, like a man who walks alone and in the dark, I resolved to go so slowly and to use so much circumspection in all things that, if I advanced only very slightly, at least I would effectively keep myself from falling. Nor did I want to begin to reject totally any of the opinions that had once been able to slip into my head without having been introduced there by reason, until I had first spent sufficient time planning the work I was undertaking and seeking the true method for arriving at the knowledge of everything of which my mind would be capable.

When I was younger, I had studied, among the parts of philosophy, a little logic, and among those of mathematics, a bit of geometrical analysis and algebra—three arts or sciences that, it seemed, ought to contribute something to my plan. But in examining them, I noticed that, in the case of logic, its syllogisms and the greater part of its other lessons served more to explain to someone else the things one knows, or even, like the art of Lully,[5] to speak without judgment concerning matters about which one is ignorant, than to learn them. And although, in effect, it might well contain many very true and very good precepts, nevertheless there are so many others mixed up with them that are either harmful or superfluous, that it is almost as difficult to separate the latter precepts from the former as it is to draw a Diana or a Minerva from a block of marble that has not yet been hewn. Then, as to the analysis of the ancients and the algebra of the moderns, apart from the fact that they apply only to very abstract matters and seem to be of no use, the former is always so closely tied to the consideration of figures that it cannot exercise the understanding without greatly fatiguing the imagination; and in the case of the latter, one is so subjected to certain rules and to certain symbols, that out of it there results a confused and obscure art that encumbers the mind rather than a science that cultivates it. That is why I thought it necessary to search for some other method embracing the advantages of these three yet free from their defects. And since the multiplicity of laws often

provides excuses for vices, so that a state is much better ruled when it has but very few laws and when these are very strictly observed; likewise, in place of the large number of precepts of which logic is composed, I believed that the following four rules would be sufficient for me, provided I made a firm and constant resolution not even once to fail to observe them:

The first was never to accept anything as true that I did not plainly know to be such; that is to say, carefully to avoid hasty judgment and prejudice; and to include nothing more in my judgments than what presented itself to my mind so clearly and so distinctly that I had no occasion to call it in doubt.

The second, to divide each of the difficulties I would examine into as many parts as possible and as was required in order better to resolve them.

The third, to conduct my thoughts in an orderly fashion, by commencing with those objects that are simplest and easiest to know, in order to ascend little by little, as by degrees, to the knowledge of the most composite things, and by supposing an order even among those things that do not naturally precede one another.

And the last, everywhere to make enumerations so complete and reviews so general that I was assured of having omitted nothing.

Those long chains of utterly simple and easy reasonings that geometers commonly use to arrive at their most difficult demonstrations had given me occasion to imagine that all the things that can fall within human knowledge follow from one another in the same way, and that, provided only that one abstain from accepting any of them as true that is not true, and that one always adheres to the order one must follow in deducing the ones from the others, there cannot be any that are so remote that they are not eventually reached nor so hidden that they are not discovered. And I was not very worried about trying to find out which of them it would be necessary to begin with; for I already knew that it was with the simplest and easiest to know. And considering that, of all those who have hitherto searched for the truth in the sciences, only the mathematicians have been able to find any demonstrations, that is to say, certain

5. Lully, that is, Ramon Lull (ca. 1235–1316), was a Catalan philosopher and Franciscan who wrote in defense of Christianity against the Moors by attempting to demonstrate the articles of faith by means of logic. Descartes seems to have encountered a Lullist in Dordrecht who could hold forth on any subject whatever for long periods of time. This encounter, more than any direct contact with the writings of Lull, seems to have colored Descartes's understanding of the "art of Lully." Cf. E. Gilson, *Discours de la méthode: texte et commentaire*, pp. 185–86.

and evident reasonings, I did not at all doubt that it was with these same things that they had examined [that I should begin]; although I expected from them no other utility but that they would accustom my mind to nourish itself on truths and not to be content with false reasonings. But it was not my plan on that account to try to learn all those particular sciences commonly called mathematical; and seeing that, even though their objects differed, these sciences did not cease to be all in accord with one another in considering nothing but the various relations or proportions which are found in their objects, I thought it would be more worthwhile for me to examine only these proportions in general, and to suppose them to be only in subjects that would help me make the knowledge of them easier, and without at the same time in any way restricting them to those subjects, so that later I could apply them all the better to everything else to which they might pertain. Then, having noted that, in order to know these proportions, I would sometimes need to consider each of them individually, and sometimes only to keep them in mind, or to grasp many of them together, I thought that, in order better to consider them in particular, I ought to suppose them to be relations between lines, since I found nothing more simple, or nothing that I could represent more distinctly to my imagination and to my senses; but that, in order to keep them in mind or to grasp many of them together, I would have to explicate them by means of certain symbols, the briefest ones possible; and that by this means I would be borrowing all that is best in geometrical analysis and algebra, and correcting all the defects of the one by means of the other.

In fact, I dare say the strict adherence to these few precepts I had chosen gave me such facility for disentangling all the questions to which these two sciences extend, that, in the two or three months I spent examining them, having begun with the simplest and most general, and each truth that I found being a rule that later helped me to find others, not only did I arrive at a solution of many problems that I had previously judged very difficult, but also it seemed to me toward the end that, even in those instances where I was ignorant, I could determine by

what means and how far it was possible to resolve them. In this perhaps I shall not seem to you to be too vain, if you will consider that, there being but one truth with respect to each thing, whoever finds this truth knows as much about a thing as can be known; and that, for example, if a child who has been instructed in arithmetic has made an addition following its rules, he can be assured of having found everything regarding the sum he was examining that the human mind would know how to find. For ultimately, the method that teaches one to follow the true order and to enumerate exactly all the circumstances of what one is seeking contains everything that gives certainty to the rules of arithmetic.

But what pleased me most about this method was that by means of it I was assured of using my reason in everything, if not perfectly, at least as well as was in my power; and in addition that I felt that in practicing this method my mind was little by little getting into the habit of conceiving its objects more rigorously and more distinctly and that, not having restricted the method to any particular subject matter, I promised myself to apply it as usefully to the problems of the other sciences as I had to those of algebra. Not that, on this account, I would have dared at the outset to undertake an examination of all the problems that presented themselves; for that would itself have been contrary to the order prescribed by the method. But having noted that the principles of these sciences must all be derived from philosophy, in which I did not yet find any that were certain, I thought it was necessary for me first of all to try to establish some there; and that, this being the most important thing in the world, and the thing in which hasty judgment and prejudice were most feared, I should not try to accomplish that objective until I had reached a much more mature age than that of merely twenty-three, which I was then, and until I had first spent a great deal of time preparing myself for it, as much in rooting out from my mind all the wrong opinions that I had accepted before that time as in accumulating many experiences, in order for them later to be the subject matter of my reasonings, and in always practicing the method I had prescribed for myself so as to strengthen myself more and more in its use.

## Part V

[. . .] I paused here in particular in order to show that, if there were such machines having the organs and the shape of a monkey or of some other animal that lacked reason, we would have no way of recognizing that they were not entirely of the same nature as these animals; whereas, if there were any such machines that bore a resemblance to our bodies and imitated our actions as far as this is practically feasible, we would always have two very certain means of recognizing that they were not at all, for that reason, true men. The first is that they could never use words or other signs, or put them together as we do in order to declare our thoughts to others. For one can well conceive of a machine being so made that it utters words, and even that it utters words appropriate to the bodily actions that will cause some change in its organs (such as if one touches it in a certain place, it asks what one wants to say to it, or, if in another place, it cries out that one is hurting it, and the like). But it could not arrange its words differently so as to respond to the sense of all that will be said in its presence, as even the dullest men can do. The second means is that, although they might perform many tasks very well or perhaps better than any of us, such machines would inevitably fail in other tasks; by this means one would discover that they were acting, not through knowledge, but only through the disposition of their organs. For while reason is a universal instrument that can be of help in all sorts of circumstances, these organs require some particular disposition for each particular action; consequently, it is for all practical purposes impossible for there to be enough different organs in a machine to make it act in all the contingencies of life in the same way as our reason makes us act.

Now by these two means one can also know the difference between men and beasts. For it is rather remarkable that there are no men so dull and so stupid (excluding not even the insane), that they are incapable of arranging various words together and of composing from them a discourse by means of which they might make their thoughts understood; and that, on the other hand, there is no other animal at all, however perfect and pedigreed it may be, that does

the like. This does not happen because they lack the organs, for one sees that magpies and parrots can utter words just as we can, and yet they cannot speak as we do, that is to say, by testifying to the fact that they are thinking about what they are saying; on the other hand, men born deaf and dumb, who are deprived just as much as, or more than, beasts of the organs that aid others in speaking, are wont to invent for themselves various signs by means of which they make themselves understood to those who, being with them on a regular basis, have the time to learn their language. And this attests not merely to the fact that the beasts have less reason than men but that they have none at all. For it is obvious it does not need much to know how to speak; and since we notice as much inequality among animals of the same species as among men, and that some are easier to train than others, it is unbelievable that a monkey or a parrot that is the most perfect of its species would not equal in this respect one of the most stupid children or at least a child with a disordered brain, if their soul were not of a nature entirely different from our own. And we should not confuse words with the natural movements that attest to the passions and can be imitated by machines as well as by animals. Nor should we think, as did some of the ancients, that beasts speak, although we do not understand their language; for if that were true, since they have many organs corresponding to our own, they could make themselves as well understood by us as they are by their fellow-creatures. It is also a very remarkable phenomenon that, although there are many animals that show more skill than we do in some of their actions, we nevertheless see that they show none at all in many other actions. Consequently, the fact that they do something better than we do does not prove that they have any intelligence; for were that the case, they would have more of it than any of us and would excel us in everything. But rather it proves that they have no intelligence at all, and that it is nature that acts in them, according to the disposition of their organs—just as we see that a clock composed exclusively of wheels and springs can count the hours and measure time more accurately than we can with all our carefulness.

After that, I described the rational soul and showed

that it can in no way be derived from the potentiality of matter, as can the other things I have spoken of, but rather that it must be expressly created; and how it is not enough for it to be lodged in the human body like a pilot in his ship, unless perhaps in order to move its members, but rather that it must be more closely joined and united to the body in order to have, in addition to this, feelings and appetites similar to our own, and thus to constitute a true man. As to the rest, I elaborated here a little on the subject of the soul because it is of the greatest importance; for, after the error of those who deny the existence of God (which I think I have sufficiently refuted), there is none at all that puts weak minds at a greater distance from the straight path of virtue than to imagine that the soul of beasts is of the same nature as ours, and that, as a consequence, we have nothing to fear or to hope for after this life any more than do flies and ants. On the other hand, when one knows how different they are, one understands much better the arguments which prove that our soul is of a nature entirely independent of the body, and consequently that it is not subject to die with it. Then, since we do not see any other causes at all for its destruction, we are naturally led to judge from this that it is immortal.

# René Descartes, *Meditations on First Philosophy* (1641)[1]

## [Letter of Dedication]

*To those Most Wise and Distinguished Men,*
*the Dean and Doctors of the Faculty of*
*Sacred Theology of Paris*
René Descartes Sends Greetings

So right is the cause that impels me to offer this work to you that I am confident you too will find it equally right and thus take up its defense, once you have understood the plan of my undertaking; so much is this the case that I have no better means of commending it here than to state briefly what I have sought to achieve in this work.

I have always thought that two issues—namely, God and the soul—are chief among those that ought to be demonstrated with the aid of philosophy rather than theology. For although it suffices for us believers to believe by faith that the human soul does not die with the body, and that God exists, certainly no unbelievers seem capable of being persuaded of any religion or even of almost any moral virtue, until these two are first proven to them by natural reason. And since in this life greater rewards are often granted to vices than to virtues, few would prefer what is right

to what is useful, if they neither feared God nor anticipated an afterlife. Granted, it is altogether true that we must believe in God's existence because it is taught in the Holy Scriptures, and, conversely, that we must believe the Holy Scriptures because they have come from God. This is because, of course, since faith is a gift from God, the very same one who gives the grace that is necessary for believing the rest can also give the grace to believe that he exists. Nonetheless, this reasoning cannot be proposed to unbelievers because they would judge it to be circular. In fact, I have observed that not only do you and all other theologians affirm that one can prove the existence of God by natural reason, but also that one may infer from Sacred Scripture that the knowledge of him is easier to achieve than the many things we know about creatures, and is so utterly easy that those without this knowledge are blameworthy. For this is clear from *Wisdom*, Chapter 13 where it is said: "They are not to be excused, for if their capacity for knowing were so great that they could think well of this world, how is it that they did not find the Lord of it even more easily?" And in *Romans*, Chapter 1, it is said that they are "without excuse." And again in the same passage it appears we are being warned with the words: "What is known of God is manifest in them," that everything that can be known about God can be shown by reasons drawn exclusively from our own

1. Translated from the Latin by Donald Cress in René Descartes, *Meditations on First Philosophy*, 3rd ed. (Indianapolis: Hackett Publishing Company, 1993).

mind. For this reason, I did not think it unbecoming for me to inquire how this may be the case, and by what path God may be known more easily and with greater certainty than the things of this world.

And as to the soul, there are many who have regarded its nature as something into which one cannot easily inquire, and some have even gone so far as to say that human reasoning convinces them that the soul dies with the body, while it is by faith alone that they hold the contrary position. Nevertheless, because the Lateran Council held under Leo X, in Session 8, condemned such people and expressly enjoined Christian philosophers to refute their arguments and to use all their powers to demonstrate the truth, I have not hesitated to undertake this task as well.

Moreover, I know that there are many irreligious people who refuse to believe that God exists and that the human mind is distinct from the body—for no other reason than their claim that up until now no one has been able to demonstrate these two things. By no means am I in agreement with these people; on the contrary, I believe that nearly all the arguments which have been brought to bear on these questions by great men have the force of a demonstration, when they are adequately understood, and I am convinced that hardly any arguments can be given that have not already been discovered by others. Nevertheless, I judge that there is no greater task to perform in philosophy than assiduously to seek out, once and for all, the best of all these arguments and to lay them out so precisely and plainly that henceforth all will take them to be true demonstrations. And finally, I was strongly urged to do this by some people who knew that I had developed a method for solving all sorts of problems in the sciences—not a new one, mind you, since nothing is more ancient than the truth, but one they had seen me use with some success in other areas. Accordingly, I took it to be my task to attempt something on this subject.

This treatise contains all that I have been able to accomplish. Not that I have attempted to gather together in it all the various arguments that could be brought forward as proof of the very same conclusions, for this does not seem worthwhile, except where no one proof is sufficiently certain. Rather, I have sought out the primary and chief arguments, so that I now

make bold to propose these as most certain and evident demonstrations. Moreover, I will say in addition that these arguments are such that I believe there is no way open to the human mind whereby better ones could ever be found. For the urgency of the cause, as well as the glory of God, to which this entire enterprise is referred, compel me here to speak somewhat more freely on my own behalf than is my custom. But although I believe these arguments to be certain and evident, still I am not thereby convinced that they are suited to everyone's grasp. In geometry there are many arguments developed by Archimedes, Apollonius, Pappus, and others, which are taken by everyone to be evident and certain because they contain absolutely nothing which, considered by itself, is not quite easily known, and in which what follows does not square exactly with what has come before. Nevertheless, they are rather lengthy and require a particularly attentive reader; thus only a small handful of people understand them. Likewise, although the arguments I use here do, in my opinion, equal or even surpass those of geometry in certitude and obviousness, nevertheless I am fearful that many people will not be capable of adequately perceiving them, both because they too are a bit lengthy, with some of them depending on still others, and also because, first and foremost, they demand a mind that is quite free from prejudices and that can easily withdraw itself from association with the senses. Certainly there are not to be found in the world more people with an aptitude for metaphysical studies than those with an aptitude for geometry. Moreover, there is the difference that in geometry everyone is of a mind that usually nothing is put down in writing without there being a sound demonstration for it; thus the inexperienced more frequently err on the side of assenting to what is false, wanting as they do to give the appearance of understanding it, than on the side of denying what is true. But it is the reverse in philosophy: Since it is believed that there is no issue that cannot be defended from either side, few look for the truth, and many more prowl about for a reputation for profundity by arrogantly challenging whichever arguments are the best.

And therefore, regardless of the force of my arguments, because they are of a philosophical nature I do not anticipate that what I will have accomplished through them will be very worthwhile unless you assist me with your patronage. Your faculty is held in such high esteem in the minds of all, and the name of the Sorbonne has such authority that not only in matters of faith has no association, with the exception of the councils of the Church, been held in such high regard as yours, but even in human philosophy nowhere is there thought to be greater insightfulness and solidity, or greater integrity and wisdom in rendering judgments. Should you deign to show any interest in this work, I do not doubt that, first of all, its errors would be corrected by you (for I am mindful not only of my humanity but also, and most especially, of my ignorance, and thus do not claim that there are no errors in it); second, what is lacking would be added, or what is not sufficiently complete would be perfected, or what is in need of further discussion would be expanded upon more fully, either by yourselves or at least by me, after you have given me your guidance; and finally, after the arguments contained in this work proving that God exists and that the mind is distinct from the body have been brought (as I am confident they can be) to such a level of lucidity that these arguments ought to be regarded as the most precise of demonstrations, you may be of a mind to make such a declaration and publicly attest to it. Indeed, should this come to pass, I have no doubt that all the errors that have ever been entertained regarding these issues would shortly be erased from the minds of men. For the truth itself will easily cause other men of intelligence and learning to subscribe to your judgment. Your authority will cause the atheists, who more often than not are dilettantes rather than men of intelligence and learning, to put aside their spirit of contrariness, and perhaps even to defend the arguments which they will come to know are regarded as demonstrations by all who are discerning, lest they appear not to understand them. And finally, everyone else will readily give credence to so many indications of support, and there no longer will be anyone in the world who would dare call into doubt either the existence of God or the real distinction between the soul and the body. Just how great the usefulness of this thing might be, you yourselves, in virtue of your singular wisdom, are

in the best position of anyone to judge; nor would it behoove me to commend the cause of God and religion at any greater length to you, who have always been the greatest pillar of the Catholic Church.

## Preface to the Reader

I have already touched briefly on the issues of God and the human mind in my *Discourse on the Method for Conducting One's Reason Well and for Seeking the Truth in the Sciences*, published in French in 1637. The intent there was not to provide a precise treatment of them, but only to offer a sample and to learn from the opinions of readers how these issues should be treated in the future. For they seemed to me to be so important that I judged they ought to be dealt with more than once. And the path I follow in order to explain them is so little trodden and so far removed from the one commonly taken that I did not think it useful to hold forth at greater length in a work written in French and designed to be read indiscriminately by everyone, lest weaker minds be in a position to think that they too ought to set out on this path.

In the *Discourse* I asked everyone who might find something in my writings worthy of refutation to do me the favor of making me aware of it. As for what I touched on regarding these issues, only two objections were worth noting, and I will respond briefly to them here before undertaking a more precise explanation of them.

The first is that, from the fact that the human mind, when turned in on itself, does not perceive itself to be anything other than a thinking thing, it does not follow that its nature or *essence* consists only in its being a thinking thing, such that the word *only* excludes everything else that also could perhaps be said to belong to the nature of the soul. To this objection I answer that in that passage I did not intend my exclusion of those things to reflect the order of the truth of the matter (I was not dealing with it then), but merely the order of my perception. Thus what I had in mind was that I was aware of absolutely nothing that I knew belonged to pertain to my essence, save that I was a thinking thing, that is, a thing having within itself the faculty of thinking. Later on, however,

I will show how it follows, from the fact that I know of nothing else belonging to my essence, that nothing else really does belong to it.

The second objection is that it does not follow from the fact that I have within me an idea of a thing more perfect than me, that this idea is itself more perfect than me, and still less that what is represented by this idea exists. But I answer that there is an equivocation here in the word "idea." For "idea" can be taken either materially, for an operation of the intellect (in which case it cannot be said to be more perfect than me), or objectively, for the thing represented by means of that operation. This thing, even if it is not presumed to exist outside the intellect, can nevertheless be more perfect than me by reason of its essence. I will explain in detail in the ensuing remarks how, from the mere fact that there is within me an idea of something more perfect than me, it follows that this thing really exists.

In addition, I have seen two rather lengthy treatises, but these works, utilizing as they do arguments drawn from atheist commonplaces, focused their attack not so much on my arguments regarding these issues, as on my conclusions. Moreover, arguments of this type exercise no influence over those who understand my arguments, and the judgments of many people are so preposterous and feeble that they are more likely to be persuaded by the first opinions to come along, however false and contrary to reason they may be, than by a true and firm refutation of them which they hear subsequently. Accordingly, I have no desire to respond here to these objections, lest I first have to state what they are. I will only say in general that all the objections typically bandied about by the atheists to assail the existence of God always depend either on ascribing human emotions to God, or on arrogantly claiming for our minds such power and wisdom that we attempt to determine and grasp fully what God can and ought to do. Hence these objections will cause us no difficulty, provided we but remember that our minds are to be regarded as finite, while God is to be regarded as incomprehensible and infinite.

But now, after having, to some degree, conducted an initial review of the judgments of men, here I begin once more to treat the same questions about God and the human mind, together with the starting points of the whole of first philosophy, but not in a way that causes me to have any expectation of widespread approval or a large readership. On the contrary, I do not advise anyone to read these things except those who have both the ability and the desire to meditate seriously with me, and to withdraw their minds from the senses as well as from all prejudices. I know all too well that such people are few and far between. As to those who do not take the time to grasp the order and linkage of my arguments, but will be eager to fuss over statements taken out of context (as is the custom for many), they will derive little benefit from reading this work. Although perhaps they might find an occasion for quibbling in several places, still they will not find it easy to raise an objection that is either compelling or worthy of response.

But because I do not promise to satisfy even the others on all counts the first time around, and because I do not arrogantly claim for myself so much that I believe myself capable of anticipating all the difficulties that will occur to someone, I will first of all narrate in the *Meditations* the very thoughts by means of which I seem to have arrived at a certain and evident knowledge of the truth, so that I may determine whether the same arguments that persuaded me can be useful in persuading others. Next, I will reply to the objections of a number of very gifted and learned gentlemen, to whom these *Meditations* were forwarded for their examination prior to their being sent to press. For their objections were so many and varied that I have dared to hope that nothing will readily occur to anyone, at least nothing of importance, which has not already been touched upon by these gentlemen. And thus I earnestly entreat the readers not to form a judgment regarding the *Meditations* until they have deigned to read all these objections and the replies I have made to them.

## Synopsis of the Following Six Meditations

In the First Meditation the reasons are given why we can doubt all things, especially material things, so long, that is, as, of course, we have no other foundations for the sciences than the ones which we have had up until now. Although the utility of so extensive a doubt is not readily apparent, nevertheless its greatest utility lies in freeing us of all prejudices, in preparing the easiest way for us to withdraw the mind from the senses, and finally, in making it impossible for us to doubt any further those things that we later discover to be true.

In the Second Meditation the mind, through the exercise of its own freedom, supposes the nonexistence of all those things about whose existence it can have even the least doubt. In so doing the mind realizes that it is impossible for it not to exist during this time. This too is of the greatest utility, since by means of it the mind easily distinguishes what things belong to it, that is, to an intellectual nature, from what things belong to the body. But because some people will perhaps expect to see proofs for the immortality of the soul in this Meditation, I think they should be put on notice here that I have attempted to write only what I have carefully demonstrated. Therefore the only order I could follow was the one typically used by geometers, which is to lay out everything on which a given proposition depends, before concluding anything about it. But the first and principal prerequisite for knowing that the soul is immortal is that we form a concept of the soul that is as lucid as possible and utterly distinct from every concept of a body. This is what has been done here. Moreover, there is the additional requirement that we know that everything that we clearly and distinctly understand is true, in exactly the manner in which we understand it; however, this could not have been proven prior to the Fourth Meditation. Moreover, we must have a distinct concept of corporeal nature, and this is formulated partly in the Second Meditation itself, and partly in the Fifth and Sixth Meditations. From all this one ought to conclude that all the things we clearly and distinctly conceive as different substances truly are substances that are really distinct from one another. (This, for example, is how mind and body are conceived.) This conclusion is arrived at in the Sixth Meditation. This same conclusion is also confirmed in this Meditation in virtue of the fact that we cannot understand a body to be anything but divisible, whereas we cannot understand the mind to be anything but indivisible. For we cannot conceive of half a mind, as we do for any body whatever, no matter how

small. From this we are prompted to acknowledge that the natures of mind and body not only are different from one another, but even, in a manner of speaking, are contraries of one another. However, I have not written any further on the matter in this work, both because these considerations suffice for showing that the annihilation of the mind does not follow from the decaying of the body (and thus these considerations suffice for giving mortals hope in an afterlife), and also because the premises from which the immortality of the mind can be inferred depend upon an account of the whole of physics. First, we need to know that absolutely all substances, that is, things that must be created by God in order to exist, are by their very nature incorruptible, and can never cease to exist, unless, by the same God's denying his concurrence to them, they be reduced to nothingness. Second, we need to realize that body, taken in a general sense, is a substance and hence it too can never perish. But the human body, insofar as it differs from other bodies, is composed of merely a certain configuration of members, together with other accidents of the same sort. But the human mind is not likewise composed of any accidents, but is a pure substance. For even if all its accidents were changed, so that it understands different things, wills different things, senses different things, and so on, the mind itself does not on that score become something different. On the other hand, the human body does become something different, merely as a result of the fact that a change in the shape of some of its parts has taken place. It follows from these considerations that a body can very easily perish, whereas the mind by its nature is immortal.

In the Third Meditation I have explained at sufficient length, it seems to me, my principal argument for proving the existence of God. Nevertheless, since my intent was to draw the minds of readers as far as possible from the senses, I had no desire to draw upon comparisons based upon corporeal things. Thus many obscurities may perhaps have remained; but these, I trust, will later be entirely removed in my Replies to the Objections. One such point of contention, among others, is the following: How can the idea that is in us of a supremely perfect being have so much objective reality that it can only come from a supremely perfect cause? This is illustrated in the Replies by a comparison with a very perfect machine, the idea of which is in the mind of some craftsman. For, just as the objective ingeniousness of this idea ought to have some cause (say, the knowledge possessed by the craftsman or by someone else from whom he received this knowledge), so too, the idea of God which is in us must have God himself as its cause.

In the Fourth Meditation it is proved that all that we clearly and distinctly perceive is true, and it is also explained what constitutes the nature of falsity. These things necessarily need to be known both to confirm what has preceded as well as to help readers understand what remains. (But here one should meanwhile bear in mind that in that Meditation there is no discussion whatsoever of sin, that is, the error committed in the pursuit of good and evil, but only the error that occurs in discriminating between what is true and what is false. Nor is there an examination of those matters pertaining to the faith or to the conduct of life, but merely of speculative truths known exclusively by the means of the light of nature.)

In the Fifth Meditation, in addition to an explanation of corporeal nature in general, the existence of God is also demonstrated by means of a new proof. But again several difficulties may arise here; however, these are resolved later in my Replies to the Objec-

tions. Finally, it is shown how it is true that the certainty of even geometrical demonstrations depends upon the knowledge of God.

Finally, in the Sixth Meditation the understanding is distinguished from the imagination and the marks of this distinction are described. The mind is proved to be really distinct from the body, even though the mind is shown to be so closely joined to the body that it forms a single unit with it. All the errors commonly arising from the senses are reviewed; an account of the ways in which these errors can be avoided is provided. Finally, all the arguments on the basis of which we may infer the existence of material things are presented—not because I believed them to be very useful for proving what they prove, namely, that there really is a world, that men have bodies, and the like (things which no one of sound mind has ever seriously doubted), but rather because, through a consideration of these arguments, one realizes that they are neither so firm nor so evident as the arguments leading us to the knowledge of our mind and of God, so that, of all the things that can be known by the human mind, these latter are the most certain and the most evident. Proving this one thing was for me the goal of these Meditations. For this reason I will not review here the various issues that are also to be treated in these Meditations as the situation arises.

# Meditations on First Philosophy in Which the Existence of God and the Distinction between the Soul and the Body Are Demonstrated

## Meditation One: Concerning Those Things That Can Be Called into Doubt

Several years have now passed since I first realized how numerous were the false opinions that in my youth I had taken to be true, and thus how doubtful were all those that I had subsequently built upon them. And thus I realized that once in my life I had to raze everything to the ground and begin again from the original foundations, if I wanted to establish anything firm and lasting in the sciences. But the task seemed enormous, and I was waiting until I reached a point in my life that was so timely that no more suitable time for undertaking these plans of

action would come to pass. For this reason, I procrastinated for so long that I would henceforth be at fault, were I to waste the time that remains for carrying out the project by brooding over it. Accordingly, I have today suitably freed my mind of all cares, secured for myself a period of leisurely tranquillity, and am withdrawing into solitude. At last I will apply myself earnestly and unreservedly to this general demolition of my opinions.

Yet to bring this about I will not need to show that all my opinions are false, which is perhaps something I could never accomplish. But reason now persuades me that I should withhold my assent no less carefully from opinions that are not completely certain and indubitable than I would from those that are patently false. For this reason, it will suffice for the rejection of all of these opinions, if I find in each of them some reason for doubt. Nor therefore need I survey each opinion individually, a task that would be endless. Rather, because undermining the foundations will cause whatever has been built upon them to crumble of its own accord, I will attack straightaway those principles which supported everything I once believed.

Surely whatever I had admitted until now as most true I received either from the senses or through the senses. However, I have noticed that the senses are sometimes deceptive; and it is a mark of prudence never to place our complete trust in those who have deceived us even once.

But perhaps, even though the senses do sometimes deceive us when it is a question of very small and distant things, still there are many other matters concerning which one simply cannot doubt, even though they are derived from the very same senses: for example, that I am sitting here next to the fire, wearing my winter dressing gown, that I am holding this sheet of paper in my hands, and the like. But on what grounds could one deny that these hands and this entire body are mine? Unless perhaps I were to liken myself to the insane, whose brains are impaired by such an unrelenting vapor of black bile that they steadfastly insist that they are kings when they are utter paupers, or that they are arrayed in purple robes when they are naked, or that they have heads made of clay, or that they are gourds, or that they are made of glass. But such people are mad, and I would appear no less mad were I to take their behavior as an example for myself.

This would all be well and good, were I not a man who is accustomed to sleeping at night, and to experiencing in my dreams the very same things, or now and then even less plausible ones, as these insane people do when they are awake. How often does my evening slumber persuade me of such ordinary things as these: that I am here, clothed in my dressing gown, seated next to the fireplace—when in fact I am lying undressed in bed! But right now my eyes are certainly wide awake when I gaze upon this sheet of paper. This head which I am shaking is not heavy with sleep.

I extend this hand consciously and deliberately, and I feel it. Such things would not be so distinct for someone who is asleep. As if I did not recall having been deceived on other occasions even by similar thoughts in my dreams! As I consider these matters more carefully, I see so plainly that there are no definitive signs by which to distinguish being awake from being asleep. As a result, I am becoming quite dizzy, and this dizziness nearly convinces me that I am asleep.

Let us assume then, for the sake of argument, that we are dreaming and that such particulars as these are not true: that we are opening our eyes, moving our head, and extending our hands. Perhaps we do not even have such hands, or any such body at all. Nevertheless, it surely must be admitted that the things seen during slumber are, as it were, like painted images, which could only have been produced in the likeness of true things, and that therefore at least these general things—eyes, head, hands, and the whole body—are not imaginary things, but are true and exist. For indeed when painters themselves wish to represent sirens and satyrs by means of especially bizarre forms, they surely cannot assign to them utterly new natures. Rather, they simply fuse together the members of various animals. Or if perhaps they concoct something so utterly novel that nothing like it has ever been seen before (and thus is something utterly fictitious and false), yet certainly at the very least the colors from which they fashion it ought to be true. And by the same token, although even these general things—eyes, head, hands and the like— could be imaginary, still one has to admit that at least certain other things that are even more simple and universal are true. It is from these components, as if from true colors, that all those images of things that are in our thought are fashioned, be they true or false.

This class of things appears to include corporeal nature in general, together with its extension; the shape of extended things; their quantity, that is, their size and number; as well as the place where they exist; the time through which they endure, and the like.

Thus it is not improper to conclude from this that physics, astronomy, medicine, and all the other disciplines that are dependent upon the consideration of composite things are doubtful, and that, on the other hand, arithmetic, geometry, and other such disciplines, which treat of nothing but the simplest and most general things and which are indifferent as to whether these things do or do not in fact exist, contain something certain and indubitable. For whether I am awake or asleep, two plus three make five, and a square does not have more than four sides. It does not seem possible that such obvious truths should be subject to the suspicion of being false.

Be that as it may, there is fixed in my mind a certain opinion of long standing, namely that there exists a God who is able to do anything and by whom I, such as I am, have been created. How do I know that he did not bring it about that there is no earth at all, no heavens, no extended thing, no shape, no size, no place, and yet bringing it about that all these things appear to me to exist precisely as they do now? Moreover, since I judge that others sometimes make mistakes in matters that they believe they know most perfectly, may I not, in like fashion, be deceived every time I add two and three or count the sides of a square, or perform an even simpler operation, if that can be imagined? But perhaps God has not willed that I be deceived in this way, for he is said to be supremely good. Nonetheless, if it were repugnant to his goodness to have created me such that I be deceived all the time, it would also seem foreign to that same goodness to permit me to be deceived even occasionally. But we cannot make this last assertion.

Perhaps there are some who would rather deny so powerful a God than believe that everything else is uncertain. Let us not oppose them; rather, let us grant that everything said here about God is fictitious. Now they suppose that I came to be what I am either by fate, or by chance, or by a connected chain of events, or by some other way. But because deceived and being mistaken appear to be a certain imperfection, the less powerful they take the author of my origin to be, the more probable it will be that I am so imperfect that I am always deceived. I have nothing to say in response to these arguments. But eventually I am forced to admit that there is nothing among the things I once believed to be true which it is not permissible to doubt—and not out of frivolity or lack of forethought, but for valid and considered arguments. Thus I must be no less careful to withhold

assent henceforth even from these beliefs than I would from those that are patently false, if I wish to find anything certain.

But it is not enough simply to have realized these things; I must take steps to keep myself mindful of them. For long-standing opinions keep returning, and, almost against my will, they take advantage of my credulity, as if it were bound over to them by long use and the claims of intimacy. Nor will I ever get out of the habit of assenting to them and believing in them, so long as I take them to be exactly what they are, namely, in some respects doubtful, as has just now been shown, but nevertheless highly probable, so that it is much more consonant with reason to believe them than to deny them. Hence, it seems to me I would do well to deceive myself by turning my will in completely the opposite direction and pretend for a time that these opinions are wholly false and imaginary, until finally, as if with prejudices weighing down each side equally, no bad habit should turn my judgment any further from the correct perception of things. For indeed I know that meanwhile there is no danger or error in following this procedure, and that it is impossible for me to indulge in too much distrust, since I am now concentrating only on knowledge, not on action.

Accordingly, I will suppose not a supremely good God, the source of truth, but rather an evil genius, supremely powerful and clever, who has directed his entire effort at deceiving me. I will regard the heavens, the air, the earth, colors, shapes, sounds, and all external things as nothing but the bedeviling hoaxes of my dreams, with which he lays snares for my credulity. I will regard myself as not having hands, or eyes, or flesh, or blood, or any senses, but as nevertheless falsely believing that I possess all these things. I will remain resolute and steadfast in this meditation, and even if it is not within my power to know anything true, it certainly is within my power to take care resolutely to withhold my assent to what is false, lest this deceiver, however powerful, however clever he may be, have any effect on me. But this undertaking is arduous, and a certain laziness brings me back to my customary way of living. I am not unlike a prisoner who enjoyed an imaginary freedom during his sleep, but, when he later begins to suspect that he is dreaming, fears being awakened and nonchalantly conspires with these pleasant illusions. In just the same way, I fall back of my own accord into my old opinions, and dread being awakened, lest the toilsome wakefulness which follows upon a peaceful rest must be spent thenceforward not in the light but among the inextricable shadows of the difficulties now brought forward.

## Meditation Two: Concerning the Nature of the Human Mind: That It Is Better Known Than the Body

Yesterday's meditation has thrown me into such doubts that I can no longer ignore them, yet I fail to see how they are to be resolved. It is as if I had suddenly fallen into a deep whirlpool; I am so tossed about that I can neither touch bottom with my foot, nor swim up to the top. Nevertheless I will work my way up and will once again attempt the same path I entered upon yesterday. I will accomplish this by putting aside everything that admits of the least doubt, as if I had discovered it to be completely false. I will stay on this course until I know something certain, or, if nothing else, until I at least know for certain that nothing is certain. Archimedes sought but one firm and immovable point in order to move the entire earth from one place to another. Just so, great things are also to be hoped for if I succeed in finding just one thing, however slight, that is certain and unshaken.

Therefore I suppose that everything I see is false. I believe that none of what my deceitful memory represents ever existed. I have no senses whatever. Body, shape, extension, movement, and place are all chimeras. What then will be true? Perhaps just the single fact that nothing is certain.

But how do I know there is not something else, over and above all those things that I have just reviewed, concerning which there is not even the slightest occasion for doubt? Is there not some God, or by whatever name I might call him, who instills these very thoughts in me? But why would I think that, since I myself could perhaps be the author of these thoughts? Am I not then at least something? But I have already denied that I have any senses and any body. Still I hesitate; for what follows from this? Am I so tied to a body and to the senses that I cannot exist without

them? But I have persuaded myself that there is absolutely nothing in the world: no sky, no earth, no minds, no bodies. Is it then the case that I too do not exist? But doubtless I did exist, if I persuaded myself of something. But there is some deceiver or other who is supremely powerful and supremely sly and who is always deliberately deceiving me. Then too there is no doubt that I exist, if he is deceiving me. And let him do his best at deception; he will never bring it about that I am nothing so long as I shall think that I am something. Thus, after everything has been most carefully weighed, it must finally be established that this pronouncement "I am, I exist" is necessarily true every time I utter it or conceive it in my mind.

But I do not yet understand sufficiently what I am—I, who now necessarily exist. And so from this point on, I must be careful lest I unwittingly mistake something else for myself, and thus err in that very item of knowledge that I claim to be the most certain and evident of all. Thus, I will meditate once more on what I once believed myself to be, prior to embarking upon these thoughts. For this reason, then, I will set aside whatever can be weakened even to the slightest degree by the arguments brought forward, so that eventually all that remains is precisely nothing but what is certain and unshaken.

What then did I formerly think I was? A man, of course. But what is a man? Might I not say a "rational animal"? No, because then I would have to inquire what "animal" and "rational" mean. And thus from one question I would slide into many more difficult ones. Nor do I now have enough free time that I want to waste it on subtleties of this sort. Instead, permit me here to focus on what came spontaneously and naturally into my thinking whenever I pondered what I was. Now it occurred to me first that I had a face, hands, arms, and this entire mechanism of bodily members: the very same as are discerned in a corpse, and which I referred to by the name "body." It next occurred to me that I took in food, that I walked about, and that I sensed and thought various things; these actions I used to attribute to the soul. But as to what this soul might be, I either did not think about it or else I imagined it a rarefied I-know-not-what, like a wind, or a fire, or ether, which had been infused into my coarser parts. But as to the body I was not in any doubt. On the contrary, I was under the impression that I knew its nature distinctly. Were I perhaps tempted to describe this nature such as I conceived it in my mind, I would have described it thus: By "body," I understand all that is capable of being bounded by some shape, of being enclosed in a place, and of filling up a space in such a way as to exclude any other body from it; of being perceived by touch, sight, hearing, taste, or smell; of being moved in several ways, not, of course, by itself, but by whatever else impinges upon it. For it was my view that the power of self-motion, and likewise of sensing or of thinking, in no way belonged to the nature of the body. Indeed I used rather to marvel that such faculties were to be found in certain bodies.

But now what am I, when I suppose that there is some supremely powerful and, if I may be permitted to say so, malicious deceiver who deliberately tries to fool me in any way he can? Can I not affirm that I possess at least a small measure of all those things which I have already said belong to the nature of the body? I focus my attention on them, I think about them, I review them again, but nothing comes to mind. I am tired of repeating this to no purpose. But what about those things I ascribed to the soul? What about being nourished or moving about? Since I now do not have a body, these are surely nothing but fictions. What about sensing? Surely, this too does not take place without a body; and I seemed to have sensed in my dreams many things that I later realized I did not sense. What about thinking? Here I make my discovery: Thought exists; it alone cannot be separated from me. I am; I exist—this is certain. But for how long? For as long as I am thinking; for perhaps it could also come to pass that if I were to cease all thinking I would then utterly cease to exist. At this time I admit nothing that is not necessarily true. I am therefore precisely nothing but a thinking thing; that is, a mind, or intellect, or understanding, or reason—words of whose meanings I was previously ignorant. Yet I am a true thing and am truly existing; but what kind of thing? I have said it already: a thinking thing.

What else am I? I will set my imagination in motion. I am not that concatenation of members we call

the human body. Neither am I even some subtle air infused into these members, nor a wind, nor a fire, nor a vapor, nor a breath, nor anything I devise for myself. For I have supposed these things to be nothing. The assumption still stands; yet nevertheless I am something. But is it perhaps the case that these very things which I take to be nothing, because they are unknown to me, nevertheless are in fact no different from that me that I know? This I do not know, and I will not quarrel about it now. I can make a judgment only about things that are known to me. I know that I exist; I ask now who is this "I" whom I know? Most certainly, in the strict sense the knowledge of this "I" does not depend upon things whose existence I do not yet know. Therefore, it is not dependent upon any of those things that I simulate in my imagination. But this word "simulate" warns me of my error. For I would indeed be simulating were I to "imagine" that I was something, because imagining is merely the contemplating of the shape or image of a corporeal thing. But I now know with certainty that I am and also that all these images—and, generally, everything belonging to the nature of the body—could turn out to be nothing but dreams. Once I have realized this, I would seem to be speaking no less foolishly were I to say, "I will use my imagination in order to recognize more distinctly who I am," than were I to say, "Now I surely am awake, and I see something true; but since I do not yet see it clearly enough, I will deliberately fall asleep so that my dreams might represent it to me more truly and more clearly." Thus I realize that none of what I can grasp by means of the imagination pertains to this knowledge that I have of myself. Moreover, I realize that I must be most diligent about withdrawing my mind from these things so that it can perceive its nature as distinctly as possible.

But what then am I? A thing that thinks. What is that? A thing that doubts, understands, affirms, denies, wills, refuses, and that also imagines and senses.

Indeed it is no small matter if all of these things belong to me. But why should they not belong to me? Is it not the very same "I" who now doubts almost everything, who nevertheless understands something, who affirms that this one thing is true, who denies other things, who desires to know more, who wishes not to be deceived, who imagines many things even against my will, who also notices many things which appear to come from the senses? What is there in all of this that is not every bit as true as the fact that I exist—even if I am always asleep or even if my creator makes every effort to mislead me? Which of these things is distinct from my thought? Which of them can be said to be separate from myself? For it is so obvious that it is I who doubt, I who understand, and I who will, that there is nothing by which it could be explained more clearly. But indeed it is also the same "I" who imagines; for although perhaps, as I supposed before, absolutely nothing that I imagined is true, still the very power of imagining really does exist, and constitutes a part of my thought. Finally, it is this same "I" who senses or who is cognizant of bodily things as if through the senses. For example, I now see a light, I hear a noise, I feel heat. These things are false, since I am asleep. Yet I certainly do seem to see, hear, and feel warmth. This cannot be false. Properly speaking, this is what in me is called "sensing." But this, precisely so taken, is nothing other than thinking.

From these considerations I am beginning to know a little better what I am. But it still seems (and I cannot resist believing) that corporeal things—whose images are formed by thought, and which the senses themselves examine—are much more distinctly known than this mysterious "I" which does not fall within the imagination. And yet it would be strange indeed were I to grasp the very things I consider to be doubtful, unknown, and foreign to me more distinctly than what is true, what is known—than, in short, myself. But I see what is happening: my mind loves to wander and does not yet permit itself to be restricted within the confines of truth. So be it then; let us just this once allow it completely free rein, so that, a little while later, when the time has come to pull in the reins, the mind may more readily permit itself to be controlled.

Let us consider those things which are commonly believed to be the most distinctly grasped of all: namely the bodies we touch and see. Not bodies in general, mind you, for these general perceptions are apt to be somewhat more confused, but one body in particular. Let us take, for instance, this piece of wax.

It has been taken quite recently from the honeycomb; it has not yet lost all the honey flavor. It retains some of the scent of the flowers from which it was collected. Its color, shape, and size are manifest. It is hard and cold; it is easy to touch. If you rap on it with your knuckle, it will emit a sound. In short, everything is present in it that appears needed to enable a body to be known as distinctly as possible. But notice that, as I am speaking, I am bringing it close to the fire. The remaining traces of the honey flavor are disappearing; the scent is vanishing; the color is changing; the original shape is disappearing. Its size is increasing; it is becoming liquid and hot; you can hardly touch it. And now, when you rap on it, it no longer emits any sound. Does the same wax still remain? I must confess that it does; no one denies it; no one thinks otherwise. So what was there in the wax that was so distinctly grasped? Certainly none of the aspects that I reached by means of the senses. For whatever came under the senses of taste, smell, sight, touch, or hearing has now changed; and yet the wax remains.

Perhaps the wax was what I now think it is: namely that the wax itself never really was the sweetness of the honey, nor the fragrance of the flowers, nor the whiteness, nor the shape, nor the sound, but instead was a body that a short time ago manifested itself to me in these ways, and now does so in other ways. But just what precisely is this thing that I thus imagine? Let us focus our attention on this and see what remains after we have removed everything that does not belong to the wax: only that it is something extended, flexible, and mutable. But what is it to be flexible and mutable? Is it what my imagination shows it to be: namely, that this piece of wax can change from a round to a square shape, or from the latter to a triangular shape? Not at all; for I grasp that the wax is capable of innumerable changes of this sort, even though I am incapable of running through these innumerable changes by using my imagination. Therefore this insight is not achieved by the faculty of imagination. What is it to be extended? Is this thing's extension also unknown? For it becomes greater in wax that is beginning to melt, greater in boiling wax, and greater still as the heat is increased. And I would not judge correctly what the wax is if I did not believe that it takes on an even greater variety of dimensions than

I could ever grasp with the imagination. It remains then for me to concede that I do not grasp what this wax is through the imagination; rather, I perceive it through the mind alone. The point I am making refers to this particular piece of wax, for the case of wax in general is clearer still. But what is this piece of wax which is perceived only by the mind? Surely, it is the same piece of wax that I see, touch, and imagine; in short it is the same piece of wax I took it to be from the very beginning. But I need to realize that the perception of the wax is neither a seeing, nor a touching, nor an imagining. Nor has it ever been, even though it previously seemed so; rather it is an inspection on the part of the mind alone. This inspection can be imperfect and confused, as it was before, or clear and distinct, as it is now, depending on how closely I pay attention to the things in which the piece of wax consists.

But meanwhile I marvel at how prone my mind is to errors. For although I am considering these things within myself silently and without words, nevertheless I seize upon words themselves and I am nearly deceived by the ways in which people commonly speak. For we say that we see the wax itself, if it is present, and not that we judge it to be present from its color or shape. Whence I might conclude straightaway that I know the wax through the vision had by the eye, and not through an inspection on the part of the mind alone. But then were I perchance to look out my window and observe men crossing the square, I would ordinarily say I see the men themselves just as I say I see the wax. But what do I see aside from hats and clothes, which could conceal automata? Yet I judge them to be men. Thus what I thought I had seen with my eyes, I actually grasped solely with the faculty of judgment, which is in my mind.

But a person who seeks to know more than the common crowd ought to be ashamed of himself for looking for doubt in common ways of speaking. Let us then go forward, inquiring on when it was that I perceived more perfectly and evidently what the piece of wax was. Was it when I first saw it and believed I knew it by the external sense, or at least by the so-called "common" sense, that is, the power of imagination? Or do I have more perfect knowledge now, when I have diligently examined both what the wax

is and how it is known? Surely, it is absurd to be in doubt about this matter. For what was there in my initial perception that was distinct? What was there that any animal seemed incapable of possessing? But indeed when I distinguish the wax from its external forms, as if stripping it of its clothing, and look at the wax in its nakedness, then, even though there can be still an error in my judgment, nevertheless I cannot perceive it thus without a human mind.

But what am I to say about this mind, that is, about myself? For as yet I admit nothing else to be in me over and above the mind. What, I ask, am I who seem to perceive this wax so distinctly? Do I not know myself not only much more truly and with greater certainty, but also much more distinctly and evidently? For if I judge that the wax exists from the fact that I see it, certainly from this same fact that I see the wax it follows much more evidently that I myself exist. For it could happen that what I see is not truly wax. It could happen that I have no eyes with which to see anything. But it is utterly impossible that, while I see or think I see (I do not now distinguish these two), I who think am not something. Likewise, if I judge that the wax exists from the fact that I touch it, the same outcome will again obtain, namely that I exist. If I judge that the wax exists from the fact that I imagine it, or for any other reason, plainly the same thing follows. But what I note regarding the wax applies to everything else that is external to me. Furthermore, if my perception of the wax seemed more distinct after it became known to me not only on account of sight or touch, but on account of many reasons, one has to admit how much more distinctly I am now known to myself. For there is not a single consideration that can aid in my perception of the wax or of any other body that fails to make even more manifest the nature of my mind. But there are still so many other things in the mind itself on the basis of which my knowledge of it can be rendered more distinct that it hardly seems worth enumerating those things which emanate to it from the body.

But lo and behold, I have returned on my own to where I wanted to be. For since I now know that even bodies are not, properly speaking, perceived by the senses or by the faculty of imagination, but by the intellect alone, and that they are not perceived through their being touched or seen, but only through their being understood, I manifestly know that nothing can be perceived more easily and more evidently than my own mind. But since the tendency to hang on to long-held beliefs cannot be put aside so quickly, I want to stop here, so that by the length of my meditation this new knowledge may be more deeply impressed upon my memory.

## Meditation Three: Concerning God, That He Exists

I will now shut my eyes, stop up my ears, and withdraw all my senses. I will also blot out from my thoughts all images of corporeal things, or rather, since the latter is hardly possible, I will regard these images as empty, false, and worthless. And as I converse with myself alone and look more deeply into myself, I will attempt to render myself gradually better known and more familiar to myself. I am a thing that thinks, that is to say, a thing that doubts, affirms, denies, understands a few things, is ignorant of many things, wills, refrains from willing, and also imagines and senses. For as I observed earlier, even though these things that I sense or imagine may perhaps be nothing at all outside me, nevertheless I am certain that these modes of thinking, which are cases of what I call sensing and imagining, insofar as they are merely modes of thinking, do exist within me.

In these few words, I have reviewed everything I truly know, or at least what so far I have noticed that I know. Now I will ponder more carefully to see whether perhaps there may be other things belonging to me that up until now I have failed to notice. I am certain that I am a thinking thing. But do I not therefore also know what is required for me to be certain of anything? Surely in this first instance of knowledge, there is nothing but a certain clear and distinct perception of what I affirm. Yet this would hardly be enough to render me certain of the truth of a thing, if it could ever happen that something that I perceived so clearly and distinctly were false. And thus I now seem able to posit as a general rule that everything I very clearly and distinctly perceive is true.

Be that as it may, I have previously admitted many things as wholly certain and evident that nevertheless I later discovered to be doubtful. What sorts of things were these? Why, the earth, the sky, the stars, and all the other things I perceived by means of the senses. But what was it about these things that I clearly perceived? Surely the fact that the ideas or thoughts of these things were hovering before my mind. But even now I do not deny that these ideas are in me. Yet there was something else I used to affirm, which, owing to my habitual tendency to believe it, I used to think was something I clearly perceived, even though I actually did not perceive it all: namely, that certain things existed outside me, things from which those ideas proceeded and which those ideas completely resembled. But on this point I was mistaken; or, rather if my judgment was a true one, it was not the result of the force of my perception.

But what about when I considered something very simple and easy in the areas of arithmetic or geometry, for example that two plus three make five, and the like? Did I not intuit them at least clearly enough so as to affirm them as true? To be sure, I did decide later on that I must doubt these things, but that was only because it occurred to me that some God could perhaps have given me a nature such that I might be deceived even about matters that seemed most evident. But whenever this preconceived opinion about the supreme power of God occurs to me, I cannot help admitting that, were he to wish it, it would be easy for him to cause me to err even in those matters that I think I intuit as clearly as possible with the eyes of the mind. On the other hand, whenever I turn my attention to those very things that I think I perceive with such great clarity, I am so completely persuaded by them that I spontaneously blurt out these words: "let him who can deceive me; so long as I think that I am something, he will never bring it about that I am nothing. Nor will he one day make it true that I never existed, for it is true now that I do exist. Nor will he even bring it about that perhaps two plus three might equal more or less than five, or similar items in which I recognize an obvious contradiction." And certainly, because I have no reason for thinking that there is a God who is a deceiver (and of course I do not yet sufficiently know whether there even is a God), the basis for doubting, depending as it does merely on the above hypothesis, is very tenuous and, so to speak, metaphysical. But in order to remove even this basis for doubt, I should at the first opportunity inquire whether there is a God, and, if there is, whether or not he can be a deceiver. For if I am ignorant of this, it appears I am never capable of being completely certain about anything else.

However, at this stage good order seems to demand that I first group all my thoughts into certain classes, and ask in which of them truth or falsity properly resides. Some of these thoughts are like images of things; to these alone does the word "idea" properly apply, as when I think of a man, or a chimera, or the sky, or an angel, or God. Again there are other thoughts that take different forms, for example, when I will, or fear, or affirm, or deny, there is always something that I grasp as the subject of my thought, yet I embrace in my thought something more than the likeness of that thing. Some of these thoughts are called volitions or affects, while others are called judgments.

Now as far as ideas are concerned, if they are considered alone and in their own right, without being referred to something else, they cannot, properly speaking, be false. For whether it is a she-goat or a chimera that I am imagining, it is no less true that I imagine the one than the other. Moreover, we need not fear that there is falsity in the will itself or in the affects, for although I can choose evil things or even things that are utterly nonexistent, I cannot conclude from this that it is untrue that I do choose these things. Thus there remain only judgments in which I must take care not to be mistaken. Now the principal and most frequent error to be found in judgments consists in the fact that I judge that the ideas which are in me are similar to or in conformity with certain things outside me. Obviously, if I were to consider these ideas merely as certain modes of my thought, and were not to refer them to anything else, they could hardly give me any subject matter for error.

Among these ideas, some appear to me to be innate, some adventitious, and some produced by me. For I understand what a thing is, what truth is, what thought is, and I appear to have derived this exclusively from

my very own nature. But say I am now hearing a noise, or looking at the sun, or feeling the fire; up until now I judged that these things proceeded from certain things outside me, and finally, that sirens, hippogriffs, and the like are made by me. Or perhaps I can even think of all these ideas as being adventitious, or as being innate, or as fabrications, for I have not yet clearly ascertained their true origin.

But here I must inquire particularly into those ideas that I believe to be derived from things existing outside me. Just what reason do I have for believing that these ideas resemble those things? Well, I do seem to have been so taught by nature. Moreover, I do know from experience that these ideas do not depend upon my will, nor consequently upon myself, for I often notice them even against my will. Now, for example, whether or not I will it, I feel heat. It is for this reason that I believe this feeling or idea of heat comes to me from something other than myself, namely from heat of the fire by which I am sitting. Nothing is more obvious than the judgment that this thing is sending its likeness rather than something else into me.

I will now see whether these reasons are powerful enough. When I say here "I have been so taught by nature," all I have in mind is that I am driven by a spontaneous impulse to believe this, and not that some light of nature is showing me that it is true. These are two very different things. For whatever is shown me by this light of nature, for example, that from the fact that I doubt, it follows that I am, and the like, cannot in any way be doubtful. This is owing to the fact that there can be no other faculty that I can trust as much as this light and which could teach that these things are not true. But as far as natural impulses are concerned, in the past I have often judged myself to have been driven by them to make the poorer choice when it was a question of choosing a good; and I fail to see why I should place any greater faith in them in other matters.

Again, although these ideas do not depend upon my will, it does not follow that they necessarily proceed from things existing outside me. For just as these impulses about which I spoke just now seem to be different from my will, even though they are in me, so too perhaps there is also in me some other faculty, one not yet sufficiently known to me, which produces these ideas, just as it has always seemed up to now that ideas are formed in me without any help from external things when I am asleep.

And finally, even if these ideas did proceed from things other than myself, it does not therefore follow that they must resemble those things. Indeed it seems I have frequently noticed a vast difference in many respects. For example, I find within myself two distinct ideas of the sun. One idea is drawn, as it were, from the senses. Now it is this idea which, of all those that I take to be derived from outside me, is most in need of examination. By means of this idea the sun appears to me to be quite small. But there is another idea, one derived from astronomical reasoning, that is, it is elicited from certain notions that are innate in me, or else is fashioned by me in some other way. Through this idea the sun is shown to be several times larger than the earth. Both ideas surely cannot resemble the same sun existing outside me; and reason convinces me that the idea that seems to have emanated from the sun itself from so close is the very one that least resembles the sun.

All these points demonstrate sufficiently that up to this point it was not a well-founded judgment, but only a blind impulse that formed the basis of my belief that things existing outside me send ideas or images of themselves to me through the sense organs or by some other means.

But still another way occurs to me for inquiring whether some of the things of which there are ideas in me do exist outside me: insofar as these ideas are merely modes of thought, I see no inequality among them; they all seem to proceed from me in the same manner. But insofar as one idea represents one thing and another idea another thing, it is obvious that they do differ very greatly from one another. Unquestionably, those ideas that display substances to me are something more and, if I may say so, contain within themselves more objective reality than those which represent only modes or accidents. Again, the idea that enables me to understand a supreme deity, eternal, infinite, omniscient, omnipotent, and creator of all things other than himself, clearly has more objective reality within it than do those ideas through which finite substances are displayed.

Now it is indeed evident by the light of nature that there must be at least as much [reality] in the efficient and total cause as there is in the effect of that same cause. For whence, I ask, could an effect get its reality, if not from its cause? And how could the cause give that reality to the effect, unless it also possessed that reality? Hence it follows that something cannot come into being out of nothing, and also that what is more perfect (that is, what contains in itself more reality) cannot come into being from what is less perfect. But this is manifestly true not merely for those effects whose reality is actual or formal, but also for ideas in which only objective reality is considered. For example, not only can a stone which did not exist previously not now begin to exist unless it is produced by something in which there is, either formally or eminently, everything that is in the stone; nor heat be introduced into a subject which was not already hot unless it is done by something that is of at least as perfect an order as heat—and the same for the rest—but it is also true that there can be in me no idea of heat, or of a stone, unless it is placed in me by some cause that has at least as much reality as I conceive to be in the heat or in the stone. For although this cause conveys none of its actual or formal reality to my idea, it should not be thought for that reason that it must be less real. Rather, the very nature of an idea is such that of itself it needs no formal reality other than what it borrows from my thought, of which it is a mode. But that a particular idea contains this as opposed to that objective reality is surely owing to some cause in which there is at least as much formal reality as there is objective reality contained in the idea. For if we assume that something is found in the idea that was not in its cause, then the idea gets that something from nothing. Yet as imperfect a mode of being as this is by which a thing exists in the intellect objectively through an idea, nevertheless it is plainly not nothing; hence it cannot get its being from nothing.

Moreover, even though the reality that I am considering in my ideas is merely objective reality, I ought not on that account to suspect that there is no need for the same reality to be formally in the causes of these ideas, but that it suffices for it to be in them objectively. For just as the objective mode of being belongs to ideas by their very nature, so the formal mode of being belongs to the causes of ideas, at least to the first and preeminent ones, by their very nature. And although one idea can perhaps issue from another, nevertheless no infinite regress is permitted here; eventually some first idea must be reached whose cause is a sort of archetype that contains formally all the reality that is in the idea merely objectively. Thus it is clear to me by the light of nature that the ideas that are in me are like images that can easily fail to match the perfection of the things from which they have been drawn, but which can contain nothing greater or more perfect.

And the longer and more attentively I examine all these points, the more clearly and distinctly I know they are true. But what am I ultimately to conclude? If the objective reality of any of my ideas is found to be so great that I am certain that the same reality was not in me, either formally or eminently, and that therefore I myself cannot be the cause of the idea, then it necessarily follows that I am not alone in the world, but that something else, which is the cause of this idea, also exists. But if no such idea is found in me, I will have no argument whatsoever to make me certain of the existence of anything other than myself, for I have conscientiously reviewed all these arguments, and so far I have been unable to find any other.

Among my ideas, in addition to the one that displays me to myself (about which there can be no difficulty at this point), are others that represent God, corporeal and inanimate things, angels, animals, and finally other men like myself.

As to the ideas that display other men, or animals, or angels, I easily understand that they could be fashioned from the ideas that I have of myself, of corporeal things, and of God — even if no men (except myself), no animals, and no angels existed in the world.

As to the ideas of corporeal things, there is nothing in them that is so great that it seems incapable of having originated from me. For if I investigate them thoroughly and examine each one individually in the way I examined the idea of wax yesterday, I notice that there are only a very few things in them that I perceive clearly and distinctly: namely, size, or extension in length, breadth, and depth; shape, which arises from the limits of this extension; position, which various things possessing shape have in relation to one another; and motion, or alteration in position. To these can be added substance, duration, and number. But as for the remaining items, such as light and colors, sounds, odors, tastes, heat and cold and other tactile qualities, I think of these only in a very confused and obscure manner, to the extent that I do not even know whether they are true or false, that is, whether the ideas I have of them are ideas of things or ideas of non-things. For although a short time ago I noted that falsity properly so called (or "formal" falsity) is to be found only in judgments, nevertheless there is another kind of falsity (called "material" falsity) which is found in ideas whenever they represent a non-thing as if it were a thing. For example, the ideas I have of heat and cold fall so far short of being clear and distinct that I cannot tell from them whether cold is merely the privation of heat or whether heat is the privation of cold, or whether both are real qualities, or whether neither is. And because ideas can only be, as it were, of things, if it is true that cold is merely the absence of heat, then an idea that represents cold to me as something real and positive will not inappropriately be called false. The same holds for other similar ideas.

Assuredly, I need not assign to these ideas an author distinct from myself. For if they were false, that is, if they were to represent non-things, I know by the light of nature that they proceed from nothing; that is, they are in me for no other reason than that something is lacking in my nature, and that my nature is not entirely perfect. If, on the other hand, these ideas are true, then because they exhibit so little reality to me that I cannot distinguish it from a non-thing, I see no reason why they cannot get their being from me.

As for what is clear and distinct in the ideas of corporeal things, it appears I could have borrowed some of these from the idea of myself: namely, substance, duration, number, and whatever else there may be of this type. For instance, I think that a stone is a substance, that is to say, a thing that is suitable for existing in itself; and likewise I think that I too am a substance. Despite the fact that I conceive myself to be a thinking thing and not an extended thing, whereas I conceive of a stone as an extended thing and not a thinking thing, and hence there is the greatest diversity between these two concepts, nevertheless they seem to agree with one another when considered under the rubric of substance. Furthermore, I perceive that I now exist and recall that I have previously existed for some time. And I have various thoughts and know how many of them there are. It is in doing these things that I acquire the ideas of duration and number, which I can then apply to other things. However, none of the other components out of which the ideas of corporeal things are fashioned (namely extension, shape, position, and motion) are contained in me formally, since I am merely a thinking thing. But since these are only certain modes of a substance, whereas I am a substance, it seems possible that they are contained in me eminently.

Thus there remains only the idea of God. I must consider whether there is anything in this idea that could not have originated from me. I understand by the name "God" a certain substance that is infinite, independent, supremely intelligent, and supremely powerful, and that created me along with everything else that exists—if anything else exists. Indeed all these are such that, the more carefully I focus my attention on them, the less possible it seems they could have arisen from myself alone. Thus, from what has been said, I must conclude that God necessarily exists.

For although the idea of substance is in me by virtue of the fact that I am a substance, that fact is not sufficient to explain my having the idea of an infinite substance, since I am finite, unless this idea proceeded from some substance which really was infinite.

Nor should I think that I do not perceive the infinite by means of a true idea, but only through a negation of the finite, just as I perceive rest and darkness by means of a negation of motion and light. On the contrary, I clearly understand that there is more reality in an infinite substance than there is in a finite one. Thus the perception of the infinite is somehow prior

in me to the perception of the finite; that is, my perception of God is prior to my perception of myself. For how would I understand that I doubt and that I desire, that is, that I lack something and that I am not wholly perfect, unless there were some idea in me of a more perfect being, by comparison with which I might recognize my defects?

Nor can it be said that this idea of God is perhaps materially false and thus can originate from nothing, as I remarked just now about the ideas of heat and cold, and the like. On the contrary, because it is the most clear and distinct and because it contains more objective reality than any other idea, no idea is in and of itself truer and has less of a basis for being suspected of falsehood. I maintain that this idea of a being that is supremely perfect and infinite is true in the highest degree. For although I could perhaps pretend that such a being does not exist, nevertheless I could not pretend that the idea of such a being discloses to me nothing real, as was the case with the idea of cold which I referred to earlier. It is indeed an idea that is utterly clear and distinct; for whatever I clearly and distinctly perceive to be real and true and to involve some perfection is wholly contained in that idea. It is no objection that I do not comprehend the infinite or that there are countless other things in God that I can in no way either comprehend or perhaps even touch with my thought. For the nature of the infinite is such that it is not comprehended by a being such as I, who am finite. And it is sufficient that I understand this very point and judge that all those things that I clearly perceive and that I know to contain some perfection—and perhaps even countless other things of which I am ignorant—are in God either formally or eminently. The result is that, of all the ideas that are in me, the idea that I have of God is the most true, the most clear and distinct.

But perhaps I am something greater than I myself understand. Perhaps all these perfections that I am attributing to God are somehow in me potentially, although they do not yet assert themselves and are not yet actualized. For I now observe that my knowledge is gradually being increased, and I see nothing standing in the way of its being increased more and more to infinity. Moreover, I see no reason why, with my knowledge thus increased, I could not acquire all the remaining perfections of God. And, finally, if the potential for these perfections is in me already, I see no reason why this potential would not suffice to produce the idea of these perfections.

Yet none of these things can be the case. First, while it is true that my knowledge is gradually being increased and that there are many things in me potentially that are not yet actual, nevertheless, none of these pertains to the idea of God, in which there is nothing whatever that is potential. Indeed this gradual increase is itself a most certain proof of imperfection. Moreover, although my knowledge may always increase more and more, nevertheless I understand that this knowledge will never by this means be actually infinite, because it will never reach a point where it is incapable of greater increase. On the contrary, I judge God to be actually infinite, so that nothing can be added to his perfection. Finally, I perceive that the objective being of an idea cannot be produced by a merely potential being (which, strictly speaking, is nothing), but only by an actual or formal being.

Indeed there is nothing in all these things that is not manifest by the light of nature to one who is conscientious and attentive. But when I am less attentive, and the images of sensible things blind the mind's eye, I do not so easily recall why the idea of a being more perfect than me necessarily proceeds from a being that really is more perfect. This being the case, it is appropriate to ask further whether I myself who have this idea could exist, if such a being did not exist.

From what source, then, do I derive my existence? Why, from myself, or from my parents, or from whatever other things there are that are less perfect than God. For nothing more perfect than God, or even as perfect as God, can be thought or imagined.

But if I got my being from myself, I would not doubt, nor would I desire, nor would I lack anything at all. For I would have given myself all the perfections of which I have some idea; in so doing, I myself would be God! I must not think that the things I lack could perhaps be more difficult to acquire than the ones I have now. On the contrary, it is obvious that it would have been much more difficult for me (that is, a thing or substance that thinks) to emerge out of

nothing than it would be to acquire the knowledge of many things about which I am ignorant (these items of knowledge being merely accidents of that substance). Certainly, if I got this greater thing from myself, I would not have denied myself at least those things that can be had more easily. Nor would I have denied myself any of those other things that I perceive to be contained in the idea of God, for surely none of them seem to me more difficult to bring about. But if any of them were more difficult to bring about, they would certainly also seem more difficult to me, even if the remaining ones that I possess I got from myself, since it would be on account of them that I would experience that my power is limited.

Nor am I avoiding the force of these arguments, if I suppose that perhaps I have always existed as I do now, as if it then followed that no author of my existence need be sought. For because the entire span of one's life can be divided into countless parts, each one wholly independent of the rest, it does not follow from the fact that I existed a short time ago that I must exist now, unless some cause, as it were, creates me all over again at this moment, that is to say, which preserves me. For it is obvious to one who pays close attention to the nature of time that plainly the same force and action are needed to preserve anything at each individual moment that it lasts as would be required to create that same thing anew, were it not yet in existence. Thus conservation differs from creation solely by virtue of a distinction of reason; this too is one of those things that are manifest by the light of nature.

Therefore, I must now ask myself whether I possess some power by which I can bring it about that I myself, who now exist, will also exist a little later on. For since I am nothing but a thinking thing—or at least since I am now dealing simply and precisely with that part of me which is a thinking thing—if such a power were in me, then I would certainly be aware of it. But I observe that there is no such power; and from this very fact I know most clearly that I depend upon some being other than myself.

But perhaps this being is not God, and I have been produced either by my parents or by some other causes less perfect than God. On the contrary, as I said before, it is obvious that there must be at least as much in the cause as there is in the effect. Thus, regardless of what it is that eventually is assigned as my cause, because I am a thinking thing and have within me a certain idea of God, it must be granted that what caused me is also a thinking thing and it too has an idea of all the perfections which I attribute to God. And I can again inquire of this cause whether it got its existence from itself or from another cause. For if it got its existence from itself, it is evident from what has been said that it is itself God, because, having the power of existing in and of itself, it unquestionably also has the power of actually possessing all the perfections of which it has in itself an idea—that is, all the perfections that I conceive to be in God. However, if it got its existence from another cause, I will once again inquire in similar fashion about this other cause: whether it got its existence from itself or from another cause, until finally I arrive at the ultimate cause, which will be God. For it is apparent enough that there can be no infinite regress here, especially since I am not dealing here merely with the cause that once produced me, but also and most especially with the cause that preserves me at the present time.

Nor can one fancy that perhaps several partial causes have concurred in bringing me into being, and that I have taken the ideas of the various perfections I attribute to God from a variety of causes, so that all of these perfections are found somewhere in the universe, but not all joined together in a single being—God. On the contrary, the unity, the simplicity, that is, the inseparability of all those features that are in God is one of the chief perfections that I understand to be in him. Certainly the idea of the unity of all his perfections could not have been placed in me by any cause from which I did not also get the ideas of the other perfections; for neither could some cause have made me understand them joined together and inseparable from one another, unless it also caused me to recognize what they were.

Finally, as to my parents, even if everything that I ever believed about them were true, still it is certainly not they who preserve me; nor is it they who in any way brought me into being, insofar as I am a thinking thing. Rather, they merely placed certain dispositions in the matter which I judged to contain me, that is,

a mind, which now is the only thing I take myself to be. And thus there can be no difficulty here concerning my parents. Indeed I have no choice but to conclude that the mere fact of my existing and of there being in me an idea of a most perfect being, that is, God, demonstrates most evidently that God too exists.

All that remains for me is to ask how I received this idea of God. For I did not draw it from the senses; it never came upon me unexpectedly, as is usually the case with the ideas of sensible things when these things present themselves (or seem to present themselves) to the external sense organs. Nor was it made by me, for I plainly can neither subtract anything from it nor add anything to it. Thus the only option remaining is that this idea is innate in me, just as the idea of myself is innate in me.

To be sure, it is not astonishing that in creating me, God should have endowed me with this idea, so that it would be like the mark of the craftsman impressed upon his work, although this mark need not be something distinct from the work itself. But the mere fact that God created me makes it highly plausible that I have somehow been made in his image and likeness, and that I perceive this likeness, in which the idea of God is contained, by means of the same faculty by which I perceive myself. That is, when I turn the mind's eye toward myself, I understand not only that I am something incomplete and dependent upon another, something aspiring indefinitely for greater and greater or better things, but also that the being on whom I depend has in himself all those greater things—not merely indefinitely and potentially, but infinitely and actually, and thus that he is God. The whole force of the argument rests on the fact that I recognize that it would be impossible for me to exist, being of such a nature as I am (namely, having in me the idea of God), unless God did in fact exist. God, I say, that same being the idea of whom is in me: a being having all those perfections that I cannot comprehend, but can somehow touch with my thought, and a being subject to no defects whatever. From these considerations it is quite obvious that he cannot be a deceiver, for it is manifest by the light of nature that all fraud and deception depend on some defect.

But before examining this idea more closely and

at the same time inquiring into other truths that can be gathered from it, at this point I want to spend some time contemplating this God, to ponder his attributes and, so far as the eye of my darkened mind can take me, to gaze upon, to admire, and to adore the beauty of this immense light. For just as we believe by faith that the greatest felicity of the next life consists solely in this contemplation of the divine majesty, so too we now experience that from the same contemplation, although it is much less perfect, the greatest pleasure of which we are capable in this life can be perceived.

## Meditation Four: Concerning the True and the False

Lately I have become accustomed to withdrawing my mind from the senses, and I have carefully taken note of the fact that very few things are truly perceived regarding corporeal things, although a great many more things are known regarding the human mind, and still many more things regarding God. The upshot is that I now have no difficulty directing my thought away from things that can be imagined to things that can be grasped only by the understanding and are wholly separate from matter. In fact the idea I clearly have of the human mind—insofar as it is a thinking thing, not extended in length, breadth or depth, and having nothing else from the body—is far more distinct than the idea of any corporeal thing. And when I take note of the fact that I doubt, or that I am a thing that is incomplete and dependent, there comes to mind a clear and distinct idea of a being that is independent and complete, that is, an idea of God. And from the mere fact that such an idea is in me, or that I who have this idea exist, I draw the obvious conclusion that God also exists, and that my existence depends entirely upon him at each and every moment. This conclusion is so obvious that I am confident that the human mind can know nothing more evident or more certain. And now I seem to see a way by which I might progress from this contemplation of the true God, in whom, namely, are hidden all the treasures of the sciences and wisdom, to the knowledge of other things.

To begin with, I acknowledge that it is impossible for God ever to deceive me, for trickery or deception are always indicative of some imperfection. And although the ability to deceive seems to be an indication of cleverness or power, the will to deceive undoubtedly attests to maliciousness or weakness. Accordingly, deception is incompatible with God.

Next I experience that there is in me a certain faculty of judgment, which, like everything else that is in me, I undoubtedly received from God. And since he does not wish to deceive me, he assuredly has not given me the sort of faculty with which I could ever make a mistake, when I use it properly.

No doubt regarding this matter would remain, but for the fact that it seems to follow from this that I am never capable of making a mistake. For if everything that is in me I got from God, and he gave me no faculty for making mistakes, it seems I am incapable of ever erring. And thus, so long as I think exclusively about God and focus my attention exclusively on him, I discern no cause of error or falsity. But once I turn my attention back on myself, I nevertheless experience that I am subject to countless errors. As I seek a cause of these errors, I notice that passing before me is not only a real and positive idea of God (that is, of a supremely perfect being), but also, as it were, a certain negative idea of nothingness (that is, of what is at the greatest possible distance from any perfection), and that I have been so constituted as a kind of middle ground between God and nothingness, or between the supreme being and non-being. Thus insofar as I have been created by the supreme being, there is nothing in me by means of which I might be deceived or be led into error; but insofar as I participate in nothingness or non-being, that is, insofar as I am not the supreme being and lack a great many things, it is not surprising that I make mistakes. Thus I certainly understand that error as such is not something real that depends upon God, but rather is merely a defect. And thus there is no need to account for my errors by positing a faculty given to me by God for the purpose. Rather, it just so happens that I make mistakes because the faculty of judging the truth, which I got from God, is not, in my case, infinite.

Still this is not yet altogether satisfactory; for error is not a pure negation, but rather a privation or a lack of some knowledge that somehow ought to be in me. And when I attend to the nature of God, it seems impossible that he would have placed in me a faculty that is not perfect in its kind or that is lacking some perfection it ought to have. For if it is true that the more expert the craftsman, the more perfect the works he produces, what can that supreme creator of all things make that is not perfect in all respects? No doubt God could have created me such that I never erred. No doubt, again, God always wills what is best. Is it then better that I should be in error rather than not?

As I mull these things over more carefully, it occurs to me first that there is no reason to marvel at the fact that God should bring about certain things the reasons for which I do not understand. Nor is his existence therefore to be doubted because I happen to experience other things of which I fail to grasp why and how he made them. For since I know now that my nature is very weak and limited, whereas the nature of God is immense, incomprehensible, and infinite, this is sufficient for me also to know that he can make innumerable things whose causes escape me. For this reason alone the entire class of causes which people customarily derive from a thing's "end," I judge to be utterly useless in physics. It is not without rashness that I think myself capable of inquiring into the ends of God.

It also occurs to me that whenever we ask whether the works of God are perfect, we should keep in view not simply some one creature in isolation from the rest, but the universe as a whole. For perhaps something might rightfully appear very imperfect if it were all by itself; and yet be most perfect, to the extent that it has the status of a part in the universe. And although subsequent to having decided to doubt everything, I have come to know with certainty only that I and God exist, nevertheless, after having taken note of the immense power of God, I cannot deny that many other things have been made by him, or at least could have been made by him. Thus I may have the status of a part in the universal scheme of things.

Next, as I focus more closely on myself and inquire into the nature of my errors (the only things that are indicative of some imperfection in me), I note that

these errors depend on the simultaneous concurrence of two causes: the faculty of knowing that is in me and the faculty of choosing, that is, the free choice of the will, in other words, simultaneously on the intellect and will. Through the intellect alone I merely perceive ideas, about which I can render a judgment. Strictly speaking, no error is to be found in the intellect when properly viewed in this manner. For although perhaps there may exist countless things about which I have no idea, nevertheless it must not be said that, strictly speaking, I am deprived of these ideas but only that I lack them in a negative sense. This is because I cannot adduce an argument to prove that God ought to have given me a greater faculty of knowing than he did. No matter how expert a craftsman I understand him to be, still I do not for that reason believe he ought to have bestowed on each one of his works all the perfections that he can put into some. Nor, on the other hand, can I complain that the will or free choice I have received from God is insufficiently ample or perfect, since I experience that it is limited by no boundaries whatever. In fact, it seems to be especially worth noting that no other things in me are so perfect or so great but that I understand that they can be still more perfect or greater. If, for example, I consider the faculty of understanding, I immediately recognize that in my case it is very small and quite limited, and at the very same time I form an idea of another much greater faculty of understanding—in fact, an understanding which is consummately great and infinite; and from the fact that I can form an idea of this faculty, I perceive that it pertains to the nature of God. Similarly, were I to examine the faculties of memory or imagination, or any of the other faculties, I would understand that in my case each of these is without exception feeble and limited, whereas in the case of God I understand each faculty to be boundless. It is only the will or free choice that I experience to be so great in me that I cannot grasp the idea of any greater faculty. This is so much the case that the will is the chief basis for my understanding that I bear a certain image and likeness of God. For although the faculty of willing is incomparably greater in God than it is in me, both by virtue of the knowledge and power that are joined to it and that render it more resolute and efficacious and by virtue of its object inasmuch as the divine will stretches over a greater number of things, nevertheless, when viewed in itself formally and precisely, God's faculty of willing does not appear to be any greater. This is owing to the fact that willing is merely a matter of being able to do or not do the same thing, that is, of being able to affirm or deny, to pursue or to shun; or better still, the will consists solely in the fact that when something is proposed to us by our intellect either to affirm or deny, to pursue or to shun, we are moved in such a way that we sense that we are determined to it by no external force. In order to be free I need not be capable of being moved in each direction; on the contrary, the more I am inclined toward one direction—either because I clearly understand that there is in it an aspect of the good and the true, or because God has thus disposed the inner recesses of my thought—the more freely do I choose that direction. Nor indeed does divine grace or natural knowledge ever diminish one's freedom; rather, they increase and strengthen it. However, the indifference that I experience when there is no reason moving me more in one direction than in another is the lowest grade of freedom; it is indicative not of any perfection in freedom, but rather of a defect, that is, a certain negation in knowledge. Were I always to see clearly what is true and good, I would never deliberate about what is to be judged or chosen. In that event, although I would be entirely free, I could never be indifferent.

But from these considerations I perceive that the power of willing, which I got from God, is not, taken by itself, the cause of my errors, for it is most ample as well as perfect in its kind. Nor is my power of understanding the cause of my errors. For since I got my power of understanding from God, whatever I understand I doubtless understand rightly, and it is impossible for me to be deceived in this. What then is the source of my errors? They are owing simply to the fact that, since the will extends further than the intellect, I do not contain the will within the same boundaries; rather, I also extend it to things I do not understand. Because the will is indifferent in regard to such matters, it easily turns away from the true and the good; and in this way I am deceived and I sin.

For example, during these last few days I was exam-ining whether anything in the world exists, and I noticed that, from the very fact that I was making this examination, it obviously followed that I exist. Nevertheless, I could not help judging that what I understood so clearly was true; not that I was coerced into making this judgment because of some external force, but because a great light in my intellect gave way to a great inclination in my will, and the less indifferent I was, the more spontaneously and freely did I believe it. But now, in addition to my knowing that I exist, insofar as I am a certain thinking thing, I also observe a certain idea of corporeal nature. It happens that I am in doubt as to whether the thinking nature which is in me, or rather which I am, is some-thing different from this corporeal nature, or whether both natures are one and the same thing. And I as-sume that as yet no consideration has occurred to my intellect to convince me of the one alternative rather than the other. Certainly in virtue of this very fact I am indifferent about whether to affirm or to deny either alternative, or even whether to make no judg-ment at all in the matter.

Moreover, this indifference extends not merely to things about which the intellect knows absolutely nothing, but extends generally to everything of which the intellect does not have a clear enough knowledge at the very time when the will is deliberating on them. For although probable guesses may pull me in one direction, the mere knowledge that they are merely guesses and not certain and indubitable proofs is all it takes to push my assent in the opposite direction. These last few days have provided me with ample experience on this point. For all the beliefs that I had once held to be most true I have supposed to be utterly false, and for the sole reason that I determined that I could somehow raise doubts about them.

But if I hold off from making a judgment when I do not perceive what is true with sufficient clarity and distinctness, it is clear that I am acting properly and am not committing an error. But if instead I were to make an assertion or a denial, then I am not using my freedom properly. Were I to select the alternative that is false, then obviously I will be in error. But were I to embrace the other alternative, it will be by sheer luck that I happen upon the truth; but I will still not be without fault, for it is manifest by the light of nature that a perception on the part of the intellect must always precede a determination on the part of the will. Inherent in this incorrect use of free will is the privation that constitutes the very essence of error: the privation, I say, present in this operation insofar as the operation proceeds from me, but not in the faculty given to me by God, nor even in its operation insofar as it depends upon him.

Indeed I have no cause for complaint on the grounds that God has not given me a greater power of understanding or a greater light of nature than he has, for it is of the essence of a finite intellect not to understand many things, and it is of the essence of a created intellect to be finite. Actually, instead of thinking that he has withheld from me or deprived me of those things that he has not given me, I ought to thank God, who never owed me anything, for what he has bestowed upon me.

Again, I have no cause for complaint on the grounds that God has given me a will that has a wider scope than my intellect. For since the will consists of merely one thing, something indivisible, as it were, it does not seem that its nature could withstand anything being removed from it. Indeed, the more ample the will is, the more I ought to thank the one who gave it to me.

Finally, I should not complain because God concurs with me in eliciting those acts of the will, that is those judgments, in which I am mistaken. For insofar as those acts depend on God, they are absolutely true and good; and in a certain sense, there is greater perfection in me in being able to elicit those acts than in not being able to do so. But privation, in which alone the defining characteristic of falsehood and wrongdoing is to be found, has no need whatever for God's concurrence, since a privation is not a thing, nor, when it is related to God as its cause, is it to be called a privation, but simply a negation. For it is surely no imperfection in God that he has given me the freedom to give or withhold my assent in those instances where he has not placed a clear and distinct perception in my intellect. But surely it is an imperfection in me that I do not use my freedom well and that I make judgments about things I do not properly understand. Nevertheless, I see that God could easily have brought it about that, while still

being free and having finite knowledge, I should nonetheless never make a mistake. This result could have been achieved either by his endowing my intellect with a clear and distinct perception of everything about which I would ever deliberate, or by simply impressing the following rule so firmly upon my memory that I could never forget it: I should never judge anything that I do not clearly and distinctly understand. I readily understand that, considered as a totality, I would have been more perfect than I am now, had God made me that way. But I cannot therefore deny that it may somehow be a greater perfection in the universe as a whole that some of its parts are not immune to error, while others are, than if all of them were exactly alike. And I have no right to complain that the part God has wished me to play is not the principal and most perfect one of all.

Furthermore, even if I cannot abstain from errors in the first way mentioned above, which depends upon a clear perception of everything about which I must deliberate, nevertheless I can avoid error in the other way, which depends solely on my remembering to abstain from making judgments whenever the truth of a given matter is not apparent. For although I experience a certain infirmity in myself, namely that I am unable to keep my attention constantly focused on one and the same item of knowledge, nevertheless, by attentive and often repeated meditation, I can bring it about that I call this rule to mind whenever the situation calls for it, and thus I would acquire a certain habit of not erring.

Since herein lies the greatest and chief perfection of man, I think today's meditation, in which I investigated the cause of error and falsity, was quite profitable. Nor can this cause be anything other than the one I have described; for as often as I restrain my will when I make judgments, so that it extends only to those matters that the intellect clearly and distinctly discloses to it, it plainly cannot happen that I err. For every clear and distinct perception is surely something, and hence it cannot come from nothing. On the contrary, it must necessarily have God for its author: God, I say, that supremely perfect being to whom it is repugnant to be a deceiver. Therefore the perception is most assuredly true. Today I have learned not merely what I must avoid so as never to make a mistake, but at the same time what I must do to attain truth. For I will indeed attain it, if only I pay enough attention to all the things that I perfectly understand, and separate them off from the rest, which I apprehend more confusedly and more obscurely. I will be conscientious about this in the future.

## Meditation Five: Concerning the Essence of Material Things, and Again Concerning God, That He Exists

Several matters remain for me to examine concerning the attributes of God and myself, that is, concerning the nature of my mind. But perhaps I will take these up at some other time. For now, since I have noted what to avoid and what to do in order to attain the truth, nothing seems more pressing than that I try to free myself from the doubts into which I fell a few days ago, and that I see whether anything certain is to be had concerning material things.

Yet, before inquiring whether any such things exist outside me, I surely ought to consider the ideas of these things, insofar as they exist in my thought, and see which ones are distinct and which ones are confused.

I do indeed distinctly imagine the quantity that philosophers commonly call "continuous," that is, the extension of this quantity, or rather of the thing quantified in length, breadth, and depth. I enumerate the various parts in it. I ascribe to these parts any sizes, shapes, positions, and local movements whatever; to these movements I ascribe any durations whatever.

Not only are these things manifestly known and transparent to me, viewed thus in a general way, but also, when I focus my attention on them, I perceive countless particulars concerning shapes, number, movement, and the like. Their truth is so open and so much in accord with my nature that, when I first discover them, it seems I am not so much learning something new as recalling something I knew beforehand. In other words, it seems as though I am noticing things for the first time that were in fact in me for a long while, although I had not previously directed a mental gaze upon them.

What I believe must be considered above all here is the fact that I find within me countless ideas of certain things, that, even if perhaps they do not exist anywhere outside me, still cannot be said to be nothing. And although, in a sense, I think them at will, nevertheless they are not something I have fabricated; rather they have their own true and immutable natures. For example, when I imagine a triangle, even if perhaps no such figure exists outside my thought anywhere in the world and never has, the triangle still has a certain determinate nature, essence, or form which is unchangeable and eternal, which I did not fabricate, and which does not depend on my mind. This is evident from the fact that various properties can be demonstrated regarding this triangle: namely, that its three angles are equal to two right angles, that its longest side is opposite its largest angle, and so on. These are properties I now clearly acknowledge, whether I want to or not, even if I previously had given them no thought whatever when I imagined the triangle. For this reason, then, they were not fabricated by me.

It is irrelevant for me to say that perhaps the idea of a triangle came to me from external things through the sense organs because of course I have on occasion seen triangle-shaped bodies. For I can think of countless other figures, concerning which there can be no suspicion of their ever having entered me through the senses, and yet I can demonstrate various properties of these figures, no less than I can those of the triangle. All these properties are patently true because I know them clearly, and thus they are something and not merely nothing. For it is obvious that whatever is true is something, and I have already demonstrated at some length that all that I know clearly is true. And even if I had not demonstrated this, certainly the nature of my mind is such that nevertheless I cannot refrain from assenting to these things, at least while I perceive them clearly. And I recall that even before now, when I used to keep my attention glued to the objects of the senses, I always took the truths I clearly recognized regarding figures, numbers, or other things pertaining to arithmetic, geometry or, in general, to pure and abstract mathematics to be the most certain of all.

But if, from the mere fact that I can bring forth from my thought the idea of something, it follows that all that I clearly and distinctly perceive to belong to that thing really does belong to it, then cannot this too be a basis for an argument proving the existence of God? Clearly the idea of God, that is, the idea of a supremely perfect being, is one I discover to be no less within me than the idea of any figure or number. And that it belongs to God's nature that he always exists is something I understand no less clearly and distinctly than is the case when I demonstrate in regard to some figure or number that something also belongs to the nature of that figure or number. Thus, even if not everything that I have meditated upon during these last few days were true, still the existence of God ought to have for me at least the same degree of certainty that truths of mathematics had until now.

However, this point is not wholly obvious at first glance, but has a certain look of a sophism about it. Since in all other matters I have become accustomed to distinguishing existence from essence, I easily convince myself that it can even be separated from God's essence, and hence that God can be thought of as not existing. But nevertheless, it is obvious to anyone who pays close attention that existence can no more be separated from God's essence than its having three angles equal to two right angles can be separated from the essence of a triangle, or than the idea of a valley can be separated from the idea of a mountain. Thus it is no less[2] contradictory to think of God (that is, a supremely perfect being) lacking existence (that is, lacking some perfection) than it is to think of a mountain without a valley.

But granted I can no more think of God as not existing than I can think of a mountain without a valley; nevertheless it surely does not follow from the fact that I think of a mountain without a valley that a mountain exists in the world. Likewise, from the fact that I think of God as existing, it does not seem to follow that God exists, for my thought imposes no necessity on things. And just as one may imagine a winged horse, without there being a horse that has wings, in the same way perhaps I can attach existence to God, even though no God exists.

2. A literal translation of the Latin text (*non magis*) is "no more." This is obviously a misstatement on Descartes's part, since it contradicts his own clearly stated views.

But there is a sophism lurking here. From the fact that I am unable to think of a mountain without a valley, it does not follow that a mountain or a valley exists anywhere, but only that, whether they exist or not, a mountain and a valley are inseparable from one another. But from the fact that I cannot think of God except as existing, it follows that existence is inseparable from God, and that for this reason he really exists. Not that my thought brings this about or imposes any necessity on anything; but rather the necessity of the thing itself, namely of the existence of God, forces me to think this. For I am not free to think of God without existence, that is, a supremely perfect being without a supreme perfection, as I am to imagine a horse with or without wings.

Further, it should not be said here that even though I surely need to assent to the existence of God once I have asserted that God has all perfections and that existence is one of these perfections, nevertheless that earlier assertion need not have been made. Likewise, I need not believe that all four-sided figures can be inscribed in a circle; but given that I posit this, it would then be necessary for me to admit that a rhombus can be inscribed in a circle. Yet this is obviously false. For although it is not necessary that I should ever happen upon any thought of God, nevertheless whenever I am of a mind to think of a being that is first and supreme, and bring forth the idea of God as it were from the storehouse of my mind, I must of necessity ascribe all perfections to him, even if I do not at that time enumerate them all or take notice of each one individually. This necessity plainly suffices so that afterwards, when I realize that existence is a perfection, I rightly conclude that a first and supreme being exists. In the same way, there is no necessity for me ever to imagine a triangle, but whenever I do wish to consider a rectilinear figure having but three angles, I must ascribe to it those properties on the basis of which one rightly infers that the three angles of this figure are no greater than two right angles, even though I do not take note of this at the time. But when I inquire as to the figures that may be inscribed in a circle, there is absolutely no need whatever for my thinking that all four-sided figures are of this sort; for that matter, I cannot even fabricate such a thing, so long as I am of a mind to admit only what I clearly and distinctly understand. Consequently, there is a great difference between false assumptions of this sort and the true ideas that are inborn in me, the first and chief of which is the idea of God. For there are a great many ways in which I understand that this idea is not an invention that is dependent upon my thought, but is an image of a true and immutable nature. First, I cannot think of anything aside from God alone to whose essence existence belongs. Next, I cannot understand how there could be two or more Gods of this kind. Again, once I have asserted that one God now exists, I plainly see that it is necessary that he has existed from eternity and will endure for eternity. Finally, I perceive many other features in God, none of which I can remove or change.

But, whatever type of argument I use, it always comes down to the fact that the only things that fully convince me are those that I clearly and distinctly perceive. And although some of these things I thus perceive are obvious to everyone, while others are discovered only by those who look more closely and inquire carefully, nevertheless, once they have been discovered, they are considered no less certain than the others. For example, in the case of a right triangle, although it is not so readily apparent that the square of the hypotenuse is equal to the sum of the squares of the other two sides as it is that the hypotenuse is opposite the largest angle, nevertheless, once the former has been ascertained, it is no less believed. However, as far as God is concerned, if I were not overwhelmed by prejudices and if the images of sensible things were not besieging my thought from all directions, I would certainly acknowledge nothing sooner or more easily than him. For what, in and of itself, is more manifest than that a supreme being exists, that is, that God, to whose essence alone existence belongs, exists?

And although I needed to pay close attention in order to perceive this, nevertheless I now am just as certain about this as I am about everything else that seems most certain. Moreover, I observe also that certitude about other things is so dependent on this, that without it nothing can ever be perfectly known.

For I am indeed of such a nature that, while I perceive something very clearly and distinctly, I cannot help believing it to be true. Nevertheless, my nature is also such that I cannot focus my mental gaze always on the same thing, so as to perceive it clearly. Often the memory of a previously made judgment may return when I am no longer attending to the arguments on account of which I made such a judgment. Thus, other arguments can be brought forward that would easily make me change my opinion, were I ignorant of God. And thus I would never have true and certain knowledge about anything, but merely fickle and changeable opinions. Thus, for example, when I consider the nature of a triangle, it appears most evident to me, steeped as I am in the principles of geometry, that its three angles are equal to two right angles. And so long as I attend to its demonstration I cannot help believing this to be true. But no sooner do I turn the mind's eye away from the demonstration, than, however much I still recall that I had observed it most clearly, nevertheless, it can easily happen that I entertain doubts about whether it is true, were I ignorant of God. For I can convince myself that I have been so constituted by nature that I might occasionally be mistaken about those things I believe I perceive most evidently, especially when I recall that I have often taken many things to be true and certain, which other arguments have subsequently led me to judge to be false.

But once I perceived that there is a God, and also understood at the same time that everything else depends on him, and that he is not a deceiver, I then concluded that everything that I clearly and distinctly perceive is necessarily true. Hence even if I no longer attend to the reasons leading me to judge this to be true, so long as I merely recall that I did clearly and distinctly observe it, no counterargument can be brought forward that might force me to doubt it. On the contrary, I have a true and certain knowledge of it. And not just of this one fact, but of everything else that I recall once having demonstrated, as in geometry, and so on. For what objections can now be raised against me? That I have been made such that I am often mistaken? But I now know that I cannot be mistaken in matters I plainly understand. That I have taken many things to be true and certain which subsequently I recognized to be false? But none of these were things I clearly and distinctly cperceived. But I was ignorant of this rule for determining the truth, and I believed these things perhaps for other reasons which I later discovered were less firm. What then remains to be said? That perhaps I am dreaming, as I recently objected against myself, in other words, that everything I am now thinking of is no truer than what occurs to someone who is asleep? Be that as it may, this changes nothing; for certainly, even if I were dreaming, if anything is evident to my intellect, then it is entirely true.

And thus I see plainly that the certainty and truth of every science depends exclusively upon the knowledge of the true God, to the extent that, prior to my becoming aware of him, I was incapable of achieving perfect knowledge about anything else. But now it is possible for me to achieve full and certain knowledge about countless things, both about God and other intellectual matters, as well as about the entirety of that corporeal nature which is the object of pure mathematics.

## Meditation Six: Concerning the Existence of Material Things, and the Real Distinction between Mind and Body

It remains for me to examine whether material things exist. Indeed I now know that they can exist, at least insofar as they are the object of pure mathematics, since I clearly and distinctly perceive them. For no doubt God is capable of bringing about everything that I am capable of perceiving in this way. And I have never judged that God was incapable of something, except when it was incompatible with my perceiving it distinctly. Moreover, from the faculty of imagination, which I notice I use while dealing with material things, it seems to follow that they exist. For to anyone paying very close attention to what imagination is, it appears to be simply a certain application of the knowing faculty to a body intimately present to it, and which therefore exists.

To make this clear, I first examine the difference between imagination and pure intellection. So, for example, when I imagine a triangle, I not only understand that it is a figure bounded by three lines, but at the same time I also envisage with the mind's eye those lines as if they were present; and this is what I call "imagining." On the other hand, if I want to think about a chiliagon, I certainly understand that it is a figure consisting of a thousand sides, just as well as I understand that a triangle is a figure consisting of three sides, yet I do not imagine those thousand sides in the same way, or envisage them as if they were present. And although in that case, because of force of habit I always imagine something whenever I think about a corporeal thing, I may perchance represent to myself some figure in a confused fashion, nevertheless this figure is obviously not a chiliagon. For this figure is really no different from the figure I would represent to myself, were I thinking of a myriagon or any other figure with a large number of sides. Nor is this figure of any help in knowing the properties that differentiate a chiliagon from other polygons. But if the figure in question is a pentagon, I surely can understand its figure, just as was the case with the chiliagon, without the help of my imagination. But I can also imagine a pentagon by turning the mind's eye both to its five sides and at the same time to the area bounded by those sides. At this point I am manifestly aware that I am in need of a peculiar sort of effort on the part of the mind in order to imagine, one that I do not employ in order to understand. This new effort on the part of the mind clearly shows the difference between imagination and pure intellection.

Moreover, I consider that this power of imagining that is in me, insofar as it differs from the power of understanding, is not required for my own essence, that is, the essence of my mind. For were I to be lacking this power, I would nevertheless undoubtedly remain the same entity I am now. Thus it seems to follow that the power of imagining depends upon something distinct from me. And I readily understand that, were a body to exist to which a mind is so joined that it may apply itself in order, as it were, to look at it any time it wishes, it could happen that it is by means of this very body that I imagine corporeal things. As a result, this mode of thinking may differ from pure intellection only in the sense that the mind, when it understands, in a sense turns toward itself and looks at one of the ideas that are in it; whereas when it imagines, it turns toward the body, and intuits in the body something that conforms to an idea either understood by the mind or perceived by sense. To be sure, I easily understand that the imagination can be actualized in this way, provided a body does exist. And since I can think of no other way of explaining imagination that is equally appropriate, I make a probable conjecture from this that a body exists. But this is only a probability. And even though I may examine everything carefully, nevertheless I do not yet see how the distinct idea of corporeal nature that I find in my imagination can enable me to develop an argument which necessarily concludes that some body exists.

But I am in the habit of imagining many other things, over and above that corporeal nature which is the object of pure mathematics, such as colors, sounds, tastes, pain, and the like, though not so distinctly. And I perceive these things better by means of the senses, from which, with the aid of the memory, they seem to have arrived at the imagination. Thus I should pay the same degree of attention to the senses, so that I might deal with them more appropriately. I must see whether I can obtain any reliable argument for the existence of corporeal things from those things that are perceived by the mode of thinking that I call "sense."

First of all, to be sure, I will review here all the things I previously believed to be true because I had perceived them by means of the senses and the causes I had for thinking this. Next I will assess the causes why I later called them into doubt. Finally, I will consider what I must now believe about these things.

So first, I sensed that I had a head, hands, feet, and other members that comprised this body which I viewed as part of me, or perhaps even as the whole of me. I sensed that this body was found among many other bodies, by which my body can be affected in various beneficial or harmful ways. I gauged what was opportune by means of a certain sensation of pleasure, and what was inopportune by a sensation of pain. In addition to pain and pleasure, I also sensed within me hunger, thirst, and other such appetites, as well as certain bodily tendencies toward mirth, sadness, anger, and other such affects. And externally, besides the extension, shapes, and motions of bodies, I also sensed their hardness, heat, and other tactile qualities. I also sensed light, colors, odors, tastes, and sounds, on the basis of whose variety I distinguished the sky, the earth, the seas, and the other bodies, one from the other. Now given the ideas of all these qualities that presented themselves to my thought, and which were all that I properly and immediately sensed, still it was surely not without reason that I thought I sensed things that were manifestly different from my thought, namely, the bodies from which these ideas proceeded. For I knew by experience that these ideas came upon me utterly without my consent, to the extent that, wish as I may, I could not sense any object unless it was present to a sense organ. Nor could I fail to sense it when it was present. And since the ideas perceived by sense were much more vivid and explicit and even, in their own way, more distinct than any of those that I deliberately and knowingly formed through meditation or that I found impressed on my memory, it seemed impossible that they came from myself. Thus the remaining alternative was that they came from other things. Since I had no knowledge of such things except from those same ideas themselves, I could not help entertaining the thought that they were similar to those ideas. Moreover, I also recalled that the use of the senses antedated the use of reason. And since I saw that the ideas that I myself fashioned were not as explicit as those that I perceived through the faculty of sense, and were for the most part composed of parts of the latter, I easily convinced myself that I had absolutely no idea in the intellect that I did not have beforehand in the sense faculty. Not without reason did I judge that this body, which by a certain special right I called "mine," belongs more to me than did any other. For I could never be separated from it in the same way I could be from other bodies. I sensed all appetites and feelings in and on behalf of it. Finally, I noticed pain and pleasurable excitement in its parts, but not in other bodies external to it. But why should a certain sadness of spirit arise from some sensation or other of pain, and why should a certain elation arise from a sensation of excitement, or why should that peculiar twitching in the stomach, which I call hunger, warn me to have something to eat, or why should dryness in the throat warn me to take something to drink, and so on? I plainly had no explanation other than that I had been taught this way by nature. For there is no affinity whatsoever, at least none I am aware of, between this twitching in the stomach and the will to have something to eat, or between the sensation of something causing pain and the thought of sadness arising from this sensation. But nature also seems to have taught me everything else as well that I judged concerning the objects of the senses, for I had already convinced myself that this was how things were, prior to my assessing any of the arguments that might prove it.

Afterwards, however, many experiences gradually weakened any faith that I had in the senses. Towers that had seemed round from afar occasionally appeared square at close quarters. Very large statues mounted on their pedestals did not seem large to someone looking at them from ground level. And in countless other such instances I determined that judgments in matters of the external senses were in error. And not just the external senses, but the internal senses as well. For what can be more intimate than pain? But I had sometimes heard it said by people whose leg or arm had been amputated that it seemed to them that they still occasionally sensed pain in the very limb they had lost. Thus, even in my own case it did not seem to be entirely certain that some bodily member was causing me pain, even though I did sense pain in it. To these causes for doubt I recently added two quite general ones. The first was that everything I ever thought I sensed while awake I could believe I also sometimes sensed while asleep, and since I do not believe that what I seem to sense in my dreams comes to me from things external to me, I saw no reason why I should hold this belief about those things I seem to be sensing while awake. The second was that, since I was still ignorant of the author of my origin (or at least pretended to be ignorant of it), I saw nothing to prevent my having been so constituted by nature that I should be mistaken even about what seemed to me most true. As to the arguments that used to convince me of the truth of sensible things, I found no difficulty responding to them. For since I seemed driven by nature toward many things about which reason tried to dissuade me, I did not think that what I was taught by nature deserved much credence. And even though the perceptions of the senses did not depend on my will, I did not think that we must therefore conclude that they came from things distinct from me, since perhaps there is some faculty in me, as yet unknown to me, that produces these perceptions.

But now, having begun to have a better knowledge of myself and the author of my origin, I am of the opinion that I must not rashly admit everything that I seem to derive from the senses; but neither, for that matter, should I call everything into doubt.

First, I know that all the things that I clearly and distinctly understand can be made by God such as I understand them. For this reason, my ability clearly and distinctly to understand one thing without another suffices to make me certain that the one thing is different from the other, since they can be separated from each other, at least by God. The question as to the sort of power that might effect such a separation is not relevant to their being thought to be different. For this reason, from the fact that I know that I exist, and that at the same time I judge that obviously nothing else belongs to my nature or essence except that I am a thinking thing, I rightly conclude that my essence consists entirely in my being a thinking thing. And although perhaps (or rather, as I shall soon say, assuredly) I have a body that is very closely joined to me, nevertheless, because on the one hand I have a clear and distinct idea of myself, insofar as I am merely a thinking thing and not an extended thing, and because on the other hand I have a distinct idea of a body, insofar as it is merely an extended thing and not a thinking thing, it is certain that I am really distinct from my body, and can exist without it.

Moreover, I find in myself faculties for certain special modes of thinking, namely the faculties of imagining and sensing. I can clearly and distinctly understand myself in my entirety without these faculties, but not vice versa: I cannot understand them clearly and distinctly without me, that is, without a substance endowed with understanding in which they inhere, for they include an act of understanding in their formal concept. Thus I perceive them to be distinguished from me as modes from a thing. I also acknowledge that there are certain other faculties, such as those of moving from one place to another, of taking on various shapes, and so on, that, like sensing or imagining, cannot be understood apart from some substance in which they inhere, and hence without which they cannot exist. But it is clear that these faculties, if in fact they exist, must be in a corporeal or extended substance, not in a substance endowed with understanding. For some extension is contained in a clear and distinct concept of them, though certainly not any understanding. Now there clearly is in me a passive faculty of sensing, that is, a faculty for receiving and knowing the ideas of sensible things; but I could not use it unless there also existed, either in me or in something else, a certain active faculty of producing or bringing about these ideas. But this faculty surely cannot be in me, since it clearly presupposes no act of understanding, and these ideas are produced without my cooperation and often even against my will. Therefore, the only alternative is that it is in some substance different from me, containing either formally or eminently all the reality that exists objectively in the ideas produced by that faculty, as I have just noted above. Hence this substance is either a body, that is, a corporeal nature, which contains formally all that is contained objectively in the ideas, or else it is God, or some other creature more noble than a body, which contains eminently all that is contained objectively in the ideas. But since God is not a deceiver, it is patently obvious that he does not send me these ideas either immediately by himself, or even through the mediation of some creature that contains the objective reality of these ideas not formally but only eminently. For since God has given me no faculty whatsoever for making this determination, but instead has given me a great inclination to believe that these ideas issue from corporeal things, I fail to see how God could be understood not to be a deceiver, if these ideas were to issue from a source other than corporeal things. And consequently corporeal things exist. Nevertheless, perhaps not all bodies exist exactly as I grasp them by sense, since this sensory grasp is in many cases very obscure and confused. But at least they do contain everything I clearly and distinctly understand—that is, everything, considered in a general sense, that is encompassed in the object of pure mathematics.

As far as the remaining matters are concerned, which are either merely particular (for example, that the sun is of such and such a size or shape, and so on) or less clearly understood (for example, light, sound, pain, and the like), even though these matters

are very doubtful and uncertain, nevertheless the fact that God is no deceiver (and thus no falsity can be found in my opinions, unless there is also in me a faculty given me by God for the purpose of rectifying this falsity) offers me a definite hope of reaching the truth even in these matters. And surely there is no doubt that all that I am taught by nature has some truth to it; for by "nature," taken generally, I understand nothing other than God himself or the ordered network of created things which was instituted by God. By my own particular nature I understand nothing other than the combination of all the things bestowed upon me by God.

There is nothing that this nature teaches me more explicitly than that I have a body that is ill-disposed when I feel pain, that needs food and drink when I suffer hunger or thirst, and the like. Therefore, I should not doubt that there is some truth in this.

By means of these sensations of pain, hunger, thirst and so on, nature also teaches that I am present to my body not merely in the way a sailor is present in a ship, but that I am most tightly joined and, so to speak, commingled with it, so much so that I and the body constitute one single thing. For if this were not the case, then I, who am only a thinking thing, would not sense pain when the body is injured; rather, I would perceive the wound by means of the pure intellect, just as a sailor perceives by sight whether anything in his ship is broken. And when the body is in need of food or drink, I should understand this explicitly, instead of having confused sensations of hunger and thirst. For clearly these sensations of thirst, hunger, pain, and so on are nothing but certain confused modes of thinking arising from the union and, as it were, the commingling of the mind with the body.

Moreover, I am also taught by nature that various other bodies exist around my body, some of which are to be pursued, while others are to be avoided. And to be sure, from the fact that I sense a wide variety of colors, sounds, odors, tastes, levels of heat, and grades of roughness, and the like, I rightly conclude that in the bodies from which these different perceptions of the senses proceed there are differences corresponding to the different perceptions—though perhaps the latter do not resemble the former. And from the fact that some of these perceptions are pleasant while others are unpleasant, it is plainly certain that my body, or rather my whole self, insofar as I am composed of a body and a mind, can be affected by various beneficial and harmful bodies in the vicinity.

Granted, there are many other things that I seem to have been taught by nature; nevertheless it was not really nature that taught them to me but a certain habit of making reckless judgments. And thus it could easily happen that these judgments are false: for example, that any space where there is absolutely nothing happening to move my senses is empty; or that there is something in a hot body that bears an exact likeness to the idea of heat that is in me; or that in a white or green body there is the same whiteness or greenness that I sense; or that in a bitter or sweet body there is the same taste, and so on; or that stars and towers and any other distant bodies have the same size and shape that they present to my senses, and other things of this sort. But to ensure that my perceptions in this matter are sufficiently distinct, I ought to define more precisely what exactly I mean when I say that I am "taught something by nature." For I am taking "nature" here more narrowly than the combination of everything bestowed on me by God. For this combination embraces many things that belong exclusively to my mind, such as my perceiving that what has been done cannot be undone, and everything else that is known by the light of nature. That is not what I am talking about here. There are also many things that belong exclusively to the body, such as that it tends to move downward, and so on. I am not dealing with these either, but only with what God has bestowed on me insofar as I am composed of mind and body. Accordingly, it is this nature that teaches me to avoid things that produce a sensation of pain and to pursue things that produce a sensation of pleasure, and the like. But it does not appear that nature teaches us to conclude anything, besides these things, from these sense perceptions unless the intellect has first conducted its own inquiry regarding things external to us. For it seems to belong exclusively to the mind, and not to the composite of mind and body, to know the truth in these matters. Thus, although a star affects my eye no more than does the flame from a small torch, still there is no real or positive tendency in my

eye toward believing that the star is no larger than the flame. Yet, ever since my youth, I have made this judgment without any reason for doing so. And although I feel heat as I draw closer to the fire, and I also feel pain upon drawing too close to it, there is not a single argument that persuades me that there is something in the fire similar to that heat, any more than to that pain. On the contrary, I am convinced only that there is something in the fire that, regardless of what it finally turns out to be, causes in us those sensations of heat or pain. And although there may be nothing in a given space that moves the senses, it does not therefore follow that there is no body in it. But I see that in these and many other instances I have been in the habit of subverting the order of nature. For admittedly I use the perceptions of the senses (which are properly given by nature only for signifying to the mind what things are useful or harmful to the composite of which it is a part, and to that extent they are clear and distinct enough), as reliable rules for immediately discerning what is the essence of bodies located outside us. Yet they signify nothing about that except quite obscurely and confusedly.

I have already examined in sufficient detail how it could happen that my judgments are false, despite the goodness of God. But a new difficulty now arises regarding those very things that nature shows me are either to be sought out or avoided, as well as the internal sensations where I seem to have detected errors, as for example, when someone is deluded by a food's pleasant taste to eat the poison hidden inside it. In this case, however, he is driven by nature only toward desiring the thing in which the pleasurable taste is found, but not toward the poison, of which he obviously is unaware. I can only conclude that this nature is not omniscient. This is not remarkable, since man is a limited thing, and thus only what is of limited perfection befits him.

But we not infrequently err even in those things to which nature impels us. Take, for example, the case of those who are ill and who desire food or drink that will soon afterwards be injurious to them. Perhaps it could be said here that they erred because their nature was corrupt. However, this does not remove our difficulty, for a sick man is no less a creature of God than a healthy one, and thus it seems no less inconsistent that the sick man got a deception-prone nature from God. And a clock made of wheels and counterweights follows all the laws of nature no less closely when it has been badly constructed and does not tell time accurately than it does when it completely satisfies the wish of its maker. Likewise, I might regard a man's body as a kind of mechanism that is outfitted with and composed of bones, nerves, muscles, veins, blood and skin in such a way that, even if no mind existed in it, the man's body would still exhibit all the same motions that are in it now except for those motions that proceed either from a command of the will or, consequently, from the mind. I easily recognize that it would be natural for this body, were it, say, suffering from dropsy and experiencing dryness in the throat (which typically produces a thirst sensation in the mind), and also so disposed by its nerves and other parts to take something to drink, the result of which would be to exacerbate the illness. This is as natural as for a body without any such illness to be moved by the same dryness in the throat to take something to drink that is useful to it. And given the intended purpose of the clock, I could say that it deviates from its nature when it fails to tell the right time. And similarly, considering the mechanism of the human body in terms of its being equipped for the motions that typically occur in it, I may think that it too is deviating from its nature, if its throat were dry when having something to drink is not beneficial to its conservation. Nevertheless, I am well aware that this last use of "nature" differs greatly from the other. For this latter "nature" is merely a designation dependent on my thought, since it compares a man in poor health and a poorly constructed clock with the ideas of a healthy man and of a well-made clock, a designation extrinsic to the things to which it is applied. But by "nature" taken in the former sense, I understand something that is really in things, and thus is not without some truth.

When we say, then, in the case of the body suffering from dropsy, that its "nature" is corrupt, given the fact that it has a parched throat and yet does not need something to drink, "nature" obviously is merely an extrinsic designation. Nevertheless, in the case of the composite, that is, of a mind joined to such a body, it is not a mere designation, but a true error of nature

that this body should be thirsty when having something to drink would be harmful to it. It therefore remains to inquire here how the goodness of God does not prevent "nature," thus considered, from being deceptive.

Now my first observation here is that there is a great difference between a mind and a body, in that a body, by its very nature, is always divisible. On the other hand, the mind is utterly indivisible. For when I consider the mind, that is, myself insofar as I am only a thinking thing, I cannot distinguish any parts within me; rather, I understand myself to be manifestly one complete thing. Although the entire mind seems to be united to the entire body, nevertheless, were a foot or an arm or any other bodily part to be amputated, I know that nothing has been taken away from the mind on that account. Nor can the faculties of willing, sensing, understanding, and so on be called "parts" of the mind, since it is one and the same mind that wills, senses, and understands. On the other hand, there is no corporeal or extended thing I can think of that I may not in my thought easily divide into parts; and in this way I understand that it is divisible. This consideration alone would suffice to teach me that the mind is wholly diverse from the body, had I not yet known it well enough in any other way.

My second observation is that my mind is not immediately affected by all the parts of the body, but only by the brain, or perhaps even by just one small part of the brain, namely, by that part where the "common" sense is said to reside. Whenever this part of the brain is disposed in the same manner, it presents the same thing to the mind, even if the other parts of the body are able meanwhile to be related in diverse ways. Countless experiments show this, none of which need be reviewed here.

My next observation is that the nature of the body is such that whenever any of its parts can be moved by another part some distance away, it can also be moved in the same manner by any of the parts that lie between them, even if this more distant part is doing nothing. For example, in the cord ABCD, if the final part D is pulled, the first part A would be moved in exactly the same manner as it could be, if one of the intermediate parts B or C were pulled, while the end part D remained immobile. Likewise, when I feel a pain in my foot, physics teaches me that this sensation takes place by means of nerves distributed throughout the foot, like stretched cords extending from the foot all the way to the brain. When these nerves are pulled in the foot, they also pull on the inner parts of the brain to which they extend, and produce a certain motion in them. This motion has been constituted by nature so as to affect the mind with a sensation of pain, as if it occurred in the foot. But because these nerves need to pass through the shin, thigh, loins, back, and neck, to get from the foot to the brain, it can happen that even if it is not the part in the foot, but merely one of the intermediate parts that is being struck, the very same movement will occur in the brain that would occur, were the foot badly injured. The inevitable result will be that the mind feels the same pain. The same opinion should hold for any other sensation.

My final observation is that, since any given motion occurring in that part of the brain immediately affecting the mind produces but one sensation in it, I can think of no better arrangement than that it produces the one sensation that, of all the ones it is able to produce, is most especially and most often conducive to the maintenance of a healthy man. Moreover, experience shows that all the sensations bestowed on us by nature are like this. Hence there is absolutely nothing to be found in them that does not bear witness to God's power and goodness. Thus, for example, when the nerves in the foot are agitated in a violent and unusual manner, this motion of theirs extends through the marrow of the spine to the inner reaches of the brain, where it gives the mind the sign to sense something, namely, the pain as if it is occurring in the foot. This provokes the mind to do its utmost to move away from the cause of the pain, since it is seen as harmful to the foot. But the nature of man could have been so constituted by God that this same motion in the brain might have indicated something else to the mind: for example, either the motion itself as it occurs in the brain, or in the foot, or in some place in between, or something else entirely different. But nothing else would have served so well the maintenance of the body. Similarly, when we need something to drink, a certain dryness arises in the throat

that moves the nerves in the throat, and, by means of them, the inner parts of the brain. And this motion affects the mind with a sensation of thirst, because in this entire affair nothing is more useful for us to know than that we need something to drink in order to maintain our health; the same holds in the other cases.

From these considerations it is utterly apparent that, notwithstanding the immense goodness of God, the nature of man, insofar as it is composed of mind and body, cannot help being sometimes mistaken. For if some cause, not in the foot but in some other part through which the nerves extend from the foot to the brain, or perhaps even in the brain itself, were to produce the same motion that would normally be produced by a badly injured foot, the pain will be felt as if it were in the foot, and the senses will naturally be deceived. For since an identical motion in the brain can only bring about an identical sensation in the mind, and it is more frequently the case that this motion is wont to arise on account of a cause that harms the foot than on account of some other thing existing elsewhere, it is reasonable that the motion should always show pain to the mind as something belonging to the foot rather than to some other part. And if dryness in the throat does not arise, as is normal, from drink's contributing to bodily health, but from a contrary cause, as happens in the case of someone with dropsy, then it is far better that it should deceive on that occasion than that it should always be deceptive when the body is in good health. The same holds for the other cases.

This consideration is most helpful, not only for my noticing all the errors to which my nature is liable, but also for enabling me to correct or avoid them without difficulty. To be sure, I know that all the senses set forth what is true more frequently than what is false regarding what concerns the welfare of the body. Moreover, I can nearly always make use of several of them in order to examine the same thing. Furthermore, I can use my memory, which connects current happenings with past ones, and my intellect, which now has examined all the causes of error. Hence I should no longer fear that those things that are daily shown me by the senses are false. On the contrary, the hyperbolic doubts of the last few days ought to be rejected as ludicrous. This goes especially for the chief reason for doubting, which dealt with my failure to distinguish being asleep from being awake. For I now notice that there is a considerable difference between these two; dreams are never joined by the memory with all the other actions of life, as is the case with those actions that occur when one is awake. For surely, if, while I am awake, someone were suddenly to appear to me and then immediately disappear, as occurs in dreams, so that I see neither where he came from nor where he went, it is not without reason that I would judge him to be a ghost or a phantom conjured up in my brain, rather than a true man. But when these things happen, and I notice distinctly where they come from, where they are now, and when they come to me, and when I connect my perception of them without interruption with the whole rest of my life, I am clearly certain that these perceptions have happened to me not while I was dreaming but while I was awake. Nor ought I have even the least doubt regarding the truth of these things, if, having mustered all the senses, in addition to my memory and my intellect, in order to examine them, nothing is passed on to me by one of these sources that conflicts with the others. For from the fact that God is no deceiver, it follows that I am in no way mistaken in these matters. But because the need to get things done does not always permit us the leisure for such a careful inquiry, we must confess that the life of man is apt to commit errors regarding particular things, and we must acknowledge the infirmity of our nature.

# René Descartes, Thomas Hobbes, and Antoine Arnauld, *Objections and Replies* (1641)[1]

*Descartes had the manuscript of the* Meditations *circulated in order to solicit objections; he then published the* Meditations, *together with the* Objections *and his* Replies. *The person distributing the manuscript for Descartes was Marin Mersenne, a Minim monk who served as Descartes's link to the learned world while Descartes lived in the Netherlands.[2] Descartes initially requested a first set of objections from friends in the Netherlands. Mersenne then collected sets from Thomas Hobbes, Antoine Arnauld, and Pierre Gassendi, and put together two sets out of the objections of various philosophers and theologians; a seventh set was received from the Jesuit Pierre Bourdin and published with the second edition of the* Meditations *(in 1642).[3] The* Objections *and* Replies *allow Descartes to* extend some of his arguments, which were so compactly given in the* Meditations. *The Second Set of Objections contains the following remark forwarded by Mersenne (probably initiated by Jean-Baptiste Morin):[4] "It would be worthwhile if you set out the entire argument in geometrical fashion, starting from a number of definitions, postulates, and axioms. You are highly experienced in employing this method, and it would enable you to fill the mind of each reader so that he could see everything as it were at a single glance. . . ." That remark produced an extended reply from Descartes about the geometrical manner of writing, the order of demonstration, and its two divisions, analysis and synthesis. Descartes further appended a rewritten portion of the* Meditations *arranged in geometric fashion.*

*Perhaps the most intriguing function of the* Objections *and* Replies *is that they enable one to see genuine philosophical debate conducted on the spot. This is especially true for Descartes's confrontation with*

1. Translated from the Latin by Donald Cress.
2. Mersenne's main contribution to the philosophy and science of his day was his tireless promotion of scientific activity. He was educated at the Jesuit College of La Flèche (which Descartes also attended). He then entered the order of the Minims, and from his cell at their convent in Paris, acted as the center of a vast correspondence network, bringing together notable philosophers, mathematicians, and scientists. He championed the new science, publishing translations (or paraphrases) of Galileo's early mechanics and his *Two New Sciences*. For more on Mersenne, see Peter Dear, *Mersenne and the Learning of the Schools* (Ithaca: Cornell University Press, 1988).
3. For more on the *Objections* and *Replies*, see Roger Ariew and Marjorie Grene, eds., *Descartes and His Contemporaries:*

*Meditations, Objections and Replies* (Chicago: University of Chicago Press, 1995).
4. Morin was an astrologer, part of the circle around Mersenne, and author of *Quod Deus Sit (That God Exists)*, a short treatise constructed on Euclidean principles, with Definitions, Axioms, and Theorems. For more on Morin, see Daniel Garber, "J.-B. Morin and the *Second Objections*," pp. 63–82, in R. Ariew and M. Grene, eds., *Descartes and His Contemporaries*.

*Hobbesian materialism in the* Third Set of Objections
and Replies.[5] *Hobbes accepts none of Descartes's arguments, and the debate gets increasingly heated. Arguably, the best set of objections is the one written by Arnauld, who at the time was a theology doctoral candidate at the University of Paris. In the critical but sympathetic exchange, one can see Arnauld's keen analytical mind working, from his criticism of Descartes's notion of material falsity, to his comments on God as positive cause of himself, to his questioning whether the Meditations are circular.*[6]

## Reply to the Second Set of Objections

[. . .] Finally, as to your suggestion that I should put forward my arguments in geometrical fashion so that the reader could perceive them, as it were, in a single intuition, it is worthwhile to indicate here how much I have already followed this suggestion and how much I think it should be followed in the future. I draw a distinction between two things in the geometrical style of writing, namely, the order and the mode [*ratio*] of the demonstration.

Order consists simply in putting forward as first what ought to be known without any help from what comes afterward and then in arranging all the rest in such a way that they are demonstrated solely by means of what preceded them. And I certainly did try to follow this order as carefully as possible in my Meditations. And it was owing to my observance of it that I treated the distinction between the mind and the body not in the Second Meditation but at the end in the Sixth Meditation. And it also explains why I deliberately and knowingly omitted many other things, since they required an explanation of a great many more.

But the mode [*ratio*] of a demonstration is of two sorts: one that proceeds by way of analysis, the other by way of synthesis.

Analysis shows the true way by which a thing has been discovered methodically, and, as it were, "a priori," so that, were the reader willing to follow it and to pay sufficient attention to everything, he will no less perfectly understand a thing and render it his own, than had he himself discovered it. However, analysis possesses nothing with which to compel belief in a less attentive or hostile reader, for if he fails to pay attention to the least thing among those that this mode [*ratio*] proposes, the necessity of its conclusions is not apparent; and it often hardly touches at all on many things that nevertheless ought to be carefully noted, since they are obvious to anyone who is sufficiently attentive.

Synthesis, on the other hand, indeed clearly demonstrates its conclusions by an opposite way, where the investigation is conducted, as it were, "a posteriori" (although it is often the case here that this proof is more "a priori" than it is in the analytic mode). And it uses a long series of definitions, postulates, axioms, theorems, and problems, so that if something in what follows is denied, this mode may at once point out that it is contained in what went before. And thus it wrests from the reader his assent, however hostile and obstinate he may be. But this mode is not as satisfactory as the other one nor does it satisfy the minds of those who desire to learn, since it does not teach the way in which the thing was discovered.

5. For Thomas Hobbes's biography and bibliography, see the selection from the *Leviathan* in Section 2 of this book.
6. Antoine Arnauld was born in Paris in 1612. He was admitted to the Paris Faculty of Theology, i.e., the Sorbonne, in 1643, and expelled from it in 1656. Throughout his life, Arnauld engaged in public controversies on philosophical and theological topics. He became the leading spokesman in France for the Jansenist movement (and against the Jesuits) and one of the more outspoken defenders of Cartesian philosophy. He was forced into exile in the Netherlands in 1679 and died in Liège in 1694. Arnauld's philosophical works included the *Port-Royal Logic* (1662), written with Pierre Nicole, and *Of True and False Ideas* (1683)—both broadly Cartesian projects. Because of the latter, he was also engaged in discussion over Malebranche's theory of ideas and doctrine of grace and divine providence (for a sample of these, see the selection from Malebranche's *Search after Truth* in Section 3); the debate produced numerous other works and letters. Arnauld maintained an important philosophical correspondence with many of the great figures of the century, including Leibniz (see Leibniz's letters to Arnauld in Section 3). English translations of Arnauld's *Objections* to Descartes's *Meditations*, *Port-Royal Logic*, and *Of True and False Ideas* are available. For more on Arnauld, see Steven Nadler, *Arnauld and the Cartesian Philosophy of Ideas* (Princeton: Princeton University Press, 1989) or E. J. Kremer, ed., *The Great Arnauld and Some of His Philosophical Correspondents* (Toronto: University of Toronto Press, 1994) and *Interpreting Arnauld* (Toronto: University of Toronto Press, 1996).

It was this mode alone that the ancient geometers were wont to use in their writings—not that they were utterly ignorant of the other mode, but rather, as I see it, they held it in such high regard that they kept it to themselves alone as a secret.

But in my Meditations I followed analysis exclusively, which is the true and best way to teach. But as to synthesis, which is undoubtedly what you are asking me about here, even though in geometry it is most suitably placed after analysis, nevertheless it cannot be so conveniently applied to these metaphysical matters.

For there is this difference, that the first notions that are presupposed for demonstrating things geometrical are readily admitted by everyone, since they accord with the use of the senses. Thus there is no difficulty there, except in correctly deducing the consequences, which can be done by all sorts of people, even the less attentive, provided only that they remember what went before. And the minute differentiation of propositions was done for the purpose of making them easy to recite and thus can be committed to memory even by the recalcitrant.

But in these metaphysical matters, on the contrary, nothing is more an object of intense effort than causing its first notions to be clearly and distinctly perceived. For although they are by their nature no less known or even more known than those studied by geometers, nevertheless, because many of the prejudices of the senses (with which we have been accustomed since our infancy) are at odds with them, they are perfectly known only by those who are especially attentive and meditative and who withdraw their minds from corporeal things as much as possible. And if these first notions were put forward by themselves, they could easily be denied by those who are eager to engage in conflict.

This was why I wrote "meditations," rather than "disputations," as the philosophers do, or theorems and problems, as the geometers do: namely, so that by this very fact I might attest that the only dealings I would have were with those who, along with myself, did not refuse to consider the matter attentively and to meditate. For the very fact that someone girds himself to attack the truth renders him less suitable for perceiving it, since he is withdrawing himself from considering the arguments that attest to the truth in order to find other arguments that dissuade him of the truth.

But perhaps someone will object here that a person should not seek arguments for the sake of being contentious when he knows that the truth is set before him. But so long as this is in doubt, all the arguments on both sides ought to be assessed in order to know which ones are the more firm. And it would be unfair of me to want my arguments to be admitted as true before they had been scrutinized, while at the same time not allowing the consideration of opposing arguments.

This would certainly be a just criticism, if any of those things which I desire in an attentive and non-hostile reader were such that they could withdraw him from a consideration of any other arguments in which there was the slightest hope of finding more truth than in my arguments. However, the greatest doubt is contained among the things I am proposing; moreover, there is nothing I more strongly urge than that each thing be scrutinized most diligently and that nothing is to be straightforwardly accepted except what has been so clearly and distinctly examined that we cannot but give our assent to it. On the other hand, the only matters from which I desire to divert the minds of my readers are things they have never sufficiently examined and which they derived not on the basis of a firm reason, but from the senses alone. As a consequence, I do not think anyone can believe that he will be in greater danger of error, were he to consider only those things that I propose to him, than were he to withdraw his mind from them and turn it toward other things—things that are opposed to them in some way and that spread darkness—that is, toward the prejudices of the senses.

And thus I am right in desiring especially close attention on the part of my readers; and I have chosen the one style of writing over all the others with which I thought it can most especially be procured, and from which I am convinced that readers will discern a greater profit than they would have thought, since, on the other hand, when the synthetic mode of writing is employed, people are likely to seem to themselves to have learned more than they actually did. But I also think it is fair for me straightforwardly to reject as worthless those criticisms made against me by those who have refused to meditate with me and who cling to their preformed opinions.

But I know how difficult it will be, even for those who pay close attention and earnestly search for the truth, to intuit the entire body of my Meditations and at the same time to discern its individual parts. I think both of these things ought to be done so that the full benefit may be derived from my Meditations. I shall therefore append here a few things in the synthetic style that I hope will prove somewhat helpful to my readers. Nevertheless, I wish they would take note of the fact that I did not intend to cover as much here as is found in my Meditations; otherwise I should then be more loquacious here than in the Meditations themselves; moreover, I will not explain in detail what I do include, partly out of a desire for brevity and partly to prevent anyone who thinks that my remarks here were sufficient from making a very cursory examination of the Meditations themselves, from which I am convinced that much more benefit is to be discerned.

# Arguments Proving the Existence of God and the Distinction of the Soul from the Body, Arranged in Geometrical Fashion.

## Definitions

I. By the word "thought" I include everything that is in us in such a way that we are immediately aware of it. Thus all the operations of the will, understanding, imagination, and senses are thoughts. But I added "immediately" to exclude those things that follow from these operations, such as voluntary motion, which surely has thought as its principle but nevertheless is not itself a thought.

II. By the word "idea" I understand that form of any thought through the immediate perception of which I am aware of that very same thought. Thus I could not express anything in words and understand what I am saying, without this very fact making it certain that there exists in me an idea of what is being signified by those words. And thus it is not the mere images depicted in the corporeal imagination that I call "ideas." In point of fact, I in no way call these images "ideas," insofar as they are in the corporeal imagination, that is, insofar as they have been depicted in some part of the brain, but only insofar as they inform the mind itself which is turned toward that part of the brain.

III. By the "objective reality of an idea" I understand the being of the thing represented by an idea, insofar as it exists in the idea. In the same way one can speak of "objective perfection," "objective skill," and so on. For whatever we perceive to exist in the objects of our ideas exists objectively in these very ideas.

IV. The same things are said to exist "formally" in the objects of our ideas when they exist in these objects in just the way we perceive them, and to exist "eminently" in the objects of our ideas when they indeed are not in these objects in the way we perceive them, but have such an amount of perfection that they could fill the role of things existing formally.

V. Everything in which there immediately inheres, as in a subject, or through which there exists, something we perceive (that is, some property, or quality, or attribute whose real idea is in us) is called a "substance." For we have no other idea of substance itself, taken in the strict sense, except that it is a thing in which whatever we perceive or whatever is objectively in one of our ideas exists either formally or eminently, since it is evident by the light of nature that no real attribute can belong to nothing.

VI. That substance in which thought immediately resides is called "mind." However, I am speaking here of the mind rather than of the soul, since the word "soul" is equivocal, and is often used for something corporeal.

VII. That substance which is the immediate subject of local extension and of the accidents that presuppose extension, such as shape, position, movement from place to place, and so on, is called "body." Whether what we call "mind" and what we call "body" are one and the same substance or two different ones must be examined later on.

VIII. That substance which we understand to be

supremely perfect and in which we conceive absolutely nothing that involves any defect or limitation upon its perfection is called "God."

IX. When we say that something is contained in the nature or concept of something, this is the same as saying that it is true of that thing or that it can be affirmed of that thing.

X. Two substances are said to be really distinct from one another when each of them can exist without the other.


## Postulates

I ask first that readers take note of how feeble are the reasons why they have up until now put their faith in their senses, and how uncertain are all the judgments that they have constructed upon them; and that they review this within themselves for so long and so often that they finally acquire the habit of no longer placing too much faith in them. For I deem this necessary for perceiving the certainty of things metaphysical.

Second, I ask that readers ponder their own mind and all its attributes. They will discover that they cannot be in doubt about these things, even though they suppose that everything they ever received from the senses is false. And I ask them not to stop pondering this point until they have acquired for themselves the habit of perceiving it clearly and of believing that it is easier to know than anything corporeal.

Third, I ask that readers weigh diligently the self-evident propositions that they find within themselves, such as that the same thing cannot be and not be at the same time, that nothingness cannot be the efficient cause of anything, and the like. And thus readers may exercise the astuteness implanted in them by nature, pure and freed from the senses, but which the objects of sense are wont to cloud and obscure as much as possible. For by this means the truth of the axioms that follow will easily be known to them.

Fourth, I ask readers to examine the ideas of those natures that contain a combination of many accidents together, such as the nature of a triangle, the

nature of a square, or of some other figure; and likewise the nature of the mind, the nature of the body, and, above all, the nature of God, the supremely perfect being. And I ask them to realize that all that we perceive to be contained in them truly can be affirmed of them. For example, the equality of its three angles to two right angles is contained in the nature of a triangle, and divisibility is contained in the nature of a body, that is, of an extended thing (for we can conceive of no extended thing that is so small that we could not at least divide it in thought). Such being the case, it is true to say of every triangle that its three angles are equal to two right angles, and that every body is divisible.

Fifth, I ask the readers to dwell long and earnestly in the contemplation of the nature of the supremely perfect being; and to consider, among other things, that possible existence is indeed contained in the ideas of all other things, whereas the idea of God contains not merely possible existence, but absolutely necessary existence. For from this fact alone and without any discursive reasoning, they will know that God exists. And it will be no less self-evident to them than that the number 2 is even or that the number 3 is odd, and the like. For there are some things that are self-evident to some and understood by others only through discursive reasoning.

Sixth, I ask the readers to get into the habit of distinguishing things that are clearly known from things that are obscure, by carefully reviewing all the examples of clear and distinct perception, and likewise of obscure and confused perception, that I have recounted in my Meditations. For this is something more easily learned from examples than from rules, and I think that therein I have either explained or at least to some extent touched upon all the examples pertaining to this subject.

Seventh and finally, when readers perceive that they have never discovered any falsity in things they clearly perceived and that, on the other hand, they have never found truth in things they only obscurely grasped, except by chance, I ask them to consider that it is utterly irrational to call into doubt things that are clearly and distinctly perceived by the pure understanding merely on account of prejudices based on the senses or on account of hypotheses in which something unknown is contained. For thus they will easily admit the following axioms as true and indubitable. Nevertheless, many of these could admittedly have been much better explained and ought to have been put forward as theorems rather than as axioms, had I wanted to be more precise.

## Axioms or Common Notions

I. Nothing exists concerning which we could not ask what the cause is of its existence. For this can be asked of God himself, not that he needs any cause in order to exist, but because the very immensity of his nature is the cause or the reason why he needs no cause in order to exist.

II. The present time does not depend on the time immediately preceding it, and therefore no less a cause is required to preserve a thing than is initially required to produce it.

III. No thing, and no perfection of a thing actually existing in it, can have nothing, or a nonexisting thing, as the cause of its existence.

IV. Whatever reality or perfection there is in a thing is formally or eminently in its first and adequate cause.

V. Whence it also follows that the objective reality of our ideas requires a cause which contains this very same reality, and not merely objectively, but either formally or eminently. And we should note that the acceptance of this axiom is so necessary that on it alone depends the knowledge of all things, sensible as well as insensible. For example, how is it we know that the sky exists? Because we see it? But this vision does not touch the mind except insofar as it is an idea: an idea, I say, inhering in the mind itself, not an image depicted in the corporeal imagination. And we are able to judge on account of this idea that the sky exists only because every idea must have a really existing cause of its objective reality; and this cause we judge to be the sky itself. The same holds for the rest.

VI. There are several degrees of reality or being; for a substance has more reality than an accident or a mode; and an infinite substance has more reality than a finite substance. Thus there is also more objective reality in the idea of a substance than there is in

the idea of an accident; and there is more objective reality in the idea of an infinite substance than there is in the idea of a finite substance.

VII. The will of a thing that thinks is surely borne voluntarily and freely (for this is of the essence of the will), but nonetheless infallibly, toward the good that it clearly knows; and therefore, if it should know of any perfections that it lacks, it will immediately give them to itself, if they are within its power.

VIII. Whatever can make what is greater or more difficult can also make what is less.

IX. It is greater to create or preserve a substance than to create or preserve the attributes or properties of a substance; however, it is not greater to create something than to preserve it, as has already been said.

X. Existence is contained in the idea or concept of everything, because we cannot conceive of something except as existing [*sub ratione existentiae*]. Possible or contingent existence is contained in the concept of a limited thing, whereas necessary and perfect existence is contained in the concept of a supremely perfect being.

Proposition I: The existence of God is known from the mere consideration of his nature.

Demonstration: To say that something is contained in the nature or concept of a thing is the same thing as saying that it is true of that thing (Def. IX). But necessary existence is contained in the concept of God (Ax. X). Therefore it is true to say of God that necessary existence is in him, or that he exists.

And this is the syllogism I already made use of above in reply to the sixth objection;[7] and its conclusion can be self-evident to those who are free of prejudices, as was stated in Postulate V. But since it is not easy to arrive at such astuteness, we will seek the same thing in other ways.

Proposition II: The existence of God is demonstrated *a posteriori* from the mere fact that the idea of God is in us.

Demonstration: The objective reality of any of our

7. Descartes's reply to the sixth point raised in the *Second Set of Objections* discusses the criterion of clarity and distinctness and the proof of the existence of God found in Meditation Five. This reply may be found in AT VII 149–52.

ideas requires a cause that contains this same reality not merely objectively but either formally or eminently (Ax. V). However, we have an idea of God (Defs. II and VII), the objective reality of which is contained in us neither formally nor eminently (Ax. VI), nor could it be contained in anything other than God (Def. VIII). Therefore, this idea of God which is in us requires God as its cause, and thus God exists (Ax. III).

Proposition III: The existence of God is also demonstrated from the fact that we ourselves who have the idea of God exist.

Demonstration: Had I the power to preserve myself, so much the more would I also have the power to give myself the perfections I lack (Axs. VIII and IX); for these are merely attributes of a substance, whereas I am a substance. But I do not have the power to give myself these perfections; otherwise I would already have them (Ax. VII). Therefore, I do not have the power to preserve myself.

Next, I cannot exist without my being preserved during the time I exist, either by myself, if indeed I have this power, or by something else which has this power (Axs. I and II). But I do exist, and yet I do not have the power to preserve myself, as has already been proved. Therefore, I am being preserved by something else.

Moreover, he who preserves me has within himself either formally or eminently all that is in me (Ax. IV). However, there is in me a perception of many of the perfections I lack, and at the same time there is in me the perception of the idea of God (Defs. II and VIII). Therefore, the perception of these same perfections is also in him who preserves me.

Finally, this same being cannot have a perception of any perfections he lacks or does not have in himself, either formally or eminently (Ax. VIII), for since he has the power to preserve me, as has already been said, so much the more would he have the power to give himself those perfections were he to lack them (Axs. VIII and IX). But he has the perception of all the perfections I lack and that I conceive to be capable

of existing in God alone, as has just been proved. Therefore, he has these perfections within himself either formally or eminently, and thus he is God.

Corollary: God created the heavens and the earth and all that is in them. Moreover, he can bring about all that we clearly perceive, precisely as we perceive it.

Demonstration: All these things clearly follow from the preceding proposition. For in that proposition I proved the existence of God from the fact that there must exist someone in whom, either formally or eminently, are all the perfections of which there is some idea in us. But there is in us an idea of such great power that the one in whom this power resides, and he alone, created the heavens and the earth and can also bring about all the other things that I understand to be possible. Thus, along with the existence of God, all these things have also been proved about him.

Proposition IV: Mind and body are really distinct.

Demonstration: Whatever we clearly perceive can be brought about by God in precisely the way we perceive it (by the preceding Corollary). But we clearly perceive the mind, that is, a substance that thinks, apart from the body, that is, apart from any extended substance (Post. II); and vice versa, we clearly perceive the body apart from the mind (as everyone readily admits). Therefore, at least by the divine power, the mind can exist without the body, and the body without the mind.

Now certainly, substances that can exist one without the other are really distinct (Def. X). But the mind and the body are substances (Defs. V, VI, and VII) that can exist one without the other (as has just been proved). Therefore, the mind and the body are really distinct.

And we should note here that I used divine power as a means of separating mind and body, not because some extraordinary power is required to achieve this separation, but because I had dealt exclusively with God in what preceded, and thus I had nothing else I could use as a means. Nor is it of any importance what power it is that separates two things for us to know that they are really distinct.

# Third Set of Objections with the Author's Replies

## Against Meditation I: Concerning Those Things That Can Be Called into Doubt

Objection I: It is sufficiently obvious from what has been said in this Meditation that there is no κρι-τήριον [criterion] by which we may distinguish our dreams from the waking state and from true sensation; and for this reason the phantasms we have while awake and using our senses are not accidents inhering in external objects, nor do they prove that such objects do in fact exist. Therefore, if we follow our senses without any other process of reasoning, we will be justified in doubting whether anything exists. There-fore, we acknowledge the truth of this Meditation. But since Plato and other ancient philosophers have discussed this same uncertainty in sensible things, and since it is commonly observed that there is a difficulty in distinguishing waking from dreams, I would have preferred the author, so very distinguished in the realm of new speculations, not to have pub-lished these old things.

Reply: The reasons for doubting, which are ac-cepted here as true by the philosopher, were proposed by me as merely probable; and I made use of them not to peddle them as something new, but partly to prepare the minds of readers for the consideration of matters geared to the understanding and for distin-guishing them from corporeal things, goals for which these arguments seem to me wholly necessary; partly to respond to these same arguments in subsequent Meditations; and partly also to show how firm those truths are that I later propose, given the fact that they cannot be shaken by these metaphysical doubts. And thus I never sought any praise for recounting them again; but I do not think I could have omitted them any more than a medical writer could omit a descrip-tion of a disease whose method of treatment he is trying to teach.

## Against Meditation II: Concerning the Nature of the Human Mind

Objection II: "I am a thing that thinks"; quite true. For from the fact that I think or have a phantasm, whether I am asleep or awake, it can be inferred that I am thinking, for "I think" means the same thing as "I am thinking." From the fact that I am thinking it follows that I am, since that which thinks is not noth-ing. But when he appends "that is, a mind, or soul, or understanding, or reason," a doubt arises. For it does not seem a valid argument to say, "I am thinking, therefore I am a thought" or "I am understanding; therefore I am an understanding." For in the same way I could just as well say, "I am walking; therefore I am an act of walking." Thus M. Descartes equates the thing that understands with an act of understand-ing, which is an act of the thing that understands. Or he at least is equating a thing that understands with the faculty of understanding, which is a power of a thing that understands. Nevertheless, all philoso-phers draw a distinction between a subject and its faculties and acts, that is, between a subject and its properties and essences; for a being itself is one thing and its essence is another. Therefore, it is possible for a thing that thinks to be the subject in which the mind, reason, or understanding inhere, and therefore this subject may be something corporeal. The oppo-site is assumed and not proved. Nevertheless, this inference is the basis for the conclusion that M. Des-cartes seems to want to establish.

In the same passage he says, "I know that I exist; I ask now who is this 'I' whom I know. Most certainly, in the strict sense, the knowledge of this 'I' does not depend upon things of whose existence I do not yet have knowledge."

Certainly the knowledge of the proposition "I exist" depends on the proposition "I think," as he rightly instructed us. But what is the source of the knowledge of the proposition "I think"? Certainly, from the mere fact that we cannot conceive any activity without its subject, for example, leaping without one who leaps, knowing without one who knows, or thinking apart from one who thinks.

And from this it seems to follow that a thing that thinks is something corporeal, for the subjects of all acts seem to be understood only in terms of matter [*sub ratione materiae*], as he later points out in the example of the piece of wax, which, while its color, hardness, shape, and other acts undergo change, is nevertheless understood always to be the same thing, that is, the same matter undergoing a number of changes. However, it is not to be concluded that I think by means of another thought; for although a person can think that he has been thinking (this sort of thinking being merely a case of remembering), nevertheless, it is utterly impossible to think that one thinks, or to know that one knows. For it would involve an infinite series of questions: How do you know that you know that you know that you know?

Therefore, since the knowledge of the proposition "I exist" depends on the knowledge of the proposition "I think," and the knowledge of this latter proposition depends on the fact that we cannot separate thought from the matter that thinks, it seems we should infer that a thing that thinks is material rather than immaterial.

Reply: Where I said "that is, a mind, or soul, or understanding, or reason," and so on, I did not understand by these terms merely the faculties, but the thing endowed with the faculty of thinking, and this is what everyone ordinarily has in mind with regard to the first two terms, and the second two terms are often understood in this sense. And I explained this so explicitly and in so many places that there does not seem to be any room for doubt.

Nor is there a parity here between walking and thinking, since walking is ordinarily taken to refer only to the action itself; whereas thought is sometimes taken to refer to an action, sometimes to refer to a faculty, and sometimes to refer to the thing that has the faculty.

Moreover, I am not asserting that the thing that understands and the act of understanding are identical, nor indeed that the identity of the thing that understands and the faculty of understanding are identical, if "understanding" is taken to refer to a faculty, but only when it is taken for the thing itself that understands. However, I also freely admit that I have used the most abstract terminology possible to signify the thing or substance, which I wanted to divest of all that did not belong to it, just as, contrariwise, the philosopher uses the most concrete terminology possible (namely, "subject," "matter," and "body") to signify a thing that thinks, in order to prevent its being separated from the body.

But I am not concerned that it may seem to someone that the philosopher's way of joining several things together may be more suitable for finding the truth than mine, wherein I distinguish each single thing as much as possible. But let us put aside verbal disputes and talk about the matter at hand.

He says that it is possible for a thing that thinks to be something corporeal, but the contrary is assumed and not proved. I did not at all assume the contrary, nor did I use it in any way as a basis for my argument. Rather, I left it completely undetermined until the Sixth Meditation, where it is proved.

Then he correctly says that we cannot conceive any act without its subject, such as an act of thinking without a thing that thinks, since that which thinks is not nothing. But then he adds, without any reason at all and contrary to the usual manner of speaking and to all logic, that hence it seems to follow that a thing that thinks is something corporeal; for the subjects of all acts are surely understood from the viewpoint of their being a substance [*sub ratione substantiae*] (or even, if you please, from the viewpoint of their being matter [*sub ratione materiae*], i.e., metaphysical matter), but it does not follow from this that it must be understood from the viewpoint of their being bodies [*sub ratione corporum*].

However, logicians and people in general are wont to say that some substances are spiritual, while others are corporeal. And the only thing I proved by means of the example of the piece of wax was that color, hardness, and shape do not belong to the essence [*rationem formalem*] of the wax. For in that passage I was treating neither the essence of the mind nor that of the body.

Nor is it relevant for the philosopher to say here that one thought cannot be the subject of another thought. For who, besides him, has ever imagined that it could be? But, to explain the matter briefly, it is certainly the case that an act of thinking cannot exist without a thing that thinks, nor in general any act or accident without a substance in which it inheres. However, since we do not immediately know this substance itself through itself, but only through its being a subject of certain acts, it is quite in keeping with the demands of reason and custom for us to call by different names those substances that we recognize to be subjects of obviously different acts or accidents, and afterwards to inquire whether these different names signify one and the same thing. But there are certain acts which we call "corporeal," such as size, shape, motion, and all the other properties that cannot be thought of apart from their being extended in space; and the substance in which they inhere we call "body." Nor is it possible to imagine that it is one substance that is the subject of shape and another substance that is the subject of movement from place to place, and so on, since all these acts have in common the one feature of being extended. In addition, there are other acts, which we call "cogitative" (such as understanding, willing, imagining, sensing, and so on), all of which have in common the one feature of thought or perception or consciousness; but the substance in which they inhere we say is "a thing that thinks," or a "mind," or any other thing we choose, provided we do not confuse it with corporeal substance, since cogitative acts have no affinity to corporeal acts, and thought, which is the feature they have in common, is utterly different in kind from extension, which is the feature [*ratio*] the others have in common. But after we have formed two distinct concepts of these two substances, it is easy, from what has been said in the Sixth Meditation, to know whether they are one and the same or different.

Objection III: "Which of these things is distinct from my thought? Which of them can be said to be separate from myself?"

Perhaps someone will answer this question thus: I myself who think am distinct from my act of thinking; and, though surely not separated from me, my act of thinking is nevertheless different from me, just as leaping is different from the one who leaps, as has been said before. But if M. Descartes were to show

that he who understands and his understanding are one and the same, we shall lapse into the parlance of the schools: The understanding understands, the sight sees, the will wills, and by an exact analogy, the act of walking or at least the faculty of walking will walk. All of this is obscure, untoward, and most unworthy of that astuteness which is typical of M. Descartes.

Reply: I do not deny that I who think am distinct from my act of thinking, as a thing is distinct from a mode. But when I ask "what then is there that is distinct from my act of thinking?" I understand this to refer to the various modes of thinking that are recounted there, and not to my substance. And when I add "what can be said to be separate from myself?" I have in mind simply that all those modes of thinking are within me. I fail to see what occasion for doubt or obscurity can be imagined here.

Objection IV: "It remains then for me to concede that I do not grasp what this piece of wax is through the imagination; rather I conceive[8] it through the mind alone."

There is a tremendous difference between imagining (that is, having some idea) and conceiving with the mind (that is, concluding by a process of reasoning that something is or exists). But M. Descartes has not explained to us the basis for their being different. Even the ancient peripatetic philosophers have taught clearly enough that a substance is not perceived by the senses, but is inferred by means of arguments.

But what are we to say now, were reasoning perhaps merely the joining together and linking of names or designations by means of the word "is"? It would follow from this that we draw no conclusions whatever by way of argument [*ratione*] about the nature of things. Rather, it is about the designations of things that we draw any conclusions, that is, whether or not we in fact join the names of things in accordance with some convention that we have arbitrarily established regarding the meanings of these terms. If this is the

---

8. Hobbes here misquotes Descartes (Meditation Two; AT VII 131). The original has "perceive" [*percipere*], whereas Hobbes has "conceive" [*concipere*].

case, as it may well be, then reasoning will depend upon names, names upon imagination, and imagination perhaps, as I see it, upon the motions of the corporeal organs. And thus the mind will be nothing but movements in certain parts of an organic body.

Reply: I have explained here the difference between imagination and a concept of the pure mind when in the example of the piece of wax I enumerated those things in the wax that we entertain in our imagination and those that we conceive with the mind alone. But I also explained elsewhere how one and the same thing, say a pentagon, can be understood by us in one way and imagined by us in another. However, in reasoning there is a joining together not of names but of things signified by these names; and I marvel that the contrary could enter anyone's mind. For who doubts that a Frenchman and a German could come to precisely the same conclusions about the very same things, even though they conceive very different words? And does not the philosopher bring about his own undoing when he speaks of conventions [*pactis*] that we have arbitrarily established regarding the significations of words? For if he admits that something is being signified by these words, why does he not want our reasonings to be about this something which is signified rather than about mere words? And certainly by the same license with which he concludes that the mind is a motion he could also conclude that the sky is the earth, or whatever else he pleases.

## Against Meditation III: Concerning God

Objection V: "Some of these thoughts are like images of things; to these alone does the word 'idea' properly apply, as when I think of a man, or a chimera, or the sky, or an angel, or God."

When I think of a man, I recognize an idea or an image made up of shape and color, concerning which I can doubt whether or not it is the likeness of a man, and likewise, when I think of the sky. When I think of a chimera, I recognize an idea or an image, concerning which I can doubt whether or not it is the likeness of some animal that does not exist but which could exist or which may or may not have existed at some other time.

But a person who is thinking of an angel at times observes in his mind the image of a flame, at other times the image of a beautiful little boy with wings. It seems certain to me that this image bears no resemblance to an angel, and thus is not the idea of an angel. But believing that there are creatures who minister unto God, who are invisible and immaterial, we ascribe the name "angel" to this thing that we believe in and suppose to exist. Nevertheless, the idea under which I imagine an angel is composed of the ideas of visible things.

It is the same with the sacred name "God": We have neither an image nor an idea of God. And thus we are forbidden to worship God under the form of an image, lest we seem to conceive him who is inconceivable.

It therefore seems there is no idea in us of God. But just as a person born blind who has often been brought close to a fire, and, feeling himself growing warm, recognizes that there is something that is warming him, and, on hearing that this is called "fire," concludes that fire exists, even though he does not know what shape or color it has, and has absolutely no idea or image of fire appearing before his mind; just so, a man who knows that there ought to be some cause of his images or ideas, and some other cause prior to this cause, and so on, is lead finally to an end of this series, namely to the supposition of some eternal cause which, since it never began to be, cannot have a cause prior to itself, and necessarily concludes that something eternal exists. Nevertheless, he has no idea that he could call the idea of this eternal something; rather he gives a name to this thing he believes in and acknowledges, calling it "God."

Now since it is from this thesis (namely, that we have an idea of God in our soul) that M. Descartes proceeds to prove this theorem (namely, that God— that is, the supremely powerful, wise creator of the world—exists), he ought to have given a better explanation of this idea of God, and he ought thence to have deduced not only the existence of God but also the creation of the world.

Reply: Here the philosopher wants the word "idea" to be understood to refer exclusively to images that are of material things and are depicted in the corporeal imagination. Once this thesis has been posited, it is easy for him to prove that there is no proper idea either of an angel or of God. But from time to time throughout the work, and especially in this passage, I point out that I take the word "idea" to refer to whatever is immediately perceived by the mind, so that, when I will or fear something, I number those very acts of willing and fearing among my ideas, since at the same time I perceive that I will and fear. And I used this word because it was common practice for philosophers to use it to signify the forms of perception proper to the divine mind, even though we acknowledge that there is no corporeal imagination in God; moreover, I had no term available to me that was more suitable. However, I think I have given a sufficient explanation of the idea of God to take care of those wishing to pay attention to my meaning; but I could never fully satisfy those preferring to understand my words otherwise than I intend. Finally, what is added here about the creation of the world is utterly irrelevant to the question at hand.

Objection VI: "Again there are other thoughts that take different forms: for example, when I will, or fear, or affirm, or deny, there is always some thing that I grasp as the subject of my thought, yet I embrace in my thought something more than the likeness of that thing. Some of these thoughts are called volitions or affects, while others are called judgments."

When someone wills or fears, he surely has an image of the thing he fears or the action he wills; but what more it is that a person who wills or fears embraces in his thought is not explained. Although fear is indeed a thought, I fail to see how it can be anything but the thought of the thing that someone fears. For what is the fear of a charging lion if not the idea of a charging lion combined with the effect that such an idea produces in the heart, which induces in a person who is frightened that animal motion we call "flight"? Now this motion of flight is not thought. It remains therefore that there is no thought in fear except the one that consists in the likeness of the thing feared. The same thing could be said of the will.

Moreover, affirmation and negation are not found without language and designations, so that brute animals can neither affirm nor deny, not even in thought, and therefore they cannot make judgments. Nevertheless, a thought can be similar in both man and beast. For when we affirm that a man is running, the thought we have is no different from the one a dog has when it sees its master running. Therefore, the only thing affirmation or negation adds to simple thoughts is perhaps the thought that the names of which an affirmation is composed are the names of the same thing in the one who affirms. This is not a matter of grasping in thought something more than the likeness of the thing, but merely the same likeness for a second time.

Reply: It is self-evident that seeing a lion and simultaneously fearing it is different from merely seeing it. Likewise seeing a man running is different from affirming to oneself that one sees him, an act which takes place without using language. And I find nothing here that requires an answer.

Objection VII: "All that remains for me is to ask how I received this idea of God. For I did not draw it from the senses; it never came upon me unexpectedly, as is usually the case with the ideas of sensible things when these things present themselves (or seem to present themselves) to the external sense organs. Nor was it made by me, for I plainly can neither subtract anything from it nor add anything to it. Thus the only option remaining is that this idea is innate in me, just as the idea of myself is innate in me."

If there is no idea of God (and it has not been proved that there is one), this entire inquiry falls apart. Moreover, if it is my body that is in question, then the idea of myself originates in me from sight; if it is my soul that is in question, then there is absolutely no idea of the soul. Rather, we infer by means of reasoning that there is something inside the human body that imparts to it the animal motion by which it senses and is moved. And this thing, whatever it is, we call the "soul," without having an idea of it.

Reply: If there is an idea of God (and it is obvious that there is), this entire objection falls apart. And when he adds that there is no idea of the soul, but rather that the soul is inferred by means of reasoning, this is the same thing as saying that there is no image of it depicted in the corporeal imagination, but that nevertheless there is such a thing as I have called an idea of it.

Objection VIII: "But there is another idea, one derived from astronomical reasoning; that is, it is elicited from certain notions innate in me. . . ."

It seems there is at any given moment but a single idea of the sun, regardless of whether it is looked at with the eyes or is understood by reasoning that it is many times larger than it appears. For this latter is not an idea of the sun, but an inference by way of arguments that the idea of the sun would be many times larger were it seen at much closer quarters.

But at different times there can be different ideas of the sun: for example, if it is looked at on one occasion with the naked eye and on another occasion through a telescope. But arguments drawn from astronomy do not make the idea of the sun any greater or smaller; rather, they show that an idea of the sun that is drawn from the senses is deceptive.

Reply: Here too what is said not to be an idea of the sun, and yet is described, is precisely what I call an idea.

Objection IX: "Unquestionably, those ideas that display [*exhibent*] substances to me are something more and, if I may say so, contain within themselves more objective reality than those which represent only modes or accidents. Again, the idea that enables me to understand a supreme deity, eternal, infinite, omniscient, omnipotent, and creator of all things other than himself, clearly has more objective reality in it than do those ideas through which finite substances are displayed."

I have frequently remarked above that there is no idea of God or of the soul. I now add that there is no idea of substance, for substance (given that it is matter subject to accidents and changes) is something concluded to solely by a process of reasoning; nevertheless, it is not conceived nor does it display any idea to us. If this is true, how can one say that the ideas that display substances to me are something

greater and have more objective reality than those ideas that display accidents to me? Moreover, would M. Descartes please give some thought once again to what he means by "more reality"? Does reality admit of degrees? Or, if he thinks that one thing is greater than another, would he please give some thought to how this could be explained to our understanding with the same level of astuteness required in all demonstrations, and such as he himself has used on other occasions.

Reply: I have frequently noted that I call an idea that very thing which is concluded to by means of reasoning, as well as anything else that is in any way perceived. Moreover, I have sufficiently explained how reality admits of degrees: namely, in precisely the way that a substance is a thing to a greater degree than is a mode. And if there are real qualities or incomplete substances, these are things to a greater degree than are modes, but to a lesser extent than are complete substances. And finally, if there is an infinite and independent substance, it is a thing to a greater degree than is a finite and dependent substance. But all of this is utterly self-evident.

Objection X: "Thus there remains only the idea of God. I must consider whether there is anything in this idea that could not have originated from me. I understand by the word 'God' a certain substance that is infinite, independent, supremely intelligent, and supremely powerful, and that created me along with everything else that exists—if anything else exists. Indeed all these are such that, the more carefully I focus my attention on them, the less possible it seems they could have arisen from myself alone. Thus, from what has been said above, I must conclude that God necessarily exists."

On considering the attributes of God in order thence to have an idea of God and to see whether there is anything in it that could not have proceeded from ourselves, I find, unless I am mistaken, that what we think of that corresponds to the word "God" does not originate with us, nor need it originate with anything but external objects. For by the word "God" I understand a "substance"; that is, I understand that

God exists. But I understand this not through an idea but through a process of reasoning. And this substance I understand to be "infinite"; that is, it is something whose boundaries or extremities I cannot conceive or imagine without imagining still more extremities beyond these. From this it follows that what emerges as the correlate of the word "infinite" is not the idea of divine infinity, but that of my own boundaries or limits. This substance I understand to be "independent"; that is, I conceive of no cause from which God proceeds. Whence it is manifest that I have no idea corresponding to the word "independent" beyond the memory of my own ideas beginning at various times and their resulting dependencies.

Hence to say that God is "independent" is merely to say that God is among the number of those things of whose origin I form no image. In like manner, saying that God is "infinite" is tantamount to our saying that he is among the number of those things whose limits we do not conceive. And thus any idea of God is out of the question, for what sort of idea is it that has neither origin nor boundaries?

God is called "supremely understanding." I ask here: Through what idea does M. Descartes understand God's act of understanding?

God is called "supremely powerful." Again, through what idea do we understand power which is of things yet to come, that is, of things that do not exist? Certainly I understand power from the image or memory of past actions, concluding to it thus: Something did thus and so; therefore it was able to do it; and therefore, if it exists as the same thing, it will again be able to do thus and so; that is, it has the power to do something. Now these are all ideas that are capable of having arisen from external objects.

God is called "creator of all that exists." I can conjure up for myself some image of creation out of what I have observed, such as a man being born or his growing from something as small as a point to the shape and size he now possesses. No one has any other idea corresponding to the word "creator." However, to prove creation it is not enough to be able to imagine that the world was created. And thus, even if it were demonstrated that something "infinite, independent, supremely powerful, and so on" exists, it still does not follow that a creator exists, unless someone were to believe it is correct to infer from the fact that something exists which we believe to have created all other things that the world has therefore been at some time created by him.

Moreover, when he says that the idea of God and of our soul is innate in us, I would like to know if the souls of those in a deep sleep are thinking. If they are not, then during that time they have no ideas. Whence no idea is innate, for what is innate is always present.

Reply: Nothing that we ascribe to God can originate from external objects, as from an exemplar, since nothing in God bears any resemblance to things found in external, that is, corporeal things. However, if we think of something that is unlike these external objects, it obviously does not originate from them but from the cause of that diversity in our thought.

And I ask here how our philosopher deduces [his conception of] God's understanding from external things. But I easily explain the idea I have of God's understanding by saying that by the word "idea" I understand everything that is the form of some perception. For who is there that does not perceive that he understands something? And thus who is there that does not have that form or idea of an act of understanding, and, by indefinitely extending it, does not form an idea of the divine act of understanding? And the same applies to the rest of God's attributes.

But we used the idea of God which is in us to demonstrate God's existence, and such immense power is contained in this idea that we understand that, if in fact God does exist, it would be contradictory for something other than God to exist without having been created by him. And because of these considerations, it plainly follows, from the fact that his existence has been demonstrated, that it has also been demonstrated that the entire world, that is, all the things other than God that exist, has been created by him.

Finally, when we assert that some idea is innate in us, we do not have in mind that we always notice it (for in that event no idea would ever be innate), but only that we have in ourselves the power to elicit the idea.

Objection XI: "The whole force of the argument rests on the fact that I recognize that it would be impossible for me to exist, being of such a nature as I am (namely, having in me the idea of God), unless God did in fact exist. God, I say, that same being the idea of whom is in me. . . ."

Since, therefore, it has not been demonstrated that we have an idea of God, and since the Christian religion requires us to believe that God is inconceivable (that is, as I see it, that we have no idea of him), it follows that the existence of God has not been demonstrated, and much less has the creation.

Reply: When it is asserted that God is inconceivable, this is understood with respect to a concept that adequately comprehends him. But I have repeated ad nauseam how it is we have an idea of God. And nothing at all is asserted here that weakens my demonstrations.

# Fourth Set of Objections

## Concerning God

The first proof of the existence of God (the one the author spells out in the Third Meditation) has two parts. The first part is that God exists if indeed there is an idea of God in me. The second part is that I who have such an idea could be derived only from God.

Regarding the first part, there is one thing that is not proved to me, namely that when the distinguished gentleman asserted that falsity properly so-called can be found only in judgments, he nevertheless admits a bit later that ideas can be false—not formally false mind you, but materially false. This seems to me to be out of keeping with his first principles.

But I fear I should not be able to explain with enough lucidity my feelings on a matter that is decidedly obscure. An example will make it clearer. The author asserts that if cold is but the privation of heat, the idea of cold which represents it to me as if it were something positive will be materially false.

Moreover, if cold is merely a privation, then there could not be an idea of cold that represents it to me as something positive, and here the author confuses a judgment with an idea.

For what is the idea of cold? Coldness itself, insofar as it exists objectively in the understanding. But if cold is a privation it cannot exist objectively in the understanding by means of an idea whose objective existence is a positive being. Thus, if cold is but a privation, there could not be a positive idea of it, and hence there could never be an idea that is materially false.

This is confirmed by the same argument the distinguished gentleman uses to prove that the idea of an infinite cannot but be true. For although one could imagine that such a being does not exist, nevertheless one could not imagine that the idea of such a being presented nothing real to me.

We can readily say the same thing about every positive idea. For although one could imagine that cold, which I think is represented by a positive idea, is not something positive, still one cannot imagine that the positive idea presents to me nothing real and positive. This is because an idea is not said to be positive in virtue of the existence it has as a mode of thinking (for on that score all ideas would be positive), but rather in virtue of the objective existence it contains and which it presents to our mind. Therefore, though it is possible that this idea is not the idea of cold, it nevertheless cannot be a false one.

But, you may say, it is false precisely in virtue of its not being the idea of cold. Actually, it is your judgment that is false, were you to judge it to be the idea of cold. But the idea, in and of itself,[9] is most true. In like manner, the idea of God surely ought not be called false, not even materially, even though someone could transfer it to something that is not God, as idolaters have done.

9. Reading *se* for *te* (AT VII 207.13).

Finally, what does this idea of cold, which you say is materially false, display to your mind? A privation? Then it is true. A positive being? Then it is not the idea of cold. Again, what is the cause of this positive objective being, which, in your opinion, renders this idea materially false? It is I, you say, insofar as I am derived from nothing. Therefore, the positive objective existence of some idea can be derived from nothing, a conclusion that destroys the principal foundations of the distinguished gentleman.

But let us move on to the second part of the demonstration, where he asks whether I myself who have the idea of an infinite being could be derived from something other than an infinite being, and especially whether I am derived from myself. The distinguished gentleman contends that I could not be derived from myself, in view of the fact that, were I myself to give myself existence, I would also give myself all the perfections an idea of which I observe to be within me. But the theologian replies with the astute observation that "being derived from itself" [*esse a se*] ought to be taken not in a positive sense, but in a negative sense, to the effect that it means the same thing as "not derived from another." "But," he says, "if something is derived from itself (that is to say, not from something else), how do I prove that this thing encompasses all things and that it is infinite? I do not follow you now if you say, 'if it is derived from itself, it would have easily given itself all things.' For neither is it derived from itself as from a cause, nor did it exist prior to itself such that it would choose beforehand what it would later be."

To refute this argument, the distinguished gentleman maintains that "being derived from itself" ought to be taken in a positive rather than a negative sense, even when it applies to God, to the effect that God "stands in the same relationship to himself as an efficient cause does to its effect." This seems to me to be a harsh statement and a false one at that.

Thus, while I am partly in agreement with the distinguished gentleman, I am partly in disagreement with him. For I confess I cannot be derived from myself except in a positive fashion, but I deny that the same may be said of God. In fact, I think it a manifest contradiction that something is derived from itself positively and as it were from a cause. Thus I bring about the same result as our author, but by way of quite another route, and it goes as follows:

For me to be derived from myself, I ought to be derived from myself in a positive fashion, and as it were from a cause. Therefore, it is impossible for me to be derived from myself.

The major premise of this syllogism is proved by the gentleman's arguments that are drawn from the doctrine that, since the various parts of time can be separated from one another, the fact that I exist now does not entail my existing in the future, unless some cause, as it were, makes me over again at each individual moment.

As to the minor premise, I believe it to be so clear by the light of nature that it is largely a waste of time to try to prove it—a matter of proving the known by means of the less known. Moreover, the author seems to have recognized the truth of this since he has not made bold to disavow it publicly. Please weigh the following statement made in reply to the theologian:[10]

". . . I did not say that it is impossible for something to be the efficient cause of itself. For although this is obviously the case when the meaning of "efficient cause" is restricted to those causes which are temporally prior to their effects or are different from them, still it does not seem that such a restriction is appropriate in this inquiry, . . . since the light of nature does not stipulate that the nature of an efficient cause requires that it be temporally prior to its effect."

Well done, as far as the first part is concerned. But why has he left out the second part? And why has he not added that the very same light of nature does not stipulate that the essence [*ratio*] of an efficient cause requires that it be different from its effect, unless it is because the very same light of nature did not permit him to assert it?

And since every effect depends upon a cause and thus receives its existence from a cause, is it not patently clear that the same thing cannot depend on itself or receive its existence from itself?

Moreover, every cause is the cause of an effect, and every effect the effect of a cause. Thus there is

---

10. Johan de Kater (Johannes Caterus), author of the *First Set of Objections*.

a reciprocal relationship between cause and effect. But a relationship must occur between two things.

Moreover, it is absurd to conceive of something receiving existence and yet having existence prior to the time we conceive it to have received existence. But this would be the case were we to ascribe the notions of cause and effect to the very same thing in respect to itself. For what is the notion of a cause? It is the giving of existence. And what is the notion of an effect? It is the receiving of existence. But the notion of a cause is prior by nature to that of an effect.

But we cannot conceive of something as a cause [sub ratione causae] (as something giving existence), unless we conceive of it as having existence; for no one gives what one does not have. Therefore we would first be conceiving a thing as having existence before conceiving of it as having received it; and yet in the case of whatever receives existence, receiving existence comes before having existence.

This argument can be put differently: no one gives what he does not have; therefore, no one can give himself existence, unless he already has it. But if he already has it, why would he give it to himself?

Finally, he claims that it is manifest by the light of nature that creation differs from preservation solely by virtue of a distinction of reason. But it is manifest by the very same light of nature that nothing can create itself. Therefore, nothing can preserve itself.

But if we descend from the general thesis to the specific instance [hypothesim] of God, the matter will, in my judgment, be even more manifest: God cannot be derived from himself positively, but only negatively, that is, in the sense of not being derived from something else.

And first, it is manifest from the argument put forward by the distinguished gentleman to prove that if a body is derived from itself, then it ought to be derived from itself in a positive fashion. For, as he says, the parts of time do not depend on one another. Thus, the fact that this body is presumed up until the present time to have been derived from itself (that is, it has no cause) does not suffice to make it exist in the future, unless there is some power in it which, as it were, continuously "remakes" it.

But so far from this argument being relevant to the case of a supremely perfect or infinite being, the opposite result could be readily deduced, and for opposite reasons. For contained in the idea of an infinite being is the fact that its duration is also infinite; that is, it is bounded by no limits; and thus it is indivisible, permanent, and possessed of all things all at once [tota simul]. Temporal sequence cannot be conceived to be in this idea except erroneously and through the imperfection of our understanding.

Whence it manifestly follows that an infinite being cannot be conceived of as existing even for a moment without at the same time being conceived of as always having existed and as existing in the future for eternity (which is what the author himself teaches in another passage). Hence it is pointless to ask why it would continue to exist.

Further—as is frequently taught by St. Augustine (than whom no one after the time of the sacred authors has ever spoken more nobly and sublimely about God)—in God there is no past or future, but an eternal present. And from this it appears quite evident that it is only with absurdity that one can ask why God continues to exist, since this question obviously involves a temporal sequence of before and after, of past and future, and this ought to be excluded from the notion of an infinite being.

Moreover, God cannot be thought of as being derived from himself positively [a se positive], as if he had initially produced himself, for in that case he would have existed before he existed. Rather, God can be thought to be derived from himself solely in virtue of the fact that he really does preserve himself, as the author frequently states.

But preservation is no more consonant with an infinite being than is an initial production. For what, pray, is preservation, except a certain continuous remaking of something? Thus every instance of preservation presupposes an initial production; and for this reason the term "continuation," like the term "preservation," implies a certain potentiality. But an infinite being is the purest actuality, without any potentiality.

Let us conclude then that God can be conceived to be derived from himself [esse a seipso] in a positive fashion only by reason of the imperfection of our understanding, which conceives of God after the manner of created things. This will be established even more firmly by means of another argument.

The efficient cause of something is sought only with respect to a thing's existence, not its essence. For example, on seeing a triangle, I may seek the efficient cause that brought about the existence of this triangle, but it would be absurd for me to seek the efficient cause of the fact that the triangle has three angles equal to two right angles. Saying that an efficient cause is the reason for this is not a proper answer to someone making an inquiry; all that can be said is that it is simply the nature of a triangle to have such a property. Thus it is that mathematicians do not demonstrate by way of efficient or final causes, since they do not concern themselves with the existence of their object. But it no less belongs to the essence of an infinite being that it exists, and even, if you will, that it continues in existence, than it is of the essence of a triangle that it have three angles equal to two right angles. Therefore, just as one cannot give an answer by way of efficient causality to the person asking why a triangle has three angles equal to two right angles but must say only that such is the eternal and unchangeable nature of a triangle, just so, to the person asking why God exists or why God continues to exist, the advice should be given that no efficient cause (either inside or outside God), no "quasi-efficient" cause (for I am in disagreement about things not words) is to be sought. Rather, this alone should be claimed as the reason: that such is the nature of a supremely perfect being.

The learned gentleman states that the light of nature dictates that there exists nothing about which it is inappropriate to ask why it exists or to inquire into its efficient cause, or, if it has none, to demand to know why it does not need one. Against this my answer to the person asking why God exists is that one should not reply in terms of an efficient cause. Rather, one should say merely that it is because he is God, that is, an infinite being. And if someone were to ask for the efficient cause of God, we should answer that God needs no efficient cause. And were the inquirer once again to ask why God does not need an efficient cause, we should answer that it is because he is an infinite being, whose existence is his essence; for the only things that need an efficient cause are those in which it is appropriate to distinguish their actual existence from their essence.

Thus is overthrown all that the author adds just after the passages cited: "Thus," he says, "if I thought that nothing could in any way be related to itself the way an efficient cause is related to its effect, it is out of the question that I then conclude that something is the first cause. On the contrary, I would again ask for the cause of that which was being called the 'first cause,' and thus I would never arrive at any first cause of all things."

On the contrary, were I to think we should seek the efficient (or quasi-efficient) cause of any given thing, I would seek a cause of each individual thing that was different from that thing, since it is most evident to me that in no way can something be in the same relation to itself as an efficient cause is to its effect.

The author, in my opinion, should be put on notice so that he can consider these things attentively and diligently, since I certainly know there can scarcely be found a theologian who would not take exception to the statement that God is derived from himself in a positive fashion, and as it were from a cause.

My only remaining concern is whether the author does not commit a vicious circle, when he says that we have no other basis on which to establish that what we clearly and distinctly perceive is true, than that God exists.

But we can be certain that God exists only because we clearly and evidently perceive this fact. Therefore, before we are certain that God exists, we ought to be certain that whatever we clearly and evidently perceive is true.

I add something that had escaped me. What the distinguished gentleman affirms as certain seems to me to be false, namely, that there can be nothing in him, insofar as he is a thing that thinks, of which he is unaware. For this "him, insofar as it is a thing that thinks," he understands to be merely his mind, insofar as it is distinct from his body. But who does not realize that there can be a great many things in the mind, of which the mind is unaware? The mind of an infant in its mother's womb has the power to think, but it is not aware of it. I pass over countless examples similar to this one.

# Reply to the Fourth Set of Objections

## Reply to the Second Part: Concerning God

Up to this point I have attempted to refute the distinguished gentleman's arguments and to withstand his attack. From here on, as is the custom for those who struggle with those stronger than themselves, I will not place myself in direct opposition to him; rather, I will dodge his blows.

He brings up only three points in this part; and these can be readily accepted if they are taken in the sense in which he understands them. But I understood what I wrote in a different sense, which also seems to me to be true.

The first point is that certain ideas are materially false. As I understand it, these ideas are such that they present matter for error to the power of judgment. But the gentleman, by considering these ideas taken formally, argues that no falsity is in them.

The second point is that God is derived from himself positively and as it were from a cause. Here I had in mind merely that the reason why God does not need any efficient cause in order to exist is founded on something positive, namely on the very immensity of God, than which there can be nothing more positive. The gentleman proves that God can never be produced or preserved by himself through some positive influence of an efficient cause. I too am in agreement with all of this.

The third and final point is that there can be nothing in our mind of which we are unaware. I understood this with respect to operations, whereas the gentleman, who understands this with respect to powers, denies this.

But let us carefully explain each of these one by one. When the gentleman says that if cold were merely a privation, there could not be an idea [of cold] that represents it as something positive, it is obvious that he is merely dealing with the idea taken formally. For since ideas are themselves forms of a certain sort and are not made up of any matter, whenever we consider them insofar as they represent something, we are taking them not materially but formally. But if we view them not insofar as they represent this

or that thing, but merely insofar as they are operations of the understanding, then we could surely say that we are taking them materially. But in that case they would bear absolutely no relationship to the truth or falsity of their objects. Hence it seems to me that we can call these ideas materially false only in the sense I have already described: Namely, whether cold be something positive or a privation, I do not on that account have a different idea of it; rather, it remains the same in me as the one I have always had. And I say that this idea provides me with matter for error if it is true that cold is a privation and does not have as much reality as heat, because, in considering either of the ideas of heat or cold just as I received them both from the senses, I cannot observe any more reality being shown me by the one idea than by the other.

And it is obviously not the case that I have confused judgment with an idea, for I have said that material falsity is to be found in the latter, whereas only formal falsity can exist in the former.

However, when the distinguished gentleman says that the idea of cold is coldness itself insofar as it exists objectively in the understanding, I think a distinction is in order. For it often happens in the case of obscure and confused ideas (and those of heat and cold should be numbered among them) that they are referred to something other than that of which they really are ideas. Thus, were cold merely a privation, the idea of cold would not be coldness itself as it exists objectively in the understanding, but something else which is wrongly taken for that privation: namely, a certain sensation having no existence outside the understanding.

But the same analysis does not hold in the case of the idea of God, or at least when the idea is clear and distinct, since it cannot be said to be referred to something with which it is not in conformity. But as to confused ideas of gods which are concocted by idolaters, I fail to see why they too cannot be called materially false, insofar as these ideas provide matter for their false judgments. Nevertheless, surely those ideas that offer the faculty of judgment little or no occasion for error are presumably less worthy of being called materially false than do those that offer it considerable occasion for error; however, it is easy to exemplify the fact that some ideas offer a greater occasion for error than others. For this occasion does not exist in confused ideas formed at the whim of the mind (such as the ideas of false gods) to the extent that it does in ideas that come to us confused from the senses (such as the ideas of heat and cold), if, as I said, it is in fact true that they display nothing real. But the greatest occasion of all for error is in ideas that arise from the sensitive appetite. For example, does not the idea of thirst in the man with dropsy in fact offer him matter for error when it provides him an occasion for judging that drinking something will do him good, when in fact it will do him harm?

But the distinguished gentleman asks what it is that is shown to me by this idea of cold, which I have said to be materially false. He says: if it shows a privation, then it is true; if it shows a positive being, then it is not the idea of cold. Quite true. However, the sole reason for my calling this idea materially false is that, since it is obscure and confused, I could not determine whether or not what it shows me is something positive outside my sensation. Thus I have an occasion for judging that it is something positive, although perhaps it is merely a privation.

Hence one should not ask what the cause is of this positive objective being that causes this idea to be materially false, since I am not claiming that this materially false idea is caused by some positive being, but rather that it is caused solely by the obscurity that nevertheless does have something positive as its subject, namely the sensation itself.

And surely this positive being is in me insofar as I am a true thing; but the obscurity, which alone provides me an occasion for judging that this idea of the sensation of cold represents something external to me which is called "cold," does not have a real cause, but arises solely from the fact that my nature is not perfect in every respect.

My basic principles are in no way weakened by this objection. However, since I never spent very much time reading the books of the philosophers, it might have been a cause for worry that I did not sufficiently take note of their manner of speaking when I asserted that ideas that provide the power of

judgment with matter for error are materially false, had it not been for the fact that I found the word "materially" used in the same sense as my own in the first author that came into my hands: namely in Francisco Suarez's *Metaphysical Disputations*, Disp. IX, sect. 2, no. 4.

But let us move on to the most significant items about which the distinguished gentleman registers his disapproval. However, in my opinion, these things seem least deserving of disapproval: namely, in the passage where I said that it is fitting for us to think that in a sense God stands in the same relationship to himself as an efficient cause does to its effect. For in that very passage I denied what the distinguished gentleman says is a harsh saying, and a false one at that: namely, that God is the efficient cause of himself. For in asserting that "in a certain sense, God stands in the same relationship to himself as an efficient cause," I did not take the two relationships to be identical. And in saying by way of preface that "it is wholly fitting for us to think . . . ," I meant that my sole explanation for these things is the imperfection of the human understanding. However, I asserted this throughout the rest of the passage; for right at the very beginning, where I said that there exists nothing about which it is inappropriate to inquire into its efficient cause, I added "or, if it does not have one, to demand why it does not need one." These words are a sufficient indication that I believed there exists something that needs no efficient cause. But what, besides God, can be of this sort? And a short time later I said that "in God there is such great and inexhaustible power, that he never needed the help of anything in order to exist. Moreover, God does not now need a cause in order to be preserved; thus, in a manner of speaking, God is the cause of himself." Here the expression "cause of himself" can in no way be understood to mean an efficient cause; rather, it is merely a matter of the inexhaustible power of God being the cause or the reason why he needs no cause. And since this inexhaustible power or immensity of essence is incomparably positive, I said that the cause or the reason why God does not need a cause is a positive one. This could not be said of anything finite, even if it is supremely perfect in its own kind. But if a finite thing were said to be derived from itself, this could only be understood in a negative sense, since no reason derived from its positive nature could be put forward, on the basis of which we might understand that it does not need an efficient cause.

And in like manner, in all the other passages in which I compared the formal cause or reason derived from God's essence (on account of which God does not need a cause, either in order to exist or to be preserved) with the efficient cause (without which finite things cannot come into existence), I always did this in such wise that the difference between the formal cause and the efficient cause may come to be known from my very own words. Nowhere have I said that God preserves himself by means of some positive influence, as is the case with created things preserved by him; on the contrary, I merely said that the immensity of power or essence, on account of which he needs no one to preserve him, is something positive.

And thus I can readily agree with everything the distinguished gentleman puts forward to prove that God is not the efficient cause of himself and that he preserves himself neither by means of any positive influence nor by means of a continuous reproduction of himself. This is the only thing that is achieved from his arguments. However, as I hope is the case, even he will not deny that this immensity of the power, on account of which God does not need a cause in order to exist, is in God something positive, and that nothing similarly positive can be understood in anything else on account of which it would not require an efficient cause in order to exist. This is all I meant when I said that, with the exception of God alone, nothing can be understood to be derived from itself unless this is understood in a negative sense. Nor was there any need for me to assume any more than this in order to resolve the difficulty that had been put forward.

However, since the distinguished gentleman warns me here with such seriousness that "there can scarcely be found a theologian who would not take exception to the proposition that God is derived from himself in a positive fashion, and as it were from a cause," I will explain a bit more carefully why this way of speaking seems to me to be extremely helpful and even necessary in treating this question, and also why

it seems to me to be quite removed from suspicion of being likely to cause someone to take offense.

I am aware that theologians of the Latin Church do not use the word *causa* [cause] in speaking of divine matters, when they are discussing the procession of persons in the Most Holy Trinity. And whereas theologians of the Greek Church use the words αἴτιον [cause] and ἀρχὴν [principle] interchangeably, theologians of the Latin Church prefer to use only the word *principium* [principle], taking it in its most general sense, lest from their manner of speaking they provide anyone an occasion on this basis for judging the Son to be less than the Father. But where no such danger of error is possible, and the discussion concerns not God considered as triune but only as one, I fail to see why the word "cause" should be shunned to such a degree, especially when we arrive at a point where it seems quite helpful and almost necessary to use it.

However, there can be no greater use for this term than if it aids in demonstrating the existence of God, and no greater necessity for it than if the existence of God manifestly could not be proved without it.

But I think it is obvious to everyone that a consideration of efficient causes is the primary and principal, not to say the only, means of proving the existence of God. However, we cannot pursue this proof with care unless we give our mind the freedom to inquire about the efficient causes of all things, including even God himself, for by what right would we thence exclude God before we have proved that he exists? We must therefore ask with respect to every single thing whether it is derived from itself or from something else. And the existence of God can indeed be inferred by this means, even if we do not provide an explicit account of how one is to understand that "something is derived from itself." For those who follow exclusively the lead of the light of nature immediately at this juncture form a certain concept common to both efficient and formal cause alike, i.e., what is derived from something else [*est ab alio*] is derived from it as it were from an efficient cause; but whatever is derived from itself [*est a se*] is derived as it were from a formal cause, that is, because it has an essence of such a type that it does not need an efficient cause. For this reason I did not explain this doctrine in my Meditations; rather I assumed it to be self-evident.

But when those who are accustomed to judging that nothing can be the efficient cause of itself and to distinguishing carefully an efficient cause from a formal cause see the question being raised as to whether something is derived from itself, it easily happens that, while thinking that this expression refers only to an efficient cause properly so-called, they do not think the expression "derived from itself" should be understood to mean "as from a cause," but only negatively as meaning "without a cause," with the result that there arises something concerning which we must not ask why it exists. Were this rendering of the expression "derived from itself" to be accepted, there could not be an argument [*ratio*] from effects to prove the existence of God, as the author of the First Set of Objections has shown. Therefore, this rendering is in no way to be accepted.

However, to give an apt reply to this, I think it is necessary to point out that there is a middle ground between an efficient cause properly so-called and no cause at all: namely the positive essence of a thing, to which we can extend the concept of an efficient cause in the same way we are accustomed in geometry to extend the concept of an exceedingly long arc to the concept of a straight line, or the concept of a rectilinear polygon with an indefinite number of sides to the concept of a circle. And I fail to see how this can be explained any better than by saying that in this query the meaning of "efficient cause" should not be restricted to those causes which are temporally prior to their effects or are different from them. For, first, the question would be pointless, since everyone knows that the same thing cannot exist prior to itself or be different from itself. Second, we could remove one of these two conditions from its concept and yet the notion of an efficient cause would remain intact.

For the fact that an efficient cause need not be temporally prior is evident from the fact that it has the defining characteristic [*rationem*] of a cause only during the time it is producing an effect, as has been said.

But from the fact that the other condition as well cannot be set aside, one ought to infer only that it is not an efficient cause taken in the strict sense, and

I grant this. However, one ought not infer that it is in no sense a positive cause which can be compared by way of analogy to an efficient cause; and this is all that is called for in my argument. For by the very same light of nature by which I perceive that I would have given myself all the perfections of which there is an idea in me (if indeed I had given myself existence), I also perceive that nothing can give itself existence in that restricted sense in which the term "efficient cause" is typically used, namely in such wise that the same thing, insofar as it gives itself existence, is different from itself, insofar as it receives existence, since being the same thing and not being the same thing (that is, being different from itself) are contradictory.

And thus, when the question arises whether something can give itself existence, one must understand this to be equivalent to asking whether the nature or essence of anything is such that it needs no efficient cause in order to exist.

And when one adds that if there were such a thing, it would give itself all the perfections of which there is some idea in it, if indeed it does not yet have them, the meaning of this is that this thing cannot fail to have in actuality all the perfections that it knows. The reason for this is that we perceive by the light of nature that a thing whose essence is so immense that it does not need an efficient cause in order to exist also does not need an efficient cause in order to possess all the perfections that it knows, and that its own proper essence gives it in an eminent fashion all that we can think an efficient cause is capable of giving to any other things.

And the words "if it does not yet have them, it will give them to itself" are helpful only in explaining the matter, since we perceive by the same light of nature that this thing cannot now have the power and the will to give itself anything new, but that its essence is such that it possesses from eternity all that we can now think it would give itself, if it did not already possess it.

Nevertheless, all these modes of speaking, which are taken from the analogy of an efficient cause, are particularly necessary in order to direct the light of nature in such wise that we pay particular attention to them. This takes place in precisely the same way in which Archimedes, by comparing the sphere and other curvilinear figures with rectilinear figures, demonstrated various properties of the sphere and other curvilinear figures that otherwise could hardly have been understood. And just as no one raises objections regarding proofs of this sort, even if during the course of them one is required to consider a sphere to be similar to a polyhedron, I likewise think I cannot be blamed here for using the analogy of an efficient cause in order to explain those things that pertain to a formal cause, that is, to the very essence of God.

And there is no possible danger of error in this matter, since that one single aspect which is a property of an efficient cause, and which cannot be extended to a formal cause, contains a manifest contradiction, and thus is incapable of being believed by anyone, namely that something is different from itself or that it simultaneously is and is not the same thing.

Moreover, one should note that we have ascribed to God the dignity inherent in being a cause in such wise that no indignity inherent in being an effect would follow thence in him. For just as theologians, in saying that the Father is the *principium* [principle] of the Son, do not on that account grant that the Son came from a principle; just so, although I have granted that God can in a certain sense be called the cause of himself, nevertheless nowhere have I in the same way called him an effect of himself. For it is customary to use the word "effect" primarily in relation to an efficient cause, and is regarded as less noble than its efficient cause, although it is often more noble than other causes.

However, when I here take the entire essence of a thing for its formal cause, I am merely following in the footsteps of Aristotle, for in his Posterior Analytics, Book II, chapter 11, having passed over the material cause, he calls the αἴταν [cause] the τὸ τί ἦν εἶναι [the what it was to be] or, as philosophers writing in Latin traditionally render it, the *causa formalis* [formal cause], and he extends this to all the essences of all things, since at this point he is dealing not with the causes of a physical composite (any more than I am here), but more generally with the causes from which some knowledge could be sought.

But it was hardly possible for me to discuss this matter without ascribing the term "cause" to God.

This can be shown from the fact that, when the distinguished gentleman attempted to do the same thing I did by a different route, he nevertheless was completely unsuccessful, at least as I see it. For after using a number of words he shows that God is not the efficient cause of himself, since the defining characteristic [*ratio*] of "efficient cause" requires it to be different from its effect. Then he shows that God is not derived from himself in a positive sense, where one understands the word "positive" to mean the positive influence of a cause. Next he shows that God does not truly preserve himself, if by "preservation" one means the continuous production of a thing. All of this I readily grant. At length he tries to prove that God cannot be said to be the efficient cause of himself because, he says, the efficient cause of a thing is sought only with respect to the thing's existence, but not at all with respect to its essence. But existing is no less of the essence of an infinite being than having three angles equal to two right angles is of the essence of a triangle. Thus, if one is asked why God exists, one should no more answer by way of an efficient cause than one should do if asked why the three angles of a triangle are equal to two right angles. This syllogism can easily be turned against the distinguished gentleman in the following way: even if an efficient cause is not sought with respect to essence, still it can be sought with respect to existence; but in God essence and existence are not distinguished; therefore, one can seek an efficient cause of God.

But in order to reconcile these two positions, someone who seeks to know why God exists should be told that one surely ought not respond in terms of an efficient cause in the strict sense, but only in terms of the very essence or formal cause of the thing. And precisely because in God existence is not distinguished from essence, the formal cause is strikingly analogous to an efficient cause, and thus can be called a "quasi-efficient cause."

Finally, he adds that the reply to be made to someone who is seeking the efficient cause of God is that he has no need of one; and to someone quizzing us further as to why God does not need one, the reply should be that this is because God is an infinite being whose existence is his essence. For only those things that need an efficient cause are those in which actual existence can be distinguished from essence. On the basis of these considerations he says he overturns what I had said, namely that were I to think that nothing could somehow be related to itself the same way that an efficient cause is related to an effect, I would never, in inquiring into the causes of things, arrive at any first cause of all things. Nevertheless, it appears to me that my position has not been overturned nor has it been shakened or weakened. Moreover, on this depends the principal force not just of my argument but of absolutely all the arguments that can be put forward to prove the existence of God from effects. Yet virtually every theologian holds that no proof can be put forward unless it is from effects.

And thus, when he disallows the analogy of an efficient cause being ascribed to God's relationship to himself, far from making the argument for God's existence transparent, he instead prevents readers from understanding it, especially at the end where he concludes that, were he to think that an efficient or quasi-efficient cause were to be sought for anything, he would be seeking a cause of that thing which is different from it. For how would those who do not yet know God inquire into the efficient cause of other things so as in this way to arrive at a knowledge of God, unless they thought that one could seek the efficient cause of anything whatever? And finally, how would they make an end of their search for God as the first cause, if they thought that for any given thing one must look for a cause that is different from it?

The distinguished gentleman certainly appears to be doing the very same thing here that he would do, were he to follow Archimedes (who spoke of the properties that he had demonstrated of a sphere by means of an analogy with rectilinear figures) and were to say, "If I thought that a sphere could not be taken for a rectilinear or quasi-rectilinear figure having an infinite number of sides, I would attach no force to this demonstration, since strictly speaking the argument holds not for a sphere as a curvilinear figure, but merely for a sphere as a rectilinear figure having an infinite number of sides." It is, I say, as if the distinguished gentleman, while not wanting to characterize the sphere thus, and nevertheless desirous of retaining Archimedes's demonstration, were to say, "If I thought that the conclusion Archimedes drew

there was supposed to be understood with respect to a rectilinear figure having an infinite number of sides, I would not admit this conclusion with respect to the sphere, since I am both certain and convinced that a sphere is in no way a rectilinear figure." Obviously, in making these remarks he would not be doing the same thing as Archimedes had done; on the contrary, he would definitely prevent himself and others from correctly understanding Archimedes's demonstration.

I have pursued these matters here at somewhat greater length than perhaps the subject required, in order to show that it is a matter of greatest importance to take care lest there be found in my writings the least thing that theologians may justly find objectionable.

Finally, as to the fact that I did not commit a vicious circle when I said that it is manifest to us that the things we clearly and distinctly perceive are true only because God exists; and that it is manifest to us that God exists only because we perceive this fact clearly, I have already given a sufficient explanation in the Reply to the Second Set of Objections, sections 3 and 4, where I drew a distinction between what we are actually perceiving clearly and what we recall having clearly perceived sometime earlier. For first of all it is manifest to us that God exists, since we are attending to the arguments that prove this; but later on, it is enough for us to recall our having clearly perceived something in order to be certain that it is true. This would not suffice, unless we knew that God exists and does not deceive us.

Now as to the doctrine that there can be nothing in the mind, insofar as it is a thing that thinks, of which it is not aware, this appears to me self-evident, because we understand that nothing is in the mind, so viewed, that is not a thought or is not dependent upon thought. For otherwise it would not belong to the mind insofar as it is a thing that thinks. Nor can there exist in us any thought of which we are not aware at the very same moment it is in us. For this reason I have no doubt that the mind begins to think immediately upon its being infused into the body of an infant, and at the same time is aware of its thought, even if later on it does not recall what it was thinking of, because the images [*species*] of these thoughts do not inhere in the memory.

However, it should be noted that although we

surely are always actually aware of the acts or operations of our mind, but this is not always the case with
regard to faculties or powers, except potentially. In
other words, when we prepare ourselves to use some
faculty, if this faculty is in the mind, we are immediately and actually aware of it. And therefore we can
deny that it is in the mind if we are unable to become
aware of it.

# René Descartes, *Principles of Philosophy* (1644–47)[1]

## Part I. The Principles of Human Knowledge

1. *For a person inquiring into the truth, it is necessary once in his life to doubt all things, as far as this is possible.*

Since we were once children and made judgments concerning things presented to our senses while we did not yet have the entire use of our reason, many judgments thus precipitately formed prevent us from arriving at the knowledge of the truth. It seems that there is no way we can deliver ourselves from these, unless we undertake once in our lives to doubt all things in which the slightest trace of uncertainty can be found.

2. *We ought to consider as false all things we can doubt.*

It will even be useful to reject as false all things in which we can imagine the least doubt, so that we may discover with greater clarity those which are absolutely true and easiest to know.

3. *We should not in the meantime use this doubt for the conduct of our life.*

1. Translated by Elizabeth S. Haldane and G. R. T. Ross in *The Philosophical Works of Descartes* (Cambridge: Cambridge University Press, 1911), substantially modified by Marjorie Grene and Roger Ariew. Significant additions from the 1647 French translation are indicated within angle brackets.

But in the meantime it is to be observed that we should use this doubt only when we are engaged in contemplating truth. For, as regards the conduct of our life, we are frequently required to follow merely probable opinions, because the opportunities for action would in most cases pass away before we could free ourselves from our doubts. And when, as frequently happens with two courses of action, we do not perceive the probability of the one more than the other, we must yet select one of them.

4. *Why we can doubt sensible things.*

But because we desire to apply ourselves only to the search after truth, we will first doubt whether sensible things or things we have imagined really exist. First, we know that our senses have deceived us before, and it is prudent not to trust too much in what has even once deceived us. Second, we continually seem to feel or imagine innumerable things in sleep which have no existence. To those who thus resolve to doubt all, there is apparently no mark by which they can distinguish with certainty being asleep from being awake.

5. *Why we can likewise doubt mathematical demonstrations.*

We will also doubt all the other things which have formerly seemed to us quite certain, even mathematical demonstrations and those principles we formerly thought quite self-evident. One reason is that those who have fallen into error in reasoning on such matters have held what we see to be false as perfectly certain and self-evident, but a yet more important reason is that we have been told that God who created us can do all that he wishes. For we are still ignorant of whether he may not have wished to create us in such a way that we will always be deceived, even in the things we believe ourselves to know best—since this does not seem less possible than our being occasionally deceived, which experience tells us is the case. And if we think that an omnipotent God is not the author of our being, and that we subsist of ourselves, or through some others, yet the less perfect we suppose the author to be, the more reason we have to believe that we are not so perfect that we cannot be continually deceived.

6. *We have free will, which allows us to withhold assent from dubious things, and thus prevents our falling into error.*

But whoever turns out to have created us, and even if he should prove to be all-powerful and deceitful, we still experience a freedom through which we may abstain from accepting as true and indisputable those things of which we do not have certain knowledge, and thus prevent ourselves from ever being deceived.

7. *We cannot doubt our existence without existing while we doubt; and this is the first thing that we can know when we philosophize in an orderly way.*

While we thus reject everything we can possibly doubt, and feign that it is false, it is easy to suppose that there is no God, no heaven, no bodies, and that we have no hands, no feet, indeed no body; but we cannot in the same way conceive that we who doubt these things are not; for there is a contradiction in conceiving that what thinks does not, at the same time as it thinks, exist. And hence this conclusion I think, therefore I am, is the first and most certain that occurs to one who philosophizes in an orderly way.

8. *This furnishes us with the distinction between the soul and the body, or between what thinks and what is corporeal.*

This, then, is the best way to discover the nature of mind and the distinction between it and the body. For, in considering what we are, we who suppose that all things apart from ourselves <and outside our thought> are false, observe very clearly that there is no extension, shape, local motion, or anything attributable to body, which pertains to our nature, but only thought alone; and consequently this notion of our thought precedes that of all corporeal things and is the most certain, since we still doubt whether there are any other things in the world, while we already perceive that we think.

9. *What thought is.*

By the word thought I understand everything we are conscious of as operating in us. And that is why not only understanding, willing, imagining, but also feeling, are here the same thing as thinking. For if I say I see, or I walk, therefore I am, and if by seeing and walking I mean the action of my eyes or my legs, which is the work of my body, my conclusion is not absolutely certain; this is because, as often happens in sleep, I think I see or I walk, although I never open my eyes or move from my place, and the same thing perhaps might occur if I had no body at all. But if I mean only to talk of my sensation, or my consciously seeming to see or to walk, it becomes quite true, because my assertion now refers only to my mind, which alone is concerned with my feeling or thinking that I see and I walk.

10. *Things perfectly simple and clear of themselves are obscured by the logical definitions <of the Schools>, and should not be counted among the things capable of being acquired by study, <but are inborn in us>.*

I do not here explain various other terms I already use or will afterwards use, because they seem to me sufficiently self-evident. And I have often noticed that philosophers err in trying to explain things that are perfectly simple and self-evident by logically constructed definitions; as a result, they render them more obscure. When I stated that this proposition *I think, therefore I am* is the first and most certain that presents itself to those who philosophize in an orderly fashion, I did not for all that deny that we must first know *what thought, existence, and certainty are,* and that *in order to think we must exist,* and such like; but because these are such simple notions that of themselves give us no knowledge of anything that exists, I did not think them worthy of being enumerated.

## 11. *How our mind is better known than our body.*

But in order to understand how the knowledge we have of our mind not only precedes that of our body, but is also more evident, it must be observed that it is well known by the natural light <in our souls>, that no qualities or properties belong to nothingness; and that where some are perceived there must necessarily be some thing or substance on which they depend. And the same light shows us that we know a thing or substance so much the better, the more properties we observe in it. And we certainly observe many more properties in our mind than in any other thing, inasmuch as there is nothing that excites us to knowledge of whatever kind which does not even much more certainly compel us to knowledge of our mind. To take an example, if I persuade myself that there is an earth because I touch or see it, by that very same fact, and by a yet stronger reason, I should be persuaded that my mind exists, because it may be that I think I touch the earth even though there is possibly no earth existing at all, but it is not possible that I who form this judgment, and my mind which judges thus, should be non-existent, and so in other cases. <We can conclude the same of all the other things that enter our minds, namely, that we who think of them exist, even though the things themselves may be false or have no existence.>

## 12. *The reason why this is not equally known to everyone.*

Those who did not philosophize in an orderly way have held other opinions on this subject because they never distinguished their mind from their body with sufficient care. For although they had no difficulty in believing that they themselves existed and that they were more certain of this than of any other thing,

they did not observe that by "themselves" they ought merely to understand their minds <when metaphysical certainty was in question>; on the contrary, since they understood by it their bodies, which they saw with their eyes, touched with their hands, and to which they wrongly attributed the power of sense-perception, they were not able to perceive the nature of the mind.

## 13. *In what sense the knowledge of all other things depends on the knowledge of God.*

But when the mind, which thus knows itself but still doubts all other things, looks around in order to try to extend its knowledge further, it first finds in itself the ideas of many things, and while it contemplates these simply and neither affirms nor denies that there is anything outside itself similar to these ideas, it is beyond any danger of falling into error. The mind likewise discovers certain common notions out of which it frames various demonstrations which absolutely convince us of their truth if we pay attention to them. For example, the mind has within itself the ideas of number and figure; it also has such common notions as "if equals are added to equals, the result is equal." From these it is easy to demonstrate that the three angles of a triangle are equal to two right angles, etc. Now the mind perceives these and similar things as true as long as it attends to the premises from which they are derived. But since it cannot always devote this attention to them <when it remembers the conclusion and does not attend to the order of its deduction>, and conceives that it may have been created of such a nature that it has been deceived even in what is most evident, it sees clearly that it has great cause to doubt the truth of such conclusions and to realize that it can have no certain knowledge until it has come to know the author of its origin.

## 14. *The existence of God may be rightly demonstrated from the fact that necessary existence is included in the conception we have of him.*

The mind afterwards considers the various ideas it has and discovers there the idea of a being who is omniscient, omnipotent, and absolutely perfect—by far the most important idea; it recognizes in it not merely possible and contingent existence, as in all the other ideas it has of things it clearly perceives, but absolutely necessary and eternal existence. And just as it perceives that it is necessarily contained in the idea of a triangle that it should have three angles that are equal to two right angles, it is absolutely persuaded that the triangle has three angles equal to two right angles. In the same way from the fact that it perceives that necessary and eternal existence is contained in the idea it has of an absolutely perfect being, it has clearly to conclude that this absolutely perfect being exists.

15. *Necessary existence is not similarly included in the notion we have of other things, but merely contingent existence.*

The mind will be the better assured of the truth of this conclusion if it observes that it does not have the idea of any other thing in which existence is necessarily contained. And from this it realizes that the idea of an absolutely perfect being is not framed in it by means of itself, nor does it represent a chimera, but that it is a true and immutable nature, which cannot but exist, since existence is necessarily contained in it.

16. *Prejudice prevents many from knowing clearly the necessity for the existence of God.*

Our mind would have no trouble in persuading itself of this truth if it were wholly free from prejudice to begin with; but inasmuch as we are accustomed to distinguish essence from existence in all other things, and as we can at will imagine many ideas of things which neither are nor have been, it may easily occur that when we do not steadily contemplate this absolutely perfect being, we will doubt whether the idea we form of him is not one of those we frame at pleasure, or one of those which do not include existence in their essence.

17. *The greater the objective perfection in our ideas, the greater its cause.*

Further, when we reflect on the various ideas that are in us, it is easy to perceive that there is not much difference between them when they are considered only as modes of thinking, but they are widely differ-

ent in another way, since the one represents one thing, and the other another; and their cause must be more perfect as what they represent of their objects is more perfect. For this is just the same as in the case of someone said to have the idea of a machine in the construction of which much skill is displayed; we have reason to ask how he obtained the idea, that is, whether he saw somewhere a similar machine made by another, or had a thorough knowledge of the science of mechanics, or his force of mind was so great that he was able to invent the machine on his own without having seen anything similar anywhere else. For the whole of the ingenuity involved in the idea which is possessed by this man objectively, as in a picture, must exist in its first and principal cause, whatever that may be, not only objectively or representatively, but also formally or eminently.

18. *From this we may demonstrate that there is a God.*

So, because we find within ourselves the idea of a God, or a supremely perfect being, we are able to investigate the cause that produces this idea in us; but after having considered the immensity of the perfection it possesses, we are constrained to admit that we can consider it only as emanating from an all-perfect being, that is, from a God who truly exists. For it is not only made manifest by the natural light that nothing can be the cause of anything whatever, and that the more perfect cannot proceed from the less perfect so as to be thus produced as by its efficient and total cause, but also that it is impossible for us to have any idea of anything whatever, if there is not within us, or outside us, an original that contains all the perfections belonging to the idea. But as we do not in any way possess all those absolute perfections of which we have the idea, we must conclude that they reside in some other nature different from ours — that is, in God; or at least that they were once in him, and it follows from this most manifestly that they are there still.

19. *Although we do not comprehend the whole nature of God, there is yet nothing we know so clearly as his perfections.*

This is quite certain and manifest to those who have accustomed themselves to contemplate God and to turn their attention to his infinite perfections. For, though we do not comprehend them because the nature of the infinite is such that we, being finite, cannot comprehend them, yet we conceive them more clearly and distinctly than any material thing, because, being simpler and not being limited by anything that may obscure them, they occupy our mind more fully.

### 20. *We are not the cause of ourselves, but are caused by God, and consequently there is a God.*

But since everyone does not notice this, and because, when we have a notion of some machine in which much skill is displayed, we know sufficiently well the manner in which we have acquired this idea, and because we cannot even recollect when the idea we have of a God has been communicated to us by God, since it has always been present in us, we must yet inquire who then is the author of our being, given that we have in us the idea of the infinite perfections of God. For the light of nature makes it very clear that whoever knows something more perfect than himself cannot be the author of his being, because then he would have given himself all the perfections of which he has the idea; and consequently he could not subsist by any other than by him who possesses all these perfections in himself, that is, by God.

### 21. *The mere duration of our life suffices to prove the existence of God.*

We cannot doubt the truth of this demonstration as long as we observe the nature of time or the duration of things; for this is of such a kind that its parts do not depend one upon the other, and never coexist; and from the fact that we now exist, it does not follow that we will exist a moment from now, if some cause — the same that first produced us — does not continue to produce us, that is to say, to conserve us. And we can easily recognize that there is no strength in us whereby we may conserve ourselves, but that he who has so much power that he can conserve us out of himself must by so much the greater reason conserve himself, or rather not require to be conserved by any other, for, in short, he is God.

### 22. *In recognizing the existence of God in the manner here explained, we also recognize all his attributes, insofar as they may be known by the natural light alone.*

There is a great advantage in proving the existence of God in this way by his idea: we recognize at the same time what he is, insofar as the weakness of our nature permits. For when we reflect on the idea of him implanted in us, we perceive that he is eternal, omniscient, omnipotent, the source of all goodness and truth, creator of all things, and finally that he has in himself everything in which we can clearly recognize some infinite perfection not limited by any imperfection.

### 23. *God is not corporeal and does not perceive by means of the senses as we do, nor is he the originator of sin.*

There are many things in the world which are in some respects imperfect or limited, although we notice in them certain perfections; it is accordingly not possible that any of these belong to God. Thus because the nature of bodies includes divisibility along with local extension, and divisibility indicates imperfection, it is certain that God is not body. And although it is of some advantage for us to have senses, yet because all sensation involves being acted upon and that indicates dependence on something else, we conclude that God does not have senses, but that he understands and wills — not indeed as we do, by operations which are in some way distinct from one another, but by a single identical and very simple action by which he understands and wills and effects everything. When I say everything, I mean all *things*; for he does not will the evil of sin because that evil is not a thing.

### 24. *In passing from the knowledge that God exists to the knowledge of his creatures, we must remember that our understanding is finite and the power of God infinite.*

Since God alone is the true cause of all that is or can be, we will doubtless follow the best method of philosophizing, if, from the knowledge we have of his nature, we pass to an explanation of the things he has created, <and if we try to deduce it from the

notions that exist naturally in our minds,> for in this way we will obtain a perfect science, that is, knowledge of the effects through their causes. But in order that we may undertake this task with most security from error, we must remember that God, the creator of all things, is infinite and that we are altogether finite.

### 25. *We must believe all that God has revealed, even though it may surpass our capacities.*

Thus if God reveals to us or to others certain things concerning himself that surpass the natural reach of our minds, such as the mysteries of the incarnation and the Trinity, we will have no difficulty in believing them, although we may not clearly understand them. For we should not think it strange that in the immensity of his nature, as also in the objects of his creation, there are many things beyond the range of our comprehension.

### 26. *We must not try to dispute about the infinite, but just consider that everything in which we find no limits is indefinite, such as the extension of the world, the divisibility of its parts, the number of the stars, etc.*

We will thus never hamper ourselves with disputes about the infinite, since it would be absurd that we who are finite should undertake to determine anything regarding it, and by this means in trying to comprehend it, regard it, so to speak, as finite. That is why we do not care to reply to those who ask whether half of an infinite line is infinite, and whether an infinite number is even or odd, and so on, because it is only those who imagine their mind to be infinite who appear to find it necessary to investigate such questions. As for us, while we regard things in which, in a certain sense, we observe no limits, we shall not for all that state that they are infinite, but merely hold them to be indefinite. Thus because we cannot imagine an extension so great that we cannot at the same time conceive that there may be one yet greater, we shall say that the magnitude of possible things is indefinite. And because we cannot divide a body into parts which are so small that each part cannot be divided into others yet smaller, we shall consider that its quantity may be divided into parts whose number

is indefinite. And because we cannot imagine so many stars that it is impossible for God to create more, we shall suppose their number to be indefinite, and so in other cases.

### 27. *The difference between the indefinite and the infinite.*

We call these things indefinite rather than infinite in order to reserve for God alone the name of infinite, first because in him alone we observe no limitation whatever, and because we are quite certain that he can have none; second, because, in regard to other things, we do not in the same way positively understand them to be in every respect unlimited, but merely negatively admit that their limits, if they exist, cannot be discovered by us.

### 28. *We must not inquire into the final, but only into the efficient causes of created things.*

Finally we will not seek the reason of natural things from the end which God or nature has set before himself in their creation <and we will entirely banish the search for final causes from our philosophy>. For we should not take so much upon ourselves as to believe that God could take us into his counsels. But regarding him as the efficient cause of all things, we shall merely try to discover by the light of nature he has placed in us, applied to those attributes of which he has been willing we should have some knowledge, what must be concluded regarding the effects that we perceive by the senses. But we must keep in mind what has been said, that we must trust this natural light only so long as nothing contrary to it is revealed by God himself.

### 29. *God is not the cause of our errors.*

The first of God's attributes that comes into consideration here is that he is supremely true and the source of all light, so that it is completely contradictory that he should deceive us, that is to say, that he should be properly and positively the cause of the errors to which we know from experience we are subject. For although among men the capacity to deceive would seem to be a mark of subtlety of mind, yet the will to deceive proceeds only from malice, or fear, or weakness, and consequently it cannot be attributed to God.

30. *As a result, all that we perceive clearly is true, and this delivers us from the doubts put forward above.*

It follows from this that the light of nature, or the faculty of knowledge God has given us, can never disclose to us any object that is not true, inasmuch as the natural light encompasses it, that is, inasmuch as it perceives it clearly and distinctly. For we would have had reason to think God a deceiver if the faculty he had given us was so perverted that <when using it properly> we would mistake the false for the true. This should deliver us from the supreme doubt that encompassed us when we did not know whether our nature had been such that we had been deceived in things that seemed most clear. It should also protect us against all the other reasons already mentioned which we had for doubting. The truths of mathematics should now be above suspicion, for they are most manifest. And if we perceive anything by our senses, either waking or sleeping, if it is clear and distinct, and if we separate it from what is obscure and confused, we will easily assure ourselves of what is the truth. There is no need to say more on this particular subject here, since I have treated of it fully in the *Meditations on Metaphysics*, and what I intend to say later will serve to explain it more accurately.

31. *Our errors are but negations in respect of God, while in respect of ourselves they are privations or defects.*

But as it happens that, although God is not a deceiver, we so frequently fall into error, if we desire to investigate the origin and cause of our errors in order to guard against them, we must take care to observe that they do not depend so much on our intellect as on our will, and that they are not such as to require the actual concurrence of God in order that they may be produced. In this way, so far as he is concerned, they are but negations, while in respect to us they are defects or privations.

32. *There are but two modes of thought in us, the perception of the intellect and the action of the will.*

For all the modes of thinking that we observe in ourselves may be related to two general modes: perception, or the operation of the intellect, and volition, or the operation of the will. Thus sense-perception, imagining, and conceiving purely intelligible things are just different methods of perceiving; but desiring, holding in aversion, affirming, denying, doubting: all these are different modes of willing.

33. *We deceive ourselves only when we form judgments about anything inadequately perceived.*

When we perceive anything, we are in no danger of misapprehending it as long as we do not judge of it in any way; and even when we judge of it we should not fall into error, provided that we do not give our assent to what we do not perceive clearly and distinctly. What usually misleads us is that we very frequently form a judgment although we do not have an accurate perception of what we judge.

34. *Not only the intellect, but also the will is requisite for judgment.*

I admit that we can judge of nothing unless our intellect intervenes, because there is no reason to suppose we can judge of what we do not perceive in any way; but the will is also essential if we are to give our assent to what we have in some manner perceived. Nor, in order to form any judgment whatever, is it necessary that we should have a perfect and entire perception of a thing; for we often give our assent to things of which we have never had any but a very obscure and confused knowledge.

35. *The will is more extended than the intellect and our errors proceed from this cause.*

Further, the perception of the intellect extends only to the few objects presented to it, and is always very limited. The will, on the other hand, may in some sense be called infinite, because we perceive nothing that may be the object of some other will, even of the immeasurable will of God, to which our will cannot also extend, so that we easily extend it beyond what we clearly perceive. And when we do this, it is no wonder if it happens that we err.

36. *Our errors cannot be imputed to God.*

And although God has not given us an omniscient intellect, we must not for that reason believe that he is the author of our errors. For all created intellect is finite, and it is of the nature of finite intellect not to extend to all things.

37. *The principal perfection of man is to have the power of acting freely or through the will, and this is what makes him deserving of either praise or blame.*

That the will should extend widely is in accordance with its nature, and it is the greatest perfection in man to be able to act by its means, that is, freely, and by so doing we are in a peculiar way masters of our actions and thereby merit praise or blame. For we do not praise automata, although they respond exactly to the movements they were designed to produce, since their actions are performed necessarily. We praise the workman who has made them because he has formed them with accuracy and has done so freely and not of necessity. And for the same reason, when we choose what is true, much more credit is due to us when the choice is made freely, than when it is made of necessity.

38. *Our errors are defects in the way we act, but not in our nature; the faults of subordinates may often be attributed to other masters, but never to God.*

It is very true that whenever we err there is some fault in the way we act, or in the manner we use our freedom, but for all that there is no defect in our nature, because our nature is the same whether we judge rightly or wrongly. And even though God could have given us so great an intellect that we should never have fallen into error, we have no right to demand this of him. For although among men, if someone had the power of preventing an impending evil and yet did not do so, we would judge him to be its cause; God is not to be regarded as responsible for our errors, even though he could have brought it about that we should not. For the power some men possess over others has been instituted for the purpose of their hindering evil from being done by others, while the power held over the universe by God is altogether absolute and free. This is why we should be grateful for the good things he has granted us and not complain that he does not bestow from his bounty all that we know he might have dispensed.

39. *The freedom of the will is self-evident.*

It is so evident that we are possessed of a free will that can give or withhold its assent, that this may be counted as one of the first and most common notions found innately in us. We have already a very clear proof of this, for at the same time as we tried to doubt all things and even supposed that he who created us employed his unlimited powers in deceiving us in every way, we perceived in ourselves a liberty such that we were able to abstain from believing what was not perfectly certain and indubitable. But that of which we could not doubt at such a time is as self-evident and clear as anything we can ever know.

40. *We likewise know certainly that everything is preordained by God.*

But because what we have already learned about God proves to us that his power is so immense that it would be a crime for us to think ourselves ever capable of doing anything he had not already preordained, we should soon be involved in great difficulties if we undertook to make his preordinations harmonize with the freedom of our will, and if we tried to comprehend them both at one time.

41. *How the freedom of the will may be reconciled with divine preordination.*

Instead of this, we will have no trouble at all if we recollect that our mind is finite, and that the power of God is infinite—the power whereby he has not only known from all eternity what is or what can be, but also willed and preordained it. In this way we may have intelligence enough to come to know clearly and distinctly that this power is in God, but not enough to comprehend how he leaves the free action of man indeterminate; and, on the other hand, we are so conscious of the liberty and indifference which are in us, that there is nothing that we comprehend more clearly and perfectly. For it would be absurd to doubt what we inwardly experience and perceive as existing within ourselves just because we do not comprehend a matter which from its nature we know to be incomprehensible.

### 42. *How, although we do not will to err, we nevertheless err by our will.*

But inasmuch as we know that all our errors depend on our will, and as no one wants to go wrong, we may wonder that we err at all. However, we must observe that there is a great difference between willing to go wrong and willing to give one's assent to opinions in which error is sometimes found. For although there is no one who expressly wants to err, there is hardly anyone who is not willing to give his assent to things in which unsuspected error is to be found. And it even frequently happens that it is the very desire to know the truth that causes those who are not fully aware of the order in which it should be sought for, to pass judgment on things of which they have no real knowledge and so to fall into error.

### 43. *We cannot err if we give our assent only to what we clearly and distinctly perceive.*

But it is certain that we will never take the false for the true if we give our assent only to what we perceive clearly and distinctly. Because God is no deceiver, the faculty of knowledge he has given us cannot incline toward the false, nor can the faculty of assenting, as long as we do not extend it beyond those things we clearly perceive. And even if this could not be rationally demonstrated, we are by nature so disposed to give our assent to what we clearly perceive that we cannot possibly doubt its truth.

### 44. *We will always judge badly when we assent to what we do not clearly perceive, although our judgment may be true; it is frequently our memory that deceives us by leading us to believe that certain things had been satisfactorily established by us.*

It is also certain that whenever we give our assent to some argument we do not exactly understand, we either go wrong or, if we arrive at the truth, it is only by chance, and thus we cannot be certain that we are not in error. It is true that it rarely happens that we assent to things we notice we have not perceived, because the light of nature teaches us that we must not make judgments of anything we do not know. But we frequently err when we presume we have perceived certain things; and once they are committed to memory, we give them our assent as if we had fully perceived them, whereas we never perceived them at all.

### 45. *What a clear and distinct perception is.*

There are even a number of people who throughout all their lives perceive nothing so correctly as to be capable of judging of it properly. For the knowledge upon which a certain and indubitable judgment can be formed should be not only clear but also distinct. I call a perception clear when it is present and apparent to an attentive mind, in the same way as we say that we see objects clearly when, being present to the regarding eye, they operate upon it with sufficient strength. But I call a perception distinct when it is clear and so different from all other objects that it contains within itself nothing but what is clear.

### 46. *It is shown from the example of pain that a perception may be clear without being distinct, but it cannot be distinct unless it is clear.*

When, for instance, a severe pain is felt, the perception of this pain may be very clear, and yet not always distinct, because people usually confuse the perception with the obscure judgment they form about its nature, assuming as they do that something exists in the affected part similar to the sensation of pain, even though it is only the sensation they perceive clearly. In this way perception may be clear without being distinct, and cannot be distinct without also being clear.

### 47. *In order to remove the prejudices of our youth, it must be considered what is clear in each of our simple notions.*

Indeed, in our early years our mind was so immersed in the body that it perceived nothing distinctly, although it perceived much sufficiently clearly; and because even then it formed many judgments, numerous prejudices were contracted from which the majority of us can hardly ever hope to become free. But in order that we may now free ourselves from them I will here enumerate all those simple notions that constitute our thoughts, and distinguish whatever is clear in each of them from what is obscure, or likely to cause us to err.

**48.** *All the objects of our perceptions are to be considered either as things or the affections of things, or else as eternal truths; the enumeration of things.*

I distinguish all the objects of our knowledge into either things or the affections of things, or eternal truths having no existence outside our thought. Of the things we consider as real, the most general are *substance, duration, order, number,* and other similar matters which extend to all classes of things. I do not, however, observe more than two ultimate classes of things: intellectual or thinking things, pertaining to the mind or to thinking substance, and material things, pertaining to extended substance or to body. Perception, volition, and every mode of perception and willing pertain to thinking substance; while to extended substance pertain magnitude or extension in length, breadth and depth, shape, motion, situation, divisibility into parts themselves divisible, and the like. Besides these, there are, however, certain things we experience in ourselves that should be attributed neither to mind nor body alone, but to the close and intimate union of body and mind, as I shall later on explain in the proper place. Such are the appetites of hunger, thirst, etc., and also the emotions or passions of the mind which do not depend on thought alone, as the emotions of anger, joy, sadness, love, etc.; and, finally all the sensations such as pain, pleasure, light and color, sounds, odors, tastes, heat, hardness, and all other tactile qualities.

**49.** *Eternal truths cannot be thus enumerated, and this is not needed.*

What I have enumerated up to now are regarded either as the qualities of things or their modes. <We must now talk of what we know as eternal truths.> When we apprehend that it is impossible that anything can come from nothing, the proposition "nothing comes from nothing" is not to be considered as an existing thing, or the mode of a thing, but as a certain eternal truth which has its seat in our mind and is a common notion or axiom. The following are of the same nature: "it is impossible that the same thing be and not be at the same time," "what has been done cannot be undone," "he who thinks must exist while he thinks," and very many other propositions which it would not be easy to enumerate completely. But <this is not necessary since> we cannot fail to recognize them when the occasion presents itself, provided we have no prejudices to blind us.

**50.** *These eternal truths are clearly perceived, but not by all, because of prejudice.*

As regards the common notions, indeed, there is no doubt that they may be clearly and distinctly perceived, for otherwise they would not deserve to bear this name; but it is also true that there are some which, in regard to all men, do not deserve the name equally with others, because they are not equally perceived by all. Not, however, that I believe the faculty of knowledge to extend further with some men than with others; it is rather that these common opinions are opposed to the prejudices of some who are thereby prevented from easily perceiving them, although they are perfectly manifest to those who are free from these prejudices.

**51.** *What substance is: a name we cannot attribute in the same sense to God and to his creatures.*

With respect to those matters we consider as being things or modes of things, it is necessary that we should examine them here one by one. By substance, we can understand nothing else than a thing which so exists that it needs no other thing in order to exist. And in fact only one substance can be understood which clearly needs nothing else, namely, God. We perceive that all other things can exist only by the help of God's concurrence. That is why the word substance does not pertain *univocally* to God and to other things, as they say in the Schools, that is, there is no meaning that can be distinctly understood as common to God and to his creatures.

## 52. *It may be attributed univocally to soul and to body; how we know substance.*

Created substances, however, whether corporeal or thinking, may be understood under this common concept; for they are things that need only the concurrence of God in order to exist. But yet substance cannot be first discovered merely from the fact that it is an existing thing, for that fact alone is not observed by us. We may, however, easily discover it by means of any one of its attributes, because it is a common notion that nothing is possessed of no attributes, properties, or qualities. For this reason, when we perceive any attribute, we can conclude that some existing thing or substance to which it may be attributed is necessarily present.

## 53. *Each substance has a principal attribute: the attribute of the mind is thought, while that of body is extension.*

But although any one attribute is sufficient to give us a knowledge of substance, there is always one principal property of substance which constitutes its nature and essence, and to which all other properties are referred. Thus extension in length, breadth, and depth constitutes the nature of corporeal substance; and thought constitutes the nature of thinking substance. For all else that may be attributed to body presupposes extension, and is but a mode of an extended thing; as everything that we find in mind is but so many diverse forms of thinking. Thus, for example, shape is unintelligible except in an extended thing, and motion likewise in an extended space; so imagination, feeling, and will are unintelligible except in a thinking thing. But, on the other hand, we can understand extension without shape or action, and thinking without imagination or sensation, and so on with the rest; as is quite clear to anyone who attends to the matter.

## 54. *How we may have clear and distinct notions of thinking substance, of corporeal substance, and of God.*

We may thus easily have two clear and distinct notions or ideas, the one of created thinking substance, the other of corporeal substance, provided we carefully separate all the attributes of thought from those of extension. We can also have a clear and distinct idea of an uncreated and independent thinking substance, that is, of God, provided that we do not suppose that this idea represents to us all things in God, and that we do not mingle anything fictitious with it, but simply attend to what is evidently contained in the idea, and which we are aware pertains to the nature of an absolutely perfect being. For no one can deny that such an idea of God is in us, unless he <groundlessly> asserts that the mind of man cannot have any knowledge of God.

## 55. *How we can also have a distinct understanding of duration, order, and number.*

We will likewise have a very distinct understanding of *duration*, *order*, and *number*, if, in place of mingling with the idea that we have of them what properly speaking pertains to the conception of substance, we merely consider that the duration of each thing is a mode under which we will consider this thing insofar as it continues to exist; and if in the same way we think that order and number are not really different from the things that are ordered and numbered, but that they are only the modes under which we consider these things.

## 56. *What are modes, qualities, and attributes.*

And, indeed, when we here speak of a *mode* we mean nothing more than what elsewhere is termed *attribute* or *quality*. But when we consider substance as modified or diversified, we use the word *mode*; and when from the disposition or variation it can be named as of such and such a kind, we use the word *quality* <to designate the different modes which cause it to be so termed>; and finally when we more generally consider that these modes or qualities are in substance we term them *attributes*. And because any variation is incomprehensible in God, we cannot ascribe to him modes or qualities, but simply attributes. And even in created things what always remains unmodified, like existence and duration in the existing and enduring thing, should not be called a quality or mode, but an attribute.

**57.** *Some attributes pertain to things and others to thought; what duration and time are.*

Some of the attributes or modes are in things themselves and others are only in our thought. Thus time, for example, which we distinguish from duration taken in its general sense and which we describe as the measure of movement, is only a mode of thinking; for we do not indeed understand the duration of things which are moved as different from that of the things which are not moved, as is evident from the fact that if two bodies are moved for the space of an hour, the one quickly, the other slowly, we do not count the time longer in one case than in the other, although there is much more movement in one of the two bodies than in the other. But in order to measure the duration of all things, we usually compare their duration with the duration of the greatest and most regular motions, which are those that create years and days, and these we call time. Hence this adds nothing to duration, taken in general, but a mode of thought.

**58.** *Number and all universals are simply modes of thought.*

Similarly, number, when considered abstractly or generally and not in created things, is but a mode of thinking; and the same is true of everything called universals <in the Schools>.

**59.** *How universals arise and the five common ones: genus, species, difference, property, and accident.*

Universals arise solely from the fact that we avail ourselves of one and the same idea in order to think of all individual things that have a certain similitude. When we understand under the same name all the objects represented by this idea, that name is universal. For example, when we see two stones, and without thinking further of their nature than that there are two, we form in ourselves an idea of a certain number we call the number two; and when afterwards we see two birds or two trees, and we observe without further thinking about their nature that there are two of them, we again take up the same idea we had before. This idea is universal; and we give to this number the universal name two. In the same way when we con-

sider a three-sided figure we form a certain idea we call the idea of a triangle, and afterwards we make use of it as a universal in representing to ourselves all the figures having three sides. But when we notice more particularly that some three-sided figures have a right angle and others do not, we form the universal idea of a right triangle, which, being related to the preceding as to a more general, may be termed a *species*; and the right angle is the universal *difference* by which right triangles are distinguished from all others. If we further observe that the square of the hypotenuse is equal to the squares of the two other sides, and that this *property* belongs only to this species of triangle, we may term it a <universal> property of the species. Finally, if we suppose that some of the triangles are moved and others are not moved, we should take that to be a universal *accident* of the same; and thus we commonly enumerate the five universals: *genus, species, difference, property,* and *accident.*

**60.** *Of distinctions, and first of real distinction.*

But as to the number in things themselves, this proceeds from the distinction between them, and distinction is of three sorts, namely, *real, modal,* and of *reason.* A *real distinction* is properly speaking found between two or more substances; and we can conclude that two substances are really distinct one from the other from the sole fact that we can clearly and distinctly understand the one without the other. For in accordance with the knowledge we have of God, we are certain that he can accomplish what we distinctly understand. That is why from the fact that we now have, for example, the idea of an extended or corporeal substance, although we do not yet know certainly whether such a thing exists at all, we can conclude that it may exist; and if it does exist, any one part of it which we can demarcate in our thought must be distinct from every other part of the same substance. Similarly, because each one of us understands that he thinks, and that in thinking he can shut off from himself every other substance, either thinking or extended, we may conclude that each of us, similarly regarded, is really distinct from every other thinking substance and from every corporeal substance. And even if we suppose that God had united a body to a soul so closely that it was impossible to bring them together more closely, and made a single thing out of the two, they would yet remain really distinct one from the other notwithstanding the union; because however closely God connected them he could not set aside the power he possessed of separating them, or conserving one of them apart from the other, and those things God can separate, or conceive in separation, are really distinct.

### 61. *Of modal distinction*.

There are two sorts of modal distinctions, namely, one between the mode properly speaking and the substance of which it is the mode, and another between two modes of the same substance. The former we recognize by the fact that we can clearly understand substance without the mode that we say differs from it, while conversely we cannot understand this mode without the substance. There is, for example, a modal distinction between shape or motion and the corporeal substance in which both exist; there is also a distinction between affirming or recollecting and the mind. As to the other kind of distinction, its characteristic is that we are able to recognize one mode without the other and *vice versa*, but we cannot know either the one or the other without recognizing that both subsist in one common substance. If, for example, a stone is moved and is square, we can understand the square figure without knowing that it is moved, and conversely, that it is moved without knowing that it is square; but we cannot understand this motion and shape without the substance of the stone. As for the distinction whereby the mode of one substance is different from another substance, or from the mode of another substance, as the motion of one body is different from another body or from mind, or else as motion is different from duration, it appears to me that we should call it real rather than modal, because we cannot clearly understand these modes apart from the substances of which they are the modes and which are really distinct.

### 62. *Of the distinction of reason*.

Finally, the distinction of reason is between substance and some one of its attributes without which it is not possible that we should have a distinct knowledge of it, or between two such attributes of the same substance. This distinction is made manifest from the fact that we cannot have a clear and distinct idea of such a substance if we exclude from it such an attribute; or we cannot have a clear idea of one of the two attributes if we separate it from the other. For example, because there is no substance that does not cease to exist when it ceases to endure, duration is only distinct from substance by thought; all the modes of thinking we consider as though they exist in the objects differ only in thought both from the objects of which they are the thought and from each other in a common object. I recollect having elsewhere conflated this sort of distinction with modal distinction (near the end of the Reply made to the First Objection to the *Meditations on First Philosophy*),[2] but then it was not necessary to treat accurately of these distinctions, and it was sufficient for my purpose at the time simply to distinguish them both from the real.

### 63. *How we may distinctly know thought and extension, inasmuch as the one constitutes the nature of mind and the other that of body*.

We may likewise consider thought and extension as constituting the natures of intelligent substance and corporeal substance; and then they must not be considered otherwise than as the very substances that think and are extended, that is, as mind and body; for we know them in this way very clearly and distinctly. It is moreover easier to know a substance that thinks, or an extended substance, than substance alone, without regarding whether it thinks or is extended. For we experience some difficulty in abstracting the notions that we have of substance from those of thought or extension, for in truth they do not differ except in thought, and our conception is more distinct not because it includes fewer properties, but because we distinguish accurately what it does include from all other notions.

2. AT VII, 120–21.

64. *How we may also distinctly know them as modes of substance.*

We may likewise consider thought and extension as modes of substance—that is, insofar as we consider that one and the same mind may have many different thoughts, and that one body, retaining the same size, may be extended in many different ways (sometimes it may be greater in length and less in breadth or depth, and sometimes on the contrary greater in breadth and less in length). We then distinguish them modally from substance, and they may be understood not less clearly and distinctly, provided that we do not think of them as substances or things separate from others, but simply as modes of things. Because when we regard them as in the substances of which they are the modes, we distinguish them from these substances, and take them for what they actually are; while, on the contrary, if we wish to consider them apart from the substances in which they are, that will have the effect of our taking them as self-subsisting things and thus confounding the ideas of mode and substance.

65. *How we may likewise know their modes.*

Similarly, we shall best apprehend the diverse modes of thought such as understanding, imagining, recollecting, willing, etc., and the diverse modes of extension, or those pertaining to extension, such as all shapes, the situation of parts, and their movements, provided that we consider them simply as modes of the things in which they are; and as for motion we shall best understand it, if we inquire only about locomotion, without taking into account the force that produces it, which I shall nevertheless endeavor to set forth in its proper place.

66. *We also have a clear knowledge of our sensations, emotions, and appetites, although we frequently err in the judgments we form of them.*

There remain our sensations, emotions, and appetites, as to which we may likewise have a clear knowledge, if we take care to include in the judgments we form of them only that which we know to be precisely contained in our perception of them, and of which we are intimately conscious. But it is most difficult to observe this condition, in regard to our senses at least, because there is no one who has not judged from our youth on that all things we were accustomed to sense existed somehow outside our thoughts, and that they were entirely similar to our sensations, that is, to the conception we had of them. Thus, when, for example, we saw a certain color, we thought we saw something that existed outside of us and clearly resembled the idea of color we were then experiencing in ourselves, and from the habit of judging in this way we seemed to see this so clearly and distinctly that we held it to be certain and indubitable.

67. *We frequently make mistakes even in judging pain.*

The same is true in regard to all our other sensations, even pleasure and pain. For although we do not believe that these things exist outside of us, we do not usually regard them as solely in our mind or our perception, but as being in our hands, feet, or some other part of our body. But there is no reason we should be required to believe that the pain, for example, that we feel as it were in our foot is anything outside our mind, any more than the light we think we see in the sun is in the sun <as it is in us>; for both these are prejudices of our youth, as will appear clearly in what follows.

68. *How we can distinguish in such matters what we know clearly from that in which we can err.*

Further, in order that we may here distinguish what is clear from what is obscure, we must note that pain, color, and other things of the sort are clearly and distinctly perceived when considered simply as sensations or thoughts. But when they are judged to be things existing outside of our mind, we can in no way understand what sort of things they are. And when anyone says that he sees color in a body or feels pain in one of his limbs, it is the same as if he told us that he saw or felt something there, but was absolutely ignorant of its nature, or else that he did not know what he was seeing or feeling. For although, perhaps, when he examines his thoughts with less attention, he easily persuades himself that he has some knowledge of it, because he supposes that there is something resembling the sensation of color or pain he is experiencing, yet if he investigates what is represented to him by this sensation of color or pain, appearing as they do to exist in a colored body or painful part, he will find that he is really ignorant of it.

### 69. *We know size, shape, etc. quite differently from color and pain, etc.*

This will be more especially evident if we consider the fact that size in a body which is seen, or shape or motion (local motion at least—for philosophers, by imagining other sorts of motion than this, have rendered its nature less intelligible to themselves), or situation, or duration, or number, and the like, which we clearly perceive in all bodies, as has been already described, are known by us in an entirely different way from that in which color is known in the same body, or pain, odor, taste, or any of the properties which, as previously mentioned, should be attributed to the senses. For although in observing a body we are not less certain of its existence from the color we perceive in its regard than from the shape that bounds it, we nevertheless know that property in it which causes us to call it shaped with much greater clarity than we know what causes us to say that it is colored.

### 70. *We can judge of sensible things in two ways, in one of which we avoid error, while in the other we fall into error.*

It is thus evident that when we say we perceive colors in objects, it is the same as though we said that we perceive something in the objects whose nature we do not know, but which produces a very clear and vivid sensation in us that we call the sensation of color. But there is a great deal of difference in our manner of judging: As long as we judge that there is something in objects of which we have no knowledge (that is in things, such as they are, from which sensation comes to us), we avoid error; indeed, we actually guard against it, for we are less likely to judge rashly of a thing we have been forewarned we do not know. But when we think we perceive a certain color in objects although we have no real knowledge of what it is we are calling a color, and we can find no intelligi-

ble resemblance between the color we suppose to be in objects and what we experience in our senses, yet, because we do not observe this or remark in these objects certain other qualities like size, shape, number, etc., that we clearly know are or may be in objects, as our senses or understanding show us, it is easy to allow ourselves to fall into the error of holding that what we call color in objects is something entirely resembling the color we perceive, and then supposing that we have a clear perception of what we do not perceive at all.

### 71. *The principal cause of error is found in the prejudices of childhood.*

It is here that the first and principal cause of our errors is to be found. For in the first years of life the mind was so closely tied to the body that it applied itself to nothing but those thoughts by which it was aware of things affecting the body; it did not yet refer these to anything existing outside itself, but merely felt pain when the body was hurt, or experienced pleasure when the body received some good, or else if the body was so <slightly> affected that it did not experience any great good or evil, it encountered different sensations, namely, those we call the senses of taste, smell, sound, heat, cold, light, colors, and the like, which in truth represent nothing to us outside of our mind, but vary in accordance with the diversity of the parts and modes in which the body is affected. The mind at the same time also perceived sizes, shapes, motions and the like, which were exhibited to it, not as sensations, but as things or the modes of things existing, or at least capable of existing, outside thought, although it did not yet observe the distinction between the two. And afterwards when the machine of the body, so constituted by nature that it can by its own inherent power turn here and there, by turning fortuitously this way and the other, pursued what was useful and avoided what was harmful, the mind which was closely tied to it, reflecting on the things it pursued or avoided, remarked first of all that they existed outside itself, and attributed to them not only sizes, shapes, motions, and other such properties it perceived as things or modes of things, but also tastes, smells, and the like, the sensations of which it perceived that these things caused in it. And as all other things were only considered insofar as they were useful for the body in which it was immersed, the mind judged that there was more or less reality in each body, as the impressions made on the body were more or less strong. Hence the belief arose that there was much more substance or corporeal reality in rocks or metals than in air or water, because the sensations of hardness and weight were much more strongly felt. And thus it was that air was only regarded as anything when it was agitated by some wind, and we experienced it to be either hot or cold. And because the stars did not give more light than tiny lighted candles, the mind did not hold them to be larger than such flames. Moreover, because it did not as yet remark that the earth turned on its own axis, and that its surface was curved like a sphere, it was more ready to apprehend that it was immobile and that its surface was flat. And we have in this way been imbued with a thousand other such prejudices from infancy, which in later youth we quite forgot we had accepted without sufficient examination, admitting them as though they were utterly true and certain, and as if they had been known by means of our senses or implanted in us by nature.

### 72. *The second cause of our errors is that we cannot forget these prejudices.*

Although in coming to years of maturity, when the mind, being no longer wholly subject to the body, does not refer everything to it, but also inquires into the truth of things as they are in themselves, we find that many of the judgments we had formed are false, yet it is not easy to eradicate false judgments from our memory, and as long as they remain there they may be the cause of many errors. Thus, for example, since from our earliest years we imagined stars to be minute bodies, we have great difficulty in imagining anything different from this first conception, although astronomical reason tells us that they are among the largest bodies—so greatly does prejudiced opinion affect our beliefs.

### 73. *The third cause is that we grow tired when we apply our attention to objects not present to the*

senses; *we are therefore in the habit of judging these, not from present perceptions, but from preconceived opinions.*

Further, our mind cannot pause to consider any one thing with attention without difficulty and fatigue, and it applies itself with the greatest difficulty to those objects present neither to the senses nor to the imagination. This may be due to the nature of the mind, because of its union with the body, or because in the first years of our life we are so much occupied with feeling and imagining that we have acquired a greater facility and habit for thinking in this way than in any other. As a result, people's understanding of substance is limited to what is imaginable and corporeal and even sensible. For they do not know that the only things imaginable are those that exist in extension, motion, and shape, while there are many others that are intelligible; and they persuade themselves that there is nothing that can subsist but body, and finally, that there is no body that is not sensible. And since in truth we do not perceive any object as it is in itself by sense alone, as will be clearly shown later on, it comes to pass that most men perceive nothing except in a confused way, throughout their whole life.

### 74. *The fourth cause is that we attach our concepts to words that do not accurately correspond to reality.*

And finally, because we attach all our concepts to words used to express them, and as we commit to memory our thought in connection with these words, and as we more easily recall to memory words than things, we can scarcely conceive of anything so distinctly as to be able to separate what we conceive completely from the words chosen to express it. In this way most men apply their attention to words rather than things, and this is the cause of their frequently giving their assent to terms they do not understand, either because they believe that they formerly understood them, or because they think that those who informed them understood their signification correctly. And although this is not the place in which to treat particularly of this matter, inasmuch as I have not yet dealt with the nature of the human body, nor even shown that any body exists at all, still it appears to me that what I have already said may serve to enable us to distinguish those of our concepts that are clear and distinct from those in which there is obscurity and confusion.

### 75. *A summary of what has to be observed in order to philosophize correctly.*

That is why, if we desire to philosophize seriously, and apply ourselves to the search for all the truths we are capable of knowing, we must in the first place rid ourselves of our prejudices, and take the greatest care to set aside all the opinions we formerly accepted, until, on applying to them further examination, we discover them to be true. We should afterwards hold an orderly review of the notions we have within us, and judge to be true those and only those which present themselves to our apprehension as clear and distinct. In this way we will know, first of all that we exist, insofar as our nature is to think, and at the same time that there is a God on whom we depend; and after having considered his attributes we shall be in a position to inquire into the truth of all other things, since God is their cause. In addition to the notions we have of God and of our thoughts, we shall likewise find within us a knowledge of many propositions that are eternally true, such as nothing comes from noth-

ing, etc. We shall also find there the idea of a corporeal or extended nature which may be moved, divided, etc., and also of the sensations that affect us, such as those of pain, color, taste, etc., although we do not as yet know the cause of our being so affected. And comparing <what we now know by examining those things in their order> with our former confused knowledge, we shall acquire the habit of forming clear and distinct concepts of all we can know. And in these few precepts it appears to me that the main principles of human knowledge are contained.

### 76. *We ought to prefer divine authority to our perceptions, but, excluding this, we should not assent to anything we do not clearly perceive.*

Above all, we should impress on our memory as an infallible rule that what God has revealed to us is incomparably more certain than anything else, and that we ought to submit to divine authority rather than to our own judgment even though the light of reason may seem to us to suggest something opposite with the utmost clearness and evidence. But in things in regard to which divine authority reveals nothing to us, it would be unworthy of a philosopher to accept anything as true that he has not ascertained to be such, and to trust more to the senses, that is, to judgments formed without consideration in childhood, than to the reasoning of maturity.

## Part II. The Principles of Material Things

### 1. *The reasons for our having a certain knowledge of the existence of material things.*

Although we are all persuaded that material things exist, yet because we have doubted this before and have placed it in the rank of the prejudices of our childhood, it is now necessary that we should inquire into the arguments by which we may accept this with certainty. To begin with we feel that without doubt all our sensations proceed from something different from our mind. For it is not in our power to have one sensation rather than another, since each one is clearly dependent on the thing affecting our senses. It is true that we may inquire whether this thing is

God or something different from God. But inasmuch as we sense, or rather are stimulated by sense to have a clear and distinct perception of matter extended in length, breadth, and depth, the various parts of which have various shapes and motions, and give rise to the sensations we have of colors, smells, pains, etc., if God immediately and of himself presented to our mind the idea of this extended matter, or merely permitted it to be caused in us by something lacking extension, shape, or motion, there would be nothing to prevent him from being regarded as a deceiver. For we clearly apprehend this matter as different from God, or ourselves, or our mind, and appear to see very clearly that the idea of it is due to things outside ourselves to which it is wholly similar. But God cannot deceive us, because deception is repugnant to his nature, as has been explained. And therefore we must conclude that there is something extended in length, breadth, and depth, and possessing all those properties we clearly perceive to pertain to extended things. And this extended thing is called by us either body or matter.

### 2. *How we likewise know that the human body is closely united to the mind.*

It may be concluded also that a certain body is more closely united to our mind than any other, from the fact that pain and other of our sensations occur without our foreseeing them; the mind is aware that these do not arise from itself alone, nor pertain to it insofar as it is a thinking thing, but only insofar as it is united to another thing, extended and mobile, which is called the human body. But this is not the place to explain this matter further.

### 3. *Sensory perceptions do not teach us what is really in things, but merely what is useful or harmful to man's composite nature.*

It will be sufficient for us to observe that sensory perceptions are related simply to the intimate union of body and mind, and that while by their means we are made aware of what in external bodies can profit or hurt this union, they do not present them to us as they are in themselves unless occasionally and accidentally. Thus, <after this observation> we will without difficulty set aside all the prejudices of the senses and in this regard rely upon our intellect alone, by reflecting carefully on the ideas implanted in it by nature.

### 4. *The nature of body does not consist in weight, hardness, color, and so on, but in extension alone.*

In this way we shall perceive that the nature of matter, or body in its universal aspect, does not consist in its being hard, or heavy, or colored, or affecting our senses in some other way, but solely in its being something extended in length, breadth, and depth. For as regards hardness, we do not know anything of it by sense, except that the portions of the hard bodies resist the motion of our hands when they come in

contact with them; but if, whenever we moved our hands in some direction, all the bodies in that part retreated with the same speed as our hands approached them, we should never feel hardness; and yet we have no reason to believe that the bodies receding in this way would on this account lose what makes them bodies. It follows that the nature of body does not consist in hardness. The same reason shows us that weight, color, and all the other qualities of the kind perceived in corporeal matter may be taken from it while it remains intact; thus it follows that the nature of body depends on none of these.

### 5. *This truth about the nature of body is obscured by prejudices regarding rarefaction and the void.*

There still remain two reasons for doubting whether the true nature of body consists solely in extension. The first is the prevalent opinion that most bodies are capable of being rarefied and condensed, so that when rarefied they have greater extension than when condensed; indeed, the subtlety of these people goes so far as to distinguish the substance of a body from its quantity, its quantity from its extension. The second reason is that if we understand there to be nothing in a place but extension in length, breadth, and depth, we are not in the habit of saying that there is a body there, but only space and further empty space, which most people persuade themselves is a mere negation.

### 6. *In what way rarefaction occurs.*

But as regards rarefaction and condensation, whoever will examine his own thoughts and refuse to admit anything he does not clearly perceive will not allow that there is anything in these processes but a change of shape — that is to say, rare bodies are those between whose parts there are many gaps filled with other bodies; and those are called dense bodies, on the other hand, whose parts, by approaching one another, either render these distances less than they were, or remove them altogether, in which case the body is rendered so dense that it cannot be denser. And yet it does not possess less extension than when the parts occupied a greater space, owing to their being further removed from one another. For the extension of the pores or the gaps which a body's parts do not occupy <when it is rarefied> should not be attributed to the body but to the other bodies occupying these gaps. Just as when we see a sponge filled with water or some other liquid, we do not suppose that for this reason each part of the sponge is more extended than when it is compressed and dry, but only that its pores are wider, and that it is therefore distributed over a larger space.

### 7. *Rarefaction cannot be intelligibly explained in any other way.*

I am indeed unable to say why this rarefaction of bodies has been explained by some as the result of augmentation of quantity rather than by the example of the sponge. For although when air and water are rarefied we do not see any pores made larger, nor any new body added to fill them, it is yet less consonant with reason to suppose something unintelligible in order to give a merely verbal explanation of how bodies are rarefied, than to conclude in consequence of that rarefaction that there are pores or gaps that become greater, and are filled with some new body, although we do not perceive this new body with the senses. For there is no reason that requires us to believe we should perceive by our senses all the bodies around us. And we see that it is very easy to explain rarefaction in this manner, though not in any other. And finally it would be undoubtedly contradictory to suppose that any body should be increased by a new quantity or new extension without the addition to it of a new extended substance, that is, a new body. This is because it is impossible to conceive any addition of extension or quantity without the addition of a substance having quantity or extension, as will be shown more clearly below.

### 8. *Quantity and number differ only in thought from what has quantity and is numbered.*

Quantity differs from extended substance, or number from what is numbered, not in reality, but only in our conception. Thus, to take an example, we may consider the whole nature of corporeal substance comprised within a space of ten feet, although we do not attend to this measure of ten feet, because it is clear that the thing conceived is the same in any one part of that space as in the whole. And vice versa, we can think of the number ten also as a continuous quantity of ten feet without attending to any particular determinate substance, because the conception of the number of ten is plainly the same, whether considered in reference to the measure of ten feet, or to any other ten; and we cannot conceive a continuous quantity of ten feet without thinking of some extended substance of which it is the quantity, but yet we can conceive it without thinking of that determinate substance. In reality, however, it is impossible that even the least part of such quantity or extension can be taken away without taking away likewise an equal amount of substance; on the other hand, not the least part of the substance can be removed without our diminishing its quantity and extension by the same amount.

### 9. *Corporeal substance, when distinguished from its quantity, is confusedly conceived as something incorporeal.*

Although some express themselves otherwise on this subject, I cannot think that they regard it otherwise than as I have just said; for when they distinguish substance from extension or quantity, either they mean nothing by the word substance, or they merely form in their minds a confused idea of incorporeal substance which they falsely attribute to corporeal substance, and leave to extension, which they nevertheless call an accident, that true idea of this corporeal substance; thus it is easy to see that their words are not in harmony with their thoughts.

### 10. *What space or internal place is.*

Space or internal place and the corporeal substance contained in it do not differ other than in the way they are conceived of by us. For, in truth, the same extension in length, breadth, and depth, which constitutes space, constitutes body; and the difference between them consists only in the fact that we consider extension as particular in body and think of it as changing whenever body changes; in space, on the contrary, we attribute to extension a generic unity, so that after having removed from a certain space the body that occupied it, we do not suppose that we have also removed the extension of that space, because it appears to us that the same extension remains so long as it is of the same size and shape, and preserves the same position in relation to certain other bodies, by which we determine this space.

### 11. *In what sense it may be said that space is not different from corporeal substance.*

And it will be easy for us to recognize that the same extension constituting the nature of body likewise constitutes the nature of space; the two do not differ, except as the nature of the genus or species differs from the nature of the individual. Suppose that, in order to discern the idea we have of any body, such as a stone, we reject from it all that is not essential to the nature of body. In the first place, then, we may reject hardness, because if the stone were liquefied or reduced to powder, it would no longer possess hardness, and yet it would not cease to be a body; let us in the next place reject color, because we have often seen stones so transparent that they had no color; again we reject weight, because we see that fire, although very light, is yet body; and finally we may reject cold, heat, and all the other qualities of the kind either because they are not thought of as in the stone, or else because with the change of their qualities the stone is not for that reason considered to have lost its nature as body. After examination we will find that there is nothing remaining in the idea of body except that it is extended in length, breadth, and depth; and this is comprised in our idea of space, not only of what is full of body, but also of what is called a void.

### 12. *How space is different from body in our mode of conceiving it.*

There is, however, some difference in our mode of conceiving them; for if we remove a stone from the space or place where it was, we think that the extension of this stone has also been removed from it, because we consider it to be singular and inseparable from the stone itself. But at the same time we suppose that the same extension of place occupied by the stone remains, though the place it formerly occupied has been taken up with wood, water, air, and any other bodies, or even has been supposed to be empty, because we now consider extension in general, and it appears to us that the same is common to stones, wood, water, air, and all other bodies, and

even to a void if there is such a thing, provided that it is of the same magnitude and shape as before, and preserves the same position in regard to the external bodies that determine this space.

### 13. *What external place is.*

The words place and space signify nothing different from the body said to be in a place, and merely designate its size, shape, and position as regards other bodies. For it is necessary in order to determine this position to observe certain others we consider to be immovable; and according as we regard different bodies we may find that the same thing at the same time changes its place, and does not change it. For example, if we consider a man seated at the stern of a vessel when it is carried out to sea, he may be said to be in one place if we regard the parts of the vessel with which he preserves the same position; and yet he will be found continually to change his position, if regard is paid to the neighboring shores in relation to which he is constantly receding from one, and approaching another. And further, if we suppose that the earth moves, and that it takes precisely the same path from west to east as the vessel does from east to west, it will again appear to us that he who is seated at the stern does not change his position, because that place is determined by certain immovable points we imagine to be in the heavens. But if at length we are persuaded that there are no points in the universe that are really immovable, as will presently be shown to be probable, we shall conclude that there is nothing that has a permanent place except insofar as it is fixed by our thought.

### 14. *The difference between place and space.*

However, the terms place and space are different, because place indicates position more expressly than size or shape, while, on the contrary, we more often think of the latter when we speak of space. For we frequently say that a thing has succeeded to the place of another, although it does not possess exactly either its size or its shape; but we do not for all that mean that it occupies the same space as the other; and when the position is changed, we say that the place also is changed, although the same size and shape exist as before. And so if we say that a thing is in a particular place, we simply mean that it is situated in a certain manner in reference to certain other things; and when we add that it occupies a certain space or place, we likewise mean that it is of a definite size or shape <so as exactly to fill the space>.

### 15. *How external place is rightly taken to be the surface of the surrounding body.*

And thus we never distinguish space from extension in length, breadth, and depth; but we sometimes consider place as internal to the thing placed, and sometimes as external to it. Internal place is indeed in no way distinguished from space; but we sometimes regard external place as the surface immediately surrounding the thing placed in it. And it is to be observed that by surface we do not here mean any portion of the surrounding body, but merely the extremity between the surrounding body and that surrounded, which is but a mode; or we mean the common surface, a surface that is not a part of one body rather than of the other and is always considered the same, as long as it retains the same size and shape. For although all the surrounding body with its surface is changed, we should not imagine that the body which was surrounded by it had for all that changed its place, if it meanwhile preserved the same position in regard to other bodies that are regarded as immovable. Thus if we suppose that a ship is carried along in one direction by the current of a stream, and is impelled by a contrary wind in another direction in an equal degree, so that its position is not changed with regard to the banks, we are ready to admit that it remains in the same place although we see that the whole surrounding surface is in a state of change.

### 16. *It is contrary to reason to say that there is a void or space in which there is absolutely nothing.*

As regards a void in the philosophic sense of the word, that is, a space in which there is no substance, it is evident that such a thing cannot exist, because the extension of space or internal place is not different from that of body. For, from the mere fact that a body is extended in length, breadth, or depth, we have reason to conclude that it is a substance; because it is absolutely inconceivable that nothing should possess extension, we ought to conclude also that the same

is true of the space which is supposed to be void—namely, that since there is extension in it, there is necessarily also substance.

### 17. *A void, in the ordinary sense, does not exclude all body.*

And when we take this word void in its ordinary sense, we do not mean a place or space in which there is absolutely nothing, but only a place in which there are none of those things we expected to find there. Thus because a pitcher is made to hold water, we say that it is empty when it contains nothing but air. Or if there are no fish in a fishpond, we say that there is nothing in it, even though it is full of water. Similarly we say a vessel is empty when, in place of the merchandise it was designed to carry, it is loaded only with sand so that it may resist the impetuous violence of the wind. Finally we say in the same way that a space is empty when it contains nothing sensible, even though it contains created matter and self-existent substance; for we do not normally consider things except those detected by our senses. And if, in place of keeping in mind what we should understand by these words—void and nothing—we afterwards suppose that in the space termed void there is not only nothing sensible, but nothing at all, we will fall into the same error as if, because a pitcher is usually termed empty when it contains nothing but air, we were therefore to judge that the air contained in it is not a substantive thing.

### 18. *How the prejudice concerning the absolute void is to be corrected.*

We have almost all lapsed into this error from the beginning of our lives, for, seeing that there is no necessary connection between the vessel and the body it contains, we thought that God at least could remove all the body contained in the vessel without its being necessary that any other body should take its place. But to correct this error, it is necessary to remark that while there is no connection between the vessel and the particular body that it contains, there is an absolutely necessary one between the concave shape of the vessel and the extension considered generally that must be contained in this cavity; so that it is not more contradictory to conceive a mountain without a valley than such a cavity without the extension it contains, or this extension without the substance which is extended, because nothing, as has already been frequently remarked, cannot have extension. And therefore, if it is asked what would happen if God removed all the body contained in a vessel without permitting its place to be occupied by another body, we shall answer that the sides of the vessel will thus come into immediate contact with one another. For two bodies must touch when there is nothing between them, because it is manifestly contradictory for these two bodies to be apart from one another, or that there should be a distance between them, and yet that this distance should be nothing; for distance is a mode of extension, and without extended substance it cannot therefore exist.

19. *This confirms what was said of rarefaction.*

After we have thus remarked that the nature of corporeal substance consists only in its being an extended thing, or that its extension is not different from what has been attributed to space, however empty, it is easy to discover that it is impossible that any one of these parts should in any way occupy more space at one time than another, and thus that it may be rarefied other than in the manner explained above; or again it is easy to perceive that there cannot be more matter or corporeal substance in a vessel when it is filled with gold or lead, or any other body that is heavy and hard, than when it only contains air and appears to be empty; for the quantity of the parts of matter does not depend on their weight or hardness, but only on the extension which is always equal in the same vessel.

20. *From this the impossibility of atoms may be demonstrated.*

We also know that there cannot be any atoms or parts of matter which are by their own nature indivisible <as some philosophers have imagined>. For however small the parts are supposed to be, yet because they are necessarily extended we are always able in thought to divide any one of them into two or more parts; and thus we know that they are divisible. For there is nothing we can divide in thought which we do not hence recognize to be divisible; and therefore

if we judge it to be indivisible, our judgment would be contrary to the knowledge we have of the matter. And even should we suppose that God had reduced some portion of matter to a smallness so extreme that it could not be divided into smaller parts, it would not for all that be properly called indivisible. For though God had rendered the particle so small that it was beyond the power of any creature to divide it, he could not deprive himself of his power of division, because it is absolutely impossible that he should lessen his own omnipotence, as was said before. And therefore, absolutely speaking, it will remain divisible <to the smallest extended particle>, because it is such from its nature.

21. *The extension of the world is likewise indefinite.*

We likewise recognize that this world, or the totality of corporeal substance, is extended without limit, because wherever we imagine a limit we are not only still able to imagine beyond that limit spaces indefinitely extended, but we perceive these to be in reality such as we imagine them, that is to say that they contain in them corporeal substance indefinitely extended. For, as has been already shown very fully, the idea of extension we perceive in any space whatever is exactly the same as the idea of corporeal substance.

22. *Thus the matter of the heavens and of the earth is one and the same, and there cannot be a plurality of worlds.*

It is thus not difficult to infer from all this, that the earth and heavens are forged of the same matter, and that even if there were an infinite number of worlds, they would all be formed of this matter; from this it follows that there cannot be a plurality of worlds, because we clearly understand that the matter whose nature consists in its being an extended substance already occupies all the imaginable spaces where these other worlds could be, and we cannot find in ourselves the idea of any other matter.

23. *All the variety in matter, or all the diversity of its forms, depends on motion.*

There is therefore but one matter in the whole universe, and we know this by the simple fact of its being extended. All the properties we clearly perceive in it may be reduced to this one: that it is divisible and thus mobile according to its parts, and hence capable of being affected in all the ways we perceive as arising from the motion of its parts. For its division by thought alone makes no difference to it; but all the variation in matter, or diversity in its forms, depends on motion. This the philosophers have doubtless observed, inasmuch as they have said that nature was the principle of motion and rest, and by nature they understood that by which all corporeal things become such as they are experienced to be.

### 24. *What motion is in common parlance.*

But motion (that is, local motion, for I can conceive no other kind, and do not think that we ought to conceive any other in nature), in the vulgar sense, is nothing more than *the action by which any body passes from one place to another.* And just as we have remarked above that the same thing may be said to change and not to change its place at the same time, we can say that it moves and does not move at the same time. For a man who is seated in a ship setting sail thinks he is moving when he looks at the shore he has left and considers as fixed, but not if he regards the vessel he is on, because he does not change his position in reference to its parts. Likewise, because

we are accustomed to think that there is no motion without action and that in rest there is cessation of action, the person thus seated may more properly be said to be at rest than in motion, since he does not feel any action in himself.

### 25. *What motion is, properly speaking.*

Not looking to popular usage, but to the truth of the matter, let us consider what should be understood by motion according to the truth of the thing; we may say, in order to attribute a determinate nature to it, that it is the transference of one part of matter or one body from the vicinity of those bodies that are in immediate contact with it, and which are regarded as at rest, into the vicinity of others. By one body or by one part of matter I understand everything transported together, although it may be composed of many parts which in themselves have other motions. And I say that it is the transference and not either the force or the action that transfers, in order to show that the motion is always in the mobile thing, not in the mover; for these two do not seem to me to be distinguished accurately enough. Further, I understand that it is a mode of the mobile thing and not a substance, just as shape is a mode of the shaped thing, and rest of that which is at rest. [ . . . ]

# Part III. The Visible World

### 1. *We cannot think too highly of the works of God.*

Having now determined certain principles of material things which were derived, not from the prejudices of the senses, but from the light of reason, so that we cannot doubt of their truth, we should examine whether we can explain all the phenomena of nature from these alone. And we shall begin with those that are the most general, and on which the others depend, such as the general structure of the visible world. But in order that we may philosophize correctly in this matter, two things are to be observed. The first is that we must always keep before our minds the infinite power and goodness of God, and not fear of falling into error by imagining his works to be too great, too beautiful, and too perfect, but that, on the contrary, we must take care lest, if we suppose any limits to

exist in them of which we have no certain knowledge, we may seem to be insufficiently sensible of the greatness and power of the Creator.

### 2. *We ought to beware lest we presume too much in supposing ourselves to understand the ends God set before himself in creating the world.*

The second is that we ought to beware lest we think too highly of ourselves. This we should appear to do if we supposed the universe to have certain limits not presented to our knowledge without at the same time being assured of it by divine revelation, which would be making our knowledge extend beyond what God has made; but this would be even more so if we persuaded ourselves that all things were created by God only for us, or even if we were to suppose that by the powers of our mind we could understand the ends he set before himself in creating the universe.

### 3. *In what sense it can be said that all things were created for man.*

For although it may be a pious thought, as far as morals are concerned, to believe that God has created all things for us to the extent that it incites us to a greater gratitude and affection toward him, and although it is true in some respect, because there is nothing created from which we cannot derive some

use, even if it is only the exercise of our minds in considering it and being incited to worship God by its means, it is yet not at all probable that all things have been created for us in such a manner that God has had no other end in creating them. And it seems to me that such a supposition would be certainly ridiculous and inept in reference to questions of physics, for we cannot doubt that an infinity of things exist, or did exist, though now they have ceased to exist, which have never been beheld or comprehended by man and which have never been of any use to him. [. . .]

## Part IV: The Earth

### 188. *What is to be borrowed from treatises on animals and man to complete the knowledge of material things.*

I would add no more to this Fourth Part of the *Principles of Philosophy*, if (as I previously intended) I was going to write two others, namely a Fifth and a Sixth Part, the fifth on living things, that is on animals and plants, and the sixth on man. But because I am not yet completely clear about all of the matters I would like to treat in these two last parts, and do not know whether I am likely to have sufficient leisure <or be able to make the necessary experiments> to complete them, I shall here add a little about the objects of the senses in order not to delay these earlier parts too long or to allow anything to be missing which I should have reserved for the others. For up to this point I have described the earth and all the visible world as if it were simply a machine in which there was nothing to consider but the shape and motion of its parts, and yet our senses cause other things to be presented to us, such as colors, smells, sounds, and other such things; if I did not speak of them, it might be thought that I had omitted the main part of the explanation of the things in nature.

### 189. *What sensation is and how it operates.*

It must be realized that although the human soul informs the whole body, it has its principal seat in the brain, and it is there that it not only understands

and imagines, but also senses. It does this by means of the nerves that stretch like filaments from the brain to all the other members, with which they are so connected that we can hardly touch any part of the human body without causing the extremities of some of the nerves spread over it to be moved; and this motion passes to the other extremities of those nerves collected in the brain around the seat of the soul, as I have explained fully enough in Discourse Four of the *Dioptrics*.[3] But the motions that are thus excited in the brain by the nerves affect the soul or mind, which is intimately connected with the brain, in diverse ways according to the variety of the motions themselves. And the various states of our mind, or thoughts that immediately arise from these motions, are called sensory perceptions, or, in common language, sensations.

### 196. *The soul does not feel except insofar as it is in the brain.*

It is, however, easily proved that the soul feels those things affecting the body not insofar as it is in each member of the body, but only insofar as it is in the brain <where the nerves by their movements convey to it the various actions of the external objects touching the parts of the body in which they are embedded>. For, in the first place, there are many illnesses

3. AT VI, 109–14.

which, although they affect the brain alone, yet either disorder or altogether take away from us the use of our senses; just like sleep itself, which affects the brain alone, and yet every day during a great part of the time takes from us our sensory faculties, which are afterwards restored to us on awakening. Secondly, from the fact that although the brain is healthy <as are the members in which the organs of the external senses are to be found>, if the paths by which the nerves pass from the external parts to the brain are obstructed, that sensation is lost in these members. And finally, we sometimes feel pain as if it were in certain of our members, and yet its cause is not in these members where it is felt, but in others through which pass the nerves extending to the brain from the parts where the pain is felt. And I could prove this by innumerable experiments; however, here one will suffice. When a girl suffering from a serious infection of the hand was seen by a surgeon, the custom was followed to bandage her eyes lest she would be upset by seeing the dressing. After some days, as gangrene set in, her arm had to be cut off from the elbow and several linen cloths tied together were substituted in place of the amputated limb, so that she was quite unaware of what had been done; meanwhile, however, she had various pains, sometimes in one of the fingers of the hand that had been cut off, and sometimes in another. This could clearly happen only because the nerves which previously had been carried all the way from the brain to the hand, and afterwards terminated in the arm near the elbow, were affected there in the same way as it was their function to be stimulated for the purpose of impressing the sensation of pain in this and that finger on the mind residing in the brain. <And this shows clearly that pain in the hand is not felt by the mind insofar as it is in the hand, but as it is in the brain.>

### 197. *Mind is of such a nature that from the motion of the body alone various sensations can be excited in it.*

It can also be proved that our mind is of such a nature that motions in the body are alone sufficient to cause it to have all sorts of thoughts with no likeness to any of the motions that give rise to them; and

especially that there may be excited in it those confused thoughts called feelings or sensations. For we see that words, whether uttered by the voice or merely written, excite in our minds all sorts of thoughts and emotions. On the same paper, with a pen and ink, by moving the point of the pen ever so little over the paper in a certain way, we can form letters that bring to the minds of our readers thoughts of battles, tempests, or furies, and the emotions of indignation and sadness; while if the pen is moved in another, hardly different way, thoughts may be given of quite a different kind, namely, those of tranquillity, peace, pleasantness, and the quite opposite emotions of love and joy. Someone will perhaps reply that writing and speech do not immediately excite any emotions in the mind, or images of things different from the letters and sounds, but as it were various acts of the understanding; and from these the mind, making them the occasions, then constructs for itself the images of various things. But what will we say of the sensations of pain and pleasure? If a sword moved toward our body cuts it, from this alone pain results which is certainly no less different from the local motion of the sword or of the part of the body that is cut, than are color or sound or smell or taste. And therefore, as we see clearly that the sensation of pain is easily excited in us merely from the local motion of our body in contact with another body, we may conclude that our mind is of such a nature that certain local motions can excite in it all the other sensations.

### 198. *There is nothing known of external objects by the senses but their shape, size, or motion.*

In addition, we observe no difference in the nerves that may cause us to judge that some convey one thing rather than another to the brain from the organs of the external sense, nor again that anything is conveyed there except the local motion of the nerves themselves. And we see that this local motion excites in us not only the sensations of pleasure or pain, but also those of sound and light. For if we receive a blow in the eye hard enough for the vibration to reach the retina, we see myriads of sparks which are still not outside our eye; and when we place our finger on our ear, we hear a murmuring sound whose cause cannot be attributed to anything but the agitation of the air trapped within it. Finally we can likewise frequently observe that heat and other sensible qualities, inasmuch as they are in objects, and also the forms of purely material things, such as those of fire, are produced in them by the motions of certain other bodies, and that these again also produce other motions in other bodies. And we can very well conceive how the motion of one body can be caused by that of another, and diversified by the size, shape, and motion of its parts, but we can in no way understand how these same things (namely, size, shape, and motion) can produce something entirely different in nature from themselves, like those substantial forms and real qualities many suppose to exist in bodies; nor likewise can we understand how these forms or qualities have the power to produce motion in other bodies. But since we know that our soul is of such a nature that the various motions of body suffice to produce in it all the various sensations it has, and as we see by experience that some of the sensations are really caused by such motions, though we do not find anything but these motions to pass through the organs of the external senses to the brain, we may conclude that we in no way likewise apprehend that in external objects like light, color, smell, taste, sound, heat, cold, and the other tactile qualities, or what are called their substantial forms, there is anything but the various dispositions of these objects which have the power of moving our nerves in various ways.

### 199. *There is no phenomenon in nature that has not been dealt with in this treatise.*

And thus by a simple enumeration it may be deduced that there is no phenomenon in nature whose treatment has been omitted in this treatise. For there is nothing that can be counted as a phenomenon of nature, except what is apprehended by the senses. And with the exception of motion, size, and shape, which are to be found in every body, we perceive nothing outside us by means of our senses, but light, color, smell, taste, sound and tactile qualities; and I have just proved that these are nothing more, as far as is known to us, than certain dispositions of objects consisting of size, shape, and motion <so that there is nothing in all the visible world, insofar as it is

merely visible or sensible, but the things I have explained there>.

### 200. *There are no principles in this treatise not accepted by all men; this philosophy is not new, but is the most ancient and most common of all.*

But I also want it to be noted that although I have tried here to give an explanation of the whole nature of material things, I have nevertheless made use of no principle that has not been approved by Aristotle and by all the other philosophers of every age; so that this philosophy, instead of being new, is the most ancient and common of all. For I have only considered the shape, motion, and size of each body, and examined what must follow from their mutual interaction according to the laws of mechanics, confirmed as they are by certain and daily experience. But no one ever doubted that bodies move and have various sizes and shapes, according to the difference of which their motions also vary, and that from mutual collision those that are larger are divided into many smaller, and thus change their shape. We have experience of this not only by a single sense, but by several, for example, by touch, sight, and hearing; we also distinctly imagine and understand this. This cannot be said of other things that come under our senses, such as colors, sounds, and the like, which are perceived not by means of several senses, but by single ones; for their images are always confused in our minds, and we do not know what they are.

### 201. *Certain sensible bodies are composed of imperceptible particles.*

I consider that in each body there are many particles that cannot be perceived by our senses, and this perhaps will not be approved by those who take their senses as a measure of the things they can know. <But it seems to me to be doing great wrong to human reason if we do not consider that knowledge goes beyond what we see>; for no one can doubt that there are bodies so small that they cannot be perceived by any of our senses, if only we consider what is added each moment to those bodies increasing little by little, and what is removed from those diminishing in the same fashion. We see a tree grow day by day, and it is impossible to understand how it becomes larger than it was before, except by conceiving that some body is added to it. But who has ever observed by means of the senses the small bodies added each day to the plant that grows? Those at least who hold quantity to be indefinitely divisible should acknowledge that the particles may become so small as to be absolutely imperceptible. And indeed it should not be wondered at that we are unable to perceive very minute bodies, for the nerves, which must be set in motion by objects in order to produce a sensation, are not very minute, but are like small cords consisting of a quantity of yet smaller fibers, and thus they cannot be moved by very minute bodies. Nor do I think that anyone who uses his reason will deny that we do much better to understand what takes place in small bodies, whose minuteness prevents us from perceiving them, by what we see occurring in those that we do perceive <and thus explain everything in nature, as I have tried to do in this treatise>. This is preferable to explaining certain things by inventing all sorts of novelties with no relation to those that are perceived <such as prime matter, substantial forms, and all the whole range of qualities which many are in the habit of assuming, any one of which is more difficult to understand than all the things they are supposed to explain>.

### 202. *The philosophy of Democritus is no less different from ours than from the commonly accepted one <of Aristotle and others>.*

But Democritus also imagined that there were certain corpuscles that had various shapes, sizes, and motions, from whose conglomeration and interaction all sensible bodies arose; and nevertheless by common consent his philosophy is universally rejected. To this I reply that it was never rejected by anyone because he considered particles smaller than those that can be perceived by the senses in bodies and attributed to them various sizes, shapes, and motions, for no one can doubt that there are in reality many such particles, as has already been shown. But this philosophy was rejected, in the first place because it presupposed certain indivisible corpuscles—a hypothesis I also completely reject; in the second place it was rejected because Democritus imagined a void around them, which I demonstrate to be an impossibility; in

the third place because he attributed to them gravity, the existence of which I deny in any body insofar as it is considered by itself, because it depends on the relation of position and motion that bodies bear to one another; and finally because he had not explained in detail how all things arose from the interaction of the corpuscles alone, or, if he explained it in regard to certain cases, his explanations were not consistent. If we may judge from those of his opinions that have been preserved, this at least is the verdict we must give on his philosophy. I leave it to others to judge as to whether what I have written in philosophy has been sufficiently coherent <and whether it is fertile enough in yielding conclusions for us. As for the consideration of shape, size, and motion, this has been admitted by Aristotle and all other philosophers, as well as by Democritus, and as I reject all of Democritus's suppositions, with this one exception, while I reject practically all that has been supposed by the others, it is clear that this method of philosophizing has no more affinity with that of Democritus than with any of the other particular sects>.

### 203. *How we may arrive at a knowledge of the shapes, <sizes>, and motions of the imperceptible particles of bodies.*

But since I assign determinate shapes, sizes, and motions to the imperceptible particles of bodies, as if I had seen them, but admit that they do not fall under the senses, someone will perhaps ask how I have come to my knowledge of them. To this I reply that I first considered generally the simplest and best understood principles implanted in our mind by nature, and examined the principal differences that could be found between the sizes, shapes, and positions of bodies imperceptible on account of their smallness alone, and what observable effects could be produced by the various ways in which they impinge on one another. And finally, when I found like effects in the bodies perceived by our senses, I considered that they might have been produced from a similar interaction of such bodies, especially as no other way of explaining them could be suggested. And for this end the example of certain artifacts was of use to me, for I can see no difference between these and natural bodies, except that the effects of machines depend for the most part on the operation of certain <tubes, springs, or other> instruments, which, since men necessarily make them, must always be large enough to be capable of being easily perceived by the senses. The effects of natural causes, on the other hand, almost always depend on certain organs minute enough to escape our senses. And it is certain that there are no rules in mechanics that do not hold good in physics, of which mechanics forms a part or species <so that all that is artificial is also natural>; for it is not less natural for a clock, made of the proper number of wheels, to indicate the hours, than for a tree which has sprung from this or that seed, to produce a particular fruit. Accordingly, just as those who apply themselves to the consideration of automata, when they know the use of a certain machine and see some of its parts, easily infer from these the manner in which others they have not seen are made, so from considering the sensible effects and parts of natural bodies, I have tried to discover the nature of the imperceptible causes and particles contained in them.

204. *With regard to the things our senses do not perceive, it is sufficient to explain their possible natures, though perhaps they are not what we describe them to be <and this is all that Aristotle has tried to do>.*

But here it may be said that although I have shown how all natural things can be formed, we have no right to conclude on this account that they were produced by these causes. For just as there may be two clocks made by the same craftsman, which although they indicate the time equally well and are externally in all respects alike, yet in no way resemble one another in the composition of their wheels, so doubtless there are many different ways in which all things we see could be formed by the great artificer <without its being possible for the mind of man to be aware which of these means he has chosen to use>. This I most freely admit; and I believe that I have done all that is required of me if the causes I have assigned are such that they correspond to all the phenomena manifested by nature <without inquiring whether it is by their means or by others that they

are produced>. And it will be sufficient for the needs of life to know such causes, for medicine and mechanics, and in general all those arts that can be developed with the use of physics, have for their end only perceptible effects that are accordingly to be counted among the phenomena of nature. And in case it is supposed that Aristotle did, or desired to do, more than this, it must be remembered that he expressly says in the first book of the *Meteorology*, in the beginning of the seventh chapter, that with regard to things not manifest to the senses, he considers that he supplies sufficient explanations and demonstrations of them, if he merely shows that they may be such as he explains them to be.

205. *Nevertheless there is a moral certainty that everything is such as it has been shown to be.*

But nevertheless, that I may not injure the truth, we must consider <two kinds of certainty and> first of all what has moral certainty; that is, a certainty that suffices for the conduct of life, though if we regard the absolute power of God, what is morally certain may be uncertain. <So those who have never visited Rome do not doubt its being a city in Italy, although it may very well be that everyone who has told them this has deceived them.> If, for instance, anyone wishing to read a letter written in Latin but encoded so that the characters are not placed in their proper order, takes it into his head to read B wherever he finds A and C where he finds B, thus substituting for each letter the one following it in the alphabet, and if in this way he finds that there are certain Latin words composed of these, he will not doubt that the true meaning of the writing is contained in these words. It is true that he discovers this by conjecture, and it is possible that the writer did not arrange the letters in this order of succession, but in some other, and thus concealed another meaning in it; this is so unlikely to occur, <especially when the coded message contains many words,> that it may seem incredible. But those who observe how many things regarding the magnet, fire, and the fabric of the whole world are here deduced from a very small number of principles, even if they thought that I took up these principles at random and without good grounds, may still acknowledge that it could hardly happen that so much would be coherent if they were false.

### 206. *We possess even more than a moral certainty*.

And further there are some, even among natural things, that we regard to be absolutely, and more than morally, certain. This certainty is founded on the metaphysical ground that as God is supremely good and cannot err, the faculty he has given us of distinguishing truth from falsehood, cannot lead us into error so long as we use it properly and thereby perceive something distinctly by means of it. Of this nature are mathematical demonstrations, the knowledge that material things exist, and the evidence of all clear reasoning that is carried on about them. Among these truths it seems to me there should be counted those conclusions which have been arrived at in this treatise, if people consider that they are derived in a continual series from the first and simplest principles of human knowledge. And this is especially so, if it is sufficiently understood that we can perceive no external objects unless some local motion is excited by them in our nerves, and that such motion cannot be excited by the fixed stars, owing to their immense distance from us, unless a motion is also produced in them, and in the whole intervening heavens; once this is accepted, all the other phenomena, at least the more general things I have advanced about the world and earth, cannot be understood except in the way I have explained them.

### 207. *Nevertheless all my opinions are submitted to the authority of the church*.

At the same time, recalling my insignificance, I affirm nothing, but submit all these things to the authority of the Catholic Church, and to the judgment of those wiser than myself; and I wish no one to believe anything I have written, unless he is personally persuaded by the force and evidence of reason.

# Baruch Spinoza, *Descartes's Principles of Philosophy*, "Prolegomenon" and "Definitions" (1663)[1]

Before giving these propositions and their demonstration, it seems best to recall briefly why Descartes came to doubt all things, how he discovered the stable foundations for the sciences, and finally how he liberated himself from all his doubts. We would have put all of this in mathematical order if we had not thought that such prolixity would have impeded our understanding of these things which should be seen as clearly as though presented in a picture.

In order to proceed with his investigation with the utmost caution, Descartes was compelled

1. To lay aside all prejudices.

2. To find the foundations on which all things ought to be built.

3. To discover the cause of error.

4. To understand everything clearly and distinctly.

In order to accomplish the first three points, he doubted all things, not, however, as a skeptic who doubts merely for the sake of doubting, but in order

to free his mind of all prejudices, so that he might find at length the firm and unshakable foundations of the sciences. By using this method, if any such foundations existed, they could not escape him. For the true principles of the sciences must be so clear that they need no proof, and cannot under any circumstances be doubted; every demonstration must presuppose them. These he found after a long period of doubt. And after he had once gained these principles, it was not difficult to distinguish the true from the false, or to detect the cause of error. And thus he could be on his guard lest he accept anything doubtful and false for what is certain and true.

To accomplish the last point, that is, to understand everything clearly and distinctly, his principal rule was to enumerate and examine separately all the simple ideas from which all others are composed. For when he could clearly and distinctly perceive these simple ideas, he would be able to understand with the same clarity and distinctness all others into which they entered as component parts. Having prefaced our remarks with these few words, we shall proceed with our purpose as stated above, namely, to explain why he doubted everything, how he found the true principles of the sciences, and how he extricated himself from the difficulties of his doubts.

*Concerning his universal doubt.* In the first place

1. Translated from the Latin by H. H. Britain in Benedict de Spinoza, *The Principles of Descartes's Philosophy* (La Salle, Ill.: Open Court, 1905), modified. For Spinoza's biography and bibliography, see Section 2 of this book.

110

he calls attention to all of those things perceived through the senses, the heavens, the earth and the like, and even his own body—all the things he had until then thought to exist in nature. And he came to doubt their certainty because he had observed that his senses sometimes deceived him, and in sleep he had often persuaded himself that many things existed in which he later found he had been deceived, and finally because he had heard others affirm that they sometimes felt pain in limbs long lost. It was not without reason, therefore, that he doubted even the existence of his own body. Hence from all these reasons he was able to conclude that the senses are not the most firm foundation on which the sciences should be built (for they can be called in doubt), but certainty rests upon some principles more certain than this. To investigate further, he next considers universal things, such as corporeal nature in general, its extension, figure, quantity, etc., as well as all mathematical truth. Although these seem more certain than the objects of sense perception, nevertheless, he finds a cause for doubting them as well. Some err even in these, and besides there is an old opinion that God, who is omnipotent, and has created us with our present faculties, has perhaps so made us that we are deceived even in those things which seem most certain. These are the causes that led him to doubt all things.

*The discovery of the foundation of all science.* In order to find the true principles of the sciences, he afterward inquired whether all things which are subjects of thought could be doubted, if perhaps there was anything which he had not yet called in question. Doubting in this way he believed that if anything was found, which, for none of the reasons given above, should be doubted, this might be considered the foundation on which all knowledge rests. And although, as it now seemed, he had doubted everything (for he had called in question all that the senses give and all that is perceived by the understanding), there was something left the certainty of which had not been doubted, namely, he himself who was doubting—not, however, insofar as he consisted of head or hands or other bodily members, for he had doubted these things, but only insofar as he was doubting, thinking, etc. Carefully examining this fact, he found that for

none of the previously mentioned reasons could it be doubted, for, whether he thinks waking or sleeping, it is true that he thinks and exists; and even though he and others might fall into error, since they were in error, they must exist. Nor could he feign a creator so skillful in deceit that he could deceive him about this. For if it is supposed that he is deceived, it must also be supposed that he exists. Finally, whatever reason for doubt may be conceived, there is none which does not at the same time make one more certain of his own existence. Indeed the more reasons for doubting, the more arguments there are which convince him of his own existence. So in whatever direction he turns in order to doubt, he is forced to exclaim, "I doubt, I think; therefore I am."

This truth discovered, he finds at the same time the foundations of all the sciences as well as the measure and rule of all other truths, namely: *Whatever is as clearly and distinctly perceived as this is true.*

That there can be no other foundation of the sciences than this is more than sufficiently evident from the preceding. For we can call all the rest in doubt with no difficulty, but we cannot doubt this in any way. Concerning this principle, "I doubt, I think; therefore I am," it should be noted in the first place that it is not a syllogism in which the major premise is omitted. If it were, the premises ought to be clearer and better known than the conclusion, "therefore I am." And if this were so, "I am" would not be the first foundation of all knowledge. Moreover, it would not be a certain conclusion, for its truth depends upon universal premises which the author had called in question. Therefore "I think, therefore I am" is a single proposition equivalent to "I am thinking."

To avoid confusion in what follows (for the matter ought to be perceived clearly and distinctly), we must know what we are. For once we do understand it clearly and distinctly, we shall not confuse our essence with others. To deduce this from what precedes, our author thus continues:

He now recalled all the thoughts he formerly held, as for example, that his soul was something very fine in texture, like the wind, or fire, or air, infused throughout with the coarser particles of the body; and that his body was better known than his soul and could be perceived more clearly and distinctly. These thoughts he now saw were clearly incompatible with what he had discovered. For he could doubt the existence of his body, but not his essence insofar as he was thinking. Moreover, he perceived these thoughts neither clearly nor distinctly, and consequently, according to the rule of his method, he was obliged to reject them as if they were false. Therefore, since he could not understand such things as pertaining to himself, so far as he was known to himself up to this point, he further inquires what there was about his essence which he could not put into doubt, and which compelled him to believe in his own existence. Such things were these: *that he had determined to be on his guard lest he be deceived; that he had desired to understand so many things; that he had doubted everything he was not able to know; that he had affirmed only one thing at a time; that he had denied all else, and even rejected it as false; that he had conceived many things though reluctantly; and finally that he had considered many things as though derived from the senses.* Since his existence was so evidently bound up with each one of these actions, and since none of them belonged to the things which he had doubted, and finally since they all can be conceived under the same attribute, it follows that these are all true and pertain to his nature. So when he said, *I think*, these modes of thought were all understood, namely, *doubting, understanding, affirming, denying, willing, not willing, imagining,* and *sensing.*

Some things must be noted here that will have importance when we come to discuss the distinction between mind and body. (1) That modes of thought may be known clearly and distinctly even though some things are still in doubt. (2) That we render a clear and distinct concept obscure and confused when we ascribe to it something concerning which we are still in doubt.

*Liberation from all doubts.* Finally, in order that he might be certain and remove all doubt from those things he had called in question, he further proceeds to inquire into the nature of the most perfect Being and whether such a Being exists. For, when he has discovered that this Being, by whose power all things are created and conserved and to whose nature it would be repugnant to be a deceiver, exists, then that reason for doubt which is found in the fact that he was ignorant of his own cause will be removed. For he will know that the power of discerning the true from the false would not have been given to him by a God of perfect goodness and truth in order that he might be deceived. Mathematical truth, therefore, and all other of like certainty cannot be suspected. To remove the other causes for doubt, he inquires next why it is we sometimes fall into error. For when he discovered how error arose, and that we use our free will to assent even to what we perceive only confusedly, he concluded immediately that we could avoid error by withholding assent from that which is seen only confusedly.

As everyone has the power of inhibiting the will, he can easily restrain it to the limits of the understanding. And since in youth we form many prejudices from which we free ourselves only with difficulty, he enumerates and examines separately all of the simple notions and ideas of which all our thoughts are composed, so that we might be freed from our prejudices and accept nothing but what we perceive clearly and distinctly. For if he could take note of what was clear and what obscure in each, he would easily be able to distinguish the clear from the obscure and to form clear and distinct thoughts. By this means he easily found the real distinction between soul and body; what was clear and what obscure in the things derived from the senses; and finally how sleep differs from waking. When this was done, he could doubt no longer concerning the waking life, nor could he be deceived by his senses. In this way he was able to free himself from all the doubts recounted above.

Before I close this part of the discussion, it seems that some satisfaction should be given to those who object that since God's existence does not become known to us through itself, we seem unable ever to be certain of anything; for from uncertain premises (and we have said that all things are uncertain so long as we are ignorant of our origin), nothing can be concluded with certainty.

In order to remove this difficulty Descartes responded in this fashion: Although we do not yet know whether the creator of our nature has created us so that we are deceived in those things which appear most evident to us, nevertheless, we cannot doubt those things we understand clearly and distinctly either through themselves or through reasoning, as long as we attend merely to them. But we only doubt those things previously demonstrated to be true and now recalled to memory when we no longer attend closely to the reasons from which they were deduced, which perhaps are even forgotten. So although God's existence cannot come to be known through itself, but only through something else, we will be able to attain a certain knowledge of his existence, provided we attend very accurately to the premises from which the conclusion is deduced. See *Principles* I, 13; *Reply to Second Objections*, 3, and Meditation Five, at the end.

But since this reply does not satisfy everybody, I shall offer another. We saw above, when speaking of the evidence and certainty of our existence, that this was found in the fact that, consider what we will, we meet no argument for doubt which does not at the same time convince us of the certainty of our existence. This is true whether we consider our own nature, or conceive of the author of our nature as a skillful deceiver, or adduce some extraneous reason for doubt. So far we have not observed this to happen regarding any other matter. For example, considering the nature of a triangle, though we are now compelled to believe that its three angles are equal to two right angles, we are not forced to the conclusion that this is really true if perhaps we are deceived by the author of our nature. In the same way we deduce the certainty of our existence. We are not here compelled to believe that under any conditions three angles of a triangle are equal to two right angles. On the contrary we find reason for doubt, for we have no idea of God which so affects us that it is impossible for us to think that God is a deceiver. It is equally easy for one who has no true idea of God (which we now suppose ourselves not to have) to think that he is a deceiver or that he is not. So for those who have no right conception of a triangle, it is equally easy for them to think that the sum of the angles is equal to two right angles, or that it is not. Therefore, we grant that we cannot be absolutely certain of anything except of our own existence, however closely we attend to the proof, until we have a clear concept of God which compels us to affirm (in the same way that the concept of a triangle compels us to affirm that the sum of its

angles is equal to two right angles) that he is supremely veracious. But we deny that we are unable to come to any certain knowledge of anything. For, as now appears, the whole matter hinges upon this, namely, whether we can form such a concept of God that it is not as easy for us to think of him as a deceiver as to think that he is not, but which compels us to affirm that he is supremely veracious. When we have formed such an idea, all reason for doubting mathematical truth is removed. For, wherever we then direct our attention in order to doubt some one of them, we shall come upon nothing from which we must not instead infer that it is most certain—as happened concerning our existence. For example, if now having obtained this concept of God we consider the nature of a triangle, we are compelled to affirm that the sum of its three angles is equal to two right angles; or if we consider the nature of God, this too compels us to affirm that he is supremely veracious and the author and continual conserver of our nature, and therefore that he does not deceive us concerning that truth. Nor is it less impossible for us to think when we once have obtained this idea of God (which we suppose to be already found) that he is a deceiver, than when we consider the nature of a triangle to think that the sum of its angles is not equal to two right angles. As we can form such an idea of a triangle although we are not certain whether the author of our nature is not deceiving us, so also we can make the idea of God clear to ourselves and put it before our eyes, even though we still doubt whether the author of our nature deceives us in all things. And, provided only that we have such an idea of God, however it may have been obtained, it is sufficient to remove all doubt, as has just been shown.

This point having been made clear, I reply as follows to the difficulty raised: We can be certain of nothing not merely as long as we are ignorant of God's existence (for I have not yet spoken of this), but as long as we do not have a clear and a distinct idea of him. Hence if anyone should desire to oppose my conclusion, his argument should be as follows: We can be certain of nothing before we have a clear and distinct idea of God. But we cannot have a clear and a distinct idea of God as long as we do not know whether or not the author of our nature is deceiving us. Therefore, we cannot be certain of anything as long as we do not know whether or not the author of our nature is deceiving us, etc. To this I reply by conceding major premise but denying the minor. For we have a clear and a distinct idea of a triangle although we do not know whether or not the author of our nature is deceiving us; and provided we have such an idea (as I have shown abundantly above), we will be able to doubt neither his existence, nor any mathematical truth.

Our prefatory remarks being thus completed, we proceed now to the main problem.

## Definitions

I. *Under the term* thought [cogitatio] *I include everything which is in us and of which we are immediately conscious.*

Thus all the operations of the will, the understanding, the imagination, and the senses are thoughts. I have added the term *immediately* to exclude those things that follow from thoughts; thus voluntary motion does have thought as its principle, but is not itself a thought.

II. *By the term* idea [idea] *I understand any form of thought of which I am conscious through immediate perception of that thought itself.*

I cannot express anything in words (when I understand what I say), therefore, without it being certain from this that I have in me an idea of what is signified by these words. Therefore, I do not call *idea* only the images depicted in fantasy; indeed, I do not call these images ideas at all, insofar as they are depicted in the corporeal imagination, i.e., in some portion of the brain, but only insofar as they inform the mind itself which is directed toward that portion of the brain.

III. *By the* objective reality of an idea, *I understand the entity of the thing represented by the idea, insofar as this entity is in the idea.*

In the same manner I may speak of objective perfection, or of an objective art, etc. For whatever we perceive in the objects of ideas is objectively in the ideas themselves.

IV. *These same things are said to be* formally [formaliter] *in the objects of ideas when they are in them as we perceive them. They are said to be* eminently [eminenter] *when they are not as we perceive them, but so great that they can take the place of such things.*

Note that when I say a cause contains the perfection of its own effect *eminently*, I mean that the cause contains the perfection of the effect more excellently than the effect itself. [. . .]

V. *Everything in which there is immediately, as in a subject, or through which there exists, something we perceive, that is, some property, quality, or attribute, of which we have a real idea, is called* substance.

Indeed we have no other idea of substance, taken precisely, than that it is something in which exists either formally or eminently that something we perceive, or which is objective in one of our ideas.

VI. *Substance in which thoughts immediately reside is called* mind.

I use the term *mind* [mens] rather than *soul* [animus] for the latter term is equivocal, often being used to mean a corporeal thing.

VII. *Substance, which is the immediate subject of extension, and of accidents which presuppose extension, like figure, position, and local motion, etc., is called* body [corpus].

Whether what is called mind is one and the same substance as what is called body, or whether they are different substances, will be inquired into later.

VIII. *Substance which we understand to be through itself supremely perfect and in which nothing can be conceived involving a defect or limitation of perfection is called* God.

IX. *When we say that something is contained in the nature of the thing itself or in its concept, it is the same as to affirm that it is true of that thing, i.e., that it can be truly affirmed of it.*

X. *Two substances are said to be really distinct when each of them can exist without the other.* [. . .]

## [Part II.] Definitions

I. *Extension is that which consists of three dimensions. We do not understand by the term the act of extending or anything else distinct from quantity.*

II. By *substance* we understand that which depends only upon the concurrence of God for its existence.

III. An *atom* is a part of matter which is indivisible by nature.

IV. *Indefinite* is that whose limits, if it has any, cannot be investigated by the human mind.

V. A *vacuum* is extension without corporeal substance.

VI. We make only a distinction of reason between *space* and *extension*; that is, they are not really distinct. See *Principles* II, article 10.

VII. That which in our thinking we understand to be divided is *divisible*, at least potentially.

VIII. *Local motion* is the transfer of one part of matter or of a body from the vicinity of other contiguous bodies considered as in a state of rest, to the vicinity of others. [. . .]

# G. W. Leibniz, On Descartes (1675–79), From the Letters to Foucher, to Elisabeth, and to Molanus[1]

*As Leibniz says in the "Letter to Foucher," he first studied Descartes's philosophy seriously when he resided in Paris from 1672 to 1676. As a result, Leibniz's letters during that period contain many incisive criticisms of Descartes's various positions. Leibniz will repeat some of these (though not all of them) in his mature work, but they never seem quite as fresh as the versions from this period, dealing with many of Descartes's basic doctrines: "I think; therefore I am" is the first principle of knowledge; God is needed to guarantee truth; God's existence follows from the idea we have of him; God wills the eternal truths; we are immortal because our soul is an unextended substance, that is, a substance that cannot perish.[2]*

## Letter to Foucher (1675)

[. . .] The principal subject of your inquiry concerns the truths that deal with what is really outside of us. Now, in the first place, we cannot deny that the very truth of hypothetical propositions is something outside of us, something that does not depend on us. For all hypothetical propositions assert what would be or what would not be if something or its contrary were posited; and consequently, they assert that the simultaneous assumption of two things in agreement with one another is possible or impossible, necessary or indifferent, or they assert that one single thing is possible or impossible, necessary or indifferent. This possibility, impossibility, or necessity (for the necessity of something is the impossibility of its contrary) is not a chimera we create, since we do nothing more than recognize it, in spite of ourselves and in a consistent manner. Thus of all things that there actually are, the very possibility or impossibility of being is the first. Now, this possibility or this necessity forms or composes what we call the essences or natures and the truths we commonly call eternal—and we are right to call them so, for there is nothing so eternal as that which is necessary. Thus the nature of the circle with its properties is something existent and eternal. That is, there is a constant cause outside us

1. Translated from the French by R. Ariew and D. Garber in G. W. Leibniz, *Philosophical Essays* (Indianapolis: Hackett Publishing Company, 1989).
2. For Leibniz's biography and bibliography, see Section 3 in this book. Leibniz's correspondents are Simon Foucher, a critic of Cartesian philosophy and proponent of Academic skepticism, whom Leibniz met in Paris; (possibly) Princess Elisabeth, Countess Palatine and sister of the Duchess Sophia of Hanover—the Duke of Hanover being Leibniz's principal employer; and (possibly) Gerhardt Molanus, abbot of Loccum, near Hanover.

which makes everyone who thinks carefully about the circle discover the same thing. It is not merely that their thoughts agree with each other, which could be attributed solely to the nature of the human mind, but even the phenomena or experiences confirm these eternal truths when the appearance of a circle strikes our senses. And these phenomena necessarily have some cause outside of us.

But even though the existence of necessities is the first of all truths in and of itself and in the order of nature, I agree that it is not first in the order of our knowledge. For you see, in order to prove their existence I took it for granted that we think and that we have sensations. Thus there are two absolute general truths, that is, two absolute general truths which speak of the actual existence of things: the first, that we think, and the second, that there is a great variety in our thoughts. From the former it follows that we exist, and from the latter it follows that there is something else besides us, that is, something else besides that which thinks, something which is the cause of the variety of our appearances. Now one of these two truths is just as incontestable and as independent as the other; and Descartes, having accepted only the former, failed to arrive at the perfection to which he had aspired in the course of his meditations. If he had followed precisely what I call the thread of meditating [*filum meditandi*], I believe that he would have achieved the first philosophy. But not even the world's greatest genius can force things, and we must necessarily enter through the entryways that nature has made, so that we do not stray. Moreover, one person alone cannot do everything at once, and for myself, when I think of everything Descartes has said that is beautiful and original, I am more astonished with what he has accomplished than with what he has failed to accomplish. I admit that I have not yet been able to read all his writings with all the care I had intended to bring to them, and my friends know that, as it happened, I read almost all the new philosophers before reading him. Bacon and Gassendi were the first to fall into my hands; their familiar and easy style was better adapted to a person who wants to read everything. It is true that I often glanced at Galileo and Descartes, but since I became a geometer only recently, I was soon repelled by their manner of writ-

ing, which requires deep meditation. As for myself, although I always liked to meditate, I always found it difficult to read books that cannot be understood without much meditation. For, when following one's own meditations one follows a certain natural inclination and gains profit along with pleasure; but one is enormously cramped when having to follow the meditations of others. I always liked books that contained some fine thoughts, but books that one could read without stopping, for they aroused ideas in me which I could follow at my fancy and pursue as I pleased. This also prevented me from reading geometry books with care, and I must admit that I have not yet brought myself to read Euclid in any other way than one commonly reads novels [*histoires*]. I have learned from experience that this method in general is a good one; but I have learned nevertheless that there are authors for whom one must make an exception—Plato and Aristotle among the ancient philosophers and Galileo and Descartes among ours. Yet what I know of Descartes's metaphysical and physical meditations is almost entirely derived from reading a number of books, written in a more familiar style, that report his opinions. So perhaps I have not yet understood him well. However, to the extent that I have leafed through his works myself, it seemed to me that I have glimpsed at very least what he has not accomplished and not even attempted to accomplish, that is, among other things, the analysis of all our assumptions. That is why I am inclined to applaud all those who examine the least truth to its deepest level; for I know that it is important to understand one perfectly, however small and however easy it may seem. This is the way to progress quite far and finally to establish the art of discovery which depends on a knowledge, but a most distinct and perfect knowledge of the easiest things. And for this reason I found nothing wrong in Roberval's attempt to demonstrate everything in geometry, including some axioms.[3] I admit that we should not demand such exactness

---

3. Roberval does attempt to demonstrate Euclid's axioms in his *Elements of Geometry*, one of Roberval's unpublished papers, which Leibniz considered publishing. See Leibniz's *New Essays on Human Understanding*, Book IV, chap. 7, sec. 1: "Of the propositions which are named maxims or axioms."

from others, but I believe that it is good to demand it from ourselves.

I return to those truths, from among those asserting that there is something outside us, which are first with respect to ourselves, namely, that we think and that there is a great variety in our thoughts. Now, this variety cannot come from that which thinks, since a single thing by itself cannot be the cause of the changes in itself. For everything would remain in the state in which it is, if there is nothing that changes it; and since it did not determine itself to have these changes rather than others, one cannot begin to attribute any variety to it without saying something which, we must admit, has no reason—which is absurd. And even if we tried to say that our thoughts had no beginning, beside the fact that we would be required to assert that each of us has existed from all eternity, we would still not escape the difficulty; for we would always have to admit that there is no reason for the particular variety which would have existed in our thoughts from all eternity, since there is nothing in us that determines us to have one kind of variety rather than another. Therefore, there is some cause outside of us for the variety of our thoughts. And since we conceive that there are subordinate causes for this variety, causes which themselves still need causes, we have established particular beings or substances certain of whose actions we recognize, that is, things from whose changes we conceive certain changes in us to follow. And we quickly proceed to construct what we call matter and body. But it is at this point that you are right to stop us a bit and renew the criticisms of the ancient Academy. For, at bottom, all our experience assures us of only two things, namely, that there is a connection among our appearances which provides us the means to predict future appearances with success, and that this connection must have a constant cause. But it does not strictly follow from all this that matter or bodies exist, but only that there is something that presents well-sequenced appearances to us. For if an invisible power took pleasure in giving us dreams that are well connected with our preceding life and in conformity among themselves, could we distinguish them from realities before having been awakened? And what prevents the course of our life from being a long well-ordered dream, a dream from which we could be wakened in a moment? And I do not see that this power would be imperfect on that account, as Descartes asserts, leaving aside the fact that it does not matter if it is imperfect. For this could be a certain subordinate power, or some genie who meddles in our affairs for some unknown reason and who has as much power over someone as had the caliph who transported a drunken man into his palace and made him taste of Mohammed's paradise when he had awakened; after this he was made drunk again and was returned to the place from which he had been taken. And when the man came to himself, he did not fail to interpret what to him appeared inconsistent with the course of his life as a vision, and spread among the people maxims and revelations that he believed he had learned in his pretended paradise—this was what the caliph wished. Now, since a reality passed for a vision, what prevents a vision from passing for a reality? It is true that the more we see some connection in what happens to us, the more we are confirmed in the opinion we have about the reality of our appearances; and it is also true that the more we examine our appearances closely, the more we find them well-sequenced, as microscopes and other aids in making experiments have shown us. This constant accord engenders great assurance, but after all, it will only be moral assurance until somebody discovers the *a priori* origin of the world we see and pursues the question as to why things are the way they appear back to the ground of essence. For having done that, he will have demonstrated that what appears to us is a reality and that it is impossible that we ever be deceived about it again. But I believe that this would nearly approach the beatific vision and that it is difficult to aspire to this in our present state. However, we would learn from this how confused the knowledge we commonly have of body and matter must be, since we believe we are certain they exist but in the end we discover that we can be mistaken. And this confirms Descartes's excellent proof of the distinction between body and soul, since we can doubt the former without being able to put the latter into question. For even if there were only appearances or dreams, we would be no less certain of the existence of that which thinks, as Descartes has said quite nicely. I add that the existence of God can be demonstrated in ways other than Descartes did, ways which, I believe, bring us farther along. For we do not need to assume a being who guarantees us against being deceived, since it is in our power to undeceive ourselves about many things, at least about the most important ones. I wish, sir, that your meditations on this have all the success you desire. But to accomplish this, it is good to proceed in order and to establish propositions; that is the way to gain ground and to make sure progress. I believe that you would oblige the public by conveying to it, from time to time, selections from the Academy and especially from Plato, for I recognize that there are things in there more beautiful and solid than commonly thought.

## Letter to Countess Elisabeth (?), On God and Formal Logic (1678?)

[. . .] I come, then, to metaphysics, and I can state that it is for the love of metaphysics that I have passed through all these stages. For I have recognized that metaphysics is scarcely different from the true logic, that is, from the art of invention in general; for, in fact, metaphysics is natural theology, and the same God who is the source of all goods is also the principle of all knowledge. This is because the idea of God contains within it absolute being, that is, what is simple in our thoughts, from which everything that we think draws its origin. Descartes did not go about it in this way. He gave two ways of proving the existence of God. The *first* is that there is an idea of God in us since, no doubt, we think about God, and we cannot think of something without having its idea.[4] Now, if we have an idea of God, and if it is true [*véritable*], that is, if it is the idea of an infinite being, and if it represents it faithfully, it could not be caused by something lesser, and consequently, God himself must be its cause. Therefore, he must exist. The *other* reasoning is even shorter. It is that God is a being who possesses all perfections, and consequently, he possesses existence, which is to be counted as one of the perfections.[5] Therefore, he exists. It must be said

4.  Cf. Descartes, Meditation III.
5.  Cf. Descartes, Meditation V.

that these reasonings are somewhat suspect, because they go too fast, and because they force themselves upon us without enlightening us. Real demonstrations, on the other hand, generally fill the mind with some solid nourishment. However, the crux of the matter is difficult to find, and I see that many able people who have formulated objections to Descartes were led astray.

*Some* have believed that there is no idea of God because he is not subject to imagination, assuming that idea and image are the same thing. I am not of their opinion, and I know perfectly well that there are ideas of thought, existence, and similar things, of which there are no images. For we think of something and when we notice in there what it is that allows us to recognize it, this is what constitutes the idea of the thing, insofar as it is in our soul. This is why there is also an idea of what is not material or imaginable.

*Others* agree that there is an idea of God, and that this idea contains all perfections, but they cannot understand how existence follows from it, either because they do not agree that existence is to be counted among the perfections, or because they do not see how a simple idea or thought can imply an existence outside us. As for me, I genuinely believe that anyone who has recognized this idea of God, and who sees that existence is a perfection, must admit that existence belongs to God. In fact, I do not question the idea of God any more than I do his existence; on the contrary, I claim to have a demonstration of it. But I do not want us to flatter ourselves and persuade ourselves that we can arrive at such a great thing with such little cost. Paralogisms are dangerous in this matter; when they occur, they reflect on us, and they strengthen the opposite side. I therefore say that we must prove with the greatest imaginable exactness that there is an idea of a completely perfect being, that is, an idea of God. It is true that the objections of those who believed that they could prove the contrary because there is no image of God are worthless, as I have just shown. But we also have to admit that the proof Descartes gives to establish the idea of God is imperfect. How, he would say, can one speak of God without thinking of him, and how can one think of him without having an idea of him? Yes, no doubt we sometimes think about impossible things and we even construct demonstrations from them. For example, Descartes holds that squaring the circle is impossible, and yet we still think about it and draw consequences about what would happen if it were given. The motion having the greatest speed is impossible in any body whatsoever, because, for example, if we assumed it in a circle, then another circle concentric to the former circle, surrounding it and firmly attached to it, would move with a speed still greater than the former, which, consequently, would not be of the greatest degree, in contradiction to what we had assumed. In spite of all that, we think about this greatest speed, something that has no idea since it is impossible. Similarly, the greatest circle of all is an impossible thing, and the number of all possible units is no less so; we have a demonstration of this. And nevertheless, we think about all this. That is why there are surely grounds for wondering whether we should be careful about the idea of the greatest of all beings, and whether it might not contain a contradiction. For I fully understand, for example, the nature of motion and speed and what it is to be greatest, but, for all that, I do not understand whether all those notions are compatible, and whether there is a way of joining them and making them into an idea of the greatest speed of which motion is capable. Similarly, although I know what being is, and what it is to be the greatest and most perfect, nevertheless I do not yet know, for all that, whether there isn't a hidden contradiction in joining all that together, as there is, in fact, in the previously stated examples. In brief, I do not yet know, for all that, whether such a being is possible, for if it were not possible, there would be no idea of it. However, I must admit that God has a great advantage, in this respect, over all other things. For to prove that he exists, it would be sufficient to prove that he is possible, something we find nowhere else, as far as I know. Moreover, I infer from that that there is a presumption that God exists. For there is always a presumption on the side of possibility, that is, everything is held to be possible unless it is proven to be impossible. There is, therefore, a presumption that God is possible, that is, that he exists, since in him existence follows from possibility. This is sufficient for practical matters in life, but it is not sufficient for a demonstration. I have strongly disputed this matter

with several Cartesians, but I finally succeeded in this with some of the most able of them who have frankly admitted, after having understood the force of my reasons, that this possibility is still to be demonstrated. There are even some who, challenged by me to do so, have undertaken this demonstration, but they have not yet succeeded.

Since Your Highness is intelligent, you see what the state of things is and you see we can do nothing unless we prove this possibility. When I consider all this, I take pity on man's weakness, and I take care not to exclude myself from it. Descartes, who was no doubt one of the greatest men of this century, erred in so visible a manner, and many illustrious people erred with him. Nevertheless, we do not question their intelligence or their care. All of this could give some people a bad opinion of the certainty of our knowledge in general. For, one can say, with so many able men unable to avoid a trap, what can I hope for, I, who am nothing compared to them? Nevertheless, we must not lose our courage. There is a way of avoiding error, which these able men have not condescended to use; it would have been contrary to the greatness of their minds, at least in appearance, and with respect to the common people. All those who wish to appear to be great figures and who set themselves up as leaders of sects have a bit of the acrobat in them. A tightrope walker does not allow himself to be braced in order to avoid falling; if he did so, he would be sure of his act, but he would no longer appear a skillful man. I will be asked, what then is this wonderful way that can prevent us from falling? I am almost afraid to say it—it appears to be too lowly. But I am speaking to Your Highness who does not judge things by their appearance. In brief, it is to construct arguments only in proper form [*in forma*]. I seem to see only people who cry out against me and who send me back to school. But I beg them to be a little patient, for perhaps they do not understand me; arguments in proper form do not always bear the stamp of *Barbara Celarent*.[6] Any rigor-

---

6. *Barbara Celarent* is a reference to the first line of some thirteenth-century mnemonic nonsense verses enabling students to remember the rules governing the validity of syllogisms; the full line would be "Barbara, Celarent, Darii, Ferioque

ous demonstration that does not omit anything necessary for the force of reasoning is of this kind, and I dare say that the account of an accountant and a calculation of analysis are arguments in proper form, since there is nothing missing in them and since the form or arrangement of the whole reasoning is the cause of their being evident. It is only the form that distinguishes an account book made according to the practice we commonly call Italian (of which Stevin has written a whole treatise) from the confused journal of someone ignorant of business. That is why I maintain that, in order to reason with evidence in all subjects, we must hold some consistent formalism [formalité constante]. There would be less eloquence, but more certainty. But in order to determine the formalism that would do no less in metaphysics, physics, and morals, than calculation does in mathematics, that would even give us degrees of probability when we can only reason probabilistically, I would have to relate here the thoughts I have on a new characteristic [characteristique], something that would take too long. Nevertheless, I will say, in brief, that this characteristic would represent our thoughts truly and distinctly, and that when a thought is composed of other simpler ones, its character would also be similarly composed. I dare not say what would follow from this for the perfection of the sciences—it would appear incredible. And yet, there is a demonstration of this. The only thing I will say here is that since that which we know is from reasoning or experience, it is certain that henceforth all reasoning in demonstrative or probable matters will demand no more skill than a calculation in algebra does; that is, one would derive from given experiments everything that can be derived, just as in algebra. But for now it is sufficient for me to note that the foundation of my characteristic is also the foundation of the demonstration of God's existence. For simple thoughts are the elements of the characteristic and simple forms are the source of things. I maintain that all simple forms are compatible among themselves. That is a proposition whose dem-

onstration I cannot give without having to explain the fundamentals of the characteristic at length. But if that is granted, it follows that God's nature, which contains all simple forms taken absolutely, is possible. Now, we have proven above that God exists, as long as he is possible. Therefore, he exists. And that is what needed to be demonstrated.

## Letter to Molanus (?), On God and the Soul (ca. 1679)

[...] Someone might tell me that Descartes established the existence of God and the immortality of soul extremely well. But I fear that we are deceived by fine words, since Descartes's God, or perfect being, is not a God like the one we imagine or hope for, that is, a God just and wise, doing everything possible for the good of creatures. Rather, Descartes's God is something approaching the God of Spinoza, namely, the principle of things and a certain supreme power or primitive nature that puts everything into motion [action] and does everything that can be done. Descartes's God has neither *will* nor *understanding*, since according to Descartes he does not have the *good* as object of the will, nor the *true* as object of the understanding. Also, he does not want his God to act in accordance with some end; this is why he eliminates the search for final causes from philosophy, under the clever pretext that we are not capable of knowing God's ends.[7] On the other hand, Plato has nicely shown that if God acts in accordance with wisdom, since God is the author of things, then the true physics consists in knowing the ends and uses of things.[8] For science consists in knowing reasons, and the reasons for what was created by an understanding are the final causes or plans of the understanding that made them. These are apparent in their use and function, which is why considering the use parts have is so helpful in anatomy. That is why a God like Descartes's allows us no consolation other than that of patience through strength. Descartes tells

---

prioris." Leibniz's statement, "arguments in proper form do not always bear the stamp of *Barbara Celarent*," indicates that there are valid arguments whose validity cannot be established by syllogistic means.

7. On the claim that the world is good because God created it, and not vice versa, see Descartes's *Replies to Objections VI*. On the denial of final causes, see *Principles of Philosophy* I, 28; Meditation IV and the *Replies to Objections V*.
8. See Plato, *Phaedo*, 97–98.

us in some places that matter passes successively through all possible forms,[9] that is, that his God created everything that can be made, and passes successively through all possible combinations, following a necessary and fated order. But for this doctrine, the necessity of matter alone would be sufficient, or rather, his God is merely this necessity or this principle of necessity acting as it can in matter. Therefore, it is impossible to believe that this God cares for intelligent creatures any more than he does for the others; each creature will be happy or unhappy depending upon how it finds itself engulfed in these great currents or vortices. Descartes has good reason to recommend, instead of felicity, patience without hope.

But one of those good people among the Cartesians, deceived by the beautiful words of his master, will tell me that Descartes has, however, quite nicely established the immortality of the soul, and consequently, a better life. When I hear such things, I am surprised by the ease with which one can deceive people merely by playing around with pleasing words, though corrupting their meaning. For as hypocrites misuse piety, heretics the Scriptures, and seditious people the word "freedom," so Descartes has misused the important words, "existence of God," and "immortality of the soul." We must therefore elucidate this mystery and show them that Descartes's immortality of soul is worth no more than his God. I believe that I will not bring pleasure to some, for people are normally unhappy to be awakened from a pleasant dream. But what should I do? Descartes wishes us to uproot false thoughts before introducing true ones.[10] We must follow his example; and I believe I would be doing the public a service if I could disabuse people of such dangerous doctrines.

I therefore assert that the immortality of soul, as established by Descartes, is useless and could not console us in any way. For let us suppose that soul is a substance and that no substance perishes; given that, the soul would not perish and, in fact, nothing would perish in nature. But just as matter, the soul will change in its way, and just as the matter that composes a man has at other times composed other plants and animals, similarly, this soul might be immortal in fact, but it might pass through a thousand changes without remembering what it once was.[11] But this immortality without memory is completely useless to morality, for it upsets all reward and punishment. What good would it do you to become the King of China under the condition that you forget what you once were? Would that not be the same as if God created a King of China at the same time as he destroyed you? That is why, in order to satisfy the hopes of humankind, we must prove that the God who governs all is wise and just, and that he will allow nothing to be without reward and without punishment; these are the great foundations of morality. But the doctrine of a God who does not act for the good, and of a soul which is immortal without any memory, serves only to deceive simple people and to undo spiritual people.

I could even show some defects in Descartes's supposed demonstration, for there is still much to be proven in order to complete it. But I believe that it would be useless to bother with this now, since these demonstrations would not be of much use for anything even if they were good demonstrations, as I have just proven. [. . .]

---

9. See Descartes, *Principles of Philosophy* III, 47; and Descartes to Mersenne, January 9, 1639. These seem to be the only passages in which Descartes makes this claim. The letter was published in Leibniz's lifetime and could well have been known to him.

10. See Descartes, Meditation I.

11. Leibniz seems to have in mind the account of memory that Descartes gives in his *Treatise of Man*; see Descartes, *Treatise of Man*, trans. Hall (Cambridge, Mass.: Harvard University Press, 1972), pp. 87ff. There Descartes conceives of memory as brain traces that cause the soul, a mental substance distinct from the brain, to perceive representations of past events. So, when a person dies and the immortal soul separates from the mortal body, it would seem that all memory would be lost. However, it should be noted that Descartes also recognizes a kind of memory that pertains to the soul alone, a kind of memory that is not lost in death. See, for example, *The Philosophical Writings of Descartes*, Vol. III, The Correspondence, ed. J. Cottingham, R. Stoothoff, D. Murdoch, and A. Kenny (Cambridge: Cambridge University Press, 1991), pp. 146–48, 151, 216, 232–33. Leibniz does not seem to take this view into account.

# Blaise Pascal, *Pensées* (1670), "The Wager"[1]

*Blaise Pascal was born in Clermont-Ferrand in 1623 and died in Paris in 1662. During his short life, he worked on mathematics, physics, and religion. He devoted himself to God and the Jansenist cause after having a mystical experience on November 23, 1654. In 1658, he began the composition of an* Apologia for the Christian Religion, *unfinished at his death and published in its incomplete form in 1670 as* Pensées. *In his lifetime, Pascal was famous for the polemical Jansenist* Provincial Letters *(1656–57); posthumously, he is best known for the* Pensées, *including the notorious "Wager." In part, the* Pensées *can be seen as a critique of Descartes, whom Pascal called "useless and uncertain"* (Pensées, *nos. 84 and 887). Pascal's tenets place him in opposition to philosophers who offer metaphysical demonstrations of God's existence: "All those who have claimed to know God and to prove his existence without Jesus Christ had only empty proofs to offer. . . . [W]ithout Scripture, without original sin, without the necessary mediator, who was promised and came, it is impossible to prove God's existence absolutely, or to teach sound doctrine and sound morality"* (Pensées, *no. 189). Thus his opposition to Descartes is not surprising; his niece reported that he "could not forgive Descartes who wanted to do without God in all of philosophy, but could not avoid having him give the first nudge to set the world in motion; after that, he had no use at all for God"* (Pensées, *no. 1001). In the "Wager," Pascal does not, of course, offer proofs for the existence of God, but an argument that it is rational to believe that God exists and a procedure for believing it: behave as if he does.*[2]

Infinity—nothing.

Our soul is cast into the body, where it finds number, time, and dimensions; it reasons about these things and calls them "nature" or "necessity," and can believe nothing else.

Unity added to infinity does not increase infinity at all, any more than a foot added to an infinite length. The finite is annihilated in the presence of the infinite and becomes pure nothingness. So it is with our mind before God and with our justice before divine justice. Yet the disproportion between our justice and God's is not as great as that between unity and infinity.

God's justice must be as vast as his compassion. Now, his justice toward the damned is less vast and

---

1. Editors' title. Translated from the French by Roger Ariew.

2. For more about Pascal, see A. J. Krailsheimer, *Pascal* (Oxford: Oxford University Press, 1980); Krailsheimer is also one of the better English translators of the *Pensées*.

should be less shocking to us than his mercy toward the chosen.

We know that there is an infinite, but do not know its nature, just as we know it to be false that numbers are finite. It is therefore true that there is an infinity in number, but we do not know what it is. It is false that it is even, false that it is odd, for the addition of a unit does not change its nature. Yet it is a number, and every number is odd or even. (It is true that this is understood of every finite number.)

So we may well know that there is a God without knowing what he is.

Is there no substantial truth, seeing that there are so many true things which are not truth itself?

Thus we know the existence and nature of the finite, because we are finite and extended like it. We know the existence of the infinite and do not know its nature, because it has extension like us, but does not have limits as we do.

But we do not know either the existence or the nature of God, because he has neither extension nor limits.

But by faith we know his existence; in glory we shall know his nature.

Now, I have already shown that we can know the existence of a thing without knowing its nature.

Let us now speak according to our natural lights.

If there is a God, he is infinitely incomprehensible, since, having neither parts nor limits, he bears no relation to us. We are therefore incapable of knowing either what he is or whether he is. This being so, who will dare undertake to resolve the question? Not we, who bear no relation to him.

Who then will blame Christians for not being able to give rational grounds for their belief, they who profess a religion for which they cannot give rational grounds? They declare, in proclaiming it to the world, that it is a folly—*stultitiam*—and then you complain that they do not prove it. If they proved it, they would not be keeping their word. It is by lacking proofs that they are not lacking sense. "Yes, but although this excuses those who offer their religion in this way and removes the blame of putting it forward without rational grounds, it does not excuse those who accept

it." Let us then examine this point, and say: Either God is or he is not. But to which side shall we incline? Reason can determine nothing here. There is an infinite chaos that separates us. At the extremity of this infinite distance a game is being played in which heads or tails will turn up. How will you wager? You have no rational grounds for choosing either way or for rejecting either alternative.

Do not, then, blame as wrong those who have made a choice, for you know nothing of the matter. "No, but I will blame them for having made, not this choice, but a choice; for although the player who chooses heads is no more at fault than the other one, they are both in the wrong—the right thing is not to wager at all."

Yes; but you must wager. It is not optional. You are committed. Which will you choose then? Let us see. Since you must choose, let us see what is the less profitable option. You have two things to lose, the true and the good; and two things to stake, your reason and your will, your knowledge and your happiness; and your nature has two things to avoid, error and misery. Since you must necessarily choose, your reason is no more offended by choosing one rather than the other. This settles one point. But your happiness? Let us weigh the gain and the loss in calling heads that God exists. Let us assess the two cases. If you win, you win everything; if you lose, you lose nothing. Wager, then, without hesitation that he exists. "This is wonderful. Yes, I must wager; but perhaps I am wagering too much." Let us see: since there is an equal chance of winning and losing, if there were two lives to win for one, you could still wager. But what if there were three lives to win?

You would have to play (since you must necessarily play), and it would be foolish, when you are forced to play, not to risk your life to win three at a game in which there is an equal chance of losing and winning. But there is an eternity of life and happiness. This being so, if there were an infinity of chances, and only one in your favor, it would still be right to wager one life in order to win two; and you would be making the wrong choice, being obliged to play, if you refused to stake one life against three in a game in which, out of an infinity of chances, there is only one in your favor, if there were an infinite life of infinite happiness to be won. But here there is an infinite life of infinite happiness to be won, one chance of winning against a finite number of chances of losing, and what you stake is finite. All bets are off wherever there is an infinity and wherever there is not an infinite number of chances of losing against the chance of winning. There is no time to hesitate, you must give everything. And thus, when you are forced to play, you must renounce reason to preserve life, rather than risk it for an infinite gain which is as likely to happen as is a loss amounting to nothing.

It is no use saying that it is uncertain whether you will win, that it is certain you are taking a risk, and that the infinite distance between the certainty of what you are risking and the uncertainty of what you stand to gain makes the finite good you are certainly staking equal to the infinite good which is uncertain. It is not so. All players take a certain risk for an uncertain gain, and yet they take a certain finite risk for an uncertain finite gain without sinning against reason. It is not true that there is an infinite distance between the certain risk and the uncertain gain. Indeed, there is an infinity between the certainty of winning and the certainty of losing. But the uncertainty of winning is proportional to the certainty of what is at risk in proportion to the chances of winning and losing. Hence, if there are as many chances on one side as on the other, you are playing for even odds, and then the certainty of what you are risking is equal to the uncertainty of what you may win — so far is it from being infinitely distant. Thus, our proposition is infinitely powerful, in which the stakes are finite in a game where the chances of winning and losing are even, and the infinite to be won.

This is conclusive and if people are capable of any truth, this is it.

"I confess it, I admit it. But, still, is there no means of seeing what is in the cards?" Yes, Scripture and the rest, etc. "Yes, but my hands are tied and my mouth is shut; I am forced to wager, and am not free. I have not been released and I am made in such a way that I cannot believe. What, then, would you have me do?" True. But at least realize that your inability to believe comes from your passions, since reason brings you to this and yet you cannot believe. Work, then, on convincing yourself, not by adding more proofs of God's existence, but by diminishing your passions. You would like to find faith and do not know the way; you would like to be cured of unbelief and ask for the remedies. Learn from those who were bound like you, and who now wager all their goods. These are people who know the way you wish to follow, and who are cured of the illness you wish to be cured. Follow the way by which they began: They acted as if they believed, took holy water, had masses said, etc. This will make you believe naturally and blunt your edges. "But this is what I am afraid of." And why? What do you have to lose? But to show you that it is the way, this diminishes the passions which are your great obstacles, etc.

## End of This Discourse

Now, what harm will come to you by taking this side? You will be faithful, honest, humble, grateful, generous, a sincere, true friend. . . . Certainly you will not be taken by unhealthy pleasures, by glory and by luxury, but will you not have others?

I will tell you that as a result you will gain in this life, and that, at each step you take on this road, you will see such a great certainty of gain and so much nothingness in what you risk, that you will at last recognize that you have wagered for something certain and infinite, for which you have given nothing.

"Oh! This discourse moves me, charms me, etc." If this discourse pleases you and seems cogent, know that it is made by a man who has knelt, both before and after it, in prayer to that being, infinite and without parts, before whom he submits all he has, so that he might bring your being to submit all you have for your own good and for his glory, and that thus strength may be reconciled with abjectness.

# 2. SPINOZA'S *ETHICS* AND ASSOCIATED TEXTS

Baruch Spinoza was born in Amsterdam in 1632. His parents had emigrated from Portugal in 1622; they were descendants of Sephardic Jews who, like all other Iberian peninsula Jews, had been forcibly converted to Catholicism many generations earlier. These "converts" who later reconverted flooded the newly independent Republic of the Netherlands and created an intellectually turbulent community of individuals whose newly expressed Jewish identity was intermixed with their Catholic origins and culture. Given the heterogeneity of this community, doctrinal tensions were prevalent, and excommunication from the synagogue became a fairly common occurrence. In Amsterdam, Spinoza went to a rabbinical school, where he learned Hebrew and read the works of Jewish thinkers, such as Moses Maimonides. He also learned Latin and sought instruction in natural philosophy and in the philosophy of Descartes. In 1656, he was excommunicated from the Jewish community, and in 1660, the Jewish authorities petitioned the Amsterdam municipal government to expel him from the city, giving as their reason that he was a menace to "all piety and morals." He moved to a village south of Amsterdam, where he supported himself by making lenses. In 1663, he moved to a town near The Hague and ultimately resided in The Hague itself until his death in 1677. During his lifetime, he published *Metaphysical Thoughts* and *Descartes' Principles of Philosophy Parts I and II, Demonstrated in the Geometrical Manner* (both 1663). He also published *Theologico-Political Treatise* in 1670, under the name of a fictitious publisher in Hamburg. The collection of his works published posthumously in 1677 included *Ethics, Demonstrated in Geometrical Order*.[1]

By the middle of the seventeenth century, philosophers had a number of fully developed philosophical systems available as alternatives to the previously dominant scholasticism. Among the more prominent ones were Hobbes's materialism (and empiricism) and Descartes's dualism (and innatism). Spinoza obviously had an affinity with Descartes's manner of philosophizing (though not with his method of doubt). After all, his first publication was a geometrical exposition of the first two parts of Descartes's *Principles*.[2] Spinoza was taken with the geometrical method and its associated perspective of the whole as opposed to

---

1. Spinoza's philosophical works and correspondence are available in English translation. For more on Spinoza, see Edwin Curley, *Behind the Geometrical Method* (Princeton: Princeton University Press, 1988); Yirmiyahu Yovel, *Spinoza and Other Heretics*, 2 vols. (Princeton: Princeton University Press, 1989); or Don Garrett, ed., *Cambridge Companion to Spinoza* (Cambridge: Cambridge University Press, 1996).
2. See Section 1 in this book.

the usual point of view of the part (cf. Letter 32 to Oldenburg, about the worm in the blood). However, even in his representation of Descartes's *Principles*, he allowed glimpses of his disagreements with Descartes; as he said to Oldenburg (Letter 2), Descartes has "gone far astray from knowledge of the first cause and origin of all things"; he has "failed to achieve an understanding of the true nature of the human mind"; and he has "never grasped the true cause of error." Spinoza's *Ethics*, then, is two steps removed from Descartes's *Principles*—Spinoza substituting his own principles and, as its subtitle indicates, exhibiting them in a geometrical presentation.

The geometrical exposition of the *Ethics* is often a source of interpretive difficulty for students of Spinoza. It is tempting to think of the work as abstract, disconnected arguments, instead of thinking about it as a paradigm of seventeenth-century thought, imbued with the concerns and aspirations of a thinker grounded in the problems of his days and writing for an audience of his peers. The geometrical apparatus also tends to make it difficult to comprehend Spinoza's philosophy itself. To conceive just a portion of those obstacles, one needs only to imagine trying to grasp Cartesian philosophy without having recourse to the *Meditations* or *Discourse*, using only the appendix to the *Second Set of Replies*, "arranged in geometrical fashion." Interestingly, it was generally agreed at the time that geometrical expositions are not best for understanding a particular philosophy. Descartes claimed that synthesis, the method of demonstration that "uses a long series of definitions, postulates, and axioms, theorems, and problems . . . is not as satisfying as the method of analysis, nor does it engage the minds of those who are eager to learn, since it does not show how the thing was discovered."[3] Spinoza agreed. He called the geometric order cumbersome (or prolix), and sometimes set it aside "so that everyone may more easily perceive" what he thinks;[4] this remark echoes an earlier one in which he said that he would have presented Descartes's *Principles* in mathematical order if he "had not thought that such prolixity would have

impeded" the understanding of such things "which should be seen as clearly as though presented in a picture."[5] So, although grateful to Spinoza for his frequent interruptions of the geometric order and for his extremely useful summations (the *scholia*), we might wish that he had provided, along with the *Ethics*, a treatise that would have revealed his doctrines according to an order of discovery.

Lacking such a treatise, one is required to construct Spinoza's steps toward the *Ethics*. Useful toward that purpose is his exposition of Descartes's *Principles*, especially his formulations of Descartes's definitions.[6] Spinoza's correspondence is also always helpful in this respect; his "Letter on the Infinite" reads more like an article for a scholarly journal than an epistle to a friendly correspondent. In any case, one way of understanding Spinoza's path of discovery is through the contrasts one can draw between his philosophy and Descartes's. Key in that enterprise is his infinitism. Spinoza's doctrine of the infinite is a radical departure from Descartes's fairly consistent finitism about everything except God, who is then termed incomprehensible, that is, beyond our mind's grasp. For Spinoza, conversely, our intellect is capable of reaching absolute knowledge, because pure understanding has the same nature in both humans and God. Another key involves Spinoza's ruminations on infinite substance and the way he interprets what Descartes would have called mental and corporeal substance. The result is a metaphysics that attempts to cleave a middle ground between Descartes's dualism and Hobbes's materialism, that is, "dual aspect" theory, with the mental and corporeal realms being two of the attributes of infinite substance, and the order and connection of ideas being the same as the order and connection of things. In the *Ethics*, Spinoza begins with a metaphysics of God and substance, and continues with the nature of the mind and its affects; this topic leads him to discuss human bondage and ultimately human freedom—or the power of the intellect. It is the end of Spinoza's journey, that is, an intellectualist morality, that gives the work its title of *Ethics*.

3. See Section 1 in this book, Descartes, *Replies to the Second Set of Objections*.
4. *Ethics IV*, prop. 18.

5. "Prolegomenon" to *Descartes's Principles* (see Section 1 in this book.)
6. See Section 1 in this book.

# Thomas Hobbes, *Leviathan* (1651)[1]

*Thomas Hobbes (1588–1679) spent most of his life as tutor, secretary, and financial manager in the service of the earls of Devonshire and Newcastle. His extensive travels in Europe brought him into contact with many of the leading thinkers of the time, including Galileo, whom he visited in 1636, and Mersenne, to whose circle he belonged while in Paris in 1635, and then again when in exile in Paris from 1640 to 1651. He had met the elderly Bacon in the 1620s. Hobbes contributed the* Third Set of Objections *to Descartes's* Meditations *in 1641 and began to publish his own philosophical system,* Elements of Philosophy, *first issuing* Section Three, Concerning Government and Society (De Cive) *in 1642, then* The First Section, Concerning Body (De Corpore) *in 1655 and* Section Two, Concerning Human Nature (De Homine) *in 1658. The work for which he is best known, in which he defends his materialist philosophy and rejects Anglicanism, is* Leviathan, or the Matter, Forme, and Power of a Commonwealth Ecclesiasticall and Civill *(1651).[2]*

## The Introduction.

Nature (the art by which God has made and governs the world) is also so imitated in this by the *art* of man, as in many other things, that it can make an artificial animal. For seeing life is but a motion of limbs, the beginning of which is in some principal part within, why may we not say that all *automata* (engines that move themselves by springs and wheels as does a watch) have an artificial life? For what is the *heart*, but a *spring*; and the *nerves*, but so many *strings*; and the *joints*, but so many *wheels*, giving motion to the whole body, such as was intended by the artificer? *Art* goes yet further, imitating that rational and most excellent work of nature, *man*. For by art is created that great LEVIATHAN called a COMMONWEALTH, or STATE (in Latin CIVITAS), which is but an artificial man, though of greater stature and strength than the natural, for whose protection and defense it was intended, and in which the *sovereignty* is an artificial soul, as giving life and motion to the whole body; the *magistrates*, and other *officers* of judi-

1. From *The English Works of Thomas Hobbes of Malmesbury*, ed. Sir William Molesworth (London, 1839–45), 11 vols., English, modified.
2. Hobbes's works are available in the original English or in translation. For more on Hobbes, see A. P. Martinich, *The Two Gods of Leviathan* (Cambridge: Cambridge University Press,

1992); Richard Tuck, *Hobbes* (Oxford: Oxford University Press, 1989); Steve Shapin and Simon Schaffer, *Leviathan and the Air-Pump* (Princeton: Princeton University Press, 1985); and Tom Sorell, ed., *Cambridge Companion to Hobbes* (Cambridge: Cambridge University Press, 1996).

cature and execution, artificial *joints*; *reward* and *punishment* (by which fastened to the seat of the sovereignty every joint and member is moved to perform his duty) are the *nerves*, that do the same in the body natural; the *wealth* and *riches* of all the particular members are the *strength*; *salus populi* (the people's safety) its *business*; *counselors*, by whom all things needful for it to know are suggested unto it, are the *memory*; *equity*, and *laws*, an artificial *reason* and *will*; *concord, health*; *sedition, sickness*; and *civil war, death*. Lastly, the *pacts* and *covenants*, by which the parts of this body politic were at first made, set together, and united, resemble that *fiat*, or the *let us make man*, pronounced by God in the creation.

To describe the nature of this artificial man, I will consider

First, the *matter* of this, and the *artificer*—both of which is *man*.

Secondly, *how*, and by what *covenants* it is made; what are the *rights* and *just power* or *authority* of a *sovereign*; and what it is that *preserves* and *dissolves* it.

Thirdly, what is a *Christian commonwealth*.

Lastly, what is the *kingdom of darkness*.

Concerning the first, there is a saying much usurped of late, that *wisdom* is acquired, not by reading of *books*, but of *men*. Consequently to which end, those persons that for the most part can give no other proof of being wise take great delight to show what they think they have read in men, by uncharitable censures of one another behind their backs. But there is another saying not of late understood, by which they might learn truly to read one another, if they would take the pains; and that is, *nosce teipsum*, read thyself: which was not meant, as it is now used, to countenance, either the barbarous state of men in power towards their inferiors, or to encourage men

of low degree to a saucy behavior towards their betters, but to teach us that for the similitude of the thoughts and passions of one man, to the thoughts and passions of another, whoever looks into himself, and considers what he does, when he does *think, opine, reason, hope, fear*, etc., and upon what grounds, he shall as a result read and know what are the thoughts and passions of all other men upon the like occasions. I say the similitude of *passions*, which are the same in all men, *desire, fear, hope*, etc., not the similitude of the objects of the passions, which are the *things desired, feared, hoped*, etc., for these the constitution individual, and particular education, do so vary, and they are so easy to be kept from our knowledge, that the characters of man's heart, blotted and confounded as they are with dissembling, lying, counterfeiting, and erroneous doctrines, are legible only to him who searches hearts. And though by men's actions we do discover their design sometimes, yet to do it without comparing them with our own, and distinguishing all circumstances by which the case may come to be altered, is to decipher without a key, and be for the most part deceived, by too much trust, or by too much diffidence, as he who reads is himself a good or evil man.

But let one man read another by his actions ever so perfectly, it serves him only with his acquaintance, which are but few. He who is to govern a whole nation must read in himself, not this or that particular man, but mankind, which though it is hard to do, harder than to learn any language or science, yet when I shall have set down my own reading orderly, and perspicuously, the pains left another, will be only to consider, if he also does not find the same in himself. For this kind of doctrine admits no other demonstration.

# Part I. Of Man

## Chapter 1. Of *Sense*.

Concerning the thoughts of man, I will consider them first *singly*, and afterwards in *train*, or dependence upon one another. *Singly*, they are every one a *representation* or *appearance* of some quality or other accident of a body without us, which is commonly called an *object*—which object works on the eyes, ears, and other parts of a man's body, and by diversity of working, produces diversity of appearances.

The origin of them all is that which we call Sense. (For there is no conception in a man's mind, which has not at first, totally, or by parts, been begotten upon the organs of sense.) The rest are derived from that origin.

To know the natural cause of sense is not very necessary to the business now in hand; and I have elsewhere written of the same at large. Nevertheless, to fill each part of my present method, I will briefly deliver the same in this place.

The cause of sense is the external body, or object, which presses the organ proper to each sense, either immediately, as in taste and touch, or mediately, as in seeing, hearing, and smelling; this pressure, by the mediation of nerves and other strings and membranes of the body, continued inwards to the brain and heart, causes there a resistance, or counterpressure, or endeavor of the heart, to deliver itself; this endeavor, because *outward*, seems to be some matter without. And this *seeming*, or *fancy*, is that which men call *sense*, and consists, as to the eye, in a *light*, or *color figured*; to the ear, in a *sound*; to the nostril, in an *odor*; to the tongue and palate, in a *savor*; and to the rest of the body, in *heat*, *cold*, *hardness*, *softness*, and such other qualities as we discern by *feeling*. All these qualities called *sensible* are in the object that causes them but so many several motions of the matter, by which it presses our organs diversely. Neither in us that are pressed are they anything else but diverse motions (for motion produces nothing but motion). But their appearance to us is fancy, the same waking as dreaming. And as pressing, rubbing, or striking the eye makes us fancy a light, and pressing the ear produces a din, so also do the bodies we see or hear produce the same by their strong, though unobserved action. For if those colors and sounds were in the bodies, or objects that cause them, they could not be severed from them, as by glasses, and in echoes by reflection, we see they are, where we know the thing we see is in one place, the appearance in another. And though at some certain distance, the real and very object seem invested with the fancy it begets in us; yet still the object is one thing, the image or fancy is another, so that sense in all cases is nothing else but original fancy, caused (as I have said) by the pressure, that is, by the motion of external things upon our eyes, ears, and other organs ordained to it.

But the philosophy schools through all the universities of Christendom, grounded upon certain texts of *Aristotle*, teach another doctrine, and say, for the cause of *vision*, that the thing seen sends forth on every side a *visible species* (in English) a *visible show*, *apparition*, or *aspect*, or *a being seen*, the receiving of which into the eye is *seeing*. And for the cause of *hearing*, that the thing heard sends forth an *audible* species, that is, an *audible aspect*, or *audible being seen*, which entering at the ear makes *hearing*. For the cause of *understanding* also, they say the thing understood sends forth *intelligible species*, that is, an *intelligible being seen* which coming into the understanding makes us understand. I do not say this as disapproving of the use of universities; but because I am to speak hereafter of their office in a commonwealth, I must let you see on all occasions by the way what things would be amended in them, among which the frequency of insignificant speech is one.

## Chapter 2. Of *Imagination*.

That when a thing lies still, unless something else stirs it, it will lie still forever is a truth that no man doubts of. But that when a thing is in motion, it will eternally be in motion, unless something else stops it, though the reason is the same (namely, that nothing can change itself), is not so easily assented to. For men measure, not only other men, but all other things, by themselves, and because they find themselves subject after motion to pain, and lassitude, think everything else grows weary of motion, and seeks repose of its own accord, little considering whether it is not some other motion in which that desire of rest they find in themselves consists. From hence it is that the schools say heavy bodies fall downwards out of an appetite to rest, and to conserve their nature in that place which is most proper for them, ascribing appetite and knowledge of what is good for their conservation (which is more than man has) to inanimate things, absurdly.

When a body is once in motion, it moves (unless something else hinders it) eternally; and whatever hinders it cannot in an instant, but in time and by degrees, quite extinguish it. And as we see in the water, though the wind ceases, the waves do not give over rolling for a long time after, so also it happens in that motion, which is made in the internal parts of a man, then, when he sees, dreams, etc. For after the object is removed or the eye shut, we still retain an image of the thing seen, though more obscure than when we see it. And this, the Latins call *imagination*, from the image made in seeing, and apply the same, though improperly, to all the other senses. But the Greeks call it *fancy*, which signifies *appearance*, and is as proper to one sense as to another. IMAGINATION therefore is nothing but *decaying sense*, and is found in men and many other living creatures, as well sleeping, as waking.

The decay of sense in men waking is not the decay of the motion made in sense, but an obscuring of it, in such manner as the light of the sun obscures the light of the stars — which stars do no less exercise their virtue, by which they are visible, in the day, than in the night. But because among many strokes which our eyes, ears, and other organs receive from external bodies, only the predominant is sensible; therefore the light of the sun being predominant, we are not affected with the action of the stars. And any object being removed from our eyes, though the impression it made in us remains, yet other objects more present succeeding and working on us, the imagination of the past is obscured and made weak, as the voice of a man is in the noise of the day. From this it follows that the longer the time is, after the sight or sense of any object, the weaker is the imagination. For the continual change of man's body destroys in time the parts which in sense were moved, so that distance of time and of place has one and the same effect in us. For as at a great distance of place, that which we look at appears dim and without distinction of the smaller parts, and as voices grow weak and inarticulate, so also, after great distance of time, our imagination of the past is weak, and we lose (for example) many particular streets of cities we have seen, and many particular circumstances of actions. This *decaying sense*, when we would express the thing itself (I mean fancy itself), we call *imagination*, as I said before, but

when we would express the *decay*, and signify that the sense is fading, old, and past, it is called *memory*. Thus, *imagination* and *memory* are but one thing which for diverse considerations have diverse names.

Much memory, or memory of many things, is called *experience*. Again, imagination being only of those things which have been formerly perceived by sense, either all at once, or by parts at several times, the former (which is the imagining the whole object, as it was presented to the sense) is *simple imagination* — as when one imagines a man, or horse, which he has seen before. The other is *compounded* — as when from the sight of a man at one time, and of a horse at another, we conceive in our mind a Centaur. So when a man compounds the image of his own person with the image of the actions of another man, as when a man imagines himself a *Hercules* or an *Alexander* (which happens often to those who are much taken with reading of romances), it is a compound imagination and properly but a fiction of the mind. There are also other imaginations that arise in men (though waking) from the great impression made in sense — as from gazing upon the sun, the impression leaves an image of the sun before our eyes a long time after, and from being long and vehemently attent upon geometrical figures, a man shall in the dark (though awake) have the images of lines and angles before his eyes — which kind of fancy has no particular name, as being a thing that does not commonly fall into men's discourse.

The imaginations of those who sleep are those we call *dreams*. And these also (as all other imaginations) have been before, either totally or by parcels in the sense. And because in sense the brain and nerves, which are the necessary organs of sense, are so benumbed in sleep, as not easily be moved by the action of external objects, there can happen in sleep no imagination, and therefore no dream, but what proceeds from the agitation of the inward parts of man's body. These inward parts, for the connection they have with the brain and other organs, when they are distempered, do keep the same in motion — by which the imaginations there formerly made appear as if a man were waking, saving that the organs of sense being now benumbed, so as there is no new object, which can master and obscure them with a more vigorous impression, a dream must necessarily be more clear, in this silence of sense, than are our waking thoughts. And hence it comes to pass that it is a hard matter, and by many thought impossible, to distinguish exactly between sense and dreaming. For my part, when I consider that in dreams, I do not often nor constantly think of the same persons, places, objects, and actions that I do waking, nor remember so long a train of coherent thoughts, dreaming, as at other times; and because waking I often observe the absurdity of dreams, but never dream of the absurdities of my waking thoughts, I am well satisfied that being awake I know I do not dream, though when I dream, I think myself awake.

And seeing dreams are caused by the distemper of some of the inward parts of the body, diverse distempers must necessarily cause different dreams. And hence it is that lying cold breeds dreams of fear and raises the thought and image of some fearful object (the motion from the brain to the inner parts, and from the inner parts to the brain being reciprocal), and that as anger causes heat in some parts of the body, when we are awake, so when we sleep the overheating of the same parts causes anger, and raises up the imagination of an enemy in the brain. In the same manner as natural kindness, when we are awake, causes desire, and desire makes heat in certain other parts of the body, so also, too much heat in those parts, while we sleep, raises an imagination of some kindness shown in the brain. In sum, our dreams are the reverse of our waking imaginations, the motion when we are awake, beginning at one end, and when we dream, at another.

The most difficult discerning of a man's dream, from his waking thoughts, is then, when by some accident we do not observe that we have slept, which easily happens to a man full of fearful thoughts and whose conscience is much troubled, and who sleeps, without the circumstances of going to bed, or putting off his clothes, as one who nods in a chair. For he who takes pains, and industriously lays himself to sleep, in case any uncouth and exorbitant fancy come unto him, cannot easily think it other than a dream. We read of *Marcus Brutus* (one who had his life given him by *Julius Caesar*, and was also his favorite, and notwithstanding murdered him), how at *Philippi*, the night before he gave battle to *Augustus Caesar*, he saw a fearful apparition, which is commonly related by historians as a vision, but considering the circumstances, one may easily judge to have been but a short dream. For sitting in his tent, pensive and troubled with the horror of his rash act, it was not hard for him, slumbering in the cold, to dream of that which most frightened him—which fear, as by degrees it made him wake, so also it must necessarily make the apparition vanish by degrees; and having no assurance that he slept, he could have no cause to think it a dream or anything but a vision. And this is no very rare accident; for even those who are perfectly awake, if they are timorous, and superstitious, possessed with fearful tales, and alone in the dark, are subject to the like fancies, and believe they see spirits and dead men's ghosts walking in churchyards; whereas it is either their fancy only, or else the knavery of such persons, as make use of such superstitious fear to pass disguised in the night to places they would not be known to haunt.

From this ignorance of how to distinguish dreams and other strong fancies from vision and sense did arise the greatest part of the religion of the Gentiles in time past, who worshipped satyrs, fawns, nymphs, and the like, and nowadays the opinion that rude people have of fairies, ghosts, and goblins, and of the power of witches. For as for witches, I do not think that their witchcraft is any real power, but yet that they are justly punished for the false belief they have that they can do such mischief, joined with their purpose to do it if they can, their trade being nearer to a new religion than to a craft or science. And for fairies and walking ghosts, the opinion of them has I think been on purpose, either taught, or not confuted, to keep in credit the use of exorcism, of crosses, of holy water, and other such inventions of ghostly men. Nevertheless, there is no doubt but God can make unnatural apparitions. But that he does it so often as men need to fear such things more than they fear the stay or change of the course of nature, which he also can stay and change, is no point of Christian faith. But evil men under the pretext that God can do anything are so bold as to say anything when it serves their turn, though they think it untrue; it is the part of a wise man to believe them no further than right reason makes that which they say appear credible. If this superstitious fear of spirits were taken away, and with it prognostics from dreams, false prophecies, and many other things depending on it, by which crafty ambitious persons abuse the simple people, men would be much more fitted than they are for civil obedience.

And this ought to be the work of the schools; but they rather nourish such doctrine. For (not knowing what imagination, or the senses are) what they receive, they teach, some saying that imaginations arise of themselves and have no cause, others that they arise most commonly from the will, and that good thoughts are blown (inspired) into a man by God, and evil thoughts by the Devil, or that good thoughts are poured (infused) into a man by God, and evil ones by the Devil. Some say the senses receive the species of things and deliver them to the common sense, and the common sense delivers them over to the fancy, and the fancy to the memory, and the memory to the judgment, like handing of things from one to another, with many words making nothing understood.

The imagination that is raised in man (or any other creature endowed with the faculty of imagining) by words or other voluntary signs is what we generally call *understanding*, and is common to man and beast. For a dog by custom will understand the call or the rating of his master, and so will many other beasts. That understanding which is peculiar to man is the understanding not only his will, but his conceptions and thoughts, by the sequel and contexture of the names of things into affirmations, negations, and other forms of speech; and of this kind of understanding I shall speak hereafter.

## Chapter 3. Of the Consequence or *Train* of Imaginations.

By *Consequence*, or TRAIN of thoughts, I understand that succession of one thought to another, which is called (to distinguish it from discourse in words) *mental discourse*.

When a man thinks on anything whatsoever, his next thought after is not altogether so casual as it seems to be. Not every thought to every thought succeeds indifferently. But as we have no imagination of which we have not formerly had sense, in whole or in parts, so we have no transition from one imagination to another of which we never had the like before in our senses. The reason of which is this: all fancies are motions within us, relics of those made in the sense, and those motions that immediately succeeded one another in the sense, continue also together after sense, inasmuch as the former coming again to take place and be predominant, the latter follows, by coherence of the matter moved, in such manner as water upon a plain table is drawn which way any one part of it is guided by the finger. But because in sense, sometimes one thing, sometimes another succeeds to one and the same thing perceived, it comes to pass in time that, in the imagining of anything, there is no certainty what we shall imagine next; only this is certain, it shall be something that succeeded the same before, at one time or another.

This train of thoughts, or mental discourse, is of two sorts. The first is *unguided, without design*, and inconstant, in which there is no passionate thought to govern and direct those that follow to itself, as the end and scope of some desire or other passion; in this case the thoughts are said to wander, and seem impertinent one to another, as in a dream. Such are commonly the thoughts of men that are not only without company, but also without care of anything, though even then their thoughts are as busy as at other times, but without harmony—as the sound which a lute out of tune would yield to any man, or in tune, to one that could not play. And yet in this wild ranging of the mind, a man may oftentimes perceive the way of it and the dependence of one thought upon another. For in a discourse of our present civil war, what could seem more impertinent than to ask (as one did) what was the value of a Roman penny? Yet the coherence was manifest enough to me. For the thought of the war introduced the thought of delivering up the king to his enemies; the thought of that brought in the thought of the delivering up of Christ; and that again the thought of the 30 pence, which was the price of that treason; and in this way easily followed that malicious question, and all this in a moment of time, for thought is quick.

The second is more constant, as being *regulated* by some desire and design. For the impression made by such things as we desire or fear is strong and permanent, or (if it ceases for a time) of quick return; so strong it is sometimes, as to hinder and break our sleep. From desire arises the thought of some means we have seen produce the like of that which we aim at; and from the thought of that, the thought of means to that mean; and so continually, until we come to some beginning within our own power. And because the end, by the greatness of the impression, comes often to mind, in case our thoughts begin to wander, they are quickly again reduced into the way; this, observed by one of the seven wise men, made him give men this precept, which is now worn out, *Respice finem*—that is to say, in all your actions, look often upon what you would have, as the thing that directs all your thoughts in the way to attain it.

The train of regulated thoughts is of two kinds: One, when of an effect imagined, we seek the causes or means that produce it; and this is common to man and beast. The other is when, imagining anything whatsoever, we seek all the possible effects that can be produced by it—that is to say, we imagine what we can do with it, when we have it. I have not at any time seen any sign of this, but in man only; for this is a curiosity hardly incident to the nature of any living creature that has no other passion but sensual, such as are hunger, thirst, lust, and anger. In sum, the discourse of the mind, when it is governed by design, is nothing but *seeking*, or the faculty of invention, which the Latins called *sagacitas* and *solertia*, a hunting out of the causes, of some effect, present or past, or of the effects of some present or past cause. Sometimes a man seeks what he has lost; and from that place and time in which he misses it, his mind runs back, from place to place, and time to time, to find where and when he had it—that is to say, to find some certain and limited time and place in which to begin a method of seeking. Again, from this his thoughts run over the same places and times, to find what action or other occasion might make him lose it. This we call *remembrance*, or calling to mind; the Latins call it *reminiscentia*, as it were a reconsideration of our former actions.

Sometimes a man knows a determinate place within the compass of which he is to seek, and then his thoughts run over all the parts of it, in the same manner as one would sweep a room to find a jewel, or as a spaniel ranges the field until he finds a scent, or as a man should run over the alphabet to start a rhyme.

Sometimes a man desires to know the event of an action, and then he thinks of some like action past, and its events one after another, supposing like events will follow like actions—as he who foresees what will become of a criminal reconsiders what he has seen follow on the like crime before, having this order of thoughts: the crime, the officer, the prison, the judge, and the gallows. This kind of thought is called *foresight*, and *prudence*, or *providence*, and sometimes *wisdom*, though such conjecture, through the difficulty of observing all circumstances, is very fallacious. But this is certain: By how much one man has more experience of things past than another, by so much also he is more prudent, and his expectations the more seldom fail him. The *present* only has a being in nature; things *past* have a being in the memory only; but things to *come* have no being at all, the *future* being but a fiction of the mind, applying the sequels of actions past to the actions that are present— which with most certainty is done by him who has most experience, but not with certainty enough. And though it is called prudence when the event answers our expectation, yet in its own nature, it is but presumption. For the foresight of things to come, which is providence, belongs only to him by whose will they are to come. From him only, and supernaturally, proceeds prophecy. The best prophet naturally is the best guesser, and the best guesser, he who is most versed and studied in the matters he guesses at, for he has most *signs* to guess by.

A *sign* is the event antecedent of the consequent, and contrarily, the consequent of the antecedent, when the like consequences have been observed before; and the more often they have been observed, the less uncertain is the sign. And therefore he who has most experience in any kind of business has most signs by which to guess at the future time, and consequently is the most prudent, and so much more prudent than he who is new in that kind of business, as not to be equaled by any advantage of natural and extemporary wit, though perhaps many young men think the contrary.

Nevertheless it is not prudence that distinguishes man from beast. There are beasts that at a year old observe more and pursue that which is for their good more prudently than a child can do at ten.

As prudence is a *presumption* of the *future*, contracted from the *experience* of time *past*, so there is a presumption of things past taken from other things (not future but) past also. For he who has seen by what courses and degrees a flourishing state has first come into civil war and then to ruin, upon the sight of the ruins of any other state will guess the like war and the like courses have been there also. But this conjecture has the same uncertainty almost with the conjecture of the future, both being grounded only upon experience.

There is no other act of man's mind that I can remember, naturally planted in him so as to need no other thing to the exercise of it, but to be born a man, and live with the use of his five senses. Those other faculties, of which I shall speak by and by, and which seem proper to man only, are acquired and increased by study and industry, and of most men learned by instruction and discipline, and proceed all from the invention of words and speech. For besides sense, and thoughts, and the train of thoughts, the mind of man has no other motion, though by the help of speech and method, the same faculties may be improved to such a height as to distinguish men from all other living creatures.

Whatever we imagine is *finite*. Therefore, there is no idea or conception of anything we call *infinite*. No man can have in his mind an image of infinite magnitude, nor conceive infinite swiftness, infinite time, or infinite force, or infinite power. When we say anything is infinite, we signify only that we are not able to conceive the ends and bounds of the things named, having no conception of the thing, but of our own inability. And therefore the name of God is used, not to make us conceive him (for he is *incomprehensible*, and his greatness and power are inconceivable), but that we may honor him. Also because whatever (as I said before) we conceive has been perceived first by sense, either all at once or by parts; a man can have no thought representing anything not subject to sense. No man therefore can conceive anything, but he must conceive it in some place, and endowed with some determinate magnitude, and which may be divided into parts; nor that anything is all in this place, and all in another place at the same time; nor that two, or more things can be in one and the same place at once; for none of these things ever have, or can be incident to sense, but are absurd speeches, taken upon credit (without any signification at all) from deceived philosophers, and deceived or deceiving schoolmen.

## Chapter 4. Of *Speech*.

The invention of *printing*, though ingenious, compared with the invention of *letters*, is no great matter. But who was the first who found the use of letters is not known. He who first brought them into *Greece*, men say was *Cadmus*, the son of *Agenor*, king of Phoenicia. A profitable invention for continuing the memory of time past and the conjunction of mankind, dispersed into so many and distant regions of the earth, and in addition difficult, as proceeding from a watchful observation of the diverse motions of the tongue, palate, lips, and other organs of speech by which to make as many differences of characters to remember them. But the most noble and profitable invention of all other was that of SPEECH, consisting of *names* or *appellations*, and their connection by which men register their thoughts, recall them when they are past, and also declare them one to another for mutual utility and conversation, without which there had been among men, neither commonwealth, nor society, nor contract, nor peace, no more than among lions, bears, and wolves. The first author of speech was *God* himself, who instructed *Adam* how to name such creatures as he presented to his sight; for the Scripture goes no further in this matter. But this was sufficient to direct him to add more names, as the experience and use of the creatures should give him occasion, and to join them in such manner by degrees as to make himself understood, and so by succession of time, so much language might be gotten as he had found use for, though not so copious as an orator or philosopher has need of. For I do not find anything in the Scripture out of which, directly or by consequence, can be gathered that *Adam* was taught the names of all figures, numbers, measures, colors, sounds, fancies, relations, much less the names of words and speech, as *general, special, affirmative, negative, interrogative, optative, infinitive*, all which are useful, and least of all, of *entity, intentionality, quiddity*, and other insignificant words of the school.

But all this language gotten and augmented by *Adam* and his posterity was again lost at the tower of *Babel*, when by the hand of God every man was stricken, for his rebellion, with an oblivion of his former language. And being as a result forced to disperse themselves into several parts of the world, it must necessarily be that the diversity of tongues that now is proceeded by degrees from them, in such manner as need (the mother of all inventions) taught them, and in tract of time grew everywhere more copious.

The general use of speech is to transfer our mental discourse into verbal, or the train of our thoughts into a train of words, and that for two commodities, of which one is the registering of the consequences of our thoughts, which being apt to slip out of our memory and put us to a new labor, may again be recalled by such words as they were marked by. So that the first use of names is to serve for *marks*, or *notes* of remembrance. Another is when many use the same words to signify (by their connection and order) one to another, what they conceive or think of each matter, and also what they desire, fear, or have any other passion for. And for this use they are called *signs*. Special uses of speech are these: first, to register what by cogitation we find to be the cause of anything, present or past, and what we find things present or past may produce or effect—which in sum is acquiring of arts. Secondly, to show to others that knowledge which we have attained, which is to counsel and teach one another. Thirdly, to make known to others our wills and purposes that we may have the mutual help of one another. Fourthly, to please and delight ourselves and others, by playing with our words, for pleasure or ornament, innocently.

To these uses, there are also four correspondent abuses: first, when men register their thoughts wrong by the inconstancy of the signification of their words, by which they register for their conceptions that which they never conceived, and so deceive themselves. Secondly, when they use words metaphorically, that is, in a sense other than that they are ordained for, and by it deceive others. Thirdly, when by words they declare that to be their will, which is not. Fourthly, when they use them to grieve one another; for seeing nature has armed living creatures, some with teeth, some with horns, and some with hands, to grieve an enemy, it is but an abuse of speech to grieve him with the tongue, unless it is one whom we are obliged to govern; and then it is not to grieve, but to correct and amend.

The manner how speech serves to the remembrance of the consequence of causes and effects consists in the imposing of *names* and the *connection* of them.

Of names, some are *proper* and singular to only one thing, as *Peter, John, this man, this tree*, and some are *common* to many things, as *man, horse, tree*—every one of which though, but one name, is nevertheless the name of diverse particular things, in respect of all which together, it is called a *universal*, there being nothing in the world universal but names; for the things named are every one of them individual and singular.

One universal name is imposed on many things for their similitude in some quality or other accident; and whereas a proper name brings to mind one thing only, universals recall any one of those many.

And of names universal, some are of more, and some of less extent, the larger comprehending the less large, and some again of equal extent, comprehending each other reciprocally—as for example, the name *body* is of larger signification than the word *man*, and comprehends it, and the names *man* and *rational* are of equal extent, comprehending mutually one another. But here we must take notice that by a name is not always understood, as in grammar, only one word, but sometimes by circumlocution many words together. For all these words, *he who observes the laws of his country in his actions*, make but one name, equivalent to this one word, *just*.

By this imposition of names, some of larger, some of stricter signification, we turn the reckoning of the consequences of things imagined in the mind into a reckoning of the consequences of appellations. For example, a man who has no use of speech at all (such as is born and remains perfectly deaf and dumb), if he sets a triangle before his eyes, and by it two right angles (such as are the corners of a square figure), he may by meditation compare and find that the three angles of that triangle are equal to those two right angles that stand by it. But if another triangle is shown him, different in shape from the former, he cannot know whether the three angles of that also are equal to the same without a new labor. But he who has the use of words, when he observes that such equality was consequent, not to the length of the sides, nor to any other particular thing in his triangle, but only to this, that the sides were straight and the angles three, and that that was all for which he named it a triangle, will boldly conclude universally that such equality of angles is in all triangles whatsoever, and register his invention in these general terms, *every triangle has its three angles equal to two right angles.* And thus the consequence found in one particular comes to be registered and remembered as a universal rule, and discharges our mental reckoning of time and place, and delivers us from all labor of the mind, saving the first, and makes that which was found true *here* and *now* be true in *all times* and *places.*

But the use of words in registering our thoughts is in nothing so evident as in numbering. A natural fool who could never learn by heart the order of numeral words, as *one*, *two*, and *three*, may observe every stroke of the clock, and nod to it, or say one, one, one, but can never know what hour it strikes. And it seems there was a time when those names of number were not in use; and men were inclined to apply their fingers of one or both hands to those things they desired to keep account of, and that as a result it proceeded that now our numeral words are but ten, in any nation, and in some but five, and then they begin again. And he who can count to ten, if he recites them out of order, will lose himself, and not know when he is done. Much less will he be able to add, and subtract, and perform all other operations of arithmetic. Thus, without words there is no possibility of reckoning of numbers, much less of magnitudes, of swiftness, of force, and other things, the reckonings of which are necessary to the being, or well-being, of mankind.

When two names are joined together into a consequence or affirmation, as thus, *a man is a living creature*, or thus, *if he is a man, he is a living creature*, if the latter name *living creature* signifies all that the former name *man* signifies, then the affirmation or consequence is *true*; otherwise *false*. For *true* and *false* are attributes of speech, not of things. And where speech is not, there is neither *truth* nor *falsehood*. *Error* there may be, as when we expect that which shall not be, or suspect what has not been; but in neither case can a man be charged with untruth.

Seeing then that *truth* consists in the right ordering of names in our affirmations, a man who seeks precise *truth* has need to remember what every name he uses stands for, and to place it accordingly, or else he will find himself entangled in words, as a bird in lime twigs, the more he struggles the more ensnared. And therefore in geometry (which is the only science that it has pleased God to bestow on mankind up to now), men begin at settling the significations of their words—which settling of significations they call *definitions*, and place them in the beginning of their reckoning.

By this it appears how necessary it is for any man who aspires to true knowledge to examine the definitions of former authors, and either to correct them, where they are negligently set down, or to make them himself. For the errors of definitions multiply themselves according as the reckoning proceeds, and lead men into absurdities, which at last they see, but cannot avoid, without reckoning anew from the beginning, in which lies the foundation of their errors. Thus it happens that they who trust to books do as they who cast up many little sums into a greater, without considering whether those little sums were rightly cast up or not, and at last finding the error visible, and not mistrusting their first grounds, do not know which way to clear themselves, but spend time in fluttering over their books—as birds that entering by the chimney, and finding themselves enclosed in a chamber, flutter at the false light of a glass window, for want of wit to consider which way they came in. Thus, in the right definition of names lies the first use of speech, which is the acquisition of science, and in wrong, or no definitions, lies the first abuse, from which proceed all false and senseless tenets, which make those men who take their instruction from the authority of books and not from their own meditation, to be as much below the condition of ignorant men as men endowed with true science are above it. For between true science and erroneous doctrines, ignorance is in the middle. Natural sense and imagination are not subject to absurdity. Nature itself cannot err; and as men abound in copiousness of language, so they become more wise or more mad than ordinary. Nor is it possible without letters for any man to become either excellently wise, or (unless his memory is hurt by disease or ill constitution of organs) excellently foolish. For words are wise men's counters—they do but reckon by them—but they are the money of fools who value them by the authority of an *Aristotle*, a *Cicero*, or a *Thomas*, or any other doctor whatsoever, if but a man.

*Subject to names* is whatever can enter into or be considered in an account, and be added one to another to make a sum, or subtracted one from another and leave a remainder. The Latins called accounts of money *rationes*, and accounting *ratiocinatio*; and that which we call *items* in bills or books of account, they call *nomina*, that is *names*; and from this it seems to proceed that they extended the word *ratio* to the faculty of reckoning in all other things. The Greeks have but one word, *logos*, for both *speech* and *reason*— not that they thought there was no speech without reason, but no reasoning without speech and the act of reasoning they called *syllogism*, which signifies the summing up of the consequences of one saying to another. And because the same things may enter into account for diverse accidents, their names are (to show that diversity) diversely wrested and diversified. This diversity of names may be reduced to four general heads.

First, a thing may enter into account for *matter* or *body*—as *living, sensible, rational, hot, cold, moved, quiet*—with all which names the word *matter*, or *body*, is understood, all such being names of matter.

Secondly, it may enter into account, or be considered, for some accident or quality, which we conceive to be in it, as for *being moved*, for *being so long*, for *being hot*, etc.; and then, of the name of the thing itself, by a little change or wresting, we make a name for that accident, which we consider; and for *living*

put into the account *life*; for *moved, motion*; for *hot, heat*; for *long, length*, and the like; and all such names are the names of the accidents and properties by which one matter and body is distinguished from another. These are called *abstract names*, because severed (not from matter, but) from the account of matter.

Thirdly, we bring into account the properties of our own bodies by which we make such distinction; as when anything is *seen* by us, we do not reckon the thing itself, but the *sight*, the *color*, the *idea* of it in the fancy; and when anything is *heard*, we do not reckon it, but the *hearing* or *sound* only, which is our fancy or conception of it by the ear—and such are names of fancies.

Fourthly, we bring into account, consider, and give *names* to names themselves, and to *speeches*. For *general, universal, special, equivocal* are names of names. And *affirmation, interrogation, commandment, narration, syllogism, sermon, oration*, and many other such are names of speeches. And this is all the variety of names *positive* which are put to mark something which is in nature, or may be feigned by the mind of man, as bodies that are, or may be conceived to be; or of bodies, the properties that are, or may be feigned to be; or words and speech.

There are also other names, called *negative*, which are notes to signify that a word is not the name of the thing in question—as these words *nothing, no man, infinite, unteachable, three want four*, and the like—which are nevertheless of use in reckoning, or in correcting of reckoning, and call to mind our past cogitations, though they are not names of anything, because they make us refuse to admit of names not rightly used.

All other names are but insignificant sounds, and those of two sorts. One when they are new, and yet their meaning not explained by definition—of which there have been abundance coined by schoolmen and puzzled philosophers.

Another, when men make a name of two names, whose significations are contradictory and inconsistent—as this name, an *incorporeal body*, or (which is all one) an *incorporeal substance*, and a great number more. For whenever any affirmation is false, the two names of which it is composed, put together and made one, signify nothing at all. For example, if it is a false affirmation to say a *quadrangle is round*, the word *round quadrangle* signifies nothing, but is a mere sound. So likewise, if it is false to say that virtue can be poured, or blown up and down, the words *in-poured virtue, in-blown virtue*, are as absurd and insignificant as a *round quadrangle*. And therefore you shall hardly meet with a senseless and insignificant word that is not made up of some Latin or Greek names. A Frenchman seldom hears our Savior called by the name of *parole*, but often by the name of *verbe*; yet *verbe* and *parole* differ no more, but that one is Latin, the other French.

When a man, upon the hearing of any speech, has those thoughts which the words of that speech and their connection were ordained and constituted to signify, then he is said to understand it, *understanding* being nothing else but conception caused by speech. And therefore if speech is peculiar to man (as for all I know it is), then is understanding peculiar to him also. And therefore of absurd and false affirmations, in case they are universal, there can be no understanding; though many think they understand then, when they do but repeat the words softly, or examine them in their mind.

What kinds of speeches signify the appetites, aversions, and passions of man's mind, and of their use and abuse, I shall speak when I have spoken of the passions.

The names of such things as affect us, that is, which please and displease us, because all men are not alike affected with the same thing, nor the same man at all times, are in the common discourses of men of *inconstant* signification. For seeing all names are imposed to signify our conceptions, and all our affections are but conceptions, when we conceive the same things differently, we can hardly avoid different naming of them. For though the nature of what we conceive is the same, yet the diversity of our reception of it, in respect of different constitutions of body and prejudices of opinion, gives everything a tincture of our different passions. And therefore in reasoning a man must take heed of words, which besides the signification of what we imagine of their nature, have a signification also of the nature, disposition, and interest of the speaker—such as are the names of virtues and vices, for one man calls *wisdom* what another calls *fear*; and one *cruelty*, what another *justice*; one *prodigality*, what another *magnanimity*; and one *gravity*, what another *stupidity*, etc. And therefore such names can never be true grounds of any ratiocination. No more can metaphors, and tropes of speech; but these are less dangerous, because they profess their inconstancy, which the others do not.

## Chapter 5. Of *Reason* and *Science*.

When a man *reasons*, he does nothing else but conceive a sum total from *addition* of parcels, or conceive a remainder from *subtraction* of one sum from another, which (if it is done by words) is conceiving of the consequence of the names of all the parts to the name of the whole, or from the names of the whole and one part to the name of the other part. And though in some things (as in numbers), besides *adding* and *subtracting*, men name other operations, as *multiplying* and *dividing*, yet they are the same; for multiplication is but adding together of things equal, and division, but subtracting of one thing as often as we can. These operations are not incident to numbers only, but to all manner of things that can be added together and taken one out of another. For as arithmeticians teach to add and subtract in *numbers*, so the geometers teach the same in *lines*, *figures* (solid and superficial), *angles*, *proportions*, *times*, degrees of *swiftness*, *force*, *power*, and the like. The logicians teach the same in *consequences of words*, adding together *two names* to make an *affirmation* and two *affirmations* to make a *syllogism*, and *many syllogisms* to make a *demonstration*; and from the *sum*, or *conclusion*, of a *syllogism*, they subtract one *proposition* to find the other. Writers of politics add together *contracts* to find men's *duties*, and lawyers, *laws* and *facts*, to find what is *right* and *wrong* in the actions of private men. In sum, in whatever matter there is place for *addition* and *subtraction*, there also is place for *reason*; and where these have no place, there *reason* has nothing at all to do.

Out of all this we may define (that is to say determine) what that is which is meant by this word *reason*, when we reckon it among the faculties of the mind. For REASON, in this sense, is nothing but *reckoning* (that is, adding and subtracting) of the consequences of general names agreed upon for the *marking* and *signifying* of our thoughts—I say marking them when we reckon by ourselves, and *signifying* when we demonstrate or approve our reckonings to other men.

And as in arithmetic, unpracticed men must, and professors themselves may, often err and cast up false, so also in any other subject of reasoning, the ablest, most attentive, and most practiced men may deceive themselves and infer false conclusions—not but that reason itself is always right reason, as well as arithmetic is a certain and infallible art, but no one man's reason, nor the reason of any one number of men, makes the certainty, no more than an account is therefore well cast up because a great many men have unanimously approved it. And therefore, as when there is a controversy in an account, the parties must by their own accord set up for right reason the reason of some arbitrator, or judge, to whose sentence they will both stand, or their controversy must either come to blows or be undecided, for want of a right reason constituted by nature, so is it also in all debates of whatever kind. And when men who think themselves wiser than all others clamor and demand right reason for judge, yet seek no more, but that things should be determined by no other men's reason but their own, it is as intolerable in the society of men as it is in play, after trump is turned, to use for trump on every occasion that suit which they have most in their hand. For they do nothing else, who will have every of their passions, as it comes to bear sway in them, be taken for right reason, and who in their own controversies, exposing their want of right reason by the claim they lay to it.

The use and end of reason is not the finding of the sum and truth of one, or a few consequences, remote from the first definitions and settled significations of names, but to begin at these, and proceed from one consequence to another. For there can be no certainty of the last conclusion without a certainty of all those affirmations and negations, on which it was grounded and inferred. As when a master of a family, in taking an account, casts up the sums of all the bills of expense into one sum, and not regarding how each bill is summed up by those that give them in account, nor what it is he pays for, he advantages himself no more than if he allowed the account in

gross, trusting to all of the accountants' skill and honesty, so also in reasoning of all other things, he that takes up conclusions on the trust of authors, and does not fetch them from the first items in every reckoning (which are the significations of names settled by definitions), loses his labor, and does not know anything, but only believes.

When a man reckons without the use of words, which may be done in particular things (as when upon the sight of any one thing, we conjecture what was likely to have preceded, or is likely to follow upon it), if that which he thought likely to follow, does not follow, or that which he thought likely to have preceded it, has not preceded it, this is called ERROR, to which even the most prudent men are subject. But when we reason in words of general signification, and fall upon a general inference which is false, though it is commonly called *error*, it is indeed an ABSURDITY, or senseless speech. For error is but a deception in presuming that something is past, or to come, of which, though it were not past, or not to come, yet there was no impossibility discoverable. But when we make a general assertion, unless it is a true one, the possibility of it is inconceivable. And words by which we conceive nothing but the sound are those we call *absurd, insignificant,* and *nonsense.* And therefore if a man should talk to me of a *round quadrangle,* or *accidents of bread in cheese;* or *immaterial substances;* or of *a free subject; a free will;* or any *free,* but free from being hindered by opposition, I should not say he was in an error, but that his words were without meaning, that is to say, absurd.

I have said before (in the second chapter) that a man did excel all other animals in this faculty, that when he conceived anything whatsoever, he was apt to inquire the consequences of it, and what effects he could do with it. And now I add this other degree of the same excellence, that he can by words reduce the consequences he finds to general rules called *theorems,* or *aphorisms*—that is, he can reason, or reckon, not only in number, but in all other things, of which one may be added unto or subtracted from another.

But this privilege is allayed by another, and that is by the privilege of absurdity, to which no living creature is subject, but man only. And of men, those are of all most subject to it who profess philosophy. For it is most true that *Cicero* said of them somewhere: that there can be nothing so absurd, but may be found in the books of philosophers. And the reason is manifest. For there is not one of them who begins his ratiocination from the definitions, or explications of the names they are to use, which is a method that has been used only in geometry, whose conclusions have in this way been made indisputable.

I. The first cause of absurd conclusions I ascribe to the want of method, in that they do not begin their ratiocination from definitions, that is, from settled significations of their words, as if they could cast accounts without knowing the value of the numeral words, *one, two,* and *three*.

And whereas all bodies enter into account upon diverse considerations (which I have mentioned in the preceding chapter), these considerations being diversely named, diverse absurdities proceed from the confusion and unfit connection of their names into assertions. And therefore,

II. The second cause of absurd assertions I ascribe to the giving of names of *bodies* to *accidents*; or of *accidents* to *bodies*; as they do who say *faith is infused*, or *inspired*; when nothing can be *poured* or *breathed* into anything but body; and that *extension is body*; that *phantasms* are *spirits*, etc.

III. The third I ascribe to the giving of the names of the *accidents* of *bodies without us* to the *accidents* of our *own bodies*; as they do who say the *color is in the body*; *the sound is in the air*, etc.

IV. The fourth, to the giving of the names of *bodies* to *names*, or *speeches*; as they do who say that *there are universal things*, that *a living creature is genus* or *a general thing*, etc.

V. The fifth, to the giving of the names of *accidents* to *names* and *speeches*; as they do who say *the nature of a thing is its definition*; *a man's command is his will*, and the like.

VI. The sixth, to the use of metaphors, tropes, and other rhetorical figures, instead of proper words. For though it is lawful to say (for example) in common speech, *the way goes, or leads here, or there; the proverb says this or that* (whereas ways cannot go, nor proverbs speak), yet in reckoning and seeking of truth such speeches are not to be admitted.

VII. The seventh, to names that signify nothing, but are taken up and learned by rote from the schools, as *hypostatical, transubstantiate, consubstantiate, eternal-now*, and the like canting of schoolmen.

To him who can avoid these things, it is not easy to fall into any absurdity, unless it is by the length of an account, where he may perhaps forget what went before. For all men by nature reason alike, and well, when they have good principles. For who is so stupid as both to make a mistake in geometry and also to persist in it, when another detects his error to him?

By this it appears that reason is not, as sense and memory, born with us, nor gotten by experience only, as prudence is, but attained by industry, first in apt imposing of names, and secondly by getting a good and orderly method in proceeding from the elements, which are names, to assertions made by connection of one of them to another, and so to syllogisms, which are the connections of one assertion to another, until we come to a knowledge of all the consequences of names appertaining to the subject in hand; and that is what men call SCIENCE. And whereas sense and memory are but knowledge of fact, which is a thing past and irrevocable, *science* is the knowledge of consequences and dependence of one fact upon another, by which, out of what we can presently do, we know how to do something else when we will, or the like, another time, because when we see how anything comes about, upon what causes, and by what manner, when the like causes come into our power, we see how to make it produce the like effects.

Children therefore are not endowed with reason at all until they have attained the use of speech, but are called reasonable creatures, for the possibility apparent of having the use of reason in time to come. And the most part of men, though they have the use of reasoning a little way, as in numbering to some degree, yet it serves them to little use in common life, in which they govern themselves, some better, some worse, according to their differences of experience, quickness of memory, and inclinations to several ends, but specially according to good or evil fortune and the errors of one another. For as for science, or certain rules of their actions, they are so far from it that they do not know what it is. Geometry they have thought conjuring; but for other sciences, they who have not been taught the beginnings and some progress in them, that they may see how they are acquired and generated, are in this point like children who, having no thought of generation, are made believe by the women that their brothers and sisters are not born, but found in the garden.

But yet they who have no *science* are in better and nobler condition with their natural prudence than men who by misreasoning, or by trusting them who reason wrong, fall upon false and absurd general rules. For ignorance of causes and of rules does not set men so far out of their way as relying on false rules, and taking for causes of what they aspire to, those that are not so, but rather causes of the contrary.

To conclude, the light of human minds is perspicuous words, but by exact definitions first made clearer and purged from ambiguity; *reason* is the *pace*; increase of *science*, the *way*; and the benefit of mankind, the *end*. And on the contrary, metaphors, and senseless and ambiguous words, are like *ignes fatui*, a fool's fire, and reasoning upon them is wandering among innumerable absurdities—and their end, contention and sedition, or contempt.

As much experience is *prudence*, so is much science *sapience*. For though we usually have one name of wisdom for them both, yet the Latins did always distinguish between *prudentia* and *sapientia*, ascribing the former to experience, the latter to science. But to make their difference appear more clearly, let us suppose one man endowed with an excellent natural use and dexterity in handling his arms, and another to have added to that dexterity an acquired science of where he can offend or be offended by his adversary, in every possible posture or guard; the ability of the former would be to the ability of the latter as prudence to sapience, both useful, but the latter infallible. But they who trusting only to the authority of books follow the blind blindly are like him who, trusting to the false rules of a master of fencing, ventures presumptuously upon an adversary who either kills or disgraces him.

The signs of science are some, certain and infallible, some, uncertain. Certain, when he who pretends the science of anything can teach the same, that is to say, demonstrate the truth of this perspicuously to another; uncertain, when only some particular events answer to his pretense, and upon many occasions prove so as he says they must. Signs of prudence are all uncertain, because to observe by experience and remember all circumstances that may alter the success is impossible. But in any business, of which a man does not have infallible science to proceed by, to forsake his own natural judgment and be guided by general sentences read in authors, and subject to many exceptions, is a sign of folly, and generally scorned by the name of pedantry. And even of those men themselves who in councils of the commonwealth love to show their reading of politics and history, very few do it in their domestic affairs, where their particular interest is concerned, having prudence enough for their private affairs; but in public they study more the reputation of their own wit than the success of another's business.

# Part III. Of a Christian Commonwealth

## Chapter 34. Of the Signification of *Spirit*, *Angel*, and *Inspiration* in the Books of Holy Scripture.

Seeing the foundation of all true ratiocination is the constant signification of words, which in the doctrine following does not depend (as in natural science) on the will of the writer, nor (as in common conversation) on vulgar use, but on the sense they carry in the Scripture, it is necessary, before I proceed any further, to determine, out of the Bible, the meaning of such words, as by their ambiguity may render what I am to infer upon them, obscure, or disputable. I will begin with the words Body and Spirit, which in the language of the Schools are termed *corporeal* and *incorporeal* substances.

The word *body*, in the most general meaning, signifies that which fills or occupies some certain room or imagined place, and does not depend on the imagination, but is a real part of what we call the *universe*.

For the *universe*, being the aggregate of all bodies, there is no real part of it that is not also *body*, nor anything properly a *body* that is not also part of (that aggregate of all *bodies*) the *universe*. The same also, because bodies are subject to change, that is to say, to variety of appearance to the sense of living creatures is called *substance*—that is to say, *subject* to various accidents, as sometimes to be moved, sometimes to stand still—and to seem to our senses sometimes hot, sometimes cold, sometimes of one color, smell, taste, or sound, sometimes of another. And we attribute this diversity of seeming (produced by the diversity of the operation of bodies on the organs of our sense) to alterations of the bodies that operate and call them *accidents* of those bodies. And according to this meaning of the word, *substance* and *body* signify the same thing; and therefore *incorporeal substance* are words which, when they are joined together, destroy one another, as if a man should say an *incorporeal body*.

But in the sense of common people, not all the universe is called body, but only such parts of it as they can discern by the sense of feeling to resist their force, or by the sense of their eyes to hinder them from a farther prospect. Therefore, in the common language of men, *air* and *aerial substances* are not typically to be taken for bodies, but (as often as men are sensible of their effects) are called *wind*, or *breath*, or (because the same are called in the Latin *spiritus*) *spirits*—as when they call that aerial substance, which, in the body of any living creature, gives it life and motion, *vital* and *animal spirits*. But for those idols of the brain, which represent bodies to us where they are not, as in a looking-glass, in a dream, or to a distempered brain waking, they are (as the apostle said generally of all idols) nothing—nothing at all, I say, there where they seem to be; and in the brain itself, nothing but tumult, proceeding either from the action of the objects, or from the disorderly agitation of the organs of our sense. And men, who are otherwise employed than to search into their causes, do not know of themselves what to call them, and may therefore easily be persuaded by those whose knowledge they much revere, some to call them *bodies*, and think them made of air compacted by a power supernatural, because the sight judges them corporeal, and some to call them *spirits*, because the sense

of touch discerns nothing in the place where they appear to resist their fingers. So that the proper signification of *spirit* in common speech is either a subtle, fluid, and invisible body, or a ghost, or other idol or phantasm of the imagination. But for metaphorical significations, there are many; for sometimes it is taken for disposition or inclination of the mind, as when for the disposition to control the sayings of other men, we say, *a spirit of contradiction*; for *a disposition to uncleanness, an unclean spirit*; for *perverseness, an obstinate spirit*; for *sullenness, a dumb spirit*, and for *inclination to godliness, and God's service, the Spirit of God*—sometimes for any eminent ability, or extraordinary passion, or disease of the mind, as when *great wisdom* is called the *spirit of wisdom*; and *madmen* are said to be *possessed with a spirit*.

I do not find anywhere any other signification of *spirit*, and where none of these can satisfy the sense of that word in Scripture, the place does not fall under human understanding, and our faith in this does not consist in our opinion, but in our submission, as in all places where God is said to be a *Spirit*; or where by the *Spirit of God*, God himself is meant. For the nature of God is incomprehensible; that is to say, we understand nothing *of what he is*, but only *that he is*; and therefore the attributes we give him are not to tell one another *what he is*, nor to signify our opinion of his nature, but our desire to honor him with such names as we conceive most honorable among ourselves. [. . .]

The disciples of Christ, seeing him walking upon the sea (Matthew 14. 26 and Mark 6. 49), supposed him to be a *Spirit*, meaning by it an aerial *body* and not a phantasm; for it is said they all saw him, which cannot be understood of the delusions of the brain (which are not common to many at once, as visible bodies are, but singular, because of the differences of fancies), but of bodies only. In like manner, where he was taken for a *spirit* by the same apostles (Luke 24. 3, 7). So also (Acts 12. 15) when St. *Peter* was delivered out of prison, it would not be believed, but when the maid said he was at the door, they said it was his *angel*; by which must be meant a corporeal substance, or we must say the disciples themselves did follow the common opinion of both Jews and Gentiles that some such apparitions were not imaginary, but real, and such as did not need the fancy of man for their existence. These the Jews called *spirits* and *angels*, good or bad, as the Greeks called the same by the name of *demons*. And some such apparitions may be real, and substantial, that is to say, subtle bodies, which God can form by the same power by which he formed all things, and make use of, as of ministers, and messengers (that is to say, angels) to declare his will and execute the same when he pleases, in extraordinary and supernatural manner. But when he has so formed them, they are substances endowed with dimensions, and take up room, and can be moved from place to place, which is peculiar to bodies; and therefore are not incorporeal ghosts, that is to say, ghosts that are in no *place*; that is to say, that are *nowhere*—that is to say, that seeming to be *somewhat* are *nothing*. But if corporeal is taken in the most vulgar manner for such substances as are perceptible by our external senses, then incorporeal substance is not an imaginary, but real thing, namely, a thin, invisible substance that has the same dimensions that are in grosser bodies.

By the name of ANGEL is signified generally a *messenger*; and most often, a *messenger of God*; and by a messenger of God is signified anything that makes known his extraordinary presence, that is to say, the extraordinary manifestation of his power, especially by a dream or vision.

Concerning the creation of *angels*, there is nothing delivered in the Scriptures. That they are spirits is often repeated, but by the name of spirit is signified both in Scripture and vulgarly, both among Jews and Gentiles, sometimes thin bodies, as the air, the wind, the spirits vital, and animal, of living creatures, and sometimes the images that arise in the fancy in dreams, and visions, which are not real substances, nor last any longer than the dream, or vision they appear in—which apparitions, though no real substances, but accidents of the brain, yet when God raises them supernaturally to signify his will, they are not improperly termed God's messengers, that is to say, his *angels*.

And as the Gentiles did vulgarly conceive the imagery of the brain for things really subsistent without them and not dependent on the fancy, and out of them framed their opinions of *demons*, good and

evil, which because they seemed to subsist really they called *substances*; and because they could not feel them with their hands, *incorporeal*, so also the Jews upon the same ground, without anything in the Old Testament that constrained them to that, had generally an opinion (except the sect of the *Sadducees*) that those apparitions (which it pleased God sometimes to produce in the fancy of men, for his own service, and therefore called them his angels) were substances, not dependent on the fancy, but permanent creatures of God; of which those which they thought were good to them, they esteemed *the angels of God*, and those they thought would hurt them they called *evil angels* or evil spirits—such as was the spirit of Python, and the spirits of madmen, of lunatics, and epileptics—for they esteemed such as were troubled with such diseases, *demoniacs*.

But if we consider the places of the Old Testament where angels are mentioned, we shall find that in most of them nothing else can be understood by the word *angel* but some image raised (supernaturally) in the fancy, to signify the presence of God in the execution of some supernatural work; and therefore in the rest, where their nature is not expressed, it may be understood in the same manner. [. . .]

To men who understand the signification of these words, *substance* and *incorporeal*, as *incorporeal* is not taken for subtle body but for *not body*, they imply a contradiction, inasmuch as to say, an angel or spirit is (in that sense) an incorporeal substance is to say in effect there is no angel nor spirit at all. Considering therefore the signification of the word *angel* in the Old Testament, and the nature of dreams and visions that happen to men by the ordinary way of nature, I was inclined to this opinion, that angels were nothing but supernatural apparitions of the fancy raised by the special and extraordinary operation of God, by that means to make his presence and commandments known to mankind, and chiefly to his own people. But the many places of the New Testament, and our Savior's own words, and in such texts where there is no suspicion of corruption of the Scripture, have extorted from my feeble reason an acknowledgment and belief that there are also substantial and permanent angels. But to believe they are in no place, that is to say, nowhere, that is to say, nothing, as they (though indirectly) say that will have them incorporeal, cannot be evinced by Scripture.

On the signification of the word *spirit* depends that of the word INSPIRATION, which must either be taken properly, and then it is nothing but the blowing into a man some thin and subtle air or wind, in such manner as a man fills a bladder with his breath or if spirits are not corporeal, but have their existence only in the fancy, it is nothing but the blowing in of a phantasm, which is improper to say and impossible; for phantasms are not, but only seem to be somewhat. That word therefore is used in the Scripture metaphorically only, as (Gen. 2. 7), where it is said that God inspired into man the breath of life, no more is meant than that God gave unto him vital motion. For we are not to think that God made first a living breath and then blew it into Adam after he was made, whether that breath were real or seeming, but only as it is (Acts 17. 25) "that he gave him life and breath," that is, made him a living creature. And where it is said (2 Tim. 3. 16) "all Scripture is given by inspiration from God," speaking there of the Scripture of the Old Testament, it is an easy metaphor to signify that God inclined the spirit or mind of those writers to write that which should be useful in teaching, reproving, correcting, and instructing men in the way of righteous living. But where St. Peter (2 Pet. 1. 21) said that "Prophecy came not in old time by the will of man, but the holy men of God spoke as they were moved by the Holy Spirit," by the Holy Spirit is meant the voice of God in a dream or supernatural vision, which is not *inspiration*: Nor when our Savior breathing on his disciples, said "Receive the Holy Spirit," was that breath the Spirit, but a sign of the spiritual graces he gave unto them. And though it is said of many, and of our Savior himself, that he was full of the Holy *Spirit*; yet that fullness is not to be understood for *infusion* of the substance of God, but for accumulation of his gifts, such as are the gift of sanctity of life, of tongues, and the like, whether attained supernaturally or by study and industry; for in all cases they are the gifts of God. So likewise where God says (Joel 2. 28) "I will pour out my Spirit upon all flesh, and your sons and your daughters shall prophesy, your old men shall dream dreams, and your young men shall see visions," we are not to understand it in the proper sense, as if his *Spirit* were like water, subject to effusion or infusion, but as if God had promised to give them prophetic dreams and visions. For the proper use of the word *infused*, in speaking of the graces of God, is an abuse of it; for those graces are virtues, not bodies to be carried hither and thither and to be poured into men as into barrels.

In the same manner, to take *inspiration* in the proper sense, or to say that good *spirits* entered into men to make them prophesy, or evil *spirits* into those that became phrenetic, lunatic, or epileptic, is not to take the word in the sense of the Scripture; for the Spirit there is taken for the power of God, working by causes to us unknown. As also (Acts 2. 2) the wind that is there said to fill the house in which the apostles were assembled on the day of Pentecost is not to be understood for the Holy Spirit, which is the Deity itself, but for an external sign of God's special working on their hearts to effect in them the internal graces and holy virtues he thought requisite for the performance of their apostleship.

# Part IV. Of the Kingdom of Darkness

## Chapter 46. Of *Darkness* from *Vain Philosophy* and *Fabulous Traditions*.

By PHILOSOPHY is understood *the knowledge acquired by reasoning from the manner of the generation of anything to the properties, or from the properties to some possible way of generation of the same, to the end to be able to produce, as far as matter and human force permit, such effects as human life requires.* So the geometer, from the construction of figures, finds out many properties of them, and from the properties, new ways of their construction by reasoning, to the end to be able to measure land and water, and for infinite other uses. So the astronomer, from the rising, setting, and moving of the sun and stars in diverse parts of the heavens, finds out the causes of day and night and of the different seasons of the year, by which he keeps an account of time—and the like of other sciences.

By this definition it is evident that we are not to account as any part of it that original knowledge called experience, in which consists prudence, because it is not attained by reasoning, but found as well in brute beasts as in man, and is but a memory of successions of events in times past, in which the omission of every little circumstance altering the effect frustrates the expectation of the most prudent; whereas nothing is produced by reasoning correctly, but general, eternal, and immutable truth.

Nor are we therefore to give that name to any false conclusions, for he who reasons correctly in words he understands can never conclude an error.

Nor to that which any man knows by supernatural revelation, because it is not acquired by reasoning.

Nor that which is gotten by reasoning from the authority of books, because it is not by reasoning from the cause to the effect, nor from the effect to the cause, and is not knowledge, but faith.

The faculty of reasoning being consequent to the use of speech, it was not possible but that there should have been some general truths found out by reasoning, as ancient almost as language itself. The savages of America are not without some good moral sentences; they also have a little arithmetic to add and divide in numbers not too great, but they are not therefore philosophers. For as there were plants of corn and wine in small quantity dispersed in the fields and woods before men knew their virtue or made use of them for their nourishment, or planted them apart in fields and vineyards, in which time they fed on acorns and drank water, so also there have been diverse true, general, and profitable speculations from the beginning, as being the natural plants of human reason. But they were at first but few in number. Men lived upon gross experience; there was no method, that is to say, no sowing, nor planting of knowledge by itself, apart from the weeds and common plants of error and conjecture. And the cause of it being the want of leisure from procuring the necessities of life and defending themselves against their neighbors, it was impossible, until the erecting of great common-

wealths, it should be otherwise. *Leisure* is the mother of *philosophy* and *Commonwealth,* the mother of *peace* and *leisure*. Where first were great and flourishing *cities*, there was first the study of *philosophy*. The *Gymnosophists* of *India*, the *Magi* of *Persia*, and the *Priests* of *Chaldea* and *Egypt* are counted the most ancient philosophers, and those countries were the most ancient of kingdoms. *Philosophy* was not risen to the *Greeks* and other people of the west, whose *commonwealths* (no greater perhaps than *Lucca* or *Geneva*) never had peace, but when their fears of one another were equal, nor the leisure to observe anything but one another. At length, when war had united many of these *Greek* lesser cities into fewer and greater, then began seven men, of several parts of *Greece*, to get the reputation of being *wise*; some of them for *moral* and *politic* sentences, and others for the learning of the *Chaldeans* and *Egyptians*, which was *astronomy* and *geometry*. But we do not yet hear of any *schools* of *philosophy*. [...]

That which is now called a University is a joining together and an incorporation under one government of many public schools, in one and the same town or city, in which the principal schools were ordained for the three professions, that is to say, of the Roman religion, of the Roman law, and of the art of medicine. And for the study of philosophy it has no place other than as a handmaid to the Roman religion; and since the authority of Aristotle is only current there, that study is not properly philosophy (the nature of which does not depend on authors) but Aristotelity. And for geometry, until of very late times it had no place at all, as being subservient to nothing but rigid truth. And if any man by the ingenuity of his own nature had attained to any degree of perfection in it, he was commonly thought a magician, and his art diabolical.

Now to descend to the particular tenets of vain philosophy derived to the Universities and as a result into the Church, partly from Aristotle, partly from blindness of understanding, I shall first consider their principles. There is a certain *philosophia prima*, on which all other philosophy ought to depend; it consists principally in right limiting of the significations of such appellations or names as are of all others the most universal—which limitations serve to avoid ambiguity and equivocation in reasoning, and are commonly called definitions, such as are the definitions of body, time, place, matter, form, essence, subject, substance, accident, power, act, finite, infinite, quantity, quality, motion, action, passion, and diverse others, necessary to the explaining of a man's conceptions concerning the nature and generation of bodies. The explication (that is, the settling of the meaning) of these and the like terms is commonly called *metaphysics* in the Schools, as being a part of the philosophy of Aristotle which has that for a title. But it is in another sense, for there it signifies as much as *books written or placed after his natural philosophy*; but the schools take them for *books of supernatural philosophy*, for the word *metaphysics* will bear both these senses. And indeed that which is there written is for the most part so far from the possibility of being understood, and so repugnant to natural reason, that whoever thinks there is anything to be understood by it must necessarily think it supernatural.

From these metaphysics, which are mingled with the Scripture to make school divinity, we are told there are in the world certain essences separated from bodies, which they call *abstract essences* and *substantial forms*. There is need of somewhat more than ordinary attention in this place for the interpreting of this *jargon*. Also I ask pardon of those who are not used to this kind of discourse, for applying myself to those who are. The world (I do not mean the earth only, that denominates the lovers of it *worldly men*, but the *universe*, that is, the whole mass of all things that are) is corporeal, that is to say, body, and has the dimensions of magnitude, namely, length, breadth, and depth. Also every part of body is likewise body, and has the like dimensions, and consequently every part of the universe is body; and that which is not body is not part of the universe. And because the universe is all, that which is no part of it is nothing, and consequently nowhere. Nor does it follow from this that spirits are nothing, for they have dimensions and are therefore really bodies, though that name in common speech is given to such bodies only as are visible or palpable, that is, that have some degree of opacity. But for spirits, they call them incorporeal, which is a name of more honor, and may therefore

with more piety be attributed to God himself, in whom we consider not what attribute expresses best his nature, which is incomprehensible, but what best expresses our desire to honor him.

To know now upon what grounds they say there are *abstract essences* or *substantial forms*, we are to consider what those words do properly signify. The use of words is to register to ourselves and make manifest to others the thoughts and conceptions of our minds. Of which words, some are the names of the things conceived, as the names of all sorts of bodies, that work upon the senses and leave an impression in the imagination. Others are the names of the imaginations themselves, that is to say, of those ideas or mental images we have of all things we see or remember. And others again are names of names, or of different sorts of speech, as *universal, plural, singular* are the names of names, and *definition, affirmation, negation, true, false, syllogism, interrogation, promise, covenant* are the names of certain forms of speech. Others serve to show the consequence or repugnance of one name to another, as when one says *a man is a body*, he intends that the name of *body* is necessarily consequent to the name of *man*, as being but several names of the same thing, *man*, which consequence is signified by coupling them together with the word *is*. And as we use the verb *is*, so the Latins use their verb *est*, and the Greeks their *esti* through all its declinations. Whether all other nations of the world have a word that answers to it or not in their several languages, I cannot tell, but I am sure they do not have need of it. For the placing of two names in order may serve to signify their consequence, if it were the custom (for custom is it, that give words their force), as well as the words *is*, or *be*, or *are*, and the like.

And if it were so, that there was a language without any verb answerable to *est*, or *is*, or *be*; yet the men who used it would not be a jot the less capable of inferring, concluding, and of all kind of reasoning than were the Greeks and Latins. But what then would become of these terms of *entity, essence, essential, essentiality* that are derived from it, and of many more that depend on these, applied as most commonly they are? They are therefore not names of things, but signs by which we make known that we conceive the consequence of one name or attribute to another, as when we say *a man is a living body*, we do not mean that the *man* is one thing, *the living body* another, and the *is*, or *being* a third, but that the *man* and the *living body* are the same thing, because the consequence, *if he is a man, he is a living body*, is a true consequence, signified by that word *is*. Therefore, *to be a body*, *to walk*, *to be speaking*, *to live*, *to see*, and the like infinitives, also *corporeity*, *walking*, *speaking*, *life*, *sight*, and the like, that signify just the same, are the names of *nothing*—as I have elsewhere more amply expressed.

But to what purpose (some man may say) is such subtlety in a work of this nature, where I pretend to nothing but what is necessary to the doctrine of government and obedience? It is to this purpose that men may no longer suffer themselves to be abused by them, that by this doctrine of *separated essences*, built on the vain philosophy of Aristotle, would fright them from obeying the laws of their country with empty names, as men frighten birds from the corn with an empty doublet, a hat, and a crooked stick. For it is upon this ground that when a man is dead and buried, they say his soul (that is his life) can walk separated from his body and is seen by night among the graves. Upon the same ground they say that the figure, and color, and taste of a piece of bread has a being there, where they say there is no bread. And upon the same ground they say that faith, and wisdom, and other virtues are sometimes *poured* into a man, sometimes *blown* into him from heaven, as if the virtuous and their virtues could be asunder, and a great many other things that serve to lessen the dependence of subjects on the sovereign power of their country. For who will endeavor to obey the laws, if he expects obedience to be poured or blown into him? Or who will not obey a priest, who can make God, rather than his sovereign, rather than God himself? Or who that is in fear of ghosts will not bear great respect to those who can make the holy water that drives them from him? And this shall suffice for an example of the errors which are brought into the Church from the *entities* and *essences* of Aristotle, which it may be he knew to be false philosophy, but wrote it as a thing consonant to and corroborative of their religion, and fearing the fate of Socrates.

Being once fallen into this error of *separated essences*, they are as a result necessarily involved in many other absurdities that follow it. For seeing they will have these forms be real, they are obliged to assign them some place. But because they hold them incorporeal, without all dimension of quantity, and all men know that place is dimension and not to be filled but by that which is corporeal, they are driven to uphold their credit with a distinction, that they are not indeed anywhere *circumscriptive*, but *definitive*— which term, being mere words, and in this occasion insignificant, pass only in Latin, that the vanity of them may be concealed. For the circumscription of a thing is nothing else but the determination or defining of its place; and so both the terms of the distinction are the same. And in particular, of the essence of a man, which (they say) is his soul, they affirm it to be all of it in his little finger, and all of it in every other part (however small) of his body; and yet no more soul in the whole body than in any one of those parts. Can any man think that God is served with such absurdities? And yet all this is necessary to believe, to those who will believe the existence of an incorporeal soul, separated from the body.

And when they come to give account, how an incorporeal substance can be capable of pain and be tormented in the fire of hell or purgatory, they have nothing at all to answer but that it cannot be known how fire can burn souls.

Again, whereas motion is change of place, and incorporeal substances are not capable of place, they are troubled to make it seem possible how a soul can go forward, without the body, to heaven, hell, or purgatory, and how the ghosts of men (and I may add of their clothes which they appear in) can walk by night in churches, churchyards, and other places of sepulture. To which I do not know what they can answer, unless they will say they walk *definitive*, not *circumscriptive*, or *spiritually*, not *temporally*, for such egregious distinctions are equally applicable to any difficulty whatsoever.

For the meaning of *eternity*, they will not have it be an endless succession of time; for then they should not be able to render a reason how God's will and preordaining of things to come should not be before his prescience of the same, as the efficient cause before the effect or agent before the action, nor of many other of their bold opinions concerning the incomprehensible nature of God. But they will teach us that eternity is the standing still of the present time, a *nunc-stans* (as the Schools call it), which neither they nor anyone else understands, no more than they would a *hic-stans* for an infinite greatness of place.

And whereas men divide a body in their thought by numbering parts of it, and in numbering those parts number also the parts of the place it filled, it cannot be but in making many parts, we make also many places of those parts—by which there cannot be conceived in the mind of any man, more or fewer parts than there are places for. Yet they will have us believe that by the almighty power of God one body may be at one and the same time in many places; and many bodies at one and the same time in one place, as if it were an acknowledgment of the Divine Power to say: that which is, is not; or that which has been, has not been. And these are but a small part of the incongruities they are forced to from their disputing philosophically, instead of admiring and adoring of the divine and incomprehensible nature, whose attributes cannot signify what he is, but ought to signify our desire to honor him with the best appellations we can think of. But they who venture to reason of his nature from these attributes of honor, losing their understanding in the very first attempt, fall from one inconvenience into another, without end and without number, in the same manner as when a man ignorant of the ceremonies of court, coming into the presence of a greater person than he is used to speak to, and stumbling at his entrance, to save himself from falling, lets slip his cloak; to recover his cloak, lets fall his hat; and with one disorder after another, discovers his astonishment and rusticity.

Then for *physics*, that is, the knowledge of the subordinate and secondary causes of natural events, they render none at all but empty words. If you desire to know why some kinds of bodies sink naturally downwards toward the earth and others go naturally from it, the Schools will tell you out of Aristotle that the bodies that sink downwards are *heavy*; and that this heaviness is what causes them to descend. But if you ask what they mean by heaviness, they will define it to be an endeavor to go to the center of the earth, so that the cause why things sink downward is an endeavor to be below, which is as much as to say that bodies descend or ascend because they do. Or they will tell you the center of the earth is the place of rest and conservation for heavy things; and therefore they endeavor to be there, as if stones and metals had a desire or could discern the place they would be at, as man does; or loved rest, as man does not; or that a piece of glass were less safe in the window than falling into the street.

If we would know why the same body seems greater (without adding to it) one time than another; they say: when it seems less, it is *condensed*; when greater, *rarefied*. What is that *condensed* and *rarefied*? Condensed is when there is in the very same matter less quantity than before; and rarefied, when more. As if there could be matter that had not some determined quantity, when quantity is nothing else but the determination of matter, that is to say, of body, by which we say one body is greater or lesser than another by thus or thus much. Or as if a body were made without any quantity at all, and that afterwards more or less were put into it, according as it is intended the body should be more or less dense.

For the cause of the soul of man, they say, *creatur infundendo* and *creando infunditur*—that is, it is created by pouring it in and poured in by creation.

For the cause of sense, an ubiquity of *species*, that is, of the *shows* or *apparitions* of objects, which, when they are apparitions to the eye, is *sight*; when to the ear, *hearing*; to the palate, *taste*; to the nostril, *smelling*; and to the rest of the body, *feeling*.

For the cause of the will to do any particular action, which is called *volitio*, they assign the faculty, that is to say, the capacity in general that men have to will sometimes one thing, sometimes another, which is called *voluntas*; making the *power* the cause of the *act*, as if one should assign for the cause of the good or evil acts of men, their ability to do them.

And in many occasions they put for the cause of natural events their own ignorance, but disguised in other words, as when they say, fortune is the cause of things contingent—that is, of things of which they know no cause—and as when they attribute many effects to *occult qualities*—that is, qualities not known

to them and therefore also (as they think) to no one
else—and to *sympathy, antipathy, antiperistasis, spe-*
*cifical qualities,* and other like terms, which signify
neither the agent that produces them, nor the operation by which they are produced.

If such *metaphysics* and *physics* as this are not *vain*
*philosophy,* there was never any, nor was St. Paul
needed to give us warning to avoid it.

# Baruch Spinoza, From the Letters to Oldenburg and to Meyer (1661–65)[1]

## To Henry Oldenburg[2] (September 1661)

Illustrious Sir,

You yourself could judge what pleasure your friendship affords me, if only your modesty would allow you to consider the estimable qualities with which you are so richly endowed. With these qualities in mind, I feel it not a little presumptuous on my part to enter into a bond of friendship with you, the more so when I reflect that between friends all things, and particularly things of the spirit, should be shared. Nevertheless, this is to be attributed to both your modesty and your kindness, rather than to me. Your modesty in so condescending and the abundant kindness that you have bestowed on me have banished any uncertainty I may have had in accepting the hand of friendship which you firmly hold out to me and deign to ask of me in return, a friendship which it shall be my earnest endeavor diligently to foster.

As for my mental endowments, such as they are, I would most willingly have you claim them for your own even if I knew that this would be to my great detriment. However, it is not my intention in this way to deny you what you ask by right of friendship, and so I shall attempt to explain my views on the subjects we spoke of, although I can scarcely believe that this will be the means of strengthening our friendship, if your kind indulgence does not intervene.

I shall therefore begin with a discussion of God, whom I define as a Being consisting of infinite attributes, each of which is infinite or supremely perfect in its own kind. Here it should be observed that by attribute I mean every thing that is conceived through itself and in itself, so that its conception does not involve the conception of anything else. For example, extension is conceived through itself and in itself, but not motion; for the latter is conceived in something else, and its conception involves extension.

That this is the true definition of God is evident from the fact that by God we understand a supremely perfect and absolutely infinite Being. The existence of such a Being is easily proved from the definition; but as this is not the place for such a proof, I shall pass it over. The points I need to prove here in order to satisfy your first inquiry, illustrious Sir, are as follows: first, that in the universe there cannot exist two substances without their differing entirely in essence;

1. Translated from the Latin by Samuel Shirley in Baruch Spinoza, *The Ethics and Selected Letters* (Indianapolis: Hackett Publishing Company, 1982), letters 2, 12, and 32 (in part).
2. Henry Oldenburg (d. 1677) was a German theologian with a scientific bent. He eventually became secretary of the London Royal Society. He met Spinoza in 1661, and when he went to London, he continued to correspond with Spinoza for many years. It was through Oldenburg that Spinoza learned of Robert Boyle's work in chemistry.

secondly, a substance cannot be produced, since to exist is of its essence; thirdly, every substance must be infinite, or supremely perfect in its kind.

With these points established, illustrious Sir, provided that at the same time you attend to the definition of God, you will readily perceive the direction of my thought, so that I need not be more explicit on this subject. However, in order to provide a clear, concise proof, I can think of no better expedient than to arrange them in geometrical style and to submit them to the bar of your judgment. I therefore enclose them separately herewith[3] and await your judgment.

Secondly, you ask me what errors I see in the philosophy of Descartes and Bacon. In this request, too, I shall try to oblige you, although it is not my custom to expose the errors of others. The first and most important error is this, that they have gone far astray from knowledge of the first cause and origin of all things. Secondly, they have failed to achieve understanding of the true nature of the human mind. Thirdly, they have never grasped the true cause of error. Only those who are completely destitute of all learning and scholarship can fail to see the critical importance of true knowledge of these three points.

How far astray they have wandered from true knowledge of the first cause and of the human mind can readily be gathered from the truth of the three propositions to which I have already referred. So I confine myself to pointing out the third error. Of Bacon I shall say little; he speaks very confusedly on this point, and simply makes assertions while proving hardly anything.[4] In the first place, he takes for granted that the human intellect, apart from the fallibility of the senses, is by its very nature liable to error, framing its assumptions on the analogy of its own nature, and not on the analogy of the universe, so that it is like a mirror of irregular surface receiving rays, mingling its own nature with the nature of reality, and so forth. Secondly, he holds that the human intellect, by reason of its own nature, is prone to abstractions, and imagines that things that are in flux are stable, and so on. Thirdly, he holds that the human intellect is

continually increasing and cannot come to a halt or rest. Whatever other causes he assigns can readily be reduced to the one Cartesian principle, that the human will is free and more extensive than the intellect, or, as Verulam himself more confusedly puts it (Aphorism 49), the intellect is not characterized by a dry light, but receives infusion from the will. (We should here observe that Verulam takes "intellect" for "mind," therein differing with Descartes.) This cause, then, disregarding the others as being of little importance, I shall show to be false. Indeed, they would easily have seen this for themselves, had they but given consideration to the fact that the will differs from this or that volition in the same way as whiteness differs from this or that white object, or as humanity differs from this or that human being. So to conceive the will to be the cause of this or that volition is as impossible as to conceive humanity to be the cause of Peter or Paul.

Since, then, the will is nothing more than a mental construct [*ens rationis*], it can in no way be said to be the cause of this or that volition. Particular volitions, since they need a cause in order to exist, cannot be said to be free; rather they are necessarily determined to be such as they are by their own causes. Lastly, according to Descartes, errors are themselves particular volitions, from which it necessarily follows that errors — that is, particular volitions — are not free, but are determined by external causes and in no way by the will. This is what I undertook to prove.

## To the learned and wise Ludwig Meyer,[5] Doctor in Philosophy and in Medicine, from Benedict de Spinoza (April 20, 1663)

[On the Nature of the Infinite]

Dearest Friend,

I have received two letters from you, one dated January 11 and delivered to me by our friend N.N.,[6] the other dated March 26 and sent to me by an unknown

---

3. See *Ethics*, Part I, from the beginning to Proposition 4.
4. Francis Bacon, *New Organon* I, sec. 41–51; Bacon was also Lord Verulam.

5. Ludwig Meyer, physician and philosopher, was a close friend of Spinoza. He participated in preparing Spinoza's writings for posthumous publication.
6. Most likely Peter Balling, another of Spinoza's close friends.

friend from Leyden. They were both very welcome, especially as I gathered from them that all is well with you and that I am often in your thoughts. My most cordial thanks are due to you for the kindness and esteem you have always shown me. At the same time I beseech you to believe that I am in no less a degree your devoted friend, and this I shall endeavor to prove whenever the occasion arises, as far as my slender abilities allow. As a first offering, I will try to answer the request made in your letters to me, in which you ask me to let you have my considered views on the question of the infinite. I am glad to oblige.

The question of the infinite has universally been found to be very difficult, indeed, insoluble, through failure to distinguish between that which must be infinite by its very nature or by virtue of its definition, and that which is unlimited not by virtue of its essence but by virtue of its cause. Then again, there is the failure to distinguish between that which is called infinite because it is unlimited, and that whose parts cannot be equated or explicated by any number, although we may know its maximum and minimum. Lastly, there is the failure to distinguish between that which we can apprehend only by intellect and not by imagination, and that which can also be apprehended by imagination. I repeat, if men had paid careful attention to these distinctions, they would never have found themselves overwhelmed by such a mountain of difficulties. They would clearly have understood what kind of infinite cannot be divided into, or possess any, parts, and what kind can be so divided without contradiction. They would also have understood what kind of infinite can be considered, without contradiction, as greater than another infinite, and what kind cannot be so conceived. This will become clear from what I am about to say. However, I shall first briefly explain these four terms: Substance, Mode, Eternity, Duration.

The points to be noted about Substance are as follows. First, existence pertains to its essence; that is, solely from its essence and definition it follows that Substance exists. This point, if my memory does not deceive me, I have proved to you in an earlier conversation without the help of any other propositions. Second, following from the first point, substance is not many; rather, there exists only one substance of the same nature. Thirdly, all Substance can be understood only as infinite.

The affections of Substance I call Modes. The definition of Modes, insofar as it is not a definition of Substance, cannot involve existence. Therefore, even when they exist, we can conceive them as not existing. It therefore follows that when we have regard only to the essence of Modes and not to the order of Nature as a whole, we cannot deduce from their present existence that they will or will not exist in the future, or that they did or did not exist in the past. Hence it is clear that we conceive the existence of Substance as of an entirely different kind from the existence of Modes. This is the source of the difference between Eternity and Duration. It is to the existence of Modes only that we can apply the term Duration; the corresponding term for the existence of Substance is Eternity, that is, the infinite enjoyment of existence or—pardon the Latin—of being [essendi].

What I have said makes it quite clear that when we have regard only to the essence of Modes and not to Nature's order, as is most frequently the case, we can arbitrarily limit the existence and duration of Modes (without thereby impairing to any degree our conception of them); and we can conceive this duration as greater or less, and divisible into parts. But Eternity and Substance, being conceivable only as infinite, cannot be thus treated without annulling our concept of them. So it is nonsense, bordering on insanity, to hold that extended Substance is composed of parts or bodies really distinct from one another. It is as if, by adding circle to circle and piling one on top of another, one were to attempt to construct a square or a triangle or any other figure of a completely different nature. Therefore the whole heap of arguments by which the common run of philosophers strive to prove that extended Substance is finite collapses of its own accord. All such arguments assume that corporeal Substance is composed of parts. A parallel case is presented by those who, having convinced themselves that a line is made up of points, have devised many arguments to prove that a line is not infinitely divisible.

However, if you ask why we have such a strong natural tendency to divide extended Substance, I answer that we conceive quantity in two ways: abstractly, or superficially, as we have it in the imagination with the help of the senses; or as substance apprehended solely by means of the intellect. If we have regard to quantity as it exists in the imagination (and this is what we most frequently and readily do), it is found to be divisible, finite, composed of parts, and multiplex. But if we have regard to it as it is in the intellect and apprehend the thing as it is in itself (and this is very difficult), then it is found to be infinite, indivisible, and one alone, as I have already sufficiently proved.

Further, from the fact that we are able to limit Duration and Quantity as we please, conceiving Quantity in abstraction from Substance and ignoring the efflux of Duration from things eternal, there arise Time and Measure: Time to limit Duration, and Measure to limit Quantity in such wise that we are thereby enabled to form images of them as best we may. Again, from the fact that we separate the Affections of Substance from Substance itself, and arrange them in classes so that we can form images of them as best we may, there arises Number, whereby we limit them. Hence it can clearly be seen that Measure, Time, and Number are nothing other than modes of thinking, or rather, modes of the imagination. It is therefore not surprising that all who have attempted to understand the workings of Nature by such concepts, and without really understanding these concepts, have tied themselves into such extraordinary knots that in the end they have been unable to extricate themselves except by breaking all laws and perpetrating the grossest absurdities. For there are many things that can in no way be apprehended by the imagination but only by the intellect, such as Substance, Eternity, and the like. If anyone tries to explicate such things by notions of this kind, which are nothing more than aids to the imagination, he will meet with no more success than if he were deliberately to encourage his imagination to run mad. The Modes of Substance, too, can never be correctly understood if they are confused with such mental constructs [*entia rationis*] or aids to the imagination. For by so doing we are abstracting them from Substance and from the manner of their efflux from Eter-

nity, and in such isolation they can never be correctly understood.

To make the matter still clearer, take the following example. If someone conceives Duration in this abstracted way and, confusing it with Time, begins dividing it into parts, he can never understand how, for instance, an hour can pass by. For in order that an hour should pass by, a half-hour must first have passed by, and then half of the remainder, and then half of what is left of the remainder; and if you go on subtracting half of the remainder to infinity, you can never reach the end of the hour. Therefore, many who are not used to distinguishing mental constructs from reality have ventured to assert that Duration is composed of moments, thus falling into the clutches of Scylla in their eagerness to avoid Charybdis. To say that Duration is made up of moments is the same as to say that Number is made up by adding noughts together.

Further, it is obvious from the above that Number, Time, and Measure, being merely aids to the imagination, cannot be infinite, for in that case Number would not be number, nor Measure measure, nor Time time. Hence one can easily see why many people, confusing these three concepts with reality because of their ignorance of the true nature of reality, have denied the actual existence of the Infinite. But let their deplorable reasoning be judged by mathematicians who, in matters that they clearly and distinctly perceive, are not to be delayed by arguments of that sort. For they not only have come upon many things inexpressible by any number, which clearly reveals the inadequacy of number to determine all things; in addition they have encountered many things that cannot be equaled by any number, and exceed any possible number. Now they do not draw the conclusion that it is because of the multitude of parts that such things exceed all number; rather, it is because the nature of the thing is such that number is inapplicable to it without manifest contradiction.

For example, all the inequalities of the space lying between the two circles ABCD in the diagram exceed any number, as do all the variations of speed of matter moving through that area. Now this conclusion is not reached because of the excessive magnitude of the

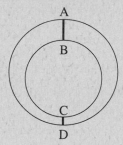

intervening space; for however small a portion of it we take, the inequalities of this small portion will still be beyond any numerical expression. Nor, again, is this conclusion reached, as happens in other cases, because we do not know the maximum and minimum; in our example we know them both, the maximum being AB and the minimum CD. Our conclusion is reached because number is not applicable to the nature of the space between the two non-concentric circles. Therefore, if anyone sought to express by number all those inequalities, he would have to bring it about that a circle should not be a circle.

Similarly, to return to our main topic of discussion, if anyone were to attempt to determine all the motions of matter that have ever been, by reducing them and their duration to a certain number and time, he would be attempting to deprive corporeal Substance, which we cannot conceive as other than existing, of its Affections, and bring it about that Substance should not possess the nature which it does possess. I could here clearly demonstrate this and many other points touched on in this letter, did I not consider it unnecessary.

From all that I have said one can clearly see that certain things are infinite by their own nature and cannot in any way be conceived as finite, while other things are infinite by virtue of the cause in which they have their being, and when the latter are conceived in abstraction, they can be divided into parts and be regarded as finite. Lastly, there are things that are called infinite, or if you prefer, indefinite, because they cannot be accurately expressed by any number, while yet being conceivable as greater or less. For it does not follow that things that cannot be accurately expressed by any number must necessarily be equal, as is evident from the given example and from many others.

To sum up, I have here briefly set before you the causes of error and of the confusions that have arisen regarding the question of the Infinite, explaining them all, unless I am mistaken, in such a way that I do not believe there is any question regarding the Infinite on which I have not touched, or which cannot be readily solved from what I have said. Therefore, I think it is pointless to detain you any longer on this matter.

However, in passing, I should like it here to be observed that in my opinion our modern Peripatetics have quite misunderstood the proof whereby scholars of old sought to prove the existence of God. According to a certain Jew named Rabbi Chasdai,[7] this proof runs as follows: "If there is granted an infinite series of causes, all things which are, are also caused. But nothing that is caused can exist necessarily by virtue of its own nature. Therefore, there is nothing in Nature to whose essence existence necessarily pertains. But this is absurd. Therefore the premise is absurd." So the force of the argument lies not in the impossibility of an actual infinite, or an infinite series of causes, but in the assumption that things which by their own nature do not necessarily exist are not determined by a thing that necessarily exists by its own nature.

I would now pass on—for I am pressed for time—to your second question, but I shall be able more conveniently to reply to the points contained there when you kindly pay me a visit. So do please try to come as soon as you can. For the time for my departure is rapidly approaching. Enough, farewell, and keep me ever in your thoughts. Yours, etc.

## To Henry Oldenburg (November 20, 1665)

Most honorable Sir,

Please accept my most grateful thanks for the kind encouragement which you and the most honorable

7. Hasdai Crescas (1340–1410), a Spanish-Jewish theologian, whose *The Light of the Lord* subjects Aristotle's physics to a "radical" critique.

Master Boyle have given me in the pursuit of philosophy. As far as my poor abilities will allow, I shall continue in this way, with the assurance of your assistance and goodwill.

When you ask for my views on "how we know the way in which each part of Nature agrees with the whole, and the manner of its coherence with the other parts," I presume you are asking for the grounds of our belief that each part of Nature agrees with the whole and coheres with the other parts. As to knowing the actual manner of this coherence and the agreement of each part with the whole, I made it clear in my previous letter that this is beyond my knowledge. To know this it would be necessary to know the whole of Nature and all its parts. So I shall attempt to give the reasoning that compels me to this belief. But I would first ask you to note that I do not attribute to Nature beauty, ugliness, order, or confusion. It is only with respect to our imagination that things can be said to be beautiful, ugly, well-ordered, or confused.

By "coherence of parts" I mean simply this, that the laws or nature of one part adapts itself to the laws or nature of another part in such wise that there is the least possible opposition between them. On the question of whole and parts, I consider things as parts of a whole to the extent that their natures adapt themselves to one another so that they are in the closest possible agreement. Insofar as they are different from one another, to that extent each one forms in our mind a separate idea and is therefore considered as a whole, not a part. For example, when the motions of particles of lymph, chyle, etc. adapt themselves to one another in accordance with size and shape so as to be fully in agreement with one another and to form all together one single fluid, to that extent only are the chyle, lymph, etc. regarded as parts of the blood. But insofar as we conceive the particles of lymph as different from the particles of chyle in respect of shape and motion, to that extent we regard them each as a whole, not a part.

Now let us imagine, if you please, a tiny worm living in the blood, capable of distinguishing by sight the particles of the blood—lymph, etc.—and of intelligently observing how each particle, on colliding with another, either rebounds or communicates some degree of its motion, and so forth. That worm would

be living in the blood as we are living in our part of the universe, and it would regard each individual particle as a whole, not a part, and it would have no idea as to how all the parts are modified by the overall nature of the blood and compelled to mutual adaptation as the overall nature of the blood requires, so as to agree with one another in a definite relation. For if we imagine that there are no causes external to the blood which would communicate new motions to the blood, nor any space external to the blood, nor any other bodies to which the particles of the blood could transfer their motions, it is beyond doubt that the blood will remain indefinitely in its present state and that its particles will undergo no changes other than those which can be conceived as resulting from the existing relation between the motion of the blood and that of the lymph, chyle, etc. Thus the blood would always have to be regarded as a whole, not a part. But since there are many other causes which do in fact modify the laws of the nature of the blood and are reciprocally modified by the blood, it follows that there occur in the blood other motions and other changes, resulting not solely from the reciprocal relation of its particles but from the relation between the motion of the blood on the one hand and external causes on the other. In this perspective the blood is accounted as a part, not as a whole. So much, then, for the question of whole and part.

Now all the bodies in Nature can and should be conceived in the same way as we have here conceived the blood; for all bodies are surrounded by others and are reciprocally determined to exist and to act in a fixed and determinate way, the same ratio of motion to rest being preserved in them taken all together, that is, in the universe as a whole. Hence it follows that every body, insofar as it exists as modified in a definite way, must be considered as a part of the whole universe and must agree with the whole and cohere with the other parts. Now since the nature of the universe, unlike the nature of the blood, is not limited, but is absolutely infinite, its parts are modified by the nature of this infinite potency in infinite ways and are compelled to undergo infinite variations. But I conceive that, in respect to substance, each individual part has a more intimate union with the whole. For, as I endeavored to prove in my first letter written some time ago, while I was living at Rhijns-burg,[8] since it is of the nature of substance to be infinite, it follows that each part pertains to the nature of corporeal substance, and can neither be nor be conceived without it.

So you see how and why I hold that the human body is a part of Nature. As regards the human mind, I maintain that it also is a part of Nature, for I hold

that in Nature there also exists an infinite power of thinking which, insofar as it is infinite, contains within itself the whole of Nature as an object of thought, and whose thoughts proceed in the same manner as does Nature, which is clearly its object of thought.

Further, I maintain that the human mind is that same power of thinking, not insofar as that power is infinite and apprehends the whole of Nature, but insofar as it is finite, apprehending the human body only. The human mind, I maintain, is in this way part of an infinite intellect. [. . .]

8. This is an allusion to Letter 2.

# Baruch Spinoza, *The Ethics* (1677)[1]

## Part I. Concerning God

### Definitions

1. By that which is self-caused I mean that whose essence involves existence; or that whose nature can be conceived only as existing.

2. A thing is said to be finite in its own kind [*in suo genere finita*] when it can be limited by another thing of the same nature. For example, a body is said to be finite because we can always conceive of another body greater than it. So, too, a thought is limited by another thought. But body is not limited by thought, nor thought by body.

3. By substance I mean that which is in itself and is conceived through itself; that is, that the conception of which does not require the conception of another thing from which it has to be formed.

4. By attribute I mean that which the intellect perceives of substance as constituting its essence.

5. By mode I mean the affections of substance, that is, that which is in something else and is conceived through something else.

6. By God I mean an absolutely infinite being, that is, substance consisting of infinite attributes, each of which expresses eternal and infinite essence.

*Explication*: I say "absolutely infinite," not "infinite in its kind." For if a thing is only infinite in its kind, one may deny that it has infinite attributes. But if a thing is absolutely infinite, whatever expresses essence and does not involve any negation belongs to its essence.

7. That thing is said to be free [*liber*] which exists solely from the necessity of its own nature, and is determined to action by itself alone. A thing is said to be necessary [*necessarius*] or rather, constrained [*coactus*], if it is determined by another thing to exist and to act in a definite and determinate way.

8. By eternity I mean existence itself insofar as it is conceived as necessarily following solely from the definition of an eternal thing.

*Explication*: For such existence is conceived as an eternal truth, just as is the essence of the thing, and therefore cannot be explicated through duration or

1. Translated from the Latin by Samuel Shirley in Baruch Spinoza, *The Ethics and Selected Letters* (Indianapolis: Hackett Publishing Company, 1982).

time, even if duration be conceived as without beginning and end.

Axioms

1. All things that are, are either in themselves or in something else.

2. That which cannot be conceived through another thing must be conceived through itself.

3. From a given determinate cause there necessarily follows an effect; on the other hand, if there be no determinate cause, it is impossible that an effect should follow.

4. The knowledge of an effect depends on, and involves, the knowledge of the cause.

5. Things which have nothing in common with each other cannot be understood through each other; that is, the conception of the one does not involve the conception of the other.

6. A true idea must agree with that of which it is the idea [*ideatum*].

7. If a thing can be conceived as not existing, its essence does not involve existence.

## Proposition 1. *Substance is by nature prior to its affections.*

Proof: This is evident from Defs. 3 and 5.

## Proposition 2. *Two substances having different attributes have nothing in common.*

Proof: This too is evident from Def. 3; for each substance must be in itself and be conceived through itself; that is, the conception of the one does not involve the conception of the other.

## Proposition 3. *When things have nothing in common, one cannot be the cause of the other.*

Proof: If things have nothing in common, then (Ax. 5) they cannot be understood through one another, and so (Ax. 4) one cannot be the cause of the other.

## Proposition 4. *Two or more distinct things are distinguished from one another either by the difference of the attributes of the substances or by the difference of the affections of the substances.*

Proof: All things that are, are either in themselves or in something else (Ax. 1); that is (Defs. 3 and 5), nothing exists external to the intellect except substances and their affections. Therefore, there can be nothing external to the intellect through which several things can be distinguished from one another except substances or (which is the same thing) (Def. 4) the attributes and the affections of substances.

## Proposition 5. *In the universe there cannot be two or more substances of the same nature or attribute.*

Proof: If there were several such distinct substances, they would have to be distinguished from one another either by a difference of attributes or by a difference of affections (Pr. 4). If they are distinguished only by a difference of attributes, then it will be granted that there cannot be more than one substance of the same attribute. But if they are distinguished by a difference of affections, then, since substance is by nature prior to its affections (Pr. 1), disregarding therefore its affections and considering substance in itself, that is (Def. 3 and Ax. 6) considering it truly, it cannot be conceived as distinguishable from another substance. That is (Pr. 4), there cannot be several such substances but only one.

## Proposition 6. *One substance cannot be produced by another substance.*

Proof: In the universe there cannot be two substances of the same attribute (Pr. 5), that is (Pr. 2), two substances having something in common. And so (Pr.

3) one cannot be the cause of the other; that is, one cannot be produced by the other.

Corollary: Hence it follows that substance cannot be produced by anything else. For in the universe there exists nothing but substances and their affections, as is evident from Ax. 1 and Defs. 3 and 5. But, by Pr. 6, it cannot be produced by another substance. Therefore, substance cannot be produced by anything else whatsoever.

Another Proof: This can be proved even more readily by the absurdity of the contradictory. For if substance could be produced by something else, the knowledge of substance would have to depend on the knowledge of its cause (Ax. 4), and so (Def. 3) it would not be substance.

## Proposition 7. *Existence belongs to the nature of substance.*

Proof: Substance cannot be produced by anything else (Cor. Pr. 6) and is therefore self-caused [*causa sui*]; that is (Def. 1), its essence necessarily involves existence; that is, existence belongs to its nature.

## Proposition 8. *Every substance is necessarily infinite.*

Proof: There cannot be more than one substance having the same attribute (Pr. 5), and existence belongs to the nature of substance (Pr. 7). It must therefore exist either as finite or as infinite. But it cannot exist as finite, for (Def. 2) it would have to be limited by another substance of the same nature, and that substance also would have to exist (Pr. 7). And so there would exist two substances of the same attribute, which is absurd (Pr. 5). Therefore, it exists as infinite.

Scholium 1: Since in fact to be finite is in part a negation and to be infinite is the unqualified affirmation of the existence of some nature, it follows from Proposition 7 alone that every substance must be infinite.

Scholium 2: I do not doubt that for those who judge things confusedly and are not accustomed to know things through their primary causes it is difficult to grasp the proof of Proposition 7. Surely, this is because they neither distinguish between the modification of substances and substances themselves, nor do they know how things are produced. And so it comes about that they ascribe to substances a beginning which they see natural things as having; for those who do not know the true causes of things confuse everything. Without any hesitation they imagine trees as well as men talking and stones as well as men being formed from seeds; indeed, any forms whatsoever are imagined to change into any other forms. So too, those who confuse the divine nature with human nature easily ascribe to God human emotions, especially so long as they are ignorant of how the latter are produced in the mind. But if men were to attend to the nature of substance, they would not doubt at all the truth of Proposition 7; indeed, this Proposition would be an axiom to all and would be ranked among universally accepted truisms. For by substance they would understand that which is in itself and is conceived through itself; that is, that the knowledge of which does not require the knowledge of any other thing. By modifications they would understand that which is in another thing, and whose conception is formed from the thing in which they are. Therefore, in the case of nonexistent modifications we can have true ideas of them since their essence is included in something else, with the result that they can be conceived through that something else, although they do not exist in actuality externally to the intellect. However, in the case of substances, because they are conceived only through themselves, their truth external to the intellect is only in themselves. So if someone were to say that he has a clear and distinct—that is, a true—idea of substance and that he nevertheless doubts whether such a substance exists, this would surely be just the same as if he were to declare that he has a true idea but nevertheless suspects that it may be false (as is obvious to anyone who gives his mind to it). Or if anyone asserts that substance is created, he at the same time asserts that a false idea has become true, than which nothing more absurd can be conceived. So it must necessarily be admitted that the existence of substance is as much an eternal truth as is its essence.

From here we can derive in another way that there

cannot be but one [substance] of the same nature, and I think it worthwhile to set out the proof here. Now to do this in an orderly fashion I ask you to note:

1. The true definition of each thing involves and expresses nothing beyond the nature of the thing defined. Hence it follows that—

2. No definition involves or expresses a fixed number of individuals, since it expresses nothing but the nature of the thing defined. For example, the definition of a triangle expresses nothing other than simply the nature of a triangle, and not a fixed number of triangles.

3. For each individual existent thing there must necessarily be a definite cause for its existence.

4. The cause for the existence of a thing must either be contained in the very nature and definition of the existent thing (in effect, existence belongs to its nature) or must have its being independently of the thing itself.

From these premises it follows that if a fixed number of individuals exist in Nature, there must necessarily be a cause why those individuals and not more or fewer exist. If, for example, in Nature twenty men were to exist (for the sake of greater clarity I suppose that they exist simultaneously and that no others existed in Nature before them), in order to account for the existence of these twenty men, it will not be enough for us to demonstrate the cause of human nature in general; it will furthermore be necessary to demonstrate the cause why not more or fewer than twenty men exist, since (Note 3) there must necessarily be a cause for the existence of each one. But this cause (Notes 2 and 3) cannot be contained in the nature of man, since the true definition of man does not involve the number twenty. So (Note 4) the cause of the existence of these twenty men, and consequently of each one, must necessarily be external to each one, and therefore we can reach the unqualified conclusion that whenever several individuals of a kind exist, there must necessarily be an external cause for their existence. Now since existence belongs to the nature of substance (as has already been shown in this Scholium) the definition of substance must involve necessary existence, and consequently the existence of substance must be concluded solely from its defini-

tion. But the existence of several substances cannot follow from the definition of substance (as I have already shown in Notes 2 and 3). Therefore, from the definition of substance it follows necessarily that there exists only one substance of the same nature, as was proposed.

## Proposition 9. *The more reality or being a thing has, the more attributes it has.*

Proof: This is evident from Definition 4.

## Proposition 10. *Each attribute of one substance must be conceived through itself.*

Proof: For an attribute is that which intellect perceives of substance as constituting its essence (Def. 4), and so (Def. 3) it must be conceived through itself.

Scholium: From this it is clear that although two attributes be conceived as really distinct, that is, one without the help of the other, still we cannot deduce therefrom that they constitute two entities, or two different substances. For it is in the nature of substance that each of its attributes be conceived through itself, since all the attributes it possesses have always been in it simultaneously, and one could not have been produced by another; but each expresses the reality or being of substance. So it is by no means absurd to ascribe more than one attribute to one substance. Indeed, nothing in Nature is clearer than that each entity must be conceived under some attribute, and the more reality or being it has, the more are its attributes which express necessity, or eternity, and infinity. Consequently, nothing can be clearer than this, too, that an absolutely infinite entity must necessarily be defined (Def. 6) as an entity consisting of infinite attributes, each of which expresses a definite essence, eternal and infinite. Now if anyone asks by what mark can we distinguish between different substances, let him read the following Propositions, which show that in Nature there exists only one substance, absolutely infinite. So this distinguishing mark would be sought in vain.

Proposition 11. *God, or substance consisting of infinite attributes, each of which expresses eternal and infinite essence, necessarily exists.*

Proof: If you deny this, conceive, if you can, that God does not exist. Therefore (Ax. 7), his essence does not involve existence. But this is absurd (Pr. 7). Therefore God necessarily exists.

Second Proof: For every thing a cause or reason must be assigned either for its existence or for its nonexistence. For example, if a triangle exists, there must be a reason, or cause, for its existence. If it does not exist, there must be a reason or cause which prevents it from existing, or which annuls its existence. Now this reason or cause must either be contained in the nature of the thing or be external to it. For example, the reason why a square circle does not exist is indicated by its very nature, in that it involves a contradiction. On the other hand, the reason for the existence of substance also follows from its nature alone, in that it involves existence (Pr. 7). But the reason for the existence or nonexistence of a circle or a triangle does not follow from their nature, but from the order of universal corporeal Nature. For it is from this latter that it necessarily follows that either the triangle necessarily exists at this moment or that its present existence is impossible. This is self-evident, and therefrom it follows that a thing necessarily exists if there is no reason or cause which prevents its existence. Therefore if there can be no reason or cause which prevents God from existing or which annuls his existence, we are bound to conclude that he necessarily exists. But if there were such a reason or cause, it would have to be either within God's nature or external to it; that is, it would have to be in another substance of another nature. For if it were of the same nature, by that very fact it would be granted that God exists. But a substance of another nature would have nothing in common with God (Pr. 2), and so could neither posit nor annul his existence. Since therefore there cannot be external to God's nature a reason or cause that would annul God's existence, then if indeed he does not exist, the reason or cause must necessarily be in God's nature, which would therefore involve a contradiction. But to affirm this of a Being

absolutely infinite and in the highest degree perfect is absurd. Therefore neither in God nor external to God is there any cause or reason which would annul his existence. Therefore, God necessarily exists.

A Third Proof: To be able to not exist is weakness; on the other hand, to be able to exist is power, as is self-evident. So if what now necessarily exists is nothing but finite entities, then finite entities are more potent than an absolutely infinite Entity—which is absurd. Therefore either nothing exists, or an absolutely infinite Entity necessarily exists, too. But we do exist, either in ourselves or in something else which necessarily exists (Ax. 1 and Pr. 7). Therefore, an absolutely infinite Entity—that is (Def. 6), God—necessarily exists.

Scholium: In this last proof I decided to prove God's existence *a posteriori* so that the proof may be more easily perceived, and not because God's existence does not follow *a priori* from this same basis. For since the ability to exist is power, it follows that the greater the degree of reality that belongs to the nature of a thing, the greater amount of energy it has for existence. So an absolutely infinite Entity or God will have from himself absolutely infinite power to exist, and therefore exists absolutely.

But perhaps many will not readily find this proof convincing because they are used to considering only such things as derive from external causes. Of these things they observe that those which come quickly into being—that is, which readily exist—likewise readily perish, while things which they conceive as more complex they regard as more difficult to bring into being—that is, not so ready to exist. However, to free them from these misconceptions I do not need at this point to show what measure of truth there is in the saying, "Quickly come, quickly go," neither need I raise the question whether or not everything is equally easy in respect of Nature as a whole. It is enough to note simply this, that I am not here speaking of things that come into being through external causes, but only of substances, which (Pr. 6) cannot be produced by any external cause. For whether they consist of many parts or few, things that are brought about by external causes owe whatever degree of perfection or reality they possess entirely to the power of the external cause, and so their existence has its origin solely in the perfection of the external cause, and not in their own perfection. On the other hand, whatever perfection substance possesses is due to no external cause; therefore its existence, too, must follow solely from its own nature, and is therefore nothing else but its essence. So perfection does not annul a thing's existence: on the contrary, it posits it; whereas imperfection annuls a thing's existence. So there is nothing of which we can be more certain than the existence of an absolutely infinite or perfect Entity; that is, God. For since his essence excludes all imperfection and involves absolute perfection, it thereby removes all reason for doubting his existence and affords the utmost certainty of it. This, I think, must be quite clear to all who give a modicum of attention to the matter.

## Proposition 12. *No attribute of substance can be truly conceived from which it would follow that substance can be divided.*

Proof: The parts into which substance thus conceived would be divided will either retain the nature of substance or they will not. In the first case each part will have to be infinite (Pr. 8) and self-caused (Pr. 6) and consist of a different attribute (Pr. 5); and so several substances could be formed from one substance, which is absurd (Pr. 6). Furthermore, the parts would have nothing in common with the whole (Pr. 2), and the whole could exist and be conceived without its parts (Def. 4 and Pr. 10), the absurdity of which none can doubt. But in the latter case in which the parts will not retain the nature of substance— then when the whole substance would have been divided into equal parts it would lose the nature of substance and would cease to be. This is absurd (Pr. 7).

## Proposition 13. *Absolutely infinite substance is indivisible.*

Proof: If it were divisible, the parts into which it would be divided will either retain the nature of absolutely infinite substance, or not. In the first case, there would therefore be several substances of the same nature, which is absurd (Pr. 5). In the second case, absolutely infinite substance can cease to be, which is also absurd (Pr. 11).

Corollary: From this it follows that no substance, and consequently no corporeal substance, insofar as it is substance, is divisible.

Scholium: The indivisibility of substance can be more easily understood merely from the fact that the nature of substance can be conceived only as infinite, and that a part of substance can mean only finite substance, which involves an obvious contradiction (Pr. 8).

## Proposition 14. *There can be, or be conceived, no other substance but God.*

Proof: Since God is an absolutely infinite being of whom no attribute expressing the essence of substance can be denied (Def. 6) and since he necessarily exists (Pr. 11), if there were any other substance but God, it would have to be explicated through some attribute of God, and so there would exist two substances with the same attribute, which is absurd (Pr. 5). So there can be no substance external to God, and consequently no such substance can be conceived. For if it could be conceived, it would have to be conceived necessarily as existing; but this is absurd (by the first part of this proof). Therefore, no substance can be or be conceived external to God.

Corollary 1: Hence it follows quite clearly that God is one: that is (Def. 6), in the universe there is only one substance, and this is absolutely infinite, as I have already indicated in Scholium Pr. 10.

Corollary 2: It follows that the thing extended and the thing thinking are either attributes of God or (Ax. 1) affections of the attributes of God.

## Proposition 15. *Whatever is, is in God, and nothing can be or be conceived without God.*

Proof: Apart from God no substance can be or be conceived (Pr. 14), that is (Def. 3), something which is in itself and is conceived through itself. Now modes (Def. 5) cannot be or be conceived without substance; therefore, they can be only in the divine nature and can be conceived only through the divine nature. But nothing exists except substance and modes (Ax. 1). Therefore, nothing can be or be conceived without God.

Scholium: Some imagine God in the likeness of man, consisting of mind and body, and subject to passions. But it is clear from what has already been proved how far they stray from the true knowledge of God. These I dismiss, for all who have given any consideration to the divine nature deny that God is corporeal. They find convincing proof of this in the fact that by body we understand some quantity having length, breadth, and depth, bounded by a definite shape; and nothing more absurd than this can be attributed to God, a being absolutely infinite.

At the same time, however, by other arguments which they try to prove their point, they show clearly that in their thinking corporeal or extended substance is set completely apart from the divine nature, and they assert that it is created by God. But they have no idea from what divine power it could have been created, which clearly shows that they don't know what they are saying. Now I have clearly proved—at any rate, in my judgment (Cor. Pr. 6 and Sch. 2 Pr. 8)—that no substance can be produced or created by anything else. Furthermore, in Proposition 14 we showed that apart from God no substance can be or be conceived, and hence we deduced that extended substance is one of God's infinite attributes.

However, for a fuller explanation I will refute my opponents' arguments, which all seem to come down to this. Firstly, they think that corporeal substance, insofar as it is substance, is made up of parts, and so they deny that it can be infinite, and consequently that it can pertain to God. This they illustrate with many examples, of which I will take one or two. They say that if corporeal substance is infinite, suppose it to be divided into two parts. Each of these parts will be either finite or infinite. If the former, then the infinite is made up of two finite parts, which is absurd. If the latter, then there is an infinite which is twice as great as another infinite, which is also absurd.

Again, if an infinite length is measured in feet, it will have to consist of an infinite number of feet; and if it is measured in inches, it will consist of an infinite number of inches. So one infinite number will be twelve times greater than another infinite number.

Lastly, if from one point in an infinite quantity two lines, AB and AC, be drawn of fixed and determinate length, and thereafter be produced to infinity, it is clear that the distance between B and C continues to increase and finally changes from a determinate distance to an indeterminate distance.

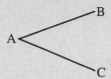

As these absurdities follow, they think, from supposing quantity to be infinite, they conclude that corporeal substance must be finite and consequently cannot pertain to God's essence.

The second argument is also drawn from God's consummate perfection. Since God, they say, is a supremely perfect being, he cannot be that which is acted upon. But corporeal substance, being divisible, can be acted upon. It therefore follows that corporeal substance does not pertain to God's essence.

These are the arguments I find put forward by writers who thereby seek to prove that corporeal substance is unworthy of the divine essence and cannot pertain to it. However, the student who looks carefully into these arguments will find that I have already replied to them, since they are all founded on the same supposition that material substance is composed of parts, and this I have already shown to be absurd (Pr. 12 and Cor. Pr. 13). Again, careful reflection will show that all those alleged absurdities (if indeed they are absurdities, which is not now under discussion) from which they seek to prove that extended substance is finite do not at all follow from the supposition that quantity is infinite, but that infinite quantity is measurable and is made up of finite parts. Therefore, from the resultant absurdities no other conclusion can be reached but that infinite quantity is not measurable and cannot be made up of finite parts. And this is exactly what we have already proved (Pr. 12). So the weapon they aimed at us is in fact turned against themselves. If therefore from this "reductio ad absurdum" argument of theirs they still seek to deduce that extended substance must be finite, they are surely just like one who, having made the supposition that a circle has the properties of a square, deduces therefrom that a circle does not have a center from which all lines drawn to the circumference are equal. For corporeal substance, which can be conceived only as infinite, one, and indivisible (Prs. 8, 5, and 12) they conceive as made up of finite parts, multiplex, and divisible, so as to deduce that it is finite. In the same way others, too, having supposed that a line is composed of points, can find many arguments to prove that a line cannot be infinitely divided. Indeed, it is just as absurd to assert that corporeal substance is composed of bodies or parts as that a body is composed of surfaces, surfaces of lines, and lines of points. This must be admitted by all who know clear reason to be infallible, and particularly those who say that a vacuum cannot exist. For if corporeal substance could be so divided that its parts were distinct in reality, why could one part not be annihilated while the others remain joined together as before? And why should all the parts be so fitted together as to leave no vacuum? Surely, in the case of things which are in reality distinct from one another, one can exist without the other and remain in its original state. Since therefore there is no vacuum in Nature (of which [more] elsewhere[2]) and all its parts must so harmonize that there is no vacuum, it also follows that the parts cannot be distinct in reality; that is, corporeal substance, insofar as it is substance, cannot be divided.

If I am now asked why we have this natural inclination to divide quantity, I reply that we conceive quantity in two ways, to wit, abstractly, or superficially—in other words, as represented in the imagination—or as substance, which we do only through the intellect. If therefore we consider quantity insofar as we represent it in the imagination—and this is what we more frequently and readily do—we find it to be finite, divisible, and made up of parts. But if we consider it intellectually and conceive it insofar as it is substance—and this is very difficult—then it will be found to be infinite, one, and indivisible, as we have already sufficiently proved. This will be quite

clear to those who can distinguish between the imagination and the intellect, especially if this point also is stressed, that matter is everywhere the same, and there are no distinct parts in it except insofar as we conceive matter as modified in various ways. Then its parts are distinct, not really but only modally.[3] For example, we conceive water to be divisible and to have separate parts insofar as it is water, but not insofar as it is material substance. In this latter respect it is not capable of separation or division. Furthermore, water, qua water, comes into existence and goes out of existence; but qua substance it does not come into existence nor go out of existence [*corrumpitur*].

I consider that in the above I have also replied to the second argument, since this too is based on the supposition that matter, insofar as it is substance, is divisible and made up of parts. And even though this were not so, I do not know why matter should be unworthy of the divine nature, since (Pr. 14) there can be no substance external to God by which it can be acted upon. All things, I repeat, are in God, and all things that come to pass do so only through the laws of God's infinite nature and follow through the necessity of his essence (as I shall later show). Therefore, by no manner of reasoning can it be said that God is acted upon by anything else or that extended substance is unworthy of the divine nature, even though it be supposed divisible, as long as it is granted to be eternal and infinite.

But enough of this subject for the present.

## Proposition 16. *From the necessity of the divine nature there must follow infinite things in infinite ways [modis], (that is, everything that can come within the scope of infinite intellect).*

Proof: This proposition should be obvious to everyone who will but consider this point, that from the given definition of any one thing the intellect infers a num-

2. If this refers to anything in Spinoza's extant works, it must be to his early *Descartes's Principles of Philosophy* II.2–3.

3. In this passage Spinoza makes use of a distinction that was frequently employed by philosophers in the Middle Ages and by Descartes as well. Indeed, it is probably the Cartesian version of the distinction that is relevant in this context. According to Descartes, a real distinction obtains between two or more substances or attributes, each one of which being clearly and

ber of properties which necessarily follow in fact from the definition (that is, from the very essence of the thing), and the more reality the definition of the thing expresses (that is, the more reality the essence of the thing defined involves), the greater the number of its properties. Now since divine nature possesses absolutely infinite attributes (Def. 6), of which each one also expresses infinite essence in its own kind, then there must necessarily follow from the necessity of the divine nature an infinity of things in infinite ways (that is, everything that can come within the scope of the infinite intellect).

Corollary 1: Hence it follows that God is the efficient cause of all things that can come within the scope of the infinite intellect.

Corollary 2: Secondly, it follows that God is the cause through himself, not however *per accidens*.

Corollary 3: Thirdly, it follows that God is absolutely the first cause.

## Proposition 17. *God acts solely from the laws of his own nature, constrained by none.*

Proof:   We have just shown that an infinity of things follow, absolutely, solely from the necessity of divine nature, or — which is the same thing — solely from the laws of that same nature (Pr. 16); and we have proved (Pr. 15) that nothing can be or be conceived without God, but that everything is in God. Therefore there can be nothing external to God by which he can be determined or constrained to act. Thus God acts solely from the laws of his own nature and is constrained by none.

Corollary 1: Hence it follows, firstly, that there is

---

distinctly conceivable without the other. Because of this clear and distinct conception of each substance, one can exist without the other. For Descartes, the mind can be clearly and distinctly conceived without the body; hence, it can exist without the latter. A modal distinction, however, is a distinction either between a mode and the substance of which it is a mode or between the various modes of a substance. There is, for example, a modal distinction between the movement of a body and the body itself; there is also a modal distinction between one movement and another movement of the same body — Descartes, *Principles of Philosophy* I, sections 60–61.

no cause, except the perfection of his nature, which either extrinsically or intrinsically moves God to act.

Corollary 2: It follows, secondly, that God alone is a free cause. For God alone exists solely from the necessity of his own nature (Pr. 11 and Cor. 1 Pr. 14) and acts solely from the necessity of his own nature (Pr. 17). So he alone is a free cause (Def. 7).

Scholium: Others take the view that God is a free cause because — so they think — he can bring it about that those things which we have said follow from his nature — that is, which are within his power — should not come about; that is, they should not be produced by him. But this is as much as to say that God can bring it about that it should not follow from the nature of a triangle that its three angles are equal to two right angles, or that from a given cause the effect should not follow, which is absurd.

Furthermore, I shall show later on without the help of this proposition that neither intellect nor will pertain to the nature of God. I know indeed that there are many who think they can prove that intellect in the highest degree and free will belong to the nature of God; for they say they know of nothing more perfect which they may attribute to God than that which is the highest perfection in us. Again, although they conceive of God as having in actuality intellect in the highest degree, they yet do not believe he can bring about the existence of everything which in actuality he understands, for they think they would thereby be nullifying God's power. If, they say, he had created everything that is within his intellect, then he would not have been able to create anything more; and this they regard as inconsistent with God's omnipotence. So they have preferred to regard God as indifferent to everything and as creating nothing but what he has decided, by some absolute exercise of will, to create. However, I think I have shown quite clearly (Pr. 16) that from God's supreme power or infinite nature an infinity of things in infinite ways — that is, everything — has necessarily flowed or is always following from that same necessity, just as from the nature of a triangle it follows from eternity to eternity that its three angles are equal to two right angles. Therefore, God's omnipotence has from eternity been actual and will remain for eternity in the same actuality. In this way, I submit, God's omnipotence is established as being far more perfect. Indeed my opponents—let us speak frankly—seem to be denying God's omnipotence. For they are obliged to admit that God understands an infinite number of creatable things which nevertheless he can never create. If this were not so, that is, if he were to create all the things that he understands, he would exhaust his omnipotence, according to them, and render himself imperfect. Thus, to affirm God as perfect they are reduced to having to affirm at the same time that he cannot bring about everything that is within the bounds of his power. I cannot imagine anything more absurd than this, or more inconsistent with God's omnipotence.

Furthermore, I have something here to say about the intellect and will that is usually attributed to God. If intellect and will do indeed pertain to the eternal essence of God, one must understand in the case of both these attributes something very different from the meaning widely entertained. For the intellect and will that would constitute the essence of God would have to be vastly different from human intellect and will, and would have no point of agreement except the name. They could be no more alike than the celestial constellation of the Dog and the dog that barks. This I will prove as follows. If intellect does pertain to the divine nature, it cannot, like man's intellect, be posterior to (as most thinkers hold) or simultaneous with the objects of understanding, since God is prior in causality to all things (Cor. 1 Pr. 16). On the contrary, the truth and formal essence of things is what it is because it exists as such in the intellect of God as an object of thought. Therefore, God's intellect, insofar as it is conceived as constituting God's essence, is in actual fact the cause of things, in respect both of their essence and their existence. This seems to have been recognized also by those who have asserted that God's intellect, will, and power are one and the same. Since therefore God's intellect is the one and only cause of things, both of their essence and their existence, as we have shown, it must necessarily be different from them both in respect of essence and existence. For that which is caused differs from its cause precisely in what it has from its cause. For example, a man is the cause of the existence of another man, but not of the other's essence; for the

essence is an eternal truth. So with regard to their essence the two men can be in full agreement, but they must differ with regard to existence; and for that reason if the existence of the one should cease, the existence of the other would not thereby cease. But if the essence of the one could be destroyed and rendered false, so too would the essence of the other. Therefore, a thing which is the cause of the essence and existence of some effect must differ from that effect both in respect of essence and existence. But God's intellect is the cause of the essence and existence of man's intellect. Therefore, God's intellect, insofar as it is conceived as constituting the divine essence, differs from man's intellect both in respect of essence and existence, and cannot agree with it in any respect other than name—which is what I sought to prove. In the matter of will, the proof is the same, as anyone can readily see.

## Proposition 18. *God is the immanent, not the transitive, cause of all things.*

Proof: All things that are, are in God, and must be conceived through God (Pr. 15), and so (Cor. 1 Pr. 16) God is the cause of the things that are in him, which is the first point. Further, there can be no substance external to God (Pr. 14); that is (Def. 3), a thing which is in itself external to God—which is the second point. Therefore, God is the immanent, not the transitive, cause of all things.

## Proposition 19. *God [is eternal], that is, all the attributes of God are eternal.*

Proof: God is substance (Def. 6) which necessarily exists (Pr. 11); that is, (Pr. 7) a thing to whose nature it pertains to exist, or—and this is the same thing—a thing from whose definition existence follows; and so (Def. 8) God is eternal. Further, by the attributes of God must be understood that which expresses the essence of the Divine substance (Def. 4), that is, that which pertains to substance. It is this, I say, which the attributes themselves must involve. But eternity pertains to the nature of substance (as I have shown in Pr. 7). Therefore, each of the attributes must involve eternity, and so they are all eternal.

Scholium: This proposition is also perfectly clear from the manner in which I proved the existence of God (Pr. 11). From this proof, I repeat, it is obvious that God's existence is, like his essence, an eternal truth. Again, I have also proved God's eternity in another way in Proposition 19 of my *Descartes's Principles of Philosophy*, and there is no need here to go over that ground again.

## Proposition 20. *God's existence and his essence are one and the same.*

Proof: God and all his attributes are eternal (Pr. 19); that is, each one of his attributes expresses existence (Def. 8). Therefore, the same attributes of God that explicate his eternal essence (Def. 4) at the same time explicate his eternal existence; that is, that which constitutes the essence of God at the same time constitutes his existence, and so his existence and his essence are one and the same.

Corollary 1: From this it follows, firstly, that God's existence, like his essence, is an eternal truth.

Corollary 2: It follows, secondly, that God is immutable; that is, all the attributes of God are immutable. For if they were to change in respect of existence, they would also have to change in respect of essence (Pr. 10); that is—and this is self-evident—they would have to become false instead of true, which is absurd.

## Proposition 21. *All things that follow from the absolute nature of any attribute of God must have existed always, and as infinite; that is, through the said attribute they are eternal and infinite.*

Proof: Suppose this proposition be denied and conceive, if you can, that something in some attribute of God, following from its absolute nature, is finite and has a determinate existence or duration; for example, the idea of God in Thought.[4] Now Thought,

being assumed to be an attribute of God, is necessarily infinite by its own nature (Pr. 11). However, insofar as it has the idea of God, it is being supposed as finite. Now (Def. 2) it cannot be conceived as finite unless it is determined through Thought itself. But it cannot be determined through Thought itself insofar as Thought constitutes the idea of God, for it is in that respect that Thought is supposed to be finite. Therefore, it is determined through Thought insofar as Thought does not constitute the idea of God, which Thought must nevertheless necessarily exist (Pr. 11). Therefore, there must be Thought which does not constitute the idea of God, and so the idea of God does not follow necessarily from its nature insofar as it is absolute Thought. (For it is conceived as constituting and as not constituting the idea of God.) This is contrary to our hypothesis. Therefore, if the idea of God in Thought, or anything in some attribute of God (it does not matter what is selected, since the proof is universal), follows from the necessity of the absolute nature of the attribute, it must necessarily be infinite. That was our first point.

Furthermore, that which thus follows from the necessity of the nature of some attribute cannot have a determinate existence, or duration. If this be denied, suppose that there is in some attribute of God a thing following from the necessity of the nature of the attribute, for example, the idea of God in Thought, and suppose that this thing either did not exist at some time, or will cease to exist in the future. Now since Thought is assumed as an attribute of God, it must necessarily exist, and as immutable (Pr. 11 and Cor. 2 Pr. 20). Therefore, outside the bounds of the duration of the idea of God (for this idea is supposed at some time not to have existed, or will at some point cease to exist) Thought will have to exist without the idea of God. But this is contrary to the hypothesis, for it is supposed that when Thought is granted the idea of God necessarily follows. Therefore, the idea of God in Thought, or anything that necessarily follows from the absolute nature of some attribute of God, cannot have a determinate existence, but is eternal through that same attribute. That was our second point. Note that the same holds for anything in an

---

4. The term "idea of God" [*idea Dei*] is one of the more difficult phrases in Spinoza's philosophical vocabulary, and it has occasioned a variety of interpretations among Spinoza's commentators. One point is agreed on by all: the term *does not* in this context signify a concept of God that any human may have, e.g., the Jewish-Muslim concept of God as distinct from the Christian concept. Rather, the "idea of God" represents an idea

that *God* has, in particular the idea that God has of himself, or of his essence (cf. Pr. 4, II).

attribute of God which necessarily follows from the absolute nature of God.

## Proposition 22. *Whatever follows from some attribute of God, insofar as the attribute is modified by a modification that exists necessarily and as infinite through that same attribute, must also exist both necessarily and as infinite.*

Proof: This proposition is proved in the same way as the preceding one.

## Proposition 23. *Every mode which exists necessarily and as infinite must have necessarily followed either from the absolute nature of some attribute of God or from some attribute modified by a modification which exists necessarily and as infinite.*

Proof:  A mode is in something else through which it must be conceived (Def. 5); that is (Pr. 15), it is in God alone and can be conceived only through God. Therefore, if a mode is conceived to exist necessarily and to be infinite, both these characteristics must necessarily be inferred or perceived through some attribute of God insofar as that attribute is conceived to express infinity and necessity of existence, or (and by Def. 8 this is the same) eternity; that is (Def. 6 and Pr. 19), insofar as it is considered absolutely. Therefore, a mode which exists necessarily and as infinite must have followed from the absolute nature of some attribute of God, either directly (Pr. 21) or through the mediation of some modification which follows from the absolute nature of the attribute; that is (Pr. 22), which exists necessarily and as infinite.

## Proposition 24. *The essence of things produced by God does not involve existence.*

Proof: This is evident from Def. 1. For only that whose nature (considered in itself) involves existence is self-caused and exists solely from the necessity of its own nature.

Corollary: Hence it follows that God is the cause not only of the coming into existence of things but also of their continuing in existence, or, to use a scholastic term, God is the cause of the being of things [*essendi rerum*]. For whether things exist or do not exist, in reflecting on their essence we realize that this essence involves neither existence nor duration. So it is not their essence which can be the cause of either their existence or their duration, but only God, to whose nature alone existence pertains (Cor. 1 Pr. 14).

## Proposition 25. *God is the efficient cause not only of the existence of things but also of their essence.*

Proof: If this is denied, then God is not the cause of the essence of things, and so (Ax. 4) the essence of things can be conceived without God. But this is absurd (Pr. 15). Therefore, God is also the cause of the essence of things.

Scholium: This proposition follows more clearly from Pr. 16; for from that proposition it follows that from the given divine nature both the essence and the existence of things must be inferred. In a word, in the same sense that God is said to be self-caused he must also be said to be the cause of all things. This will be even clearer from the following Corollary.

Corollary: Particular things are nothing but affections of the attributes of God, that is, modes wherein the attributes of God find expression in a definite and determinate way. The proof is obvious from Pr. 15 and Def. 5.

## Proposition 26. *A thing which has been determined to act in a particular way has necessarily been so determined by God; and a thing which has not been determined by God cannot determine itself to act.*

Proof: That by which things are said to be determined to act in a particular way must necessarily be something positive (as is obvious). So God, from the necessity of his nature, is the efficient cause both of its essence and its existence (Prs. 25 and 16)—which was the first point. From this the second point quite clearly follows as well. For if a thing which has not been determined by God could determine itself, the first part of this proposition would be false, which, as I have shown, is absurd.

### Proposition 27. *A thing which has been determined by God to act in a particular way cannot render itself undetermined.*

Proof: This proposition is evident from Axiom 3.

### Proposition 28. *Every individual thing, i.e., anything whatever which is finite and has a determinate existence, cannot exist or be determined to act unless it be determined to exist and to act by another cause which is also finite and has a determinate existence, and this cause again cannot exist or be determined to act unless it be determined to exist and to act by another cause which is also finite and has a determinate existence, and so* ad infinitum.

Proof: Whatever is determined to exist and to act has been so determined by God (Pr. 26 and Cor. Pr. 24). But that which is finite and has a determinate existence cannot have been produced by the absolute nature of one of God's attributes, for whatever follows from the absolute nature of one of God's attributes is infinite and eternal (Pr. 21). It must therefore have followed from God or one of his attributes insofar as that is considered as affected by some mode; for nothing exists but substance and its modes (Ax. 1 and Defs. 3 and 5), and modes (Cor. Pr. 25) are nothing but affections of God's attributes. But neither could a finite and determined thing have followed from God or one of his attributes insofar as that is affected by a modification which is eternal and infinite (Pr. 22). Therefore, it must have followed, or been determined to exist and to act, by God or one of his attributes insofar as it was modified by a modification which is finite and has a determinate existence. That was the first point. Then again this cause or this mode (the reasoning is the same as in the first part of this proof) must also have been determined by another cause, which is also finite and has a determinate existence, and again this last (the reasoning is the same) by another, and so *ad infinitum*.

Scholium: Since some things must have been produced directly by God (those things, in fact, which necessarily follow from his absolute nature) and others through the medium of these primary things (which other things nevertheless cannot be or be conceived without God), it follows, firstly, that God is absolutely the proximate cause of things directly produced by him. I say "absolutely" [*absolute*], and not "within their own kind" [*suo genere*], as some say. For the effects of God can neither be nor be conceived without their cause (Pr. 15 and Cor. Pr. 24). It follows, secondly, that God cannot properly be said to be the remote cause of individual things, unless perchance for the purpose of distinguishing these things from things which he has produced directly, or rather, things which follow from his absolute nature. For by "remote cause" we understand a cause which is in no way conjoined with its effect. But all things that are, are in God, and depend on God in such a way that they can neither be nor be conceived without him.

### Proposition 29. *Nothing in nature is contingent, but all things are from the necessity of the divine nature determined to exist and to act in a definite way.*

Proof: Whatever is, is in God (Pr. 15). But God cannot be termed a contingent thing, for (Pr. 11) he exists necessarily, not contingently. Again, the modes of the divine nature have also followed from it necessarily, not contingently (Pr. 16), and that, too, whether insofar as the divine nature is considered absolutely (Pr. 21) or insofar as it is considered as determined to act in a definite way (Pr. 27). Furthermore, God is the cause of these modes not only insofar as they simply exist (Cor. Pr. 26), but also insofar as they are considered as determined to a particular action (Pr. 26). Now if they are not determined by God (Pr. 26), it is an impossibility, not a contingency, that they should determine themselves. On the other hand (Pr. 27), if they are determined by God, it is an impossibility, not a contingency, that they should render themselves undetermined. Therefore, all things are determined from the necessity of the divine nature not only to exist but also to exist and to act in a definite way. Thus, there is no contingency.

Scholium: Before I go any further, I wish to explain at this point what we must understand by "Natura naturans" and "Natura naturata." I should perhaps say not "explain," but "remind the reader," for I consider that it is already clear from what has gone before that by "Natura naturans" we must understand that which is in itself and is conceived through itself; that is, the attributes of substance that express eternal and infinite essence; or (Cor. 1 Pr. 14 and Cor. 2 Pr. 17), God insofar as he is considered a free cause. By "Natura naturata" I understand all that follows from the necessity of God's nature, that is, from the necessity of each one of God's attributes; or all the modes of God's attributes insofar as they are considered as things which are in God and can neither be nor be conceived without God.

## Proposition 30: *The finite intellect in act or the infinite intellect in act must comprehend the attributes of God and the affections of God, and nothing else.*[5]

Proof: A true idea must agree with its object [*ideatum*] (Ax. 6); that is (as is self-evident), that which is contained in the intellect as an object of thought must necessarily exist in Nature. But in Nature (Cor. 1 Pr. 14) there is but one substance—God—and no other affections (Pr. 15) than those which are in God and that can neither be nor be conceived (Pr. 15) without God. Therefore, the finite intellect in act or the infinite intellect in act must comprehend the attributes of God and the affections of God, and nothing else.

## Proposition 31. *The intellect in act, whether it be finite or infinite, as also will, desire, love, etc., must be related to Natura naturata, not to Natura naturans.*

Proof: By intellect (as is self-evident) we do not understand absolute thought, but only a definite mode of thinking which differs from other modes such as desire, love, etc., and so (Def. 5) must be conceived through absolute thought—that is (Pr. 15 and Def. 6), an attribute of God which expresses the eternal and infinite essence of thought—in such a way that without this attribute it can neither be nor be conceived; and therefore (Sch. Pr. 29) it must be related to Natura naturata, not to Natura naturans, just like the other modes of thinking.

Scholium: The reason for my here speaking of the intellect in act is not that I grant there can be any intellect in potentiality, but that, wishing to avoid any confusion, I want to confine myself to what we perceive with the utmost clarity, to wit, the very act of understanding, than which nothing is more clearly apprehended by us. For we can understand nothing that does not lead to a more perfect cognition of the understanding.

## Proposition 32. *Will cannot be called a free cause, but only a necessary cause.*

Proof: Will, like intellect, is only a definite mode of thinking, and so (Pr. 28) no single volition can exist or be determined to act unless it is determined by another cause, and this cause again by another, and so *ad infinitum*. Now if will be supposed infinite, it

---

5. In Propositions 30 and 31, Spinoza makes use of several terms that were widely employed in medieval psychology and metaphysics. Aristotle originally suggested that human thinking is such that we need to distinguish three phases in its development. First, there is the mere capacity for thinking, say, for doing mathematics. All humans, except those who are unfortunately diseased or mutilated, have this capacity. This kind of intellect was called by the medieval Aristotelians the material, or the potential, intellect [*intellectus in potentia*]. Second, when this capacity is exercised and brought into play, it is called the intellect in act [*intellectus in actu*], since now the intrinsic capacity for thinking possessed by all humans is "actualized." Another expression then for this aspect of intellection is the actual intellect. Finally, the medievals, influenced by Aristotle, introduced a third character into this story to account for the stimulation, or energizing, of the potential intellect so that it actually thinks, i.e., the agent, or active, intellect [*intellectus agens*]. This latter entity was identified by some philosophers as a suprahuman, supranatural power akin to or identical with God, or by others as a distinct power in the human intellect that acts on the mere capacity for thought, or the potential intellect. In any case, the agent, or active, intellect is *always actual*, whereas the human intellect is only *actual at times*. As Spinoza himself confesses in the Scholium to Proposition 31, he isn't really committed to this whole way of talking about

thought, for he holds that intellect is always in act. If this is so, there is nothing to contrast it to, so this entire conceptual apparatus and its vocabulary become idle.

must also be determined to exist and to act by God, not insofar as he is absolutely infinite substance, but insofar as he possesses an attribute which expresses the infinite and eternal essence of Thought (Pr. 23). Therefore, in whatever way will is conceived, whether finite or infinite, it requires a cause by which it is determined to exist and to act; and so (Def. 7) it cannot be said to be a free cause, but only a necessary or constrained cause.

Corollary 1: Hence it follows, firstly, that God does not act from freedom of will.

Corollary 2: It follows, secondly, that will and intellect bear the same relationship to God's nature as motion-and-rest and, absolutely, as all natural phenomena that must be determined by God (Pr. 29) to exist and to act in a definite way. For will, like all the rest, stands in need of a cause by which it may be determined to exist and to act in a definite manner. And although from a given will or intellect infinite things may follow, God cannot on that account be said to act from freedom of will any more than he can be said to act from freedom of motion-and-rest because of what follows from motion-and-rest (for from this, too, infinite things follow). Therefore, will pertains to God's nature no more than do other natural phenomena. It bears the same relationship to God's nature as does motion-and-rest and everything else that we have shown to follow from the necessity of the divine nature and to be determined by that divine nature to exist and to act in a definite way.

## Proposition 33. *Things could not have been produced by God in any other way or in any other order than is the case.*

Proof: All things have necessarily followed from the nature of God (Pr. 16) and have been determined to exist and to act in a definite way from the necessity of God's nature (Pr. 29). Therefore, if things could have been of a different nature or been determined to act in a different way so that the order of Nature would have been different, then God's nature, too, could have been other than it now is, and therefore (Pr. 11) this different nature, too, would have had to exist, and consequently there would have been two or more Gods, which (Cor. 1 Pr. 14) is absurd. Therefore, things could not have been produced by God in any other way or in any other order than is the case.

Scholium 1: Since I have here shown more clearly than the midday sun that in things there is absolutely nothing by virtue of which they can be said to be "contingent," I now wish to explain briefly what we should understand by "contingent"; but I must first deal with "necessary" and "impossible." A thing is termed "necessary" either by reason of its essence or by reason of its cause. For a thing's existence necessarily follows either from its essence and definition or from a given efficient cause. Again, it is for these same reasons that a thing is termed "impossible"— that is, either because its essence or definition involves a contradiction or because there is no external cause determined to bring it into existence. But a thing is termed "contingent" for no other reason than the deficiency of our knowledge. For if we do not know whether the essence of a thing involves a contradiction, or if, knowing full well that its essence does not involve a contradiction, we still cannot make any certain judgment as to its existence because the chain of causes is hidden from us, then that thing cannot appear to us either as necessary or as impossible. So we term it either "contingent" or "possible."

Scholium 2: It clearly follows from the above that things have been brought into being by God with supreme perfection, since they have necessarily followed from a most perfect nature. Nor does this imply any imperfection in God, for it is his perfection that has constrained us to make this affirmation. Indeed, from its contrary it would clearly follow (as I have just shown) that God is not supremely perfect, because if things had been brought into being in a different way by God, we should have to attribute to God another nature different from that which consideration of a most perfect Being has made us attribute to him.

However, I doubt not that many will ridicule this view as absurd and will not give their minds to its examination, and for this reason alone, that they are in the habit of attributing to God another kind of freedom very different from that which we (Def. 7) have assigned to him, that is, an absolute will. Yet I do not doubt that if they were willing to think the matter over and carefully reflect on our chain of proofs they would in the end reject the kind of freedom which they now attribute to God not only as nonsensical but as a serious obstacle to science. It is needless for me here to repeat what was said in the Scholium to Proposition 17. Yet for their sake I shall proceed to show that, even if it were to be granted that will pertains to the essence of God, it would nevertheless follow from his perfection that things could not have been created by God in any other way or in any other order. This will readily be shown if we first consider—as they themselves grant—that on God's decree and will alone does it depend that each thing is what it is. For otherwise God would not be the cause of all things. Further, there is the fact that all God's decrees have been sanctioned by God from eternity, for otherwise he could be accused of imperfection and inconstancy. But since the eternal does not admit of "when" or "before" or "after," it follows merely from God's perfection that God can never decree otherwise nor ever could have decreed otherwise; in other words, God could not have been prior to his decrees nor can he be without them. "But," they will say, "granted the supposition that God had made a different universe, or that from eternity he had made a different decree concerning Nature and her order, no imperfection in God would follow therefrom." But if they say this, they will be granting at the same time that God can change his decrees. For if God's decrees had been different from what in fact he has decreed regarding Nature and her order—that is, if he had willed and conceived differently concerning Nature—he would necessarily have had a different intellect and a different will from that which he now has. And if it is permissible to attribute to God a different intellect and a different will without any change in his essence and perfection, why should he not now be able to change his decrees concerning created things, and nevertheless remain equally perfect? For his intellect and will regarding created things and their order have the same relation to his essence and perfection, in whatever manner it be conceived.

Then again, all philosophers whom I have read grant that in God there is no intellect in potentiality

but only intellect in act. Now since all of them also grant that his intellect and will are not distinct from his essence, it therefore follows from this, too, that if God had had a different intellect in act and a different will, his essence too would necessarily have been different. Therefore—as I deduced from the beginning—if things had been brought into being by God so as to be different from what they now are, God's intellect and will—that is (as is granted), God's essence—must have been different, which is absurd. Therefore, since things could not have been brought into being by God in any other way or order—and it follows from God's supreme perfection that this is true—surely we can have no sound reason for believing that God did not wish to create all the things that are in his intellect through that very same perfection whereby he understands them.

"But," they will say, "there is in things no perfection or imperfection; that which is in them whereby they are perfect or imperfect, and are called good or bad, depends only on the will of God. Accordingly, if God had so willed it he could have brought it about that that which is now perfection should be utmost imperfection, and vice versa." But what else is this but an open assertion that God, who necessarily understands that which he wills, can by his will bring it about that he should understand things in a way different from the way he understands them—and this, as I have just shown, is utterly absurd. So I can turn their own argument against them, as follows. All things depend on the power of God. For things to be able to be otherwise than as they are, God's will, too, would necessarily have to be different. But God's will cannot be different (as we have just shown most clearly from the consideration of God's perfection). Therefore, neither can things be different.

I admit that this view which subjects everything to some kind of indifferent will of God and asserts that everything depends on his pleasure diverges less from the truth than the view of those who hold that God does everything with the good in mind. For these people seem to posit something external to God that does not depend upon him, to which in acting God looks as if it were a model, or to which he aims, as if it were a fixed target. This is surely to subject God to fate; and no more absurd assertion can be made about God, whom we have shown to be the first and the only free cause of both the essence and the existence of things. So I need not spend any more time in refuting this absurdity.

## Proposition 34. *God's power is his very essence.*

Proof: From the sole necessity of God's essence it follows that God is self-caused (Pr. 11) and the cause of all things (Pr. 16 and Cor.). Therefore, God's power, whereby he and all things are and act, is his very essence.

## Proposition 35. *Whatever we conceive to be within God's power necessarily exists.*

Proof: Whatever is within God's power must be so comprehended in his essence (Pr. 34) that it follows necessarily from it, and thus necessarily exists.

## Proposition 36. *Nothing exists from whose nature an effect does not follow.*

Proof: Whatever exists expresses God's nature or essence in a definite and determinate way (Cor. Pr. 25); that is (Pr. 34), whatever exists expresses God's power, which is the cause of all things, in a definite and determinate way, and so (Pr. 16) some effect must follow from it.

## Appendix

I have now explained the nature and properties of God: that he necessarily exists, that he is one alone, that he is and acts solely from the necessity of his own nature, that he is the free cause of all things and how so, that all things are in God and are so dependent on him that they can neither be nor be conceived without him, and lastly, that all things have been predetermined by God, not from his free will or absolute pleasure, but from the absolute nature of God, his infinite power. Furthermore, whenever the opportunity arose I have striven to remove prejudices that might hinder the apprehension of my proofs. But since there still remain a considerable number of prejudices, which have been, and still are, an obstacle—indeed, a very great obstacle—to the acceptance of the concatenation of things in the manner which I have expounded, I have thought it proper at this point to bring these prejudices before the bar of reason.

Now all the prejudices which I intend to mention here turn on this one point, the widespread belief among men that all things in Nature are like themselves in acting with an end in view. Indeed, they hold it as certain that God himself directs everything to a fixed end; for they say that God has made everything for man's sake and has made man so that he should worship God. So this is the first point I shall consider, seeking the reason why most people are victims of this prejudice and why all are so naturally disposed to accept it. Secondly, I shall demonstrate its falsity; and lastly I shall show how it has been the source of misconceptions about good and bad, right and wrong, praise and blame, order and confusion, beauty and ugliness, and the like.

However, it is not appropriate here to demonstrate the origin of these misconceptions from the nature of the human mind. It will suffice at this point if I take as my basis what must be universally admitted, that all men are born ignorant of the causes of things, that they all have a desire to seek their own advantage, a desire of which they are conscious. From this it follows, firstly, that men believe that they are free, precisely because they are conscious of their volitions and desires; yet concerning the causes that have determined them to desire and will they do not think, not even dream about, because they are ignorant of them. Secondly, men act always with an end in view, to wit, the advantage that they seek. Hence it happens that they are always looking only for the final causes of things done, and are satisfied when they find them, having, of course, no reason for further doubt. But if they fail to discover them from some external source, they have no recourse but to turn to themselves, and to reflect on what ends would normally determine them to similar actions, and so they necessarily judge other minds by their own. Further, since they find within themselves and outside themselves a considerable number of means very convenient for the pursuit of their own advantage—as, for instance, eyes for seeing, teeth for chewing, cereals and living creatures for food, the sun for giving light, the sea for breeding fish—the result is that they look on all the things of Nature as means to their own advantage. And realizing that these were found, not produced by them, they come to believe that there is someone else who produced these means for their use. For looking on things as means, they could not believe them to be self-created, but on the analogy of the means which they are accustomed to produce for themselves, they were bound to conclude that there was some governor or governors of Nature, endowed with human freedom, who have attended to all their needs and made everything for their use. And having no information on the subject, they also had to estimate the character of these rulers by their own, and so they asserted that the gods direct everything for man's use so that they may bind men to them and be held in the highest honor by them. So it came about that every individual devised different methods of worshipping God as he thought fit in order that God should love him beyond others and direct the whole of Nature so as to serve his blind cupidity and insatiable greed. Thus it was that this misconception developed into superstition and became deep-rooted in the minds of men, and it was for this reason that every man strove most earnestly to understand and to explain the final causes of all things. But in seeking to show that Nature does nothing in vain—that is, nothing that is not to man's advantage—they seem to have shown only this, that Nature and the gods are as crazy as mankind.

Consider, I pray, what has been the upshot. Among so many of Nature's blessings they were bound to discover quite a number of disasters, such as storms, earthquakes, diseases and so forth, and they maintained that these occurred because the gods were angry at the wrongs done to them by men, or the faults committed in the course of their worship. And although daily experience cried out against this and showed by any number of examples that blessings and disasters befall the godly and the ungodly alike without discrimination, they did not on that account

abandon their ingrained prejudice. For they found it easier to regard this fact as one among other mysteries they could not understand and thus maintain their innate condition of ignorance rather than to demolish in its entirety the theory they had constructed and devise a new one. Hence they made it axiomatic that the judgment of the gods is far beyond man's understanding. Indeed, it is for this reason, and this reason only, that truth might have evaded mankind forever had not Mathematics, which is concerned not with ends but only with the essences and properties of figures, revealed to men a different standard of truth. And there are other causes too—there is no need to mention them here—which could have made men aware of these widespread misconceptions and brought them to a true knowledge of things.

I have thus sufficiently dealt with my first point. There is no need to spend time in going on to show that Nature has no fixed goal and that all final causes are but figments of the human imagination. For I think that this is now quite evident, both from the basic causes from which I have traced the origin of this misconception and from Proposition 16 and the Corollaries to Proposition 32, and in addition from the whole set or proofs I have adduced to show that all things in Nature proceed from all eternal necessity and with supreme perfection. But I will make this additional point, that this doctrine of Final Causes turns Nature completely upside down, for it regards as an effect that which is in fact a cause, and vice versa. Again, it makes that which is by nature first to be last; and finally, that which is highest and most perfect is held to be the most imperfect. Omitting the first two points as self-evident, Propositions 21, 22, and 23 make it clear that that effect is most perfect which is directly produced by God, and an effect is the less perfect in proportion to the number of intermediary causes required for its production. But if the things produced directly by God were brought about to enable him to attain an end, then of necessity the last things for the sake of which the earlier things were brought about would excel all others. Again, this doctrine negates God's perfection; for if God acts with an end in view, he must necessarily be seeking something that he lacks. And although theologians and metaphysicians may draw a distinction between a purpose arising from want and an assimilative purpose,[6] they still admit that God has acted in all things for the sake of himself, and not for the sake of the things to be created. For prior to creation they are not able to point to anything but God as a purpose for God's action. Thus they have to admit that God lacked and desired those things for the procurement of which he willed to create the means—as is self-evident.

I must not fail to mention here that the advocates of this doctrine, eager to display their talent in assigning purpose to things, have introduced a new style of argument to prove their doctrine, i.e., a reduction, not to the impossible, but to ignorance, thus revealing the lack of any other argument in its favor. For example, if a stone falls from the roof on somebody's head and kills him, by this method of arguing they will prove that the stone fell in order to kill the man; for if it had not fallen for this purpose by the will of God, how could so many circumstances (and there are often many coinciding circumstances) have chanced to concur? Perhaps you will reply that the event occurred because the wind was blowing and the man was walking that way. But they will persist in asking why the wind blew at that time and why the man was walking that way at that very time. If you again reply that the wind sprang up at that time because on the previous day the sea had begun to toss after a period of calm and that the man had been invited by a friend, they will again persist—for there is no end to questions—"But why did the sea toss, and why was the man invited for that time?" And so they will

go on and on asking the causes of causes, until you take refuge in the will of God—that is, the sanctuary of ignorance. Similarly, when they consider the structure of the human body, they are astonished, and being ignorant of the causes of such skillful work they conclude that it is fashioned not by mechanical art but by divine or supernatural art, and is so arranged that no one part shall injure another.

As a result, he who seeks the true causes of miracles and is eager to understand the works of Nature as a scholar, and not just to gape at them like a fool, is universally considered an impious heretic and denounced by those to whom the common people bow down as interpreters of Nature and the gods. For these people know that the dispelling of ignorance would entail the disappearance of that astonishment, which is the one and only support for their argument and for safeguarding their authority. But I will leave this subject and proceed to the third point that I proposed to deal with.

When men become convinced that everything that is created is created on their behalf, they were bound to consider as the most important quality in every individual thing that which was most useful to them, and to regard as of the highest excellence all those things by which they were most benefited. Hence they came to form these abstract notions to explain the natures of things: Good, Bad, Order, Confusion, Hot, Cold, Beauty, Ugliness; and since they believed that they are free, the following abstract notions came into being: Praise, Blame, Right, Wrong. The latter I shall deal with later on after I have treated of human nature; at this point I shall briefly explain the former.

All that conduces to well being and to the worship of God they call Good, and the contrary, Bad. And since those who do not understand the nature of things, but only imagine things, make no affirmative judgments about things themselves and mistake their imagination for intellect,[7] they are firmly convinced

---

6. Spinoza alludes here to a late scholastic distinction between two kinds of purposes, or goals: a purpose that satisfies some internal need or lack [*fines indigentiae*]; and a purpose that aims to share what one already has with others who lack it [*fines assimilationis*]. In the present case, this distinction implies that when God does something purposively, he acts not to fulfill a need he has, but to benefit creatures. In their commentaries on the *Ethics*, both Lewis Robinson and Harry Wolfson refer to the seventeenth-century Dutch theologian A. Heereboord as Spinoza's source for this distinction (L. Robinson, *Kommentar zu Spinoza's Ethik* (Leipzig, 1928), pp. 234–35; H. Wolfson, *The Philosophy of Spinoza* (New York, 1969), vol. 1, p. 432).

   The theologians derided by Spinoza hoped to avoid by means of this distinction the suggestion that if God acts purposively, he does so because of a need on his part.

7. One of the more fundamental doctrines in Spinoza's theory of knowledge is the radical distinction between imagination and understanding, a point that will be developed in detail in Part II, Propositions 40–49. A corollary of this distinction is the important difference for Spinoza between images and ideas. The former are virtually identical with pictures, which the etymology of the word "imagine" indicates. The capacity of

that there is order in things, ignorant as they are of things and of their own nature. For when things are in such arrangement that, being presented to us through our senses, we can readily picture them and thus readily remember them, we say that they are well arranged; if the contrary, we say that they are ill arranged, or confused. And since those things we can readily picture we find pleasing compared with other things, men prefer order to confusion, as though order were something in Nature other than what is relative to our imagination. And they say that God has created all things in an orderly way, without realizing that they are thus attributing human imagination to God—unless perchance they mean that God, out of consideration for the human imagination, arranged all things in the way that men could most easily imagine. And perhaps they will find no obstacle in the fact that there are any number of things that far surpass our imagination, and a considerable number that confuse the imagination because of its weakness.

But I have devoted enough time to this. Other notions, too, are nothing but modes of imagining whereby the imagination is affected in various ways, and yet the ignorant consider them as important attributes of things because they believe—as I have said—that all things were made on their behalf, and they call a thing's nature good or bad, healthy or rotten and corrupt, according to its effect on them. For instance, if the motion communicated to our nervous system by objects presented through our eyes is conducive to our feeling of well being, the objects which are its cause are said to be beautiful, while the objects which provoke a contrary motion are called ugly. Those things that we sense through the nose are called fragrant or fetid; through the tongue, sweet or bitter, tasty or tasteless; those that we sense by touch are called hard or soft, rough or smooth, and so on. Fi-

nally, those that we sense through our ears are said to give forth noise, sound, or harmony, the last of which has driven men to such madness that they used to believe that even God delights in harmony. There are philosophers who have convinced themselves that the motions of the heavens give rise to harmony. All this goes to show that everyone's judgment is a function of the disposition of his brain, or rather, that he mistakes for reality the way his imagination is affected. Hence it is no wonder—as we should note in passing—that we find so many controversies arising among men, resulting finally in skepticism. For although human bodies agree in many respects, there are very many differences, and so one man thinks good what another thinks bad; what to one man is well ordered, to another is confused; what to one is pleasing, to another is displeasing, and so forth. I say no more here because this is not the place to treat at length of this subject, and also because all are well acquainted with it from experience. Everybody knows those sayings: "So many heads, so many opinions," "everyone is wise in his own sight," "brains differ as much as palates," all of which show clearly that men's judgment is a function of the disposition of the brain, and they are guided by imagination rather than intellect. For if men understood things, all that I have put forward would be found, if not attractive, at any rate convincing, as Mathematics attests.

We see therefore that all the notions whereby the common people are wont to explain Nature are merely modes of imagining, and denote not the nature of any thing but only the constitution of the imagination. And because these notions have names as if they were the names of entities existing independently of the imagination I call them "entities of imagination" [*entia imaginationis*] rather than "entities of reason" [*entia rationis*]. So all arguments drawn from such notions against me can be easily refuted. For many are wont to argue on the following lines: If everything has followed from the necessity of God's most perfect nature, why does Nature display so many imperfections, such as rottenness to the point of putridity, nauseating ugliness, confusion, evil, sin, and so on? But, as I have just pointed out, they are easily refuted. For the perfection of things should be measured solely from their own nature and power; nor

---

imagination, or better the act of imagining, is for Spinoza the ability we have to represent to ourselves things, which may or may not exist, without regard to truth. In this sense the imagination is always "free" and "spontaneous": reality doesn't tie it down. Understanding, or intellect, however, is not so "fancy free." It is concerned with reality and truth. Ideas, for Spinoza, are the products of the intellect, or understanding: they are not pictures of things but judgments about them, and hence are true or false (Part II, Proposition 43, Scholium).

are things more or less perfect to the extent that they please or offend human senses, serve or oppose human interests. As to those who ask why God did not create men in such a way that they should be governed solely by reason, I make only this reply, that he lacked not material for creating all things from the highest to the lowest degree of perfection; or, to speak more accurately, the laws of his nature were so comprehensive as to suffice for the production of everything that can be conceived by an infinite intellect, as I proved in Proposition 16.

These are the misconceptions which I undertook to deal with at this point. Any other misconception of this kind can be corrected by everyone with a little reflection.

## Part II. Of the Nature and Origin of the Mind

I now pass on to the explication of those things that must necessarily have followed from the essence of God, the eternal and infinite Being; not indeed all of them—for we proved in Proposition 16, Part I that from his essence there must follow infinite things in infinite ways—but only those things that can lead us as it were by the hand to the knowledge of the human mind and its utmost blessedness.

### Definitions

1. By "body" I understand a mode that expresses in a definite and determinate way God's essence insofar as he is considered as an extended thing. (See Cor. Pr. 25, I.)

2. I say that there pertains to the essence of a thing that which, when granted, the thing is necessarily posited, and by the annulling of which the thing is necessarily annulled; or that without which the thing can neither be nor be conceived, and, vice versa, that which cannot be or be conceived without the thing.

3. By idea I understand a conception of the Mind which the Mind forms because it is a thinking thing.
   *Explication:* I say "conception" rather than "perception" because the term perception seems to indi-

cate that the Mind is passive to its object whereas conception seems to express an activity of the Mind.

4. By an adequate idea I mean an idea which, insofar as it is considered in itself without relation to its object, has all the properties, that is, intrinsic characteristics, of a true idea [*ideatum*].
   *Explication:* I say "intrinsic" so as to exclude the extrinsic characteristic—to wit the agreement of the idea with that of which it is an idea.

5. Duration is the indefinite continuance of existing.
   *Explication:* I say "indefinite" because it can in no wise be determined through the nature of the existing thing, nor again by the thing's efficient cause which necessarily posits, but does not annul, the existence of the thing

6. By reality and perfection I mean the same thing.

7. By individual things [*res singulares*] I mean things that are finite and have a determinate existence. If several individual things concur in one act in such a way as to be all together the simultaneous cause of one effect, I consider them all, in that respect, as one individual.

### Axioms

1. The essence of man does not involve necessary existence; that is, from the order of Nature it is equally possible that a certain man exists or does not exist.

2. Man thinks.

3. Modes of thinking such as love, desire, or whatever emotions are designated by name, do not occur unless there is in the same individual the idea of the thing loved, desired, etc. But the idea can be without any other mode of thinking.

4. We feel a certain body to be affected in many ways.

5. We do not feel or perceive any individual things except bodies and modes of thinking. [N.B.: For Postulates, see after Proposition 13.]

## Proposition 1. *Thought is an attribute of God; i.e., God is a thinking thing.*

Proof: Individual thoughts, or this and that thought, are modes expressing the nature of God in a definite and determinate way (Cor. Pr. 25, I). Therefore, there belongs to God (Def. 5, I) an attribute the conception of which is involved in all individual thoughts, and through which they are conceived. Thought, therefore, is one of God's infinite attributes, expressing the eternal and infinite essence of God (Def. 6, I); that is, God is a thinking thing.

Scholium: This Proposition is also evident from the fact that we can conceive of an infinite thinking being. For the more things a thinking being can think, the more reality or perfection we conceive it to have. Therefore, a being that can think infinite things in infinite ways is by virtue of its thinking necessarily infinite. Since therefore by merely considering Thought we conceive an infinite being, Thought is necessarily one of the infinite attributes of God (Defs. 4 and 6, I), as we set out to prove.

## Proposition 2. *Extension is an attribute of God; i.e., God is an extended thing.*

Proof: This Proposition is proved in the same way as the preceding proposition.

## Proposition 3. *In God there is necessarily the idea both of his essence and of everything that necessarily follows from his essence.*

Proof: For God can (Pr. 1, II) think infinite things in infinite ways, or (what is the same thing, by Pr. 16, I) can form the idea of his own essence and of everything that necessarily follows from it. But all that is in God's power necessarily exists (Pr. 35, I). Therefore, such an idea necessarily exists, and only in God (Pr. 15, I).

Scholium: By God's power the common people understand free will and God's right over all things that are, which things are therefore commonly considered as contingent. They say that God has power to destroy everything and bring it to nothing. Further-

more, they frequently compare God's power with that of kings. But this doctrine we have refuted in Cors. 1 and 2, Pr. 32, I; and in Pr. 16, I, we proved that God acts by the same necessity whereby he understands himself; that is, just as it follows from the necessity of the divine Nature (as is universally agreed) that God understands himself, by that same necessity it also follows that God acts infinitely in infinite ways. Again, we showed in Pr. 34, I that God's power is nothing but God's essence in action, and so it is as impossible for us to conceive that God does not act as that God does not exist. Furthermore if one wished to pursue the matter, I could easily show here that the power that common people assign to God is not only a human power (which shows that they conceive God as a man or like a man) but also involves negation of power. But I am reluctant to hold forth so often on the same subject. I merely request the reader most earnestly to reflect again and again on what we said on this subject in Part I from Proposition 16 to the end. For nobody will rightly apprehend what I am trying to say unless he takes great care not to confuse God's power with a king's human power or right.

## Proposition 4. *The idea of God, from which infinite things follow in infinite ways, must be one, and one only.*

Proof: Infinite intellect comprehends nothing but the attributes of God and his affections (Pr. 30, I). But God is one, and one only (Cor. 1, Pr. 14, I). Therefore, the idea of God, from which infinite things follow in infinite ways, must be one, and one only.

## Proposition 5. *The formal being of ideas recognizes God as its cause only insofar as he is considered as a thinking thing, and not insofar as he is explicated by any other attribute; that is, the ideas both of God's attributes and of individual things recognize as their efficient cause not the things of which they are ideas, that is, the things perceived, but God himself insofar as he is a thinking thing.*

Proof: This is evident from Pr. 3, II. For there our conclusion that God can form the idea of his own essence and of everything that necessarily follows therefrom was inferred solely from God's being a thinking thing, and not from his being the object of his own idea. Therefore, the formal being of ideas recognizes God as its cause insofar as he is a thinking thing. But there is another proof, as follows. The formal being of ideas is a mode of thinking (as is self-evident); that is (Cor. Pr. 25, I), a mode which expresses in a definite manner the nature of God insofar as he is a thinking thing, and so does not involve (Pr. 10, I) the conception of any other attribute of God. Consequently (Ax. 4, I), it is the effect of no other attribute but thought; and so the formal being of ideas recognizes God as its cause only insofar as he is considered as a thinking thing.

## Proposition 6. *The modes of any attribute have God for their cause only insofar as he is considered under that attribute, and not insofar as he is considered under any other attribute.*

Proof: Each attribute is conceived through itself independently of any other (Pr. 10, I). Therefore, the modes of any attribute involve the conception of their own attribute, and not that of any other. Therefore, they have God for their cause only insofar as he is considered under the attribute of which they are modes, and not insofar as he is considered under any other attribute (Ax. 4, I).

Corollary: Hence it follows that the formal being of things that are not modes of thinking does not follow from the nature of God by reason of his first having known them; rather, the objects of ideas follow and are inferred from their own attributes in the same way and by the same necessity as we have shown ideas to follow from the attribute of Thought.

## Proposition 7. *The order and connection of ideas is the same as the order and connection of things.*

Proof: This is evident from Ax. 4, I; for the idea of what is caused depends on the knowledge of the cause of which it is the effect.

Corollary: Hence it follows that God's power of thinking is on par with his power of acting. That is, whatever follows formally from the infinite nature of God, all this follows from the idea of God as an object of thought in God according to the same order and connection.

Scholium: At this point, before proceeding further, we should recall to mind what I have demonstrated above—that whatever can be perceived by infinite intellect as constituting the essence of substance pertains entirely to the one sole substance. Consequently, thinking substance and extended substance are one and the same substance, comprehended now under this attribute, now under that. So, too, a mode of Extension and the idea of that mode are one and the same thing, expressed in two ways. This truth seems to have been glimpsed by some of the Hebrews, who hold that God, God's intellect, and the things understood by God are one and the same. For example, a circle existing in Nature and the idea of the existing circle—which is also in God—are one and the same thing, explicated through different attributes. And so, whether we conceive Nature under the attribute of Extension or under the attribute of Thought or under any other attribute, we find one and the same order, or one and the same connection of causes—that is, the same things following one another. When I said that God is the cause, e.g., of the idea of a circle only insofar as he is a thinking thing, and of a circle only insofar as he is an extended thing, my reason was simply this, that the formal being of the idea of a circle can be perceived only through another mode of thinking as its proximate cause, and that mode through another, and so *ad infinitum*, with the result that as long as things are considered as modes of thought, we must explicate the order of the whole of Nature, or the connection of causes, through the attribute of Thought alone; and insofar as things are considered as modes of Extension, again the order of the whole of Nature must be explicated through the attribute of Extension only. The same applies to other attributes. Therefore God, insofar as he consists of infinite attributes, is in fact the cause of things as they are in themselves. For the present, I cannot give a clearer explanation.

Proposition 8. *The ideas of nonexisting individual things or modes must be comprehended in the infinite idea of God in the same way as the formal essences of individual things or modes are contained in the attributes of God.*

Proof: This proposition is obvious from the preceding one, but may be understood more clearly from the preceding Scholium.

Corollary: Hence it follows that as long as individual things do not exist except insofar as they are comprehended in the attributes of God, their being as objects of thought—that is, their ideas—do not exist except insofar as the infinite idea of God exists; and when individual things are said to exist not only insofar as they are comprehended in the attributes of God but also insofar as they are said to have duration, their ideas also will involve the existence through which they are said to have duration.

Scholium: Should anyone want an example for a clearer understanding of this matter, I can think of none at all that would adequately explicate the point with which I am here dealing, for it has no parallel. Still, I shall try to illustrate it as best I can. The nature of a circle is such that the rectangles formed from

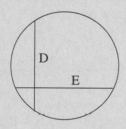

the segments of its intersecting chords are equal. Hence an infinite number of equal rectangles are contained in a circle, but none of them can be said to exist except insofar as the circle exists, nor again can the idea of any one of these rectangles be said to exist except insofar as it is comprehended in the idea of the circle. Now of this infinite number of intersecting chords let two, E and D, exist. Now indeed their ideas also exist not only insofar as they are merely comprehended in the idea of the circle but

also insofar as they involve the existence of those rectangles, with the result that they are distinguished from the other ideas of the other rectangles.

Proposition 9. *The idea of an individual thing existing in actuality has God for its cause not insofar as he is infinite but insofar as he is considered as affected by another idea of a thing existing in actuality, of which God is the cause insofar as he is affected by a third idea, and so ad infinitum.*

Proof: The idea of an individual actually existing thing is an individual mode of thinking distinct from other modes (Cor. and Sch. Pr. 8, II), and so (Pr. 6, II) it has God as its cause only insofar as he is a thinking thing. But not (Pr. 28, I) insofar as he is a thinking thing absolutely, but insofar as he is considered as affected by another definite mode of thinking. And of this latter God is also the cause insofar as he is affected by another definite mode of thinking, and so *ad infinitum*. But the order and connection of ideas is the same as the order and connection of causes (Pr. 7, II). Therefore, an individual idea is caused by another idea; i.e., God insofar as he is considered as affected by another idea. And this last idea is caused by God, insofar as he is affected by yet another idea, and so *ad infinitum*.

Corollary: Whatsoever happens in the individual object of any idea, knowledge of it is in God only insofar as he has the idea of that object.

Proof: Whatsoever happens in the object of any idea, the idea of it is in God (Pr. 3, II) not insofar as he is infinite, but insofar as he is considered as affected by another idea of an individual thing (preceding Pr.). But the order and connection of ideas is the same as the order and connection of things (Pr. 7, II). Therefore, the knowledge of what happens in an individual object is in God only insofar as he has the idea of that object.

Proposition 10. *The being of substance does not pertain to the essence of man; i.e., substance does not constitute the form [forma] of man.*

Proof: The being of substance involves necessary existence (Pr. 7, I). So if the being of substance pertained to the essence of man, man would necessarily be granted together with the granting of substance (Def. 2, II) and consequently man would necessarily exist, which is absurd (Ax. 1, II). Therefore . . . etc.

Scholium: This Proposition is also proved from Pr. 5, I, which states that there cannot be two substances of the same nature. Now since many men can exist, that which constitutes the form of man is not the being of substance. This Proposition is furthermore evident from the other properties of substance—that substance is by its own nature infinite, immutable, indivisible, etc., as everyone can easily see.

Corollary: Hence it follows that the essence of man is constituted by definite modifications of the attributes of God.

Proof: For the being of substance does not pertain to the essence of man (preceding Pr.), which must therefore be something that is in God, and which can neither be nor be conceived without God; i.e., an affection or mode (Cor. Pr. 25, I) which expresses the nature of God in a definite and determinate way.

Scholium: All must surely admit that nothing can be or be conceived without God. For all are agreed that God is the sole cause of all things, both of their essence and of their existence; that is, God is the cause of things not only in respect of their coming into being [*secundum fieri*], as they say, but also in respect of their being. But at the same time many assert that that without which a thing can neither be nor be conceived pertains to the essence of the thing, and so they believe that either the nature of God pertains to the essence of created things or that created things can either be or be conceived without God; or else, more probably, they hold no consistent opinion. I think that the reason for this is their failure to observe the proper order of philosophical inquiry. For the divine nature, which they should have considered before all else—it being prior both in cognition and in Nature—they have taken to be last in the order of cognition, and the things that are called objects of sense they have taken as prior to everything. Hence it has come about that in considering natural phenomena, they have completely disregarded the divine

nature. And when thereafter they turned to the contemplation of the divine nature, they could find no place in their thinking for those fictions on which they had built their natural science, since these fictions were of no avail in attaining knowledge of the divine nature. So it is little wonder that they have contradicted themselves on all sides.

But I pass over these points, for my present purpose is restricted to explaining why I have not said that that without which a thing can neither be nor be perceived pertains to the essence of the thing. My reason is that individual things can neither be nor be conceived without God, and yet God does not pertain to their essence. But I did say that that necessarily constitutes the essence of a thing which, when posited, posits the thing, and by the annulling of which the thing is annulled; i.e., that without which the thing can neither be nor be conceived, and vice versa, that which can neither be nor be conceived without the thing.

## Proposition 11. *That which constitutes the actual being of the human mind is basically nothing else but the idea of an individual actually existing thing.*

Proof: The essence of man (Cor. Pr. 10, II) is constituted by definite modes of the attributes of God, to wit (Ax. 2, II), modes of thinking. Of all these modes the idea is prior in nature (Ax. 3, II), and when the idea is granted, the other modes—modes to which the idea is prior by nature—must be in the same individual (Ax. 3, II). And so the idea is that which basically constitutes the being of the human mind. But not the idea of a nonexisting thing; for then (Cor. Pr. 8, II) the idea itself could not be said to exist. Therefore, it is the idea of an actually existing thing. But not the idea of an infinite thing, for an infinite thing (Prs. 21 and 22, I) must always necessarily exist, and this is absurd (Ax. 1, II). Therefore, that which first constitutes the actual being of the human mind is the idea of an individual actually existing thing.

Corollary: Hence it follows that the human mind is part of the infinite intellect of God; and therefore when we say that the human mind perceives this or that, we are saying nothing else but this: that God—

not insofar as he is infinite but insofar as he is expli-cated through the nature of the human mind, that is, insofar as he constitutes the essence of the human mind—has this or that idea. And when we say that God has this or that idea not only insofar as he consti-tutes the essence of the human mind but also insofar as he has the idea of another thing simultaneously with the human mind, then we are saying that the human mind perceives a thing partially or inade-quately.

Scholium: At this point our readers will no doubt find themselves in some difficulty and will think of many things that will give them pause. So I ask them to proceed slowly step by step with me, and to post-pone judgment until they have read to the end.

## Proposition 12. *Whatever happens in the object of the idea constituting the human mind is bound to be perceived by the human mind; i.e., the idea of that thing will necessarily be in the human mind. That is to say, if the object of the idea constituting the human mind is a body, nothing can happen in that body without its being perceived by the mind.*

Proof: Whatever happens in the object of any idea, knowledge thereof is necessarily in God (Cor. Pr. 9, II) insofar as he is considered as affected by the idea of that object; that is, (Pr. 11, II) insofar as he consti-tutes the mind of some thing. So whatever happens in the object of the idea constituting the human mind, knowledge thereof is necessarily in God insofar as he constitutes the nature of the human mind; that is (Cor. Pr. 11, II), knowledge of that thing is necessarily in the mind; i.e., the mind perceives it.

Scholium: This Proposition is also obvious, and is more clearly understood from Sch. Pr. 7, II, above.

## Proposition 13. *The object of the idea constituting the human mind is the body— i.e., a definite mode of extension actually existing, and nothing else.*

Proof: If the body were not the object of the human mind, the ideas of the affections of the body would not be in God (Cor. Pr. 9, II) insofar as he constitutes

our mind, but insofar as he constitutes the mind of another thing; that is (Cor. Pr. 11, II), the ideas of the affections of the body would not be in our mind. But (Ax. 4, II) we do have ideas of the affections of a body. Therefore, the object of the idea constituting the human mind is a body, a body actually existing (Pr. 11, II). Again, if there were another object of the mind apart from the body, since nothing exists from which some effect does not follow (Pr. 36, I), there would necessarily have to be in our mind the idea of some effect of it (Pr. 12, II). But (Ax. 5, II) there is no such idea. Therefore, the object of our mind is an existing body, and nothing else.

Corollary: Hence it follows that man consists of mind and body, and the human body exists according as we sense it.

Scholium: From the above we understand not only that the human Mind is united to the Body but also what is to be understood by the union of Mind and Body. But nobody can understand this union ade-quately or distinctly unless he first gains adequate knowledge of the nature of our body. For what we have so far demonstrated is of quite general applica-tion, and applies to men no more than to other indi-viduals, which are all animate, albeit in different de-grees. For there is necessarily in God an idea of each thing whatever, of which idea God is the cause in the same way as he is the cause of the idea of the human body. And so whatever we have asserted of the idea of the human body must necessarily be as-serted of the idea of each thing. Yet we cannot deny, too, that ideas differ among themselves as do their objects, and that one is more excellent and contains more reality than another, just as the object of one idea is more excellent than that of another and con-tains more reality. Therefore, in order to determine the difference between the human mind and others and in what way it surpasses them, we have to know the nature of its object, (as we have said) that is, the nature of the human body. Now I cannot here explain this nature, nor is it essential for the points that I intend to demonstrate. But I will make this general assertion, that in proportion as a body is more apt than other bodies to act or be acted upon simultaneously in many ways, so is its mind more apt than other minds to perceive many things simultaneously; and in proportion as the actions of one body depend on itself alone and the less that other bodies concur with it in its actions, the more apt is its mind to understand distinctly. From this we can realize the superiority of one mind over others, and we can furthermore see why we have only a very confused knowledge of our body, and many other facts which I shall deduce from this basis in what follows. Therefore, I have thought it worthwhile to explicate and demonstrate these things more carefully. To this end there must be a brief preface concerning the nature of bodies.

Axiom 1: All bodies are either in motion or at rest.

Axiom 2: Each single body can move at varying speeds.

Lemma 1: Bodies are distinguished from one another in respect of motion-and-rest, quickness and slowness, and not in respect of substance.

Proof: The first part of this Lemma I take to be self-evident. As to bodies not being distinguished in respect of substance, this is evident from both Pr. 5 and Pr. 8, Part I, and still more clearly from Sch. Pr. 15, Part I.

Lemma 2: All bodies agree in certain respects.

Proof: All bodies agree in this, that they involve the conception of one and the same attribute (Def. 1, II), and also in that they may move at varying speeds, and may be absolutely in motion or absolutely at rest.

Lemma 3: A body in motion or at rest must have been determined to motion or rest by another body, which likewise has been determined to motion or rest by another body, and that body by another, and so *ad infinitum*.

Proof: Bodies are individual things (Def. 1, II) which are distinguished from one another in respect of motion-and-rest (Lemma 1), and so (Pr. 28, I) each body must have been determined to motion or rest by another individual thing, namely, another body (Pr. 6, II), which is also in motion or at rest (Ax. 1). But this body again—by the same reasoning—could not have been in motion or at rest unless it had been determined to motion or rest by another body, and this body again—by the same reasoning—by another body, and so on, *ad infinitum*.

Corollary: Hence it follows that a body in motion

will continue to move until it is determined to rest by another body, and a body at rest continues to be at rest until it is determined to move by another body. This, too, is self-evident; for when I suppose, for example, that a body A is at rest and I give no consideration to other moving bodies, I can assert nothing about body A but that it is at rest. Now if it should thereafter happen that body A is in motion, this surely could not have resulted from the fact that it was at rest; for from that fact nothing else could have followed than that body A should be at rest. If on the other hand A were supposed to be in motion, as long as we consider only A, we can affirm nothing of it but that it is in motion. If it should thereafter happen that A should be at rest, this surely could not have resulted from its previous motion; for from its motion nothing else could have followed but that A was in motion. So this comes about from a thing that was not in A, namely, an external cause by which the moving body A was determined to rest.

Axiom 1: All the ways in which a body is affected by another body follow from the nature of the affected body together with the nature of the body affecting it, so that one and the same body may move in various ways in accordance with the various natures of the bodies causing its motion; and, on the other hand, different bodies may be caused to move in different ways by one and the same body.

Axiom 2: When a moving body collides with a body at rest and is unable to cause it to move, it is

reflected so as to continue its motion, and the angle between the line of motion of the reflection and the plane of the body at rest with which it has collided is equal to the angle between the line of incidence of motion and the said plane.

So far we have been discussing the simplest bodies, those which are distinguished from one another solely by motion-and-rest, quickness and slowness. Now let us advance to composite bodies.

Definition: When a number of bodies of the same or different magnitude form close contact with one another through the pressure of other bodies upon them, or if they are moving at the same or different rates of speed so as to preserve an unvarying relation of movement among themselves, these bodies are said to be united with one another and all together to form one body or individual thing, which is distinguished from other things through this union of bodies.

Axiom 3: The degree of difficulty with which the parts of an individual thing or composite body can be made to change their position and consequently the degree of difficulty with which the individual takes on different shapes is proportional to the extent of the surface areas along which they are in close contact. Hence bodies whose parts maintain close contact along large areas of their surfaces I term hard; those whose parts maintain contact along small surface areas I term soft; while those whose parts are in a state of motion among themselves I term liquid.

Lemma 4: If from a body, or an individual thing composed of a number of bodies, certain bodies are separated, and at the same time a like number of other bodies of the same nature take their place, the individual thing will retain its nature as before, without any change in its form [*forma*].

Proof: Bodies are not distinguished in respect of substance (Lemma 1). That which constitutes the form of the individual thing consists in a union of bodies (preceding definition). But this union, by hypothesis, is retained in spite of the continuous change of component bodies. Therefore, the individual thing will retain its own nature as before, both in respect of substance and of mode.

Lemma 5: If the parts of an individual thing become greater or smaller, but so proportionately that they all preserve the same mutual relation of motion-and-rest as before, the individual thing will likewise retain its own nature as before without any change in its form.

Proof: The reasoning is the same as in the preceding Lemma.

Lemma 6: If certain bodies composing an individual thing are made to change the existing direction of their motion, but in such a way that they can continue their motion and keep the same mutual relation as before, the individual thing will likewise preserve its own nature without any change of form.

Proof: This is evident; for, by hypothesis, the individual thing retains all that we, in defining it, asserted as constituting its form.

Lemma 7: Furthermore, the individual thing so composed retains its own nature, whether as a whole it is moving or at rest, and in whatever direction it moves, provided that each constituent part retains its own motion and continues to communicate this motion to the other parts.

Proof: This is evident from its definition, which you will find preceding Lemma 4.

Scholium: We thus see how a composite individual can be affected in many ways and yet preserve its nature. Now previously we have conceived an individual thing composed solely of bodies distinguished from one another only by motion-and-rest and speed of movement; that is, an individual thing composed of the simplest bodies. If we now conceive another individual thing composed of several individual things of different natures, we shall find that this can be affected in many other ways while still preserving its nature. For since each one of its parts is composed of several bodies, each single part can therefore (preceding Lemma), without any change in its nature, move with varying degrees of speed and consequently communicate its own motion to other parts with varying degrees of speed. Now if we go on to conceive a third kind of individual things composed of this second kind, we shall find that it can be affected in many other ways without any change in its form. If we thus continue to infinity, we shall readily conceive the whole of Nature as one individual whose parts—that is, all the constituent bodies— vary in infinite ways without any change in the individual as a whole.

If my intention had been to write a full treatise on body, I should have had to expand my explications and demonstrations. But I have already declared a different intention, and the only reason for my dealing with this subject is that I may readily deduce therefrom what I have set out to prove.

## Postulates

1. The human body is composed of very many individual parts of different natures, each of which is extremely complex.

2. Of the individual components of the human body, some are liquid, some are soft, and some are hard.

3. The individual components of the human body, and consequently the human body itself, are affected by external bodies in a great many ways.

4. The human body needs for its preservation a great many other bodies, by which, as it were (*quasi*), it is continually regenerated.

5. When a liquid part of the human body is determined by an external body to impinge frequently on another part which is soft, it changes the surface of that part and impresses on it certain traces of the external body acting upon it.

6. The human body can move external bodies and dispose them in a great many ways.

## Proposition 14. *The human mind is capable of perceiving a great many things, and this capacity will vary in proportion to the variety of states which its body can assume.*

Proof: The human body (Posts. 3 and 6) is affected by external bodies in a great many ways and is so structured that it can affect external bodies in a great many ways. But the human mind must perceive all that happens in the human body (Pr. 12, II). Therefore, the human mind is capable of perceiving very many things, and . . . etc.

## Proposition 15. *The idea which constitutes the formal being of the human mind is not simple, but composed of very many ideas.*

Proof: The idea which constitutes the formal being of the human mind is the idea of the body (Pr. 13, II), which is composed of a great number of very

composite individual parts (Postulate 1). But in God there is necessarily the idea of every individual component part (Cor. Pr. 8, II). Therefore (Pr. 7, II), the idea of the human body is composed of these many ideas of the component parts.

## Proposition 16. *The idea of any mode wherein the human body is affected by external bodies must involve the nature of the human body together with the nature of the external body.*

Proof: All the modes wherein a body is affected follow from the nature of the body affected together with the nature of the affecting body (Ax. 1 after Cor. Lemma 3). Therefore, the idea of these modes will necessarily involve the nature of both bodies (Ax. 4, I). So the idea of any mode wherein the human body is affected by an external body involves the nature of the human body and the external body.
    Corollary 1: Hence it follows that the human mind perceives the nature of very many bodies along with the nature of its own body.
    Corollary 2: Secondly, the ideas that we have of external bodies indicate the constitution of our own body more than the nature of external bodies. This I have explained with many examples in Appendix, Part I.

## Proposition 17. *If the human body is affected in a way* [modo] *that involves the nature of some external body, the human mind will regard that same external body as actually existing, or as present to itself, until the human body undergoes a further modification which excludes the existence or presence of the said body.*

Proof: This is evident; for as long as the human body is thus affected, so long will the human mind (Pr. 12, II) regard this affection of the body that is (by the preceding Proposition), so long will it have the idea of a mode existing in actuality, an idea involving the nature of an external body; that is, an idea which does not exclude but posits the existence or presence of the nature of the external body. So the mind (Cor. 1

of the preceding proposition) will regard the external body as actually existing, or as present, until . . . etc.

Corollary: The mind is able to regard as present external bodies by which the human body has been once affected, even if they do not exist and are not present.

Proof: When external bodies so determine the fluid parts of the human body that these frequently impinge on the softer parts, they change the surfaces of these softer parts (Post. 5). Hence it comes about (Ax. 2 after Cor. Lemma 3) that the fluid parts are reflected therefrom in a manner different from what was previously the case; and thereafter, again coming into contact with the said changed surfaces in the course of their own spontaneous motion, they are reflected in the same way as when they were impelled towards those surfaces by external bodies. Consequently, in continuing this reflected motion they affect the human body in the same manner, which manner will again be the object of thought in the mind (Pr. 12, II); that is (Pr. 17, II), the mind will again regard the external body as present. This will be repeated whenever the fluid parts of the human body come into contact with those same surfaces in the course of their own spontaneous motion. Therefore, although the external bodies by which the human body has once been affected may no longer exist, the mind will regard them as present whenever this activity of the body is repeated.

Scholium: So we see how it comes about that we regard as present things which are not so, as often happens. Now it is possible that there are other causes for this fact, but it is enough for me at this point to have indicated one cause through which I can explicate the matter just as if I had demonstrated it through its true cause. Yet I do not think that I am far from the truth, since all the postulates that I have assumed contain scarcely anything inconsistent with experience; and after demonstrating that the human body exists just as we sense it (Cor. Pr. 13, II), we may not doubt experience.

In addition (preceding Cor. and Cor. 2 Pr. 16, II), this gives a clear understanding of the difference between the idea, e.g., of Peter which constitutes the essence of Peter's mind, and on the other hand the idea of Peter which is in another man, say Paul. The former directly explicates the essence of Peter's body, and does not involve existence except as long as Peter exists. The latter indicates the constitution of Paul's body rather than the nature of Peter; and so, while that constitution of Paul's body continues to be, Paul's mind will regard Peter as present to him although Peter may not be in existence. Further, to retain the usual terminology, we will assign the word "images" [*imagines*] to those affections of the human body the ideas of which set forth external bodies as if they were present to us, although they do not represent shapes. And when the mind regards bodies in this way, we shall say that it "imagines" [*imaginari*].

At this point, to begin my analysis of error, I should like you to note that the imaginations of the mind, looked at in themselves, contain no error; i.e., the mind does not err from the fact that it imagines, but only insofar as it is considered to lack the idea which excludes the existence of those things which it imagines to be present to itself. For if the mind, in imagining nonexisting things to be present to it, knew at the same time that those things did not exist in fact, it would surely impute this power of imagining not to the defect but to the strength of its own nature, especially if this faculty of imagining were to depend solely on its own nature; that is, (Def. 7, I) if this faculty of imagining were free.

## Proposition 18. *If the human body has once been affected by two or more bodies at the same time, when the mind afterwards imagines one of them, it will straightway remember the others too.*

Proof: The mind imagines (preceding Cor.) any given body for the following reason, that the human body is affected and conditioned by the impressions of an external body in the same way as it was affected when certain of its parts were acted upon by the external body. But, by hypothesis, the human mind was at that time conditioned in such a way that the mind imagined two bodies at the same time. Therefore, it will now also imagine two bodies at the same time, and the mind, in imagining one of them, will straightway remember the other as well.

Scholium: Hence we clearly understand what memory is. It is simply a linking of ideas involving the nature of things outside the human body, a linking which occurs in the mind parallel to the order and linking of the affections of the human body. I say, firstly, that it is only the linking of those ideas that involve the nature of things outside the human body, not of those ideas that explicate the nature of the said things. For they are in fact (Pr. 16, II) ideas of the affections of the human body which involve the nature both of the human body and of external bodies. Secondly, my purpose in saying that this linking occurs in accordance with the order and linking of the affections of the human body is to distinguish it from the linking of ideas in accordance with the order of the intellect whereby the mind perceives things through their first causes, and which is the same in all men.

Furthermore, from this we clearly understand why the mind, from thinking of one thing, should straightway pass on to thinking of another thing which has no likeness to the first. For example, from thinking of the word "pomum" [apple] a Roman will straightway fall to thinking of the fruit, which has no likeness to that articulated sound nor anything in common with it other than that the man's body has often been affected by them both; that is, the man has often heard the word "pomum" while seeing the fruit. So everyone will pass on from one thought to another according as habit in each case has arranged the images in his body. A soldier, for example, seeing the tracks of a horse in the sand will straightway pass on from thinking of the horse to thinking of the rider, and then thinking of war, and so on. But a peasant, from thinking of a horse, will pass on to thinking of a plough, and of a field, and so on. So every person will pass on from thinking of one thing to thinking of another according as he is in the habit of joining together and linking the images of things in various ways.

## Proposition 19. *The human mind has no knowledge of the body, nor does it know it to exist, except through ideas of the affections by which the body is affected.*

Proof: The human mind is the very idea or knowledge of the human body (Pr. 13, II), and this idea is in God (Pr. 9, II) insofar as he is considered as affected by another idea of a particular thing; or, since (Post. 4) the human body needs very many other bodies by which it is continually regenerated, and the order and connection of ideas is the same (Pr. 7, II) as the order and connection of causes, this idea is in God insofar as he is considered as affected by the ideas of numerous particular things. Therefore, God has the idea of the human body, or knows the human body, insofar as he is affected by numerous other ideas, and not insofar as he constitutes the nature of the human mind; that is (Cor. Pr. 11, II), the human mind does not know the human body. But the ideas of the affections of the body are in God insofar as he does constitute the nature of human mind; i.e., the human mind perceives these affections (Pr. 12, II) and consequently perceives the human body (Pr. 16, II), and perceives it as actually existing (Pr. 17, II). Therefore, it is only to that extent that the human mind perceives the human body.

## Proposition 20. *There is also in God the idea or knowledge of the human mind, and this follows in God and is related to God in the same way as the idea or knowledge of the human body.*

Proof: Thought is an attribute of God (Pr. 1, II), and so (Pr. 3, II) the idea of both Thought and its affections—and consequently of the human mind as well—must necessarily be in God. Now this idea or knowledge of the mind does not follow in God insofar as he is infinite, but insofar as he is affected by another idea of a particular thing (Pr. 9, II). But the order and connection of ideas is the same as the order and connection of causes (Pr. 7, II). Therefore, the idea or knowledge of the mind follows in God and is related to God in the same way as the idea or knowledge of the body.

## Proposition 21. *This idea of the mind is united to the mind in the same way as the mind is united to the body.*

Proof: That the mind is united to the body we have shown from the fact that the body is the object of the mind (Prs. 12 and 13, II), and so by the same reasoning the idea of the mind must be united to its object—that is, to the mind itself—in the same way as the mind is united to the body.

Scholium: This proposition is understood far more clearly from Sch. Pr. 7, II. There we showed that the idea of the body and the body itself—that is, (Pr. 13, II) mind and body—are one and the same individual thing, conceived now under the attribute of Thought and now under the attribute of Extension. Therefore, the idea of the mind and the mind itself are one and the same thing, conceived under one and the same attribute, namely, Thought. The idea of the mind, I repeat, and the mind itself follow in God by the same necessity and from the same power of thought. For in fact the idea of the mind—that is, the idea of an idea—is nothing other than the form [*forma*] of the idea insofar as the idea is considered as a mode of thinking without relation to its object. For as soon as anyone knows something, by that very fact he knows that he knows, and at the same time he knows that he knows that he knows, and so on *ad infinitum*. But I will deal with this subject later.

## Proposition 22. *The human mind perceives not only the affections of the body but also the ideas of these affections.*

Proof: The ideas of ideas of affections follow in God and are related to God in the same way as ideas of affections, which can be proved in the same manner as Pr. 20, II. But the ideas of affections of the body are in the human mind (Pr. 12, II); that is (Cor. Pr. 11, II), in God insofar as he constitutes the essence of the human mind. Therefore, the ideas of these ideas will be in God insofar as he has knowledge or the idea of the human mind; that is (Pr. 21, II), they will be in the human mind itself, which therefore perceives not only the affections of the body but also the ideas of these affections.

## Proposition 23. *The mind does not know itself except insofar as it perceives ideas of affections of the body.*

Proof: The idea or knowledge of the mind (Pr. 20, II) follows in God and is related to God in the same way as the idea or knowledge of the body. But since (Pr. l9, II) the human mind does not know the human body—that is, (Cor. Pr. 11, II) since the knowledge of the human body is not related to God insofar as he constitutes the nature of the human mind—therefore neither is knowledge of the mind related to God insofar as he constitutes the essence of the human mind. And so (Cor. Pr. 11, II) the human mind to that extent does not know itself. Again, the ideas of the affections by which the body is affected involve the nature of the human body (Pr. 16, II); that is, (Pr. 13, II) they are in agreement [*conveniunt*] with the nature of the mind. Therefore, the knowledge of these ideas will necessarily involve knowledge of the mind. But (preceding Pr.) the knowledge of these ideas is in the human mind. Therefore, the human mind knows itself but only to that extent.

## Proposition 24. *The human mind does not involve an adequate knowledge of the component parts of the human body.*

Proof: The component parts of the human body do not pertain to the essence of the body itself save insofar as they preserve an unvarying relation of motion with one another (Def. after Cor. Lemma 3), and not insofar as they can be considered as individual things apart from their relation to the human body. For the parts of the human body (Post. 1) are very composite individual things, whose parts can be separated from the human body (Lemma 4) without impairing in any way its nature and specific reality [*forma*], and can establish a quite different relation of motion with other bodies (Ax. 1 after Lemma 3). Therefore (Pr. 3, II), the idea or knowledge of any component part will be in God, and will be so (Pr. 9, II) insofar as he is considered as affected by another idea of a particular thing, a particular thing which is prior in Nature's order to the part itself (Pr. 7, II). Further, the same holds good of any part of an individual component part of the human body, and so of any component part of the human body there is knowledge in God insofar as he is affected by very many ideas of things, and not insofar as he has the idea only of the human body, that is (Pr. 13, II), the idea that constitutes the nature of the human mind. So (Cor. Pr. 11, II) the human mind does not involve adequate knowledge of the component parts of the human body.

## Proposition 25. *The idea of any affection of the human body does not involve an adequate knowledge of an external body.*

Proof: We have shown that the idea of an affection of the human body involves the nature of an external body insofar as the external body determines the human body in some definite way (Pr. 16, II). But insofar as the external body is an individual thing that is not related to the human body, the idea or knowledge of it is in God (Pr. 9, II) insofar as God is considered as affected by the idea of another thing which is (Pr. 7, II) prior in nature to the said external body. Therefore, an adequate knowledge of the external body is not in God insofar as he has the idea of an affection of the human body; i.e., the idea of an affection of the human body does not involve an adequate knowledge of an external body.

## Proposition 26. *The human mind does not perceive any external body as actually existing except through the ideas of affections of its own body.*

Proof: If the human body is not affected in any way by an external body, then (Pr. 7, II) neither is the idea of the human body—that is (Pr. 13, II), the human mind—affected in any way by the idea of the existence of that body; i.e., it does not in any way perceive the existence of that external body. But insofar as the human body is affected in some way by an external body, to that extent it perceives the external body (Pr. 16, II, with Cor. 1).

   Corollary: Insofar as the human mind imagines [*imaginatur*] an external body, to that extent it does not have an adequate knowledge of it.

Proof: When the human mind regards external bodies through the ideas of affections of its own body, we say

that it imagines [*imaginatur*] (see Sch. Pr. 17, II), and in no other way can the mind imagine external bodies as actually existing (preceding Pr.). Therefore, insofar as the mind imagines external bodies (Pr. 25, II), it does not have adequate knowledge of them.

## Proposition 27. *The idea of any affection of the human body does not involve adequate knowledge of the human body.*

Proof: Any idea whatsoever of any affection of the human body involves the nature of the human body only to the extent that the human body is considered to be affected in some definite way (Pr. 16, II). But insofar as the human body is an individual thing that can be affected in many other ways, the idea . . . etc. (See Proof Pr. 25, II).

## Proposition 28. *The ideas of the affections of the human body, insofar as they are related only to the human mind, are not clear and distinct, but confused.*

Proof: The ideas of the affections of the human body involve the nature both of external bodies and of the human body itself (Pr. 16, II), and must involve the nature not only of the human body but also of its parts. For affections are modes in which parts of the human body (Post. 3), and consequently the body as a whole, are affected. But (Prs. 24 and 25, II) an adequate knowledge of external bodies, as also of the component parts of the human body, is not in God insofar as he is considered as affected by the human mind, but insofar as he is considered as affected by other ideas. Therefore, these ideas of affections, insofar as they are related only to the human mind, are like conclusions without premises; that is, as is self-evident, confused ideas.

   Scholium: The idea that constitutes the nature of the human mind is likewise shown, when considered solely in itself, not to be clear and distinct, as is also the idea of the human mind and the ideas of affections of the human body insofar as they are related only to the human mind, as everyone can easily see.

**Proposition 29.** *The idea of the idea of any affection of the human body does not involve adequate knowledge of the human mind.*

Proof: The idea of an affection of the human body (Pr. 27, II) does not involve adequate knowledge of the body itself; in other words, it does not adequately express the nature of the body; that is (Pr. 13, II), it does not adequately agree [*convenit*] with the nature of the mind. So (Ax. 6, I) the idea of this idea does not adequately express the nature of the human mind; i.e., it does not involve an adequate knowledge of it.

Corollary: Hence it follows that whenever the human mind perceives things after the common order of nature, it does not have an adequate knowledge of itself, nor of its body, nor of external bodies, but only a confused and fragmentary knowledge. For the mind does not know itself save insofar as it perceives ideas of the affections of the body (Pr. 23, II). Now it does not perceive its own body (Pr. 19, II) except through ideas of affections of the body, and also it is only through these affections that it perceives external bodies (Pr. 26, II). So insofar as it has these ideas, it has adequate knowledge neither of itself (Pr. 29, II) nor of its own body (Pr. 27, II) nor of external bodies (Pr. 25, II), but only a fragmentary [*mutilatam*] and confused knowledge (Pr. 28, II and Sch.).

Scholium: I say expressly that the mind does not have an adequate knowledge, but only a confused and fragmentary knowledge, of itself, its own body, and external bodies whenever it perceives things from the common order of nature, that is, whenever it is determined externally—namely, by the fortuitous run of circumstance—to regard this or that, and not when it is determined internally, through its regarding several things at the same time, to understand their agreement, their differences, and their opposition. For whenever it is conditioned internally in this or in another way, then it sees things clearly and distinctly, as I shall later show.

**Proposition 30.** *We can have only a very inadequate knowledge of the duration of our body.*

Proof: The duration of our body does not depend on its essence (Ax. 1, II), nor again on the absolute nature of God (Pr. 21, I), but (Pr. 28, I) it is determined to exist and to act by causes which are also determined by other causes to exist and to act in a definite and determinate way, and these again by other causes, and so *ad infinitum*. Therefore, the duration of our body depends on the common order of nature and the structure of the universe. Now there is in God adequate knowledge of the structure of the universe insofar as he has ideas of all the things in the universe, and not insofar as he has only the idea of the human body (Cor. Pr. 9, II). Therefore, knowledge of the duration of our body is very inadequate in God insofar as he is considered only to constitute the nature of the human mind. That is (Cor. Pr. 11, II), this knowledge is very inadequate in the human mind.

**Proposition 31.** *We can have only a very inadequate knowledge of the duration of particular things external to us.*

Proof: Each particular thing, just like the human body, must be determined by another particular thing to exist and to act in a definite and determinate way, and this latter thing again by another, and so on *ad infinitum* (Pr. 28, I). Now since we have shown in the preceding Proposition that from this common property of particular things we can have only a very inadequate knowledge of the duration of the human body, in the case of the duration of particular things we have to come to the same conclusion: that we can have only a very inadequate knowledge thereof.

Corollary: Hence it follows that all particular things are contingent and perishable. For we can have no adequate knowledge of their duration (preceding Pr.), and that is what is to be understood by contingency and perishability (Sch. 1, Pr. 33, I). For apart from this there is no other kind of contingency (Pr. 29, I).

**Proposition 32.** *All ideas are true insofar as they are related to God.*

Proof: All ideas, which are in God, agree completely with the objects of which they are ideas (Cor. Pr. 7, II), and so they are all true (Ax. 6, I).

**Proposition 33.** *There is nothing positive in ideas whereby they can be said to be false.*

Proof: If this be denied, conceive, if possible, a positive mode of thinking which constitutes the form [*forma*] of error or falsity. This mode of thinking cannot be in God (preceding Pr.), but neither can it be or be conceived externally to God (Pr. 15, I). Thus there can be nothing positive in ideas whereby they can be called false.

**Proposition 34.** *Every idea which in us is absolute, that is, adequate and perfect, is true.*

Proof: When we say that there is in us an adequate and perfect idea, we are saying only this (Cor. Pr. 11, II), that there is adequate and perfect idea in God insofar as he constitutes the essence of our mind. Consequently, we are saying only this, that such an idea is true (Pr. 32, II).

**Proposition 35.** *Falsity consists in the privation of knowledge which inadequate ideas, that is, fragmentary and confused ideas, involve.*

Proof: There is nothing positive in ideas which constitutes the form [*forma*] of falsity (Pr. 33, II). But falsity cannot consist in absolute privation (for minds, not bodies, are said to err and be deceived), nor again in absolute ignorance, for to be ignorant and to err are different. Therefore, it consists in that privation of knowledge which inadequate knowledge, that is, inadequate and confused ideas, involves.

Scholium: In Sch. Pr. 17, II I explained how error consists in the privation of knowledge, but I will give an example to enlarge on this explanation. Men are deceived in thinking themselves free, a belief that consists only in this, that they are conscious of their actions and ignorant of the causes by which they are determined. Therefore, the idea of their freedom is simply the ignorance of the cause of their actions. As to their saying that human actions depend on the will, these are mere words without any corresponding idea. For none of them knows what the will is and

how it moves the body, and those who boast otherwise and make up stories of dwelling places and habitations of the soul provoke either ridicule or disgust.

As another example, when we gaze at the sun, we see it as some two hundred feet distant from us. The error does not consist in simply seeing the sun in this way but in the fact that while we do so we are not aware of the true distance and the cause of our seeing it so. For although we may later become aware that the sun is more than six hundred times the diameter of the earth distant from us, we shall nevertheless continue to see it as close at hand. For it is not our ignorance of its true distance that causes us to see the sun to be so near; it is that the affection of our body involves the essence of the sun only to the extent that the body is affected by it.

**Proposition 36.** *Inadequate and confused ideas follow by the same necessity as adequate, or clear and distinct, ideas.*

Proof: All ideas are in God (Pr. 15, I), and insofar as they are related to God, they are true (Pr. 32, II) and adequate (Cor. Pr. 7, II). So there are no inadequate or confused ideas except insofar as they are related to the particular mind of someone (see Prs. 24 and 28, II). So all ideas, both adequate and inadequate, follow by the same necessity (Cor. Pr. 6, II).

**Proposition 37.** *That which is common to all things (see Lemma 2 above) and is equally in the part as in the whole does not constitute the essence of any one particular thing.*

Proof: If this is denied, conceive, if possible, that it does constitute the essence of one particular thing, B. Therefore, it can neither be nor be conceived without B (Def. 2, II). But this is contrary to our hypothesis. Therefore, it does not pertain to B's essence, nor does it constitute the essence of any other particular thing.

**Proposition 38.** *Those things that are common to all things and are equally in the part as in the whole can be conceived only adequately.*

Proof: Let A be something common to all bodies, and equally in the part of any body as in the whole. I say that A can be conceived only adequately. For its idea (Cor. Pr. 7, II) will necessarily be in God both insofar as he has the idea of the human body and insofar as he has the ideas of affections of the human body, affections which partly involve the natures of both the human body and external bodies (Prs. 16, 25, and 27, II). That is (Prs. 12 and 13, II), this idea will necessarily be adequate in God insofar as he constitutes the human mind; that is, insofar as he has the ideas which are in the human mind. Therefore, the mind (Cor. Pr. 11, II) necessarily perceives A adequately, and does so both insofar as it perceives itself and insofar as it perceives its own body or any external body; nor can A be perceived in any other way.

Corollary: Hence it follows that there are certain ideas or notions common to all men. For (by Lemma 2) all bodies agree in certain respects, which must be (preceding Pr.) conceived by all adequately, or clearly and distinctly.


## Proposition 39. *Of that which is common and proper to the human body and to any external bodies by which the human body is customarily affected, and which is equally in the part as well as in the whole of any of these bodies, the idea also in the mind will be adequate.*

Proof: Let A be that which is common and proper to the human body and to any external bodies and which is equally in the human body as in those same external bodies, and which is finally equally in the part of any external body as in the whole. There will be in God an adequate idea of A (Cor. Pr. 7, II) both insofar as he has the idea of the human body and insofar as he has ideas of those posited external bodies. Let it now be supposed that the human body is affected by an external body through that which is common to them both, that is, A. The idea of this affection will involve the property A (Pr. 16, II), and so (Cor. Pr. 7, II) the idea of this affection, insofar as it involves the property A, will be adequate in God insofar as he is affected by the idea of the human

body; that is (Pr. 13, II), insofar as he constitutes the nature of the human mind. So this idea will also be adequate in the human mind (Cor. Pr. 11, II).

Corollary: Hence it follows that the mind is more capable of perceiving more things adequately in proportion as its body has more things in common with other bodies.


## Proposition 40. *Whatever ideas follow in the mind from ideas that are adequate in it are also adequate.*

Proof: This is evident. For when we say that an idea follows in the human mind from ideas that are adequate in it, we are saying no more than that there is in the divine intellect an idea of which God is the cause, not insofar as he is infinite nor insofar as he is affected by ideas of numerous particular things, but only insofar as he constitutes the essence of the human mind.

Scholium I: I have here set forth the causes of those notions that are called "common," and which are the basis of our reasoning processes. Now certain axioms or notions have other causes which it would be relevant to set forth by this method of ours; for thus we could establish which notions are useful compared with others, and which are of scarcely any value. And again, we could establish which notions are common to all, which ones are clear and distinct only to those not laboring under prejudices [*praejudiciis*] and which ones are ill-founded. Furthermore, this would clarify the origin of those notions called "secondary"—and consequently the axioms which are based on them—as well as other related questions to which I have for some time given thought. But I have decided not to embark on these questions at this point because I have set them aside for another treatise,[8] and also to avoid wearying the reader with too lengthy a discussion of this subject. Nevertheless, to omit nothing that it is essential to know, I shall briefly deal with the question of the origin of the so-called "transcendental terms," such as "entity," "thing," "something" [*ens, res, aliquid*].

8. This is Spinoza's incomplete essay, *On the Improvement of the Understanding*.

These terms originate in the following way. The human body, being limited, is capable of forming simultaneously in itself only a certain number of distinct images. (I have explained in Sch. Pr. 17, II what an image is.) If this number be exceeded, these images begin to be confused, and if the number of distinct images which the body is capable of forming simultaneously in itself be far exceeded, all the images will be utterly confused with one another. This being so, it is evident from Cor. Pr. 17 and Pr. 18, II that the human mind is able to imagine simultaneously and distinctly as many bodies as there are images that can be formed simultaneously in its body. But when the images in the body are utterly confused, the mind will also imagine all the bodies confusedly without any distinction, and will comprehend them, as it were, under one attribute, namely, that of entity, thing, etc. This conclusion can also be reached from the fact that images are not always equally vivid, and also from other causes analogous to these, which I need not here explicate. For it all comes down to this, that these terms signify ideas confused in the highest degree.

Again, from similar causes have arisen those notions called "universal," such as "man," "horse," "dog," etc.; that is to say, so many images are formed in the human body simultaneously (e.g., of man) that our capacity to imagine them is surpassed, not indeed completely, but to the extent that the mind is unable to imagine the unimportant differences of individuals (such as the complexion and stature of each, and their exact number) and imagines distinctly only their common characteristic insofar as the body is affected by them. For it was by this that the body was affected most repeatedly, by each single individual. The mind expresses this by the word "man," and predicates this word of an infinite number of individuals. For, as we said, it is unable to imagine the determinate number of individuals.

But it should be noted that not all men form these notions in the same way; in the case of each person the notions vary according as that thing varies whereby the body has more frequently been affected, and which the mind more readily imagines or calls to mind. For example, those who have more often regarded with admiration the stature of men will understand by the word "man" an animal of upright stature, while those who are wont to regard a different aspect will form a different common image of man, such as that man is a laughing animal, a featherless biped, or a rational animal. Similarly, with regard to other aspects, each will form universal images according to the conditioning of his body. Therefore, it is not surprising that so many controversies have arisen among philosophers who have sought to explain natural phenomena through merely the images of these phenomena.

Scholium 2: From all that has already been said it is quite clear that we perceive many things and form universal notions:

1. From individual objects presented to us through the senses in a fragmentary [*mutilate*] and confused manner without any intellectual order (see Cor. Pr. 29, II); and therefore I call such perceptions "knowledge from casual experience."

2. From symbols. For example, from having heard or read certain words we call things to mind and we form certain ideas of them similar to those through which we imagine things (Sch. Pr. 18, II).

Both these ways of regarding things I shall in future refer to as "knowledge of the first kind," "opinion" or "imagination."

3. From the fact that we have common notions and adequate ideas of the properties of things (see Cor. Pr. 38 and 39 with its Cor., and Pr. 40, II). I shall refer to this as "reason" and "knowledge of the second kind."

Apart from these two kinds of knowledge there is, as I shall later show, a third kind of knowledge, which I shall refer to as "intuition." This kind of knowledge proceeds from an adequate idea of the formal essence of certain attributes of God to an adequate knowledge of the essence of things. I shall illustrate all these kinds of knowledge by one single example. Three numbers are given; it is required to find a fourth which is related to the third as the second to the first. Tradesmen have no hesitation in multiplying the second by the third and dividing the product by the first, either because they have not yet forgotten the rule they learnt without proof from their teachers, or because they have in fact found this correct in the case of very simple numbers, or else from the force of the proof of Proposition 19 of the Seventh Book of Euclid, to wit, the common property of proportionals.

But in the case of very simple numbers, none of this is necessary. For example, in the case of the given numbers 1, 2, 3, everybody can see that the fourth proportional is 6, and all the more clearly because we infer in one single intuition the fourth number from the ratio we see the first number bears to the second.

## Proposition 41. *Knowledge of the first kind is the only cause of falsity; knowledge of the second and third kind is necessarily true.*

Proof: In the preceding Scholium we asserted that all those ideas which are inadequate and confused belong to the first kind of knowledge; and thus (Pr. 35, II) this knowledge is the only cause of falsity. Further, we asserted that to knowledge of the second and third kind there belong those ideas which are adequate. Therefore (Pr. 34, II), this knowledge is necessarily true.

## Proposition 42. *Knowledge of the second and third kind, and not knowledge of the first kind, teaches us to distinguish true from false.*

Proof: This Proposition is self-evident. For he who can distinguish the true from the false must have an adequate idea of the true and the false; that is (Sch. 2 Pr. 40, II), he must know the true and the false by the second or third kind of knowledge.

## Proposition 43. *He who has a true idea knows at the same time that he has a true idea, and cannot doubt its truth.*

Proof: A true idea in us is one which is adequate in God insofar as he is explicated through the nature of the human mind (Cor. Pr. 11, II). Let us suppose, then, that there is in God, insofar as he is explicated through the nature of the human mind, an adequate idea, A. The idea of this idea must also necessarily be in God, and is related to God in the same way as the idea A (Pr. 20, II, the proof being of general application). But by our supposition the idea A is related to God insofar as he is explicated through the

nature of the human mind. Therefore, the idea of the idea A must be related to God in the same way; that is (Cor. Pr. 11, II), this adequate idea of the idea A will be in the mind which has the adequate idea A. So he who has an adequate idea, that is, he who knows a thing truly (Pr. 34, II), must at the same time have an adequate idea, that is, a true knowledge of his knowledge; that is, (as is self-evident) he is bound at the same time to be certain.

Scholium: I have explained in the Scholium to Pr. 21, II what is an idea of an idea; but it should be noted that the preceding proposition is sufficiently self-evident. For nobody who has a true idea is unaware that a true idea involves absolute certainty. To have a true idea means only to know a thing perfectly, that is, to the utmost degree. Indeed, nobody can doubt this, unless he thinks that an idea is some dumb thing like a picture on a tablet, and not a mode of thinking, to wit, the very act of understanding. And who, pray, can know that he understands some thing unless he first understands it? That is, who can know that he is certain of something unless he is first certain of it? Again, what standard of truth can there be that is clearer and more certain than a true idea? Indeed, just as light makes manifest both itself and darkness, so truth is the standard both of itself and falsity.

I think I have thus given an answer to those questions which can be stated as follows: If a true idea is distinguished from a false one only inasmuch as it is said to correspond with that of which it is an idea, then a true idea has no more reality or perfection than a false one (since they are distinguished only by an extrinsic characteristic) and consequently neither is a man who has true ideas superior to one who has only false ideas. Secondly, how do we come to have false ideas? And finally, how can one know for certain that one has ideas which correspond with that of which they are ideas? I have now given an answer, I repeat, to these problems. As regards the difference between a true and a false idea, it is clear from Pr. 35, II that the former is to the latter as being to nonbeing. The causes of falsity I have quite clearly shown from Propositions 19 to 35 with the latter's Scholium, from which it is likewise obvious what is the difference between a man who has true ideas and one who has only false ideas. As to the last question, how can a man know that he has an idea which corresponds to that of which it is an idea, I have just shown, with abundant clarity, that this arises from the fact that he does have an idea that corresponds to that of which it is an idea; that is, truth is its own standard. Furthermore, the human mind, insofar as it perceives things truly, is part of the infinite intellect of God (Cor. Pr. 11, II), and thus it is as inevitable that the clear and distinct ideas of the mind are true as that God's ideas are true.

## Proposition 44. *It is not in the nature of reason to regard things as contingent, but as necessary.*

Proof: It is in the nature of reason to perceive things truly (Pr. 41, II), to wit, (Ax. 6, I) as they are in themselves; that is (Pr. 29, I), not as contingent, but as necessary.

Corollary I: Hence it follows that it solely results from imagination [*imaginatio*] that we regard things, both in respect of the past and of the future, as contingent.

Scholium: I shall explain briefly how this comes about. We have shown above (Pr. 17, II and Cor.) that although things may not exist, the mind nevertheless always imagines them as present unless causes arise which exclude their present existence. Further, we have shown (Pr. 18, II) that if the human body has once been affected by two external bodies at the same time, when the mind later imagines one of them, it will straightway call the other to mind as well; that is, it will regard both as present to it unless other causes arise which exclude their present existence. Furthermore, nobody doubts that time, too, is a product of the imagination, and arises from the fact that we see some bodies move more slowly than others, or more quickly, or with equal speed. Let us therefore suppose that yesterday a boy saw Peter first of all in the morning, Paul at noon, and Simon in the evening, and that today he again sees Peter in the morning. From Pr. 18, II it is clear that as soon as he sees the morning light, forthwith he will imagine the sun as traversing the same tract of sky as on the previous day, that is, he will imagine a whole day, and he will imagine Peter together with morning, Paul with midday, and Simon with evening; that is, he will

imagine the existence of Paul and Simon with reference to future time. On the other hand, on seeing Simon in the evening he will refer Paul and Peter to time past by imagining them along with time past. This train of events will be the more consistent the more frequently he sees them in that order. If it should at some time occur that on another evening he sees James instead of Simon, then the following morning he will imagine along with evening now Simon, now James, but not both together. For we are supposing that he has seen only one of them in the evening, not both at the same time. Therefore, his imagination will waver, and he will imagine, along with a future evening, now one, now the other; that is, he will regard neither of them as going to be there for certain, but both of them contingently. This wavering of the imagination occurs in the same way if the imagination be of things which we regard with relation to past or present time, and consequently we shall imagine things, as related both to present and past or future time, as contingent.

Corollary 2: It is in the nature of reason to perceive things in the light of eternity [*sub quadam specie aeternitatis*].

Proof: It is in the nature of reason to regard things as necessary, not as contingent (previous Pr.). Now it perceives this necessity truly (Pr. 41, II); that is, as it is in itself (Ax. 6, I). But (Pr. 16, I) this necessity is the very necessity of God's eternal nature. Therefore, it is in the nature of reason to regard things in this light of eternity. Furthermore, the basic principles of reason are those notions (Pr. 38, II) which explicate what is common to all things, and do not explicate (Pr. 37, II) the essence of any particular thing, and therefore must be conceived without any relation to time, but in the light of eternity.

## Proposition 45. *Every idea of any body or particular thing existing in actuality necessarily involves the eternal and infinite essence of God.*

Proof: The idea of a particular thing actually existing necessarily involves both the essence and the existence of the thing (Cor. Pr. 8, II). But particular things cannot be conceived without God (Pr. 15, I).

Now since they have God for their cause (Pr. 6, II) insofar as he is considered under that attribute of which the things themselves are modes, their ideas (Ax. 4, I) must necessarily involve the conception of their attribute; that is (Def. 6, I), the eternal and infinite essence of God.

Scholium: Here by existence I do not mean duration, that is, existence insofar as it is considered in the abstract as a kind of quantity. I am speaking of the very nature of existence, which is attributed to particular things because they follow in infinite numbers in infinite ways from the eternal necessity of God's nature (Pr. 16, I). I am speaking, I repeat, of the very existence of particular things insofar as they are in God. For although each particular thing is determined by another particular thing to exist in a certain manner, the force by which each perseveres in existing follows from the eternal necessity of God's nature. See Cor. Pr. 24, I.

## Proposition 46. *The knowledge of the eternal and infinite essence of God which each idea involves is adequate and perfect.*

Proof: The proof of the preceding proposition is universally valid, and whether a thing be considered as a part or a whole, its idea, whether of whole or part, involves the eternal and infinite essence of God (preceding Pr.). Therefore, that which gives knowledge of the eternal and infinite essence of God is common to all things, and equally in the part as in the whole. And so this knowledge will be adequate (Pr. 38, II).

## Proposition 47. *The human mind has an adequate knowledge of the eternal and infinite essence of God.*

Proof: The human mind has ideas (Pr. 22, II) from which (Pr. 23, II) it perceives itself, its own body (Pr. 19, II), and external bodies (Cor. 1, Pr. 16 and Pr. 17, II) as actually existing, and so it has an adequate knowledge of the eternal and infinite essence of God (Prs. 45 and 46, II).

Scholium: Hence we see that God's infinite essence and his eternity are known to all. Now since all things are in God and are conceived through God,

it follows that from this knowledge we can deduce a great many things so as to know them adequately and thus to form that third kind of knowledge I mentioned in Sch. 2 Pr. 40, II, of the superiority and usefulness of which we shall have occasion to speak in Part V. That men do not have as clear a knowledge of God as they do of common notions arises from the fact that they are unable to imagine God as they do bodies, and that they have connected the word "God" with the images of things which they commonly see; and this they can scarcely avoid, being affected continually by external bodies. Indeed, most errors result solely from the incorrect application of words to things. When somebody says that the lines joining the center of a circle to its circumference are unequal, he surely understands by circle, at least at that time, something different from what mathematicians understand. Likewise, when men make mistakes in arithmetic, they have different figures in mind from those on paper. So if you look only to their minds, they indeed are not mistaken; but they seem to be wrong because we think that they have in mind the figures on the page. If this were not the case, we would not think them to be wrong, just as I did not think that person to be wrong whom I recently heard shouting that his hall had flown into his neighbor's hen, for I could see clearly what he had in mind. Most controversies arise from this, that men do not correctly express what is in their mind, or they misunderstand another's mind. For, in reality, while they are hotly contradicting one another, they are either in agreement or have different things in mind, so that the apparent errors and absurdities of their opponents are not really so.

## Proposition 48. *In the mind there is no absolute, or free, will. The mind is determined to this or that volition by a cause, which is likewise determined by another cause, and this again by another, and so* ad infinitum.

Proof: The mind is a definite and determinate mode of thinking (Pr. 11, II), and thus (Cor. 2, Pr. 17, I) it cannot be the free cause of its actions: that is, it cannot possess an absolute faculty of willing and non-willing. It must be determined to will this or that (Pr. 28, I) by a cause, which likewise is determined by another cause, and this again by another, etc.

Scholium: In the same way it is proved that in the mind there is no absolute faculty of understanding, desiring, loving, etc. Hence it follows that these and similar faculties are either entirely fictitious or nothing more than metaphysical entities or universals which we are wont to form from particulars. So intellect and will bear the same relation to this or that idea, this or that volition, as stoniness to this or that stone, or man to Peter and Paul. As to the reason why men think they are free, we explained that in the Appendix to Part I.

But before proceeding further, it should here be noted that by the will I mean the faculty of affirming and denying, and not desire. I mean, I repeat, the faculty whereby the mind affirms or denies what is true or what is false, not the desire whereby the mind seeks things or shuns them. But now that we have proved that these faculties are universal notions which are not distinct from the particulars from which we form them, we must inquire whether volitions themselves are anything more than ideas of things. We must inquire, I say, whether there is in the mind any other affirmation and denial apart from that which the idea, insofar as it is an idea, involves. On this subject see the following proposition and also Def. 3, II, lest thought becomes confused with pictures. For by ideas I do not mean images such as are formed at the back of the eye—or if you like, in the middle of the brain—but conceptions of thought.

## Proposition 49. *There is in the mind no volition, that is, affirmation and negation, except that which an idea, insofar as it is an idea, involves.*

Proof: There is in the mind (preceding Pr.) no absolute faculty of willing and non-willing, but only particular volitions, namely, this or that affirmation, and this or that negation. Let us therefore conceive a particular volition, namely, a mode of thinking whereby the mind affirms that the three angles of a triangle are equal to two right angles. This affirmation involves the conception, or idea, of a triangle; that

is, it cannot be conceived without the idea of a triangle. For to say that A must involve the conception of B is the same as to say that A cannot be conceived without B. Again, this affirmation (Ax. 3, II) cannot even be without the idea of a triangle. Therefore, this idea can neither be nor be conceived without the idea of a triangle. Furthermore, this idea of a triangle must involve this same affirmation, namely, that its three angles are equal to two right angles. Therefore, vice versa, this idea of a triangle can neither be nor be conceived without this affirmation, and so (Def. 2, II) this affirmation belongs to the essence of the idea of a triangle, and is nothing more than the essence itself. And what I have said of this volition (for it was arbitrarily selected) must also be said of every volition, namely, that it is nothing but an idea.

Corollary: Will and intellect are one and the same thing.

Proof: Will and intellect are nothing but the particular volitions and ideas (Pr. 48, II and Sch.). But a particular volition and idea are one and the same thing (preceding Pr.). Therefore, will and intellect are one and the same thing.

Scholium: By this means we have removed the cause to which error is commonly attributed. We have previously shown that falsity consists only in the privation that fragmentary and confused ideas involve. Therefore, a false idea, insofar as it is false, does not involve certainty. So when we say that a man acquiesces in what is false and has no doubt thereof, we are not thereby saying that he is certain, but only that he does not doubt, or that he acquiesces in what is false because there is nothing to cause his imagination to waver. On this point see Sch. Pr. 44, II. So however much we suppose a man to adhere to what is false, we shall never say that he is certain. For by certainty we mean something positive (Pr. 43, II and Sch.), not privation of doubt. But by privation of certainty we mean falsity.

But for a fuller explanation of the preceding proposition some things remain to be said. Then, again, there is the further task of replying to objections that may be raised against this doctrine of ours. Finally, to remove every shred of doubt, I have thought it worthwhile to point out certain advantages of this doctrine. I say certain advantages, for the most important of them will be better understood from what we have to say in Part V.

I begin, then, with the first point, and I urge my readers to make a careful distinction between an idea — i.e., a conception of the mind — and the images of things that we imagine. Again, it is essential to distinguish between ideas and the words we use to signify things. For since these three — images, words, and ideas — have been utterly confused by many, or else they fail to distinguish between them through lack of accuracy, or, finally, through lack of caution, our doctrine of the will, which it is essential to know both for theory and for the wise ordering of life, has never entered their minds. For those who think that ideas consist in images formed in us from the contact of external bodies are convinced that those ideas of things whereof we can form no like image are not ideas, but mere fictions fashioned arbitrarily at will. So they look on ideas as dumb pictures on a tablet, and misled by this preconception they fail to see that an idea, insofar as it is an idea, involves affirmation or negation. Again, those who confuse words with idea, or with the affirmation which an idea involves, think that when they affirm or deny something merely by words contrary to what they feel, they are able to will contrary to what they feel. Now one can easily dispel these misconceptions if one attends to the nature of thought, which is quite removed from the concept of extension. Then one will clearly understand that an idea, being a mode of thinking, consists neither in the image of a thing nor in words. For the essence of words and images is constituted solely by corporeal motions far removed from the concept of thought. With these few words of warning, I turn to the aforementioned objections.

The first of these rests on the confident claim that the will extends more widely than the intellect, and therefore is different from it. The reason for their belief that the will extends more widely than the intellect is that they find — so they say — that they do not need a greater faculty of assent, that is, of affirming and denying, than they already possess, in order to assent to an infinite number of other things that we do not perceive, but that we do need an increased faculty of understanding. Therefore, will is distinct

from intellect, the latter being finite and the former infinite.

Second, it may be objected against us that experience appears to tell us most indisputably that we are able to suspend judgment so as not to assent to things that we perceive, and this is also confirmed by the fact that nobody is said to be deceived insofar as he perceives something, but only insofar as he assents or dissents. For instance, he who imagines a winged horse does not thereby grant that there is a winged horse; that is, he is not thereby deceived unless at the same time he grants that there is a winged horse. So experience appears to tell us most indisputably that the will, that is, the faculty of assenting, is free, and different from the faculty of understanding.

Third, it may be objected that one affirmation does not seem to contain more reality than another; that is, we do not seem to need greater power in order to affirm that what is true is true than to affirm that what is false is true. On the other hand, we do perceive that one idea has more reality or perfection than another. For some ideas are more perfect than others in proportion as some objects are superior to others. This, again, is a clear indication that there is a difference between will and intellect.

Fourth, it may be objected that if man does not act from freedom of will, what would happen if he should be in a state of equilibrium like Buridan's ass? Will he perish of hunger and thirst? If I were to grant this, I would appear to be thinking of an ass or a statue, not of a man. If I deny it, then the man will be determining himself, and consequently will possess the faculty of going and doing whatever he wants.

Besides these objections there may possibly be others. But since I am not obliged to quash every objection that can be dreamed up, I shall make it my task to reply to these objections only, and as briefly as possible.

To the first objection I reply that, if by the intellect is meant clear and distinct ideas only, I grant that the will extends more widely than the intellect, but I deny that the will extends more widely than perceptions, that is, the faculty of conceiving. Nor indeed do I see why the faculty of willing should be termed infinite any more than the faculty of sensing. For just as by the same faculty of willing we can affirm an infinite number of things (but in succession, for we cannot affirm an infinite number of things simultaneously), so also we can sense or perceive an infinite number of bodies (in succession) by the same faculty of sensing. If my objectors should say that there are an infinite number of things that we cannot sense, I retort that we cannot grasp them by any amount of thought, and consequently by any amount of willing. But, they say, if God wanted to bring it about that we should perceive these too, he would have had to give us a greater faculty of perceiving, but not a greater faculty of willing than he has already given us. This is the same as saying that if God wishes to bring it about that we should understand an infinite number of other entities, he would have to give us a greater intellect than he already has, so as to encompass these same infinite entities, but not a more universal idea of entity. For we have shown that the will is a universal entity, or the idea whereby we explicate all particular volitions; that is, that which is common to all particular volitions. So if they believe that this common or universal idea of volitions is a faculty, it is not at all surprising that they declare this faculty to extend beyond the limits of the intellect to infinity. For the term "universal" is applied equally to one, to many, and to an infinite number of individuals.

To the second objection I reply by denying that we have free power to suspend judgment. For when we say that someone suspends judgment, we are saying only that he sees that he is not adequately perceiving the thing. So suspension of judgment is really a perception, not free will. To understand this more clearly, let us conceive a boy imagining a winged horse and having no other perception. Since this imagining involves the existence of a horse (Cor. Pr. 17, II), and the boy perceives nothing to annul the existence of the horse, he will regard the horse as present and he will not be able to doubt its existence, although he is not certain of it. We experience this quite commonly in dreams, nor do I believe there is anyone who thinks that while dreaming he has free power to suspend judgment regarding the contents of his dream, and of bringing it about that he should not dream what he dreams that he sees. Nevertheless, it does happen that even in dreams we suspend judg-

ment, to wit, when we dream that we are dreaming. Furthermore, I grant that nobody is deceived insofar as he has a perception; that is, I grant that the imaginings of the mind, considered in themselves, involve no error (see Sch. Pr. 17, II). But I deny that a man makes no affirmation insofar as he has a perception. For what else is perceiving a winged horse than affirming wings of a horse? For if the mind should perceive nothing apart from the winged horse, it would regard the horse as present to it, and would have no cause to doubt its existence nor any faculty of dissenting, unless the imagining of the winged horse were to be connected to an idea which annuls the existence of the said horse, or he perceives that the idea which he has of the winged horse is inadequate. Then he will either necessarily deny the existence of the horse or he will necessarily doubt it.

In the above I think I have also answered the third objection by my assertion that the will is a universal term predicated of all ideas and signifying only what is common to all ideas, namely, affirmation, the adequate essence of which, insofar as it is thus conceived as an abstract term, must be in every single idea, and the same in all in this respect only. But not insofar as it is considered as constituting the essence of the idea, for in that respect particular affirmations differ among themselves as much as do ideas. For example, the affirmation which the idea of a circle involves differs from the affirmation which the idea of a triangle involves as much as the idea of a circle differs from the idea of a triangle. Again, I absolutely deny that we need an equal power of thinking to affirm that what is true is true as to affirm that what is false is true. For these two affirmations, if you look to their meaning and not to the words alone, are related to one another as being to non-being. For there is nothing in ideas that constitutes the form of falsity (see Pr. 35, II with Sch. and Sch. Pr. 47, II). Therefore, it is important to note here how easily we are deceived when we confuse universals with particulars, and mental constructs [*entia rationis*] and abstract terms with the real.

As to the fourth objection, I readily grant that a man placed in such a state of equilibrium (namely, where he feels nothing else but hunger and thirst and perceives nothing but such-and-such food and drink at equal distances from him) will die of hunger and thirst. If they ask me whether such a man is not to be reckoned an ass rather than a man, I reply that I do not know, just as I do not know how one should reckon a man who hangs himself, or how one should reckon babies, fools, and madmen.

My final task is to show what practical advantages accrue from knowledge of this doctrine, and this we shall readily gather from the following points:

1. It teaches that we act only by God's will, and that we share in the divine nature, and all the more as our actions become more perfect and as we understand God more and more. Therefore, this doctrine, apart from giving us complete tranquillity of mind, has the further advantage of teaching us wherein lies our greatest happiness or blessedness, namely, in the knowledge of God alone, as a result of which we are induced only to such actions as are urged on us by love and piety. Hence we clearly understand how far astray from the true estimation of virtue are those who, failing to understand that virtue itself and the service of God are happiness itself and utmost freedom, expect God to bestow on them the highest rewards in return for their virtue and meritorious actions as if in return for the basest slavery.

2. It teaches us what attitude we should adopt regarding fortune, or the things that are not in our power, that is, the things that do not follow from our nature; namely, to expect and to endure with patience both faces of fortune. For all things follow from God's eternal decree by the same necessity as it follows from the essence of a triangle that its three angles are equal to two right angles.

3. This doctrine assists us in our social relations, in that it teaches us to hate no one, despise no one, ridicule no one, be angry with no one, envy no one. Then again, it teaches us that each should be content with what he has and should help his neighbor, not from womanish pity, or favor, or superstition, but from the guidance of reason as occasion and circumstance require. This I shall demonstrate in Part IV.

4. Finally, this doctrine is also of no small advantage to the commonwealth, in that it teaches the manner in which citizens should be governed and led; namely, not so as to be slaves, but so as to do freely what is best.

And thus I have completed the task I undertook in this Scholium, and thereby I bring to an end Part II, in which I think I have explained the nature of the human mind and its properties at sufficient length and as clearly as the difficult subject matter permits, and that from my account can be drawn many excellent lessons, most useful and necessary to know, as will partly be disclosed in what is to follow.

## Part V. Of the Power of the Intellect, or of Human Freedom

### Preface

I pass on finally to that part of the *Ethics* which concerns the method or way leading to freedom. In this part, then, I shall be dealing with the power of reason, pointing out the degree of control reason has over the emotions, and then what is freedom of mind, or blessedness, from which we shall see how much to be preferred is the life of the wise man to the life of the ignorant man. Now we are not concerned here with the manner or way in which the intellect should be perfected, nor yet with the science of tending the body so that it may correctly perform its functions. The latter is the province of medicine, the former of logic. Here then, as I have said, I shall be dealing only with the power of the mind or reason. Above all I shall be showing the degree and nature of its command over the emotions in checking and controlling them. For I have already demonstrated that we do not have absolute command over them. [. . .]

## Proposition 21. *The mind can exercise neither imagination nor memory save while the body endures.*

Proof: It is only while the body endures that the mind expresses the actual existence of its body and conceives the affections of the body as actual (Cor. Pr. 8, II). Consequently (Pr. 26, II), it does not conceive any body as actually existing save while its own body endures. Therefore (see Def. Imagination in Sch. Pr. 17, II), it cannot exercise either imagination or memory save while the body endures (see Def. of Memory in Sch. P 18, II).

**Proposition 22.** *Nevertheless, there is necessarily in God an idea which expresses the essence of this or that human body under a form of eternity* [sub specie aeternitatis].

Proof: God is the cause not only of the existence of this or that human body but also of its essence (Pr. 25, I), which must therefore necessarily be received through God's essence (Ax. 4, I) by a certain eternal necessity (Pr. 16, I), and this conception must necessarily be in God (Pr. 3, II).

**Proposition 23.** *The human mind cannot be absolutely destroyed along with body, but something of it remains, which is eternal.*

Proof: In God there is necessarily a conception, or idea, which expresses the essence of the human body (preceding Pr.) and which therefore is necessarily something that pertains to the essence of the human mind (Pr. 13, II). But we assign to the human mind the kind of duration that can be defined by time only insofar as the mind expresses the actual existence of the body, an existence that is explicated through duration and can be defined by time. That is, we do not assign duration to the mind except while the body endures (Cor. Pr. 8, II). However, since that which is conceived by a certain eternal necessity through God's essence is nevertheless a something (preceding Pr.), this something, which pertains to the essence of mind, will necessarily be eternal.

Scholium: As we have said, this idea, which expresses the essence of the body under a form of eternity, is a definite mode of thinking which pertains to the essence of mind, and which is necessarily eternal. Yet it is impossible that we should remember that we existed before the body, since neither can there be any traces of this in the body nor can eternity be defined by time, or be in any way related to time. Nevertheless, we feel and experience that we are eternal. For the mind senses those things that it conceives by its understanding just as much as those which it has in its memory. Logical proofs are the eyes of the mind, whereby it sees and observes things. So

although we have no recollection of having existed before the body, we nevertheless sense that our mind, insofar as it involves the essence of the body under a form of eternity, is eternal, and that this aspect of its existence cannot be defined by time, that is, cannot be explicated through duration. Therefore, our mind can be said to endure, and its existence to be defined by a definite period of time, only to the extent that it involves the actual existence of the body, and it is only to that extent that it has the power to determine the existence of things by time and to conceive them from the point of view of duration.

**Proposition 24.** *The more we understand particular things, the more we understand God.*

Proof: This is evident from Cor. Pr. 25, I.

**Proposition 25.** *The highest conatus of the mind and its highest virtue is to understand things by the third kind of knowledge.*

Proof: The third kind of knowledge proceeds from the adequate idea of certain of God's attributes to the adequate knowledge of the essence of things (see its definition in Sch. 2, Pr. 40, II), and the more we understand things in this way, the more we understand God (preceding Pr.). Therefore (Pr. 28, IV),[9] the highest virtue of the mind, that is (Def. 8, IV),[10] its power or nature, or its highest conatus (Pr. 7, III),[11] is to understand things by this third kind of knowledge.

9. Pr. 28, IV: The mind's highest good is the knowledge of God, and the mind's highest virtue is to know God.
10. Def. 8, IV: By "virtue" and "power" I mean the same thing; that is (Pr. 7, III [see note 11]), virtue, insofar as it is related to man, is man's very essence, or nature, insofar as he has power by some other thing. Whatsoever thing there is, there is another more powerful by which the same thing can be destroyed.
11. Pr. 7, III: The conatus with which each thing endeavors to persist in its own being is nothing but the actual essence of the thing itself.

**Proposition 26.** *The more capable the mind is of understanding things by the third kind of knowledge, the more it desires to understand things by this same kind of knowledge.*

Proof: This is evident; for insofar as we conceive the mind to be capable of understanding things by the third kind of knowledge, to that extent we conceive it as determined to understand things by that same kind of knowledge. Consequently (Def. of Emotions 1),[12] the more the mind is capable of this, the more it desires it.

**Proposition 27.** *From this third kind of knowledge there arises the highest possible contentment of mind.*

Proof: The highest virtue of the mind is to know God (Pr. 28, IV),[13] that is, to understand things by the third kind of knowledge (Pr. 25, V), and this virtue is all the greater the more the mind knows things by the third kind of knowledge (Pr. 24, V). So he who knows things by this third kind of knowledge passes to the highest state of human perfection, and consequently (Def. of Emotions 2)[14] is affected by the highest pleasure, this pleasure being accompanied (Pr. 43, II) by the idea of himself and his own virtue. Therefore (Def. of Emotions 25),[15] from this kind of knowledge there arises the highest possible contentment.

**Proposition 28.** *The conatus, or desire, to know things by the third kind of knowledge cannot arise from the first kind of knowledge, but from the second.*

Proof: This proposition is self-evident. For whatever we understand clearly and distinctly, we understand either through itself or through something else which is conceived through itself. That is, ideas which are clear and distinct in us or which are related to the third kind of knowledge (Sch. 2, Pr. 40, II) cannot follow from fragmentary or confused ideas which (same Sch.) are related to the first kind of knowledge, but from adequate ideas, that is (same Sch.), from the second or third kind of knowledge. Therefore (Def. of Emotions 1),[16] the desire to know things by the third kind of knowledge cannot arise from the first kind of knowledge, but from the second.

**Proposition 29.** *Whatever the mind understands under a form of eternity it does not understand from the fact that it conceives the present actual existence of the body, but from the fact that it conceives the essence of the body under a form of eternity.*

Proof: Insofar as the mind conceives the present existence of its body, to that extent it conceives a duration that can be determined by time, and only to that extent does it have the power to conceive things in relation to time (Pr. 21, V and Pr. 26, II). But eternity cannot be explicated through duration (Def. 8, I and its explication). Therefore, to that extent the mind does not have the power to conceive things under a form of eternity. But since it is the nature of reason to conceive things under a form of eternity (Cor. 2, Pr. 44, II), and since it belongs to the nature of mind, too, to conceive the essence of the body under a form of eternity (Pr. 23, V), and since there belongs to the essence of mind nothing but these two ways of conceiving (Pr. 13, II), it follows that this power to conceive things under a form of eternity pertains to the mind only insofar as it conceives the essence of the body under a form of eternity.

Scholium: We conceive things as actual in two ways: either insofar as we conceive them as related to a fixed time and place, or insofar as we conceive them to be contained in God and to follow from the necessity of the divine nature. Now the things that are conceived as true or real in this second way, we conceive under a form of eternity, and their ideas

---

12. Def. of Emotions 1: Desire is the very essence of man insofar as his essence is conceived as determined to any action from a given affection of itself.
13. Pr. 28, IV: See note 9.
14. Def. of Emotions 2: Pleasure is man's transition from a state of less perfection to a state of greater perfection.
15. Def. of Emotions 25: Self-contentment is pleasure arising from a man's contemplation of himself and his power of activity.
16. Def. of Emotions 1: See note 12.

involve the eternal and infinite essence of God, as we demonstrated in Pr. 45, II. See also its Scholium.

## Proposition 30. *Our mind, insofar as it knows both itself and the body under a form of eternity, necessarily has a knowledge of God, and knows that it is in God and is conceived through God.*

Proof: Eternity is the very essence of God insofar as this essence involves necessary existence (Def. 8, I). Therefore, to conceive things under a form of eternity is to conceive things insofar as they are conceived through God's essence as real entities; that is, insofar as they involve existence through God's essence. Therefore, our mind, insofar as it knows itself and the body under a form of eternity, necessarily has knowledge of God, and knows . . . etc.

## Proposition 31. *The third kind of knowledge depends on the mind as its formal cause insofar as the mind is eternal.*

Proof: The mind conceives nothing under a form of eternity except insofar as it conceives the essence of its body under a form of eternity (Pr. 29, V), that is (Prs. 21 and 23, V), except insofar as the mind is eternal. Therefore (preceding Pr.), insofar as it is eternal, it has knowledge of God, knowledge which is necessarily adequate (Pr. 46, II). Therefore, the mind, insofar as it is eternal, is capable of knowing all the things that can follow from this given knowledge of God (Pr. 40, II): that is, of knowing things by the third kind of knowledge (see its definition in Sch. 2, Pr. 40, II), of which the mind is therefore (Def. 1, III)[17] the adequate or formal cause insofar as it is eternal.

Scholium: So the more each man is advanced in this kind of knowledge, the more clearly conscious he is of himself and of God, that is, the more perfect and blessed he is, as will become even more evident from what is to follow. But here it should be noted

that although we are at this point certain that the mind is eternal insofar as it conceives things under a form of eternity, yet, to facilitate the explanation and render more readily intelligible what I intend to demonstrate, we shall consider the mind as if it were now beginning to be and were now beginning to understand things under a form of eternity, as we have been doing up to now. This we may do without any danger of error, provided we are careful to reach no conclusion except from premises that are quite clear.

## Proposition 32. *We take pleasure in whatever we understand by the third kind of knowledge, and this is accompanied by the idea of God as cause.*

Proof: From this kind of knowledge there arises the highest possible contentment of mind (Pr. 27, V), that is (Def. of Emotions 25),[18] the highest possible pleasure, and this is accompanied by the idea of oneself, and consequently (Pr. 30, V) also by the idea of God, as cause.

Corollary: From the third kind of knowledge there necessarily arises the intellectual love of God [*amor Dei intellectualis*]. For from this kind of knowledge there arises (preceding Pr.) pleasure accompanied by the idea of God as cause, that is (Def. of Emotions 6),[19] the love of God not insofar as we imagine him as present (Pr. 29, V) but insofar as we understand God to be eternal. And this is what I call the intellectual love of God.

## Proposition 33. *The intellectual love of God which arises from the third kind of knowledge is eternal.*

Proof: The third kind of knowledge is eternal (Pr. 31, V and Ax. 3, I), and therefore (by the same Ax. 3, I) the love that arises from it is also necessarily eternal.

Scholium: Although this love towards God has had no beginning (preceding Pr.), it yet has all the perfec-

17. Def. 1, III: I call that an adequate cause whose effect can be clearly and distinctly perceived through the said cause. I call that an inadequate or partial cause whose effect cannot be understood through the same cause alone.

18. Def. of Emotions 25: See note 15.
19. Def. of Emotions 6: Love is pleasure accompanied by the idea of external cause.

tions of love just as if it had originated in the manner we supposed in the Corollary to the preceding Proposition. There is no difference, except that the mind has possessed from eternity those perfections which we then supposed to be accruing to it, accompanied by the idea of God as eternal cause. If pleasure consists in the transition to a state of greater perfection, blessedness must surely consist in this, that the mind is endowed with perfection itself.

## Proposition 34. *It is only while the body endures that the mind is subject to passive emotions.*

Proof: Imagining is the idea whereby the mind regards some thing as present (see its definition in Sch. Pr. 17, II), an idea which, however, indicates the present state of the body rather than the nature of an external thing (Cor. 2, Pr. 16, II). Therefore, an emotion (Gen. Def. of Emotions)[20] is an imagining insofar as it indicates the present state of the body. So (Pr. 21, V) it is only while the body endures that the mind is subject to passive emotions.

Corollary: Hence it follows that no love is eternal except for intellectual love [*amor intellectualis*].

Scholium: If we turn our attention to the common belief entertained by men, we shall see that they are indeed conscious of the eternity of the mind, but they confuse it with duration and assign it to imagination or to memory, which they believe to continue after death.

## Proposition 35. *God loves himself with an infinite intellectual love.*

Proof: God is absolutely infinite (Def. 6, I); that is (Def. 6, II), God's nature enjoys infinite perfection, accompanied (Pr. 3, II) by the idea of itself, that is (Pr. 11 and Def. 1, I), by the idea of its own cause; and that is what, in Cor. Pr. 32. V, we declared to be intellectual love.

## Proposition 36. *The mind's intellectual love towards God is the love of God wherewith God loves himself not insofar as he is infinite, but insofar as he can be explicated through the essence of the human mind considered under a form of eternity. That is, the mind's intellectual love towards God is part of the infinite love wherewith God loves himself.*

Proof: This, the mind's love, must be related to the active nature of the mind (Cor. Pr. 32, V and Pr. 3, III),[21] and is therefore an activity whereby the mind regards itself, accompanied by the idea of God as cause (Pr. 32, V and Cor.); that is (Cor. Pr. 25, I and Cor. Pr. 11, II), an activity whereby God, insofar as he can be explicated through the human mind, regards himself, accompanied by the idea of himself. And therefore (preceding Pr.) this love of God is part of the infinite love wherewith God loves himself.

Corollary: Hence it follows that God, insofar as he loves himself, loves mankind, and, consequently, that the love of God towards men and the mind's intellectual love towards God are one and the same.

Scholium: From this we clearly understand in what our salvation or blessedness or freedom consists, namely, in the constant and eternal love towards God, that is, in God's love towards men. This love or blessedness is called glory in the Holy Scriptures, and rightly so. For whether this love be related to God or to the mind, it can properly be called spiritual contentment, which in reality cannot be distinguished from glory (Def. of Emotions, 25 and 30).[22] For insofar as it is related to God, it is (Pr. 35, V) pleasure (if we may still use this term) accompanied by the idea of himself, and this is also the case insofar as it is related to the mind (Pr. 27, V). Again, since the essence of our mind consists solely in knowledge, whose principle and basis is God (Pr. 15, I and Sch. Pr. 47, II), it follows that we see quite clearly how

20. Gen. Def. of Emotions: The emotion called a passive experience is a confused idea whereby the mind affirms a greater or lesser force of existence of its body, or part of its body, than was previously the case, and by the occurrence of which the mind is determined to think of one thing rather than another.

21. Pr. 3, III: The active states [*actiones*] of the mind arise only from adequate ideas; its passive states depend solely on inadequate ideas.
22. Def. of Emotions, 25: See note 15; Def. of Emotions 30: Honor is pleasure accompanied by the idea of some action of ours which we think that others praise.

and in what way our mind, in respect of essence and existence, follows from the divine nature and is continuously dependent on God.

I have thought this worth noting here in order to show by this example the superiority of that knowledge of particular things which I have called "intuitive" or "of the third kind," and its preferability to that abstract knowledge which I have called "knowledge of the second kind."

For although I demonstrated in a general way in Part I that everything (and consequently the human mind, too) is dependent on God in respect of its essence and of its existence, that proof, although legitimate and exempt from any shadow of doubt, does not so strike the mind as when it is inferred from the essence of each particular thing which we assert to be dependent on God.

## Proposition 37. *There is nothing in Nature which is contrary to this intellectual love, or which can destroy it.*

Proof: This intellectual love follows necessarily from the nature of the mind insofar as that is considered as an eternal truth through God's nature (Prs. 33 and 29, V). Therefore, if there were anything that was contrary to this love, it would be contrary to truth, and consequently that which could destroy this love could cause truth to be false, which, as is self-evident, is absurd. Therefore, there is nothing in Nature . . . etc.

Scholium: The Axiom in Part IV is concerned with particular things insofar as they are considered in relation to a definite time and place, of which I think no one can be in doubt.

## Proposition 38. *The greater the number of things the mind understands by the second and third kinds of knowledge, the less subject it is to emotions that are bad, and the less it fears death.*

Proof: The essence of the mind consists in knowledge (Pr. 11, II). Therefore, the greater the number of things the mind knows by the second and third kinds of knowledge, the greater is the part of it that survives

(Prs. 23 and 29,V), and consequently (preceding Pr.) the greater is that part of it that is not touched by emotions contrary to our nature; that is (Pr. 30, IV),[23] by emotions that are bad. Therefore, the greater the number of things the mind understands by the second and third kinds of knowledge, the greater is that part of it that remains unimpaired, and consequently the less subject it is to emotions . . . etc.

Scholium: Hence we understand that point which I touched upon in Sch. Pr. 39, IV and which I promised to explain in this part, namely that death is less hurtful in proportion as the mind's clear and distinct knowledge is greater, and consequently the more the mind loves God. Again, since (Pr. 27, V) from the third kind of knowledge there arises the highest possible contentment, hence it follows that the human mind can be of such a nature that that part of it that we have shown to perish with the body (Pr. 21, V) is of no account compared with that part of it that survives. But I shall be dealing with this at greater length in due course.

## Proposition 39. *He whose body is capable of the greatest amount of activity has a mind whose greatest part is eternal.*

Proof: He whose body is capable of the greatest amount of activity is least assailed by emotions that are evil (Pr. 38, IV),[24] that is (Pr. 30, IV),[25] by emotions that are contrary to our nature. Thus (Pr. 10, V)[26] he has the capacity to arrange and associate the affections

23. Pr. 30, IV: No thing can be evil for us through what it possesses in common with our nature, but insofar as it is evil for us, it is contrary for us.
24. Pr. 38, IV: That which so dispenses the human body that it can be affected in more ways, or which renders it capable of affecting external bodies in more ways, is advantageous to man, and proportionately more advantageous as the body is thereby rendered more capable of being affected in more ways and of affecting other bodies in more ways. On the other hand, that which renders the body less capable in these respects is harmful.
25. Pr. 30, IV: See note 23.
26. Pr. 10, V: As long as we are not assailed by emotions that are contrary to our nature, we have the power to arrange and associate the affections of the body according to the order of the intellect.

of the body according to intellectual order and consequently to bring it about (Pr. 14, V)[27] that all the affections of the body are related to God. This will result (Pr. 15, V)[28] in his being affected with love towards God, a love (Pr. 16, V)[29] that must occupy or constitute the greatest part of the mind. Therefore (Pr. 33, V), he has a mind whose greatest part is eternal.

Scholium: Since human bodies are capable of a great many activities, there is no doubt that they can be of such a nature as to be related to minds which have great knowledge of themselves and of God, and whose greatest and principal part is eternal, with the result that they scarcely fear death. But in order that this may be more clearly understood, it should here be remarked that our lives are subject to continual variation, and as the change is for the better or worse, so we are said to be fortunate or unfortunate. For he who passes from being a baby or child into being a corpse is said to be unfortunate; while, on the other hand, to have been able to pass the whole of one's life with a healthy mind in a healthy body is regarded as a mark of good fortune. And in fact he who, like a baby or a child, has a body capable of very little activity and is most dependent on external causes, has a mind which, considered solely in itself, has practically no consciousness of itself, of God, or of things, while he whose body is capable of very considerable activity has a mind which, considered solely in itself, is highly conscious of itself and of God and of things. In this life, therefore, we mainly endeavor that the body of childhood, as far as its nature allows and is conducive thereto, should develop into a body that is capable of a great many activities and is related to a mind that is highly conscious of itself, of God, and of things, and in such a way that everything relating to its memory or imagination should be of scarcely any importance in comparison with its intellect, as I have already stated in the Scholium to the preceding Proposition.

**Proposition 40.** *The more perfection a thing has, the more active and the less passive it is. Conversely, the more active it is, the more perfect it is.*

Proof: The more perfect a thing is, the more reality it has (Def. 6, II); consequently (Pr. 3, III and Sch.),[30] the more active it is and the less passive. This proof proceeds in the same manner in inverse order, from which it follows that a thing is the more perfect as it is more active.

Corollary: Hence it follows that the part of the mind that survives, of whatever extent it may be, is more perfect than the rest. For the eternal part of the mind (Prs. 23 and 29, V) is the intellect, through which alone we are said to be active (Pr. 3, III),[31] whereas that part which we have shown to perish is the imagination (Pr. 21, V), through which alone we are said to be passive (Pr. 3, III and Gen. Def. of Emotions).[32] Therefore, the former (preceding Pr.), of whatever extent it be, is more perfect than the latter.

Scholium: This is what I had resolved to demonstrate concerning the mind insofar as it is considered without reference to the existence of the body. It is clear from this, and also from Pr. 21, I and other propositions, that our mind, insofar as it understands, is an eternal mode of thinking which is determined by another eternal mode of thinking, and this again by another, and so on *ad infinitum*, with the result that they all together constitute the eternal and infinite intellect of God.

**Proposition 41.** *Even if we did not know that our mind is eternal, we should still regard as being of prime importance piety and religion and, to sum up completely, everything which in Part IV we showed to be related to courage and nobility.*

---

27. Pr. 14, V: The mind can bring it about that all the affections of the body—i.e., images of things—be related to the idea of God.
28. Pr. 15, V: He who clearly and distinctly understands himself and his emotions loves God, and the more so the more he understands himself and his emotions.
29. Pr. 16, V: The love towards God is bound to hold chief place in the mind.

30. Pr. 3, III: See note 21.
31. Pr. 3, III: See note 21.
32. Pr. 3, III and Gen. Def. of Emotions: See notes 21 and 20.

Proof: The first and only basis of virtue, that is, of the right way of life (Cor. Pr. 22 and Pr. 24, IV),[33] is to seek one's own advantage. Now in order to determine what reason prescribes as advantageous we took no account of the mind's eternity, a topic which we did not consider until Part V. So although at that point we were unaware that the mind is eternal, we regarded as being of prime importance whatever is related to courage and nobleness. So even if now we were unaware of the mind's eternity, we should still regard the said precepts of reason as being of prime importance.

Scholium: The common belief of the multitude seems to be quite different. For the majority appear to think that they are free to the extent that they can indulge their lusts, and that they are giving up their rights to the extent that they are required to live under the commandments of the divine law. So they believe that piety and religion, in fact everything related to strength of mind, are burdens which they hope to lay aside after death, when they will receive the reward of their servitude, that is, of piety and religion. And it is not by this hope alone, but also and especially by fear of incurring dreadful punishment after death, that they are induced to live according to the commandments of the divine law as far as their feebleness and impotent spirit allows. And if men did not have this hope and this fear, and if they believed on the contrary that minds perish with bodies and that they, miserable creatures, worn out by the burden of piety, had no prospect of further existence, they would return to their own inclinations and decide to shape their lives according to their lusts, and to be ruled by fortune rather than by themselves. This seems to me no less absurd than if a man, not believing that he can sustain his body on good food forever, were to decide to glut himself on poisons and deadly fare; or, on realizing that the mind is not eternal or immortal, he preferred to be mad and to live without reason.

Such attitudes are so absurd that they are scarcely worth recounting.

## Proposition 42. *Blessedness is not the reward of virtue, but virtue itself. We do not enjoy blessedness because we keep our lusts in check. On the contrary, it is because we enjoy blessedness that we are able to keep our lusts in check.*

Proof: Blessedness consists in love towards God (Pr. 36, V and Sch.), a love that arises from the third kind of knowledge (Cor. Pr. 32. V), and so this love (Prs. 59 and 3, III)[34] must be related to the mind insofar as the mind is active; and therefore it is virtue itself (Def. 8, IV).[35] That is the first point. Again, the more the mind enjoys this divine love or blessedness, the more it understands (Pr. 32, V); that is (Cor. Pr. 3, V),[36] the more power it has over the emotions and (Pr. 38, V) the less subject it is to emotions that are bad. So the mind's enjoyment of this divine love or blessedness gives it the power to check lusts. And since human power to keep lusts in check consists solely in the intellect, nobody enjoys blessedness because he has kept his emotions in check. On the contrary, the power to keep lusts in check arises from blessedness itself.

Scholium: I have now completed all that I intended to demonstrate concerning the power of the mind over the emotions and concerning the freedom of the mind. This makes clear how strong the wise man is and how much he surpasses the ignorant man whose motive force is only lust. The ignorant man, besides being driven hither and thither by external causes, never possessing true contentment of spirit, lives as if he were unconscious of himself, God, and things, and as soon as he ceases to be passive, he at once ceases to be at all. On the other hand, the wise man, insofar as he is considered as such, suffers

---

33. Cor. Pr. 22, IV: The conatus to preserve oneself is the primary and sole basis of virtue. No other principle can be conceived as prior to this one (by Pr. 22, IV), and no virtue can be conceived independently of it (Pr. 21, IV); Pr. 24, IV: Nobody can desire to be happy, to do well, and to live well without at the same time desiring to be, to do, and to live; that is, actually to exist.

34. Pr. 59, III: Among all the emotions that are related to the mind insofar as it is active, there are none that are not related to pleasure and desire; Pr. 3, III: See note 21.
35. Def. 8, IV: See note 10.
36. Cor. Pr. 3, V: So the more an emotion is known to us, the more it is within our control, and the mind is the less passive in respect of it.

scarcely any disturbance of spirit, but being conscious, by virtue of a certain eternal necessity, of himself, of God and of things, never ceases to be, but always possesses true spiritual contentment.

If the road I have pointed out as leading to this goal seems very difficult, yet it can be found. Indeed, what is so rarely discovered is bound to be hard. For if salvation were ready to hand and could be discovered without great toil, how could it be that it is almost universally neglected? All things excellent are as difficult as they are rare.

End

# 3. LEIBNIZ'S MONADOLOGY AND ASSOCIATED TEXTS

Gottfried Wilhelm Leibniz (1646–1716) attended the universities of Leipzig (1661–66) and Altdorf (1666–67), graduating with degrees in law and in philosophy. Invited to join the faculty at Altdorf, he chose instead to enter the service of the elector of Mainz. He was sent on diplomatic business to Paris (1672-76); there he met Antoine Arnauld and Nicolas Malebranche, among others, and accomplished the basic work on his differential and integral calculus. Leibniz returned to Germany, in 1676, in the service of the court of Hanover, and along the way, he stopped in Holland to meet Baruch Spinoza. In Hanover he became counselor and served in numerous roles: as mining engineer (unsuccessfully supervising the draining of the silver mines in the Harz mountains), head librarian, adviser and diplomat, and court historian. His chosen literary form was the occasional article or essay in a learned journal. Among the important essays he wrote but did not publish are "Discourse on Metaphysics" (1686), *Dynamics* (1689–91), and "Monadology" (1714). In 1705, he finished his *New Essays on Human Understanding*, a book-length commentary on John Locke's *Essay*, but did not issue the work. He did publish several significant philosophical essays: "New System of Nature" (*Journal des Sçavants*, 1695); "Specimen of Dynamics" (*Acta Eruditorum*, 1695); and *Theodicy* (1710). The latter is a loosely structured work, consisting largely of responses to Pierre Bayle's skepticism. Leibniz maintained an extensive circle of correspondents, including Simon Foucher, Arnauld, Malebranche, and Samuel Clarke.[1]

There is nothing in Leibniz's enormous body of work that resembles, let us say, Descartes's *Meditations* or Spinoza's *Ethics*, no authoritative expression of Leibniz's philosophy in a single volume. In part, that lack must be due to his desire not to set himself up as head of a sect and to produce what he would

---

1. There are a number of collections of Leibniz's philosophical essays as well as editions of the *Theodicy* and *New Essays* in English translation. For more on Leibniz, see C. D. Broad, *Leibniz: An Introduction* (Cambridge: Cambridge University Press, 1975); Stuart Brown, *Leibniz* (Minneapolis: University of Minnesota Press, 1984); Catherine Wilson, *Leibniz's Metaphysics: A Historical and Comparative Study* (Princeton: Princeton University Press, 1989); Robert Sleigh, *Leibniz and Arnauld* (New Haven: Yale University Press, 1990); Donald Rutherford, *Leibniz and the Rational Order of Nature* (Cambridge: Cambridge University Press, 1995); and Nicholas Jolley, ed., *The Cambridge Companion to Leibniz* (Cambridge: Cambridge University Press, 1995).

disparagingly call a "learned magician's book."[2] In part, it must also be due to his manner of philosophizing. Leibniz usually wrote essays, small treatises, and letters to learned correspondents. With the rise of intellectual journals in the second half of the seventeenth century (*Journal des Sçavants, Acta Eruditorum*, etc.), he had a ready means of disseminating his thought. But Leibniz's chosen form must be handled gingerly. One finds approximately the same set of typical Leibnizian theses in Leibniz's various essays (from the "Discourse on Metaphysics" and "Primary Truths" to the "New System of Nature" and ultimately to the Preface to the *New Essays* and "Monadology"). However, the formulations of the theses and the relations they have with one another vary from essay to essay; these are not always minor differences.

Take, for example, the "Discourse on Metaphysics." Leibniz intended the work as a philosophical framework within which theological disputes between Protestants and Catholics might be resolved. The structure of the "Discourse" displays this purpose. It begins with God, with an account of his perfection and the creation, as well as an application of the principle of sufficient reason, and it ends with God, with his relation to finite spirits, including humans. In between, Leibniz discusses the metaphysics required for those doctrines. Section 8 of the "Discourse" explains the notion of an individual substance so as to distinguish the actions of God from those of creatures. For that purpose, Leibniz introduces the concept-containment theory of truth: a proposition is true if and only if the concept of the predicate is contained in the concept of the subject. A consequence of this account is that "the nature of an individual substance or of a complete being is to have a notion so complete that it is sufficient to contain and to allow us to deduce from it all the predicates of the subject to which this notion is attributed." As Leibniz says in section 9, "several notable paradoxes follow from this"; the "paradoxes," however, are metaphysical doctrines Leibniz actually holds: the identity of indiscernibles — that two substances cannot resemble each other completely and differ only in number; the

indestructibility of substances — that a substance can begin only by creation and end only by annihilation; and the complete-world view of substance — that every substance is like a complete world and like a mirror of the whole universe, expressing, however confusedly, everything that happens in the universe, whether past, present, or future. As further consequences of his theory of substance, Leibniz argues against Descartes that extension cannot constitute the essence of any substance and rehabilitates substantial forms as the essence of extended substances (sec. 10–12). He distinguishes between certainty and necessity: the truth of each event, however certain, is nevertheless contingent, being based on the free will of God, whose choice always has its reasons, which incline without necessitating (sec. 13, which provokes the correspondence between Leibniz and Arnauld). And he further argues a thesis of spontaneity (sec. 14–16) — that everything that happens to a substance is a consequence of its idea or of its being, and that nothing determines it, except God alone — applying the thesis to the relation between mind and body (sec. 33).

By the "New System of Nature," Leibniz's concept-containment account of truth and his complete-concept theory of substance disappear. The essay begins with a consideration of the labyrinth of the continuum: the principles of a true unity cannot be found in matter alone, since everything in matter is only an aggregation of parts to infinity. A multitude can derive its reality only from true unities. This explanation requires Leibniz to postulate formal atoms and to rehabilitate substantial forms, which, in turn, requires the indestructibility of substances: every substance that has a true unity can begin only by creation and end only by annihilation. It also requires the thesis of spontaneity: God originally created the soul (and any other real unity) in such a way that everything must arise for it from its own depths through a perfect spontaneity relative to itself, and yet with a perfect conformity relative to external things. Moreover, spontaneity entails that every substance represents the whole universe, from a certain point of view, in virtue of its own laws, as if in a world apart. Ultimately, the thesis of pre-established harmony also follows: there will be a perfect agreement among all these sub-

2. See Brown, *Leibniz*, pp. 6–8.

stances, producing the same effect that would be noticed if they communicated through the transmission of species or qualities.

The Preface to the *New Essays*[3] also contains Leibniz's characteristic set of theses, but again they are reworked. Reflecting on Locke's opinion that there is nothing in our mind that we are not actually conscious of perceiving, Leibniz develops his doctrine of *petites perceptions*: at every moment there is an infinity of perceptions in us that we do not consciously perceive. These small perceptions involve infinity; as a result, the present is filled with the future and laden with the past, everything conspires together, and the whole sequence of the universe could be read in the smallest of substances. The insensible perceptions also constitute the individual, which is individuated by the traces that these perceptions preserve of its previous states, connecting it up with the individual's present state. That is why, according to Leibniz, death might only be a state like that of sleep. Leibniz also explains the pre-established harmony holding between the soul and the body by means of these insensible perceptions. Moreover, the thesis of the identity

of indiscernibles follows as well: because of insensible variations, two individual things cannot be perfectly alike and must always differ in something over and above number. According to Leibniz, the identity of indiscernibles would "put an end to such doctrines as the empty tablets of the soul, a soul without thought, a substance without action, void space, atoms, and even particles in matter not actually divided, complete uniformity in a part of time, place, or matter, [. . .] and a thousand other fictions of philosophers which arise from their incomplete notions"—about which he disputed with Locke in the *New Essays* and subsequently debated (indirectly) with Isaac Newton in the Letters to Clarke.

As is clear, the particular interpretive challenge Leibniz poses is that his characteristic doctrines change through time, depending perhaps on the purpose of the essay, the issues he is addressing, and the audience to which he is speaking—whether he is seeking reconciliation between Catholic and Protestant churches in the "Discourse on Metaphysics," discussing Cartesian problems in learned journals such as the *Journal des Sçavants*, or commenting on Lockean themes in the *New Essays* (or even when he is unfolding logical consequences in "Primary Truths" or explicating the foundations of his *Theodicy* in the "Monadology").

---

3. For Leibniz's Preface to the *New Essays*, see *Modern Philosophy* (Indianapolis: Hackett Publishing Company, 1998).

# Nicolas Malebranche, *The Search after Truth* (1674–75)[1]

*Nicolas Malebranche (1638–1715) was a philosopher and priest. He had a traditional scholastic education, including three years at the Sorbonne. He entered the Oratory in 1660 and was ordained in 1664. The Oratory was surely responsible for the Augustinian influence on his philosophy, but an accidental discovery in 1664 of Descartes's* Treatise on Man *provided Malebranche with his other major influence. His first and most significant work,* The Search after Truth, *was published initially in 1674–75 and subsequently printed with an increasingly long set of* Elucidations. *The work elicited critiques by Foucher and Arnauld; although he denied having a taste for polemics, Malebranche engaged in lengthy debates with these two critics, as well as others (Leibniz and the Cartesian Pierre-Sylvain Régis, for example). In* The Search after Truth, *Malebranche presents and defends the two doctrines for which he is best known, the occasionalism that denies causation between any finite substances and the claim that we see all things in God.[2]*

1. Translated from the French by Roger Ariew and Marjorie Grene.
2. For more on Malebranche, see Charles J. McCracken, *Malebranche and British Philosophy* (Oxford: Oxford University Press, 1983); Nicholas Jolley, *The Light of the Soul: Theories of Ideas in Leibniz, Malebranche, and Descartes* (Oxford: Oxford University Press, 1990); Steven Nadler, *Malebranche and Ideas* (Oxford: Oxford University Press, 1992); Tad Schmaltz, *Malebranche's Theory of the Soul: A Cartesian Interpretation* (Oxford:

## Book III. Part II: The Pure Understanding. The Nature of Ideas

### Chapter 1

*I. What is understood by ideas. That they truly exist and are necessary to perceive all material objects.* I think everyone agrees that we do not perceive objects outside of us by themselves. We see the sun, the stars, and an infinity of objects outside of us; it is not likely that the soul leaves the body and, as it were, goes wandering about the heavens in order to contemplate all these objects. It does not therefore see them by themselves; the immediate object of our mind when it sees the sun, for example, is not the sun, but is something intimately united to our soul, and this is what I call an *idea*. Thus, by the word *idea*, I understand here nothing other than the immediate object, or the object closest to the mind, when it perceives something, namely, what touches and modifies the mind with the perception it has of an object.

It must be noted that for the mind to perceive an object, it is absolutely necessary for the idea of that object to be actually present to it—it is not possible to doubt this—but it is not necessary for there to be

Oxford University Press, 1996); and Steven Nadler, ed., *Cambridge Companion to Malebranche* (Cambridge: Cambridge University Press, 1997).

something similar to that idea outside it. For it very often happens that we perceive things which do not exist and even which have never existed; thus, we often have in the mind real ideas of things that have never existed. When, for example, a man imagines a golden mountain, it is absolutely necessary that the idea of this mountain be really present to his mind. When a madman, or someone with a high fever or who is sleeping, sees some animal as if before his eyes, it is certain that what he sees is not nothing, and that, thus, the idea of this animal really exists— but this golden mountain and this animal have never existed.

However, since men are led as if by nature to believe that only corporeal objects exist, they judge of the reality and existence of things in a completely different way than they should. For once they perceive an object, they want it to be quite certain that the object exists, even though it often happens that there is nothing outside. They want, in addition, for the object to be exactly as they see it, which never happens. But, with respect to the idea that exists necessarily and that cannot be other than as it is seen, they ordinarily judge without reflection that it is nothing— as if ideas did not have a great number of properties— as if the idea of a square, for example, were not quite different from that of a circle or of a number and did not represent completely different things—which can never happen for nothingness, since nothingness has no properties. It is therefore indubitable that ideas have a very real existence. But now let us examine what their nature is, and their essence, and let us see what in the soul can be capable of representing all things to it.

All the things the soul perceives are of two kinds: they are either in the soul or outside the soul. Those in the soul are its own thoughts, that is, all its different modifications, for by the words *thought, manner of thinking,* or *modification of the soul,* I understand generally all those things that cannot be in the soul without the soul perceiving them through the internal sensation it has of itself—such as its own sensations, imaginings, pure intellections, or simply its conceptions, even its passions and natural inclinations. Now, our soul does not need ideas in order to perceive all these things in the way it perceives them, because

these things are inside the soul, or rather because they are only the soul itself in this or that fashion, just as the actual roundness and motion of a body are only that body shaped and moved in this or that fashion.

But as for things outside the soul, we can perceive them only by means of ideas, assuming that these things cannot be intimately united to the soul. There are two kinds of these, spiritual and material. As for the spiritual ones, it seems that they can be revealed to the soul without ideas and by themselves. For although experience teaches us that we cannot communicate our thoughts to one another immediately and by ourselves, but only through speech or other sensible signs to which we have attached our ideas, it might be said that God has decreed it thus only for the duration of this life, in order to prevent the disorder that would happen if people could communicate as it pleased them. But when justice and order reign and we are delivered from the captivity of our body, we shall perhaps be able to communicate through the intimate union among ourselves, as the angels seem to be able to do in heaven. Thus, it does not seem to be absolutely necessary to have ideas represent spiritual things to the soul, because it can happen that they are seen through themselves, though in a very imperfect fashion.

I shall not examine here how two minds can be united to one another and whether they can in this way reveal their thoughts to each other. I believe, however, that there is no purely intelligible substance other than God's, that nothing can be discovered with evidence except in its light, and that the union of minds cannot make them visible to each other. For although we are closely united to ourselves, we are and will be unintelligible to ourselves until we see ourselves in God, and until he presents to us the perfectly intelligible idea he has of our being contained in his being. Thus, although it seems I am here allowing that angels can by themselves make known to one another both what they are and what they are thinking—which at bottom I do not believe to be true—I warn that this is only because I do not want to argue about it, as long as you grant me what is incontestable, namely, that material things cannot be seen by themselves and without ideas.

In the seventh chapter I will explain my opinion on the way we know minds and I will show that for now we cannot know them completely by themselves, even though they might be able to be united with us. But I am speaking here primarily about material things, which certainly cannot be united to our soul in the way it is necessary for it to perceive them, because, since they are extended and the soul is not so, there is no relation between them. Moreover, our souls do not leave the body to measure the size of the heavens and, as a result, they cannot see bodies on the outside except through the ideas representing them. This is what everyone must agree with.

*II. Division of all the ways according to which objects can be seen from the outside.* We assert, therefore, that it is absolutely necessary that the ideas we have of bodies and of all the other objects we do not perceive by themselves come from these very bodies or from these objects; or else that our soul has the power of producing these ideas; or that God has produced them with it while creating it or produces them every time we think about some object; or that the soul has in itself all the perfections it sees in these bodies; or finally that it is united to a completely perfect being which contains generally all intelligible perfections, or all the ideas of created beings.

We are not able to see objects except in one of these ways. Let us examine which of these is the most likely without prejudice and without fearing the difficulty of the question. Perhaps we will resolve it clearly enough, even though we do not claim here to give incontestable demonstrations for all people, but rather very persuasive proofs for those who will at least meditate about them with serious care, for we would perhaps appear presumptuous if we were to speak otherwise.

## Chapter 2

*That material objects do not transmit species resembling them.* The most common opinion is that of the Peripatetics, who claim that external objects transmit species which resemble them, and that these species are carried by the external senses to the common sense. They call these species *impressed* because ob-

jects impress them on the external senses. These impressed species, being material and sensible, are made intelligible by the *agent* or *active intellect* and are capable of being received in the *passive intellect*. These species, thus spiritualized, are called *expressed* species, because they are expressed from the impressed species, and through them the *passive intellect* knows all material things.

We shall not pause here to explicate further these fine things and the various ways different philosophers conceive of them. For although they do not agree about the number of faculties they attribute to the interior sense and to the understanding, and there are even many of them who strongly doubt whether an *agent intellect* is needed to know sensible objects, still they almost all agree that external objects transmit species or images resembling them; and it is only on this foundation that they multiply their faculties and defend their *agent intellect*. Since this foundation has no solidity, as we will show, it is not necessary to pause further in order to overthrow everything that has been built on it.

We assert, then, that it is not likely that objects transmit images or species resembling them; and here are some reasons why. The first is derived from the impenetrability of bodies. All objects, such as the sun, the stars, and all those close to our eyes, are unable to transmit species of another nature than theirs. This is why philosophers commonly say that these species are gross and material, in contrast to the expressed species, which are spiritualized. These impressed species of objects are therefore little bodies; thus, they cannot penetrate each other or all the spaces from the earth to the heavens, which must be full of them. From this it is easy to conclude that they must rub against and damage each other from every side, and that thus they cannot make objects visible.

Moreover, a great number of objects in the heavens and on earth can be seen from the same place or the same point; therefore, the species of all these objects would have to be capable of being reduced to a point. Now since they are extended, they are impenetrable; therefore, etc.

But not only can we see a great number of very large and vast objects from the same point, there is even no point in all these great spaces of the world from which an almost infinite number of objects cannot be discovered, even objects as large as the sun, moon, and heavens. There is therefore no point in the whole world where the species of all these things cannot meet—which goes against all semblance of truth.

The second reason is taken from the change that happens in the species. It is certain that the closer an object is, the larger its species must be, since we see the object as larger. Now, we do not see what can make this species diminish or what can happen to the parts composing it when it was larger. But what is even harder to conceive of according to their view is how, if we look at this object with a telescope or a microscope, the species suddenly becomes five or six hundred times larger than it was, for still less do we see with what parts it can be so greatly increased in an instant.

The third reason is that when we look at a perfect cube, all the species of its sides are unequal, and yet we still see all its sides as equally square. And, similarly, when we consider ovals and parallelograms in a picture, which can transmit only species of the same shape, we see only circles and squares there. This clearly shows that it is not necessary for the object we are looking at to produce species similar to it in order for us to see it.

Finally, we are not able to conceive of how it can happen that a body which does not sensibly diminish can always emit species in all directions and continually fill the great spaces around it—and do this with inconceivable speed. For a hidden object can be seen at the very instant of its discovery from several million leagues away and from all sides. And, what seems even more strange, very active bodies, such as air and some others, do not have the force to emit images resembling them—which coarser and less active bodies, such as earth, stones, and almost all hard bodies do.

But we do not wish to linger further and bring forth all the reasons opposed to this opinion, because it cannot be done, since the least mental effort yields such a great number of them that they cannot be exhausted. The reasons we have just related are enough; they were not even needed, given what we have said about this subject in book I, where we explained the errors of the senses. But such a great number of philosophers hold this opinion that we thought it necessary to say something about it in order to make them reflect upon their thoughts.

## Chapter 3

*That the soul has no power to produce ideas. Cause of the error we make concerning this matter.* The second opinion belongs to those who believe that our souls have the power of producing the ideas of the things about which they want to think—that they are moved to produce them by the impressions objects make on the body, even though these impressions are not images resembling the objects that cause them. They claim that this is how man is made in the image of God and how he participates in God's power. Further, just as God has created all things from nothing and can annihilate them and create new ones, so can man create and annihilate ideas of all things as it pleases him. But there is good reason to distrust all these opinions that elevate man. They are normally thoughts arising from his pride and vanity, which the Father of lights did not issue.

This participation in God's power that men boast of for representing objects to themselves, and for performing several other particular actions, seems to involve a certain independence, as it is generally explained. But it is also a chimerical participation, which the ignorance and vanity of men makes them imagine. Their dependence on God's power and goodness is much greater than they think, but here is not the place to explain this. Let us try only to show that men do not have the power to form ideas of the things they perceive.

No one can doubt that ideas are real beings, since they have real properties, that they differ from one another, and that they represent completely different things. Nor can we reasonably doubt that they are spiritual and very different from the bodies they represent. This seems sufficient to make us doubt whether the ideas by means of which we see bodies are not more noble than the bodies themselves. Indeed, the intelligible world must be more perfect than the material and terrestrial world, as we will see in what follows. Thus, when someone claims that men have the power to form such ideas as please them, he runs the risk of claiming that men have the power of creating beings more noble and more perfect than the world God has created. Yet we never reflect upon this, because we imagine that an idea is nothing, since it cannot be sensed, or if it is considered as a being, it is only as a meager and insignificant being, because we imagine that it is annihilated as soon as it is no longer present to the mind.

But even if it were true that ideas are only lesser and insignificant beings, they are nevertheless beings, and spiritual beings; since men do not have the power to create, it follows that they cannot produce these beings. For the production of ideas in the way it is explained is a true creation, and although they may try to palliate and soften the audacity and harshness of this view by saying that the production of ideas presupposes something existing, whereas creation presupposes nothing, still they have not resolved the difficulty.

For we ought to take heed that it is no more difficult to produce something from nothing than to produce it by supposing another thing from which it cannot be made and which can contribute nothing to its production. For example, it is no more difficult to create an angel than to produce it from a stone, because a stone is something of a totally contrary kind and cannot serve in any way toward the production of an angel. But it can contribute toward the production of bread, of gold, etc., because stone, gold, and bread are just the same extension differently configured, and all of these are material things.

It is even more difficult to produce an angel from a stone than to produce it from nothing, because to make an angel from a stone, insofar as that can be done, the stone must first be annihilated and then the angel must be created, and nothing needs to be annihilated simply to create an angel. Therefore, if the mind produces its ideas from the material impressions the brain receives from objects, it is always doing the same thing, or something as difficult, or even more difficult, than if it created them. Since ideas are spiritual, they cannot be produced from material images, which are in the brain and have no common measure with them.

If it is said that an idea is not a substance, I would

agree; but still it is a spiritual thing, and just as it is not possible to make a square out of a mind, even though a square is not a substance, it is also not possible to form a spiritual idea from a material substance, even though an idea would not be a substance.

But even if we granted to the mind of man a supreme power to annihilate and to create the ideas of things, it would still not be adequate to produce them. For just as a painter, no matter how skillful he is in his art, cannot represent an animal he has never seen and of which he has no idea (in such a way that the picture he would be required to produce could not be similar to this unknown animal), so a man cannot form the idea of an object unless he knew it beforehand, that is, unless he already has the idea of it, which does not depend on his will. But if he already has an idea of it, he knows the object, and it is useless for him to form a new idea of it. It is therefore useless to attribute to the mind of man the power to produce its ideas.

We could perhaps say that the mind has general and confused ideas it does not produce, and that those it produces are plainer and more distinct particular ideas. But this is still the same thing. For just as a painter cannot draw the portrait of a particular person in such a way that he is certain of having succeeded if he does not have a distinct idea of him (even if the person is present), so also a mind that has, for example, only the idea of being or of animal in general, cannot represent a horse to itself, or form a very distinct idea of it, or be sure that the idea exactly resembles a horse, if it does not already have a first idea to which it refers the second. And if it already has a first idea, it is useless to form a second, and therefore the question concerns the first idea; therefore, etc.

It is true that when we conceive of a square through pure intellection, we can still imagine it, that is to say, perceive it in us by tracing an image in the brain. But it should be noted, first, that we are neither the true nor the principal cause of that image (but it would take too long to explain this here) and second, that far from the second idea accompanying the image being more distinct and more accurate than the first idea, on the contrary, it is accurate only because it resembles the first, which serves as rule for the second.

For finally, we must not believe that the imagination and even the senses represent objects to us more distinctly than does the pure understanding, but only that they affect and move the mind more. For the ideas of the senses and of the imagination are distinct only through the conformity they have with the ideas of pure intellection. The image of a square that the imagination traces in the brain, for example, is only accurate and well formed through the conformity it has with the idea of a square that we conceive through pure intellection. It is this idea that rules the image. It is the mind that leads the imagination and requires it, so to speak, to consider from time to time whether the image it depicts is a figure composed of four straight and equal lines, whose angles are exactly ninety degrees—in a word, whether what one imagines is similar to what one conceives.

After what we have said, I do not think we can doubt that those who assert that the mind can itself form ideas of objects are mistaken, since they attribute to the mind the power to create, and even to create with wisdom and order, even though it does not have knowledge of what it does—for this is not conceivable. But the cause of their error is that people never fail to judge that a thing is the cause of some effect when the two are joined together, assuming that the true cause of the effect is unknown to them. This is why everyone concludes that a moving ball meeting another is the true and principal cause of the motion it communicates to the other, and that the soul's will is the true and principal cause of motion of the arm, and other such similar prejudices, because it always happens that a ball moves when it is struck by another, that our arms move almost every time we want them to, and that we do not sensibly see what other thing could be the cause of these motions.

Even when an effect does not so often follow something which is not its cause, still, there are a great number of people who believe that the thing is the cause of the effect that happens, though not everyone falls into this error. For example: a comet appears and afterwards a prince dies; stones are exposed to the moon and they are eaten by worms; the sun is in conjunction with Mars at the birth of a child and something extraordinary happens to the child. This is enough to convince many people that the comet,

the moon, and the conjunction of the sun with Mars are the causes of the effects just noted and others similar to them; and the reason why not everyone is of the same belief is that these effects are not always observed to follow these things.

But since all persons normally have ideas of things present to the mind as soon as they want them, and this happens to them many times a day, almost everyone concludes that the will accompanying the production, or rather, the presence of ideas is their true cause, because they see nothing at the time they can attribute to them as their cause, and because they imagine that ideas no longer exist once the mind no longer sees them and begin to exist again when they are represented to the mind. This is also why some people judge that external objects transmit images resembling them, as we have just pointed out in the previous chapter. Since it is not possible to see objects by themselves, but only through their ideas, they judge that the object produces the idea: once it is present, they see it; as soon as it is absent, they no longer see it; and the presence of the object almost always accompanies the idea representing it to us.

Yet if people were not so precipitous in their judgments, from the fact that the ideas of things are present to their mind as soon as they want, they would conclude only that according to the order of nature their will is generally necessary for them to have these ideas, and not that the will is the true and principal cause that makes them present to their mind, and still less that the will produces them from nothing (or in the way they explain it). Nor should they conclude that objects transmit species resembling them because the soul ordinarily perceives them only when they are present, but only that the object is ordinarily necessary for the idea to be present to the mind. Finally, they should not judge that a moving ball is the true and principal cause of the motion of the ball it finds in its path, since the former ball does not have the power to move itself. They can only judge that the collision of two balls is the occasion for the Author of all the motion of matter to execute the decree of his will, which is the universal cause of all things. This he does by communicating to the second ball part of the motion of the first—that is, to speak more clearly, by willing that the latter ball should acquire as much motion in the same direction as the former loses—for the motive force of bodies can only be the will of the one who preserves them, as we shall show elsewhere.

## Chapter 4

*That we do not see objects by means of ideas created with us. That God does not produce ideas in us at each moment we need them.* The third opinion is held by those who claim that all ideas are innate or created with us.

To recognize the implausibility of this opinion, it should be considered that there are many completely different things in the world of which we have ideas. But to mention only simple figures, it is certain that their number is infinite, and even if we attend only to one, such as the ellipse, we cannot doubt that the mind conceives of an infinite number of different kinds of them when it conceives that one of the diameters may be lengthened to infinity while the other remains always the same.

In the same way, since the height of a triangle can be increased or decreased to infinity while the base remains always the same, we conceive that there can be an infinite number of different kinds of triangles; moreover, and this is what I beg to have considered here, the mind perceives this infinite number in some way, even though we can imagine only a very few and cannot at the same time have particular and distinct ideas of many triangles of different kinds. But what should be especially noted is that the mind's general idea of this infinite number of different kinds of triangles sufficiently proves that if we do not conceive of all these different triangles by particular ideas—in short, if we do not comprehend the infinite—it is not through our lack of ideas or because the infinite is not present to us, but only through the mind's lack of capacity and scope. If a person applied himself to considering the properties of all the different kinds of triangles, and even if he should forever continue this kind of investigation, he would never lack new and particular ideas, but his mind would exhaust itself uselessly.

What I have just said about triangles can be applied to figures of five, six, a hundred, a thousand, ten thousand sides, and so on to infinity. And if the sides of a triangle can have infinite relations with one another, making an infinity of kinds of triangles, it is easy to see that figures of four, five, or a million sides can have even greater differences, since they can have a greater number of relations and combinations of their sides than simple triangles.

The mind, therefore, sees all these things; it has ideas of them. It is certain that these ideas will never be unavailable to it, even if it should spend infinite centuries considering even a single figure; and if it does not perceive these infinite figures all at once, or if it does not comprehend the infinite, it is only because its scope is quite limited. It therefore has an infinite number of ideas—I do not mean just an infinite number: it has as many infinite numbers of ideas as there are different figures, such that, since there is an infinite number of different figures, in order to know the figures alone, the mind must have an infinity of infinite numbers of ideas.

Now, I ask whether it is likely that God has created so many things along with the mind of man. It does not appear to me to be so, mainly because all this could be done in another very simple and very easy way, as we shall see shortly. For as God always acts in the simplest ways, it does not seem reasonable to explain how we know objects by assuming the creation of an infinity of beings, since this difficulty can be resolved in an easier and more natural fashion.

But even if the mind had a store of all the ideas necessary for it to see objects, nevertheless it would be impossible to explain how the soul could choose them to represent them to itself—how, for example, the soul could make itself perceive all the different objects whose size, figure, distance and motion it discovers the instant it opens its eyes in the country-side. It could not even perceive by this means a single object such as the sun when it is present to the eyes of the body. For, since the image the sun impresses in the brain does not at all resemble the idea we have of it (as we have proved elsewhere) and the soul does not perceive the motion the sun produces in the back of the eyes and in the brain, it is not conceivable that it can rightly predict, among the infinite number of its ideas it would have, which one must be represented for the sun to be imagined or seen, and seen as having this or that determinate size. We cannot therefore say that the ideas of things are created with us and that this suffices for us to see the objects surrounding us.

Nor can we say that God produces at every moment as many new ideas as we perceive different things. This view is sufficiently refuted by what we have just said in this chapter. Moreover, it is necessary that at all times we actually have in us the ideas of all things, since we can at all times will to think about all things—which we could not do if we did not already perceive them confusedly, that is to say, if an infinite number of ideas were not present to our mind; for, after all, we cannot will to think about objects of which we have no idea. Moreover, it is evident that the idea or immediate object of our mind, when we think of immense spaces, or of a circle in general, or of indeterminate being, is not a created thing. For created reality can be neither infinite nor even general, such as what we perceive there. But all this will be seen more clearly in what follows.

## Chapter 6

*That we see all things in God.* In the previous chapters we have examined four different ways in which the soul might see external objects, none of which appears to us likely. There remains only the fifth way, which alone appears to conform to reason and to be most appropriate for allowing us to know the dependence that minds have on God in all their thoughts.

To understand this fifth way adequately, we must remember what we have just said in the previous chapter: It is absolutely necessary for God to have in himself the ideas of all the beings he has created, since otherwise he could not have produced them, and thus he sees all these beings by considering those perfections he contains to which they have a relation. We must know, further, that God is very closely united to our souls through his presence, so that we can say that he is the place of minds in the same way that spaces are, in a sense, the place of bodies. Assuming these two things, it is certain that the mind can see what in God represents created beings, since the latter is very spiritual, intelligible, and present to the mind. Thus, the mind can see in God the works of God,

assuming that God does indeed will to reveal to the mind what it is in him that represents them. Now, here are the reasons that seem to prove that he wills this rather than the creation of an infinite number of ideas in each mind.

Not only is it in strict conformity with reason, but it is also apparent in the economy of all of nature, that God never does by very difficult means what can be done by very simple and easy means. For God never does anything in vain and without reason. What shows his wisdom and his power is not his doing small things with great means—this goes against reason and indicates a limited intelligence—on the contrary, it is doing great things with very simple and easy means. Thus, it was with extension alone that he produced everything we see that is admirable in nature and even what gives life and motion to animals. Those who absolutely insist on substantial forms, faculties, and souls in animals to perform their functions (different from their blood and bodily organs) at the same time would have it that God lacks intelligence, or that he cannot make all these admirable things with extension alone. They measure the power and supreme wisdom of God by the smallness of their mind. Thus, since God can reveal everything to minds simply by willing that they see what is in their midst, that is to say, what is in him which is related to and represents these things, there is no likelihood that he does it otherwise and that he produces for this as many infinities of infinite numbers of ideas as there are created minds.

But it should be carefully noted that we cannot conclude that minds see the essence of God from the fact of their seeing all things in God in this way. God's essence is his own absolute being, and minds do not see the divine substance taken absolutely, but only as relative to creatures or as they are able to participate in it. What they see in God is very imperfect and God is most perfect. They see matter shaped, divisible, and so forth, but in God there is nothing divisible or shaped, for God is all being, because he is infinite and comprises everything; but he is no particular being. However, what we see is only one or several particular beings and we do not understand this perfect simplicity of God, which contains all beings. In addition, it might be said that we do not so much see ideas of things as things themselves represented by ideas; when we see a square, for example, we do not say that we see the idea of the square united to the mind, but only the square outside it.

The second reason for thinking that we see beings because God wills that what is in him representing them be revealed to us—and not because we have as many ideas created with us as we can see things—is that this puts created minds in a position of complete dependence on God, the most complete possible. For this being so, not only would we see nothing unless God wills that we see it, but we would see nothing unless God himself made us see it. [. . .]

For, after all, it is difficult enough to understand distinctly the dependence that our minds have on God in all their particular actions, assuming that they have everything we distinctly know to be necessary for them to act, or all the ideas of things present to their mind. And that general and confused word *concourse*, by means of which we claim to explain the dependence of creatures on God, does not awaken any distinct idea in an attentive mind; and yet it is good that people know very distinctly that they can do nothing without God.

But the strongest argument of all is the way the mind perceives all things. It is certain, and everyone knows it from experience, that when we want to think about some particular thing, we first glance over all beings and then apply ourselves to considering the object we wish to think about. Now, it is indubitable that we could not desire to see a particular object we had not already seen, though confusedly and in general. Thus, since we are able to desire to see all beings, sometimes one, sometimes another, it is certain that all beings are present to our mind; and it seems that all beings cannot be present to our mind without God—he who contains all things in the simplicity of his being—being present to it.

It even seems that the mind would not be capable of representing to itself universal ideas of genus, species, etc., had it not seen all the beings contained in one. Since every creature is a particular being, we cannot say that we see something created when, for example, we see a triangle in general. Finally, I do not think

that we can account for the way the mind knows abstract and general truths, except through the presence of him who can illuminate the mind in an infinity of different ways.

Finally, the most beautiful, highest, most solid, primary proof of God's existence (or the one that makes the fewest assumptions) is the idea we have of the infinite. For it is certain that the mind perceives the infinite, though it does not comprehend it, and that it has a very distinct idea of God, which it can have only by means of its union with him, since we cannot conceive that the idea of an infinitely perfect being—the one we have of God—should be something created.

But not only does the mind have the idea of the infinite, it even has it before that of the finite. For we conceive of infinite being merely by conceiving of being, without thinking whether it is finite or infinite. But, in order for us to conceive of a finite being, we must necessarily subtract something from this general notion of being, which consequently must come first. Thus, the mind perceives nothing except in the idea it has of the infinite; and as for this idea being formed from the confused assemblage of all our ideas of particular beings, as philosophers think, on the contrary, every particular idea is only a participation in the general idea of the infinite: In the same way, God does not derive his being from creatures, while every creature is only an imperfect participation in the divine being.

Here is a proof that may constitute a demonstration for those accustomed to abstract reasoning. It is certain that ideas are efficacious, since they act in the mind and illuminate it, and since they make it happy or unhappy through the pleasant or unpleasant perceptions by which they affect it. Now nothing can act in the mind immediately unless it is superior to the mind; nothing but God alone can do this. For only the Author of our being can change its modifications. Therefore, it is necessary that all our ideas are located in the efficacious substance of the divinity, which alone is intelligible or capable of illuminating us, because it alone can affect intelligences. [. . .]

Finally, it is not possible for God to have any other principal end for his actions than himself. This is a notion common to all people capable of some reflection; and Sacred Scripture does not allow us to doubt that God has made all things for himself. It is therefore necessary that not only our natural love—I am referring to the impulse he produces in our mind—tends toward him, but also the knowledge and light he gives the mind must allow us to know something in him, for everything coming from God can only be for God. If God made a mind and gave it the sun as an idea, or as an immediate object of knowledge, it seems to me that God would be making this mind and the idea of this mind for the sun and not for himself.

God, therefore, cannot make a mind in order for it to know his works without that mind in some way being able to see God in seeing his works. Thus, it might be said that if we did not see God in some way, we would not see anything, just as if we did not love God—I mean if God did not continuously impress upon us the love of good in general—we would not love anything. For, this love being our will, we cannot love or will anything without it, since we cannot love particular goods except by determining toward these goods the motion of love God has given us for himself. Thus, in the same way that we do not love anything except through the necessary love we have for God, we do not see anything except through the natural knowledge we have of God; all the particular ideas we have of creatures are only limitations of the idea of the Creator, just as all the motions of the will toward creatures are only determinations of the motion toward the Creator. [. . .]

Therefore, we think that truths, even the eternal truths such as twice two is four, are not absolute beings, much less do we think that they are God himself. For, clearly, this truth consists only in the relation of equality between twice two and four. Thus, we do not say, as does Saint Augustine, that we see God in seeing truths, but in seeing the *ideas* of these truths—for the ideas are real, whereas the equality between the ideas, which is the truth, is nothing real. When we say, for example, that the cloth we are measuring is three ells long, the cloth and the ells are real. But the equality between the three ells and the cloth is not at all a real being; the equality is only a relation holding between the three ells and the cloth. When we say that twice two is four, the ideas

of the numbers are real, but the equality between them is only a relation. Thus, according to our view, we see God when we see eternal truths, not because these truths are God, but because the ideas on which these truths depend are in God; perhaps Saint Augustine also understood it that way. We also believe that we know changeable and corruptible things in God, even though Saint Augustine speaks only of immutable and incorruptible things; it is not necessary to posit some imperfection in God for this, since it is sufficient, as we have already said, that God should reveal to us what in him is related to these things.

But although I may say that we see material and sensible things in God, we must take note that I am not saying that we have sensations of them in God, but only that it is God who acts in us; for God surely knows sensible things, but he does not sense them. When we perceive something sensible, two things are found in our perception: *sensation* and pure *idea*. The sensation is a modification of our soul, and God causes it in us. He can cause this modification even though he does not have it himself, because he sees in the idea he has of our soul that it is capable of it. As for the idea united to the sensation, it is in God, and we see it because it pleases God to reveal it to us. God unites the sensation to the idea when objects are present so that we may believe them to be thus and enter into the sensations and passions we should have in relation to them. [. . .]

## Chapter 7

In order to summarize and clarify the view I have just established about the way the mind perceives all the various objects of its knowledge, it is necessary that I distinguish in it four ways of knowing.

*I. Four ways of seeing things.* The first is to know things by themselves.

The second is to know them through their ideas, that is, as I understand it here, through something different from them.

The third is to know them through *consciousness*, or internal awareness.

The fourth is to know them through conjecture.

We know things by themselves and without ideas

when they are intelligible by themselves, that is, when they can act on the mind and thereby reveal themselves to it. For the understanding is a purely passive faculty of the soul, and activity is found only in the will. Even its desires are not the true causes of ideas; they are only the occasional or natural causes of their presence, following the natural laws of the union of our soul with universal Reason, as I shall explain elsewhere. We know things through their ideas when they are not intelligible by themselves, either because they are corporeal or because they cannot affect the mind or reveal themselves to it. We know through consciousness all things not distinct from ourselves. Finally, we know through conjecture those things different from ourselves and from the ones we know in themselves or through ideas, when we think that certain things are similar to others we know.

*II. How we know God.* Only God is known through himself, for while there are other spiritual beings that seem intelligible by their nature, only he can act in the mind and reveal himself to it. Only God is seen by a direct and immediate view. Only he can illuminate the mind with his own substance. Finally, only through the union we have with him are we capable in this life of knowing what we know, as we have explained in the previous chapter; for he is the only Master, according to Saint Augustine, presiding over our mind without the intermediary of any creature.

We cannot conceive that something created can represent the infinite—that being, without restriction, immense and universal being, can be perceived through an idea, that is, through a particular being, one different from universal and infinite being. But as for particular beings, it is not difficult to conceive that they can be represented by the infinite being containing them in his most efficacious and, consequently, most intelligible substance. Thus, it is necessary to say that we know God through himself, even though our knowledge of him in this life is very imperfect, and we know corporeal things through their ideas, that is, in God, since only God contains the intelligible world, in which the ideas of all things are found.

But while we can see all things in God, it does not follow that we do see them all: We see in God only the things of which we have ideas, and there are things we see without ideas, or know only through sensation.

*III. How we know bodies.* All the things in this world of which we have knowledge are either bodies or minds, properties of minds or properties of bodies. Undoubtedly, we see bodies with their properties only through their ideas, because, not being intelligible by themselves, we can see them only in that being which contains them in an intelligible way. Thus, it is in God and through their ideas that we see bodies and their properties, and for this reason, the knowledge we have of them is quite perfect—I mean that our idea of extension suffices to enable us to know all the properties of which extension is capable, and we could not wish to have a more distinct and more fruitful idea of extension, figure, and motion than the one God gives us of them.

Since the ideas of things in God contain all their properties, he who sees their ideas can also see all their properties successively; for, when we see things as they are in God, we always see them in perfect fashion, and the way we see them would be infinitely perfect if the mind seeing them were infinite. What is lacking from the knowledge we have of extension, figures, and motion is not a defect of the idea representing it, but of our mind considering it.

*IV. How we know our soul.* It is not the same for the soul: We do not at all know it through its idea; we do not at all see it in God; we know it only through *consciousness* and because of this, the knowledge we have of it is imperfect. We know of our soul only what we sense taking place in us. If we never sensed pain, heat, light, etc., we could not know whether our soul was capable of it, because we do not know it through its idea. But if we saw in God the idea relating to our soul, we would at the same time know, or could know, all the properties of which it is capable—as we know, or can know, all the properties of which extension is capable, because we know extension through its idea.

It is true that we know enough through our consciousness, or the internal awareness we have of ourselves, that our soul is something great; but it might be that what we know of it is almost nothing compared to what it is in itself. If we knew of matter only some twenty or thirty figures by which it had been modified, we certainly would know almost nothing of it in comparison with what we can know of it through the idea representing it; therefore, to know the soul perfectly, it is not enough to know only what we know through internal awareness, since the consciousness we have of ourselves shows us perhaps only the least part of our being.

We might conclude from what we have just said that, although we know the existence of our soul more distinctly than the existence of our body and those surrounding us, still we do not have as perfect a knowledge of the nature of the soul as that of the nature of bodies; this might serve to reconcile the differing views of those who say that nothing is known better than the soul and those who assert that there is nothing they know less.

This might also serve to prove that ideas representing to us things outside us are not modifications of our soul. For if the soul saw all things by considering its own modifications, it would have to know more clearly its essence or nature than that of bodies, and all the sensations or modifications of which it is capable more clearly than the figures or modifications of which bodies are capable. However, it does not at all know itself capable of such a sensation through the view it has of itself in consulting its idea, but only through experience; instead it knows that extension is capable of an infinite number of figures through the idea it has of extension. There are even certain sensations like colors and sounds which are such that most people cannot tell whether or not they are modifications of the soul, but there is no figure that everyone, through the idea he has of extension, does not recognize as the modification of a body.

What I have just said also shows us the reason why we cannot give a definition that allows us to know modifications of the soul; for, since we know neither the soul nor its modifications through ideas, but only through sensations, and since such sensations as, for example, pleasure, pain, heat, etc., are not attached to words, it is clear that if someone had never seen color nor felt heat, we could not make him know those sensations through any definition of them we might give him. Now, since people have their sensa-

tions only because of their bodies, which are not all disposed in the same way, it often happens that words are equivocal, that the words we use to express the modifications of our soul signify just the contrary of what we mean, and that we often make people think of bitterness, for example, when we believe we are making them think of sweetness.

While we do not have complete knowledge of our soul, what we do have of it through consciousness or internal awareness suffices to demonstrate its immortality, spirituality, freedom, and several other attributes that it is necessary for us to know; and it is apparently for this reason that God does not have us know the soul through its idea, as he has us know bodies. Granted that the knowledge that we have of our soul through consciousness is imperfect, but it is not false. In contrast, the knowledge we have of bodies through sensation or consciousness—if we can call consciousness the confused sensation we have of what happens in our body—is not only imperfect, but also false. We therefore needed an idea of bodies to correct our sensations of them, but we do not need an idea of our soul, since the consciousness we have of it does not involve us in error, and since to avoid being mistaken in our knowledge of it, it suffices that we do not confuse it with the body—which we can do through reason, since the idea we have of the body reveals to us that the modalities of which it is capable are very different from those we feel. Finally, if we had an idea of the soul as clear as the one we have of the body, that idea would have us overly consider the soul as separated from the body. It would have thus diminished the union between our soul and our body by preventing us from regarding it as dispersed through all our members—a point I shall not explain any further.

*V. How we know the souls of other men.* Of all the objects of our knowledge, only the souls of other men and pure intelligences remain; it is manifest that we know them only through conjecture. At present we do not know them either in themselves or through their ideas, and as they are different from us, it is not possible to know them through consciousness. We conjecture that the souls of other men are of the same kind as our own. We claim that they feel what we feel in ourselves, and even when these sensations have no relation to the body, we are certain we are not mistaken because we see in God certain ideas and immutable laws according to which we know with certainty that God acts uniformly in all minds. [. . .]

## Book VI. Part II: On Method

### Chapter 3

*The most dangerous error of the philosophy of the ancients.* Not only do philosophers say what they do not at all conceive when they explain natural effects through certain beings of which they have no particular idea, they even furnish a principle from which very false and very dangerous conclusions can be drawn directly.

For if we assume, according to their view, that there are entities distinct from matter in bodies, then, having no distinct idea of these entities, we can easily imagine that they are the true or principal causes of the effects we see happening. This is even the general opinion of ordinary philosophers: For it is principally to explain these effects that they think there are substantial forms, real qualities, and other similar entities. Next, if we consider carefully the idea we have of cause or of power to act, we cannot doubt that this idea represents something divine. For the idea of a supreme power is the idea of a supreme divinity and the idea of a subalternate power is the idea of an inferior, but genuine, divinity, at least according to the pagans, assuming that it is the idea of a genuine power or cause. We therefore admit something divine in all the bodies around us when we admit forms, faculties, qualities, virtues, or real beings capable of producing certain effects through the force of their nature; and thus we insensibly adopt the view of the pagans because of our respect for their philosophy. It is true that faith corrects us, but perhaps it can be said that if the heart is Christian, the mind is at bottom pagan. Perhaps it will be said that substantial forms— for example, those *plastic* forms which produce animals and plants—do not know what they are doing and that, thus, lacking intelligence, they have no relation to the divinities of the pagans. But who will be

able to believe that what produces works manifesting a wisdom surpassing that of all the philosophers produces them without intelligence? [. . .]

In order that we shall no longer be able to doubt the falsity of this unfortunate philosophy and recognize with evidence the soundness of the principles and the distinctness of the ideas we use, it is necessary to establish clearly the truths that are opposed to the errors of the ancient philosophers, and to prove in a few words that: there is only one true cause because there is only one true God; the nature or power of each thing is but the will of God; all natural causes are not at all *true* causes but only *occasional* causes; and some other truths following from these.

It is evident that bodies, large and small, do not have the power to move themselves. A mountain, a house, a rock, a grain of sand—in brief, the smallest or largest body conceivable—does not have the power to move itself. We have only two sorts of ideas, ideas of minds and ideas of bodies; and since we should say only what we conceive of, we should reason only according to these two. Thus, since the idea we have of all bodies makes us know that they cannot move themselves, it must be concluded that it is minds which move them. But when we examine the idea we have of all finite minds, we do not see any necessary connection between their will and the motion of any body whatsoever. On the contrary, we see that there is none and that there can be none. We must also conclude, if we wish to reason according to our lights, that no created mind can move any body whatsoever as a true or principal cause, just as we have said that no body could move itself.

But when we think of the idea of God, that is, of an infinitely perfect and consequently omnipotent being, we know that there is such a connection between his will and the motion of all bodies, that it is impossible to conceive that he wills a body be moved and that this body not be moved. We must therefore say that only his will can move bodies if we wish to say things as we conceive of them and not as we sense them. The motive force of bodies is therefore not in the bodies that are moved, for this motive force is nothing other than the will of God. Thus, bodies have no action; and when a moving ball collides with and moves another, it communicates to it nothing of its own, for it does not itself have the force it communicates. However, a ball is the natural cause of the motion it communicates. A natural cause is therefore not a real and true, but only an occasional, cause, one that determines the Author of nature to act in such and such a manner in such and such a situation.

It is certain that all things are produced through the motion of bodies, visible or invisible, for experience teaches us that bodies whose parts have more motion are always those that act more and produce more change in the world. All natural forces are therefore nothing but the always efficacious will of God. God created the world because he willed it—"He spoke and it was done"—and he moves all things, and thus produces all the effects we see happening, because he also willed certain laws according to which motions are communicated upon the collision of bodies; because these laws are efficacious, they act, and bodies cannot act. There are therefore no forces, powers, or true causes in the material and sensible world; and we must not admit forms, faculties, and real qualities for producing effects that bodies do not produce and for sharing with God the force and power that are essential to him.

Not only can bodies not be the true causes of anything whatsoever, but the most noble minds are similarly powerless. They can know nothing unless God illuminates them. They can sense nothing unless God modifies them. They are capable of willing nothing if God does not move them toward good in general, that is, toward himself. I admit that they can determine toward objects other than himself the impression God gives them toward himself, but I do not know if that can be called power. If the ability to sin is a power, it will be a power that the Almighty does not have, as Saint Augustine says somewhere. If people held of themselves the power to love the good, we could say they had some power; but people can love only because God wills that they love and because his will is efficacious. People can love only because God constantly pushes them toward the good in general, that is, toward himself; for God having created them only for himself, he never preserves them without turning and pushing them toward him. It is not they who move toward the good in general,

it is God who moves them. They merely follow this impression through an entirely free choice according to the law of God, or they determine it toward false goods, according to the law of the flesh, but they can determine it only through their view of the good; since they can do only what God makes them do, they can only love the good.

But if we were to assume what is true in one sense—that minds have in themselves the power to know the truth and to love the good—if their thoughts and wills produced nothing externally, we could always say that they can do nothing. Now it appears to me quite certain that the will of minds is not capable of moving the smallest body in the world; for it is evident that there is no necessary connection between the will we have to move our arm, for example, and the motion of our arm. It is true that the arm moves when we will it, and that we are thus the natural cause of the motion of our arm. But *natural* causes are not at all true causes; they are merely *occasional* causes acting only through the force and efficacy of the will of God, as I have just explained.

For how could we move our arm? To move it, we must have animal spirits, we must send them through certain nerves toward certain muscles to inflate and contract them, for that is how the arm attached to them moves; or according to some other views, we still do not know how that happens. And we see people who do not even know that they have spirits, nerves, and muscles move their arm, and move it even with more skill and ease than those who know anatomy best. Therefore, people will to move their arm, and only God is able and knows how to move it. If a person is not able to knock down a tower, at least he knows what must be done to knock it down; but no person knows what must be done to move just one of his fingers by means of animal spirits. How, then, could people move their arm? These things appear evident to me and, it seems, to all those willing to think, though they are perhaps incomprehensible to all those willing only to sense.

But not only are men not at all the true causes of the motions they produce in their body, it even seems contradictory that they could be. As I understand it, a true cause is a cause such that the mind perceives a necessary connection between it and its effect. Now the mind perceives a necessary connection only between the will of an infinitely perfect being and its effects. Therefore, only God is the true cause who truly has the power to move bodies. In addition, I say that it is inconceivable that God could communicate to people or to angels the power he has to move bodies, and that those who claim that the power we have to move our arm is a true power must admit that God can also give minds the power to create, annihilate, and to do all possible things—in short, that he can render them omnipotent, as I shall show.

God needs no instruments to act; it suffices that he wills[3] in order for a thing to be, because it is contradictory that he should will and that what he wills should not be. Therefore, his power is his will, and to communicate his power is to communicate the efficacy of his will. But to communicate this efficacy to a person or an angel can signify nothing other than to will that, for example, when a person or angel shall will this or that body be moved, the body will actually be moved. Now in this case, I see two wills concurring when an angel moves a body—that of God and that of the angel—and in order to know which of the two is the true cause of the motion of this body, we must know which cause is efficacious. There is a necessary connection between the will of God and the thing he wills. God wills in this case that, when an angel wills this or that body be moved, the body will be moved. Therefore, there is a necessary connection between the will of God and the motion of the body; and consequently God is the true cause of the motion of the body and the will of the angel is only an occasional cause.

But to show this still more clearly, let us suppose that God wills to produce the opposite of what some minds would will, as might be thought for demons or some other minds deserving of this punishment. We could not say in this case that God would communicate his power to them, since they could do nothing they wished to do. However, the wills of these minds would be the natural causes of the effects produced. Such bodies would be moved to the right only because these minds willed them to be moved to the left; and the desires of these minds would determine the will of God to act, as our will to move the parts of our bodies determines the first cause to move them. In this way, all the volitions of minds are only occasional causes.

But if after all these arguments someone still wanted to maintain that the will of an angel who moved a body would be a true and not an occasional cause, it is evident that this same angel could be the true cause of the creation and annihilation of all things. For God could communicate his power to create and annihilate bodies to the angel, in the same way he does the power to move them, if he willed all things to be created and annihilated—in short, if he willed all things to happen as the angel would wish it, just as he willed bodies to be moved as the angel would will. Therefore, if someone claims that an angel and a person are truly movers because God moves bodies when they wish it, he must also say that a person and an angel can truly be creators, since God can create beings when they would will it. Perhaps he could even say that the most vile animal, or matter all alone, would effectively cause the creation of some substance, if he assumed, as do the philosophers, that God produced substantial forms when required by matter. Finally, because God resolved from all eternity to create certain things in certain times, he could also say that these times would be the causes of the creation of these beings—just as he claims that one ball colliding with another is the true cause of the motion it communicates to the latter, because God willed through his general will, which causes the order of nature, that when two bodies collide, such a communication of motion would occur.

There is therefore only a single true God and a single cause which is truly a cause, and we should not imagine that what precedes an effect is its true cause. God cannot even communicate his power to creatures, if we follow the light of reason: He cannot make true causes of them; he cannot make them gods. But even if he could, we cannot conceive of why he would. Bodies, minds, pure intelligences, all these can do nothing. It is he who makes minds, who illuminates and moves them. It is he who created heaven and earth, and who regulates their motions.

---

3. Malebranche: It is clear that I am speaking here about practical volitions, or those God has when he claims to act.

In the end, it is the Author of our being who executes our wills: "Once God judges, the will always obeys." He even moves our arm when we use it against his orders; for he complains through his prophet (Isa. 43.24) that we make him serve our unjust and criminal desires. [. . .]

## Elucidation Fifteen

*On Book VI, Part II, Chapter 3. Concerning the efficacy attributed to secondary causes.* [. . .] There are many reasons preventing me from attributing to *secondary* or *natural* causes a force, a power, an efficacy to produce anything whatsoever. But the principal one is that this opinion does not even appear conceivable to me. Whatever effort I make to comprehend it, I cannot find in me any idea representing to me what might be the force or power attributed to creatures. And I do not even think I am making an overly bold judgment when I assert that those who maintain that creatures have force and power in themselves advance something they do not conceive of clearly. For, in the end, if philosophers conceived clearly that secondary causes have a true force to act and produce things similar to them, then being a man as much as they are and participating like them in supreme Reason, I could apparently discover the idea representing this force to them. But whatever effort of mind I make, I can find force, efficacy, power, only in the will of the infinitely perfect being.

In addition, when I think about the different opinions of philosophers on this subject, I cannot doubt what I am proposing. For, if they saw clearly what the power of creatures is, or what is truly powerful in them, they would agree about it. When people who have no special interest preventing them from doing so cannot agree, it is a sure sign that they simply do not have a clear idea of what they are saying and do not understand each other—especially if they are disputing about subjects not overly complex or difficult to discuss, such as the question at hand, for there would be no difficulty in resolving it, if people had some clear idea of a created force or power. [. . .]

When I see one ball strike another, my eyes tell me, or seem to tell me, that the first ball is truly the cause of the motion it impresses on the second; for the true cause that moves bodies does not appear to my eyes. But when I examine my reason, I see evidently that, since bodies cannot move themselves and their motive force is only the will of God conserving them successively in different places, they cannot communicate a power they do not have and could not even communicate if it was in their possession. For the mind will never conceive that a body, a purely passive substance, can in any way whatsoever transmit to another body the power moving it.

When I open my eyes, it appears evident to me that the sun is bursting with light, that not only is it visible by itself, but that it renders visible all the bodies around it; it covers the earth with flowers and fruits, gives life to animals, and, penetrating even into the bowels of the earth by its heat, produces stones, marble, and metals there. But when I consult Reason, I see nothing of all this; and when I consult it faithfully, I recognize clearly that my senses are seducing me, and that it is God who does everything in all things. For, knowing that all the changes happening in bodies have no other principle than the different communications of motion taking place in visible and invisible bodies, I see that it is God who does everything, since it is his will that causes, and his wisdom that regulates, all these communications.

I assume that local motion is the principle of generation, corruption, alteration, and generally of all the changes occurring in bodies; this opinion is accepted well enough among the learned. But it does not matter what view is held about it. For it seems even easier to conceive that a body pushes another when it collides with the other than it is to understand that fire produces heat and light and draws from the power of matter a substance that was not previously there. And if it is necessary to recognize God alone as the true cause of the different communications of motion, so much the more must we judge that only he can create and annihilate real qualities and substantial forms. I say *create* and *annihilate*, because it seems to me at least as difficult to draw from matter a substance that was not there, or to have it return without its having been there, as it is to create or annihilate it. But I do not pause over terms; I make use of these because I know of no others that express clearly and unequivocally the changes philosophers assume are happening at every moment through the force of secondary causes.

I am somewhat troubled by reporting here the other proofs commonly given about the force and efficacy of natural causes, for they seem so weak to those who resist prejudices and prefer their reason to their senses, that it does not seem likely they could have persuaded reasonable people. However, I am reporting and replying to them because there are many philosophers who make use of them.

First Proof of the Efficacy of Secondary Causes: If secondary causes did nothing, say Suarez, Fonseca, and a few others,[4] we could not distinguish living things from those not living, for neither would have an internal principle of their actions.

Reply: I reply that men would still have the same sensible proofs which convinced them of the distinction they draw between living and non living things. They would still see animals perform certain actions such as eating, growing, crying, running, jumping, etc., and they would observe nothing similar in stones. This alone causes ordinary philosophers to believe that beasts are alive and stones are not. For we should not imagine that they know what the life of a dog is through a clear and distinct view of the mind; it is their senses that govern their decisions on this question.

If necessary, I would prove here that the principle of the life of a dog is not very different from that of the motion of a watch. For the life of bodies, whatever they are, can consist only in the motion of their parts; and it is not difficult to judge that the same subtle matter producing in a dog the fermentation of blood and animal spirits which is the principle of its life, is no more perfect than the one giving motion to the mechanism of watches or causing the heaviness in the weights of clocks which is the principle of their life, or, to speak as others do, of their motion.

It is up to the Peripatetics to give those they call Cartesians a clear idea of what they entitle *the life of beasts, corporeal soul, body that perceives, desires, sees, senses, wills*, and then we will clearly resolve their difficulties, if they still continue to produce them.

4. Malebranche: Suarez, *Metaphysical Disputations*, Disputation 18, sec. 1, assert. 12; Fonseca, *Commentary on Aristotle's Metaphysics*, quest. 7, sec. 2.

Second Proof: We could not recognize the differences or the virtues of the elements. It could happen that fire would cool in the same way that water does; the nature of individual things would not be fixed and determinate.

Reply: I reply that, nature remaining as it is, that is, the laws of the communication of motion still remaining the same, it is contradictory that fire does not burn or separate the parts of certain bodies. Fire cannot cool like water unless it becomes water, for fire being only wood whose parts have been agitated with a violent motion by an invisible matter surrounding them, as is easy to demonstrate, it is impossible for these parts not to communicate some of their motion to the bodies with which they collide. Now, since these laws are constant, the nature of fire, its virtues, and its qualities do not change. But this nature and these virtues are only consequences of the general and efficacious will of God, who does everything in all things. As a result, it is false and useless in every way when we seek in the study of nature true causes other than the volitions of the Almighty or the general laws according to which he constantly acts.

I grant that we should not have recourse to God or to the universal cause when we seek the reason for particular effects. For it would be ridiculous to say, for example, that God dries the roads or freezes the water of rivers. We should say that the air dries the earth because it stirs and takes up the water drenching the earth, and that the air or subtle matter freezes the river in winter, because during winter it ceases to communicate enough motion to the parts making up the water to render it fluid. In a word, we must give, if we can, the natural and particular cause of the effects in question. But since the action of these causes consists only in the motive force activating them, and since this motive force is only the will of God, we should not say that in themselves they have force or power to produce some effects. And when we finally come to a general effect whose cause we seek when we reason, if we imagine any other cause of it than the general cause, we are still philosophizing badly. We must not feign a certain *nature*, a *first mobile*, a *universal soul*, or some similar *chimera* of which we have no clear and distinct idea; that would be to reason like a pagan philosopher. For example, when we ask how it happens that bodies are in motion, that agitated air communicates its motion to water, or rather that bodies push one another, we answer: since motion and its communication are a general effect on which all other effects depend, to be a philosopher (I do not say to be a Christian) it is necessary to have recourse to God, who is the universal cause, because his will is the motive force of bodies and also produces the communication of their motion. If he had willed to produce nothing new in the world, he would not have put its parts in motion. And if he wills some day to render incorruptible some of the beings he has formed—our bodies after the resurrection, for example—he will cease to will certain communications of motion with respect to these beings.

Third Proof: It would be useless to cultivate, water, and give certain dispositions to bodies so as to prepare them for what we hope will happen to them. For God has no need to prepare the subjects on which he acts.

Reply: I reply that God can absolutely do anything that pleases him without finding dispositions in the subjects on which is he acting. But, he cannot do it without a miracle, or by natural means, that is, according to the general laws of the communication of motion he has established, and according to those by which he almost always acts. God does not multiply his volitions without reason; he always acts through the simplest ways. This is why he uses the collision of bodies to move them, not because their impact is absolutely necessary for their motion, as our senses tell us, but because very few natural laws are needed to produce all the admirable effects we see, given that impact is the occasion for the communication of motion.

It is necessary to water a plant for it to grow because, according to the laws of the communication of motion, hardly anything other than the parts of water can, by their motion and shape, slide around and climb up between the fibers of plants, carry with them some salts and other small bodies, and by congealing or attaching themselves variously to one another, take the shape necessary to nourish them. The subtle matter the sun constantly propagates can raise water in plants by agitating it, but it does not have enough motion to raise the coarse parts of earth. However,

earth and even air are necessary for the growth of plants—earth to keep water at their roots and air to excite a moderate fermentation in the same water. Since the action of the sun, air, and water consists only in the motion of their parts, only God is acting, properly speaking. For, as I have just said, only he, through the efficacy of his volitions and through the infinite extent of his knowledge, can produce and regulate the infinitely infinite communications of motion occurring at each instant and conserving in the universe all the beautiful things we observe in it.

Fourth Proof: We do not struggle against ourselves; we do not resist ourselves. Bodies collide, strike, and resist each other. Therefore, God does not act in them, except through his *concourse*. If God alone produced and conserved motion in bodies, he would make them turn aside before their impact, for he knows well enough that they are impenetrable. Why push bodies to make them rebound, why make them advance to make them withdraw, why produce and conserve useless motion? Is it not an extravagant thing to say that God struggles against himself and that he destroys his works when a bull fights with a lion, when a wolf devours a sheep, and when a sheep eats the grass that God makes grow? Therefore, there are secondary causes.

Reply: Therefore, secondary causes do everything and God does nothing. For God cannot act against himself, and *concourse* is action. *To concur* with contrary actions is to give contrary *concourse*, and consequently to perform contrary actions. To concur with the actions of creatures resisting each other is to act against oneself. To concur with useless motions is to act uselessly. Now, God does nothing uselessly; he performs no contrary action at all; he does not at all struggle against himself. Therefore, he does not concur with the action of creatures, which often destroy one another and perform useless actions or motions. That is where this proof of secondary causes leads us. But here is what reason teaches us.

God does everything in all things, and nothing resists him. He does everything in all things, for his volitions produce and regulate all motions, and nothing resists him because he does everything he wills. But here is how we must conceive this. In greater conformity with the immutable order of his attributes, having resolved to produce through the simplest ways this infinite variety of creatures we admire, he willed that bodies move in a straight line because that line is the simplest. Since bodies are impenetrable and their motions occur along opposing or intersecting lines, it is necessary that they strike each other and that, consequently, they stop moving in the same way. God foresaw this, and still he positively willed the collision or impact of bodies, not because it pleases him to struggle against himself, but because he intended to use this impact of bodies as an occasion to establish the general law of the communication of motion, by which he foresaw that an infinity of admirable effects must be produced. For I am persuaded that these two natural laws, which are the simplest of all—namely, that all motion occurs or tends to occur in a straight line and that in impact motions are communicated in proportion to, and along the line of, their pressure—are sufficient, the initial motions being wisely distributed to produce the world such as we see it, that is, the heaven, stars, planets, comets, earth and water, air and fire, in a word, the elements, and all bodies not organized or living; for organized bodies depend on the initial construction of those from which they arise, and it is likely that they were formed at the creation of the world (not however such as they appear to our eyes) and that they receive with time nothing more than the growth necessary to become visible. Nevertheless, it is certain that they receive this growth only through the general laws of nature according to which all other bodies are formed; this results in their growth not always being regular and monsters being engendered. [. . .]

When a house crushes a right-thinking man, there occurs a greater evil than when one beast devours another, or when a body is required to rebound by the impact of the body it strikes; but God does not multiply his volitions to remedy the true or apparent disorders that are the necessary consequences of natural laws. God must neither correct nor change these laws, even though they sometimes produce monsters. He must not trouble the uniformity of his conduct and the simplicity of his ways. He must neglect insignificant things—I mean that he must not have particular volitions to produce effects that are not worth his willing them or that are unworthy of the action of the one producing them. God produces miracles only when it is required by the order he always fol-

lows—by this I understand the immutable order of justice he wills to give his attributes. And this order requires that he act in the simplest ways and that there are exceptions to his volitions only when it is absolutely necessary for his intentions, only when the simplicity and uniformity of his conduct do not as much honor his immutability and foreknowledge as miraculous conduct would honor his wisdom, justice, goodness, or other of his attributes; in short, only on certain occasions that are entirely unknown to us. Even though we are all united to the order or wisdom of God, we do not know all its rules. We see in it what we must do, but do not understand in it everything God must will, and we must not make too much effort to understand it. [. . .]

Sixth Proof: The main proof that the philosophers bring forth for the efficacy of secondary causes is drawn from the will and freedom of man. Man wills, he determines himself by himself, and to will and to determine oneself is to act. It is certain that man commits sin. God is no more its author than he is that of concupiscence and error. Therefore, man acts through his own efficacy.

Reply: I have explained sufficiently in several passages of the *Search after Truth* (particularly in chapter 1 of book I, and in Elucidation One on the same chapter) what man's will and freedom are; it is useless to repeat this. I grant that man wills and that he determines himself, but it is because God makes him will by constantly bringing him toward the good. He determines himself, but it is because God gives him all the ideas and feelings that are the motives by which he determines himself. I also grant that man alone commits sin. But I deny that in this he does something, for sin, error, and even concupiscence are nothing. They are only deficiencies. I have sufficiently explained myself on this in Elucidation One.

Man wills, but his volitions are powerless in themselves; they produce nothing. They do not at all prevent God's doing everything, because God himself produces our volitions in us through the pressure he exerts on us toward the good in general, for without this pressure we could not will anything. Man has from himself only error and sin, which are nothing.

There is a great difference between our minds and the bodies surrounding us. Our mind wills, acts, determines itself; I do not doubt this in any way. We are convinced of it by the internal awareness we have of ourselves. If we had no freedom at all, there would be no punishments or future rewards, for without freedom there are neither good nor bad actions. As a result, religion would be an illusion and a phantom. But what we do not clearly see is that bodies have the power to act; this is what appears incomprehensible, and it is also what we deny when we deny the efficacy of secondary causes.

The mind itself does not act as much as we imagine. I know that I will and that I will freely; I have no reason to doubt this any more than I have to doubt the internal awareness I have of myself. Nor do I deny the latter. But I deny that my will is the true cause of the motion of my arm, of the ideas in my mind, and of other things accompanying my volitions, for I do not see any relation between such different things. I even see very clearly that there can be no relation between the volition I have to move my arm and the agitation of the animal spirits, that is, of certain small bodies whose motion and shape I do not know; the latter choose certain nerve canals from a million others I do not know, so as to cause in me the motion I desire through an infinity of motions I do not desire. I deny that my will produces my ideas in me, for I do not even see how it could produce them, because my will, which cannot act or will without knowledge, presupposes my ideas and does not produce them. I do not even know precisely what an idea is. I do not know whether they are produced from nothing and whether they return to nothingness as soon as we stop seeing them. I am speaking according to the view of some people.

I produce my own ideas, they will say, by the faculty God has given me for thinking. I move my arm because of the *union* God has established between my mind and my body. *Faculty* and *union* are terms of logic; they are vague and indeterminate words. No particular being or mode of being can be a *faculty* or a *union*; these terms must be explained. If they say that the union of my mind with my body consists in God's willing that when I will my arm to move, animal spirits spread in the muscles making it up, so as to move it in the way I wish, I clearly understand this explanation and I accept it. But this is to say exactly what I maintain; for my will specifying God's practical will, it is evident that my arm will be moved,

not by my will, which is powerless in itself, but by God's, which can never fail to have its effect.

But if they say that the union of my mind with my body consists in God's having given me the *force*[5] to move my arm, just as he has also given my body the force to make me feel pleasure and pain in order that I apply myself to this body and interest myself in its preservation, then surely they are supposing what is in question and going in a circle. They have no clear idea of this force that the soul has over the body, nor of the force that the body has over the soul; they do not know well enough what they are saying when they assert this positively. They have arrived at this view through prejudice: They believed this view from infancy as soon as they were capable of sensing; but mind, reason, and reflection have no part in it at all. This is clear enough from the things I have said in the *Search after Truth*.

But, they will say, I know through the internal awareness of my action that I truly have this force; therefore, I am not at all mistaken in believing it. I reply that when they move their arm they have an internal awareness of the actual volition by which they move it, and they are not mistaken in believing that they have this volition. In addition, they have an internal sensation of a certain effort accompanying this volition, and they must also believe that they are making this effort. Finally, I grant[6] that they have an internal sensation of the arm moving at the moment of this effort; on this assumption I also agree to what they say, that the motion of the arm occurs at the instant we feel this effort, or that they have a *practical* volition to move it. But I deny that this effort, which is only a modification or sensation of the soul given to us to make us understand our weakness and to give

---

5. Malebranche: I still mean a true and efficacious power.
6. Malebranche: It seems evident to me that the mind does not even know, through internal sensation or consciousness, the motion of the arm it animates. It only knows its own sensation through consciousness, for the soul is *conscious* only of its own thoughts. The sensation we have of the motion of our arm is known through internal sensation or consciousness, but it is not through consciousness that we are informed of the motion of our arm, the pain we suffer there, any more than the colors we see on objects. Or if we do not wish to agree with this, I say that internal sensation is not infallible, for error is almost always found in these sensations when they are compound. I have sufficiently proven this in book I of the *Search after Truth*.

us an obscure and confused sensation of our power, is by itself capable of giving motion to animal spirits or determining them. I deny that there is a relation between our thoughts and the motions of matter. I deny that the soul has the least knowledge of the animal spirits it uses to move the body it animates. Finally, even if the soul had an exact knowledge of the animal spirits and if it were capable of moving them or of determining their motion, I still deny that it could select the nerve ducts, of which it has no knowledge, in order to push the spirits into them and thus move the body with the promptness, exactness, and force we observe even in those who have the least knowledge of the structure of their body.

For, assuming even that our volitions are truly the moving force of bodies (even though this seems incomprehensible), how are we able to conceive that the soul moves its body? The arm, for example, moves only because spirits distend some of the muscles making it up. Now, in order that the motion the soul impresses on the spirits in the brain can be communicated to those in the nerves, and the latter to others in the muscles of the arm, the volitions of the soul must multiply or change in proportion to the almost infinite collisions or impacts that would occur in the small bodies making up the spirits; for bodies cannot by themselves move those they meet, as I believe I have sufficiently shown. But we cannot conceive this, if we do not allow in the soul an infinite number of volitions for the least motion of the body, because an infinite number of communications of motion necessarily takes place in order to move the body. For, finally, since the soul is a particular cause and cannot know exactly the size and agitation of an infinite number of small bodies colliding with one another when the spirits spread out in the muscles, it could neither establish a general law of the communication of motion of these spirits, nor follow it exactly if it had established it. Thus, it is evident that the soul could not move its arm, even if it had the power of determining the motion of the animal spirits in the brain. These things are too clear to pause any longer over them.

The same is true of the faculty we have for thinking. We know through internal awareness that we will to think about something, that we make an effort to do this, and that at the moment of our desire and effort the idea of that thing presents itself to our mind. But we do not know through internal awareness that our will or effort produces our idea. We do not see through reason that this could happen. It is through prejudice that we believe that our attention or our desires are the cause of our ideas; it is because we experience a hundred times a day that our ideas follow or accompany them. Since God and his operations contain nothing sensible and we sense nothing else preceding the presence of ideas than our desires, we think there can be no other cause of these ideas than our desires. But let us take care: We do not see in ourselves any force to produce them; reason and the internal awareness we have of ourselves tell us nothing about this. [ . . . ]

# G. W. Leibniz, *Discourse on Metaphysics* (1686)[1]

*1. On divine perfection, and that God does everything in the most desirable way.* The most widely accepted and meaningful notion we have of God is expressed well enough in these words, that God is an absolutely perfect being; yet the consequences of these words are not sufficiently considered. And, to penetrate more deeply into this matter, it is appropriate to remark that there are several entirely different perfections in nature, that God possesses all of them together, and that each of them belongs to him in the highest degree.

We must also know what a perfection is. A fairly sure test for being a perfection is that forms or natures that are not capable of a highest degree are not perfections, as for example, the nature of number or figure. For the greatest of all numbers (or even the number of all numbers), as well as the greatest of all figures, imply a contradiction, but the greatest knowledge and omnipotence do not involve any impossibility. Consequently, power and knowledge are perfections, and, insofar as they belong to God, they do not have limits.

Whence it follows that God, possessing supreme and infinite wisdom, acts in the most perfect manner, not only metaphysically, but also morally speaking, and that, with respect to ourselves, we can say that the more enlightened and informed we are about God's works, the more we will be disposed to find them excellent and in complete conformity with what we might have desired.

*2. Against those who claim that there is no goodness in God's works, or that the rules of goodness and beauty are arbitrary.* Thus I am far removed from the opinion of those who maintain that there are no rules of goodness and perfection in the nature of things or in the ideas God has of them and who say that the works

1. Translated from the French by R. Ariew and D. Garber in G. W. Leibniz, *Philosophical Essays* (Indianapolis: Hackett Publishing Company, 1989). In February 1686, Leibniz wrote a letter to the Landgrave Ernst von Hessen-Reinfels, saying: "being somewhere having nothing to do for a few days, I have lately composed a short discourse on metaphysics about which I would be very happy to have Mr. Arnauld's opinion. For questions on grace, God's concourse with creatures, the nature of miracles, the cause of sin and the origin of evil, the immortality of the soul, ideas, etc. are touched upon in a manner which seems to provide new openings capable of illuminating some very great difficulties," *Philosophische Schriften*, ed. C. I. Gerhardt (Berlin, 1875–90) II, 11. Leibniz does not appear to have sent out the full "Discourse," as it later came to be known, following Leibniz's own characterization, though he did append "summaries" of it to his letter (which the landgrave transmitted to Arnauld); the summaries are also preserved as the titles of each article of the "Discourse" (in a later version of the "Discourse" than the manuscript in Leibniz's handwriting discov-

ered by Henri Lestienne). Arnauld replied with a letter criticizing section 13, and the Leibniz-Arnauld correspondence began.

of God are good solely for the formal reason that God has made them.[2] For, if this were so, God, knowing that he is their author, would not have had to consider them afterwards and find them good, as is testified by the Sacred Scriptures—which seem to have used such anthropomorphic expressions only to make us understand that the excellence of God's works can be recognized by considering them in themselves, even when we do not reflect on this empty external denomination which relates them to their cause. This is all the more true, since it is by considering his works that we can discover the creator. His works must therefore carry his mark in themselves. I confess that the contrary opinion seems to me extremely dangerous and very near to the opinion of the recent innovators[3] who hold that the beauty of the universe and the goodness we attribute to the works of God are but the chimeras of those who conceive of God in terms of themselves. Thus, in saying that things are not good by virtue of any rule of goodness but solely by virtue of the will of God, it seems to me that we unknowingly destroy all of God's love and all his glory. For why praise him for what he has done if he would be equally praiseworthy in doing the exact contrary? Where will his justice and wisdom reside if there remains only a certain despotic power, if will holds the place of reason, and if, according to the definition of tyrants, justice consists in whatever pleases the most powerful? Besides, it seems that all acts of will presuppose a reason for willing and that this reason is naturally prior to the act of will. That is why I also find completely strange the expression of some other philosophers[4] who say that the eternal truths of metaphysics and geometry and consequently also the rules of goodness, justice, and perfection are merely the effects of the will of God; instead, it seems to me, they are only the consequences of his understanding, which, assuredly, does not depend on his will, any more than does his essence.

3. *Against those who believe that God might have made things better.* Nor can I approve of the opinion of some moderns who maintain boldly that what God has made is not of the highest perfection and that he could have done much better.[5] For it seems to me that the consequences of this opinion are wholly contrary to the glory of God: As a lesser evil is relatively good, so a lesser good is relatively evil. And to act with less perfection than one could have is to act imperfectly. To show that an architect could have done better is to find fault with his work. This opinion is also contrary to the Sacred Scripture, which assures us of the goodness of God's works. For, if their view were sufficient, then since the series of imperfections descends to infinity, God's works would always have been good in comparison with those less perfect, no matter how he created them, but something is hardly praiseworthy if it can be praised only in this way. I also believe that a great many passages from Sacred Scripture and the holy fathers will be found favoring my opinion, but scarcely any will be found favoring the opinion of these moderns, an opinion which is, in my judgment, unknown to all antiquity and which is based only on the inadequate knowledge we have of the general harmony of the universe and of the hidden reasons for God's conduct. This enables us to judge audaciously that many things could have been rendered better. Besides, these moderns insist on certain dubious subtleties, for they imagine that nothing is so perfect that there is not something more perfect—this is an error.

They also believe that in this way they are able to safeguard God's freedom, as though it were not freedom of the highest sort to act in perfection following sovereign reason. For to believe that God does something without having any reason for his will—overlooking the fact that this seems impossible—is an opinion that conforms little to his glory. Let us assume, for example, that God chooses between A and B and that he takes A without having any reason to prefer it to B. I say that this action of God is at the very least not praiseworthy; for all praise must be

2. This is Descartes's view. See, e.g., the *Sixth Replies, Oeuvres,* ed. C. Adam and A. Tannery (Paris: Vrin, 1964–74), vol. VII, pp. 432, 435–36.
3. Spinoza, and by extension, Descartes. The earlier draft explicitly mentions the Spinozists alone in this regard. See Spinoza, Appendix to *Ethics,* Part I.
4. Descartes is mentioned in an earlier draft, but deleted.

5. See, e.g., Malebranche, *Traité de la nature et de la grace,* Pr. disc., sec. xiv. Malebranche's *Traité* seems to be one of the main targets of this essay.

based on some reason, and by hypothesis there is none here. Instead I hold that God does nothing for which he does not deserve to be glorified.

4. *That the love of God requires our complete satisfaction and acquiescence with respect to what he has done without our being quietists*[6] *as a result.* The general knowledge of this great truth, that God acts always in the most perfect and desirable way possible, is, in my judgment, the foundation of the love that we owe God in all things, since he who loves seeks his satisfaction in the happiness or perfection of the object loved and in his actions. To will the same and dislike the same is true friendship. And I believe that it is difficult to love God well when we are not disposed to will what God wills, when we might have the power to change it. In fact, those who are not satisfied with what God does seem to me like dissatisfied subjects whose attitudes are not much different from those of rebels.

I hold, therefore, that, according to these principles, in order to act in accordance with the love of God, it is not sufficient to force ourselves to be patient; rather, we must truly be satisfied with everything that has come to us according to his will. I mean this acquiescence with respect to the past. As for the future, we must not be quietists and stand ridiculously with arms folded, awaiting that which God will do, according to the sophism that the ancients called *logon aergon*, the lazy reason. But we must act in accordance with what we presume to be the *will of God*, insofar as we can judge it, trying with all our might to contribute to the general good and especially to the embellishment and perfection of that which affects us or that which is near us, that which is, so to speak, in our grasp. For, although the outcome might perhaps demonstrate that God did not wish our good will to have effect at present, it does not follow that he did not wish us to act as we have. On the contrary, since he is the best of all masters, he

never demands more than the right intention, and it is for him to know the proper hour and place for letting the good designs succeed.

5. *What the rules of the perfection of divine conduct consist in, and that the simplicity of the ways is in balance with the richness of the effects.* Therefore, it is sufficient to have the confidence that God does everything for the best and that nothing can harm those who love him. But to know in detail the reasons that could have moved him to choose this order of the universe—to allow sins, to dispense his saving grace in a certain way—surpasses the power of a finite mind, especially when it has not yet attained the enjoyment of the vision of God.

However, we can make some general remarks concerning the course of providence in the governance of things. We can therefore say that one who acts perfectly is similar to an excellent geometer who can find the best constructions for a problem; or to a good architect who makes use of his location and the funds set aside for a building in the most advantageous manner, allowing nothing improper or lacking in the beauty of which it is capable; or to a good householder, who makes use of his holdings in such a way that there remains nothing uncultivated and sterile; or to a skilled machinist who produces his work in the least difficult way possible; or to a learned author who includes the greatest number of truths [*realités*] in the smallest possible volume. Now, the most perfect of all beings, those that occupy the least volume, that is, those that least interfere with one another, are minds, whose perfections consist in their virtues. That is why we mustn't doubt that the happiness of minds is the principal aim of God and that he puts this into practice to the extent that general harmony permits it. We shall say more about this below.

As for the simplicity of the ways of God, this holds properly with respect to his means, as opposed to the variety, richness, and abundance, which holds with respect to his ends or effects. And the one must be in balance with the other, as are the costs of a building and the size and beauty one demands of it. It is true that nothing costs God anything—even less than it costs a philosopher to build the fabric of his imaginary

---

6. The quietists were followers of Miguel de Molinos (ca. 1640–97), author of the *Guida spirituale* (1675), and others, who stressed passive contemplation and complete resignation to the will of God.

world out of hypotheses—since God has only to make decrees in order that a real world come into being. But in matters of wisdom, decrees or hypotheses take the place of expenditures to the extent that they are more independent of one another, because reason requires that we avoid multiplying hypotheses or principles, in somewhat the same way that the simplest system is always preferred in astronomy.

6. *God does nothing which is not orderly and it is not even possible to imagine events that are not regular.* The volitions or acts of God are commonly divided into ordinary or extraordinary. But it is good to consider that God does nothing which is not orderly. Thus, what passes for extraordinary is extraordinary only with some particular order established among creatures; for everything is in conformity with respect to the universal order. This is true to such an extent that not only does nothing completely irregular occur in the world, but we would not even be able to imagine such a thing. Thus, let us assume, for example, that someone jots down a number of points at random on a piece of paper, as do those who practice the ridiculous art of geomancy.[7] I maintain that it is possible to find a geometric line whose notion is constant and uniform, following a certain rule, such that this line passes through all the points in the same order in which the hand jotted them down.

And if someone traced a continuous line which is sometimes straight, sometimes circular, and sometimes of another nature, it is possible to find a notion, or rule, or equation common to all the points of this line, in virtue of which these very changes must occur. For example, there is no face whose contours are not part of a geometric line and cannot be traced in one stroke by a certain regular movement. But, when a rule is extremely complex, what is in conformity with it passes for irregular.

Thus, one can say, in whatever manner God might have created the world, it would always have been regular and in accordance with a certain general order. But God has chosen the most perfect world, that is, the one which is at the same time the simplest in

hypotheses and the richest in phenomena, as might be a line in geometry whose construction is easy and whose properties and effects are extremely remarkable and widespread. I use these comparisons to sketch an imperfect likeness of divine wisdom and to point out something that can at least elevate our minds to conceive in some way what cannot be sufficiently expressed. But I do not claim to explain in this way the great mystery upon which the entire universe depends.

7. *That miracles conform to the general order, even though they may be contrary to the subordinate maxims; and about what God wills or permits by a general or particular volition.* Now, since nothing can happen which is not in the order, one can say that miracles are as much within the order as are natural operations, operations which are called natural because they are in conformity with certain subordinate maxims that we call the nature of things. For one can say that this nature is only God's custom, with which he can dispense for any stronger reason than the one which moved him to make use of these maxims.

As for the general or particular volitions, depending upon how the matter is understood, we can say that God does everything following his most general will, which is in conformity with the most perfect order he has chosen, but we can also say that he has particular volitions which are exceptions to these aforementioned subordinate maxims. For the most general of God's laws, the one that rules the whole course of the universe, is without exception.

We can say also that God wills everything that is an object of his particular volition. But we must make a distinction with respect to the objects of his general volition, such as the actions of other creatures, particularly the actions of those that are reasonable, actions with which God wishes to concur. For, if the action is good in itself, we can say that God wills it and sometimes commands it, even when it does not take place. But if the action is evil in itself and becomes good only by accident, because the course of things (particularly punishment and atonement) corrects its evilness and repays the evil with interest in such a way that in the end there is more perfection in the

7. Geomancy is the art of divination by means of lines or figures.

whole sequence than if the evil had not occurred, then we must say that God permits this but does not will it, even though he concurs with it because of the laws of nature he has established and because he knows how to draw a greater good from it.

8. *To distinguish the actions of God from those of creatures we explain the notion of an individual substance.* It is rather difficult to distinguish the actions of God from those of creatures; for some believe that God does everything, while others imagine that he merely conserves the force he has given to creatures. What follows will let us see the extent to which we can say the one or the other. And since actions and passions properly belong to individual substances [*actiones sunt suppositorum*],[8] it will be necessary to explain what such an individual substance is.

It is indeed true that when several predicates are attributed to a single subject and this subject is attributed to no other, it is called an individual substance; but this is not sufficient, and such an explanation is merely nominal. We must therefore consider what it is to be attributed truly to a certain subject.

Now it is evident that all true predication has some basis in the nature of things and that, when a proposition is not an identity, that is, when the predicate is not explicitly contained in the subject, it must be contained in it virtually. That is what the philosophers call *in-esse*, when they say that the predicate is in the subject. Thus the subject term must always contain the predicate term, so that one who understands perfectly the notion of the subject would also know that the predicate belongs to it.

Since this is so, we can say that the nature of an individual substance or of a complete being is to have a notion so complete that it is sufficient to contain and to allow us to deduce from it all the predicates of the subject to which this notion is attributed. An accident, on the other hand, is a being whose notion does not include everything that can be attributed to

the subject to which the notion is attributed.[9] Thus, taken in abstraction from the subject, the quality of being a king which belongs to Alexander the Great is not determinate enough to constitute an individual and does not include the other qualities of the same subject, nor does it include everything that the notion of this prince includes. On the other hand, God, seeing Alexander's individual notion or haecceity,[10] sees in it at the same time the basis and reason for all the predicates which can be said truly of him, for example, that he vanquished Darius and Porus; he even knows *a priori* (and not by experience) whether he died a natural death or whether he was poisoned, something we can know only through history. Thus when we consider carefully the connection of things, we can say that from all time in Alexander's soul there are vestiges of everything that has happened to him and marks of everything that will happen to him and even traces of everything that happens in the universe, even though God alone could recognize them all.[11]

9. *That each singular substance expresses the whole universe in its own way, and that all its events, together with all their circumstances and the whole sequence of external things, are included in its notion.* Several notable paradoxes follow from this; among others, it follows that it is not true that two substances can resemble each other completely and differ only in number [*solo numero*],[12] and that what Saint Thomas asserts on this point about angels or intelligences (that

---

8. Leibniz is making use of scholastic logical terminology: a *suppositum* is an individual subsistent substance; *actiones sunt suppositorum* therefore means that actions are of individual subsistent substances.

9. An earlier draft of the following passage read: "Thus the circular shape of the ring of [Gyges] [Polycrates] does not contain everything that the notion of this particular ring contains, unlike God [knowing] seeing the individual notion of this ring [seeing, for example, that it will be swallowed by a fish and yet returned to its owner]." (Words in brackets were deleted by Leibniz.)

10. The word *haecceitas* (or *hecceïté*, what we are translating as "haecceity") was coined by John Duns Scotus (ca. 1270–1308) to refer to an individual essence or "thisness"—what *haecceitas* means literally.

11. An earlier draft added: "I speak here as if it were assumed that this ring [has consciousness] [is a substance]."

12. An earlier draft added the following: "Also, that if bodies are substances, it is not possible that their nature consists only in size, shape, and motion, but that something else is needed."

here every individual is a lowest species)[13] is true of all substances, provided that one takes the specific difference as the geometers do with respect to their figures. It also follows that a substance can begin only by creation and end only by annihilation; that a substance is not divisible into two; that one substance cannot be constructed from two; and that thus the number of substances does not naturally increase and decrease, though they are often transformed.

Moreover, every substance is like a complete world and like a mirror of God or of the whole universe, which each one expresses in its own way, somewhat as the same city is variously represented depending upon the different positions from which it is viewed. Thus the universe is in some way multiplied as many times as there are substances, and the glory of God is likewise multiplied by as many entirely different representations of his work. It can even be said that every substance bears in some way the character of God's infinite wisdom and omnipotence and imitates him as much as it is capable. For it expresses, however confusedly, everything that happens in the universe, whether past, present, or future—this has some resemblance to an infinite perception or knowledge. And since all other substances in turn express this substance and accommodate themselves to it, one can say that it extends its power over all the others, in imitation of the creator's omnipotence.

*10. That the belief in substantial forms has some basis, but that these forms do not change anything in the phenomena and must not be used to explain particular effects.* It seems that the ancients, as well as many able men accustomed to deep meditation who have taught theology and philosophy some centuries ago (some of whom are respected for their saintliness) have had some knowledge of what we have just said; this is why they introduced and maintained the substantial forms which are so decried today. But they are not so distant from the truth nor so ridiculous as the common lot of our new philosophers imagines.

I agree that the consideration of these forms serves no purpose in the details of physics and must not be used to explain particular phenomena. That is where the Scholastics failed, as did the physicians of the past who followed their example, believing that they could account for the properties of bodies by talking about forms and qualities without taking the trouble to examine their manner of operation. It is as if we were content to say that a clock has a quality of clockness derived from its form without considering in what all of this consists; that would be sufficient for the person who buys the clock, provided that he turns over its care to another.

But this misunderstanding and misuse of forms must not cause us to reject something whose knowledge is so necessary in metaphysics that, I hold, without it one cannot properly know the first principles or elevate our minds sufficiently well to the knowledge of incorporeal natures and the wonders of God.

However, just as a geometer does not need to burden his mind with the famous labyrinth of the composition of the continuum, there is no need for any moral philosopher and even less need for a jurist or statesman to trouble himself with the great difficulties involved in reconciling free will and God's providence, since the geometer can achieve all his demonstrations and the statesman can complete all his deliberations without entering into these discussions, discussions that remain necessary and important in philosophy and theology. In the same way, a physicist can explain some experiments, at times using previous simpler experiments and at times using geometric and mechanical demonstrations, without needing[14] general considerations from another sphere. And if he uses God's concourse, or else a soul, animating force [*archée*], or something else of this nature, he is raving just as much as the person who, in the course of an important practical deliberation, enters into a lofty discussion concerning the nature of destiny and the nature of our freedom. In fact, people often commit this fault without thinking when they encumber their minds with the consideration of fatalism and sometimes are even diverted from a good resolution or a necessary duty in this way.

13. See St. Thomas Aquinas, *Summa Theologiae* I, q. 50, art. 4.

14. An earlier draft continued "[forms and other] [considerations of substantial forms]."

*11. That the thoughts of the theologians and philosophers who are called Scholastics are not entirely to be disdained.* I know that I am advancing a great paradox by attempting to rehabilitate the old philosophy in some fashion and to restore the almost banished substantial forms to their former place.[15] But perhaps I will not be condemned so easily when it is known that I have long meditated upon the modern philosophy, that I have given much time to experiments in physics and demonstrations in geometry, and that I had long been persuaded about the futility of these beings, which I finally was required to embrace in spite of myself and, as it were, by force, after having myself carried out certain studies. These studies made me recognize that our moderns do not give enough credit to Saint Thomas and to the other great men of his time and that there is much more solidity than one imagines in the opinions of the Scholastic philosophers and theologians, provided that they are used appropriately and in their proper place. I am even convinced that, if some exact and thoughtful mind took the trouble to clarify and summarize their thoughts after the manner of the analytic geometers, he would find there a great treasure of extremely important and wholly demonstrative truths.

*12. That the notions involved in extension contain something imaginary and cannot constitute the substance of body.* But, to resume the thread of our discussion, I believe that anyone who will meditate about the nature of substance, as I have explained it above, will find[16] that the nature of body does not consist merely in extension, that is, in size, shape, and motion, but that we must necessarily recognize in body something related to souls, something we commonly call substantial form, even though it makes no change in the phenomena, any more than do the souls of animals, if they have any. It is even possible to demonstrate that the notions of size, shape, and motion are not as distinct as is imagined and that they contain

something imaginary and relative to our perception, as do (though to a greater extent) color, heat, and other similar qualities, qualities about which one can doubt whether they are truly found in the nature of things outside ourselves. That is why qualities of this kind cannot constitute any substance. And if there were no other principle of identity in body other than the one just mentioned, a body could not subsist for more than a moment.

Yet the souls and substantial forms of other bodies are entirely different from intelligent souls, which alone know their actions. Not only don't intelligent souls perish naturally, but they also always preserve the basis for the knowledge of what they are; this is what renders them alone susceptible to punishment and reward and makes them citizens of the republic of the universe, whose monarch is God. It also follows that all other creatures must serve them—something which we will later discuss more fully.

*13. Since the individual notion of each person includes once and for all everything that will ever happen to him, one sees in it the a priori proofs of the truth of each event, or, why one happened rather than another, but these truths, however certain, are nevertheless contingent, being based on the free will of God or of his creatures, whose choice always has its reasons, which incline without necessitating.* But before going further, we must attempt to resolve a great difficulty that can arise from the foundations we have set forth above. We have said that the notion of an individual substance includes once and for all everything that can ever happen to it and that, by considering this notion, one can see there everything that can truly be said of it, just as we can see in the nature of a circle all the properties that can be deduced from it. But it seems that this would eliminate the difference between contingent and necessary truths, that there would be no place for human freedom, and that an absolute fatalism would rule all our actions as well as all the other events of the world. To this I reply that we must distinguish between what is certain and what is necessary. Everyone grants that future contingents are certain, since God foresees them, but we do not concede that they are necessary on that account. But (someone will say) if a conclusion can be

---

15. A marginal note in an earlier draft: "I do this, however, only under an hypothesis, insofar as one can say that bodies are substances."
16. An earlier draft interpolates: "either that bodies are not substances in metaphysical rigor (which was, in fact, the view of the Platonists), or."

deduced infallibly from a definition or notion, it is necessary. And it is true that we are maintaining that everything that must happen to a person is already contained virtually in his nature or notion, just as the properties of a circle are contained in its definition; thus the difficulty still remains. To address it firmly, I assert that connection or following [*consécution*] is of two kinds. The one whose contrary implies a contradiction is absolutely necessary; this deduction occurs in the eternal truths, for example, the truths of geometry. The other is necessary only *ex hypothesi* and, so to speak, accidentally, but it is contingent in itself, since its contrary does not imply a contradiction. And this connection is based not purely on ideas and God's simple understanding, but on his free decrees and on the sequence of the universe.

Let us take an example. Since Julius Caesar will become perpetual dictator and master of the republic and will overthrow the freedom of the Romans, this action is contained in his notion, for we assume that it is the nature of such a perfect notion of a subject to contain everything, so that the predicate is included in the subject, *ut possit inesse subjecto*.[17] It could be said that it is not in virtue of this notion or idea that he must perform this action, since it pertains to him only because God knows everything. But someone might insist that his nature or form corresponds to this notion, and, since God has imposed this personality on him, it is henceforth necessary for him to satisfy it. I could reply by citing future contingents, since they have no reality as yet, save in God's understanding and will, and, because God gave them this form in advance, they must in the same way correspond to it.

But I much prefer to overcome difficulties rather than to excuse them by giving some other similar difficulties, and what I am about to say will illuminate the one as well as the other. It is here, then, that we must apply the distinction concerning connections, and I say that whatever happens in conformity with these predeterminations [*avances*] is certain but not necessary, and if one were to do the contrary, he would not be doing something impossible in itself,

17. The Latin is an approximate paraphrase of the preceding clause.

even though it would be impossible [*ex hypothesi*] for this to happen. For if someone were able to carry out the whole demonstration by virtue of which he could prove this connection between the subject, Caesar, and the predicate, his successful undertaking, he would in fact be showing that Caesar's future dictatorship is grounded in his notion or nature, that there is a reason why he crossed the Rubicon rather than stopped at it and why he won rather than lost at Pharsalus and that it was reasonable, and consequently certain, that this should happen. But this would not show that it was necessary in itself nor that the contrary implies a contradiction. It is reasonable and certain in almost the same way that God will always do the best, even though what is less perfect does not imply a contradiction.

For it will be found that the demonstration of this predicate of Caesar is not as absolute as those of numbers or of geometry, but that it supposes the sequence of things that God has freely chosen, a sequence based on God's first free decree always to do what is most perfect and on God's decree with respect to human nature, following out of the first decree, that man will always do (although freely) that which appears to be best. But every truth based on these kinds of decrees is contingent, even though it is certain; for these decrees do not change the possibility of things, and, as I have already said, even though it is certain that God always chooses the best, this does not prevent something less perfect from being and remaining possible in itself, even though it will not happen, since it is not its impossibility but its imperfection which causes it to be rejected. And nothing is necessary whose contrary is possible.

We will therefore be in a position to satisfy these sorts of difficulties, however great they may appear (and in fact they are not made any the less pressing by considering the other thinkers who have ever treated this matter), as long as we recognize that all contingent propositions have reasons to be one way rather than another or else (what comes to the same thing) that they have *a priori* proofs of their truth which render them certain and which show that the connection between subject and predicate of these propositions has its basis in the natures of both. But they do not have necessary demonstrations, since these reasons are based only on the principle of contingency or the principle of the existence of things, that is, based on what is or appears to be best from among several equally possible things. On the other hand, necessary truths are based on the principle of contradiction and on the possibility or impossibility of essences themselves, without regard to the free will of God or his creatures.

14. *God produces various substances according to the different views he has of the universe, and through God's intervention the proper nature of each substance brings it about that what happens to one corresponds with what happens to all the others, without their acting upon one another directly.* After having seen, in some way, what the nature of substances consists in, we must try to explain the dependence they have upon one another and their actions and passions. Now, first of all, it is very evident that created substances depend upon God, who preserves them and who even produces them continually by a kind of emanation, just as we produce our thoughts. For God, so to speak, turns on all sides and in all ways the general system of phenomena which he finds it good to produce in order to manifest his glory, and he views all the faces of the world in all ways possible, since there is no relation that escapes his omniscience. The result of each view of the universe, as seen from a certain position, is a substance which expresses the universe in conformity with this view, should God see fit to render his thought actual and to produce this substance. And since God's view is always true, our perceptions are always true; it is our judgments, which come from ourselves, that deceive us.

Now we said above, and it follows from what we have just said, that each substance is like a world apart, independent of all other things, except for God; thus all our phenomena, that is, all the things that can ever happen to us, are only consequences of our being. And since these phenomena maintain a certain order in conformity with our nature or, so to speak, in conformity with the world which is in us, an order which enables us to make useful observations to regulate our conduct, observations justified by the success of future phenomena, an order which thus allows us

often to judge the future from the past without error, this would be sufficient to enable us to say that these phenomena are true without bothering with whether they are outside us and whether others also perceive them. Nevertheless, it is very true that the perceptions or expressions of all substances mutually correspond in such a way that each one, carefully following certain reasons or laws it has observed, coincides with others doing the same—in the same way that several people who have agreed to meet in some place at some specified time can really do this if they so desire. But although they all express the same phenomena, it does not follow that their expressions are perfectly similar; it is sufficient that they are proportional. In just the same way, several spectators believe that they are seeing the same thing and agree among themselves about it, even though each sees and speaks in accordance with his view.

And God alone (from whom all individuals emanate continually and who sees the universe not only as they see it but also entirely differently from all of them) is the cause of this correspondence of their phenomena and makes that which is particular to one of them public to all of them; otherwise, there would be no interconnection. We could therefore say in some way and properly speaking, though not in accordance with common usage, that one particular substance never acts upon another particular substance nor is acted upon by it, if we consider that what happens to each is solely a consequence of its complete idea or notion alone, since this idea already contains all its predicates or events and expresses the whole universe. In fact, nothing can happen to us except thoughts and perceptions, and all our future thoughts and perceptions are merely consequences, though contingent, of our preceding thoughts and perceptions, in such a way that, if I were capable of considering distinctly everything that happens or appears to me at this time, I could see in it everything that will ever happen or appear to me. This would never fail, and it would happen to me regardless, even if everything outside of me were destroyed, provided there remained only God and me. But since we attribute what we perceive in a certain way to other things as causes acting on us, we must consider the basis for this judgment and the element of truth there is in it.

15. *The action of one finite substance on another consists only in the increase of degree of its expression together with the diminution of the expression of the other, insofar as God requires them to accommodate themselves to one another.* But, without entering into a long discussion, in order to reconcile the language of metaphysics with practice, it is sufficient for now to remark that we ascribe to ourselves—and with reason—the phenomena that we express most perfectly and that we attribute to other substances the phenomena that each expresses best. Thus a substance, which is of infinite extension insofar as it expresses everything, becomes limited in proportion to its more or less perfect manner of expression. This, then, is how one can conceive that substances impede or limit each other, and consequently one can say that, in this sense, they act upon one another and are required, so to speak, to accommodate themselves to one another. For it can happen that a change that increases the expression of one diminishes that of another. Now, the efficacy [*vertu*] a particular substance has is to express well the glory of God, and it is by doing this that it is less limited. And whenever something exercises its efficacy or power, that is, when it acts, it improves and extends itself insofar as it acts. Therefore, when a change takes place by which several substances are affected (in fact every change affects all of them), I believe one may say that the substance which immediately passes to a greater degree of perfection or to a more perfect expression exercises its power and acts, and the substance which passes to a lesser degree shows its weakness and *is acted upon* [*pâtit*]. I also hold that every action of a substance which has perfection involves some *pleasure*, and every passion some pain and vice versa. However, it can happen that a present advantage is destroyed by a greater evil in what follows, whence one can sin in acting, that is, in exercising one's power and finding pleasure.

16. *God's extraordinary concourse is included in that which our essence expresses, for this expression extends to everything. But this concourse surpasses the powers of our nature or of our distinct expression, which is finite and follows certain subordinate maxims.* It now only remains to explain how God can sometimes influence men and other substances by an extraordinary and miraculous concourse, since it seems that nothing extraordinary and supernatural can happen to them, given that all their events are only consequences of their nature. But we must remember what we have said above concerning miracles in the universe—that they are always in conformity with the universal law of the general order, even though they may be above the subordinate maxims. And to the extent that every person or substance is like a small world expressing the large world, we can say equally that the extraordinary action of God on this substance does not fail to be miraculous, despite the fact that it is included in the general order of the universe insofar as it is expressed by the essence or individual notion of this substance. That is why, if we include in our nature everything that it expresses, nothing is supernatural to it, for our nature extends everywhere, since an effect always expresses its cause and God is the true cause of substances. But what our nature expresses more perfectly belongs to it in a particular way, since it is in this that its power consists. But since it is limited, as I have just explained, there are many things that surpass the powers of our nature and even surpass the powers of all limited natures. Thus, to speak more clearly, I say that God's miracles and extraordinary concourse have the peculiarity that they cannot be foreseen by the reasoning of any created mind, no matter how enlightened, because the distinct comprehension of the general order surpasses all of them. On the other hand, everything that we call natural depends on the less general maxims that creatures can understand. Thus, in order that my words may be as irreproachable as my meaning, it would be good to connect certain ways of speaking with certain thoughts. We could call that which includes everything we express our essence or idea; since this expresses our union with God himself, it has no limits and nothing surpasses it. But that which is limited in us could be called our nature or our power; and in that sense, that which surpasses the natures of all created substances is supernatural.

17. *An example of a subordinate maxim or law of nature; in which it is shown, against the Cartesians and many others, that God always conserves the same*

*force but not the same quantity of motion.* I have already mentioned the subordinate maxims or laws of nature often enough, and it seems appropriate to give an example of one. Our new philosophers commonly make use of the famous rule that God always conserves the same quantity of motion in the world. In fact, this rule is extremely plausible, and, in the past, I held it as indubitable. But I have since recognized what is wrong with it. It is that Descartes and many other able mathematicians have believed that the quantity of motion, that is, the speed multiplied by the size of the moving body, coincides exactly with the moving force, or, to speak geometrically, that the forces are proportional to the product of the speeds and [sizes of] bodies. Now, it is extremely reasonable that the same force is always conserved in the universe. Also, when we attend to the phenomena, we see that there is no perpetual mechanical motion, because then the force of a machine, which is always diminished somewhat by friction and which must sooner or later come to an end, would restore itself, and consequently would increase by itself without any new external impulsion. We observe also that the force of a body is diminished only in proportion to the force it imparts to some bodies contiguous to it or to its own parts, insofar as they have separate motion.

Thus they believed that what can be said about force can also be said about the quantity of motion. But to show the difference between them, I assume that a body falling from a certain height acquires the force to rise up that height, if its direction carries it that way, at least, if there are no impediments. For example, a pendulum would rise again exactly to the height from which it descended, if the resistance of the air and some other small obstacles did not diminish its acquired force a little.

*I assume* also that as much force is required to elevate A, a body of one pound, to CD, a height of four fathoms, as to elevate B, a body of four pounds, to EF, a height of one fathom. All this is admitted by our new philosophers.

It is therefore evident that, having fallen from height CD, body A acquired exactly as much force as did body B, which fell from height EF; for since body (B) reached F and acquired the force to rise to E (by the first assumption), it has the force to carry

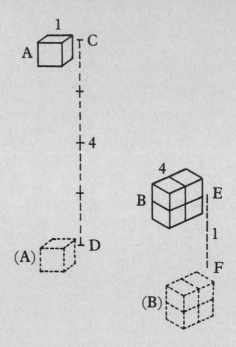

a body of four pounds, that is, itself, to EF, the height of one fathom; similarly, since body (A) reached D and acquired the force to rise to C, it has the force to carry a body of one pound, that is, itself, to CD, a height of four fathoms. Therefore (by the second assumption), the force of these two bodies is equal.

Let us now see whether the quantity of motion is also the same in each. But here we will be surprised to find a very great difference. For Galileo demonstrated that the speed acquired by the fall CD is twice the speed acquired by the fall EF, even though the one height is four times the other. Let us therefore multiply body A, proportional to 1, with its speed, proportional to 2; the product or quantity of motion will be proportional to 2. On the other hand, let us multiply body B, proportional to 4, by its speed, proportional to 1; the product or quantity of motion will be proportional to 4. Therefore, the quantity of motion of body (A) at point D is half of the quantity of motion of body (B) at point F; yet their forces are equal. Hence, there is a great difference between quantity of motion and force—which is what needed to be proved.

Thus we see that force must be calculated from the quantity of the effect it can produce, for example, by the height to which a heavy body of a certain size and kind can be raised; this is quite different from the speed that can be imparted to it. And to give it double the speed, it must be given more than double the force.

Nothing is simpler than this proof. Descartes fell into error here only because he had too much confidence in his own thoughts, even when they were not sufficiently ripe. But I am surprised that his followers have not since then discovered this mistake; and I fear that they are beginning, little by little, to imitate some of the Peripatetics, whom they ridicule, like them gradually acquiring the habit of consulting their master's writings rather than reason and nature.[18]

18. *The distinction between force and quantity of motion is important, among other reasons, for judging that one must have recourse to metaphysical considerations distinct from extension in order to explain the phenomena of bodies.* This consideration, the distinction between force and quantity of motion, is rather important, not only in physics and mechanics, in order to find the true laws of nature and rules of motion and even to correct the several errors of practice which have slipped into the writings of some able mathematicians, but also in metaphysics, in order to understand the principles better. For if we consider only what motion contains precisely and formally, that is, change of place, motion is not something entirely real, and when several bodies change position among themselves, it is not possible to determine, merely from a consideration of these changes, to which body we should attribute motion or rest, as I could show geometrically, if I wished to stop and do this now.

But the force or proximate cause of these changes is something more real, and there is sufficient basis to attribute it to one body more than to another. Also,

it is only in this way that we can know to which body the motion belongs. Now, this force is something different from size, shape, and motion, and one can therefore judge that not everything conceived in body consists solely in extension and in its modifications, as our moderns have persuaded themselves. Thus we are once again obliged to reestablish some beings or forms they have banished. And it becomes more and more apparent that, although all the particular phenomena of nature can be explained mathematically or mechanically by those who understand them, nevertheless the general principles of corporeal nature and of mechanics itself are more metaphysical than geometrical, and belong to some indivisible forms or natures as the causes of appearances, rather than to corporeal mass or extension. This is a reflection capable of reconciling the mechanical philosophy of the moderns with the caution of some intelligent and well-intentioned persons who fear, with some reason, that we are withdrawing too far from immaterial beings, to the disadvantage of piety.

19. *The utility of final causes in physics.* Since I do not like to judge people wrongly, I do not accuse our new philosophers, who claim to banish final causes from physics.[19] But I am nevertheless obliged to confess that the consequences of this opinion appear dangerous to me, especially if I combine it with the one I refuted at the beginning of this discourse, which seems to go so far as to eliminate final causes altogether, as if God proposed no end or good in acting or as if the good were not the object of his will. As for myself, I hold, on the contrary, that it is here we must seek the principle of all existences and laws of nature, because God always intends the best and most perfect.

I am quite willing to admit that we are subject to deception when we wish to determine God's ends or counsels. But this is only when we try to limit them to some particular design, believing that he had only

18. This section is a summary of an important paper Leibniz published in the *Acta Eruditorum* on January 6, 1686, "A Brief Demonstration of a Notable Error of Descartes," in which he argues against the conservation of quantity of motion, size times speed, a law first framed by Descartes (*Principles of Philosophy* II, art. 36), and widely held by his followers. This essay began a long exchange in the learned journals that came to be known as the *vis viva* controversy, over the quantity, living force or *vis viva*, that Leibniz held was conserved. See "A Specimen of Dynamics," part I.

19. The "new philosophers" Leibniz has in mind include Descartes and Spinoza, who explain everything mechanically and reject final causes. See Descartes, *Principles of Philosophy* I, art. 28, and the Appendix to Part I of Spinoza's *Ethics*. In an earlier draft, it is impiety that Leibniz is not accusing them of, but the phrase was deleted.

one thing in view, when instead he regards everything at the same time. For instance, it is a great mistake to believe that God made the world only for us, although it is quite true that he made it in its entirety for us and that there is nothing in the universe which does not affect us and does not also accommodate itself in accordance with his regard for us, following the principles set forth above. Thus when we see some good effect or perfection occurring or ensuing from God's works, we can say with certainty that God had proposed it. For he does nothing by chance and is not like us, who sometimes fail to do the good. That is why, far from being able to fall into error in this, as do extreme politicians who imagine too much subtlety in the designs of princes or as do commentators who look for too much erudition in their author, we cannot attribute too much reflection to this infinite wisdom, and there is no subject in which error is to be feared less, provided we limit ourselves to affirmations and avoid negative propositions that limit God's designs.

Anyone who sees the admirable structure of animals will find himself forced to recognize the wisdom of the author of things. And I advise those who have any feelings of piety and even feelings of true philosophy to keep away from the phrases of certain would-be freethinkers who say that we see because it happens that we have eyes and not that eyes were made for seeing. When one seriously holds these opinions ascribing everything to the necessity of matter or to some chance (even though both must appear ridiculous to those who understand what we have explained above), it is difficult to recognize an intelligent author of nature. For the effect must correspond to its cause; indeed, the effect is best recognized through a knowledge of the cause. Moreover, it is unreasonable to introduce a supreme intelligence as orderer of things and then, instead of using his wisdom, use only the properties of matter to explain the phenomena. This is as if, in order to account for the conquest of an important place by a great prince, a historian were to claim that it occurred because the small particles of gunpowder, set off by the contact of a spark, escaped with sufficient speed to push a hard and heavy body against the walls of the place, while the little particles that make up the brass of the cannon were so firmly

interlaced that this speed did not separate them, instead of showing how the foresight of the conqueror enabled him to choose the suitable means and times and how his power overcame all obstacles.

20. A *noteworthy passage by Socrates in Plato against the philosophers who are overly materialistic.* This reminds me of a beautiful passage by Socrates in Plato's *Phaedo.* This passage agrees marvelously with my opinions on this point and seems to be directed expressly against our overly materialistic philosophers. Thus I have been tempted to translate this account, even though it is a little long; perhaps this sample will give an incentive to some of us to share in many of the other beautiful and solid thoughts which can be found in the writings of this famous author.[20]

20. Leibniz's marginal note: "The passage from Plato's *Phaedo* where Socrates ridicules Anaxagoras, who introduces mind but does not make use of it, is to be inserted." Leibniz repeats the passage in "Two Sects of Naturalists":

"I heard one day (he said) someone reading in a book of Anaxagoras, in which it was said *that an intelligent being was the cause of all things and that he had disposed and arranged them.* That pleased me greatly, for I believed that if the world were the effect of an intelligence, everything would be done in the most perfect manner possible. That is why I believed that anyone who wanted to account for why things are produced or perish, or why they subsist, must look for what would be appropriate to the perfection of any given thing. And so, a man would need to consider in himself or in something else only that which would be the best or the most perfect. One who knows the most perfect could easily judge what is imperfect from this, for knowing the one amounts to knowing the other [Literally: "there is only a single science for both the one and the other"].

"Considering all this, I rejoiced in having found a teacher who could teach the reasons for things—for example, whether the earth is round rather than flat, and why it was better that it be this way rather than otherwise. Moreover, I expected that when saying that the earth is at the center of the universe, or that it is not, he would explain to me why it was most appropriate for it to be this way, and I expected he would tell me as much about the sun, moon, stars, and their motions. And finally, after having shown what was most suitable for each thing in particular, he would have shown what was best in general. Filled with this hope, I quickly got hold of the books of Anaxagoras and ran through them with great haste. But I found myself far from my expectation, for I was surprised to see that he did not make use of the governing intelligence that he had first posited, that he no longer spoke of the arrangement nor of the perfection of things, and that he introduced certain ethereal matters that are hardly probable. In this he seemed like someone who, having said that Socrates does things through intelligence, and

*21. If mechanical rules depended only on geometry without metaphysics, the phenomena would be entirely different.* Now, since we have always recognized God's wisdom in the detail of the mechanical structure of some particular bodies, it must also be displayed in the general economy of the world and in the constitution of the laws of nature. This is true to such an extent that one can observe the counsels of this wisdom in the laws of motion in general. For if there were nothing in bodies but extended mass and nothing in motion but change of place and if everything should and could be deduced solely from these definitions by geometrical necessity, it would follow, as I have shown elsewhere, that, upon contact, the smallest body would impart its own speed to the largest body without losing any of this speed; and we would have to accept a number of such rules which are completely contrary to the formation of a system.[21] But the decree of divine wisdom always to conserve the same total force and the same total direction has provided for this.

I even find that several effects of nature can be demonstrated doubly, that is, by considering first the efficient cause and then by considering the final cause, making use, for example, of God's decree always to produce his effect by the easiest and most determinate ways, as I have shown elsewhere in accounting for the rules of catoptrics and dioptrics;[22] I shall say more about this soon.

*22. Reconciliation of two ways of explaining things, by final causes and by efficient causes, in order to satisfy both those who explain nature mechanically and those who have recourse to incorporeal natures.* It is appropriate to make this remark in order to reconcile those who hope to explain mechanically the formation of the first tissue of an animal and the whole machinery of its parts, with those who account for this same structure using final causes. Both ways are good and both can be useful, not only for admiring the skill of the Great Worker, but also for discovering something useful in physics and in medicine. And the authors who follow these different routes should not malign each other.

For I see that those who apply themselves to explaining the beauty of the divine anatomy laugh at others who imagine that a movement of certain fluids that seems fortuitous could have produced such a beautiful variety of limbs, and call these people rash and profane. And the latter, on the other hand, call the former simple and superstitious, comparing them to the ancients who regarded physicists as impious when they maintained that it is not Jupiter that thunders, but some matter present in the clouds. It would be best to join together both considerations, for if it is permitted to use a humble comparison, I recognize and praise the skill of a worker not only by showing his designs in making the parts of his machine, but also by explaining the instruments he used in making each part, especially when these instruments are simple and cleverly contrived. *And God is a skillful enough artisan* to produce a machine which is a thousand times more ingenious than that of our body, while using only some very simple fluids explicitly

---

then going on to explain in particular the causes of his actions, says that he is seated here because he has a body composed of bones, flesh, and sinews, that his bones are hard, but that they are separated by intervals or junctures, that the sinews can be tightened or relaxed, and that this is why the body is flexible and finally why I am seated here. Or, if, wishing to account for this present discourse, he were to refer to the air, to the organs of voice and hearing, and the like, forgetting, however, the true causes, namely that the Athenians believed that it would be better to condemn me rather than to absolve me, and that I believed that it was better to sit here rather than to flee. For, by my faith, without this, these sinews and bones would long have been among the Boeotians and Megarians, if I hadn't thought it more just and more honorable [*honneste*] of me to suffer the penalty imposed by my native land rather than to live elsewhere as a wanderer and an exile. That is why it is unreasonable to call these bones and sinews and their motion causes. It is true that whoever would say that I could not do all this without bones and sinew would be right. But something else is the true cause, and they constitute only a condition without which the cause could not be a cause. Those who only say, for example, that motions of bodies around the earth keep it here, where it is, forget that divine power disposes everything in the finest way, and do not understand that it is the good and the beautiful that join, form, and maintain the world."

21. See, e.g., "On the Nature of Body and the Laws of Motion" (ca. 1678–82) for the full argument.

22. The reference is to the "Unicum Opticae, Catoptricae et Dioptricae Principium, Autore G. G. L.," from the *Acta Eruditorum* (June 1682).

concocted in such a way that only the ordinary laws of nature are required to arrange them in the right way to produce so admirable an effect; but it is also true that this would not happen at all unless God were the author of nature.

However, I find that the way of efficient causes, which is in fact deeper and in some sense more immediate and *a priori*, is, on the other hand, quite difficult when one comes to details, and I believe that, for the most part, our philosophers are still far from it. But the way of final causes is easier, and is not infrequently of use in divining important and useful truths which one would be a long time in seeking by the other, more physical way; anatomy can provide significant examples of this. I also believe that Snell, who first discovered the rules of refraction, would have waited a long time before discovering them if he first had to find out how light is formed. But he apparently followed the method which the ancients used for catoptrics, which is in fact that of final causes. For, by seeking the easiest way to lead a ray from a given point to another point given by reflection on a given plane (assuming that this is nature's design), they discovered the equality of angles of incidence and angles of reflection, as can be seen in a little treatise by Heliodorus of Larissa, and elsewhere.[23] That is what, I believe, Snell and Fermat after him (though without knowing anything about Snell) have most ingeniously applied to refraction. For when, in the same media, rays observe the same proportion between sines (which is proportional to the resistances of the media), this happens to be the easiest or, at least, the most determinate way to pass from a given point in a medium to a given point in another. And the demonstration Descartes attempted to give of this same theorem by way of efficient causes is not nearly as good. At least there is room for suspicion that he would never have found the law in this way, if he had learned nothing in Holland of Snell's discovery.[24]

23. *To return to immaterial substances, we explain how God acts on the understanding of minds and whether we always have the idea of that about which we think.* I found it appropriate to insist a bit on these considerations of final causes, incorporeal natures, and an intelligent cause with respect to bodies, in order to show their use even in physics and mathematics: on the one hand, to purge the mechanical philosophy of the impiety with which it is charged and, on the other hand, to elevate the minds of our philosophers from material considerations alone to nobler meditations. It is now appropriate to return from bodies to immaterial natures, in particular to minds, and to say something of the means God uses to enlighten them and act on them. In this matter, too, we must not doubt that there are certain laws of nature, of which I could speak more fully elsewhere. But for now it will be sufficient to touch somewhat on ideas, whether we see all things in God and how God is our light.[25]

It may be appropriate to observe that the improper use of ideas gives rise to several errors. For when we reason about something, we imagine ourselves to have the idea of that thing; and that is the foundation upon which certain ancient and new philosophers have built a certain extremely imperfect demonstration of God. For, they say, I must have an idea of God or of a perfect being since I think of him, and one cannot think without an idea. Now, the idea of this being contains all perfections, and existence is a perfection, so consequently he exists. But since we often think of impossible chimeras—for example, of the highest degree of speed, of the greatest number, of the intersection of the conchoid with its base or rule—this reasoning is insufficient. It is therefore in this sense that we can say that there are true and false ideas, depending upon whether the thing in question is possible or not. And it is only when we are certain

---

23. Heliodorus of Larissa, or Damianos, was a Greek mathematician who flourished after Ptolemy. He was probably known to Leibniz through an edition, *De opticis libri duo*, published by Erasmus Bartholinus in Paris in 1657.
24. The law of refraction was first published in the second discourse of Descartes's *Dioptrics*. Descartes does indeed at-

tempt to derive the law from hypotheses about the nature of light. Snell discovered the same laws at roughly the same time as Descartes, and there was (and continues to be) a lively dispute about who discovered the law first, and whether Descartes actually discovered the law or learned it from Snell. Leibniz seems to favor Snell.
25. See Malebranche, *Search after Truth*, Book III, pt. II, chap. 6.

of its possibility that we can boast of having an idea of the thing. Thus the argument above proves, at least, that God exists necessarily, if he is possible. It is indeed a prerogative of divine nature, one that surpasses all others, that divine nature needs only its possibility or essence in order actually to exist, and it is precisely this that is called *ens a se*.

24. *What is clear or obscure, distinct or confused, adequate and intuitive or suppositive*[26] *knowledge; nominal, real, causal, and essential definition.* In order to understand better the nature of ideas, we must to some extent touch on the varieties of knowledge. When I can recognize a thing from among others without being able to say what its differences or properties consist in, the knowledge is *confused*. It is in this way that we sometimes know something *clearly*, without being in any doubt whether a poem or a picture is done well or badly, simply because it has a certain something, I know not what, that satisfies or offends us. But when I can explain the marks which I have, the knowledge is called *distinct*. And such is the knowledge of an assayer, who discerns the true from the false by means of certain tests or marks which make up the definition of gold.

But distinct knowledge has degrees, for ordinarily the notions that enter into the definition would themselves need definition and are known only confusedly. But when everything that enters into a distinct definition or distinct knowledge is known distinctly, down to the primitive notions, I call this knowledge *adequate*. And when my mind understands all the primitive ingredients of a notion at once and distinctly, it has intuitive knowledge of it; this is extremely rare, since the greater part of human knowledge is only confused or *suppositive*.[27]

It is also good to distinguish nominal and real definitions. I call a definition nominal when one can still doubt whether the notion defined is possible, as, for example, if I say that an endless helix is a solid line

whose parts are congruent or can be superimposed on one another; anyone who does not know from elsewhere what an endless helix is could doubt whether such a line is possible, even though having such congruent parts is in fact one of the reciprocal properties of the endless helix, for other lines whose parts are congruent (which are only the circumference of a circle and the straight line) are planar; that is, they can be inscribed on a plane. This shows that any reciprocal property can serve as a nominal definition; but when the property makes known the possibility of the thing, it constitutes a real definition. As long as we have only a nominal definition, we cannot be certain of the consequences we derive, for if it concealed some contradiction or impossibility, the opposite conclusions could be derived from it. That is why truths do not depend upon names and are not arbitrary, as some new philosophers have believed.[28]

Furthermore, there are still great differences between the kinds of real definitions. For when possibility is proved only by experience, as in the definition of quicksilver, whose possibility we know because we know that there actually is such a body which is an extremely heavy but rather volatile fluid, the definition is merely real and nothing more; but when the proof of the possibility is *a priori*, the definition is both real and *causal*, as when it contains the possible generation of the thing. And when a definition pushes the analysis back to the primitive notions without assuming anything requiring an *a priori* proof of its possibility, it is perfect or *essential*.

25. *In what case our knowledge is joined to the contemplation of the idea.* Now, it is evident that we have no idea of a notion when it is impossible. And in the case in which knowledge is only *suppositive*, even when we have the idea, we do not contemplate it, for such a notion is only known in the way in which we know notions involving a hidden impossibility [*occultement impossibles*]; and if a notion is possible, we do not learn its possibility in this way. For example, when I think of a thousand or of a chiliagon, I often do this without contemplating the idea—as when I

26. Cf. "Meditations on Knowledge, Truth, and Ideas" (1684). Instead of "suppositive" Leibniz there uses the term "symbolic."
27. In the margin: "A notion intermediate between intuitive and clear is when I have been deprived of clear knowledge of all surrounding notions."

28. Leibniz probably has Hobbes in mind here.

say that a thousand is ten times a hundred without bothering to think of what 10 and 100 are because I suppose I know it and do not believe I need to stop now and conceive it. Thus, it could happen, as in fact it often happens, that I am mistaken with respect to a notion I suppose or believe that I understand, although in fact the notion is impossible, or at least incompatible with those to which I join it. And whether I am mistaken or not, this suppositive way of conceiving remains the same. Therefore, only in confused notions when our knowledge is clear or in distinct notions when it is intuitive do we see the entire idea in them.[29]

26. *That we have all ideas in us; and of Plato's doctrine of reminiscence.* In order properly to conceive what an idea is, we must prevent an equivocation. For some take the idea to be the form or difference of our thoughts, and thus we have an idea in the mind only insofar as we think of it; every time we think of it again, we have other ideas of the same thing, though similar to the preceding ideas. But it seems that others take the idea as an immediate object of thought or as some permanent form that remains when we are not contemplating it. And, in fact, our soul always has in it the quality of representing to itself any nature or form whatsoever, when the occasion to think of it presents itself. And I believe that this quality of our soul, insofar as it expresses some nature, form, or essence, is properly the idea of the thing, which is in us and which is always in us, whether we think of it or not. For our soul expresses God, the universe, and all essences, as well as all existences.

This agrees with my principles, for nothing ever enters into our mind naturally from the outside; and we have a bad habit of thinking of our soul as if it received certain species as messengers and as if it has doors and windows. We have all these forms in our mind; we even have forms from all time, for the mind always expresses all its future thoughts and already thinks confusedly about everything it will ever think about distinctly. And nothing can be taught to us

whose idea we do not already have in our mind, an idea which is like the matter of which that thought is formed.

This is what Plato so excellently recognized when he proposed his doctrine of reminiscence, a very solid doctrine, provided that it is taken rightly and purged of the error of preexistence and provided that we do not imagine that at some earlier time the soul must already have known and thought distinctly what it learns and thinks now. Plato also strengthened his view by way of a fine experiment, introducing a little boy, whom he leads insensibly to extremely difficult truths of geometry concerning incommensurables without teaching him anything, merely by asking appropriate questions in proper order.[30] This demonstrates that our soul knows all these things virtually and requires only attention to recognize truths, and that, consequently, it has, at very least, the ideas upon which these truths depend. One can even say that it already possesses these truths, if they are taken as relations of ideas.

27. *How our soul can be compared to empty tablets and how our notions come from the senses.* Aristotle preferred to compare our soul to tablets that are still blank, where there is room for writing,[31] and he maintained that nothing is in our understanding that does not come from the senses. That agrees better with the popular notions, as is Aristotle's way, but Plato goes deeper. However, these kinds of doxologies or practicologies may be acceptable in ordinary usage, much as we see that those who follow Copernicus do not stop saying that the sun rises and sets. I even find that they can be given a good sense, a sense according to which they have nothing false in them, just as I have already noted how one can truly say that particular substances act on one another. In this same way, one can also say that we receive knowledge

---

29. An earlier draft continues: "However, we actually have in our mind all possible ideas, and we always think of them in a confused way."

30. This is a reference to Plato's *Meno*, 82b et seq., where, in a familiar passage, Socrates leads a young slave boy through some geometrical arguments.

31. Aristotle, *De Anima*, Book II, chap. 4. The doctrine that nothing is in the intellect that was not first in the senses, attributed to Aristotle by the Scholastics, does not actually occur in Aristotle; perhaps it is a rendering of *Posterior Analytics*, Book II, chap. 19, or *Nicomachean Ethics*, Book VI, chap. 3, sec. 3.

from the outside by way of the senses, because some external things contain or express more particularly the reasons that determine our soul to certain thoughts. But when we are concerned with the exactness of metaphysical truths, it is important to recognize the extent and independence of our soul, which goes infinitely further than is commonly thought, though in ordinary usage in life we attribute to it only what we perceive most manifestly and what belongs to us most particularly, for it serves no purpose to go any further.

However, it would be good to choose terms proper to each conception [*sens*] in order to avoid equivocation. Thus, the expressions in our soul, whether we conceive them or not, can be called ideas, but those we conceive or form can be called notions, concepts [*conceptus*]. But however we take these expressions, it is always false to say that all our notions come from the external senses, for the notions I have of myself and of my thoughts, and consequently of being, substance, action, identity, and of many others, arise from an internal experience.

28. *God alone is the immediate object of our perceptions, which exist outside of us, and he alone is our light.* Now, in rigorous metaphysical truth, there is no external cause acting on us except God alone, and he alone communicates himself to us immediately in virtue of our continual dependence. From this it follows that there is no other external object that touches our soul and immediately excites our perception. Thus we have ideas of everything in our soul only by virtue of God's continual action on us, that is to say, because every effect expresses its cause, and thus the essence of our soul is a certain expression, imitation or image of the divine essence, thought, and will, and of all the ideas comprised in it. It can then be said that God is our immediate external object and that we see all things by him. For example, when we see the sun and the stars, it is God who has given them to us and who conserves the ideas of them in us, and it is God who determines us really to think of them by his ordinary concourse while our senses are disposed in a certain manner, according to the laws he has established. God is the sun and the light of souls, the light that lights every man that comes

into this world,[32] and this is not an opinion new to our times. After Holy Scripture and the Church Fathers, who have always preferred Plato to Aristotle, I remember having previously noted that from the time of the Scholastics, several believed that God is the light of the soul and, in their way of speaking, the active intellect of the rational soul. The Averroists gave the sense of this a bad turn,[33] but others, among whom was, I believe, William of St. Amour, and several mystical theologians, have taken it in a manner worthy of God and capable of elevating the soul to the knowledge of its good.

29. *Yet we think immediately through our own ideas and not through those of God.* However, I am not of the opinion of certain able philosophers who seem to maintain that our very ideas are in God and not at all in us.[34] In my opinion, this arises from the fact that they have not yet considered sufficiently either what we have just explained about substances or the full extent and independence of our soul, which makes it contain everything that happens to it, and makes it express God and, with him, all possible and actual beings, just as an effect expresses its cause. Also, it is inconceivable that I think through the ideas of others. The soul must actually be affected in a certain way when it thinks of something, and it must already have in itself not only the passive power of being able to be affected in this way (which is already wholly determined) but also an active power, a power by virtue of which there have always been in its nature marks of the future production of this thought and dispositions to produce it in its proper time. And all this already involves the idea included in this thought.

30. *How God inclines our soul without necessitating it; that we do not have the right to complain and that we must not ask why Judas sins but only why Judas*

---

32. John 1:9.
33. Averroists were Christian followers of Averroës (or Ibn Rushd—1126–98), the great Arabic commentator on Aristotle, who held that the active intellect in each man is part of a single active intellect. The doctrine of a single world-soul was condemned as heresy.
34. Malebranche, again, is Leibniz's primary target, as earlier in sec. 23.

*the sinner is admitted to existence in preference to some other possible persons. On original imperfection before sin and on the degrees of grace.* There are a number of considerations with respect to the action of God on human will which are so difficult that it would be inordinately lengthy to pursue them here. Roughly speaking, however, here is what can be said. In concurring with our actions, God ordinarily does no more than follow the laws he has established, that is, he continually conserves and produces our being in such a way that thoughts come to us spontaneously or freely in the order that the notion pertaining to our individual substance contains them, a notion in which they could be foreseen from all eternity. Moreover, in virtue of his decree that the will always tend toward the apparent good, expressing or imitating his will in certain particular respects (so that this apparent good always has some truth in it), God determines our will to choose what seems better, without, however, necessitating it. For, absolutely speaking, the will is in a state of indifference, as opposed to one of necessity, and it has the power to do otherwise or even to suspend its action completely; these two alternatives are possible and remain so.

Therefore, the soul must guard itself against deceptive appearances [*les surprises des apparences*] through a firm will to reflect and neither to act nor to judge in certain circumstances except after having deliberated fully. But it is true, and it is even assured from all eternity, that a certain soul will not make use of this power in such a situation. But who is to blame? Can the soul complain about anything other than itself? All these complaints after the fact are unjust, if they would have been unjust before the fact. Now, could this soul, a little before sinning, complain about God in good faith, as if God determined it to sin? Since God's determinations in these matters cannot be foreseen, how does the soul know that it is determined to sin, unless it is actually sinning already? It is only a matter of not willing, and God could not put forth an easier and more just condition; thus judges do not seek the reasons which have disposed a man to have a bad will, but only stop to consider the extent to which this particular will is bad. But perhaps it is certain from all eternity that I shall sin? Answer this question for yourself: perhaps not; and without con-

sidering what you cannot know and what can give you no light, act according to your duty, which you do know.

But someone else will say, why is it that this man will assuredly commit this sin? The reply is easy: Otherwise, it would not be this man. For God sees from all time that there will be a certain Judas whose notion or idea (which God has) contains this free and future action. Therefore, only this question remains, why does such a Judas, the traitor, who is merely possible in God's idea, actually exist? But no reply to this question is to be expected on earth, except that, in general, one must say that, since God found it good that he should exist, despite the sin that God foresaw, it must be that this sin is paid back with interest in the universe, that God will derive a greater good from it, and that it will be found that, in sum, the sequence of things in which the existence of that sinner is included is the most perfect among all the possible sequences. But we cannot always explain the admirable economy of this choice while we are travelers in this world; it is enough to know it without understanding it. And here is the occasion to recognize the *altitudinem divitarum*, the depth and abyss of divine wisdom, without seeking a detail that involves infinite considerations.[35]

Yet one sees clearly that God is not the cause of evil. For not only did original sin take possession of the soul after the innocence of men had been lost, but even before this, there was an original imperfection or limitation connatural to all creatures, which makes them liable to sin or capable of error. Thus, the supralapsarians[36] raise no more problems than the others do. And it is to this, in my view, that we must reduce the opinion of Saint Augustine and other authors, the opinion that the root of evil is in nothingness, that is to say, in the privation or limitation of creatures, which God graciously remedies by the degree of perfection it pleases him to give. This grace of God, whether ordinary or extraordinary, has its degrees and its measures; in itself, it is always effica-

---

35. The Latin translates: "depth of riches," a reference to Romans 11:33.
36. Calvinists who held that God's decrees of election and reprobation preceded the fall. Cf. *Theodicy* I, sec. 77–84.

cious in producing a certain proportionate effect, and, further, it is always sufficient, not only to secure us from sin, but even to produce salvation, assuming that man unites himself to it by what derives from him.[37] But it is not always sufficient to overcome man's inclinations, for otherwise he would have nothing more to strive for; this is reserved solely for the absolutely efficacious grace which is always victorious, whether it is so by itself or by way of appropriate circumstances.

31. *On the motives of election, on faith foreseen, on middle knowledge, on the absolute decree and that it all reduces to the reason why God has chosen for existence such a possible person whose notion includes just such a sequence of graces and free acts; this puts an end to all difficulties at once.* Finally, God's graces are wholly pure graces, upon which creatures have no claim. However, just as it is not sufficient to appeal to God's absolute or conditional foresight into the future actions of men in order to account for his choice in the dispensation of these graces, we also must not imagine absolute decrees that have no reasonable motive. As for God's foreknowledge of faith or good works, it is very true that he has elected only those whose faith and charity he foresaw, whom he foreknew he would endow with faith. But the same question returns, why will God give the grace of faith or of good works to some rather than to others? And as for this knowledge God has, which is the foresight not of faith and good works, but of their grounds [*matière*] and predisposition, that is, foresight of what a man would contribute to them on his side (for it is true that there are differences among men whenever there are differences in grace and that, in fact, although a man needs to be stimulated to the good and be converted, he must also act in that direction afterward), it seems to several people that one could say that God, seeing what a man would do without grace or extraordinary assistance, or at least seeing the sort of person he is, leaving grace aside, might resolve to give grace to those whose natural dispositions were better or, at least, less imperfect or less

bad. But even if that were the case, one can say that these natural dispositions, insofar as they are good, are still the effect of grace, although ordinary grace, since God has favored some more than others. And since he knows that these natural advantages he gives will serve as motives for grace or extraordinary assistance, is it not true, according to this doctrine, that in the end everything is completely reduced to his mercy?

Since we do not know how much and in what way God takes account of natural dispositions in the dispensation of grace, I believe, then, that the most exact and surest thing to say, according to our principles, as I have already noted, is that among the possible beings there must be the person of Peter or John, whose notion or idea contains this entire sequence of ordinary and extraordinary graces and all the rest of these events with their circumstances, and that it pleased God to choose him for actual existence from among an infinity of equally possible persons. After this it seems that there is nothing more to ask and that all difficulties vanish.

For, with respect to this single great question, why it pleased God to choose him from among so many other possible persons, one would have to be very unreasonable not to be content with the general reasons we have given, reasons whose details lie beyond us. Thus, instead of having recourse to an absolute decree which is unreasonable, since it is without reason, or to reasons which do not solve the difficulty completely and are in need of further reasons, it would be best to say with Saint Paul, that God here followed certain great reasons of wisdom or appropriateness, unknown to mortals and based on the general order, whose aim is the greatest perfection of the universe. It is to this that the motives of the glory of God and the manifestation of his justice are reduced, as well as of his mercy and generally of his perfections and finally the immense depth of his riches, with which the soul of Saint Paul was enraptured.

32. *The utility of these principles in matters of piety and religion.* For the rest, it seems that the thoughts we have just explained, particularly the great principle of the perfection of the operations of God and the principle that the notion of a substance contains all its

---

37. The text also contains "by his will" as a possible ending for the sentence.

events with all their circumstances, far from harming, serve to confirm religion, to dispel enormous difficulties, to enflame souls with a divine love, and to elevate minds to the knowledge of incorporeal substances, much more than hypotheses we have seen until now. For one sees clearly that all other substances depend on God, in the same way as thoughts emanate from our substance, that God is all in all, and that he is intimately united with all creatures, in proportion to their perfection, that it is he alone who determines them from the outside by his influence, and, if to act is to determine immediately, it can be said in this sense, in the language of metaphysics, that God alone operates on me, and God alone can do good or evil to me; the other substances contribute only by reason of these determinations, because God, having regard for all, shares his blessings and requires them to accommodate themselves to one another. Hence God alone brings about the connection and communication among substances, and it is through him that the phenomena of any substance meet and agree with those of others and consequently, that there is reality in our perceptions. But, in practice, one ascribes an action to particular reasons[38] in the sense that I have explained above, because it is not necessary always to mention the universal cause in particular cases.

We also see that every substance has a perfect spontaneity (which becomes freedom in intelligent substances), that everything that happens to it is a consequence of its idea or of its being, and that nothing determines it, except God alone. And that is why a person of very exalted mind, revered for her saintliness, was in the habit of saying that the soul must often think as if there were nothing but God and itself in the world.[39]

Now, nothing gives us a stronger understanding of immortality than the independence and extent of the soul in question here, which shelters it absolutely from all external things, since the soul alone makes up its whole world and is sufficient to itself with God. And it is as impossible that it should perish without annihilation, as it is that the world (of which it is a perpetual living expression) should destroy itself; hence, it is impossible that the changes in this extended mass called our body should do anything to the soul or that the dissolution of this body should destroy what is indivisible.

33. *Explanation of the union of soul and body, a matter which has been considered as inexplicable or miraculous, and on the origin of confused perceptions.* We also see the unexpected illumination of this great mystery of the union of the soul and the body, that is, how it happens that the passions and actions of the one are accompanied by the actions and passions, or by the corresponding phenomena, of the other. For there is no way to conceive that the one has any influence on the other, and it is unreasonable simply to appeal to the extraordinary operation of the universal cause in an ordinary and particular thing. But here is the true reason: We have said that everything that happens to the soul and to each substance follows from its notion, and therefore the very idea or essence of the soul carries with it the fact that all its appearances or perceptions must arise spontaneously from its own nature and precisely in such a way that they correspond by themselves to what happens in the whole universe. But they correspond more particularly and more perfectly to what happens in the body assigned to it, because the soul expresses the state of the universe in some way and for some time, according to the relation other bodies have to its own body. This also allows us to know how our body belongs to us, without, however, being attached to our essence. And I believe that persons who can meditate will judge our principles favorably, because they will be able to see easily what the connection between the soul and the body consists in, a connection which seems inexplicable in any other way.

We also see that the perceptions of our senses, even when they are clear, must necessarily contain some

---

38. An earlier draft had "occasional causes" rather than "particular reasons."

39. Leibniz probably had St. Theresa in mind here. In a letter from 1696 he wrote: "In [her writings] I once found this lovely thought, that the soul should conceive of things as if there were only God and itself in the world. This even provides a considerable object to reflect upon in philosophy, which I usefully employed in one of my hypotheses," G. Grua, *Textes inédits d'après les manuscrits de la Bibliothèque provinciale de Hanovre* (Paris: PUF, 1948), p. 103.

confused feeling [*sentiment*], for our body receives the impression of all other bodies, since all the bodies of the universe are in sympathy, and, even though our senses are related to everything, it is impossible for our soul to attend to everything in particular; that is why our confused sensations are the result of a truly infinite variety of perceptions. This is almost like the confused murmur coming from the innumerable set of breaking waves heard by those who approach the seashore. Now, if from several perceptions (which do not come together to make one), there is none which stands out before the others and if they make impressions that are almost equally strong or equally capable of gaining the attention of the soul, the soul can only perceive them confusedly.

34. *On the difference between minds and other substances, souls or substantial forms, and that the immortality required includes memory.* Assuming[40] that the bodies that make up an *unum per se*, as does man, are substances, that they have substantial forms, and that animals have souls, we must admit that these souls and these substantial forms cannot entirely perish, no more than atoms or the ultimate parts of matter can, on the view of other philosophers. For no substance perishes, although it can become completely different. They also express the whole universe, although more imperfectly than minds do. But the principal difference is that they do not know what they are nor what they do, and consequently, since they do not reflect on themselves, they cannot discover necessary and universal truths. It is also because they lack reflection about themselves that they have no moral qualities. As a result, though they may pass through a thousand transformations, like those we see when a caterpillar changes into a butterfly, yet from the moral or practical point of view, the result is as if they had perished; indeed, we may even say that they have perished physically, in the sense in which we say that bodies perish through their corruption.

But the intelligent soul, knowing what it is — having the ability to utter the word " I," a word so full of meaning — does not merely remain and subsist metaphysically, which it does to a greater degree than the others, but also remains the same morally and constitutes the same person. For it is memory or the knowledge of this self that renders it capable of punishment or reward. Thus the immortality required in morality and religion does not consist merely in this perpetual subsistence common to all substances, for without the memory of what one has been, there would be nothing desirable about it. Suppose that some person all of a sudden becomes the king of China, but only on the condition that he forgets what he has been, as if he were born anew; practically, or as far as the effects could be perceived, wouldn't that be the same as if he were annihilated and a king of China created at the same instant in his place? That is something this individual would have no reason to desire.

35. *The excellence of minds and that God considers them preferable to other creatures. That minds express God rather than the world, but that the other substances express the world rather than God.* But so that we may judge by natural reasons that God will always preserve not only our substance, but also our person, that is, the memory and knowledge of what we are (though distinct knowledge is sometimes suspended during sleep and fainting spells), we must join morals to metaphysics, that is, we must not only consider God as the principle and cause of all substances and all beings, but also as the leader of all persons or intelligent substances and as the absolute monarch of the most perfect city or republic, which is what the universe composed of all minds together is, God himself being the most perfect of all minds and the greatest of all beings. For certainly minds are the most perfect beings[41] and best express divinity. And since the whole nature, end, virtue, and function of substance is merely to express God and the universe,

---

40. An earlier draft began with this first sentence: "I do not attempt to determine if bodies are substances in metaphysical rigor or if they are only true phenomena like the rainbow and, consequently, if there are true substances, souls, or substantial forms which are not intelligent."

41 An earlier draft of this sentence began: ". . . minds are either the only substances one finds in the world, in the case in which bodies are only true phenomena, or else they are at least the most perfect. . . ."

as has been sufficiently explained, there is no reason to doubt that the substances which express the universe with the knowledge of what they are doing and which are capable of knowing great truths about God and the universe, express it incomparably better than do those natures, which are either brutish and incapable of knowing truths or completely destitute of sensation and knowledge. And the difference between intelligent substances and substances that have no intelligence at all is just as great as the difference between a mirror and someone who sees.

Since God himself is the greatest and wisest of all minds, it is easy to judge that the beings with whom he can, so to speak, enter into conversation, and even into a society—by communicating to them his views and will in a particular manner and in such a way that they can know and love their benefactor—must be infinitely nearer to him than all other things, which can only pass for the instruments of minds. So we see that all wise persons value a man infinitely more than any other thing, no matter how precious it is, and it seems that the greatest satisfaction that a soul, content in other ways, can have is to see itself loved by others. With respect to God, though, there is the difference that his glory and our worship cannot add anything to his satisfaction, since knowledge of creatures is only a consequence of his supreme and perfect happiness—far from contributing to it or being its partial cause. However, what is good and reasonable in finite minds is found preeminently in him, and, just as we would praise a king who would prefer to preserve the life of a man rather than the most precious and rarest of his animals, we should not doubt that the most enlightened and most just of all monarchs is of the same opinion.

36. *God is the monarch of the most perfect republic, composed of all minds, and the happiness of this city of God is his principal purpose.* Indeed, minds are the most perfectible substances, and their perfections are peculiar in that they interfere with each other the least, or rather they aid one another the most, for only the most virtuous can be the most perfect friends. Whence it obviously follows that God, who always aims for the greatest perfection in general, will pay the greatest attention to minds and will give them the greatest perfection that universal harmony can allow, not only in general, but to each of them in particular.

One can even say that God, insofar as he is a mind, is the originator of existences; otherwise, if he lacked the will to choose the best, there would be no reason for a possible thing to exist in preference to others. Thus the quality that God has of being a mind himself takes precedence over all the other considerations he can have toward creatures; only minds are made in his image and are, as it were, of his race or like children of his household, since they alone can serve him freely and act with knowledge in imitation of the divine nature; a single mind is worth a whole world, since it does not merely express the world but it also knows it and it governs itself after the fashion of God. In this way we may say that, although all substances express the whole universe, nevertheless the other substances express the world rather than God, while minds express God rather than the world. And this nature of minds, so noble that it brings them as near to divinity as it is possible for simple creatures, has the result that God draws infinitely more glory from them than from all other beings, or rather the other beings only furnish minds the matter for glorifying him.

That is why this moral quality God has, which makes him the lord or monarch of minds, relates to him, so to speak, personally and in a quite singular manner. It is because of this that he humanizes himself, that he is willing to allow anthropomorphism, and that he enters into society with us, as a prince with his subjects; and this consideration is so dear to him that the happy and flourishing state of his empire, which consists in the greatest possible happiness of its inhabitants, becomes the highest of his laws. For happiness is to people what perfection is to beings. And if the first principle of the existence of the physical world is the decree to give it the greatest perfection possible, the first intent of the moral world or the City of God, which is the noblest part of the universe, must be to diffuse in it the greatest possible happiness.

Therefore, we must not doubt that God has ordered everything in such a way that minds not only may live always, which is certain, but also that they may always preserve their moral quality, so that the city does not lose a single person, just as the world does not lose any substance. And consequently they will always know what they are; otherwise they would not be susceptible to reward or punishment, something, however, essential to a republic, but above all essential to the most perfect republic, in which nothing can be neglected.

Finally, since God is at the same time the most just and most good-natured of monarchs and since he demands only a good will, as long as it is sincere and serious, his subjects cannot wish for a better condition, and, to make them perfectly happy, he wants only for them to love him.

37. *Jesus Christ has revealed to men the mystery and admirable laws of the kingdom of heaven and the greatness of the supreme happiness that God prepares for those who love him.* The ancient philosophers knew very little of these important truths; Jesus Christ alone has expressed them divinely well and in a manner so clear and familiar that the coarsest of minds have grasped them. Thus his gospel has entirely changed the course of human affairs; he has brought us to know the kingdom of heaven, or that perfect republic of minds which deserves the title of City of God, whose admirable laws he has disclosed to us. He alone has made us see how much God loves us and with what exactitude he has provided for everything that concerns us; that, caring for sparrows, he will not neglect the rational beings which are infinitely more dear to him; that all the hairs on our head are numbered; that heaven and earth will perish rather than the word of God and what pertains to the economy of our salvation; that God has more regard for the least of the intelligent souls than for the whole machinery of the world; that we must not fear those who can destroy bodies but cannot harm souls, because God alone can make souls happy or unhappy; and that the souls of the just, in his hands, are safe from all the upheavals of the universe, God alone being able to act upon them; that none of our actions are forgotten; that everything is taken account of, even idle words or a spoonful of water well used; finally, that everything must result in the greatest welfare of those who are good; that the just will be like suns; and that neither our senses nor our mind has ever tasted anything approaching the happiness that God prepares for those who love him.

# G. W. Leibniz, From the Letters to Arnauld (1686–87)[1]

Remarks on Arnauld's Letter about My
Proposition That the Individual Notion of
Each Person Includes Once and for All
Everything That Will Ever Happen to
Him [May 1686].

*I thought* (says Arnauld) *that we might infer that God
was free to create or not to create Adam, but assuming
that he wanted to create him, everything that has
happened to humankind had to happen, or ought to
happen, by a fatal necessity, or at least, I thought that,
assuming he wanted to create Adam, God is no more
free, with respect to all this, than he would be not to
create a creature capable of thought, assuming that
he wanted to create me.* I first replied that we must
distinguish between absolute and hypothetical necessity. To this, Arnauld replies here that *he is speaking
only of hypothetical necessity.* After this assertion, the
argument takes a different turn. The terms he used,

*fatal necessity*, are ordinarily understood only as applied to absolute necessity, so I was required to make
this distinction, which, however, is no longer called
for, inasmuch as Arnauld does not insist upon this
fatal necessity, since he uses alternative phrases: by
a fatal necessity or at least, etc. It would be useless
to dispute about the word. But, as for the thing itself,
Arnauld still finds it strange that I seem to maintain
*that all human events occur necessitate ex hypothesi,
given the single assumption that God wanted to create
Adam.* To this I have *two replies* to make. The *first*
is that my assumption is not merely that God wanted
to create an Adam whose notion was vague and incomplete, but that God wanted to create a particular
Adam, sufficiently determined as an individual. And
according to me, this complete individual notion involves relations to the whole series of things. This
should appear more reasonable, given that Arnauld
grants here the interconnections among God's resolutions; that is, he grants that God, having resolved to
create Adam, takes into consideration all the resolutions he has concerning the whole series of the universe; this is somewhat like a wise man who, making
a decision about one part of his plan and having the
whole plan in view, would decide so much the better,
if his decision could settle all the parts at once.

*The other reply* is that the conclusion [*conséquence*],
by virtue of which all the events follow from the

---

1. Translated from the French by R. Ariew and D. Garber
in G. W. Leibniz, *Philosophical Essays* (Indianapolis: Hackett
Publishing Company, 1989). Arnauld's critique of section 13
of the "Discourse on Metaphysics" started off a correspondence
with Leibniz. Leibniz summarizes adequately the debate that
ensued (from February to May 1686) in the first selection we
have chosen from that correspondence. Passages in double
brackets that follow are not in the copies Arnauld received and
may be either earlier thoughts or later additions. Only selected
variants are noted.

hypothesis, is indeed always certain, but it is not always necessary with metaphysical necessity as is the one found in Arnauld's example: that God in resolving to create me cannot fail to create a nature capable of thought. The conclusion is often only physical and assumes God's free decrees, as do conclusions which depend on the laws of motion or which depend on the moral principle that all minds will pursue what appears best to them. It is true that, when the assumption of those decrees that yield the conclusion is added to the first assumption which had constituted the antecedent, namely, God's resolution to create Adam, to make up a single antecedent out of all these assumptions or resolutions; then, I say, it is true in that case that the conclusion follows.

Since I have already touched upon these two replies in some way in the letter I sent to the Landgrave, Arnauld brings forward replies to them that must be considered. He admits in good faith that he took my view to be that all the events of an individual can be deduced from his individual notion in the same way and with the same necessity as the properties of a sphere can be deduced from its specific notion or definition; he also supposed that I considered the notion of the individual in itself, without taking account of the way in which it exists in the divine understanding or will. *For* (he says) *it seems to me that we don't usually consider the specific notion of a sphere in relation to its representation in God's understanding, but in relation to what it is in itself, and I thought that it was the same for the individual notion of each person. But,* he adds, *now that he knows what I think about this, that is sufficient to enable him to accept it for the purpose of asking whether it overcomes all the difficulties;* he is still doubtful of this. I see that Arnauld has not remembered, or at least did not concern himself with, the view of the Cartesians, who maintain that it is through his will that God establishes the eternal truths, like those concerning the properties of the sphere. But since I am not of their opinion any more than Arnauld is, I will only say why I think that we must philosophize differently about the notion of an individual substance than about the specific notion of the sphere. The reason is because the notion of a *species* includes only eternal or necessary truths, but the notion of an individual includes considered

as possible what, in fact, is true, that is, considerations related to the existence of things and to time, and consequently it depends upon God's free decrees considered as possible; for truths of fact or existence depend upon God's decrees. Thus the notion of sphere in general is incomplete or abstract; that is, we consider in it only the essence of a sphere in general or in theory, without regard to particular circumstances, and consequently it does not in any way include what is required for the existence of a certain sphere. But the notion of the sphere Archimedes had placed on his tomb is complete and must include everything belonging to the subject of that shape. That is why, in individual or practical considerations, which are concerned with singulars, in addition to the shape of the sphere, we must consider the matter of which it is made, the place, the time, and the other circumstances, considerations which, by a continual linkage, would in the end include the whole series of the universe, if everything these notions included could be pursued. For the notion of the piece of matter of which this sphere is made involves all the changes it has undergone and will undergo one day. And according to me, each individual substance always contains traces of what has ever happened to it and marks of what will ever happen to it. But what I have just said can suffice to explain my line of thought.

Now, Arnauld states that, by taking the individual notion of a person in relation to the knowledge God had of it when he resolved to create it, what I have said about this notion is quite certain. And similarly, he even grants that the volition to create Adam was not detached from God's volition concerning what would happen to him and to his posterity. But he now asks whether the link between Adam and what happens to his posterity is dependent on or independent of God's free decrees; *that is,* as he explains, *whether God knew what would happen to Adam and his posterity only as a consequence of the free decrees by which God ordained everything that will happen, or whether there is an intrinsic and necessary connection, independent of these decrees, between Adam and the events in question.* He does not doubt that I would choose the latter alternative, and in fact I could not choose the first as he explained it, but it seems to me that there is a middle ground. However, he proves that I must choose the latter, because I consider the individual notion of Adam as possible when I maintain that, among an infinity of possible notions, God has chosen the notion of an Adam such as this, and notions possible in themselves do not depend upon God's free decrees.

But here I must explain myself a little better. Therefore, I say that the connection between Adam and human events is not independent of all of God's free decrees, but also, that it does not depend upon them so completely that each event could happen or be foreseen only in virtue of a particular primitive decree made about it. I therefore think that there are only a few free primitive decrees that regulate the course of things, decrees that can be called laws of the universe, and which, joined to the free decree to create Adam, bring about the consequence. This is a bit like needing few hypotheses to explain phenomena — something I will explain more distinctly in what follows. As for the objection that possibles are independent of God's decrees, I grant it with respect to actual decrees (even though the Cartesians do not agree with this), but I hold that possible individual notions include some possible free decrees. For example, if this world were only possible, the individual notion of some body in this world, which includes certain motions as possible, would also include our laws of motion (which are free decrees of God), but also only as possible. For, since there is an infinity of possible worlds, there is also an infinity of possible laws, some proper to one world, others proper to another, and each possible individual of a world includes the laws of its world in its notion.

The same things can be said about miracles or God's extraordinary operations. These belong to the general order and conform to God's principal plans and, consequently, are included in the notion of this universe, which is a result of these plans; just as the idea of a building results from the ends or plans of the builder, so the idea or notion of this world is a result of one of God's plans considered as possible. For everything must be explained by its cause, and God's ends are the cause of the universe. Now, in my opinion, each individual substance expresses the whole universe from a certain point of view, and consequently it also expresses the miracles in ques-

tion. All this must be understood of the general order, of God's plans, of the course of this universe, of individual substance, and of miracles, whether they are taken in the actual state or whether they are considered *sub ratione possibilitatis*. For another possible world will also have all this in its own way, though the plans of our world have been preferred.

It can also be seen from what I have just said about God's plans and primitive laws that this universe has a certain principal or primitive notion, a notion of which particular events are merely the result, with the exception of what is free and contingent, to which certainty does no harm, since the certainty of events is based in part upon free acts. Now, each individual substance of this universe expresses in its notion the universe into which it enters. And not only does the assumption that God has resolved to create this Adam include resolutions for all the rest, but so does the assumption that he created any other individual substance whatsoever, because it is the nature of an individual substance to have a notion so complete that everything that can be attributed to it can be deduced from it, even the whole universe, because of the interconnection of things. Nevertheless, to proceed carefully, it must be said that it is not so much because God decided to create this Adam that he decided on all the rest. Rather, both the decision he made with regard to Adam and the one he made with regard to other particular things are the result of the decision he made with regard to the whole universe and a result of the principal plans that determine its primitive notion and establish in it this general and inviolable order. Everything is in conformity with this order, even miracles, which are, no doubt, in conformity with God's principal plans, although they do not always observe the particular maxims that are called laws of nature.

I have said that all human events can be deduced not simply by assuming the creation of a vague Adam, but by assuming the creation of an Adam determined with respect to all these circumstances, chosen from among an infinity of possible Adams. This has given Arnauld the occasion to object, not without reason, that it is as difficult to conceive of several Adams, taking Adam as a particular nature, as it is to conceive of several mes. I agree, but when speaking of several

Adams, I was not taking Adam as a determinate individual. I must therefore explain myself. This is what I meant. When one considers in Adam a part of his predicates, for example, that he is the first man, set in a garden of pleasure, from whose side God fashioned a woman, and similar things conceived *sub ratione generalitatis*, in a general way (that is to say, without naming Eve, Paradise, and other circumstances that fix individuality), and when one calls Adam the person to whom these predicates are attributed, all this is not sufficient to determine the individual, for there can be an infinity of Adams, that is, an infinity of possible persons, different from one another, whom this fits. Far from disagreeing with what Arnauld says against this multiplicity of the same individual, I myself used this to make it better understood that the nature of an individual must be complete and determinate. I am even quite convinced of what Saint Thomas had already taught about intelligences, which I hold to apply generally, namely, that it is not possible for there to be two individuals entirely alike, or differing only numerically.[2] Therefore, we must not conceive of a vague Adam, that is, a person to whom certain attributes of Adam belong, when we are concerned with determining whether all human events follow from positing his existence; rather, we must attribute to him a notion so complete that everything that can be attributed to him can be deduced from it. Now, there is no room for doubting that God can form such a notion of him, or rather that he finds it already formed in the realm of possibles, that is, in his understanding.

It, therefore, also follows that he would not have been our Adam, but another Adam, had other events happened to him, for nothing prevents us from saying that he would be another. Therefore, he is another. It seems obvious to us that this block of marble brought from Genoa would have been altogether the same if it had been left there, because our senses allow us to judge only superficially. But at bottom, because of the interconnection of things, the whole universe with all its parts would be quite different

and would have been different from the beginning, if the least thing in it had happened differently than it did. It does not follow from this that events are necessary, but rather that they are certain, given God's choice of this possible universe, whose notion contains this series of things. I hope that what I am going to say will enable Arnauld himself to agree with this. Let there be a straight line ABC representing a certain time. And let there be an individual substance, for example, I, enduring or subsisting during that time. Let us first take me subsisting during time AB, and then me subsisting during time BC. Then, since the assumption is that it is the same individual substance that endures throughout, or rather that it is I who subsists in time AB, being then in Paris, and that it is still I who subsists in time BC, being then in Germany, there must necessarily be a reason allowing us truly to say that we endure, that is to say that I, who was in Paris, am now in Germany. For if there were no such reason, we would have as much right to say that it is someone else. It is true that my internal experience convinces me *a posteriori* of this identity; but there must also be an *a priori* reason. Now, it is not possible to find any reason but the fact that both my attributes in the preceding time and state and my attributes in the succeeding time and state are predicates of the same subject—they are in the subject. Now, what is it to say that the predicate is in the same subject, except that the notion of the predicate is in some way included in the notion of the subject? And since, once I began existing, it was possible truly to say of me that this or that would happen to me, it must be admitted that these predicates were laws included in the subject or in my complete notion, which constitutes what is called I, which is the foundation of the connection of all my different states and which God has known perfectly from all eternity. After this, I think that all doubts should disappear, for, when I say that the individual notion of Adam includes everything that will ever happen to him, I don't mean to say anything other than what all philosophers mean when they say that the predicate is included in the subject in a true proposition. It is true that the results of so evident a doctrine are paradoxical, but that is the fault of the philosophers who do not sufficiently pursue the clearest notions.

2. The reference is to St. Thomas's doctrine that, with intelligences, every individual is a lowest species; cf. the "Discourse on Metaphysics," sec. 9.

I now think that Arnauld, being as penetrating and fair-minded as he is, will no longer find my proposition so strange, even if he is not able to approve of it entirely (though I almost flatter myself that I have his approval). I agree with what he so judiciously adds about the circumspection we must use when appealing to divine knowledge [*la science divine*] in order to find out what we ought to judge concerning the notions of things. But, properly understood, what I have just said must hold, even though we should speak of God only as much as is necessary. For even if we did not say that God, when considering Adam whom he is resolving to create, sees in him everything that will happen to him, it suffices that one can always prove that there must be a complete notion of this Adam which contains them. For all the predicates of Adam either depend upon other predicates of the same Adam or they do not. Then, setting aside all of those predicates that depend upon the others, we need only gather together all the primitive predicates in order to form Adam's complete notion, a notion sufficient for deducing everything that will ever happen to him, and this is as much as we need for us to be able to explain it. It is evident that God can construct—and even actually conceive—a notion sufficient to explain all the phenomena pertaining to Adam; but it is no less evident that this notion is possible in itself. It is true that we should not enter unnecessarily into an investigation of the divine knowledge and will, because of the great difficulties involved. Nevertheless, we can explain what we have derived from such an investigation relevant to our question without entering into the difficulties Arnauld mentions—for example, the difficulty of understanding how God's simplicity is reconcilable with what we must distinguish in it. It is also very difficult to explain perfectly how God has knowledge he might not have had, namely, the knowledge by intuition [*la science de la vision*]; for, if things that exist contingently in the future didn't exist, God would not have any intuition of them. It is true that he would have simple knowledge of them, which would become intuition when it is joined to his will, so that this difficulty is perhaps reduced to a difficulty concerning his will, namely, how God is free to will. No doubt this is beyond us, but it is not necessary to understand it in order to resolve our question.[3]

As for the way in which we conceive that God acts by choosing the best among several possibles, Arnauld is right in finding some obscurity there. He seems, nevertheless, to recognize that we are led to conceive that there is an infinity of possible first men, each connected to a long sequence of persons and events, and that God has chosen from them the one who, together with his sequence, pleased him. So this is not as strange as it had first appeared to him. It is true that Arnauld testifies that he is strongly led to think that these purely possible substances are only chimeras. I do not wish to dispute this, but I hope that, in spite of this, he will grant me what I need. I agree that there is no other reality in pure possibles than the reality they have in the divine understanding, and we see from this that Arnauld himself will be required to fall back on divine knowledge to explain them, whereas it seemed earlier that he thought that we should seek them in themselves. When I also grant what Arnauld is convinced of and what I do not deny—that we conceive no possibles except through the ideas actually found in the things God has created—it does no harm to me. For when speaking of possibilities, I am satisfied that we can form true propositions about them. For example, even if there were no perfect square in the world, we would still see that it does not imply a contradiction. And if we wished absolutely to reject pure possibles, contingency would be destroyed; for, if nothing were possible except what God actually created, then what God created would be necessary, in the case he resolved to create anything.

Finally, I agree that in order to determine the notion of an individual substance it is good to consult the one I have of myself, just as one must consult the specific notion of the sphere in order to determine its properties. Yet there is a considerable difference,

3. Knowledge of simple understanding [*scientia simplicis intelligentiae*] is God's knowledge of possibles; knowledge by intuition [*scientia visionis*] is God's knowledge of actuals, which differs from the former only in God's reflexive knowledge of his own decrees. Cf. *Philosophische Schriften*, ed. C. I. Gerhardt (Berlin, 1875–90) IV 440–41, C 16–17.

for my notion and the notion of every other individual substance is infinitely broader and more difficult to understand than a specific notion, like that of the sphere, which is only incomplete. It is not enough that I sense myself [*je me sente*] to be a substance that thinks; I must distinctly conceive what distinguishes me from all other minds, and I have only a confused experience of this. The result is that, though it is easy to determine that the number of feet in the diameter is not included in the notion of sphere in general, it is not so easy to judge whether the trip I intend to make is included in my notion; otherwise, it would be as easy for us to be prophets as to be geometers. I am uncertain whether I will make the trip, but I am not uncertain that, whether I go or not, I will always be me. This is a presumption that must not be confused with a distinct notion or item of knowledge. These things appear undetermined to us only because the foreshadowings or marks which are in our substance are not recognizable to us. This is a bit like those who, consulting only the senses, would ridicule someone who says that the least motion is also communicated as far as matter extends, because experience alone cannot demonstrate this; but, when the nature of motion and matter are considered, one is convinced of this. It is the same here: when someone consults the confused experience he has of his individual notion in particular, he is far from perceiving this interconnection of events; but when the general and distinct notions which enter into it are considered, it is discovered. In fact, in considering the notion I have of every true proposition, I find that every predicate necessary or contingent, past, present, or future is included in the notion of the subject; and I ask no more of it.

Indeed, I believe that this will open up to us a way of reconciling our views. For I suspect that Arnauld did not want to grant me this proposition only because he took the connection I am maintaining to be both intrinsic and necessary, whereas I hold it to be intrinsic, but in no way necessary; for now, I have sufficiently explained that it is founded on free decrees and acts. I do not intend any connection between the subject and the predicate other than that which holds in the most contingent of truths, that is, that we can always conceive something in the subject which serves to provide a reason why this predicate or event belongs to it, or why this happened rather than not. But these reasons for contingent truths incline, rather than necessitate. Therefore, it is true that I could fail to go on this trip, but it is certain that I shall go. This predicate or event is not connected with certainty to my other predicates, conceived incompletely or *sub ratione generalitatis*; but it is connected with certainty to my complete individual notion, since I suppose that this notion was constructed explicitly so that everything that happens to me can be deduced from it. No doubt, this notion is found *a parte rei*, and it is properly the notion that belongs to me, who finds myself in different states, since this notion alone is capable of including all of them.

I have so much deference for Arnauld and such a good opinion of his judgment that I easily give up my opinions, or at least my way of expressing them as soon as I see that he finds something objectionable in them. That is why I precisely followed the difficulties he proposed, and having attempted to satisfy them in good faith, it seems to me that I am not far removed from his opinions.

The proposition at issue is of great importance and deserves to be firmly established, for from this it follows that every soul is like a world apart, independent of every other thing outside of God, that it is not only immortal and, so to speak, undisturbable, but that it holds in its substance the traces of everything that happens to it. From this also follows that in which the interaction [*commerce*] of substances consists, particularly the union of soul and body. This interaction does not occur in accordance with the ordinary hypothesis of physical influence of one substance on another, since every present state of a substance happens to it spontaneously and is only a result of its preceding state. This interaction also does not occur in accordance with the hypothesis of occasional causes, according to which God ordinarily intervenes in some way other than conserving each substance in its course, and according to which God on the occasion of something happening in the body arouses thoughts in the soul which change the course it would have taken without this intervention. It occurs in accordance with the hypothesis of concomitance, which appears demonstrative to me. That is, each substance expresses the whole series of the universe according to the point of view or relation proper to it, from which it happens that they agree perfectly; and when we say that one acts upon another, we mean that the distinct expression of the one acted upon is diminished, and that of the one acting is augmented, in conformity with the series of thoughts involved in its notion. For although every substance expresses everything, in common usage we correctly attribute to it only the most evident expressions in accordance to its relation to us.

Finally, I believe that after this, the propositions contained in the summary sent to Arnauld will appear not only more intelligible, but perhaps also more solid and more important than might have been thought at first.[4]

## To Arnauld (28 November/8 December 1686) [excerpts][5]

As I found something extraordinary in the frankness and sincerity with which you accepted some arguments I used, I cannot avoid recognizing and admiring it. I suspected that the argument taken from the general nature of propositions would make some impression on your mind; but I also confess that there are few people able to appreciate truths so abstract, and that perhaps no one else would have been able to perceive its cogency so readily.

I should like to be informed of your meditations about the possibilities of things; they can only be

profound and important since they are concerned with speaking of these possibilities in a way worthy of God. But this will be at your convenience. As for the two difficulties you found in my letter, the one concerning the hypothesis of concomitance, that is, the hypothesis of the agreement of substances among themselves, and the other concerning the nature of the forms of corporeal substances, I confess that they are considerable, and if I were able to satisfy them completely, I think that I would be able to decipher the greatest secrets of nature in its entirety. But it is something to advance to a certain point.[6] As for the first, I find that you yourself have sufficiently explained the obscurity you found in my thought concerning the hypothesis of concomitance; for when the soul has a sensation of pain at the same time that the arm is injured, I think that the situation is, in fact, as you say, Sir, that the soul itself forms this pain, which is a natural result of its state or notion. I admire Saint Augustine for having apparently recognized the same thing (as you have remarked) when he said that the pain the soul has in these encounters is nothing but a sadness that accompanies the ill disposition of the body. In fact, this great man had very solid and very profound thoughts. But (it will be asked), how does the soul know this ill disposition of the body? I reply that it is not by any impression or action of bodies on the soul, but because the nature of every substance carries a general expression of the whole universe and because the nature of the soul carries, more particularly, a more distinct expression of that which is now happening with regard to its body. That is why it is natural for the soul to mark and know the accidents of its body through accidents of its own. The situation is the same for the body when it accommodates itself to the thoughts of the soul. And when I wish to raise my arm, it is exactly at the moment when everything in the body is disposed for that effect, so that the body moves by virtue of its own laws. But through the wondrous though unfailing agreement of things among themselves, it happens that these laws work together exactly at the moment that the will is so inclined, since God took this into account in advance when he formed his

---

4. Again, Arnauld seems not to have been sent the whole "Discourse," but only a summary that corresponds closely to the titles of successive sections.

5. Arnauld wrote to Leibniz on September 28, 1686, saying that he sees "no other difficulties except about the possibility of things, and about this way of conceiving God as having chosen the universe he created from an infinity of other possible universes he saw at the same time and did not wish to create" (*Philosophische Schriften* II, 64). Arnauld then asked Leibniz to explain himself further about the hypothesis of concomitance and about the nature of the form of corporeal substance; he formulated a series of seven queries on the latter problem. Leibniz's response takes up each query individually.

6. Horace, *Epistles*, I. 1. 32.

resolution about this series of all the things in the universe. All these things are only consequences of the notion of an individual substance, which contains all its phenomena in such a way that nothing can happen to a substance that does not come from its own depths, though in conformity to what happens to another, despite the fact that the one acts freely and the other without choice. [[And this agreement is one of the best proofs that can be given of the necessity for there to be a substance which is the supreme cause of everything.]]

I should like to be able to explain myself as clearly and decisively about the other question, concerning the substantial forms. The first difficulty you indicated, Sir, is that our soul and our body are two really distinct substances; therefore, it seems that the one is not the substantial form of the other. I reply that, in my opinion, our body in itself or the *cadaver*, setting the soul apart, can be called a substance only in an improper sense, just as in the case of a machine or a pile of stones, which are only beings by aggregation; for regular or irregular arrangement does not constitute substantial unity. Besides, the last Lateran council declares that the soul is truly the substantial form of our body.

As for the second difficulty,[7] I grant that the substantial form of the body is indivisible, and it seems to me that this is also Saint Thomas's opinion; and I further grant that every substantial form or, indeed, every substance is indestructible and even ingenerable—which was also the opinion of Albertus Magnus and, among the ancients, the opinion of the author of the book *De diaeta*, attributed to Hippocrates.[8] Therefore, they can only come into being by an act

of creation. And I am greatly inclined to believe that all reproduction among animals deprived of reason, reproduction which does not deserve a new act of creation, is only the transformation of another animal already living but sometimes imperceptible, like the changes that happen to a silkworm and other similar animals; nature is accustomed to reveal its secrets in some cases and hide them in others. Thus the souls of brutes would have all been created from the beginning of the world, in accordance with the fruitfulness in seed mentioned in Genesis. But the rational soul is created only at the time of the formation of its body, being entirely different from the other souls we know, because it is capable of reflection and it imitates the divine nature on a small scale.

Third,[9] I think that a block of marble is, perhaps, only like a pile of stones, and thus cannot pass as a single substance, but as an assemblage of many. Suppose that there were two stones, for example, the diamond of the Great Duke and that of the Great Mogul. One could impose the same collective name for the two, and one could say that they constitute a pair of diamonds, although they are far apart from one another; but one would not say that these two diamonds constitute a substance. More and less do not make a difference here. Even if they were brought nearer together and made to touch, they would not be substantially united to any greater extent. And if, after they had touched, one joined to them another body capable of preventing their separation—for example, if they had been set in the same ring—all this would make only what is called an *unum per accidens*.[10] For it is as by accident that they are required to perform the same motion. Therefore, I hold that a block of marble is not a complete single substance, any more than the water in a pond together with all the fish it contains would be, even if all the water and all the fish were frozen, or any more than a flock of sheep would be, even if these sheep were tied together so that they could only walk in step and so that one could not be touched without all the others

7. Arnauld asked: If the substantial form of the body is divisible, "we would not gain anything with respect to the unity of body [literally: to body being a *unum per se*]" (*Philosophische Schriften* II, 66); if it is indivisible, "it seems that body would be as indestructible as our soul" (ibid.).

8. The reference to St. Thomas might be to *Summa Theologica* I, q. 76, art. 8, but Leibniz is probably not representing Aquinas accurately. See below, the "New System of Nature," for a different set of attributions. The reference to Albertus Magnus is too vague to be specified. On Hippocrates, see *The Regimen* I.4. Although the text is part of the Hippocratic corpus, it is probably not by Hippocrates himself. See "Letter to Samuel Masson," in which Leibniz's claims about this text are modified.

9. Arnauld asked: "What happens to this substantial form [of a block of marble] when it stops being one, because someone has broken it in two?" (*Philosophische Schriften* II, 66).

10. Accidental unity.

crying out. There is as much difference between a substance and such a being as there is between a man and a community, such as a people, an army, a society, or a college; these are moral beings, beings in which there is something imaginary and dependent on the fabrication [*fiction*] of our mind. A substantial unity requires a thoroughly indivisible and naturally indestructible being, since its notion includes everything that will happen to it, something which can be found neither in shape nor in motion (both of which involve something imaginary, as I could demonstrate), but which can be found in a soul or substantial form, on the model of what is called *me*. These are the only thoroughly real beings, as was recognized by the ancients, and above all, by Plato, who clearly showed that matter alone is not sufficient to form a substance. Now, the aforementioned I, or that which corresponds to it in each individual substance, can neither be made nor destroyed by the bringing together or separation of parts, which is a thing entirely external to what constitutes a substance. I cannot say precisely whether there are true corporeal substances other than those that are animated, but souls at least serve to give us some knowledge of others by analogy.

All this can contribute to clearing up the fourth difficulty.[11] For without bothering with what the Scholastics have called the form of corporeity [*formam corporeitatis*], I assign substantial forms to all corporeal substances that are more than mechanically united. But fifth,[12] if I am asked in particular what I say about the sun, the earthly globe, the moon, trees, and other similar bodies, and even about beasts, I cannot be absolutely certain whether they are animated, or even whether they are substances, or, indeed, whether they are simply machines or aggregates of several substances. But at least I can say that if

there are no corporeal substances such as I claim, it follows that bodies would only be true phenomena, like the rainbow. For the continuum is not merely divisible to infinity, but every part of matter is actually divided into other parts as different among themselves as the two aforementioned diamonds. And since we can always go on in this way, we would never reach anything about which we could say, here is truly a being, unless we found animated machines whose soul or substantial form produced a substantial unity independent of the external union arising from contact. And if there were none, it then follows that, with the exception of man, there is nothing substantial in the visible world.

Sixth,[13] since the notion of individual substance in general, which I have given, is as clear as that of truth, the notion of corporeal substance will also be clear and, consequently, so will that of substantial form. But even if this were not so, we are required to admit many things whose knowledge is not sufficiently clear and distinct. I hold that the notion of extension is much less clear and distinct—witness the strange difficulties of the composition of the continuum. And it can indeed be said that *because of the actual subdivision of parts, there is no definite and precise shape in bodies*. As a result, *bodies would doubtless be only imaginary and apparent, if there were only matter and its modifications*. However, it is useless to mention the unity, notion, or substantial form of bodies when we are concerned with explaining the particular phenomena of nature, just as it is useless for the geometers to examine the difficulties concerning the composition of the continuum when they are working on resolving some problem. These things are still important and worthy of consideration in their place. All the phenomena of bodies can be explained mechanically, that is, by the corpuscular philosophy, following certain principles of mechanics posited without troubling oneself over whether there are souls or not. But in the final analysis of the principles of physics and even of mechanics, we find that

---

11. Arnauld asked: "Do you give to extension a general substantial form, such as certain Scholastics admitted when they called it *forma corporeitatis*, or do you want there to be as many different substantial forms as there are different bodies, and different species when these are bodies of different species?" (*Philosophische Schriften* II, 66).
12. Arnauld asked: "Where do you situate the unity we attribute to the earth, the sun, the moon . . . ?" (*Philosophische Schriften* II, 66).

13. Arnauld asked: "Finally, it will be said that it is not worthy of a philosopher to admit entities of which we have no clear and distinct idea" (*Philosophische Schriften* II, 67).

these principles cannot be explained by the modifications of extension alone, and that the nature of force already requires something else.

Finally, in the seventh place[14] I remember that Cordemoy, in his treatise, *On the Distinction between Body and Soul*, thought he needed to admit atoms, or extended indivisible bodies, to save substantial unity in bodies, so as to find something fixed to constitute a simple being. But you rightly concluded that I am not of that opinion. It appears that Cordemoy recognized something of the truth, but he did not yet see what the true notion of substance consists in; but this is the key to the most important knowledge. The atom which contains only a shaped mass of infinite hardness (which I hold not to be in conformity with divine wisdom, any more than the void is) cannot contain in itself all its past and future states, and even less all those of the entire universe.

## To Arnauld (April 30, 1687)

Since your letters are of considerable benefit to me and the marks of your genuine liberality, I have no right to ask for them, and consequently your reply is never too late. However agreeable and useful they may be to me, I take into consideration what you owe to the public good, and thus I suppress my wishes. Your reflections are always instructive for me and I will take the liberty to go through them in order.

I do not think that there is any difficulty in my saying that *the soul expresses more distinctly, other things being equal, that which belongs to its body*, since it expresses the whole universe in a certain sense, in particular in accordance with the relation other bodies have to its own, since it cannot express all things equally well; otherwise there would be no differences among souls. But it does not follow from this that it must perceive perfectly everything occurring in the parts of its body, since there are degrees of relation between these very parts, parts which are

not all expressed equally, any more than external things are. The greater distance of external bodies is compensated for by the smallness, or some other hindrance, with respect to the internal parts—Thales saw the stars, though he did not see the ditch at his feet.

For us the nerves are more sensitive than the other parts of our bodies, and perhaps it is only through them that we perceive the others. This apparently happens because the motions of the nerves or of the fluids in them imitate the impressions better and confuse them less, and the most distinct expressions in the soul correspond to the most distinct impressions of the body. This is not because the nerves act on the soul, or the other bodies on the nerves, metaphysically speaking, but because the former represent the state of the latter through a spontaneous relation [*spontanea relatione*]. We must also take into account that too many things take place in our bodies for us to be able to perceive them all individually. What we sense is only a certain resultant to which we are habituated, and we are not able to distinguish the things that enter into the resultant because of their multitude, just as when one hears the noise of the sea from afar, one does not discern what each wave does, even though each wave has an effect on our ears. But when a striking change happens in our body, we soon notice it and notice it more clearly than external changes which are not accompanied by a notable change in our organs.

*I do not say that the soul knows the pricking before it has the sensation of pain*, except insofar as it knows or expresses confusedly all things in accordance with my previously established principles. But this expression which the soul has of the future in advance, although obscure and confused, is the true cause of what will happen to it and of the clearer perception it will have afterwards, when the obscurity is lifted, since the future state is a result of the preceding one.

I said that God created the universe in such a way that the soul and the body, each acting according to its laws, agree in their phenomena. You judge that *this is in accord with the hypothesis of occasional causes*. If this were so, I would not be sorry, and I am always glad to find others who hold my positions.

14. Arnauld wrote: "There are Cartesians who, in order to find unity in bodies, have denied that matter is divisible to infinity, and [have asserted] that one must admit indivisible atoms. But I do not think that you share their opinion" (*Philosophische Schriften* II, 67).

But I have only a glimpse of your reason for thinking this; you suppose that I wouldn't say that a body can move by itself, and thus, since the soul is not the real cause of the motion of the arm, and neither is the body, the cause must therefore be God. But I am of another opinion. I hold that what is real in the state called motion proceeds as much from the corporeal substance as thought and will proceed from the mind. Everything happens to each substance as a consequence of the first state God gave to it in creating it, and, extraordinary concourse apart, his ordinary concourse consists only in the conservation of the same substance, in conformity with its preceding state and the changes it brings about. Yet it is rightly said that one body pushes another, that is, that it never happens that a body begins to have a certain tendency unless another body touching it has a proportionate loss, in accordance with the unvarying laws that we observe in phenomena. And in fact, since motions are real phenomena rather than beings, a motion considered as a phenomenon is the immediate result or effect of another phenomenon in my mind, and similarly in the minds of others, but the state of a substance is not the immediate result of the state of another particular substance.

I do not dare assert that plants have no soul, life, or substantial form, for although a part of a tree planted or grafted can produce a tree of the same kind, it is possible that there is a seminal part in it that already contains a new vegetative thing, as perhaps there are already some living animals, though extremely small, in the seeds of animals, which can be transformed within a similar animal. Therefore, I don't yet dare assert that only animals are living and endowed with a substantial form. Perhaps there is an infinity of degrees in the forms of corporeal substances.

You say that those who maintain the hypothesis of occasional causes, saying that *my will is the occasional cause and God is the real cause of the motion of my arm, do not claim that God does this in time by means of a new volition he has each time I wish to raise my arm, but through the unique act of eternal will, by which he willed to do everything he foresaw it would be necessary for him to do.* To this I reply that one could say, for the same reason, that even miracles are not accomplished by a new volition of God, since they are in conformity with his general plan, and I already remarked that each volition of God involves all the others, but in a certain order of priority. In fact, if I properly understand the views of the authors of occasional causes, they introduce a miracle which is no less miraculous for being continual. For it seems to me that the notion of miracle does not consist in rarity. One might say that in this matter God acts only according to a general rule, and consequently he acts without miracle. But I do not grant that consequence, and I believe that God can make general rules for himself even with respect to miracles. For example, if God had resolved to give his grace immediately or to perform some other action of this nature every time a certain condition was satisfied, this action, though ordinary, would nevertheless still be a miracle. I admit that the authors of occasional causes might give another definition of the term, but, according to common usage, it seems that a miracle differs internally and substantively from the performance of an ordinary action, and not by the external accident of frequent repetition; properly speaking, God performs a miracle when he does something that surpasses the forces he has given to creatures and conserves in them. [[For example, if God made a body, put into circular motion by means of a sling, freely to go in a circular path when released from the sling, without it being pushed or retained by anything whatever, that would be a miracle, for according to the laws of nature, it should continue in a straight line along a tangent; and if God decided that this should always happen, he would be performing natural miracles, since this motion could not be explained by anything simpler.]] Thus, in the same way, we must say, in accordance with the received view, that if continuing the motion exceeds the force of bodies, then the continuation of the motion is a true miracle. But I believe that corporeal substance has the ability [*force*] to continue its changes in accordance with the laws God put into its nature and conserves there. To make myself better understood, I believe that the actions of minds change nothing at all in the nature of bodies, nor do bodies change anything in the nature of minds, and even that God changes nothing on their occasion, except when he performs a miracle.

In my opinion, things are so interconnected that the mind never wills anything efficaciously except when the body is ready to accomplish it in virtue of its own laws and forces; [[but, according to the authors of occasional causes, God changes the laws of bodies on the occasion of the action of the soul, and vice versa. That is the essential difference between our opinions.]] Thus, on my view, we should not worry about how the soul can give some motion or some new determination to animal spirits, since, in fact, it never gives them any at all, insofar as there is no proportion between mind and body, and there is nothing that can determine what degree of speed a mind can give a body, nor even what degree of speed God would want to give to a body on the occasion of the action of the mind in accordance with a certain law. The same difficulty found in the hypothesis of a real influence of soul on body, and *vice versa*, is also found in the hypothesis of occasional causes, insofar as we can see no connection nor can we see a foundation for any rule. And if someone were to say, as, it seems, Descartes wishes to say, that the soul, or God on its occasion, changes only the direction or determination of a motion and not the force which is in bodies (since it does not seem probable to him that at every moment God would violate the general law of nature that the same force must persist, on the occasion of every volition minds have), I would reply that it would still be quite difficult to explain what connection there can be between the thoughts of the soul and the paths or angles of the direction of bodies. Furthermore, there is in nature yet another general law which Descartes did not perceive, a law no less important, namely, that the same sum of determination or direction must always persist. For I find that if one were to draw any straight line, for example, from east to west through a given point, and if one were to calculate all the directions of all the bodies in the world insofar as they advance or recede in lines parallel to this line, the difference between the sum of all the easterly directions and of all the westerly directions would always be the same. This holds both for certain particular bodies, assuming that at present they have interactions only among themselves, and for the whole universe, in which the difference is always zero, since everything is perfectly balanced, and easterly and westerly directions are perfectly equal in the universe. If God does something in violation of this rule, it is a miracle.[15]

It is therefore infinitely more reasonable and more worthy of God to suppose that, from the beginning, he created the machinery of the world in such a way that, without at every moment violating the two great laws of nature, namely, those of force and direction, but rather, by following them exactly (except in the case of miracles), it happens that the springs in bodies are ready to act of themselves, as they should, at precisely the moment the soul has a suitable volition or thought; the soul, in turn, has this volition or thought only in conformity with the preceding states of the body. Thus the union of the soul with the machinery of the body and with the parts entering into it, and the action of the one on the other, consist only in this concomitance that marks the admirable wisdom of the creator far better than any other hypothesis. It cannot be denied that this hypothesis is at least possible and that God is a sufficiently great craftsman to be able to execute it; hence, we can easily judge that this hypothesis is the most probable, being the simplest, the most beautiful, and most intelligible, at once avoiding all difficulties—to say nothing of criminal actions, in which it seems more reasonable to have God concur only through the conservation of created forces.

To use a comparison I will say that this concomitance I maintain is like several different bands of musicians or choirs separately playing their parts, and placed in such a way that they do not see and do not even hear each other, though they nevertheless can agree perfectly, each following his own notes, so that someone hearing all of them would find a marvelous harmony there, one more surprising than if there were a connection among them. It is quite possible that someone next to one of two such choirs could judge from the one what the other was doing (particularly if we supposed that he could hear his choir without seeing it and see the other without hearing

---

15. The rule in question here is what is now called the conservation of momentum, mass times velocity, which, Leibniz claims here, holds both for the universe as a whole and for any closed system within the universe.

it), he would, as a result, form such a habit that, with the help of his imagination, he would no longer think of the choir where he was, but of the other, and he would mistake his own choir for an echo of the other, attributing to his own only certain interludes in which some rules of composition [*symphonie*], by which he distinguished the other, were not satisfied. Or, attributing to his own choir a certain beating of the tempo, performed on his side according to certain plans, he might think, because of the agreement on this he finds as the melody continues, that the beating of the tempo is being imitated by the others, since he doesn't know that those on the other side are also acting in accordance with their own plans, though in agreement with his.

Yet I do not disapprove at all of the assertion that minds are in some way the occasional causes, and even the real causes, of the movements of bodies. For, with respect to divine resolutions, what God foresaw and pre-established with regard to minds was the occasion for his regulating bodies from the beginning so that they might fit together in accordance with the laws and forces he will give them. And since the state of the one is an unfailing, though frequently contingent, and even free, consequence of the state of the other, we can say that God brings about that there is a real connection by virtue of this general notion of substances, which entails that substances express one another perfectly. This connection is not, however, immediate, since it is founded only upon what God has done in creating substances.

If my opinion that substance requires a true unity were founded only on a definition I had formulated in opposition to common usage, *then the dispute would be only one of words*.[16] But besides the fact that most philosophers have taken the term in almost the same fashion, distinguishing between a unity in itself and an accidental unity, between substantial and accidental form, and between perfect and imperfect, natural and artificial mixtures, I take things to a much

higher level, and setting aside the question of terminology, *I believe that where there are only beings by aggregation, there aren't any real beings.* For every being by aggregation presupposes beings endowed with real unity, because every being derives its reality only from the reality of those beings of which it is composed, so that it will not have any reality at all if each being of which it is composed is itself a being by aggregation, a being for which we must still seek further grounds for its reality, grounds which can never be found in this way, if we must always continue to seek for them. I agree, Sir, that there are only machines (that are often animated) in all of corporeal nature, but I do not agree *that there are only aggregates of substances*; and if there are aggregates of substances, there must also be true substances from which all the aggregates result.[17] We must, then, necessarily come down either to mathematical points, of which some authors constitute extension, or to the atoms of Epicurus and Cordemoy (which are things you reject along with me), or else we must admit that we do not find any reality in bodies; or finally, we must recognize some substances that have a true unity. I have already said in another letter that the composite made up of the diamonds of the Grand Duke and of the Great Mogul can be called a pair of diamonds, but this is only a being of reason. And when they are brought closer to one another, it would be a being of the imagination or perception, that is to say, a phenomenon. For contact, common motion, and participation in a common plan have no effect on substantial unity. It is true that there are sometimes more, and sometimes fewer, grounds for supposing that several things constitute a single thing, in proportion to the extent to which these things are connected. But this serves only to abbreviate our thoughts and to represent the phenomena.

It also seems that what constitutes the essence of a being by aggregation is only a mode [*manière d'être*] of the things of which it is composed. For example, what constitutes the essence of an army is only a mode of the men who compose it. This mode therefore presupposes a substance whose essence is not a mode

---

16. Arnauld had written that Leibniz's arguments "amount to saying that all bodies whose parts are mechanically united are not substances, but only machines or aggregates of many substances," and that "there is only a quibble over words here; for Saint Augustine feels no difficulties about recognizing that bodies have no true unity" (*Philosophische Schriften* II, 86).

17. The version Arnauld received concludes: ". . . of which all aggregates are made."

of a substance.[18] Every machine also presupposes some substance in the pieces of which it is made, and there is no plurality without true unities. To put it briefly, I hold this identical proposition, differentiated only by the emphasis, to be an axiom, namely, *that what is not truly* one *being is not truly one* being *either.* It has always been thought that one and being are mutually supporting. Being is one thing and beings are another; but the plural presupposes the singular, and where there is no being still less will there be several beings. What could be clearer? [[I therefore believed that I would be allowed to distinguish beings by aggregation from substances, since these beings have their unity in our mind only, a unity founded on the relations or modes [modes] of true substances. If a machine is one substance, a circle of men holding hands will also be one substance, and so will an army, and finally, so will every multitude of substances.]]

I do not say that there is nothing substantial or nothing but appearance in things that do not have a true unity, for I grant that they always have as much reality or substantiality as there is true unity in that which enters into their composition.

You object that it might be of the essence of body not to have a true unity. But it would then be of the essence of body to be a phenomenon, deprived of all reality, like an ordered dream, for phenomena themselves, like the rainbow or a pile of stones, would be completely imaginary if they were not composed of beings with a true unity.

You say that you do not see what leads me to admit these substantial forms, or rather, these corporeal substances endowed with a true unity; but that is because I conceive no reality without a true unity. On my view, the notion of singular substance involves consequences incompatible with a being by aggregation. I conceive properties in substance that cannot be explained by extension, shape, and motion, besides the fact that there is no exact and fixed shape in bodies due to the actual subdivision of the continuum to infinity, and the fact that motion involves something imaginary insofar as it is only a modification of extension and change of location, so that we cannot

determine which of the changing subjects it belongs to, unless we have recourse to the force which is the cause of motion and which is in corporeal substance. I confess that we do not need to mention these substances and qualities to explain particular phenomena, but for this we also do not need to examine God's concourse, the composition of the continuum, the plenum, and a thousand other things. I confess that we can explain the particularities of nature mechanically, but that can happen only after we recognize or presuppose the very principles of mechanics, principles which can only be established *a priori* by metaphysical reasonings. And even the difficulties concerning the composition of the continuum will never be resolved as long as extension is considered as constituting the substance of the bodies, and as long as we entangle ourselves in our own chimeras.

I also think that to want to limit true unity or substance almost exclusively to man is to be as shortsighted in metaphysics as were those in physics who wanted to confine the world in a sphere. And since there are as many true substances as there are expressions of the whole universe, and as many as there are replications of divine works, it is in conformity with the greatness and beauty of the works of God for him to produce as many substances as there can be in this universe, and as many as higher considerations allow, for these substances hardly get in one another's way. By assuming mere extension we destroy all this marvelous variety, since mass [*massa*] by itself (if it is possible to conceive it) is as far beneath a substance which is perceptive and representative of the whole universe, according to its point of view and according to the impressions (or rather the relations) its body receives mediately or immediately from all others, as a cadaver is beneath an animal, or rather, it is as far beneath a substance as a machine is beneath a man. It is also because of this that the features of the future are formed in advance, and that the features of the past are conserved forever in each thing, and that cause and effect give way to one another exactly up to the least detail of the least circumstance, even though every effect depends on an infinity of causes, and every cause has an infinity of effects; it would not be possible for this to happen if the essence of body consisted in a certain determinate shape, motion, or

18. In the draft Arnauld received, Leibniz wrote: "of another substance."

modification of extension. Thus, there is nothing of the kind in nature. Everything is strictly indefinite with respect to extension, and the extensions we attribute to bodies are merely phenomena and abstractions; this enables us to see how easily we fall into error when we do not reflect in this way, something so necessary for recognizing the true principles and for having a proper idea of the universe. [[And it seems to me that there is as much prejudice in refusing such a reasonable idea as there is in not recognizing the greatness of the world, the subdivision to infinity, and mechanical explanations in nature. It is as great an error to conceive of extension as a primitive notion without conceiving the true notion of substance or action as it was to be content considering substantial forms as a whole without entering into the details of the modifications of extension.]]

The multitude of souls (to which, in any case, I do not always attribute pleasure or pain) should not trouble us, any more than does the multitude of Gassendi's atoms, which are as indestructible as these souls. On the contrary, it is a perfection of nature to have many of them, a soul or animated substance being infinitely more perfect than an atom, which is without variety or subdivision, whereas every animated thing contains a world of diversity in a true unity. Now, experience favors this multitude of animated things. We find that there is a prodigious quantity of animals in a drop of water imbued with pepper;[19] and with one blow millions of them can be killed [[neither the frogs of the Egyptians nor the quails of the Israelites, of which you spoke, Sir, approach this number.]] Now, if these animals have souls, we would have to say of their souls what we can probably say of the animals themselves, namely, that they were already alive from the creation of the world, and that they will live to its end, and that since generation is apparently only a change consisting in growth, so death will only be a change consisting in diminution, which causes this animal to reenter the recesses of a world of minute creatures where perceptions are more limited, until the order comes, perhaps calling them to return to the stage. The ancients were

mistaken in introducing the transmigration of souls instead of the transformations of the same animal which always preserves the same soul; they put *metempsychoses pro metaschematismis*.[20] But minds are not subject to these revolutions [[or rather, the revolutions in bodies must serve the divine economy with respect to minds.]] God creates them when it is time and detaches them from the body [[[at least the coarse body]]] by death, since they must always keep their moral qualities and their memory, in order to be [[perpetual]] citizens of this universal, perfect republic, of which God is the monarch; this republic can never lose any of its members and its laws are superior to those of bodies. I confess that the body by itself, without the soul, has only a unity of aggregation, but that the reality inhering in it derives from the parts composing it, which retain their [[substantial]] unity [[through the countless living bodies included in them.]]

Nevertheless, although a soul can have a body made up of parts animated by other souls, the soul or form of the whole is not, as a consequence, composed of the souls or forms of its parts. It is not necessary for the two parts of an insect cut in half to remain animated, although there may be some movement in them. At very least, the soul of the whole insect will remain only on one side. And since, in the formation and growth of the insect, the soul was, from the beginning, in a certain part that was already living, after the destruction of the insect it will still remain in a certain part that is still alive, a part as small as is necessary for it to be protected from the action of someone tearing or destroying the body of that insect. Hence, we do not need to imagine, with the Jews, that there is a little bone of insurmountable hardness in which the soul takes refuge.

I agree that there are degrees of accidental unity,[21] that an ordered society has more unity than a confused mob, and that an organized body, or rather a machine,

---

19. Leeuwenhoek experimented with pepper water.

20. Change of souls in place of change of shape.
21. Arnauld stated that "although it is true that there is true unity only in intelligent natures, all of which can say I [*moi*], there are nevertheless various degrees in this improper unity suitable to the body" (*Philosophische Schriften* II, 88).

has more unity than a society; that is to say, it is more appropriate to conceive them as a single thing, because there are more relations among the constituents. But in the end, all these unities become realized only by thoughts and appearances; like colors and other phenomena, which, nevertheless, are called real. The tangibility of a heap of stones or a block of marble does not prove its substantial reality any more than the visibility of a rainbow proves its substantial reality; and since nothing is so solid that it does not have some degree of fluidity, perhaps this block of marble is only a heap of an infinite number of living bodies, or like a lake full of fish, even though these animals cannot ordinarily be distinguished by the eye except in partially decayed bodies. We can therefore say of these composites and similar things what Democritus said so well of them; namely, they depend for their being on opinion or custom.[22] And Plato held the same opinion about everything which is purely material. Our mind notices or conceives some true substances which have certain modes; these modes involve relations to other substances, so the mind takes the occasion to join them together in thought and to make one name account for all these things together. This is useful for reasoning, but we must not allow ourselves to be misled into making substances or true beings of them; this is suitable only for those who stop at appearances, or for those who make realities out of all abstractions of the mind, and who conceive number, time, place, motion, shape, [[and sensible qualities]] as so many separate beings. Instead I hold that philosophy cannot be better reestablished and reduced to something precise, than by recognizing only substances or complete beings endowed with a true unity, together with the different states that succeed one another; everything else is only phenomena, abstractions, or relations.

No regularity will ever be found which can make a true substance out of several beings by aggregation. For example, if parts fitting together in the same plan are more suitable for composing a true substance than those touching, then all the officers of the Dutch East India Company will make up a real substance, far better than a heap of stones. But what is a common plan other than a resemblance, or an order of actions and passions that our mind notices in different things? But if we prefer the unity of contact, we will find other difficulties. Perhaps solid bodies have nothing uniting their parts except the pressure of the surrounding bodies, and have no more union in themselves and in their substance than does a pile of sand without lime.[23] Why should several rings, interlaced so as to make a chain, compose a genuine substance any more than if they had openings so that they could be separated? It may be that no part of the chain touches another, and even that none encloses another, and that, nevertheless, they are so interlaced that, unless they are approached in a certain way, they cannot be separated, as in the enclosed figure.

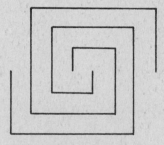

Are we to say, in this case, that the substance composed of these things is, as it were, in abeyance and dependent on the future skill of whoever may wish to disentangle them? These are all fictions of the mind, and as long as we do not discern what a complete being, or rather a substance, really is, we will never have something at which we can stop; [[and this is the only way of establishing solid and real principles.]] In conclusion, nothing should be posited without good grounds. Therefore, those who imagine beings and substances without genuine unity are left to prove that there is more reality than what we have just said,[24] and I am waiting for a notion of substance or of being which can include all these things—

22. See Diogenes Laertius, *Lives of the Eminent Philosophers,* IX 45.
23. I.e., shifting sands with nothing to bind them.
24. Writing to Arnauld, Leibniz continued: "and to show what it consists in."

after which mock suns and perhaps even dreams will someday lay claim to reality, unless very precise limits are set for this *droit de bourgeoisie*[25] that is to be granted to beings formed by aggregation.

I have treated these matters so that you may be able to judge not only my opinions, but also, the arguments which forced me to adopt them. I submit them to your judgment, whose fairness and exactness I know. I also send something which you could have found in the *Nouvelles de la république des lettres*, to serve as a response to the Abbé Catelan.[26] I consider

him an able man, given what you say of him; but what he has written against Huygens and against me makes it clear that he goes a little too fast. We will see what use he will make of this now.

I am delighted to learn of the good state of your health, and I hope for its continuation with all the zeal and all the passion which makes me what I am, etc.

P.S. I reserve for another time some other matters you have touched upon in your letter.

---

25. A kind of inferior citizenship.
26. The paper in question is probably the "Réplique de M. L. à M. l'Abbé D. C. . . . ," published in the *Nouvelles* in February

1687. It was part of the so-called *vis-viva* controversy. See the "Discourse on Metaphysics," sec. 18.

# G. W. Leibniz, *Primary Truths* (1689)[1]

The primary truths are those which assert the same thing of itself or deny the opposite of its opposite. For example, "A is A," "A is not not-A," or "if it is true that A is B, then it is false that A is not B or that A is not-B." Also "every thing is as it is," "every thing is similar or equal to itself," "nothing is greater or less than itself," and others of this sort. Although they themselves may have their degrees of priority, nonetheless they can all be included under the name "identities."

Moreover, all remaining truths are reduced to primary truths with the help of definitions, that is, through the resolution of notions; in this consists *a priori* proof, proof independent of experience. As an example, I shall give this proposition from among the axioms accepted equally by mathematicians and all others alike: "the whole is greater than its part," or "the part is less than the whole," something easily demonstrated from the definition of "less" or "greater," with the addition of the primitive axiom, that is, the axiom of identity. For the *less* is that which is equal to a part of the other (the *greater*), a definition easy to understand and in agreement with the practice of the human race, when people compare things with one another and, taking away from the greater something equal to the lesser, they find something that remains. Hence there is an argument of this sort: the part is equal to a part of the whole (it is, of course, equal to itself through the axiom of identity, that each and every thing is equal to itself), and what is equal to a part of a whole is less than the whole (from the definition of "less"). Therefore, the part is less than the whole.

Therefore, the predicate or consequent is always in the subject or antecedent, and the nature of truth in general or the connection between the terms of a statement, consists in this very thing, as Aristotle also observed. The connection and inclusion of the predicate in the subject is explicit in identities, but in all other propositions it is implicit and must be shown through the analysis of notions; *a priori* demonstration rests on this.

Moreover, this is true for every affirmative truth, universal or particular, necessary or contingent, and in both an intrinsic and extrinsic denomination. And here lies hidden a wonderful secret, a secret that contains the nature of contingency, that is, the essential difference between necessary and contingent truths, a secret that eliminates the difficulty concerning the fatal necessity of even those things that are free.

Many things of great importance follow from these considerations, considerations insufficiently attended

1. Translated from the Latin by R. Ariew and D. Garber in G. W. Leibniz, *Philosophical Essays* (Indianapolis: Hackett Publishing Company, 1989). Editors' title.

to because of their obviousness. For the received axiom that *nothing is without reason,* or *there is no effect without a cause,* directly follows from these considerations; otherwise there would be a truth which could not be proved *a priori,* that is, a truth which could not be resolved into identities, contrary to the nature of truth, which is always an explicit or implicit identity. It also follows that, when in the givens everything on the one side is the same as it is on the other side, then everything will be the same in the unknowns, that is, in the consequents. This is because no reason can be given for any difference, a reason which certainly must derive from the givens. And a corollary of this, or better, an example, is Archimedes's postulate at the beginning of the book on statics, that, given equal weights on both sides of a balance with equal arms, everything is in equilibrium.[2] And hence *there is even a reason for eternal things.* If we imagine that the world has been from eternity, and we imagine only little balls in it, then we would have to explain why there are little balls rather than cubes.

From these considerations it also follows that, *in nature, there cannot be two individual things that differ in number alone.* For it certainly must be possible to explain why they are different, and that explanation must derive from some difference they contain. And so what St. Thomas recognized concerning separated intelligences, which, he said, never differ by number alone,[3] must also be said of other things, for never do we find two eggs or two leaves or two blades of grass in a garden that are perfectly similar. And thus, perfect similarity is found only in incomplete and abstract notions, where things are considered [*in rationes veniunt*] only in a certain respect, but not in every way, as, for example, when we consider shapes alone, and neglect the matter that has shape. And so it is justifiable to consider two similar triangles in geometry, even though two perfectly similar material triangles are nowhere found. And although gold and other metals, also salts and many liquids might be taken to

be homogeneous, this can only be admitted with regard to the senses, and it is not true that they are, in all rigor.

It also follows that *there are no purely extrinsic denominations,* denominations which have absolutely no foundation in the very thing denominated. For it is necessary that the notion of the subject denominated contain the notion of the predicate. And consequently, whenever the denomination of a thing is changed, there must be a variation in the thing itself.

The complete or perfect notion of an individual substance contains all of its predicates, past, present, and future. For certainly it is now true that a future predicate will be, and so it is contained in the notion of a thing. And thus everything that will happen to Peter or Judas, both necessary and free, is contained in the perfect individual notion of Peter or Judas, considered in the realm of possibility by withdrawing the mind from the divine decree for creating him, and is seen there by God. And from this it is obvious that God chose from an infinite number of possible individuals those he thought most in accord with the supreme and hidden ends of his wisdom. Properly speaking, he did not decide that Peter sin or that Judas be damned, but only that Peter who would sin with certainty, though not with necessity, but freely, and Judas who would suffer damnation would attain existence rather than other possible things; that is, he decreed that the possible notion become actual. And, although the future salvation of Peter is also contained in his eternal possible notion, it is, however, not without the concurrence of grace, for in the same perfect notion of that possible Peter, even the aid of divine grace to be given him is found, under the notion of possibility.

*Every individual substance contains in its perfect notion the entire universe* and everything that exists in it, past, present, and future. For there is no thing on which one cannot impose some true denomination from another thing, at very least a denomination of comparison and relation. Moreover, there is no purely extrinsic denomination. I have shown the same thing in many other ways, all in harmony with one another.

Indeed, *all individual created substances are different expressions of the same universe* and different ex-

---

2. See Archimedes, *On the Equilibrium of Planes,* Book I, postulate 1, in Heath, *The Works of Archimedes* (Cambridge: Cambridge University Press, 1897 and 1912), p. 189.
3. See St. Thomas, *Summa Theologiae* I, q. 50, art. 4.

pressions of the same universal cause, namely God. But the expressions vary in perfection, just as different representations or drawings of the same town from different points of view do.

Every individual created substance exerts physical action and passion on all the others. From a change made in one, some corresponding change follows in all the others, since the denomination[4] is changed. And this is in agreement with our experience of nature. For, in a vessel filled with a liquid (and the whole universe is just such a vessel) motion made in the middle is propagated to the edges, although it is rendered more and more insensible, the more it recedes from its origin.

Strictly speaking, one can say that *no created substance exerts a metaphysical action or influx on any other thing*. For, not to mention the fact that one cannot explain how something can pass from one thing into the substance of another, we have already shown that from the notion of each and every thing follows all of its future states. What we call causes are only concurrent requisites, in metaphysical rigor. This is also illustrated by our experience of nature. For bodies really rebound from others through the force of their own elasticity, and not through the force of other things, even if another body is required in order for the elasticity (which arises from something intrinsic to the body itself) to be able to act.

Also, *assuming the distinction between soul and body, from this we can explain their union* without the common hypothesis of an influx, which is unintelligible, and without the hypothesis of an occasional cause, which appeals to a *Deus ex machina*. For God from the beginning constituted both the soul and the body with such wisdom and such workmanship that, from the first constitution or notion of a thing, everything that happens through itself [*per se*] in the one corresponds perfectly to everything that happens in the other, just as if something passed from one to the other. This is what I call the hypothesis of concomitance. This hypothesis is true in all substances in the whole universe but cannot be sensed in all of them, unlike the case of the soul and the body.

*There is no vacuum.* For the different parts of empty

space would then be perfectly similar and mutually congruent and could not be distinguished from one another. And so they would differ in number alone, which is absurd. One can also prove that time is not a thing in the same way as we did for space.[5]

*There is no atom*, indeed, there is no body so small that it is not actually subdivided. Because of that, while it is acted upon by everything else in the whole universe and receives some effect from everything (an effect which must cause change in a body), it also preserves all past impressions and contains, before they happen, all future impressions. And if anyone were to say that that effect is contained in the motions impressed on the atom, which receives the effect as a whole without being divided, one can respond that not only must there be effects produced in an atom from all the impressions of the universe, but also, in turn, the state of the whole universe must be inferred from the atom, from the effect, the cause. But since the same motion can come about through different impressions, through no regress can one infer the impressions by means of which it [i.e., the atom] had come to its present state, from the shape and motion of an atom alone—not to mention the fact that one cannot explain why bodies of a certain smallness cannot be divided further.

From this it follows that *every particle of the universe contains a world of an infinity of creatures.* However, the continuum is not divided into points, nor is it divided in all possible ways—not into points, since points are not parts but boundaries, and not in all possible ways, since not all creatures are in a given thing, but there is only a certain progression of them *ad infinitum*, just as one who assumes a straight line and any part derived by bisection sets up divisions different from someone who trisects it.

*There is no determinate shape in actual things*, for none can be appropriate for an infinite number of impressions. And so neither a circle, nor an ellipse,

---

4. Originally Leibniz wrote "extrinsic denomination."

5. The following passage was deleted here: "*There is no corporeal substance in which there is nothing but extension or size, shape, and their variations*, for in this way two substances perfectly similar to one another could exist, which would be absurd. From this it follows that there is something in corporeal substances analogous to the soul which they [i.e., the Scholastics] call form."

nor any other line we can define exists except in the intellect, nor do lines exist before they are drawn, nor parts before they are separated off.[6]

Extension and motion, as well as bodies themselves (insofar as only motion and extension are placed in bodies) are not substances, but true phenomena, like rainbows and parhelia. For there are no shapes in things, and if we consider their extension alone, then bodies are not substances, but many substances.

Something lacking extension is required for the substance of bodies; otherwise there would be no source [*principium*] for the reality of phenomena or for true unity. There is always a plurality of bodies, and never one, and therefore, in reality, there is not even a plurality. Cordemoy proved atoms using a similar argument.[7] But since atoms are excluded, what remains is something lacking extension, analogous to the soul, which they once called form or species.

*Corporeal substance can neither arise nor perish except through creation or annihilation.* For when corporeal substance once endures, it will always endure, since there is no reason for any difference, and the dissolution of parts of a body has nothing in common with its destruction. Therefore, *animate things neither arise nor perish, but are only transformed.*

6. Leibniz deleted the following here: "Space, time, extension, and motion are not things, but modes of contemplating things that have a foundation."

7. See Cordemoy, *Le discernement du corps et de l'ame*, premier discours, in Cordemoy, *Oeuvres philosophiques*, ed. P. Clair and F. Girbal (Paris: PUF, 1968).

# G. W. Leibniz, A New System of the Nature and Communication of Substances, and of the Union of the Soul and Body (1695)[1]

A few years have already passed since I conceived this system and communicated with some learned men about it, especially with one of the greatest theologians and philosophers of our time,[2] who had learned about some of my opinions through a person of the highest nobility, and had found them extremely paradoxical. But having received my explanations, he changed his attitude in the most generous and edifying way possible; and, having approved some of my propositions, he withdrew his censure regarding the others, with which he still disagreed. Since that time I have continued my meditations, as circumstances allow, so as to give the public only well-examined opinions; I have also tried to satisfy objections raised against my essays on dynamics, which are connected with this system.[3] Finally, since some important persons have desired to see my opinions further clarified, I have risked publishing these meditations, even though they are not at all popular, nor can they be appreciated by all sorts of minds. I have decided upon this mainly to profit from the judgments of persons enlightened in these matters, since it would be too troublesome to seek out and call individually upon all those who would be disposed to give me instruction—which I shall always be glad to receive, provided that it contains the love of truth, rather than a passion for preconceived opinions.

Although I am someone who has done much work on mathematics, I have continued to meditate on philosophy since my youth, for it always seemed to me that one can establish something solid there through clear demonstrations. I had penetrated far into the territory of the Scholastics, when mathematics and the modern authors made me withdraw from it, while I was still young. I was charmed by their beautiful ways of explaining nature mechanically, and I rightly despised the method of those who use only forms or faculties, from which one can learn nothing. But

1. Translated from the French by R. Ariew and D. Garber in G. W. Leibniz, *Philosophical Essays* (Indianapolis: Hackett Publishing Company, 1989). Leibniz published the "New System of Nature" anonymously in 1695, in the *Journal des Sçavants*. It was the first public statement of his philosophy, a particularly interesting statement because of the autobiographical or historical style adopted by Leibniz. The publication of the "New System of Nature" stimulated much discussion, with Foucher, de Beauval, Bayle, and others publishing criticisms of it, and Leibniz answering them. Leibniz's manuscript copy contains some material thought to be later additions that does not appear in the published version. These are given in the double-bracketed passages, when possible, and otherwise in the notes.

2. Leibniz indicates in his copy that he is referring to Arnauld.

3. See the "Preliminary Specimen to the Dynamics" and the "Specimen of Dynamics" in Leibniz, *Philosophical Essays*.

since then, having attempted to examine the very principles of mechanics in order to explain the laws of nature we learn from experience, I perceived that considering *extended mass* alone was not sufficient, and that it was necessary, in addition, to make use of the notion of *force*, which is very intelligible, despite the fact that it belongs in the domain of metaphysics. It also seemed to me that although the opinion of those who transform or degrade animals into pure machines may be possible, it is improbable, and even contrary to the order of things.

In the beginning, when I had freed myself from the yoke of Aristotle, I accepted the void and atoms, for they best satisfy the imagination. But on recovering from that, after much reflection, I perceived that it is impossible to find the *principles of a true unity* in matter alone, or in what is only passive, since everything in it is only a collection or aggregation of parts to infinity. Now, a multitude can derive its reality only from *true unities*, which have some other origin and are considerably different from [[mathematical]] points [[which are only the extremities and modifications of extension,]] which all agree cannot make up the *continuum*. Therefore, in order to find these *real entities* I was forced to have recourse to a formal atom, since a material thing cannot be both material and, at the same time, perfectly indivisible, that is, endowed with a true unity.[4] Hence, it was necessary to restore, and, as it were, to rehabilitate the *substantial forms* which are in such disrepute today, but in a way that would render them intelligible, and separate the use one should make of them from the abuse that has been made of them. I found then that their nature consists in force, and that from this there follows something analogous to sensation and appetite, so that we must conceive of them on the model of the notion we have of *souls*. But just as soul must not be used to explain the particular details of the economy of the animal's body, I judged that we must not use

these forms to explain the particular problems of nature, even though they are necessary to establish the true general principles. Aristotle calls them *first entelechies*; I call them, perhaps more intelligibly, *primitive forces*, which contain not only act or the completion of possibility, but also an original *activity*.

I saw that these forms and souls must be indivisible, as our mind is; I remembered that this was Saint Thomas's view on the souls of animals.[5] But this truth revived the great difficulties about the origin and duration of souls and forms. For, since every [[*simple*]] *substance* which has a true unity can begin and end only by miracle, it follows that they can begin only by creation and end only by annihilation. Thus I was forced to recognize that, except for the souls that God wishes to create expressly, the forms constitutive of substances must have been created together with the world, and must always subsist. Moreover, certain Scholastics, like Albertus Magnus and John Bacon,[6] glimpsed a part of the truth about the origin of these forms. This should not appear extraordinary, since we ascribe to forms only duration, which the Gassendists grant their atoms.

I judged, however, that we must not indiscriminately confuse minds or rational souls [[with other forms or souls]], for they are of a higher order, and have incomparably greater perfection than the forms thrust into matter [[(which, in my view, are found everywhere)]], minds being like little gods in comparison with them, made in the image of God, and having in them some ray of the light of divinity. That is why God governs minds as a prince governs his subjects, and even as a father cares for his children, whereas he disposes of other substances as an engineer handles

---

4. A later version read as follows: "Therefore, in order to find these real unities, I was forced to have recourse to a *real and animated point*, so to speak, or to an atom of substance which must include something of form or activity to make a complete being."

5. Leibniz seems to have in mind the *Summa Theologiae* I, q. 76, art. 8, in which St. Thomas states that the souls of animals are "not able to be divided accidentally, that is, by a quantitative division." But it would not be accurate to attribute the immortality of animal souls to St. Thomas. See, e.g., *Summa Contra Gentiles* II, chap. 82: That the souls of brute animals are not immortal.

6. Albertus Magnus, Bishop of Ratisbon, and John Bacon of Baconthorpe were, respectively, thirteenth- and fourteenth-century Scholastics. Leibniz's statement is too vague to enable one to fix a reference to precise passages of which he might be thinking.

his machines. Thus minds have particular laws, which place them above the upheavals [revolutions] in matter, [[through the very order which God has put in them]]; and we can say that everything else is made only for them, and that these tumultuous motions themselves are adjusted for the happiness of the good and the punishment of the wicked.

However, returning to ordinary forms, or to material souls,[7] the duration that we must attribute to them, in place of the duration that had been attributed to atoms, might make us suspect that they pass from body to body—which would be *metempsychosis*— somewhat as some philosophers have believed in the transmission of motion and species. But this fancy is far removed from the nature of things. There is no such passage; this is where the transformations of Swammerdam, Malpighi, and Leeuwenhoek, the best observers of our time, have come to my aid, and have made it easier for me to admit that animals and all other organized substances have no beginning, although we think they do, and that their apparent generation is only a development, a kind of augmentation. I have also noticed that the author of the *Search after Truth*,[8] Régis, Hartsoeker, and other able persons have held opinions not far removed from this.

But the greatest question still remained: What becomes of these souls or forms at the death of the animal or at the destruction of the individual organized substance? This question is most perplexing, since it hardly seems reasonable that souls should remain uselessly in a chaos of confused matter. This made me judge that there is only one reasonable view to take—namely, the conservation not only of the soul, but also of the animal itself and its organic machine, even though the destruction of its larger parts reduces it to a smallness which escapes our senses, just as it was before its birth. Moreover, no one can specify the true time of death, which for a long time may pass for a simple suspension of noticeable actions, and is basically never anything else in simple animals—witness the *resuscitations* of drowned flies buried under pulverized chalk, and

several other similar examples which are sufficient to show that there would be many other resuscitations, and greater ones, if men were in a position to restore the machine. This may be similar to something the great Democritus discussed, complete atomist that he was, though Pliny made fun of him.[9] It is therefore natural that an animal, having always been alive and organized (as some persons of great insight are beginning to recognize), always remains so. And since there is no first birth or entirely new generation of an animal, it follows that there will not be any final extinction or complete death, in a strict metaphysical sense. Consequently, instead of the *transmigration* of souls, there is only a *transformation* of the same animal, according to whether its organs are differently enfolded and more or less developed.

However, rational souls follow much higher laws, and are exempt from anything that might make them lose the quality of being citizens of the society of minds; God has provided so well that no changes of matter can make them lose the moral qualities of their personhood. And we can say that everything tends not only toward the perfection of the universe in general, but also toward the perfection of these creatures in particular, creatures who are destined for such a degree of happiness that the universe finds itself benefited by virtue of the divine goodness that is communicated to each, to the extent that supreme wisdom can allow.

With respect to ordinary animal bodies and other corporeal substances, whose complete extinction has been accepted until now, and whose changes depend on mechanical rules rather than moral laws, I noted with pleasure that the ancient author of the book *De diaeta*, attributed to Hippocrates,[10] had glimpsed something of the truth when he stated explicitly that animals are not born and do not die, and that things we believe to begin and perish merely appear and

---

7. A later version reads: "brute souls."
8. Nicolas Malebranche.

9. In Book vii, chap. 55, of his *Natural History*, Pliny mocks Democritus's theory of resuscitation, referring to "the false opinion of resuscitation, promulgated by Democritus, who himself did not come back to life."
10. See *The Regimen*, I.4: "So of all things nothing perishes and nothing comes into being that did not exist before. Things change merely by mingling and being separated."

disappear. This was also the opinion of Parmenides and Melissus, according to Aristotle.[11] For these ancients were much more solid than people believe.

I am the most readily disposed person to do justice to the moderns, yet I find that they have carried reform too far, among other things, by confusing natural things with artificial things, because they have lacked sufficiently grand ideas of the majesty of nature. They think that the difference between natural machines and ours is only the difference between great and small. Recently this led a very able man, the author of the *Conversations on the Plurality of Worlds*,[12] to assert that when we examine nature more closely we find it less admirable than previously thought and more like the workshop of a craftsman. I believe that this conception does not give us a sufficiently just or worthy idea of nature, and that my system alone allows us to understand the true and immense distance between the least productions and mechanisms of divine wisdom and the greatest masterpieces that derive from the craft of a limited mind; this difference is not simply a difference of degree, but a difference of kind. We must then know that the machines of nature have a truly infinite number of organs, and are so well supplied and so resistant to all accidents that it is not possible to destroy them. A natural machine still remains a machine in its least parts, and moreover, it always remains the same machine that it has been, being merely transformed through the different enfolding it undergoes, sometimes extended, sometimes compressed and concentrated, as it were, when it is thought to have perished.

In addition, by means of the soul or form there is a true unity corresponding to what is called the *self* [*moy*] in us. Such a unity could not occur in the machines made by a craftsman or in a simple mass of matter, however organized it may be; such a mass can only be considered as an army or a herd, or a pond full of fish, or like a watch composed of springs and wheels. Yet if there were no true *substantial unities*, there would be nothing substantial or real in

the collection. That was what forced Cordemoy to abandon Descartes and to embrace the Democritean doctrine of atoms in order to find a true unity. But *atoms of matter* are contrary to reason. Furthermore, they are still composed of parts, since the invincible attachment of one part to another (if we can reasonably conceive or assume this) would not eliminate diversity of those parts. There are only *atoms of substance*, that is, real unities absolutely destitute of parts, which are the source of actions, the first absolute principles of the composition of things, and, as it were, the final elements in the analysis of substantial things. We could call them *metaphysical points*: They have *something vital*, a kind of *perception*, and *mathematical points* are the *points of view* from which they express the universe. But when corporeal substances are contracted, all their organs together constitute only a *physical point* relative to us. Thus physical points are indivisible only in appearance; mathematical points are exact, but they are merely modalities. Only metaphysical points or points of substance (constituted by forms or souls) are exact and real, and without them there would be nothing real, since without true unities there would be no multitude.

After I established these things, I thought I was entering port; but when I began to meditate about the union of soul and body, I felt as if I were thrown again into the open sea. For I could not find any way of explaining how the body makes anything happen in the soul, or vice versa, or how one substance can communicate with another created substance. Descartes had given up the game at this point, as far as we can determine from his writings. But his disciples, seeing that the common opinion is inconceivable, judged that we sense the qualities of bodies because God causes thoughts to arise in the soul on the occasion of motions of matter, and that when our soul, in turn, wishes to move the body, it is God who moves the body for it. And since the communication of motions also seemed inconceivable to them, they believed that God imparts motion to a body on the occasion of the motion of another body. That is what they call the *system of occasional causes*, which has been made very fashionable by the beautiful reflections of the author of the *Search after Truth*.

I must admit that they have penetrated the difficulty

---

11. Parmenides of Elea and his follower, Melissus of Samos, were two Presocratic philosophers (ca. 450 B.C.) who denied the reality of all change.
12. Bernard de Fontenelle.

by articulating what could not possibly be the case, but their explanation of what actually happens does not appear to eliminate the difficulty. It is quite true that, speaking with metaphysical rigor, there is no real influence of one created substance on another, and that all things, with all their reality, are continually produced by the power [*vertu*] of God. But in solving problems it is not sufficient to make use of the general cause and to invoke what is called a *Deus ex machina*. For when one does that without giving any other explanation derived from the order of secondary causes, it is, properly speaking, having recourse to a miracle. In philosophy we must try to give reasons by showing how things are brought about by divine wisdom, but in conformity with the notion of the subject in question.

Therefore, since I was forced to agree that it is not possible for the soul or any other true substance to receive something from without, except by divine omnipotence, I was led, little by little, to a view that surprised me, but which seems inevitable, and which, in fact, has very great advantages and rather considerable beauty. That is, we must say that God originally created the soul (and any other real unity) in such a way that everything must arise for it from its own depths [*fonds*], through a perfect *spontaneity* relative to itself, and yet with a perfect *conformity* relative to external things. And thus, since our internal sensations (meaning those in the soul itself, and not those in the brain or in other subtle parts of the body) are merely phenomena which follow upon external beings, or better, they are true appearances and like well-ordered dreams, these internal perceptions in the soul itself must arise because of its own original constitution; that is, they must arise through the representative nature (capable of expressing external things as they relate to its organs) given to the soul from its creation, which constitutes its individual character. This is what makes every substance represent the whole universe exactly and in its own way, from a certain point of view, and makes the perceptions or expressions of external things occur in the soul at a given time, in virtue of its own laws, as if in a world apart, and as if there existed only God and itself (to make use of the manner of speaking used by a certain person of great spiritual elevation whose piety is re-

nowned).[13] There will be a perfect agreement among all these substances, producing the same effect that would be noticed if they communicated through the transmission of species or qualities, as the common philosophers imagine they do. In addition, the organized mass, in which the point of view of the soul lies, being expressed more closely by the soul, is in turn ready to act by itself, following the laws of the corporeal machine, at the moment when the soul wills it to act, without disturbing the laws of the other—the spirits and blood then having exactly the motions that they need to respond to the passions and perceptions of the soul. It is this mutual relation, regulated in advance in each substance of the universe, which produces what we call their *communication*, and which alone brings about the *union of soul and body*. We can thus understand how the soul has its seat in the body by an immediate presence which could not be greater, since the soul is in the body as unity is in the resultant of unities, which is a multitude.

This hypothesis is entirely possible. For why should God be unable to give substance, from the beginning, a nature or an internal force that can produce in it, in an orderly way (as would happen in a *spiritual or formal* automaton, but *free* in the case in which it has a share of reason), everything that will happen to it, that is, all the appearances or expressions it will have, without the help of any created being? This is especially so since the nature of substance necessarily requires and essentially involves progress or change, without which it would not have the force to act. And since this nature that pertains to the soul is representative of the universe in a very exact manner (though more or less distinctly), the series of representations produced by the soul will correspond naturally to the series of changes in the universe itself, just as the body, in turn, has also been accommodated to the soul for the situations in which the soul is thought to act externally. This is all the more reasonable insofar as bodies are made only for minds capable of entering into community with God and celebrating his glory. Thus, once we see the possibility of this

13. Leibniz probably has St. Theresa in mind here. See the note to sec. 32 of the "Discourse on Metaphysics."

*hypothesis of agreements*, we also see that it is the most reasonable hypothesis, and that it gives us a marvelous idea of the harmony of the universe and the perfection of the works of God.

It also has this great advantage, that instead of saying that we are free only in appearance and in a way sufficient for practical purposes, as several intelligent persons have believed,[14] we should rather say that we are determined only in appearance, and that, in rigorously metaphysical language, we have a perfect independence relative to the influence of every other creature. This also throws a marvelous light on the immortality of our soul and the always uniform conservation of our individual being, which is perfectly well regulated by its own nature and protected from all external accidents, appearances to the contrary notwithstanding. Never has any system made our eminence more evident. Since every mind is like a world apart, self-sufficient, independent of any other creature, containing infinity, and expressing the universe, it is as durable, subsistent, and absolute as the universe of creatures itself. Thus we should judge that it must always behave in the way most proper to contribute to the perfection of the society of all minds, which is their moral union in the City of God. There is also a new proof for the existence of God in our system, one which has extraordinary clarity. For the perfect agreement of so many substances which have no communication among them can only come from the common source.

Besides all the advantages that recommend this hypothesis, we can say that it is something more than a hypothesis, since it hardly seems possible to explain things in any other intelligible way, and since several

14. Leibniz probably has Spinoza in mind here. See the Appendix to Ethics I.

serious difficulties which, until now, have troubled minds, seem to disappear by themselves when we properly understand the system. Ordinary ways of speaking are also preserved. For we can say that the substance, whose disposition accounts for change intelligibly, in the sense that we may judge that the other substances have been accommodated to this one in this regard from the beginning, according to the order of God's decree, is the substance we must consequently conceive as acting upon the others. Furthermore, the action of one substance on another is neither the emission nor the transplanting of an entity, as commonly conceived, and can reasonably be taken only in the manner just stated. It is true that we readily conceive emissions and receptions of parts in matter, by which we can reasonably explain all the phenomena of physics mechanically. But since material mass is not a substance, it is clear that action with respect to substance itself can only be as I have just described.

These considerations, however metaphysical they may seem, have yet another marvelous use in physics, in order to establish the laws of motion, as our *Dynamics* will be able to show. For we can say that in the impact of bodies, each body suffers only through its own elasticity, caused by the motion already in it. And as for absolute motion, nothing can fix it with mathematical rigor, since everything terminates in relations. This makes for the perfect equivalence of hypotheses, as in astronomy, so that no matter how many bodies we take, we may arbitrarily assign rest or a particular degree of speed to any body we choose, without being refuted by the phenomena of rectilinear, circular, or composite motion. However, it is reasonable to attribute some true motions to bodies, in accordance with the assumption that accounts for the phenomena in the most intelligible way, this denomination being in conformity with the notion of action we have just established.

# G. W. Leibniz, *The Principles of Philosophy, or, the Monadology* (1714)[1]

1. The monad, which we shall discuss here, is nothing but a simple substance that enters into composites—simple, that is, without parts (*Theodicy*, sec. 10).

2. And there must be simple substances, since there are composites; for the composite is nothing more than a collection, or *aggregate*, of simples.

3. But where there are no parts, neither extension, nor shape, nor divisibility is possible. These monads are the true atoms of nature and, in brief, the elements of things.

4. There is also no dissolution to fear, and there is no conceivable way in which a simple substance can perish naturally.

5. For the same reason, there is no conceivable way a simple substance can begin naturally, since it cannot be formed by composition.

6. Thus, one can say that monads can only begin or end all at once—that is, they can only begin by creation and end by annihilation—whereas composites begin or end through their parts.

7. There is also no way of explaining how a monad can be altered or changed internally by some other creature, since one cannot transpose anything in it, nor can one conceive of any internal motion that can be excited, directed, augmented, or diminished within it, as can be done in composites, where there can be change among the parts. The monads have no windows through which something can enter or leave. Accidents cannot be detached, nor can they go about outside of substances, as the sensible species of the Scholastics once did. Thus, neither substance nor accident can enter a monad from without.[2]

8. However, monads must have some qualities; otherwise they would not even be beings.[3] And if simple substances did not differ at all in their qualities, there would be no way of perceiving any change in things, since what there is in a composite can only come from its simple ingredients; and if the monads had no qualities, they would be indiscernible from one another, since they also do not differ in quantity. As a result, assuming a plenum, in motion, each place

1. Translated from the French by R. Ariew and D. Garber in G. W. Leibniz, *Philosophical Essays* (Indianapolis: Hackett Publishing Company, 1989). "Principles..." was probably Leibniz's title. References to the *Theodicy* are not found in the final copy but are taken from an earlier draft. It should be stressed that the "Monadology" was not intended as an introduction to Leibniz's philosophy but rather as a condensed statement of the main principles of his philosophy and an elucidation of some of the passages of his *Theodicy*.

2. Deleted from the first draft: "Monads are not mathematical points. For these points are only extremities, and the line cannot be composed of points."
3. Deleted from earlier drafts: "and if simple substances were nothings, the composites would reduce to nothing."

would always receive only the equivalent of what it already had, and one state of things would be indistinguishable from another[4] (Pref. 2.b).

9. It is also necessary that each monad be different from each other. For there are never two beings in nature that are perfectly alike, two beings in which it is not possible to discover an internal difference, that is, one founded on an intrinsic denomination.

10. I also take for granted that every created being, and consequently the created monad as well, is subject to change, and even that this change is continual in each thing.

11. It follows from what we have just said that the monad's natural changes come from an *internal principle*, since no external cause can influence it internally (sec. 396, 400).

12. But, besides the principle of change, there must be *diversity [un détail] in that which changes*, which produces, so to speak, the specification and variety of simple substances.

13. This diversity must involve a multitude in the unity or in the simple. For, since all natural change is produced by degrees, something changes and something remains. As a result, there must be a plurality of properties [*affections*] and relations in the simple substance, although it has no parts.

14. The passing state which involves and represents a multitude in the unity or in the simple substance is nothing other than what one calls *perception*, which should be distinguished from apperception, or consciousness, as will be evident in what follows. This is where the Cartesians have failed badly, since they took no account of the perceptions that we do not apperceive. This is also what made them believe that minds alone are monads and that there are no animal souls or other entelechies. With the common people, they have confused a long stupor with death, properly speaking, which made them fall again into the scholastic prejudice of completely separated souls, and they have even confirmed unsound minds in the belief in the mortality of souls.[5]

15. The action of the internal principle which brings about the change or passage from one perception to another can be called *appetition*; it is true that the appetite cannot always completely reach the whole perception toward which it tends, but it always obtains something of it, and reaches new perceptions.

16. We ourselves experience a multitude in a simple substance when we find that the least thought we ourselves apperceive involves variety in its object. Thus, all those who recognize that the soul is a simple substance should recognize this multitude in the monad; and Mr. Bayle should not find any difficulty in this as he has done in his *Dictionary* article, "Rorarius."[6]

17. Moreover, we must confess that the *perception*, and what depends on it, *is inexplicable in terms of mechanical reasons*, that is, through shapes and motions. If we imagine that there is a machine whose structure makes it think, sense, and have perceptions, we could conceive it enlarged, keeping the same proportions, so that we could enter into it, as one enters into a mill. Assuming that, when inspecting its interior, we will only find parts that push one another, and we will never find anything to explain a perception. And so, we should seek perception in the simple substance and not in the composite or in the machine. Furthermore, this is all one can find in the simple substance—that is, perceptions and their changes. It is also in this alone that all the internal actions of simple substances can consist.

18. One can call all simple substances or created monads entelechies, for they have in themselves a certain perfection [*echousi to enteles*]; they have a sufficiency [*autarkeia*] that makes them the sources of their internal actions, and, so to speak, incorporeal automata (sec. 87).

19. If we wish to call *soul* everything that has *percep-*

---

4. Cf. "On Nature Itself," sec. 13, in Leibniz, *Philosophical Essays*.
5. For Leibniz's critique of Descartes on the immortality of the soul, see the "Letter to Molanus," in the section in this book on Descartes's *Meditations*.

6. Leibniz's *Theodicy* was, to a large extent, an attempt to answer the skeptical arguments, from Bayle's *Historical and Critical Dictionary*, regarding the impossibility of reconciling faith with reason. "Rorarius," an article of the *Dictionary*, was Bayle's occasion for a discussion of the problem of the souls of animals: Jerome Rorarius (1485–1566) wrote a treatise maintaining that men are less rational than the lower animals. In "Rorarius," Bayle criticizes Leibniz's views; see Bayle, "Rorarius," notes H and L.

*tions* and *appetites* in the general sense I have just explained, then all simple substances or created monads can be called souls. But, since sensation is something more than a simple perception, I think that the general name of monad and entelechy is sufficient for simple substances which only have perceptions, and that we should only call those substances *souls* where perception is more distinct and accompanied by memory.

20. For we experience within ourselves a state in which we remember nothing and have no distinct perception; this is similar to when we faint or when we are overwhelmed by a deep, dreamless sleep. In this state the soul does not differ sensibly from a simple monad; but since this state does not last, and since the soul emerges from it, our soul is something more (sec. 64).

21. And it does not at all follow that in such a state the simple substance is without any perception. This is not possible for the previous reasons; for it cannot perish, and it also cannot subsist without some property [*affection*], which is nothing other than its perception. But when there is a great multitude of small perceptions in which nothing is distinct, we are stupefied. This is similar to when we continually spin in the same direction several times in succession, from which arises a dizziness that can make us faint and does not allow us to distinguish anything. Death can impart this state to animals for a time.

22. And since every present state of a simple substance is a natural consequence of its preceding state, the present is pregnant with the future (sec. 360).

23. Therefore, since on being awakened from a stupor, we apperceive our perceptions, it must be the case that we had some perceptions immediately before, even though we did not apperceive them; for a perception can only come naturally from another perception, as a motion can only come naturally from a motion (secs. 401–3).

24. From this we see that if, in our perceptions, we had nothing distinct or, so to speak, in relief and stronger in flavor, we would always be in a stupor. And this is the state of bare monads.

25. We also see that nature has given heightened perceptions to animals, from the care she has taken to furnish them organs that collect several rays of light or several waves of air, in order to make them more effectual by bringing them together. There is something similar to this in odor, taste, and touch, and perhaps in many other senses which are unknown to us. I will soon explain how what occurs in the soul represents what occurs in the organs.

26. Memory provides a kind of sequence in souls, which imitates reason, but which must be distinguished from it. We observe that when animals have the perception of something which strikes them, and when they previously had a similar perception of that thing, then, through a representation in their memory, they expect that which was attached to the thing in the preceding perception, and are led to have sensations similar to those they had before. For example, if we show dogs a stick, they remember the pain that it caused them and they flee (Prelim., sec. 65).

27. And the strong imagination that strikes and moves them comes from the magnitude or the multitude of the preceding perceptions. For often a strong impression produces, all at once, the effect produced by a long *habit* or by many lesser, reiterated perceptions.

28. Men act like beasts insofar as the sequence of their perceptions results from the principle of memory alone; they resemble the empirical physicians who practice without theory. We are all mere Empirics in three fourths of our actions. For example, when we expect that the day will dawn tomorrow, we act like an Empiric,[7] because until now it has always been thus. Only the astronomer judges this by reason (Prelim., sec. 65).

29. But the knowledge of eternal and necessary truths is what distinguishes us from simple animals and furnishes us with *reason* and the sciences, by raising us to a knowledge of ourselves and of God. And that is what we call the rational soul, or *mind*, in ourselves.

30. It is also through the knowledge of necessary truths and through their abstractions that we rise to

7. The Empirics were a sect of physicians before Galen (ca. A.D. 150). In later times, the epithet "Empiric" was given to physicians who despised theoretical study and trusted tradition and their own experience.

*reflective* acts, which enable us to think of that which is called "I" and enable us to consider that this or that is in us. And thus, in thinking of ourselves, we think of being, of substance, of the simple and of the composite, of the immaterial and of God himself, by conceiving that that which is limited in us is limitless in him. And these reflective acts furnish the principal objects of our reasonings (*Theod.* Preface 4.a).

31. Our reasonings are based on *two great principles, that of contradiction*, in virtue of which we judge that which involves a contradiction to be false, and that which is opposed or contradictory to the false to be true (sec. 44, 169).

32. And *that of sufficient reason*, by virtue of which we consider that we can find no true or existent fact, no true assertion, without there being a sufficient reason why it is thus and not otherwise, although most of the time these reasons cannot be known to us (sec. 44, 196).

33. There are also two kinds of *truths*, those of *reasoning* and those of *fact*. The truths of reasoning are necessary and their opposite is impossible; the truths of fact are contingent, and their opposite is possible. When a truth is necessary, its reason can be found by analysis, resolving it into simpler ideas and simpler truths until we reach the primitives (sec. 170, 174, 189, 280–82, 367, Abridgment, objection 3).

34. This is how the speculative *theorems* and practical *canons* of mathematicians are reduced by analysis to *definitions*, *axioms*, and *postulates*.

35. And there are, finally, *simple ideas*, whose definition cannot be given. There are also axioms and postulates, in brief, *primitive principles*, which cannot be proved and which need no proof. And these are *identical propositions*, whose opposite contains an explicit contradiction.

36. But there must also be a *sufficient reason* in *contingent truths*, or *truths of fact*, that is, in the series of things distributed throughout the universe of creatures, where the resolution into particular reasons could proceed into unlimited detail because of the immense variety of things in nature and because of the division of bodies to infinity. There is an infinity of past and present shapes and motions that enter into the efficient cause of my present writing, and there is an infinity of small inclinations and disposi-

tions of my soul, present and past, that enter into its final cause (sec. 36, 37, 44, 45, 49, 52, 121, 122, 337, 340, 344).

37. And since all this *detail* involves nothing but other prior or more detailed contingents, each of which needs a similar analysis in order to give its reason, we do not make progress in this way. It must be the case that the sufficient or ultimate reason is outside the sequence or *series* of this multiplicity of contingencies, however infinite it may be.

38. And that is why the ultimate reason of things must be in a necessary substance in which the diversity of changes is only eminent, as in its source. This is what we call *God* (*Theod.* sec. 7).

39. Since this substance is a sufficient reason for all this diversity, which is utterly interconnected, *there is only one God, and this God is sufficient.*

40. We can also judge that this supreme substance which is unique, universal, and necessary must be incapable of limits and must contain as much reality as is possible, insofar as there is nothing outside it which is independent of it, and insofar as it is a simple consequence of its possible existence.

41. From this it follows that God is absolutely perfect—*perfection* being nothing but the magnitude of positive reality considered as such, setting aside the limits or bounds in the things which have it. And here, where there are no limits, that is, in God, perfection is absolutely infinite (*Theod.* sec. 22; *Theod.* Preface, sec. 4.a).

42. It also follows that creatures derive their perfections from God's influence, but that they derive their imperfections from their own nature, which is incapable of being without limits. For it is in this that they are distinguished from God (*Theod.* sec. 20, 27–31, 153, 167, 377 et seq.; sec. 30, 380, Abridgment, objection 5).[8]

43. It is also true that God is not only the source of existences, but also that of essences insofar as they are real, that is, or the source of that which is real in possibility. This is because God's understanding is the realm of eternal truths or that of the ideas on

---

8. The following appears in the second draft, but is missing in the final copy: "This *original imperfection* of creatures is noticeable in the *natural inertia* of bodies."

which they depend; without him there would be nothing real in possibles, and not only would nothing exist, but also nothing would be possible (*Theod.* sec. 20).

44. For if there is reality in essences or possibles, or indeed, in eternal truths, this reality must be grounded in something existent and actual, and consequently, it must be grounded in the existence of the necessary being, in whom essence involves existence, that is, in whom possible being is sufficient for actual being (sec. 184–89, 335).

45. Thus God alone (or the necessary being) has this privilege, that he must exist if he is possible. And since nothing can prevent the possibility of what is without limits, without negation, and consequently without contradiction, this by itself is sufficient for us to know the existence of God *a priori*. We have also proved this by the reality of the eternal truths. But we have also just proved it *a posteriori* since there are contingent beings, which can only have their final or sufficient reason in the necessary being, a being that has the reason of its existence in itself.

46. However, we should not imagine, as some do, that since the eternal truths depend on God, they are arbitrary and depend on his will, as Descartes appears to have held, and after him Mr. Poiret.[9] This is true only of contingent truths, whose principle is *fitness* [*convenance*] or the choice of the *best*. But necessary truths depend solely on his understanding, and are its internal object (sec. 180, 184, 185, 335, 351, 380).

47. Thus God alone is the primitive unity or the first [*originaire*] simple substance; all created or derivative monads are products, and are generated, so to speak, by continual fulgurations of the divinity from moment to moment, limited by the receptivity of the creature, to which it is essential to be limited (sec. 382–91, 398, 395).

48. God has *power*, which is the source of everything, *knowledge*, which contains the diversity of ideas, and finally *will*, which brings about changes or products in accordance with the principle of the best (sec. 7, 149, 150). And these correspond to what, in created monads, is the subject or the basis, the perceptive faculty and the appetitive faculty. But in God these attributes are absolutely infinite or perfect, while in the created monads or in entelechies (or *perfectihabies*, as Hermolaus Barbarus translated that word)[10] they are only imitations of it, in proportion to the perfection that they have (sec. 87).

49. The creature is said to act externally insofar as it is perfect, and *to be acted upon* [*patir*] by another, insofar as it is imperfect. Thus we attribute *action* to a monad insofar as it has distinct perceptions, and *passion*, insofar as it has confused perceptions (*Theod.* sec. 32, 66, 386).

50. And one creature is more perfect than another insofar as one finds in it that which provides an *a priori* reason for what happens in the other; and this is why we say that it acts on the other.

51. But in simple substances the influence of one monad over another can only be ideal, and can only produce its effect through God's intervention, when in the ideas of God a monad reasonably asks that God take it into account in regulating the others from the beginning of things. For, since a created monad cannot have an internal physical influence upon another, this is the only way in which one can depend on another (*Theod.* sec. 9, 54, 65, 66, 201, Abridgment, objection 3).

52. It is in this way that actions and passions among creatures are mutual. For God, comparing two simple substances, finds in each reasons that require him to adjust the other to it; and consequently, what is active in some respects is passive from another point of view: *active* insofar as what is known distinctly in one serves to explain what happens in another; and *passive* insofar as the reason for what happens in one is found in what is known distinctly in another (sec. 66).

53. Now, since there is an infinity of possible universes in God's ideas, and since only one of them can exist, there must be a sufficient reason for God's

9. For Leibniz's critique of Descartes's concept of God, see the "Letter to Molanus" in section 1. Pierre Poiret (1646–1719) was initially one of Descartes's followers; he published a book of reflections on God, soul, and evil, *Cogitationum rationalium de Deo, anima, et malo libri quattuor* (1677), which was attacked by Bayle.

10. Hermolaus Barbarus (1454–93) was an Italian scholar who attempted, through retranslations of Aristotle, to recover Aristotle's original doctrine from under the layers of scholastic interpretations. His works include popular compendia of ethics and natural philosophy, drawn from the writings of Aristotle.

choice, a reason which determines him towards one thing rather than another (*Theod.* sec. 8, 10, 44, 173, 196 & seq., 225, 414–16).

54. And this reason can only be found in *fitness*, or in the degree of perfection that these worlds contain, each possible world having the right to claim existence in proportion to the perfection it contains (sec. 74, 167, 350, 201, 130, 352, 345 & seq., 354).[11]

55. And this is the cause of the existence of the best, which wisdom makes known to God, which his goodness makes him choose, and which his power makes him produce (*Theod.* sec. 8, 78, 80, 84, 119, 204, 206, 208; Abridgment, objection 1, objection 8).

56. This interconnection or accommodation of all created things to each other, and each to all the others, brings it about that each simple substance has relations that express all the others, and consequently, that each simple substance is a perpetual, living mirror of the universe (sec. 130, 360).

57. Just as the same city viewed from different directions appears entirely different and, as it were, multiplied perspectively, in just the same way it happens that, because of the infinite multitude of simple substances, there are, as it were, just as many different universes, which are, nevertheless, only perspectives on a single one, corresponding to the different points of view of each monad (sec. 147).

58. And this is the way of obtaining as much variety as possible, but with the greatest order possible, that is, it is the way of obtaining as much perfection as possible (sec. 120, 124, 241 & seq., 214, 243, 275).

59. Moreover, this is the only hypothesis (which I dare say is demonstrated) that properly enhances God's greatness. Mr. Bayle recognized this when, in his *Dictionary* (article "Rorarius"), he set out objections to it; indeed, he was tempted to believe that I ascribed too much to God, more than is possible. But he was unable to present any reason why this universal harmony, which results in every substance expressing exactly all the others through the relations it has to them, is impossible.[12]

60. Furthermore, in what I have just discussed, we

can see the *a priori* reasons why things could not be otherwise. Because God, in regulating the whole, had regard for each part, and particularly for each monad, and since the nature of the monad is representative, nothing can limit it to represent only a part of things. However, it is true that this representation is only confused as to the detail of the whole universe, and can only be distinct for a small portion of things, that is, either for those that are closest, or for those that are greatest with respect to each monad; otherwise each monad would be a divinity. Monads are limited, not as to their objects, but with respect to the modifications of their knowledge of them. Monads all go confusedly to infinity, to the whole; but they are limited and differentiated by the degrees of their distinct perceptions.

61. In this respect, composites are analogous to simples. For everything is a plenum, which makes all matter interconnected. In a plenum, every motion has some effect on distant bodies, in proportion to their distance. For each body is affected, not only by those in contact with it, and in some way feels the effects of everything that happens to them, but also, through them, it feels the effects of those in contact with the bodies with which it is itself immediately in contact. From this it follows that this communication extends to any distance whatsoever. As a result, every body is affected by everything that happens in the universe, to such an extent that he who sees all can read in each thing what happens everywhere, and even what has happened or what will happen, by observing in the present what is remote in time as well as in space. "All things conspire [*sympnoia panta*]," said Hippocrates. But a soul can read in itself only what is distinctly represented there; it cannot unfold all its folds at once, because they go to infinity.

62. Thus, although each created monad represents the whole universe, it more distinctly represents the body which is particularly affected by it, and whose entelechy it constitutes. And just as this body expresses the whole universe through the interconnection of all matter in the plenum, the soul also represents the whole universe by representing this body, which belongs to it in a particular way (sec. 400).

63. The body belonging to a monad (which is the entelechy or soul of that body) together with an

---

11. The following appears in the second draft: "Thus there is nothing that is completely arbitrary."
12. See note to sec. 16.

entelechy constitutes what may be called a *living being*, and together with a soul constitutes what is called an *animal*. Now, the body of a living being or an animal is always organized; for, since every monad is a mirror of the universe in its way, and since the universe is regulated in a perfect order, there must also be an order in the representing being, that is, in the perceptions of the soul, and consequently, in the body in accordance with which the universe is represented therein (sec. 403).

64. Thus each organized body of a living being is a kind of divine machine or natural automaton, which infinitely surpasses all artificial automata. For a machine constructed by man's art is not a machine in each of its parts. For example, the tooth of a brass wheel has parts or fragments which, for us, are no longer artificial things, and no longer have any marks to indicate the machine for whose use the wheel was intended. But natural machines, that is, living bodies, are still machines in their least parts, to infinity. That is the difference between nature and art, that is, between divine art and our art (sec. 134, 146, 194, 483).

65. And the author of nature has been able to practice this divine and infinitely marvelous art, because each portion of matter is not only divisible to infinity, as the ancients have recognized, but is also actually subdivided without end, each part divided into parts having some motion of their own; otherwise, it would be impossible for each portion of matter to express the whole universe (Prelim., sec. 70, *Theodicy*, sec. 195).

66. From this we see that there is a world of creatures, of living beings, of animals, of entelechies, of souls in the least part of matter.

67. Each portion of matter can be conceived as a garden full of plants, and as a pond full of fish. But each branch of a plant, each limb of an animal, each drop of its humors, is still another such garden or pond.

68. And although the earth and air lying between the garden plants, or the water lying between the fish of the pond, are neither plant nor fish, they contain yet more of them, though of a subtleness imperceptible to us, most often.

69. Thus there is nothing fallow, sterile, or dead in the universe, no chaos and no confusion except in appearance, almost as it looks in a pond at a distance, where we might see the confused and, so to speak, teeming motion of the fish in the pond, without discerning the fish themselves (Preface 5.b, 6).

70. Thus we see that each living body has a dominant entelechy, which in the animal is the soul; but the limbs of this living body are full of other living beings, plants, animals, each of which also has its entelechy, or its dominant soul.

71. But we must not imagine, as some who have misunderstood my thought do, that each soul has a mass or portion of matter of its own, always proper to or allotted by it, and that it consequently possesses other lower living beings, forever destined to serve it. For all bodies are in a perpetual flux, like rivers, and parts enter into them and depart from them continually.

72. Thus the soul changes body only little by little and by degrees, so that it is never stripped at once of all its organs. There is often metamorphosis in animals, but there is never metempsychosis nor transmigration of souls; there are also no completely *separated souls*, nor spirits [*Génies*] without bodies. God alone is completely detached from bodies (sec. 90, 124).

73. That is why there is never total generation nor, strictly speaking, perfect death, death consisting in the separation of the soul. And what we call *generations* are developments and growths, as what we call deaths are enfoldings and diminutions.

74. Philosophers have been greatly perplexed about the origin of forms, entelechies, or souls. But today, when exact inquiries on plants, insects, and animals have shown us that organic bodies in nature are never produced from chaos or putrefaction, but always through seeds in which there is, no doubt, some *preformation*, it has been judged that, not only the organic body was already there before conception, but there was also a soul in this body; in brief, the animal itself was there, and through conception this animal was merely prepared for a great transformation, in order to become an animal of another kind. Something similar is seen outside generation, as when worms become flies, and caterpillars become butterflies (sec. 86, 89; Preface 5.b ff; sec. 90, 187, 188, 403, 86, 397).

75. Those *animals*, some of which are raised by

conception to the level of the larger animals, can be called *spermatic*. But those of them that remain among those of their kind, that is, the majority, are born, multiply, and are destroyed, just like the larger animals. There are but a small number of Elect that pass onto a larger stage [*théâtre*].

76. But this was only half the truth. I have, therefore, held that if the animal never begins naturally, it does not end naturally, either; and not only will there be no generation, but also no complete destruction, nor any death, strictly speaking. These *a posteriori* reasonings, derived from experience, agree perfectly with my principles deduced *a priori*, as above (sec. 90).

77. Thus one can state that not only is the soul (mirror of an indestructible universe) indestructible, but so is the animal itself, even though its mechanism often perishes in part, and casts off or puts on its organic coverings.

78. These principles have given me a way of naturally explaining the union, or rather the conformity of the soul and the organic body. The soul follows its own laws and the body also follows its own; and they agree in virtue of the harmony pre-established between all substances, since they are all representations of a single universe (Preface 6; sec. 340, 352, 353, 358).

79. Souls act according to the laws of final causes, through appetitions, ends, and means. Bodies act according to the laws of efficient causes or of motions. And these two kingdoms, that of efficient causes and that of final causes, are in harmony with each other.

80. Descartes recognized that souls cannot impart a force to bodies because there is always the same quantity of force in matter. However, he thought that the soul could change the direction of bodies. But that is because the law of nature, which also affirms the conservation of the same total direction in matter, was not known at that time. If he had known it, he would have hit upon my system of pre-established harmony (Preface; *Theod.* sec. 22, 59, 60, 61, 63, 66, 345, 346 & seq., 354, 355).

81. According to this system, bodies act as if there were no souls (though this is impossible); and souls act as if there were no bodies; and both act as if each influenced the other.

82. As for *minds* or rational souls, I find that, at bottom, what we just said holds for all living beings and animals, namely that animals and souls begin only with the world and do not end any more than the world does. However, rational animals have this peculiarity, that their little spermatic animals, as long as they only remain in this state, have only ordinary or sensitive souls. But that as soon as the Elect among them, so to speak, attain human nature by actual conception, their sensitive souls are elevated to the rank of reason and to the prerogative of minds (sec. 91, 397).

83. Among other differences which exist between ordinary souls and minds, some of which I have already noted, there are also the following: that souls, in general, are living mirrors or images of the universe of creatures, but that minds are also images of the divinity itself, or of the author of nature, capable of knowing the system of the universe, and imitating something of it through their schematic representations [*échantillons architectoniques*] of it, each mind being like a little divinity in its own realm (sec. 147).

84. That is what makes minds capable of entering into a kind of society with God, and allows him to be, in relation to them, not only what an inventor is to his machine (as God is in relation to the other creatures) but also what a prince is to his subjects, and even what a father is to his children.

85. From this it is easy to conclude that the collection of all minds must make up the city of God, that is, the most perfect possible state under the most perfect of monarchs (see 146, Abridgment, Objection 2).

86. This city of God, this truly universal monarchy, is a moral world within the natural world, and the highest and most divine of God's works. The glory of God truly consists in this city, for he would have none if his greatness and goodness were not known and admired by minds. It is also in relation to this divine city that God has goodness, properly speaking, whereas his wisdom and power are evident everywhere.

87. Since earlier we established a perfect harmony between two natural kingdoms, the one of efficient causes, the other of final causes, we ought to note here yet another harmony between the physical king-

dom of nature and the moral kingdom of grace, that is, between God considered as the architect of the mechanism of the universe, and God considered as the monarch of the divine city of minds (sec. 62, 74, 118, 248, 112, 130, 247).

88. This harmony leads things to grace through the very paths of nature. For example, this globe must be destroyed and restored by natural means at such times as the governing of minds requires it, for the punishment of some and the reward of others (sec. 18 & seq., 110, 244, 245, 340).

89. It can also be said that God the architect pleases in every respect God the legislator, and, as a result, sins must carry their penalty with them by the order of nature, and even in virtue of the mechanical structure of things. Similarly, noble actions will receive their rewards through mechanical means with regard to bodies, even though this cannot, and must not, always happen immediately.

90. Finally, under this perfect government, there will be no good action that is unrewarded, no bad action that goes unpunished, and everything must result in the well being of the good, that is, of those who are not dissatisfied in this great state, those who trust in providence, after having done their duty, and who love and imitate the author of all good, as they should, finding pleasure in the consideration of his perfections according to the nature of genuinely *pure love*, which takes pleasure in the happiness of the beloved. This is what causes wise and virtuous persons to work for all that appears to be in conformity with the presumptive or antecedent divine will, and nevertheless, to content themselves with what God brings about by his secret, consequent, or decisive will, since they recognize that if we could understand the order of the universe well enough, we would find that it surpasses all the wishes of the wisest, and that it is impossible to make it better than it is.[13] This is true not only for the whole in general, but also for ourselves in particular, if we are attached, as we should be, to the author of the whole, not only as the architect and efficient cause of our being, but also as to our master and final cause; he ought to be the whole aim of our will, and he alone can make us happy (sec. 134 end, Preface 4.a.b.; *Theodicy*, sec. 278, Preface 4.b).

13. The distinction between God's antecedent and consequent will can be found in Thomas Aquinas, *Summa Theologiae* I, q. 23, art. 2, ad 1.

# Isaac Newton, *Natural Philosophy* (1687–1718), *Principia,* "Scholium to Definitions" and "General Scholium," and *Optics,* "Query 31"[1]

*Isaac Newton (1642–1727) was the foremost mathematician and natural philosopher of the late seventeenth century. He attended Trinity College, Cambridge, was elected a Fellow in 1667, and succeeded Isaac Barrow as Lucasian Professor of Mathematics in 1669. Newton's great work,* The Mathematical Principles of Natural Philosophy *(or* Principia*), published in 1687, was a revision and expansion of several treatises he had previously composed but did not publish. He was elected President of the Royal Society in 1703 and knighted in 1705. During his life, he engaged in several bitter priority disputes about scientific and mathematical discoveries—for example, with Robert Hooke in 1686–88 over the inverse square law, and with Leibniz in 1703–15 over the calculus. His influence in the history of science is unequaled and extends well beyond* science; of particular consequence are his cosmological remarks from the *Principia.*[2]

## Scholium

Up to now I have defined terms that are less known and explained the sense I would have them understood in the following discourse. I do not define time, space, place, and motion, since they are well known to all. Only I must observe that the common people conceive those quantities under no other notions than from their relation to sensible objects. And from this certain prejudices arise, for the removing of which it will be convenient to distinguish the terms into absolute and relative, true and apparent, mathematical and common.

---

1. *Principia* (that is, *Philosophiae naturalis principia mathematica*), translated from the Latin by A. Motte in *The Mathematical Principles of Natural Philosophy . . .* (London, 1729), modified. Passages added in the third edition (1726) are indicated by angle brackets in the text. *Optics* from *Opticks: or, A treatise of the reflexions, refractions, inflexions and colours of light* (second ed. with additions, London, 1718; first ed., 1704; Latin trans. by Samuel Clarke), modified. Passages added in the second edition are indicated by angle brackets in the text.

2. For more on Newton, see Richard W. Westfall, *Never at Rest* (Cambridge: Cambridge University Press, 1980); I. Bernard Cohen, *The Newtonian Revolution* (Cambridge: Cambridge University Press, 1980); or B. J. Dobbs, *The Janus Faces of Genius: The Role of Alchemy in Newton's Thought* (Cambridge: Cambridge University Press, 1991). For an account of the dispute between Newton and Leibniz on the calculus, see A. Rupert Hall, *Philosophers at War* (Cambridge: Cambridge University Press, 1980).

I. Absolute, true, and mathematical time, of itself, and from its own nature, flows uniformly without relation to anything external, and by another name is called *duration*. Relative, apparent, and common time is some sensible and external (whether accurate or varying in rate) measure of duration by the means of motion, which is commonly used instead of true time, such as an hour, a day, a month, a year.

II. Absolute space, in its own nature, without relation to anything external, always remains similar and immovable. Relative space is some movable dimension or measure of the absolute spaces, which our senses determine by its position to bodies and is commonly taken for immovable space, such as the dimension of subterraneous, aerial, or celestial space, determined by its position with respect to earth. Absolute and relative space are the same in form and magnitude, but they do not always remain numerically the same. For if the earth, for instance, moves, a space of our air, which relatively and with respect to the earth always remains the same, will at one time be one part of the absolute space into which the air passes, at another time it will be another part of the same, and so, absolutely understood, it will be continually changed.

III. Place is a part of space which a body takes up, and is absolute or relative according to the space. I say, a part of space, not the situation nor the external surface of the body. For the places of equal solids are always equal, but their surfaces, by reason of their dissimilar figures, are often unequal. Positions properly have no quantity, nor are they so much the places themselves as the properties of places. The motion of the whole is the same as the sum of the motions of the parts; that is, the translation of the whole out of its place is the same thing as the sum of the translations of the parts out of their places; and therefore the place of the whole is the same as the sum of the places of the parts, and for that reason it is internal and in the whole body.

IV. Absolute motion is the translation of a body from one absolute place into another, and relative motion the translation from one relative place into another. Thus in a ship under sail, the relative place of a body is that part of the ship the body possesses, or that part of the cavity the body fills, and which therefore moves together with the ship; and relative rest is the continuance of the body in the same part of the ship or of its cavity. But real, absolute rest is the continuance of the body in the same part of that immovable space, in which the ship itself, its cavity, and all that it contains, is moved. For that reason, if the earth is really at rest, the body which relatively rests in the ship will really and absolutely move with the same velocity which the ship has on the earth. But if the earth also moves, the true and absolute motion of the body will arise, partly from the true motion of the earth in immovable space, partly from the relative motion of the ship on the earth; and if the body moves also relatively in the ship, its true motion will arise, partly from the true motion of the earth in immovable space, and partly from the relative motions as well of the ship on the earth as of the body in the ship; and from these relative motions will arise the relative motion of the body on the earth. As if that part of the earth, where the ship is, was truly moved towards the east with a velocity of 10,010 units, while the ship itself, with a fresh gale and full sails, is carried towards the west with a velocity expressed by ten of those units, while a sailor walks in the ship towards the east, with one unit of the said velocity, then the sailor will be moved truly in immovable space towards the east with a velocity of 10,001 units, and relatively on the earth towards the west with a velocity of nine of those units.

Absolute time is distinguished from relative in astronomy by the equation or correction of the apparent time. For the natural days are truly unequal, though they are commonly considered as equal and used for a measure of time; astronomers correct this inequality that they may measure the celestial motions by a more accurate time. It may be that there is no such thing as a uniform motion by which time may be accurately measured. All motions may be accelerated and retarded, but the flowing of absolute time is not liable to any change. The duration or perseverance of the existence of things remains the same, whether the motions are swift or slow or none at all; and therefore this duration ought to be distinguished from what are only sensible measures of it, and from which we deduce it by means of the astronomical equation. The necessity of this equation for determining the times of a phenomenon is established as well from the experiments of the pendulum clock as by eclipses of the satellites of Jupiter.

As the order of the parts of time is immutable, so also is the order of the parts of space. Suppose those parts to be moved out of their places, and they will be moved (if the expression may be allowed) out of themselves. For times and spaces are, as it were, the places as well of themselves as of all other things. All things are placed in time as to order of succession, and in space as to order of situation. It is from their essence or nature that they are places, and it is absurd that the primary places of things should be movable. These are therefore the absolute places, and translations out of those places are the only absolute motions.

But because the parts of space cannot be seen or distinguished from one another by our senses, we use sensible measures of them in their stead. For from the positions and distances of things from any body considered as immovable, we define all places, and then with respect to such places, we estimate all motions, considering bodies as transferred from some of those places into others. And so, instead of absolute places and motions, we use relative ones, and that without any inconvenience in common affairs; but in philosophical disquisitions, we ought to abstract from our senses and consider things themselves, distinct from what are only sensible measures of them. For it may be that there is no body really at rest to which the places and motions of others may be referred.

But we may distinguish rest and motion, absolute and relative, one from the other by their properties, causes, and effects. It is a property of rest that bodies really at rest do rest in respect to one another. And therefore as it is possible that in the remote regions of the fixed stars, or perhaps far beyond them, there may be some body absolutely at rest, but impossible to know, from the position of bodies to one another in our regions, whether any of these do keep the same position to that remote body, it follows that absolute

rest cannot be determined from the position of bodies in our regions.

It is a property of motion that the parts, which retain given positions to their wholes, do partake of the motions of those wholes. For all the parts of revolving bodies endeavor to recede from the axis of motion, and the impetus of bodies moving forwards arises from the joint impetus of all the parts. Therefore, if surrounding bodies are moved, those that are relatively at rest within them will partake of their motion. Because of this, the true and absolute motion of a body cannot be determined by the translation of it from those which only seem to rest; for the external bodies should not only appear at rest, but be really at rest. For otherwise, all included bodies, besides their translation from near the surrounding ones, partake likewise of their true motions; and though that translation were not made, they would not be really at rest, but only seem to be so. For the surrounding bodies stand in the like relation to the surrounded as the exterior part of a whole does to the interior, or as the shell does to the kernel; but if the shell moves, the kernel will also move, as being part of the whole, without any removal from near the shell.

A property related to the preceding is that if a place is moved, whatever is placed in it moves along with it; and therefore a body which is moved from a place in motion partakes also of the motion of its place. Upon which account, all motions, from places in motion, are no other than parts of entire and absolute motions, and every entire motion is composed of the motion of the body out of its first place, and the motion of this place out of its place, and so on, until we come to some immovable place, as in the aforementioned example of the sailor. Because of this, entire and absolute motions can be no otherwise determined than by immovable places; and for that reason I did before refer those absolute motions to immovable places, but relative ones to movable places. Now no other places are immovable but those that, from infinity to infinity, do all retain the same given position one to another, and upon this account must ever remain unmoved, and do as a result constitute immovable space.

The causes by which true and relative motions are distinguished from one another are the forces impressed upon bodies to generate motion. True motion is neither generated nor altered, but by some force impressed upon the body moved; but relative motion may be generated or altered without any force impressed upon the body. For it is sufficient only to impress some force on other bodies with which the former is compared, that by their giving way, that relation in which the relative rest or motion of this other body did consist may be changed. Again, true motion always suffers some change from any force impressed upon the moving body; but relative motion does not necessarily undergo any change by such forces. For if the same forces are likewise impressed on those other bodies, with which the comparison is made, that the relative position may be preserved, then that condition will be preserved in which the relative motion consists. And therefore any relative motion may be changed when the true motion remains unaltered, and the relative may be preserved when the true suffers some change. Thus, true motion by no means consists in such relations.

The effects which distinguish absolute from relative motion are the forces of receding from the axis of circular motion. For there are no such forces in a circular motion purely relative, but in a true and absolute circular motion, they are greater or less, according to the quantity of the motion. If a vessel hung by a long cord is so often turned about that the cord is strongly twisted, then filled with water and held at rest together with the water, at once, by the sudden action of another force, it is whirled about the contrary way, and while the cord is untwisting itself, the vessel continues for some time in this motion, the surface of the water will at first be even, as before the vessel began to move; but after that the vessel, by gradually communicating its motion to the water, will make it begin to revolve sensibly and recede gradually from the middle, and ascend to the sides of the vessel, forming itself into a concave figure (as I have experienced); and the swifter the motion becomes, the higher will the water rise, until at last, performing its revolutions in the same times with the vessel, it becomes relatively at rest in it. This ascent of the water shows its endeavor to recede from the axis of its motion, and the true and absolute circular motion of the water, which is here directly contrary to the relative, becomes known and may be measured by this endeavor. At first, when the relative motion of the water in the vessel was greatest, it produced no endeavor to recede from the axis; the water showed no tendency to the circumference, nor any ascent towards the sides of the vessel, but remained of an even surface, and therefore its true circular motion had not yet begun. But afterwards, when the relative motion of the water had decreased, its ascent towards the sides of the vessel proved its endeavor to recede from the axis; and this endeavor showed the real circular motion of the water continually increasing, until it had acquired its greatest quantity when the water rested relatively in the vessel. And therefore this endeavor does not depend upon any translation of the water in respect of the ambient bodies, nor can true circular motion be defined by such translation. There is only one real circular motion of any one revolving body corresponding to only one power of endeavoring to recede from its axis of motion as its proper and adequate effect; but relative motions in one and the same body are innumerable, according to the various relations it bears to external bodies, and like other relations are altogether destitute of any real effect, except insofar as they may perhaps partake of that unique true motion. And therefore in the system of those who suppose that our heavens revolving below the sphere of the fixed stars carry the planets along with them, the several parts of those heavens and the planets, which are indeed relatively at rest in their heavens, do yet really move. For they change their position one to another (which never happens to bodies truly at rest), and being carried together with their heavens, partake of their motions, and as parts of revolving wholes, endeavor to recede from the axis of their motions. For that reason relative quantities are not the quantities themselves, whose names they bear, but those sensible measures of them (either accurate or inaccurate), which are commonly used instead of the measured quantities themselves. And if the meaning of words is to be determined by their use, then by the names time, space, place, and motion, their sensible measures are properly to be understood; and the expression will be unusual, and purely mathematical, if the measured quantities themselves are meant. On this account, those who interpret these words for the measured quantities violate the accuracy of language, which ought to be kept precise. Nor do those who confound real quantities with their relations and sensible measure defile the purity of mathematical and philosophical truths any less.

It is indeed a matter of great difficulty to discover and effectually to distinguish the true motions of particular bodies from the apparent, because the parts of that immovable space in which those motions are performed do by no means come under the observation of our senses. Yet the thing is not altogether desperate; for we have some arguments to guide us, partly from the apparent motions, which are the differences of the true motions, partly from the forces, which are the causes and effects of the true motions. For instance, if two globes, kept at a given distance one from the other by means of a cord that connects them, were revolved about their common center of gravity, we might, from the tension of the cord, discover the endeavor of the globes to recede from the axis of their motion, and from thence we might compute the quantity of their circular motions. And then if any equal forces should be impressed at once on the alternate faces of the globes to augment or diminish their circular motions, from the increase or decrease of the tension of the cord, we might infer the increment or decrement of their motions; and hence would be found on what faces those forces ought to be impressed, that the motions of the globes might be most augmented; that is, we might discover their hindmost faces, or those which do follow in the circular motion. But the faces which follow being known, and consequently the opposite ones that precede, we should likewise know the determination of their motions. And thus we might find both the quantity and the determination of this circular motion, even in an immense vacuum, where there was nothing external or sensible with which the globes could be compared. But now, if some remote bodies that kept always a given position one to another were placed in that space, as the fixed stars do in our regions, we could not indeed determine from the relative translation of the globes among those bodies, whether the motion did belong to the globes or to the bodies. But if we observed the cord and found that its tension was that very tension which the motions of the globes required, we might conclude the motion to be in the globes and the bodies to be at rest; and then, lastly, from the translation of the globes among the bodies, we should find the determination of their motions. But how we are to obtain the true motions from their causes, effects, and apparent differences, and the converse, shall be explained more at large in the following treatise. For to this end it was that I composed it.

## *Principia* (2nd ed., 1713), "General Scholium"

The hypothesis of vortices is pressed by many difficulties. In order that any planet may describe areas proportional to the time by a radius drawn to the sun, the periodic times of the parts of the vortices should observe the square of their distances from the sun; but in order that the periodic times of the planets may obtain the 3/2th power of their distances from the sun, the periodic times of the parts of the vortex ought to be as the 3/2th power of their distances. In order that the smaller vortices may maintain their lesser revolutions about Saturn, Jupiter, and other planets, and float quietly and undisturbed in the greater vortex of the sun, the periodic times of the parts of the solar vortex should be equal. But the rotation of the sun and planets about their axes, which ought to correspond with the motions of their vortices, are in disagreement with all these ratios. The motions of the comets are exceedingly regular, are governed by the same laws as the motions of the planets, and cannot be accounted for by the hypothesis of vortices. For comets are carried in highly eccentric motions through all parts of the heavens, which is incompatible with the notion of a vortex.

Projectiles in our air feel only the resistance of the air. If the air is removed, as is done in Mr. Boyle's vacuum, the resistance ceases, for a bit of fine down and a piece of solid gold fall with equal velocity in this void. And the same argument must apply to the celestial spaces above the earth's atmosphere; in these spaces, where there is no air to resist their motions, all bodies will move with complete freedom and the planets and comets will constantly revolve in orbits given in shape and position, according to the laws above explained. But although these bodies may, indeed, carry on in their orbits by the mere laws of gravity, they could by no means have attained the regular position of the orbits through these laws.

The six primary planets revolve about the sun in circles concentric with the sun, in the same direction of motion and almost in the same plane. Ten moons revolve about the earth, Jupiter, and Saturn in concentric circles, in the same direction of motion, and nearly in the planes of the orbits of those planets. But it is not to be conceived that mere mechanical causes could give birth to so many regular motions, since the comets range over all parts of the heavens in very eccentric orbits. In this kind of motion, the comets pass easily through the orbits of the planets and with great rapidity; and at their aphelions, where they move the slowest and delay the longest, they recede to the greatest distances from each other, and hence suffer the least disturbance from their mutual attractions. This most beautiful system of the sun, planets, and comets could only proceed from the counsel and dominion of an intelligent and powerful Being. And if the fixed stars are the centers of similar other systems, since these are formed by the same counsel, they must all be subject to the dominion of One, especially since the light of the fixed stars is of the same nature as the light of the sun and light passes into all the other systems from every system <; and so that the systems of the fixed stars should not fall on each other by their gravity, he has placed those systems at immense distances from one another>.

This Being governs all things, not as the soul of the world, but as Lord over all; and because of his dominion he is usually called Lord God *Pantokrator*, or Universal Ruler. For God is a relative word, and is relative to servants, and Deity is the dominion of God, not over his own body, as those imagine who imagine God to be the world soul, but over servants. The supreme God is a Being eternal, infinite, absolutely perfect; but a being, however perfect, without dominion, cannot be said to be Lord God. For we say, my God, your God, the God of Israel, <the God of Gods, and Lord of Lords,> but we do not say, my Eternal, your Eternal, the Eternal of Israel <,the Eternal of Gods; we do not say, my Infinite or my

Perfect>. These are titles which have no relation to servants. The word God[3] usually signifies Lord, but not every Lord is God. It is the dominion of a spiritual being that constitutes God—a true, supreme, or imaginary dominion makes a true, supreme, or imaginary God. From his true dominion it follows that the true God is a living, intelligent, and powerful Being, and, from his other perfections, that he is supreme or most perfect. He is eternal and infinite, omnipotent and omniscient; that is, he endures from eternity to eternity and is present from infinity to infinity; he governs all things and knows all things that are or can be done. He is not eternity and infinity, but eternal and infinite; he is not duration and space, but he endures and is present. He endures forever and is present everywhere, and, by existing always and everywhere, he constitutes duration and space. Since every particle of space is always, and every indivisible moment of duration is everywhere, certainly the Maker and Lord of all things cannot be never and nowhere. <Every sentient soul is still the same indivisible person at different times and in different organs of sense and motion. Successive parts are given in duration, coexistent parts in space, but neither is given in the person of a man or his thinking principle, and much less can they be found in the thinking substance of God. Every person, insofar as he is a sentient being, is one and the same person during his whole life, in each and all of his organs of sense. God is the same God always and everywhere.> God is omnipresent not only virtually, but also substantially, for virtues cannot subsist without substance. In him[4] are all things contained

---

3. Newton's marginal note: "Dr. Pocock derives the Latin word *Deus* from the Arabic *du* (in the oblique case *di*), which signifies the Lord. And in this sense princes are called gods, Psalm 84.6 and John 10:45. And Moses is called a god to his brother Aaron and a god to Pharaoh (Exodus 4.16 and 7.1). And in the same sense the souls of dead princes were formerly called gods by the heathens, but falsely, because of their lack of dominion."
4. Newton's marginal note: "This was the opinion of the ancients, such as Pythagoras (in Cicero, *On the Nature of the Gods*, book 1), Thales, Anaxagoras, Virgil (*Georgics* 4.220 and *Aeneid* 6.721), Philo (*Allegories*, at the beginning of book 1), Aratus (*Phenomena*, at the beginning). So also the sacred writers, as Saint Paul (*Acts* 17.27–28), Saint John 14.2, Moses (*Deuteronomy* 4.39 and 10.14), David (Psalm 139.7–9), Solomon (1 *Kings* 8.27), Job 22.12–14, Jeremiah 23.23–24. Moreover, the idolaters supposed that the sun, moon, and stars, the souls of

and moved, yet neither affects the other. God is not affected by the motion of bodies and bodies do not experience any resistance from God's omnipresence. It is allowed by all that the supreme God exists necessarily, and by the same necessity he exists always and everywhere. Hence also he is all similar, all eye, all ear, all brain, all arm, all power to perceive, to understand, and to act, but in a manner not at all human, in a manner not at all corporeal, in a manner entirely unknown to us. As a blind man has no idea of colors, so have we no idea of the manner by which the all-wise God perceives and understands all things. He is entirely void of all body and bodily shape, and therefore cannot be seen, nor heard, nor touched; nor ought he be worshipped under the image of any corporeal thing. We have ideas of his attributes, but we do not know what the real substance of anything is. We see only the shapes and colors of bodies, we hear only sounds, we touch only the external surfaces, we smell only the odors, and taste the flavors; we do not know the inmost substances by our senses or by any act of reflection; much less, then, do we have any idea of the substance of God. We know him only through his most wise and excellent contrivances of things and final causes; we admire him for his perfections, but we revere and adore him on account of his dominion. <For we adore him as his servants, and a god without dominion, providence, and final causes is nothing else but fate and nature. No variation of things can arise from blind metaphysical necessity, which is certainly the same always and everywhere. All the diversity of natural things that we find suited to different times and places could only have arisen from the ideas and will of a Being existing necessarily. But, by way of allegory, God is said to see, to speak, to laugh, to love, to hate, to desire, to give, to receive, to rejoice, to be angry, to fight, to frame, to work, to build. For all our notions of God are taken from the ways of mankind by a certain similitude, which, though not perfect, has some likeness, however>. And this much concerning God, about whom a discourse from the appearances of things does certainly belong to natural philosophy.

_____

men, and other parts of the world are parts of the Supreme God, and are therefore to be worshipped, but falsely."

Up to now we have explained the phenomena of the heavens and of our sea through the force of gravity, but have not yet assigned the cause for this. It is certain that it must proceed from a cause that penetrates to the very centers of the sun and planets with no diminution of force, and that operates, not according to the quantity of the surfaces of the particles upon which it acts (as mechanical causes usually do), but according to the quantity of the solid matter they contain, and which acts at immense distances, extended everywhere, always decreasing as the inverse square of the distances. Gravitation toward the sun is made up out of the gravitations toward the individual particles of the body, and in receding from the sun decreases precisely as the inverse square of the distances as far as the orbit of Saturn, as is evident from the aphelions of the planets being at rest, and even to the remotest aphelions of the comets, if those aphelions are also at rest. But up to now I have not been able to deduce the reason for these properties of gravity from phenomena, and I frame no hypotheses. For whatever is not deduced from the phenomena is to be called a hypothesis, and hypotheses, whether metaphysical or physical, whether of occult qualities or mechanical, have no place in experimental philosophy. In this philosophy, particular propositions are deduced from the phenomena and are rendered general by induction. The impenetrability, mobility, and impetus of bodies, and the laws of motion and of gravitation, were discovered in this way. And it is enough that gravity does really exist and acts according to the laws we have explained, and abundantly serves to account for all the motions of the celestial bodies and of our sea.

And now we might add something about a certain extremely subtle spirit that pervades and lies hidden in all gross bodies, by whose force and action the particles of bodies attract one another at near distances and cohere, if brought into contact, and electric bodies act at greater distances, both repelling and attracting neighboring corpuscles, and light is emitted, reflected, refracted, inflected, and heats bodies, and all sensation is aroused, and the members of animals move by the will, that is, by the vibrations of this spirit, propagated through the solid filaments of the nerves from the external organs of sense to the brain, and from the brain to the muscles. But these things cannot be explained in a few words, nor do we have at hand sufficient experiments by which the laws of action of this electric and elastic spirit can accurately be determined and demonstrated.

## *Optics*, "Query 31"

[. . .] And thus nature will be very conformable to herself and very simple, performing all the great motions of the heavenly bodies by the attraction of gravity that intercedes between those bodies, and almost all the small ones of their particles by some other attractive and repelling powers which intercede between the particles. The *vis inertiae* is a passive principle by which bodies persist in their motion or rest, receive motion in proportion to the force impressing it, and resist as much as they are resisted. By this principle alone there never could have been any motion in the world. Some other principle was necessary for putting bodies into motion; and now that they are in motion, some other principle is necessary for conserving the motion. For from the various composition of two motions, it is very certain that there is not always the same quantity of motion in the world. For if two globes joined by a slender rod revolve about their common center of gravity with a uniform motion, while that center moves on uniformly in a right line drawn in the plane of their circular motion, the sum of the motions of the two globes, as often as the globes are in the right line described by their common center of gravity, will be bigger than the sum of their motions, when they are in a line perpendicular to that right line. By this instance it appears that motion may be gotten or lost. But by reason of the tenacity of fluids and attrition of their parts, and the weakness of elasticity in solids, motion is much more apt to be lost than gotten, and is always upon the decay. For bodies which are either absolutely hard or so soft as to be void of elasticity will not rebound from one another. Impenetrability makes them only stop. If two equal bodies meet directly *in vacuo*, they will by the laws of motion stop where they meet and lose all their motion, and remain in rest unless they are elastic and receive new motion from their spring. If they have so much elasticity as suffices to make them rebound

with a quarter, or half, or three quarters of the force with which they come together, they will lose three quarters or half or a quarter of their motion. And this may be tried by letting two equal pendulums fall against one another from equal heights. If the pendulums are of lead or soft clay, they will lose all or almost all their motions; if they are of elastic bodies they will lose all but what they recover from their elasticity. If it is said that they can lose no motion but what they communicate to other bodies, the consequence is that *in vacuo* they can lose no motion, but when they meet they must go on and penetrate one another's dimensions. If three equal round vessels are filled, the one with water, the other with oil, the third with molten pitch, and the liquors are stirred about alike to give them a vortical motion, the pitch by its tenacity will lose its motion quickly, the oil being less tenacious will keep it longer, and the water being less tenacious will keep it longest but yet will lose it in a short time. From this it is easy to understand that if many contiguous vortices of molten pitch were each of them as large as those which some suppose to revolve about the sun and fixed stars, as large as the Cartesian vortices, yet these and all their parts would, by their tenacity and stiffness, communicate their motion to one another until they all rested among themselves. Vortices of oil or water, or some more fluid matter, might continue longer in motion, but unless the matter were void of all tenacity and attrition of parts, and communication of motion (which is not to be supposed), the motion would constantly decay. Seeing therefore the variety of motion that we find in the world is always decreasing, there is a necessity of conserving and recruiting it by active principles, such as are the cause of gravity, by which planets and comets keep their motions in their orbs and bodies acquire great motion in falling, and the cause of fermentation, by which the heart and blood of animals are kept in perpetual motion and heat, the inward parts of the earth are constantly warmed and in some places grow very hot, bodies burn and shine, mountains take fire, the caverns of the earth are blown up, and the sun continues violently hot and lucid and warms all things by his light. For we meet with very little motion in the world besides what is owing either to these active principles or to the dictates of a will. <And if it were not for these principles, the bodies of the earth, planets, comets, sun, and all things in them, would grow cold and freeze and become inactive masses, and all putrefaction, generation, vegetation, and life would cease, and the planets and comets would not remain in their orbs.>

All these things being considered, it seems probable to me that God in the beginning formed matter in solid, massy, hard, impenetrable, moveable particles, of such sizes and figures, and with such other properties and in such proportion to space as was most conducive to the end for which he formed them; and that these primitive particles being solids are incomparably harder than any porous bodies compounded of them, even so very hard as never to wear or break in pieces, no ordinary power being able to divide what God himself made one in the first creation. While the particles continue entire, they may compose bodies of one and the same nature and texture in all ages; but should they wear away or break in pieces, the nature of things depending on them would be changed. Water and earth, composed of old worn particles and fragments of particles, would not be of the same nature and texture now, with water and earth composed of entire particles in the beginning. And, therefore, that nature may be lasting, the changes of corporeal things are to be placed only in the various separations and new associations and motions of these permanent particles since compound bodies are apt to break, not in the midst of solid particles, but where those particles are laid together and only touch in a few points.

It seems to me further that these particles have not only a *vis inertia* accompanied with such passive laws of motion as naturally result from that force, but also that they are moved by certain active principles, such as is that of gravity and that which causes fermentation and the cohesion of bodies. These principles I consider, not as occult qualities supposed to result from the specific forms of things, but as general laws of nature, by which the things themselves are formed, their truth appearing to us by phenomena, though their causes are not yet discovered. <For these are manifest qualities and their causes are only occult. And the Aristotelians gave the name of occult qualities not to manifest qualities, but to such qualities only

as they supposed to lie hidden in bodies and to be the unknown causes of manifest effects, such as would be the causes of gravity, and of magnetic and electric attractions, and of fermentations, if we should suppose that these forces or actions arose from qualities unknown to us and incapable of being discovered and made manifest. Such occult qualities put a stop to the improvement of natural philosophy, and therefore of late years have been rejected.> To tell us that every species of things is endowed with an occult specific quality by which it acts and produces manifest effects is to tell us nothing, but to derive two or three general principles of motion from phenomena, and afterwards to tell us how the properties and actions of all corporeal things follow from those manifest principles, would be a very great step in philosophy, though the causes of those principles were not yet discovered; and therefore I do not hesitate to propose the principles of motion above mentioned, since they are of very general extent <, and leave their causes to be found out>.

Now by the help of these principles all material things seem to have been composed of the hard and solid particles mentioned above, variously associated in the first creation by the counsel of an intelligent agent. For it became him who created them to set them in order. And if he did so, it is unphilosophical to seek for any other origin of the world, or to pretend that it might arise out of a chaos by the mere laws of nature, though being once formed it may continue by those laws for many ages. For while comets move in very eccentric orbs in all manner of positions, blind fate could never make all the planets move one and the same way in concentric orbs, some inconsiderable irregularities excepted which may have arisen from the mutual actions of comets and planets upon one another, and which will be apt to increase until this system needs a reformation. Such a wonderful uniformity in the planetary system must be allowed the effect of choice. And so must the uniformity in the bodies of animals, they having generally a right and a left side shaped similarly, and on either side of their bodies two legs behind and either two arms or two legs or two wings before upon their shoulders, and between their shoulders a neck running down into a backbone and a head upon it, and in the head two ears, two eyes, a nose, a mouth, and a tongue, similarly situated. Also the first contrivance of those very artificial parts of animals, the eyes, ears, brain, muscles, heart, lungs, midriff, glands, larynx, hands, wings, swimming bladders, natural spectacles, and other organs of sense and motion, and the instinct of brutes and insects can be the effect of nothing else than the wisdom and skill of a powerful ever-living agent, who, being in all places, is more able by his will to move the bodies within his boundless uniform sensorium, and thereby to form and reform the parts of the universe, than our spirit, which is in us the image of God, is able by our will to move the parts of our own bodies. <And yet we are not to consider the world as the body of God, or the several parts of it as the parts of God. He is a uniform being, void of organs, members, or parts, and they are his creatures subordinate to him, and subservient to his will; and he is no more the soul of them than the soul of man is the soul of the species of things carried through the organs of sense into the place of its sensation, where it perceives them by means of its immediate presence, without the intervention of any third thing. The organs of sense are not for enabling the soul to perceive the species of things in its sensorium, but only for conveying them there; and God has no need of such organs, he being everywhere present to the things themselves.> And since space is divisible *in infinitum* and matter is not necessarily in all places, it may be also allowed that God is able to create particles of matter of several sizes and figures, and in several proportions to space, and perhaps of different densities and forces, and thereby to vary the laws of nature and make worlds of several sorts in several parts of the universe. At least, I see no contradiction in all this.

As in mathematics, so in natural philosophy, the investigation of difficult things by the method of analysis ought ever to precede the method of composition. This analysis consists in making experiments and observations, and in drawing general conclusions from them by induction, and admitting of no objections against the conclusions but such as are taken from experiments or other certain truths. For hypotheses are not to be regarded in experimental philosophy. And although the arguing from experiments and observations by induction is no demonstration of general conclusions, yet it is the best way of arguing which the nature of things admits of, and may be looked upon as so much the stronger by how much the induction is more general. And if no exception occurs from phenomena, the conclusion may be pronounced generally. But if at any time afterwards any exception shall occur from experiments, it may then begin to be pronounced with such exceptions as occur. By this way of analysis we may proceed from compounds to ingredients and from motions to the forces producing them, and in general from effects to their causes and from particular causes to more general ones, until the argument ends in the most general. This is the method of analysis; and the synthesis consists in assuming the causes discovered and established as principles, and by them explaining the phenomena proceeding from them and proving the explanations.

In the two first books of these *Optics* I proceeded by this analysis to discover and prove the original differences of the rays of light in respect of refrangibility, reflexibility, and color, and their alternate fits of easy reflection and easy transmission, and the properties of bodies, both opaque and pellucid, on which their reflections and colors depend. And these discoveries being proved may be assumed in the method of composition for explaining the phenomena arising from them; I gave an instance of this method in the end of the First Book. In this Third Book I have only begun the analysis of what remains to be discovered about light and its effects on the frame of nature, hinting several things about it and leaving the hints to be examined and improved by the further experiments and observations of such as are inquisitive. And if natural philosophy in all its parts, by pursuing this method, shall at length be perfected, the bounds of moral philosophy will be also enlarged. For so far as we can know by natural philosophy what is the first cause, what power he has over us, and what benefits we receive from him, so far our duty toward him as well as that toward one another will appear to us by the light of nature. And no doubt, if the worship of false gods had not blinded the heathen, their moral philosophy would have gone further than to the four cardinal virtues; and instead of teaching the transmigration of souls, and to worship the sun and moon and dead heroes, they would have taught us to worship our true author and benefactor, as their ancestors did under the government of Noah and his sons before they corrupted themselves.

# G. W. Leibniz, From the Letters to Clarke (1715–16)[1]

## I. Leibniz's First Paper, Being an Extract of a Letter (November 1715)

1. Natural religion itself seems to decay [in England] very much. Many will have human souls to be material; others make God himself a corporeal being.

2. Mr. Locke and his followers are uncertain, at least, whether the soul is not material and naturally perishable.

3. Sir Isaac Newton says that space is an organ which God makes use of to perceive things by. But if God stands in need of an organ to perceive things by, it will follow that they do not depend altogether on him, nor were produced by him.

4. Sir Isaac Newton and his followers also have a very odd opinion concerning the work of God. According to them, God Almighty needs to wind up his watch from time to time;[2] otherwise it would cease to move. He had not, it seems, sufficient foresight to make it a perpetual motion. No, the machine of God's making is so imperfect, according to these gentlemen, that he is obliged to clean it now and then by an extraordinary concourse, and even to mend it, as a clockmaker mends his work, who must consequently be so much the more unskillful a workman as he is more often obliged to mend his work and to set it right. According to my opinion, the same force and vigor remains always in the world and only passes from one part of matter to another agreeably to the laws of nature and the beautiful pre-established order. And I hold that when God works miracles, he does not do it in order to supply the wants of nature, but those of grace. Whoever thinks otherwise must necessarily have a very mean notion of the wisdom and power of God.

1. Translated from the French by Samuel Clarke in *A Collection of Papers which passed between the late learned Mr. Leibnitz and Dr. Clarke in the years 1715 and 1716 relating to the Principles of Natural Philosophy and Religion* (London, 1717), modified. Leibniz's first four papers are given in their entirety. Samuel Clarke was a philosopher and theologian, a friend and follower of Newton. In 1697, he translated Jacques Rohault's Cartesian physics textbook, adding to it extensive annotations that "corrected" Descartes, often by incorporating Newtonian principles. It is clear that Newton collaborated with Clarke, in his replies to Leibniz's letters, and contributed some of the arguments (there is a manuscript in Newton's hand that found its way into one of Clarke's letters). However, given that some of the arguments are to be found in Clarke's previous and contemporaneous work, one would have to conclude that much of the letters are by Clarke himself.

2. Leibniz here calls attention to a passage in Newton's *Opticks*, Query 31: "For while comets move in very eccentric orbs in all manner of position, blind fate could never make all planets move one and the same way in orbs concentric, some inconsiderable irregularities excepted which may have arisen from the mutual actions of comets and planets upon one another, and

## II. Leibniz's Second Letter

1. It is rightly observed in the paper delivered to the Princess of Wales, which Her Royal Highness has been pleased to communicate to me, that next to corruption of manners, the principles of the materialists do very much contribute to keep up impiety. But I believe that one has no reason to add that the mathematical principles of philosophy are opposite to those of the materialists. On the contrary, they are the same, only with this difference—that the materialists, in imitation of Democritus, Epicurus, and Hobbes, confine themselves altogether to mathematical principles and admit only bodies, whereas the Christian mathematicians admit also immaterial substances. Wherefore, not mathematical principles (according to the usual sense of that word) but *metaphysical principles* ought to be opposed to those of the materialists. Pythagoras, Plato, and Aristotle in some measure had a knowledge of these principles, but I claim to have established them demonstratively in my *Theodicy*, though I have done it in a popular manner. The great foundation of mathematics is the *principle of contradiction or identity*, that is, that a proposition cannot be true and false at the same time, and that therefore A is A and cannot be not A. This single principle is sufficient to demonstrate every part of arithmetic and geometry, that is, all mathematical principles. But in order to proceed from mathematics to natural philosophy, another principle is required, as I have observed in my *Theodicy*; I mean the *principle of sufficient reason*, namely, that nothing happens without a reason why it should be so rather than otherwise. And therefore Archimedes, being desirous to proceed from mathematics to natural philosophy, in his book *De aequilibro*, was obliged to make use of a particular case of the great principle of sufficient reason. He takes it for granted that if there is a balance in which everything is alike on both sides, and if equal weights are hung on the two ends of that balance, the whole will be at rest. That is because no reason can be given why one side should weigh down rather than the other. Now by that single principle, namely, that there ought to be a sufficient reason why things should be so and not otherwise, one may demonstrate the being of God and all the other parts of metaphysics or natural theology and even, in some measure, those principles of natural philosophy that are independent of mathematics; I mean the dynamic principles or the principles of force.

2. The author proceeds and says that according to the *mathematical principles*, that is, according to Sir Isaac Newton's philosophy (for *mathematical principles* determine nothing in the present case), matter is the most inconsiderable part of the universe. The reason is because he admits empty space besides matter and because, according to his notions, matter fills up a very small part of space. But Democritus and Epicurus maintained the same thing; they differed from Sir Isaac Newton only as to the quantity of matter, and perhaps they believed there was more matter in the world than Sir Isaac Newton will allow; wherein I think their opinion ought to be preferred, for the more matter there is, the more God has occasion to exercise his wisdom and power. This is one reason, among others, why I maintain that there is no void at all.

3. I find, in express words in the Appendix to Sir Isaac Newton's *Opticks*, that space is the sensorium of God. But the word "sensorium" has always signified the organ of sensation. He and his friends may now, if they think fit, explain themselves quite otherwise; I shall not be against it.

4. The author supposes that the presence of the soul is sufficient to make it consciously perceive what passes in the brain. But this is the very thing which Father Malebranche and all the Cartesians deny; and they rightly deny it. More is required besides bare presence to enable one thing to represent what passes in another. Some communication that may be explained, some sort of influence, or a common source [*cause*] is requisite for this purpose. Space, according to Sir Isaac Newton, is intimately present to the body contained in it and commensurate with it. Does it follow from thence that space perceives consciously what passes in a body and remembers it when that body is gone away? Besides, the soul being indivisible, its immediate presence, which may be imagined in the body, would only be in one point. How then

___

which will be apt to increase, until this system wants a reformation."

could it perceive consciously what happens out of that point? I claim to be the first who has shown how the soul perceives consciously what passes in the body.

5. The reason why God perceives everything consciously is not his bare presence, but also his operation. It is because he preserves things by an action which continually produces whatever is good and perfect in them. But the soul having no immediate influence over the body, nor the body over the soul, their mutual correspondence cannot be explained by their being present to each other.

6. The true and principal reason why we commend a machine is rather taken from the effects of the machine than from its cause. We don't inquire so much about the power of the artist as we do about his skill in his workmanship. And therefore, the reason alleged by the author for extolling God's machine, that he made it entirely, without borrowing any materials from outside—that reason, I say, is not sufficient. It is a mere shift the author has been forced to have recourse to, and the reason why God exceeds any other artisan is not only because he makes the whole, whereas all other artisans must have matter to work upon. This excellency in God would only be on the account of power. But God's excellency also arises from another cause, namely, wisdom, whereby his machine lasts longer and moves more regularly than those of any other artisan whatsoever. He who buys a watch does not mind whether the workman made every part of it himself, or whether he got the several parts made by others and only put them together— provided the watch goes right. And if the workman had received from God even the gift of creating the matter of the wheels, yet the buyer of the watch would not be satisfied unless the workman had also received the gift of putting them together well. In like manner, he who will be pleased with God's work cannot be so without some other reason than that which the author has here alleged.

7. Thus the skill of God must not be inferior to that of a workman; no, it must go infinitely beyond it. The bare production of everything would indeed show the power of God, but it would not sufficiently show his wisdom. They who maintain the contrary will fall exactly into the error of the materialists and of Spinoza, from whom they profess to differ. They would, in such case, acknowledge power but not sufficient wisdom in the principle or cause of things.

8. I do not say the material world is a machine or watch that goes without God's interposition, and I have sufficiently insisted that creatures need his continual influence. But I maintain it to be a watch that goes without needing to be mended by him; otherwise we must say that God revises himself. No, God has foreseen everything. He has provided a remedy for everything beforehand. There is in his works a harmony, a beauty, already pre-established.

9. This opinion does not exclude God's providence or his government of the world; on the contrary, it makes it perfect. A true providence of God requires a perfect foresight. But then it requires, moreover, not only that he should have foreseen everything but also that he should have provided for everything beforehand with proper remedies; otherwise he must either want wisdom to foresee things or power to provide for them. He will be like the God of the Socinians who lives only from day to day, as Mr. Jurieu says. Indeed, God, according to the Socinians, does not so much as foresee inconveniences, whereas the gentlemen I am arguing with, who oblige him to mend his work, say only that he does not provide against them.[3] But this seems to me to still be a very great imperfection. According to this doctrine, God must either want power or good will.

10. I don't think I can be rightly blamed for saying that God is *intelligentia supramundana*. Will they say that he is *intelligentia mundana*, that is, the soul of the world? I hope not. However, they will do well to take care not to fall into that notion unawares.

11. The comparison of a king under whose reign everything should go on without his interposition is by no means to the present purpose, since God continually preserves everything and nothing can subsist without him. His kingdom therefore is not a nominal one. It is just as if one should say that a king who should originally have taken care to have his subjects

3. This is a reference to Pierre Jurieu's *Le tableau du Socinianisme* (The Hague, 1960). Socinianism was a Protestant sect, a forerunner of Unitarianism, founded by Laelius and Faustus Socinius; one of the Socinian doctrines was that God's foreknowledge was limited to what was necessary and did not apply to the possible.

so well raised, and should, by his care in providing for their subsistence, preserve them so well in their fitness for their several stations and in their good affection toward him, as that he should have no occasion ever to be amending anything among them, would be only a nominal king.

12. To conclude. If God is obliged to mend the course of nature from time to time, it must either be done supernaturally or naturally. If it is done supernaturally, we must have recourse to miracles in order to explain natural things, which is reducing a hypothesis *ad absurdum*, for everything may easily be accounted for by miracles. But if it is done naturally, then God will not be *intelligentia supramundana*; he will be comprehended under the nature of things; that is, he will be the soul of the world.

## III. Leibniz's Third Letter

1. According to the usual way of speaking, *mathematical principles* concern only pure mathematics, namely, numbers, figures, arithmetic, geometry. But *metaphysical principles* concern more general notions, such as cause and effect.

2. The author grants me this important principle, that nothing happens without a sufficient reason why it should be so rather than otherwise. But he grants it only in words and in reality denies it. This shows that he does not fully perceive the strength of it. And therefore, he makes use of an instance, which exactly falls in with one of my demonstrations against real absolute space, the idol of some modern Englishmen. I call it an idol, not in a theological sense, but in a philosophical one, as Chancellor Bacon says that there are idols of the tribe and idols of the cave.[4]

3. These gentlemen maintain, therefore, that space is a real absolute being. But this involves them in great difficulties, for it appears that such a being must be eternal and infinite. Hence some have believed it to be God himself, or one of his attributes, his immensity. But since space consists of parts, it is not a thing which can belong to God.

4. As for my own opinion, I have said more than once that I hold space to be something merely rela-

tive, as time is, that I hold it to be an order of coexistences, as time is an order of successions. For space denotes, in terms of possibility, an order of things which exist at the same time, considered as existing together, without entering into their particular manners of existing. And when many things are seen together, one perceives this order of things among themselves.

5. I have many demonstrations to confute the fancy of those who take space to be a substance, or, at least, an absolute being. But I shall only use, at present, one demonstration, which the author here gives me occasion to insist upon. I say, then, that if space were an absolute being, something would happen for which it would be impossible that there should be a sufficient reason—which is against my axiom. And I can prove it thus. Space is something absolutely uniform, and without the things placed in it, one point of space absolutely does not differ in anything from another point of space. Now, from hence it follows (supposing space to be something in itself, besides the order of bodies among themselves) that is impossible there should be a reason why God, preserving the same situations of bodies among themselves, should have placed them in space after one certain particular manner and not otherwise—why everything was not placed the quite contrary way, for instance, by changing east into west. But if space is nothing else but this order or relation, and is nothing at all without bodies but the possibility of placing them, then those two states, the one such as it is now, the other supposed to be the quite contrary way, would not at all differ from one another. Their difference therefore is only to be found in our chimerical supposition of the reality of space in itself. But in truth, the one would exactly be the same thing as the other, they being absolutely indiscernible, and consequently there is no room to inquire after a reason for the preference of the one to the other.

6. The case is the same with respect to time. Supposing anyone should ask why God did not create everything a year sooner, and the same person should infer from this that God has done something concerning which it is not possible that there should be a reason why he did it so and not otherwise; the answer is that his inference would be right if time was any-

4. See Bacon, *New Organon*, Book I, aphorisms 38–42.

thing distinct from things existing in time. For it would be impossible that there should be any reason why things should be applied to such particular instants rather than to others, their succession continuing the same. But then the same argument proves that instants, considered without the things, are nothing at all and that they consist only in the successive order of things; this order remaining the same, one of the two states, namely, that of a supposed anticipation, would not at all differ, nor could be discerned from the other which now is.

7. It appears from what I have said that my axiom has not been well understood and that the author denies it, though he seems to grant it. It is true, says he, that there is nothing without a sufficient reason why it is, and why it is thus rather than otherwise, but he adds that this sufficient reason is often the simple or mere will of God—as when it is asked why matter was not placed otherwise in space, the same situations of bodies among themselves being preserved. But this is plainly to maintain that God wills something without any sufficient reason for his will, against the axiom or the general rule of whatever happens. This is falling back into the loose indifference which I have amply refuted and showed to be absolutely chimerical, even in creatures, and contrary to the wisdom of God, as if he could operate without acting by reason.

8. The author objects against me that, if we don't admit this simple and mere will, we take away from God the power of choosing and bring in a fatality. But quite the contrary is true. I maintain that God has the power of choosing, since I ground that power upon the reason of a choice agreeable to his wisdom. And it is not this fatality (which is only the wisest order of providence) but a blind fatality or necessity void of all wisdom and choice which we ought to avoid.

9. I had observed that by lessening the quantity of matter, the quantity of objects upon which God may exercise his goodness will be lessened. The author answers that instead of matter there are other things in the void on which God exercises his goodness. Be it so, though I don't grant it, for I hold that every created substance is attended with matter. However, let it be so. I answer that more matter was consistent with those same things, and consequently the said objects will still be lessened. The instance of a greater

number of men or animals is not to the purpose, for they would fill up place in exclusion of other things.

10. It will be difficult to make me believe that sensorium does not, in its usual meaning, signify an organ of sensation. See the words of Rudolphus Goclenius in his *Dictionarium philosophicum* under *sensiterium*. "Barbarum Scholasticorum," says he, "qui interdum sunt simae Graecorum. Hi dicunt *aitheterion*. Ex quo illi fecerunt *sensiterium* pro sensorio, id est, organo sensationis."[5]

11. The mere presence of a substance, even an animated one, is not sufficient for perception. A blind man, and even someone distracted, does not see. The author must explain how the soul perceives what is outside itself.

12. God is not present to things by situation but by essence; his presence is manifest by his immediate operation. The presence of the soul is quite of another nature. To say that it is diffused all over the body is to make it extended and divisible. To say it is, the whole of it, in every part of the body is to make it divisible of itself. To fix it to a point, to diffuse it all over many points, are only abusive expressions, idols of the tribe.[6]

13. If active force should diminish in the universe by the natural laws which God has established, so that there should be need for him to give a new impression in order to restore that force, like an artisan's mending the imperfections of his machine, the disorder would not only be with respect to us but also with respect to God himself. He might have prevented it and taken better measures to avoid such an inconvenience, and therefore, indeed, he has actually done it.

14. When I said that God has provided remedies beforehand against such disorders, I did not say that God suffers disorders to happen and then finds remedies for them, but that he has found a way beforehand to prevent any disorders happening.

---

5. Rudolph Goclenius, *Lexicon Philosophicum* (Frankfurt, 1613). Goclenius was a standard reference work for seventeenth-century school philosophers, an alphabetical compendium of standard definitions and distinctions. The passage translates: "[Sensiterium is] a barbarism due to the scholastics, who sometimes aped the Greeks. The Greeks said 'aitheterion', from which the scholastics made up 'sensiterium', in place of 'sensorium', that is, the organ of sensation."

6. See Bacon, *New Organon*, Book I, aphorism 41.

15. The author strives in vain to criticize my expression that God is *intelligentia supramundana*. To say that God is above the world is not denying that he is in the world.

16. I never gave any occasion to doubt but that God's conservation is an actual preservation and continuation of the beings, powers, orders, dispositions, and motions [of all things], and I think I have perhaps explained it better than many others. But, says the author, this is all I contended for. To this I answer: [I am] your humble servant for that, Sir. Our dispute consists in many other things. The question is whether God does not act in the most regular and most perfect manner; whether his machine is liable to disorder, which he is obliged to mend by extraordinary means; whether the will of God can act without reason; whether space is an absolute being; also concerning the nature of miracles; and many such things, which make a wide difference between us.

17. Theologians will not grant the author's position against me, namely, that there is no difference, with respect to God, between natural and supernatural; and it will be still less approved by most philosophers. There is an infinite difference between these two things, but it plainly appears that it has not been duly considered. The supernatural exceeds all the powers of creatures. I shall give an instance which I have often made use of with good success. If God wanted to cause a body to move free in the aether round about a certain fixed center, without any other creature acting upon it, I say it could not be done without a miracle, since it cannot be explained by the nature of bodies. For a free body naturally recedes from a curve in the tangent. And therefore, I maintain that the attraction of bodies, properly so called, is a miraculous thing, since it cannot be explained by the nature of bodies.

## IV. Leibniz's Fourth Letter

1. In absolutely indifferent things there is [no foundation for] choice,[7] and consequently no election or will, since choice must be founded on some reason or principle.

2. A mere will without any motive is a fiction, not

only contrary to God's perfection, but also chimerical and contradictory, inconsistent with the definition of the will, and sufficiently confuted in my *Theodicy*.

3. It is an indifferent thing to place three bodies, equal and perfectly alike, in any order whatsoever, and consequently they will never be placed in any order by him who does nothing without wisdom. But then, he being the author of things, no such things will be produced by him at all, and consequently, there are no such things in nature.

4. There is no such thing as two individuals indiscernible from each other. An ingenious gentleman of my acquaintance, discoursing with me in the presence of Her Electoral Highness, the Princess Sophia, in the garden of Herrenhausen, thought he could find two leaves perfectly alike. The princess defied him to do it, and he ran all over the garden a long time to look for some; but it was to no purpose. Two drops of water or milk, viewed with a microscope, will appear distinguishable from each other. This is an argument against atoms, which are confuted, as well as the void, by the principles of true metaphysics.

5. Those great principles of sufficient reason and of the identity of indiscernibles change the state of metaphysics. That science becomes real and demonstrative by means of these principles, whereas before it did generally consist in empty words.

6. To suppose two things indiscernible is to suppose the same thing under two names. And therefore, the hypothesis that the universe could have had at first another position of time and place than that which it actually had, and yet that all the parts of the universe should have had the same situation among themselves as that which they actually had—such a supposition, I say, is an impossible fiction.

7. The same reason which shows that extramundane space is imaginary proves that all empty space is an imaginary thing, for they differ only as greater and less.

8. If space is a property or attribute, it must be the property of some substance. But of what substance will that bounded empty space be an affection or property, which the persons I am arguing with suppose to be between two bodies?

9. If infinite space is immensity, finite space will be the opposite to immensity; that is, it will be mensurability, or limited extension. Now extension must be

---

7. The bracketed remark is Clarke's addition.

the affection of something extended. But if that space is empty, it will be an attribute without a subject, an extension without anything extended. Wherefore, by making space a property, the author falls in with my opinion, which makes it an order of things and not anything absolute.

10. If space is an absolute reality, far from being a property or an accident opposed to substance, it will have a greater reality than substances themselves. God cannot destroy it, nor even change it in any respect. It will be not only immense in the whole but also immutable and eternal in every part. There will be an infinite number of eternal things besides God.

11. To say that infinite space has no parts is to say that it is not composed of finite spaces, and that infinite space might subsist though all finite space should be reduced to nothing. It would be as if one should say, in accordance with the Cartesian supposition of a material extended unlimited world, that such a world might subsist, though all the bodies of which it consists should be reduced to nothing.

12. The author attributes parts to space, on page 19 of the third edition of his *Defense of the Argument against Mr. Dodwell*, and makes them inseparable one from another. But on page 30 of his *Second Defense* he says they are parts improperly so called — which may be understood in a good sense.

13. To say that God can cause the whole universe to move forward in a right line or in any other line, without otherwise making any alteration in it, is another chimerical supposition. For two states indiscernible from each other are the same state, and consequently, it is a change without any change. Besides, there is neither rhyme nor reason in it. But God does nothing without reason, and it is impossible that there should be any here. Besides, it would be *agendo nihil agere*, as I have just now said, because of the indiscernibility.

14. These are idols of the tribe, mere chimeras, and superficial imaginations. All this is only grounded upon the supposition that imaginary space is real.[8]

15. It is a like fiction (that is) an impossible one,

to suppose that God might have created the world some millions of years sooner. They who run into such kind of fictions can give no answer to those who would argue for the eternity of the world. For since God does nothing without reason, and no reason can be given why he did not create the world sooner, it will follow either that he has created nothing at all, or that he created the world before any assignable time, which is to say that the world is eternal. But when once it has been shown that the beginning, whenever it was, is always the same thing, the question why it was not otherwise becomes needless and insignificant.

16. If space and time were anything absolute, that is, if they were anything else besides certain orders of things, then indeed my assertion would be a contradiction. But since it is not so, the hypothesis [that space and time are anything absolute][9] is contradictory; that is, it is an impossible fiction.

17. And the case is the same as in geometry, where by the very supposition that a figure is greater than it really is, we sometimes prove that it is not greater. This indeed is a contradiction, but it lies in the hypothesis, which appears to be false for that very reason.

18. Space being uniform, there can neither be any external nor internal reason by which to distinguish its parts and to make any choice among them. For any external reason to discern between them can only be grounded upon some internal one. Otherwise we should discern what is indiscernible or choose without discerning. A will without reason would be the chance of the Epicureans. A God who should act by such a will would be a God only in name. The cause of these errors proceeds from want of care to avoid what derogates from the divine perfections.

19. When two incompatible things are equally good, and neither in themselves, nor by their combination with other things, has the one any advantage over the other, God will produce neither of them.

20. God is never determined by external things but always by what is in himself, that is, by his knowledge, before anything exists outside himself.

21. There is no possible reason that can limit the

8. See Bacon, *New Organon*, Book I, aphorism 41.

9. The bracketed remark is Clarke's addition.

quantity of matter, and therefore, such limitation can have no place.

22. And supposing this arbitrary limitation of the quantity of matter, something might always be added to it without derogating from the perfection of the things which do already exist, and consequently, something must always be added, in order to act according to the principle of the perfection of the divine operations.

23. And therefore, it cannot be said that the present quantity of matter is the fittest for the present constitution of things. And even supposing it is, it would follow that this present constitution of things would not be the fittest absolutely, if it hinders God from using more matter. It is therefore better to choose another constitution of things, capable of something more.

24. I should be glad to see a passage of any philosopher who takes *sensorium* in any other sense than Goclenius does.

25. If Scapula says that sensorium is the place in which the understanding resides, he means by it the organ of internal sensation. And therefore, he does not differ from Goclenius.[10]

26. *Sensorium* has always signified the organ of sensation. The pineal gland would be, according to Descartes, the *sensorium* in the above-mentioned sense of Scapula.

27. There is hardly any less appropriate expression on this subject than that which makes God have a *sensorium*. It seems to make God the soul of the world. And it will be a hard matter to put a justifiable sense upon this word, according to the use Sir Isaac Newton makes of it.

28. Though the question is about the sense put upon that word by Sir Isaac Newton, and not by Goclenius, yet I am not to blame for quoting the *Philosophical Dictionary* of that author, because the design of dictionaries is to show the use of words.

29. God perceives things in himself. Space is the place of things and not the place of God's ideas, unless we look upon space as something that makes

the union between God and things in imitation of the imagined union between the soul and the body, which would still make God the soul of the world.

30. And indeed, the author is much in the wrong when he compares God's knowledge and operation with the knowledge and operation of souls. The soul knows things because God has put into it a principle representative of things without. But God knows things because he continually produces them.

31. The soul does not act upon things, according to my opinion, any otherwise than because the body adapts itself to the desires of the soul, by virtue of the harmony which God has pre-established between them.

32. But they who fancy that the soul can give a new force to the body, and that God does the same in the world to mend the imperfections of his machine, make God too much like the soul by ascribing too much to the soul and too little to God.

33. For none but God can give a new force to nature, and he does it only supernaturally. If there was need for him to do it in the natural course of things, he would have made a very imperfect work. At that rate, he would be, with respect to the world, what the soul, in the vulgar notion, is with respect to the body.

34. Those who undertake to defend the vulgar opinion concerning the soul's influence over the body by instancing God's operating on things external, still make God too much like the soul of the world. The author's affecting to find fault with the words *intelligentia supramundana* seems also to incline that way.

35. The images with which the soul is immediately affected are within itself, but they correspond to those of the body. The presence of the soul is imperfect and can only be explained by that correspondence. But the presence of God is perfect and manifested by his operation.

36. The author wrongly supposes against me that the presence of the soul is connected with its influence over the body, for he knows I reject that influence.

37. The soul's being diffused through the brain is no less inexplicable than its being diffused through

10. Johann Scapula, *Lexicon Graeco-Latinum* (Basel, 1580). Clarke had attempted to counter Goclenius with Scapula.

the whole body. The difference is only in more and less.

38. They who fancy that active forces decrease of themselves in the world do not well understand the principal laws of nature and the beauty of the works of God.

39. How will they be able to prove that this defect is a consequence of the dependence of things?

40. The imperfection of our machines, which is the reason why they need to be mended, proceeds from this very thing, that they do not sufficiently depend upon the workman. And therefore, the dependence of nature upon God, far from being the cause of such an imperfection, is rather the reason why there is no such imperfection in nature, because nature is so dependent upon an artist too perfect to make a work that needs to be mended. It is true that every particular machine of nature is in some measure liable to be disordered, but not the entire universe, which cannot diminish in perfection.

41. The author contends that space does not depend upon the situation of bodies. I answer: It is true, it does not depend upon such or such a situation of bodies, but it is that order which renders bodies capable of being situated, and by which they have a situation among themselves when they exist together, as time is that order with respect to their successive position. But if there were no creatures, space and time would only be in the ideas of God.

42. The author seems to acknowledge here that his notion of a miracle is not the same as that which theologians and philosophers usually have. It is therefore sufficient for my purpose that my adversaries are obliged to have recourse to what is commonly called a miracle, which one attempts to avoid in philosophy.

43. I am afraid the author, by altering the sense commonly put upon the word "miracle," will fall into an inconvenient opinion. The nature of a miracle does not at all consist in usualness or unusualness, for then monsters would be miracles.

44. There are miracles of an inferior sort which an angel can work. He can, for instance, make a man walk upon the water without sinking. But there are miracles which none but God can work, they exceeding all natural powers. Of this kind are creating and annihilating.

45. It is also a supernatural thing that bodies should attract one another at a distance without any intermediate means, and that a body should move around without receding in the tangent, though nothing hinders it from so receding. For these effects cannot be explained by the nature of things.

46. Why should it be impossible to explain the motion of animals by natural forces? Though, indeed, the beginning of animals is no less inexplicable by natural forces than the beginning of the world.

P.S. All those who maintain a vacuum are more influenced by imagination than by reason. When I was a young man, I also gave in to the notion of the void and atoms, but reason brought me into the right way. It was a pleasing imagination. Men carry their inquiries no further than those two things: They (as it were) nail down their thoughts to them; they fancy they have found out the first elements of things, a *non plus ultra*. We would have nature to go no further, and to be finite as our minds are; but this is being ignorant of the greatness and majesty of the author of things. The least corpuscle is actually subdivided *in infinitum* and contains a world of other creatures which would be wanting in the universe if that corpuscle were an atom, that is, a body of one entire piece without subdivision. In like manner, to admit the void in nature is ascribing to God a very imperfect work; it is violating the grand principle of the necessity of a sufficient reason, which many have talked of without understanding its true meaning; as I have lately shown in proving, by that principle, that space is only an order of things, as time also is, and not at all an absolute being. To omit many other arguments against the void and atoms, I shall here mention those which I ground upon God's perfection and upon the necessity of a sufficient reason. I lay it down as a principle that every perfection which God could impart to things, without derogating from their other perfections, has actually been imparted to them. Now let us fancy a space wholly empty. God could have placed some matter in it without derogating, in any respect, from all other things; therefore, he has actually placed some matter in that space; therefore, there is no space wholly empty; therefore, all is full. The same argument proves that there is no corpuscle but what is subdivided. I shall add another argument grounded upon the necessity of a sufficient reason. It is impossible there should be any principle to determine what proportion of matter there ought to be, out of all the possible degrees from a plenum to a void, or from a void to a plenum. Perhaps it will be said that the one should be equal to the other, but, because matter is more perfect than the void, reason requires that a geometrical proportion should be observed and that there should be as much more matter than void, as the former deserves to be preferred. But then, there must be no void at all, for the perfection of matter is to that of the void as something to nothing. And the case is the same with atoms: What reason can anyone assign for confining nature in the progression of subdivision? These are fictions, merely arbitrary and unworthy of true philosophy. The reasons alleged for the void are mere sophisms.